THE VICTORIAN GARDEN

– CATALOGUE –

BY
APPOINTMENT TO
HIS MAJESTY
THE KING
W. A. Gell
1909

THE VICTORIAN GARDEN – CATALOGUE –

A Treasure Trove of Horticultural Paraphernalia

Introduction by Daphne Ledward

Acknowledgements

The Publishers are particularly grateful to Mr Carol Hogben, to the Sutton's Seeds Archive and to Mr Webb of Webbs of Wychbold for making available the original material from which this volume has been compiled.

First published in 1995 by Studio Editions Ltd. Princess House, 50 Eastcastle Street, London W1N 7AP, England

ISBN 1 85891 267 9

Printed and bound in the UK

Contents

Introduction

Today, with a large number of retail outlets and easy motorised transport, it is possible for anyone to see and buy a huge range of plants and equipment from local garden centres, nurseries, shops and supermarkets. With a range of broadcasting media to choose from, information about garden products is readily accessible, and virtually every national and local newspaper and magazine, radio station and television channel runs a regular gardening feature. Wholesalers and retailers have a range of options to reach potential customers through media advertising, and, as with many other commodities, direct mail has also proved an invaluable method of enticing the gardening audience.

A century ago, such diverse methods of communication and public access to gardening goods did not exist. There were few gardening magazines, and newspapers rarely devoted space to what is now an area of leisure interest. Plant nurseries sold what they produced; they were not retail outlets comparable with today's garden centres and home improvement stores. Producers of garden catalogues were aiming at a specialist readership, rather than the general public. The catalogue customer was generally a committed plant grower, often of some financial substance, or the professional gardeners employed by people of means. While the cost of seeds, plants, furniture and garden architecture a hundred years ago may seem incredibly low to the 1990s reader, it was far too high for many poorly paid labourers, who relied on saving and swapping garden seeds and plants. It is interesting to note that some public-spirited seed companies made available heavily-discounted or sometimes even free vegetable seed to clergymen and others, for distribution amongst the cottage tenants in the parish, in order to encourage them in the worthy pursuit of cultivating their gardens.

In the absence of present day mass-media advertising, the catalogues had to be their own testimonials, leaning heavily on extracts from the letters of satisfied customers, a practice often viewed with suspicion nowadays, and therefore seldom used by suppliers. Then such testimony was a conventional practice deemed essential, and if the writer had a title, so much the better. Since complete success and satisfaction was then, as now, the desire of the seed companies, it was essential to provide detailed instructions on how to grow and care for plants, and cultivate the garden as a whole. Not only is such information unnecessary these days (though how convenient it would be!) with so many other sources of advice, but its omission allows for valuable pictorial space, and in our modern, image-focused world, colour photographs sell.

Thus it was that the Victorian gardening catalogues were not just brochures for the seeds, plants, equipment and sundries on offer, but also a jolly good read, so much so that were often thought of as gardening manuals in themselves. Some seed merchants went as far as including a comprehensive gardening calendar, from which it can be seen that the tasks of a century ago were not that dissimilar to those of today, though many weekend gardeners today may find the nineteenth-century prose a little heavy-going! Cultivating instructions in many cases were very detailed, and in some cases compare admirably with our modern reference books.

Gardening under glass featured very prominently. The choice of glass structures for plant cultivation and protection was extremely wide, though this aspect of amateur gardening would mainly be confined to those with larger homes and gardens. Today, with the average plot becoming increasingly modest in size, a new market has been created for small, mass-produced greenhouses, vertical cold-frames and miniature lean-to glass structures, and there is a resurgence in popularity of Victorian-style conservatories, now of scaled-down proportions.

Catalogue articles often extended to discussions on wider aspects of the contemporary garden scene. These were frequently written in lofty prose, printed in solid text uninterrupted with images, and were much longer than the 1990s reader would be prepared to devote undivided attention to. The compilers of Victorian seed catalogues also went to great lengths to assure prospective customers of the quality of their products, often describing and illustrating the laboratory processes and trials to which they were subjected, and usually going into some detail about the breeding techniques and origins of notable new varieties. Most modern seed catalogues hardly, if ever, touch on this information, though now it is so easy for the public to travel large distances, most companies organise public open days with conducted tours of all processes of seed production and technical staff on hand to answer individual queries. The telephone also enables the present-day customer to gain, first-hand and quickly, information that would have been necessary to provide in print, or at least as a response to a formal letter of enquiry, a hundred years ago.

Colour printing was still in its infancy in the second half of the last century, although garden catalogues were beginning to benefit from the colour lithography pioneered by the acclaimed Victorian Yorkshire printer, Alf Cooke, whose delightful lithographs were also gracing the pages of many prestigious journals and other publications of the time. However, what the catalogues lacked in colour was certainly made up for by the superb artwork. The line drawings accompanying the comprehensive descriptions of the 1800s were each a work of art, not necessarily a reliable record of a particular plant, but nevertheless beautiful, and somehow more inspirational than the ubiquitous colour photographs of modern catalogues.

Perhaps the most noticeable difference between the Victorian gardening catalogues and those of today is the quantity of items offered. There would have been no difficulty in finding exactly the right item for the job from those listing garden architecture, furniture and ornaments, but for the really exacting customer, most firms would also provide custom-made items to individual requirements. The novice gardener today may find modern seed catalogues confusing in the choice of varieties offered, but this is only a fraction of what he or she would have been presented with in Victorian times. For example, the Sutton's 1892 catalogue offered ten individual varieties of double hollyhocks, whereas the Sutton's 1995 catalogue lists only two mixtures. The Sutton's 1863 catalogue had thirty-eight named potatoes and offered 'other sorts' as well, but the 1995 catalogue shows only four, and Marshalls of Wisbech, with perhaps the widest choice of the popular catalogues, lists only twenty-four.

The plants themselves were also subject to prevailing fashion. Double and striped flowers abounded in the last century, but in the intervening years they have largely disappeared. Recently there has been a revival and some old varieties are being reintroduced under new, more modern 'gardener-friendly' names, while easy-to-grow, all-weather bedding plants such as *mimulus, impatiens* and French marigolds are now available in varieties that would have surprised the Victorian gardener.

Ordering everything from seeds to furniture through garden catalogues may not be common practice as it once was, but as the following pages show, for the Victorian gardener and householder, catalogues not only acted as precious postal advertising, but offered useful information and advice. It is fortunate that so many have been preserved, providing an invaluable record of nineteenth century garden practice, and a source of delight for gardeners and historians today.

WEBBS'
Boxes of Floral Gems.
SPECIALLY RECOMMENDED FOR THE GARDENS OF LADIES AND AMATEURS.
2s. 6d., 5s., 7s. 6d., 10s. 6d., 15s., 21s., 31s. 6d., 42s., & 63s. each.
FREE BY POST OR RAIL.
WEBBS' Popular Boxes of Floral Gems contain Collections of Flower Seeds that are highly desirable to every admirer of an abundant succession of exquisite bloom, as they consist of selections from our Kinver Trial Grounds of the choicest and most universal favourites of the garden, liberally arranged for the various prices.
WEBBS' 2s. 6d. BOX contains:—
3 varieties Hardy Annuals.
3 ,, Half-hardy Annuals.
1 packet Everlasting Flowers.
1 packet Ornamental Grasses.
1 ,, Aster, mixed.
1 ,, Ten-week Stock, mixed.
1 packet Mignonette.
1 ,, Balsam, mixed.
1 ,, Sweet Pea, mixed.
WEBBS' 5s. BOX contains:—
6 varieties Half-hardy Annuals.
1 packet Zinnia Elegans.
6 varieties Hardy Annuals.
1 packet Aster, mixed.
3 varieties Hardy Perennials.
1 packet Mignonette.
1 ,, Sweet Pea, mixed.
1 ,, Ornamental Grasses.
1 packet Everlasting Flowers.
1 ,, Ten-week Stock, mixed.
1 ,, Petunia, mixed.
1 ,, Balsam, mixed.
WEBBS' 10s. 6d. BOX contains:—
12 varieties Half-hardy Annuals.
6 ,, Hardy Perennials.
8 ,, Aster.
12 ,, Hardy Annuals.
1 packet Petunia, mixed.
6 varieties Ten-week Stock.
1 packet Zinnia Elegans.
½ ounce Mignonette.
1 ounce Sweet Pea.
3 varieties Ornamental Grasses.
3 ,, Everlasting Flowers.
1 packet Balsam, mixed.
WEBBS' 21s. BOX contains:—
12 varieties Half-hardy Annuals.
6 ,, Zinnia Elegans.
6 ,, Phlox Drummondi.
12 ,, Aster.
12 ,, Ten-week Stock.
1 packet Petunia, mixed.
12 varieties Hardy Annuals.
6 ,, Hardy Perennials.
1 ounce Mignonette.
2 ounces Sweet Pea, mixed.
1 packet Balsam, mixed.
6 varieties Brompton Stock.
3 ,, Ornamental Grasses.
3 ,, Everlasting Flowers.
6 ,, Seeds for Greenhouse.
6 ,, Quilled Asters.
Particulars of Contents of other Boxes on application.
For Complete List of the best Flower Seeds see WEBBS' SPRING CATALOGUE for 1895,
Beautifully Illustrated with
nd hundreds of Engravings. Post free 1s.
Gratis to

THE FLOWER GARDEN AND PLEASURE GROUNDS

The aims of the seedsman and plant breeder — to develop improved strains and techniques and enable the gardener to produce a constant supply of new and unusual stock — have differed little since Victorian times. Then, as now, fashion played a large part in horticultural purchasing habits, with, incidentally, the same controversy raging over the acceptability of various bedding schemes. But for the many Victorian gardeners and florists who believed that colour rather than form was essential, there was certainly no shortage of choice in contemporary catalogues. It is clear, however, from the number of seed, rose and other plant collections of unspecified varieties on offer, that nineteenth century gardeners were somewhat more willing to leave the selection to somebody else.

Those of us who began our gardening careers in the 1960s, when simplicity was stylish and anything leaning towards the ornamentation and geometric intricacies of Victoriana was generally despised, even when eminently suited to the surroundings, are often surprised at the strength of the Victorian influence on present-day landscape architecture. Today, such decorative accessories as flower border edgings, iron furniture, elaborate treillage and fencing, and conventions such as pillar-training and formal shaping of climbing plants and roses are enjoying a revival as a vital part of a well-designed garden.

The Victorians took their turf seriously. Garden lawns were only a small part of the grassland scene, as many large houses and estates also had their own tennis courts, cricket pitches, croquet lawns, putting and bowling greens. It was therefore necessary for the seedsmen to provide suitable mixes for a variety of uses, and supply the gardener or groundsman with adequate instructions on how to maintain the relevant swards to perfection. Yet the lawn fanatic of today would be horrified with Sutton's promotion in their 1880s catalogue for a 'close, velvety garden lawn' of trefoil and yellow suckling clover — surely a modern lawn connoisseur's nightmare.

FLOWER GARDEN CALENDAR,

WRITTEN EXPRESSLY FOR

THE ILLUSTRATED GUIDE FOR AMATEUR GARDENERS.

JANUARY.

Little can be done among Flowers in the open air during January, unless the weather be exceptionally open and mild, in that case Autumn-sown annuals must be attended to, relieved of dead rubbish that may have fallen or been blown on their tops. Those that are too thick might likewise be thinned, and the thinnings replanted elsewhere if room can be found. It frequently happens that the thinnings stand through the Winter best and flower first. The check to growth, in so far as it limits the flow of sap, strengthens the power of resisting cold. Should the ground and the weather prove sufficiently dry, run a hoe through all early Annuals and Spring flowers, and break the crust over the crowns of bulbs, before they get to the surface. See that mice or rats do not visit Crocuses or Tulips, and feast on their undeveloped beauty underground. Favourite beds of Tulips and Hyacinths should be thatched or hooped over, should severe weather set in. After a frost too many plants are in more danger of perishing than while it lasts, the expansion of the soil in freezing upheaves young plants of Annuals—Pinks, Polyanthuses, Cloves, Pansies. When the ground thaws the plants are left lying almost on the surface; therefore after each frost examine all choice plants, and replace them by a firm pressure of finger and thumb. The monster who takes his heel to them is not worthy to be satisfied by their fragrance, nor cheered by their beauty. Possibly the weather will check all this and in fact all operations, by binding the soil hard in the iron fetters of frost. Even then, however, much work may be done if not among the flowers, the garden and beds may need draining or enriching, and this is the season to do the one and prepare material for the other; no flowers, tender or hardy, will continue to thrive on saturated soil. Thorough drainage is even more essential in Floriculture than in Horti or Agriculture. And then as to Manure, flowers can neither paint their beauty nor elaborate their fragrance on dead rocks or barren soil. To prevent disappointment begin the year by enriching the earth for a crop of flowers, much as you would for a crop of rich fruits, as Strawberries; and vegetables, as Cauliflowers. The manures should be more decomposed, that is all. During frosty weather get manures or composts ready, unless both were applied in the Autumn, at which season all flower beds and borders should have been dressed and dug.

Ground-work may also be pushed forward in open weather, and alterations of walks, flower beds, lawns, &c., carried on. Ground may also be levelled, and turf relaid or renewed; the best turf for the purpose is that found on a common or by the road side. Mark the turves out a yard long and a foot wide, then run the long spade under them, an inch from the surface, and roll up firmly. These rolled turves are easily conveyed from place to place, and run out on the new lawn, which should first be made firm and even.

Under glass, shelter Auriculas, Carnations, Pinks, Pansies, Polyanthus, and protect seedling Pelargoniums, Verbenas, &c., from frost. Also Double Stocks, Wallflowers, choice Sweet Williams, Humea elegans, Fuschias, &c., for planting out in Spring and Summer, protect from severe cold. Seedling Hollyhocks in pots and pans pick over, and syringe with Gishurst's compost, as an antidote to disease.

Roots of Marvel of Peru, Dahlias, Salvia Patens, old Pelargoniums, protect from frosts. Calceolarias, Pinks, and seedlings, pot off small plants, attend to cuttings.

Roses may still be planted in open weather, mulching over the surface to prevent the frost reaching the roots. Sow Sweet Peas of all sorts, if not done in November, they are perfectly hardy.

FEBRUARY.

Push forward all ground work, such as draining, digging, and all alterations of form. As a rule turf ought not to be disturbed after the end of February; a dry March is almost sure to open the spaces between the turves, and at times it takes them several months to close again. Ground may be got ready this month for sowing with grass seeds early in March. The ground should be firm, and if possible dry, and the seeds well trod or rolled in. This is a good time to renovate and top-dress exhausted lawns, filling in the patchy places with turf, sowing seeds, and top-dressing with guano, or some manure rotted down into fine looking soil; rake these in, and then roll heavily, and the lawn will spring forth with a new life and a deeper verdure. Prepare ground for planting, and continue to plant Deciduous Trees and Shrubs, also Evergreens, if forced to do so, but neither, if the first can stand till next November and the second till April. Of the twelve, these two months are the best for planting.

Make up hot-beds for the sowing of tender and half-hardy Annuals, and also prepare cold frames, &c., for the sowing of seeds. Tender Annuals should have a hot-bed of sufficient mass to furnish and maintain, for two months

or more, a bottom heat of 70 degrees; this will require from three to five feet of fermenting material. For half-hardy Annuals in frames, about half the above depth will suffice, and a temperature of 55 or 60 degrees; cold frames, without bottom heat, are admirably adapted for the sowing of hardy Annuals, to succeed those sown in the Autumn. It is quite true that many Annuals are hardy, but this hardly applies to seeds caught in the first attempts at growth by a biting March wind, or from 15 to 20 degrees of frost. Therefore while hardy Annuals may be sown in a sheltered place, or on a warm border, out of doors, in February, it would be prudent to sow a portion of each packet in a pot, pan, or box, under glass, or on the ground of a cold frame. The seeds here would be safe from birds and vermin, and requires no further attention than a mat in severe weather, and an occasional sprinkling over with water.

Such hardy Annuals as Clarkia, Collinsia, Silene, Erysimum, Godetia, Isotoma, Calliopsis, Bartonia, Eschscholtzia, Leptosiphon, Lupinus, Nemophila, Malope, Poppy, Sanvitalia, Chrysanthemum, &c., should now be sown outside or in, at least in.

Half-hardy Annuals vegetate best in a gentle heat. Of those that are better sown thus early are Helichrysum, Mesembryanthemum, Schizanthus, Schizopetalon, Salpiglossis, Portulacca, Rhodanthe, Phlox Drummondi, Petunia, Linum, Lobelia, Ageratum, Anagallis.

Sow such half-hardy or hardy perennials or biennials as Acacia lophantha, Centaurea, Campanula, Cineraria maritima, Convolvulus Mauritanicus, Dahlias, Eccremocarpus, Gazania, Pelargoniums, Golden feather Pyrethrum, Linum flavum, Lophospermum, Maurandia, Mimulus, Nierembergia, Salvia coccinea, or Patens, Verbenas, &c. A few very tender Annuals, and what are popularly called sub-tropical plants require a temperature of 65 to 70 degrees, to cause them to vegetate freely and pass rapidly through their youthful stages of growth. The effectiveness of these plants in beds and borders depend upon the size and strength they have attained before being planted out. Some of these grow rather slowly and others very fast, the sooner the former are sown the better, the second class will be in good time next month. The following should be sown in pots and plunged into a hot-bed at once, Aralias, Eucalyptus Globosus, Variegated Maize, Cannas, of which a hundred varieties may be had, Centaurea, Ricinus, Sanguineus, Giant Tobacco, Solanums, Wigandias, these, with others to be sown next month, will make a fine show. Anemones may now be planted. By planting some in the Autumn and others now, the season is much prolonged. Early Crocuses and Scillas will now be showing above ground. It is a useful aid to growth, as well as a protection from mice and birds, to dust these over with soot and lime or wood ashes. Protect choice tulips and Hyacinths from severe weather. As Snowdrops and Golden Aconites will now be silvering over and dappling with gold the flower border or beds, and a few early wind flowers, Violets, and perhaps Pansies, and Forget-me-nots will be coming into blossom, the flower garden should be hoed and fresh raked to give early flowers the benefit of a clean base and surroundings. The roller should also be run over the walks, and the roller and mowing-machine over the turf. Good keeping adds immensely to the beauty of Spring flowers, and also seems to make them grow better. In some exposed and cold gardens, Spring flowers and Autumn-sown Annuals, such as Saponarias, Virginian Stock, Limnanthes, Alyssum, Collinsias, Nemophilas, etc., and Spring flowers, such as Heartsease, Daisies, Primroses, Aubretias, Myosotis, Arabis, Omphaloides, &c., are not planted in their blooming quarters till now. Transplanted with care, and with a ball of earth to each plant, they flower as well, or better often, than if planted or sown in their flowering places in the Autumn. Many also who do not attempt Spring gardening make their first sowings of hardy Annuals in the open beds or borders now. February sown Annuals generally come up well and remain long in bloom. The great secret of having a garden gay the year round with Annuals is to sow often, a few only at one time, and sow the seed fleetly and thinly. The habit of sowing all at once, and thick sowing, does much to lower undeservedly the reputation of Annuals for furnishing the flower garden.

MARCH.

All ground works, the levelling and relaying of turf, alterations and regravelling of walks, &c., should be completed early this month. Likewise all planting, in fact March is almost the worst month in the year for the planting of shrubs and trees. All digging and manuring or top-dressing of beds and borders should also have been completed. Work sufficient and more than enough, will be found in keeping and furnishing the garden, without any new or arrears of old work. Finish pruning Deciduous Shrubs, and prune Roses, finishing by the end of the month. The chance of a good bloom of Roses is much better by pruning now than in the early Autumn or Winter. Leave the shoots full length, and the first rush of the sap flows to the extremities, and breaks the buds there into leaf. This involves some loss of force, but that loss proves the salvation of the buds nearer the base of the shoots. The pruner now cuts back to these, and before they break into flowers the last lagging Spring frosts have passed away. Prepare beds for planting Tea Roses. They are so exquisite in colour, form, and fragrance, that they deserve a place in every garden. A rich deep soil, less heavy than for other Roses, suits them best; and most of them are so far hardy as to stand the Winter with no further protection than a few spruce or other boughs or fern fronds placed over them.

Plant Gladioli. No bulb has been so much improved and multiplied in recent years as the Gladioli. Over a thousand named varieties are in the trade; and new varieties are raised by thousands and tens of thousands every year. This, unless for enthusiasts or skilful hybridisers, is hardly worth the trouble, as capital flowering bulbs, of the finest varieties, are offered at prices ranging from 6s. to 48s. per doz., and seedlings, old enough to flower, from the finest strains, at £5 per hundred. The Gladiolus, like most bulbs, prefers a deep, rich, rather light soil, if trenched a yard deep all the better, no rank manure should be used, but a liberal dressing of well decomposed farm-yard manure, thoroughly incorporated with the soil, will assist the plants very much; the roots run deeply, but the bulb ought to be kept close to the surface. Deep planting has been a frequent cause of failure; plant about three inches deep, filling up to the level with a handful of sand, or light

compost, on the crown of each bulb. Place a stake by the side of each at planting, so that the bulb may not be staked through afterwards, and also that the stake may be ready to fasten the plant to, as soon as the leaves begin to grow. The bulbs should not be placed closer than from nine to twelve or fifteen inches apart. They form splendid masses and lines in the garden and borders, or in mixed borders; they look well planted closely together, in groups of three, five, &c. They have a grand effect mixed with American plants, planted in beds of dwarf Roses, massed among shrubs, or in beds near to Evergreens. They are of easy culture, delight in manure water in dry weather, and if planted at different times, from February to May, may be had in flower throughout most of the summer and Autumn months. Nameless mixtures of good varieties may be had at 20s. per 100, and others, such as Brenchleyensis at 15s. per 100. Hardy **Lilies also** make magnificent groups in beds and borders. The glorious golden-rayed Japan Lily, Auratum, is quite hardy, as also are Lilium speciosum, longiflorum, Brownii, gigantea, and the well-known and more generally grown candidum, or common white; Chalcedonicum, or scarlet Martagon; and several varieties of Tigrinum, or tiger lily. These are all easily cultivated, and will thrive and flower well in any good garden earth; they are even less trouble than Gladiolus, which require to be taken up in Autumn and stored in sand or dry earth till planting time returns, whereas most of the Lilies thrive best left undisturbed for years.

Anemones and Ranunculus may still be planted.

Hyacinths and Tulips, stake or tie as soon as the flower stems appear, and covering kept in readiness, to shelter choice beds during snow storms and rough weather.

Crocuses—Protect from birds by running a small piece of white thread or string along, six inches above the plants, thin, and almost invisible; the bird does not see it till it alights for a feast, and before proceeding to make a meal of the budding Crocus it looks up, sees the string, pipes out danger, and away it goes, and familiarity with the thread does not breed indifference, for the same process is repeated again and again, to the safety of the Crocuses; coloured string is of no use as a preventive.

Take off cuttings of Dahlias, Petunias, &c., and strike in heat; also divide the roots of the former, and multiply dwarf varieties for the flower beds and borders in quantity.

Hardy Annuals—Make another sowing in the open ground. Plant all Autumn-sown Annuals, from the reserve gardens, to their blooming quarters. Prick off singly in pots and pans, or in frames, those sown under glass last month.

Half-hardy Annuals, sub-tropical plants, perennials, &c., prick off as soon as large enough to handle, and pot off the larger varieties singly. If seeds are sown too thickly, or remain too long without being singled out, they are apt to rot off in the mass, and if once decomposition sets in it is difficult to arrest it, therefore early singling out is of the greatest moment.

Finish sowing all half-hardy and tender Annuals at once, such as Perillas, Amaranthus. Chilian Beet, which though hardy, is best sown under glass, potted off, and forced into good size with the plants here indicated, Nicotiana, or Tobacco plant; Ricinus, or Castor Oil plant; Zeas, or Maize of different sorts, especially the silver-striped Japanese. Likewise sow a batch of Everlasting plants, some of these are not only among the most beautiful in the garden, but they are exquisite for bouquets and for drying. The Rhodanthes—Manglesii, maculata, and maculata alba, are among the most useful and popular plants in cultivation. The Helichrysum, Xeranthemums, Waitzia, Gnaphaliums, Acroclinium, Gomphrenas or Globe Amaranthus, are likewise extremely pretty and useful, and should be sown forthwith.

Sow on a very slight bottom heat Asters, Ten-week, and other Stocks, Zinnias, double and single; Marigolds, African and French; Balsams, for early flowering in pots, or planting in beds or borders, in which they do exceedingly well in sheltered positions. Celosia, Larkspur, double Sunflower; also sow Ornamental Grasses for bouquets, &c., in pans in a cold frame, and plant out early in May where wanted to flower.

Sow Tropæolum, Canary Creepers, tall Convolvulus. Plant out Hollyhocks, Sweet Williams, Pinks, Carnations, Cloves, Seedling Pansies, Violas, double Primroses, Auriculas, Antirrhinums, Columbines, Delphiniums, &c.

APRIL

This is a good time to re-lay box edgings, if not done last month, and being about to start into growth, it will quickly lay hold of the new soil and establish itself. Thrift and other edgings are sometimes laid in April, but it is better to do so in the Autumn, then the plants will have time to get a good root hold before they throw up flowers. The grass of the lawns will now be growing fast, and will need to be mown once a week. Gravel walks should likewise be cleaned, top-dressed, and thoroughly rolled, so as to put a gloss on the garden as leaves and flowers burst into beauty.

Plant Tea Roses and Evergreen Shrubs, and finish pruning both. In planting shrubs, see that the plants are so graduated in height that the front row will speedily rest upon the turf, and so hide that greatest disfigurement of modern shrubberies—the raw edge of earth or weeds between them and the grass. For the formation of new shrubberies it is a good plan to sow this space and the interstices between with Annuals, to furnish a glow of colour while the shrubs are massing out into beauty. Gladioli, Lilies, Fritillarias, and other bulbs are also well adapted for such situations.

The flower beds and borders will now be aglow with hardy Annuals, early Spring Herbaceous plants and Bulbs, such as Crocuses, Tulips, Hyacinths. Squills, Anemones, Hepaticas, Leucojums, Daisies, Primroses, of all shades of colour, double and single Pansies, Auriculas, Aubrietias, Arabis, Phloxes, Cheiranthus, Adonis, Alyssums, Myosotis, Golden Thyme, Golden Feather, Gentians, and hardy Sedums, Saxifragas, &c., &c. The cultivator must see to its preservation and the producing of a succession. To this end all glass at command is overflowing with plants preparing for the open air; and the great business of this month is to multiply the number of plants to the utmost—push them into growth, and harden them off. The former is done by seeds and cuttings. Our purpose has been to show what may be done by seed chiefly, though in all gardens cuttings of Pelargoniums, Calceolarias, Coleus, Iresines,

Petunias, Verbenas, Ageratums, Alternantheras, Salvias, &c., have been put in and are growing.

It matters little how the plants are raised; most of them will now have to be treated alike, bulked out into finishing size, and prepared for the open air. Continue to prick out, pot, and shift seedlings as they advance in growth, and take special care of such indispensable plants as Lobelias, Ageratums, Petunias, Verbenas, and Pelargoniums, &c., raised from seeds, the latter, unless sown in the Autumn, it is almost impossible to get forward enough to flower the first year. Pot off sub-tropical plants, and keep them in a temperature of 60 to 65 or 70 degrees, to get them strongly established. Everlastings, and especially Rhodanthes, pot off the moment they are fairly ready; it is one of the most delicate plants grown. Keep Stocks, Asters, &c., cool as soon as they are fairly up, to induce a strong sturdy growth, prick out into other pots and pans, and pot singly if room can be found, so that the plants may go out without check. Pot and keep Marigolds and Stocks in small pots long enough for them to show their character, and then throw out all the worthless and single ones, and thus have beds and masses all good and all double alike Plant out all hardy Annuals from pots or pits into the blooming quarters at once, and sow Mignonette, Poppies, Venus's Looking-glass, Lupinus, Larkspurs, Convolvulus, Dianthus, Candytuft, Clarkias, Collinsias, Nemophilas, Sweet Alyssum, &c., in beds or borders where they are to bloom. It is almost impossible to have an excess of Mignonette. Ten-week and other Stocks should likewise be sown for succession on the open borders where they are to bloom.

Much attention will now be necessary to give each class of plants the special treatment best adapted for it. As to soil, all may fare alike. A light, sweet, sandy soil is the best for raising all seeds of flower-garden plants. But each class of plants almost has its own individuality in regard to the temperature and treatment that suits it best through its earlier stages, the sub-tropical plants and tender Annuals requiring most heat, the half-hardy Annuals less, and the hardy no artificial heat, only protection from cold. But at last they must all go into the open air, though the more tender need not do so till June. As the hardy Annuals get planted out, the half-hardy take their places; and when these go, the tenderest of all, by that time grown into strong plants, will occupy all available space formerly filled by the others. At the last shift of the seedlings, a little rough dung might be used for drainage for all the stronger growing sorts, in lieu of the usual potsherds. This will be occupied by the roots and afford the plants a useful stimulus at starting, and in after-growth.

MAY.

This is, or rather has been, the great furnishing month of the year. But the Springs of late have been so fickle, that the planting of the flower beds and borders with half-hardy Annuals and Perennials has mostly been deferred till the end of the month, and of the more tender plants until the first and second week of June. For a succession of years, frosts of unusual severity have visited us, from the 5th to the 25th of May, and hardly any plant at all likely to be injured or killed by frost can be considered safe till after that time. Nothing is gained by precipitate planting, but much by judicious preparation. The soil should be well prepared for the plants, and the plants for the change of place and condition. Where a full crop of bulbs and Spring-flowering Annuals or other plants have been grown, it would be well to clear the beds or borders as much as practicable; top-dress and manure, and dig slightly, and scarify deeply for the forthcoming plants. In any case, Spring-flowering plants that have finished flowering, might be taken up, and reduced and propagated for another season elsewhere, and the beds and borders cleared of dead leaves and other rubbish; hoed and raked clean, and then the plants should be prepared for the open air by a course of careful cultivation and gradual hardening off. What is called hardening off, is mostly sheer reckless ill-usage. Plants are thrust suddenly from an Italian climate under glass, into the semi arctic atmosphere of an English May. And then they shrivel up, are three-fourths killed and chilled, so that they do but little good afterwards. This process of killing by inches is called hardening off. There are more plants crippled for life, if not killed outright, during the month of May than in all the other months of the year; and all for want of thought. Better wait a whole month than harden off and turn out plants prematurely.

Begin with the hardiest plants, and end with those that are most tender—Calceolarias, Verbenas, properly prepared, Petunias, and Pelargoniums, are among the hardiest of bedding plants; Ageratums, Perillas, Amaranthus, Iresines, Alternantheras, Lobelias, Mesembryanthemums, are much more tender, whilst Coleus are tenderest of all, excepting the large leaves of Solanums, Wigandia, and Tobacco. Then again, edgings are frequently formed of hardy plants, such as Veronica, Campanula, Cerastium, Golden Feather, Sedum, Saxifragas, Thrift, Violas; and all these can be planted first.

Again, there are differences between Asters and Stocks, Marigolds and Zinnias. Asters and Marigolds being more hardy than the other two.

The final planting can hardly be performed with too much care. Not only should each plant be placed in the best position for effect, but it ought to be allowed sufficient space to grow, and be transferred to it with the slightest possible loss of roots or check of any sort. As soon as planted all should be watered home, to prevent their flagging, and to so pack the soil in around the roots as to enable them to lay hold of it at once. Even showery weather must not be trusted to perform this most useful service to newly-planted flowers. By planting Annuals and sub-tropical plants, and even ornamental grasses, in groups, almost as striking effects may be produced with these, chiefly or alone, as with the usual bedding plants. The great secret of continuous blooming are good soil, a fair start, with fine plants, skilful planting and culture, and no seed-bearing. Better far buy seeds than cut short the beauty of the garden for the seed that would probably be purchased for a few pence. Of course, in planting in the mixed style the tallest plants will be placed at the back, and foliage and flowering plants should be nicely balanced, and tastefully arranged, each to heighten the effect of the other. Hardly will the garden be filled, however, until

some things will probably want to be taken up, and preparations begin for a display of beauty next Spring. Hyacinths, Tulips, Jonquils, Narcissus, Autumn Crocuses, Early Anemones, had better be harvested as soon as the leaves begin to decay, be dried in the shade, cleaned, and stored. If room can be found, a few more Annual seeds may still be sown on the flower border. These afford a succession, and continue the season of beauty until it is reaped by the frost; and a little seed, more or less, costs but little.

In planting, always reserve a few plants of all that are placed in important positions, in order to be prepared to make good, blanks caused by accidents or losses Propagate by cuttings, Double Rockets, Lychnis, Wallflowers, and some of the best Brompton Stocks. These may be rooted in a cool frame or a shady situation out of doors.

Sow such Biennials in the open air as Brompton and other Spring-flowering Stocks, Wallflowers, Antirrhinums, Sweet Williams, Pansies, Mimulus, Myosotis, Centaureas, &c.

JUNE.

Finish the planting out of all plants intended for the flower garden and borders. Coleus and Dahlias should be last. The former are very tender in the Spring, though they will bear a fair degree of frost in the Autumn. Water newly-planted flowers, should the weather continue dry. Replace any weakly plants with stronger ones. Run a hoe through the surface of the beds, to check the loss of moisture, and preserve the roots in a more even temperature. Choose a showery day for thinning out the patches, mostly sown in circles, of hardy Annuals, and planting the thinnings wherever there may be a vacant space. Plant out the remainder of succulents, such as Echeveria metallica, or others raised from seed.

Tree, and other large Ferns, Palms, Aloes, Cactus, Dracenas, New Zealand Flax, and other choice and striking foliage plants, may now either be placed out singly on the turf or in groups, where they would be most telling.

Take up and dry bulbs as they die off, such as Tulips, Jonquils, Crown Imperials, Hyacinths, Guernsey Lilies, Anemones, Autumnal Crocuses, Belladonna Lilies, &c. Autumn-flowering bulbs must not, however, be kept out of the ground longer than August. Hepatica should not be disturbed at all, and Crocuses not oftener than once in three years. The propagation of Spring-flowering plants, as Violets, Daisies, Aubretias, Arabis, must be pushed forward at once. Brompton, Emperor, Giant, and Queen Stocks, sow for flowering next Spring, on an open, dry, somewhat hard piece of ground; also make another sowing of Wallflowers.

JULY.

The flower beds and borders will now be getting covered with their Summer-tide beauty. Many of the plants will need staking and regulating. Coarse growing plants are apt to overrun the weak, and such Annuals as Mignonette, Œnotheras, &c., to smother choice herbaceous plants and delicate Annuals. The cultivator must prevent this, and keep each plant in its place. If Double Zinnias, Asters, Marigolds, &c., are wanted fine, the flowers must be thinned, and only a few left on a plant and a shoot. These flowers can also be very much increased in size by liberal waterings with house sewage and other manure water. All sub-tropical plants thrive on the same diet. Weeds are sure to thrive also if they have a chance; therefore they must be carefully looked after and instantly destroyed. The surface, where any is visible, should be kept loose. Thin the buds and shoots of Dahlias, also of Hollyhocks, where size of individual blossom, as well as length and duration of spike is valued. When too thickly set, as they often are on the stems, the rain cannot get out from among the flowers, and the excessive moisture causes them to rot. Sow Hollyhock seed and seed of Crocus and other bulbs as soon as ripe. Tie up Gladiolus; apply manure water in dry weather. Take up and store all bulbs as soon as their leaves decay. Prick off Perennials, such as Brompton Stocks, Wallflowers, Pansies, Picotees, &c., as soon as fairly up. Shift Pelargonium seedlings, Balsams and Cockscombs, Layer Carnations, Picotees, and Pinks. Bud Roses, dwarf and standards; also work any common variety with the finest sorts. Many Roses do exceedingly well thus double worked; for instance, a Gloire de Dijon on the Briar is, perhaps, the best stock for Maréchal Niel, and so of other sorts. Notably the Banksian Rose makes a capital stock for Teas. Saponarias and Succulents make nice carpetings for rose beds. As the rose beauty will soon be on the wane, it would be worth while to sow the surface with Saponarias, or transplant some from the reserve garden to the rose beds. Some of the smaller Echeverias and Sedums and Alternantheras also do well for this purpose, and do not seem to draw virtue out of the rose beds like most other plants.

AUGUST.

Much staking and training will be needful in the garden this month. Hollyhocks must be carefully secured with large strong stakes. Dahlias and other tall, strong growing plants must also be strongly supported. Verbenas, Phlox Drummondi, Ageratums, Petunias, pegged down. Salvia Patens also form a splendid bed of quite a distinct character when treated thus. Many other Annuals, such as Saponaria, Sanvitalia, double or single, naturally hug the ground. Zinnias, again, stand without stakes, as also do Ten-week and other Stocks; but Asters in exposed situations, or during wet weather, require support. Watering, training, and keeping without spot will now be the chief work in the flower garden.

Plant Autumn-flowering bulbs, such as the Guernsey Lily, and Autumnal, or very early flowering Narcissus and Crocuses. By planting in succession for two and three months past, part of each, the season of flowering will be proportionately prolonged. Propagate by division, Gentians, Polyanthus, Primroses, Daisies, Forget-me-nots, Pansies. Put in cuttings of Hollyhocks, Phloxes, Pentstemons, Delphiniums, in a cold close frame.

Attend to the pricking out of hardy Perennials: keep clean, water in dry weather. Sow Primula, Cineraria, Calceolaria, Pansy, Hollyhock, Giant, Brompton, and Ten-week Stocks and Wallflowers. Attend to seedlings of all kinds in reserve garden, and finally prick off and out most of these for the Winter. Water Violets, Violas, Primulas, &c., in dry weather. Continue to plant out rooted layers of

Carnations, Cloves, Picotees, Pinks, and to plant out seedlings on light rich soil. Bud late Briars. Attend to the tying and stopping of those budded early. Cut back roses for late bloom. Top dress with guano or rich manure.

SEPTEMBER.

Continue to stake and train, water and keep clean. Pick seeds off all plants, Annuals, and others that are required to continue growing and flowering; if any have failed it is not too late to fill up with such Annuals as Nemophilia, Virginian Stocks, Collinsias, etc., from the reserve garden. Continue to stimulate Stocks, Asters, Marigolds, Dahlias, late Hollyhocks, &c., with manure-water; thin the buds and shoots of Dahlias, and maintain order among the plants on the mixed borders and beds. Let all be fully clothed without crowding or confusion. Propagate, by cuttings, some of the finest strains of Phlox Drummondi, Petunias, Ageratums, Salvia patens, Salvia Coccinea, Salvia fulgens.

About the middle of the month make a sowing of hardy Annuals, for flowering next Spring; choose a dry, firm piece of ground, open fully to light and air, and sow such hardy Annuals as Limnanthes, Collinsias, Clarkias, Gilias, Candytufts, Godetias, Catchfly, Calliopsis, Silenes, &c., very thinly; let all rooted cuttings, of whatever kind, intended to stand the Winter in the open air, be at once planted out, and all seedlings finally thinned and planted. None of the plants must be put into rich soil at this season, as Winter pride is almost synonymous with certain ruin.

Plant bulbs of Hyacinths, Tulips, Anemones, Ixias, Iris, Bulbocodiums, Crown Imperials, Narcissus, Jonquils, Aconites, Snowdrops, Crocuses. The ground should be well drained for these early bulbs, and moderately rich; plant the bulbs from two inches to six inches deep, the Crocuses rather the deepest, as they soon rise if left to themselves, a few inches a year, by the young bulbs constantly mounting on the crowns of the old.

Pansies, for late flowering, may still be planted out, and young plants placed in prepared beds for the Winter. Take up the earliest Gladioli as the leaves die, and store the roots as they are, and with a good bit of soil adhering, in dry sand or earth. Later batches, planted in succession from February to May, will not be fit to take up.

OCTOBER.

As the heavy hand of decay presses more and more severely on the flowers, and leaves a deep imprint behind, see to the safety and security of any plants that are to be saved from the approaching wreck, before the frost destroys all. Dahlias, Salvias, Marvel of Peru, and other bulbous plants will bear several degrees of frost, as long as sheltered by their tops; but when the top is gone, the plant, roots, and all, are almost sure to be destroyed. Therefore save such as Pelargoniums, or other plants, at once, and place all tender and half-hardy Annuals in pots under glass, as soon as possible. Few things are more useful or welcome, at this season, than a few dozen pots of Mignonette, Stocks, Asters, Double Zinnias, or even French Marigolds in full beauty.

Cuttings of shrubby Calceolarias may also be put in, and a few of these plants potted up now are also exceedingly useful bye-and-bye. Heliotropes, Alternantheras, Iresines do well lifted in the same way. As the garden is cleared it should be manured, dug, and planted with bulbs and other Spring-flowering plants, small flowering or foliage shrubs, miniature trees, &c., for the Winter. Roses may now be transplanted with more success than later in the season, as the descending sap heals and repairs the wounds, bruises, and losses of the roots, and helps to start the plant at once into a growing state.

NOVEMBER.

This month mostly puts a night-cap of fog upon the flowers, and utterly extinguishes their beauty; but for Violets, Christmas Roses, Chrysanthemums and Laurustinus, the garden would run serious risk of being without a flower at all this month. Remove all tender plants in pots and boxes under glass. Clear Annuals and young Perennials of all leaves and litter. These, by lying on the crowns of young plants, utterly ruin them, and give them a prey to the first severe frost. The gardens and borders may now be cleared of all rubbish, top-dressed, manured, dug, and the remainder of the bulbs and Perennials planted. Hardy Annuals may either be added from the reserve garden, or sown direct on to the beds or borders. Should the weather permit of their breaking through the ground and the frost, forbear to nip them at that critical period of their life, late sown Annuals often Winter well, and flower with great strength and beauty in the Spring. Roses—Finish planting and top-dressing all varieties excepting Teas and Bourbons. Shrubs and Trees—finish planting this month if possible; also all turf-laying and ground-work alterations. Sweep and roll grass and ground; and should the grass on lawns keep on growing, as it often does, stimulated by November fogs, mow at least once a week till the end of the year.

DECEMBER.

There is little to be done in the open air among flowers in this the last month of the year. The few flowers, such as the Golden Aconite and Christmas Roses, that come forth and blossom are mostly too hardy to need our care. And yet the Christmas Rose is grateful for a covering of glass, and blossoms larger and with a more spotless blanched purity in consequence. Protect bulbs from the ravages of rats and mice, and trap the latter; also dust off slugs and worms with hot dressings of soot, lime, or hot ashes. See that Annuals, young Perennials, &c., in the open are not displaced nor loosened by the frost: consolidate the earth around them after thaws. Protect Annuals by inserting a few boughs among them, or in very severe weather hooping over the beds, and covering with mats. Complete all planting of roses, shrubs, trees, turf-layings, ground-changes, as soon as possible, and hasten to get all the old year's work completed with the year, so that with a fair start, a good stock of healthy material, and work and furnishing matter well on hand, the flower garden in 1877 may be adorned with a higher grace, and clothed with a richer beauty.

Sutton's Flower Seeds—Complete List for 1892 continued.

GROUP OF ASTERS.

1 DWARF CHRYSANTHEMUM-FLOWERED ASTER. (*See page* 75.)
2 TRUFFAUT'S FRENCH PÆONY-FLOWERED ASTER. (*See page* 77.)
3 SUTTON'S QUILLED VICTORIA ASTER. (*See page* 77.)
4 SUTTON'S COCKADE OR CROWN-FLOWERED ASTER. (*See page* 77.)
5 SUTTON'S VICTORIA ASTER, STRIPED. (*See page* 77.)

Drawn from flowers grown in Messrs. Sutton's Experimental Grounds.

SUTTON & SONS, Seed Growers and Merchants, READING, ENGLAND.

ASTER—continued. TALL VARIETIES.

Comet. A beautiful and favourite class, which has carried off many prizes at leading Shows. Much resembles the Japanese Chrysanthemum. Height 15 inches.

Rose and white, striped ... ... per packet, 1*s.* 6*d.*
Lilac and white, striped ... ... „ 1*s.* 6*d.*
Blue. Bright shining blue flowers ... ... „ 1*s.* 6*d.*
Mixed ... ... „ 1*s.* 6*d.*

'I gained the Bronze Medal of the Petersfield Horticultural Society for 12 Asters with "Comet," besides taking First Prize in the next class with 9 of the same variety.'—Mr. T. GOLDRING, Stodham Park Gardens.

'I have a grand bed of "Comet." It is a beautiful Aster.'—Mr. H. C. DENTON, *Gardener to* Major EGERTON.

Jewel. A charming new class of Aster, almost perfectly globular in form and with incurved petals, resembling the finest of the Pæony-flowered varieties. The plants attain a height of about 20 inches, and carry numerous flowers measuring nearly 3 inches in diameter. Valuable for cutting. We offer two colours—both very charming.

Apple-blossom...per packet, 2*s.* 6*d.* | **Bright rose**...per packet, 2*s.* 6*d.*

Sutton's Mont Blanc. Plants of good habit, producing an enormous number of well-shaped pure white flowers, of great value for bouquets and general decorative purposes. Height 18 inches ... per packet, 2*s.* 6*d.*

Sutton's Crimson Globe. Very handsome, the petals overlapping each other so as to form a complete sphere. Colour rich crimson. Height 2 feet ... ... per packet, 2*s.* 6*d.*

Washington. A beautiful variety, somewhat resembling the Victoria Aster, but the flowers are larger and more perfectly formed, after the manner of a double Zinnia. One of the most useful strains for exhibition. Height 18 inches.

Four varieties ... separate, 3*s.* 6*d.* | **Mixed** ... per packet, 1*s.* 6*d.*

Sutton's Harbinger. Produces an immense number of large flowers, blooming four weeks before any other class of Aster. Height 18 inches.

Pure white ... per packet, 1*s.* 6*d.* | **Mixed** ... per packet, 1*s.* 6*d.*

'Aster Harbinger.—One of Messrs. Sutton's introductions, and quite correctly named. To those by whom white Asters are required as early as possible in the summer the variety under notice should commend itself. The seeds in this instance were sown on March 30 in a frame with only a slight bottom heat from a partially spent hotbed, and the first blooms were ready for cutting by the first week in July. The habit of the plants is extremely free and branching, every bloom being supported by a rather long stem, which is an advantage for cutting purposes. The flowers are a pure white and reflexed, like the Chrysanthemum-flowered, but are larger. Considering how late Asters as a rule are this year, it must be readily understood how valuable Harbinger is for decorative work in a cut state or even in pots.—W. S.'—JOURNAL OF HORTICULTURE, *August* 20, 1891.

Sutton's Giant French. A splendid exhibition variety; specially selected for its immense flowers and exquisite colours. Height 2 feet.

Six varieties	... separate, 3*s.* 6*d.*	**Scarlet and white, striped**	... per packet, 1*s.* 6*d.*
Blue	... per packet, 1*s.* 6*d.*	**Pure white** ...	„ 1*s.* 6*d.*
Blue & wh. strpd.	„ 1*s.* 6*d.*	**Mixed** ...	„ 1*s.* 6*d.*
Rose	„ 1*s.* 6*d.*		

Sutton's selection of brilliant colours, mixed, large packet, 2*s.* 6*d.*

'I exhibited at the Shipton Flower Show last year your Giant and Victoria Asters, taking First Prize.'—E. E. BRADLEY, Esq., Milton.

'Many of the Giant French Asters had as many as 20 to 30 flowers on a plant.'—Mr. A. MURRAY, *Gardener to* J. O. MACQUEEN, Esq.

'None could beat your Giant French Asters in size, colour, and perfect form.'—Mr. T. HOOPER, Crediton.

'I took First Prize at our Show with your Giant French Aster, which was very fine.'—Mr. G. SHARP, *Gardener to* S. WELLS, Esq.

'The Asters were really a grand show, the finest I have ever seen.' MR. J. HENRY, *Gardener to* the Hon. Mrs. BAILLIE-HAMILTON.

Sutton's Victoria. One of the finest classes for exhibition; flowers very large and globular. As the petals curve outward instead of folding in, the Victoria makes a splendid contrast to the Pæony-flowered varieties. Height 18 inches.

Twelve varieties,	separate, 4*s.* 6*d.*	**Dark blue** ...	...per packet, 1*s.*
Six „	„ 2*s.* 6*d.*	**Light blue** ...	„ 1*s.*
Crimson ...	per packet, 1*s.*	**Peach-blossom** ...	„ 1*s.*
Crimson & white, striped. (*See illustration page* 76)	per packet, 1*s.*	**Rosy carmine** ...	„ 1*s.*
		White	„ 1*s.* 6*d.*
		Mixed	„ 1*s.*

Sutton's selection of brilliant colours, mixed, large packet, 2*s.* 6*d.*

'The Victoria Asters were perfectly lovely—everyone admired them.'—Mr. JOHN DOREY, Alresford.

'With your Victoria Asters we have won every Aster prize we have competed for. The number of years we have been rewarded with similar honours makes me feel that too much cannot be said in praise of your strain.'—Mr. ROBERT ELLIOTT, *Gardener*, Harbottle Castle.

'Your Victoria Asters are the finest I have ever seen, and I have taken two First Prizes against nine competitors.'—Mr. W. DANN, *Gardener to* C. H. SIMMONS, Esq.

Sutton's Quilled Victoria. A beautiful and distinct class, having perfectly tubular petals. Height 1 foot. (*See illustration page* 76.)

Eight varieties separate, 3*s.* 6*d.* | **Four varieties** ... separate, 2*s.* 6*d.*
Mixed ... ... per packet, 1*s.* 6*d.*

Sutton's Cockade, or Crown-flowered. Extremely showy, each flower having a white centre bordered with some distinct colour; valuable for bouquets. Height 2 feet. (*See illustration page* 76.)

Six varieties ... separate, 2*s.* 6*d.* | **Mixed** ... ... per packet, 1*s.*

Sutton's Pompone. Very free-blooming, with beautifully-formed compact flowers; valuable for bouquets. Height 18 inches.

Eight varieties separate, 2*s.* 6*d.* | **Mixed** ... ... per packet, 1*s.*

Sutton's Exhibition Globe. The finest quilled English Globe Aster in existence, the centre petals being closely set, and the outer guard petals broad and flat. This class of Aster is invaluable to those who exhibit, and it is also greatly prized for bouquets; but the plants are somewhat loose in habit, and are therefore unsuited for bedding. Height 2 feet.

Twelve varieties ... separate, 5*s.* | **Mixed** ... ... per packet, 2*s.* 6*d.*

Truffaut's French Pæony-flowered. One of the best and most extensively cultivated classes, having large incurved flowers of the brightest colours. Height 2 feet. (*See illustration page* 76.)

Eighteen varieties,	separate, 3*s.* 6*d.*	**White** ...	per packet, 1*s.* 6*d.*
Twelve „	„ 2*s.* 6*d.*	**Dark blue** ...	„ 1*s.*
Six „	„ 1*s.* 6*d.*	**Scarlet** ...	„ 1*s.*
Black Prince. The darkest Aster yet raised. This and the White make a charming bouquet.	Per packet, 1*s.* 6*d.*	**Crimson & white**	„ 1*s.*
		Bright rose ...	„ 1*s.*
		Mixed ...	„ 1*s.* & 6*d.*

German Globe. Quilled flowers and branching habit. A showy class for mixed borders; large and free-flowering. Height 2 feet.

Six varieties,	separate, 1*s.* 6*d.*	**Purple**	per packet, 6*d.*
White ...	... per packet, 6*d.*	**Mixed**	„ 6*d.*
Crimson ...	„ 6*d.*		

English Globe (Betteridge's), mixed ... ... per packet, 1*s.*

German, mixed. Height 2 feet. Per ounce, 2*s.* 6*d.*; per packet, 6*d.* and 3*d.*

Sutton's Half-guinea Collection of Asters, including a packet (mixed colours) of each of the following varieties:—Sutton's Dwarf Bouquet, Sutton's Reading Beauty, Dwarf Chrysanthemum-flowered, Dwarf Pæony Perfection, Dwarf Victoria, Sutton's Giant French, Sutton's Tall Victoria, Sutton's Crown-flowered, Sutton's Quilled Victoria, German Globe.

CULTURE.—Several sowings of Aster will ensure a long succession of flowers. In frames seed may be raised from the end of March to the middle of April, and the heat should be only moderate. When the plants attain the third leaf, prick them off round the edges of pots filled with rich compost. From these transfer to other pots singly, or direct to blooming quarters. Gradually harden before planting out. In the open ground towards the end of April, sowings on a good seed bed will result in stout plants if properly managed. Sow thinly in drills; thin early and put the seedlings into final positions while small, or they can be thinned and flowered where sown. Sutton's Book 'The Culture of Vegetables and Flowers' gives full details on the treatment of Asters. Price 5*s.*

New Edition of Mr. M. H. Sutton's Essay on Pastures, post-free for 12 stamps.

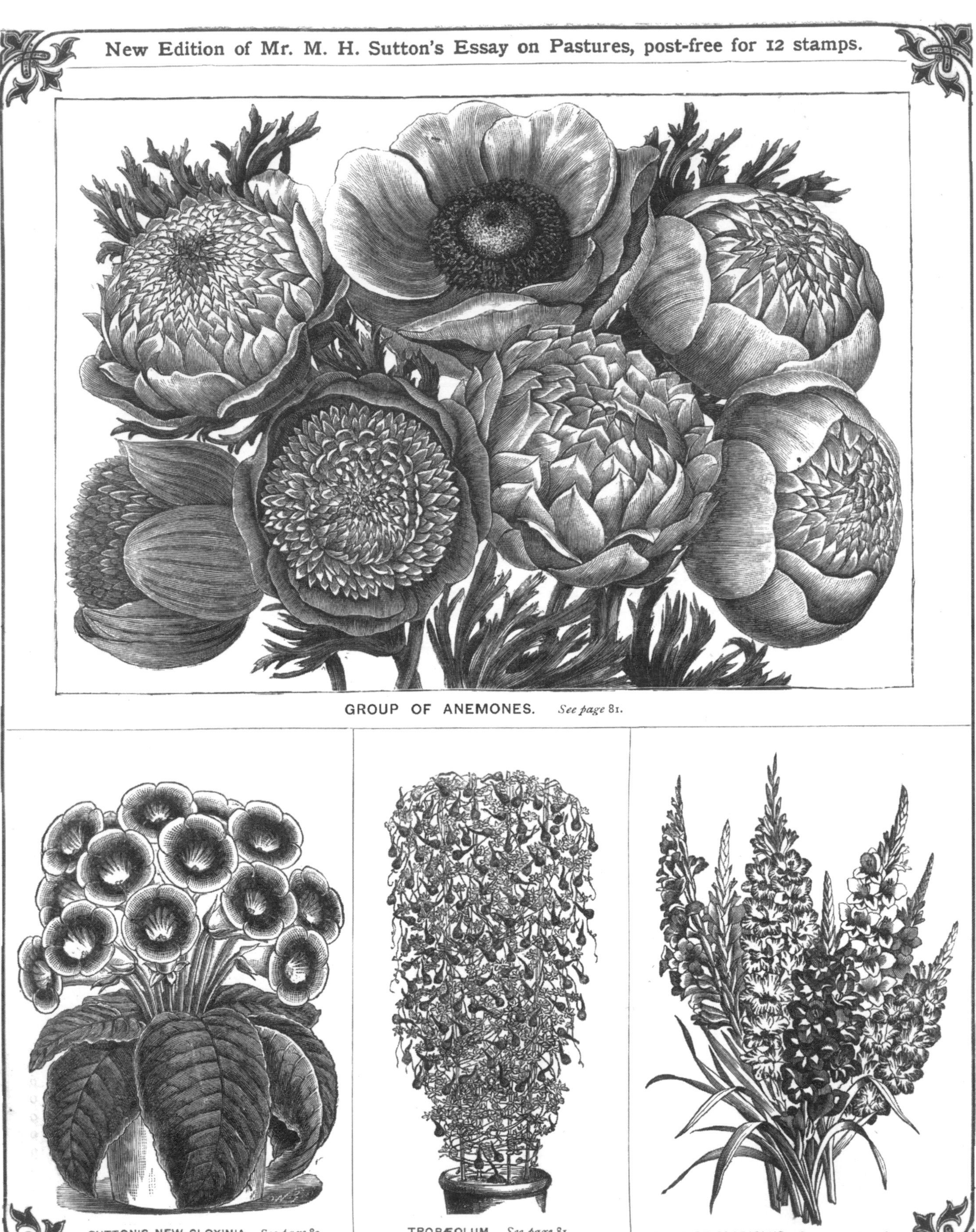

GROUP OF ANEMONES. *See page* 81.

SUTTON'S NEW GLOXINIA. *See page* 80.

TROPÆOLUM. *See page* 81.

GROUP OF GLADIOLUS. *See pages* 78 *and* 79.

Sutton's Flower Seeds—Complete List for 1892 continued.

PETUNIA.

Half-hardy perennial.

SUTTON'S SUPERB DOUBLE PETUNIA. *Per packet, 2s. 6d.*

SUTTON'S SUPERB SINGLE PETUNIA. *Per packet, 1s. 6d.*

SUTTON'S STRIPED BEDDING PETUNIA. *Per packet, 2s. 6d. and 1s. 6d.*

DOUBLE VARIETIES.

Our seed has been saved from the very finest single blooms, carefully fertilised with pollen of the best double flowers, which is the only way of obtaining double seedlings. The strain may be confidently relied on to produce from 20 to 40 per cent. of double flowers of exquisite beauty and great size, and the blossoms that come single will be of the Grandiflora type.

Sutton's Superb, mixed. One of the finest strains in existence. The double flowers are very large, full, and beautifully formed, and the edges of the petals well fringed. Height 2 feet. (*See accompanying illustration.*) Per packet, 2*s.* 6*d.*

'Double Petunias are usually grown from cuttings struck in the spring, but this spring I had a packet of double seed from Messrs. Sutton & Sons, of Reading, which has produced several plants fully equal to the finest named kinds. Of course there are some singles among them, but even these are beautifully fringed.—S. T.'—FARM, FIELD AND FIRESIDE, *July* 31, 1891.

'The Petunias I have are really beautiful, and people are continually asking where I got the seed. A great many of them are very double, and make beautiful pot plants.'—Mr. A. FRY, *Gardener to* C. W. CATT, Esq.

Sutton's Dwarf Compact. A valuable strain; plants dwarf and compact, very free flowering. Flowers quite as fine as those of our Superb strain, and beautifully fringed. Height 1 foot... ... per packet, 2*s.* 6*d.*

'Over 50 per cent. of the plants produced double flowers, really exquisite.'—Mr. B. TOWN, Guiseley.

Lady of the Lake. Some magnificent pure white beautifully fringed flowers can be obtained from this strain. Invaluable for taking cuttings from for greenhouse decoration or bedding, but the percentage of flowers true to character is not so great as in the other varieties ... per packet, 5*s.*

SINGLE VARIETIES.

Height $1\frac{1}{2}$ or 2 feet.

Sutton's Leviathan, mixed. The largest of all Petunias, having gigantic flowers with beautifully veined throats. Habit robust. Per packet, 2*s.* 6*d.*

'The Petunias are magnificent; some of the blooms measure 5 inches in diameter.'—Miss GOFFE, Fringford.

Sutton's Superb, mixed. Exceedingly handsome free-flowering varieties; brilliant and effective in beds and borders. (*See accompanying illustration.*)

Fringed flowers, per pkt., 1*s.* 6*d.* | **Plain-edged** ... per packet, 1*s.*

Sutton's Superb White. A charming variety. Planted in a bed alone, it produces a mass of pure white flowers.

Fringed flowers, per pkt., 2*s.* 6*d.* | **Plain-edged** ... per packet, 1*s.*

Sutton's Superb Crimson. Fine rich colour, valuable for bedding in conjunction with the White... ... ... per packet, 1*s.*

Sutton's Superb Rose. A charming colour. A few plants in pots add greatly to the beauty of a greenhouse or conservatory per packet, 1*s.*

Sutton's Superb, six varieties ... ... 5*s.*

Sutton's Large-flowered Striped. Twice the size of ordinary Petunias, and beautifully striped and blotched, per packet, 5*s.* and 2*s.* 6*d.*

Sutton's Striped Bedding. Distinct and perfectly marked Petunias of robust habit, and yielding a profusion of bloom, of brilliant colours; valuable for bedding. (*See accompanying illustration.*) Per packet, 2*s.* 6*d.* and 1*s.* 6*d.*

'Your Striped Bedding Petunia is a great acquisition, and I can strongly recommend it for bedding.'—Mr. J. A. COLTHORPE, *Gardener to the* Hon. D. F. FORTESCUE.

Sutton's Dwarf. A perfectly distinct variety, very compact, seldom growing more than 5 to 8 inches in height, with brilliant cherry-red blossoms, each distinctly striped with white ... ... per packet, 5*s.* and 2*s.* 6*d.*

Yellow-throated, effective ... ... per packet, 2*s.* 6*d.*

Superbissima, large-veined throat ... ... 1*s.* 6*d.*

OLDER VARIETIES.

Height 2 feet.

Alba ... ... per packet, 6*d.*	**Fine striped** (small flowered), pkt. 1*s.*
Atroviolacea ,, 6*d.*	**Three varieties,** separate ... 1*s.*
Countess of Ellesmere ,, 6*d.*	**Mixed single,** per pkt., 1*s.* and 6*d.*

CULTURE.—For culture in pots, Petunia seed may be sown either in pans or pots in January or February. Sow thinly on an even surface, and barely cover the seed with sand. Maintain moisture and an even temperature of 60°. Prick off the seedlings into pans an inch apart, using a light compost. In April transfer to small pots, and then pot on until the flowering size is reached. For bedding, the end of February or beginning of March is time enough to sow, and there is no necessity for using pots beyond the 60-size.

SUTTON & SONS, Seedsmen by Royal Warrant to H.R.H. the Prince of Wales.

Gloxinias. **No. 272.** *Cyclamen.* **No. 229.**

No.	Name.	Hard Dur.	Ht in feet.	Colour.	Months of Flowering	Per Pkt.	Observations.
						s. d.	
193	Cistus, rock, finest mixed ...	hP	1	various	,,	3	*Rock Rose.* Very handsome.
194	Clarkia elegans fl. pl.	hA	2	rose	Jy to Sp	3	An exceedingly useful class of hardy annuals, admirably suited for sowing in patches, &c. in mixed borders, and are very easy of cultivation. Integripetala varieties, and C. pulchella marginata, are very handsome.
195	,, **integripetala** fl. pl. ...	,,	1	pink	Ju to Oc	3	
196	,, ,, **alba** fl. pl. ...	,,	,,	pure white	,,	3	
197	,, ,, **limbata** ...	,,	,,	white & crim.	,,	6	
198	,, pulchella	,,	,,	pink	,,	3	
199	,, alba	,,	,,	white	,,	3	
200	,, **marginata** fl. pl.	,,	,,	pink & white	,,	3	
201	,, mixed	,,	,,	various	,,	3	
202	Clematis, choice mixed	hP	cl.	,,	Ju to Sp	6	Valuable hardy climbers.
203	Clianthus Dampierii	gs	4	scarlet & blk.	Ap to Jy	1 0	Parrot-beak plant, magnificent
204	**Clintonia pulchella**... ...	hhA	½	blue & white	Ju to Sp	4	Beautiful little plant for pots, borders, &c.
205	*Cobœa scandens	hhP	cl.10	purple	My to Oc	6	Well known useful climber.
206	**Cockscomb dwarf crimson** ...	tA	1	rich crimson	Jy to Sp	6	Splendid varieties for pot culture
207	,, **gold and crimson var.**	,,	2½	gold & crim.	,,	1 0	
208	,, **crimson feathered**	tA	3	crimson	Jy to Sp	6	Splendid plants for the greenhouse or conservatory, producing noble plume-like spikes of bloom.
209	,, **golden feathered** ...	,,	,,	golden yellow	,,	6	
						6	
210	,, choicest mixed... ...	,,	1	various	,,	6	Fine dwarf varieties.
211	**Coleus,** choicest mixed... ...	tP	2	,,	Jy & Au	1 6	Saved from the newest varieties.
212	**Collinsia bicolor**	hA	1	lilac & white	My to Au	3	Much admired and useful annuals. Exceedingly hardy and very easy of cultivation, C. verna is a new and charming variety, seeds of which must be sown in August as soon as ripe or will not vegetate.
213	,, candidissima	,,	,,	white	,,	3	
214	,, marmorata	,,	,,	marbled	,,	3	
215	,, multicolor	,,	,,	var. coloured	,,	3	
216	,, verna	,,	,,	sky bl. & wh.	Ap & My	4	
217	Collomia coccinea	,,	1½	scarlet	Jy to Oc	3	Useful for bees, pretty.
	Columbine. See Aquilegia.						

From Mr. JAMES WOOD, Rothwell, Yorkshire.

August 12th, 1875.

"I am pleased to inform you the **Gloxinias,** raised from the Seed I had of you, have taken the First and Second Prizes where exhibited this year. Your **Improved Pæony Asters** have also taken First Prize."

Double Dahlia. No. 230.

Cockscomb, crimson-feathered. No. 208.

No.	Name.	Hard Dur.	Ht in feet.	Colour.	Months of Flowering	Per pkt. s. d.	Observations.
218	**Convolvulus major.** choice mixed	hA	cl.	various	Jy to Oc	3	In splendid variety, well known.
219	,, **minor**	,,	1	dark purple	,,	3	The true dark purple varieties exceedingly rich coloured.
220	,, ,, **unicaulis** ...	,,	,,	,,	,,	3	
221	,, ,, **new crimson-violet** *(see coloured plate.)*	,,	,,	crim.-violet	,,	1 6	Splendid new variety.
222	,, aureus superbus ...	hhA	cl.	yellow	Jy to Sp	4	Suitable for greenhouse or warm border.
223	,, Cantabricus stellatus ...	hhP	trl.	pink & white	Ap to Sp	4	Useful varieties for hanging baskets, rockwork, &c.
224	,, Mauritanicus	,,	,,	lavender	Jy to Sp	3	
225	Cowslip, common field	hP	¾	yellow	My & Ju	4	*Primula elatior.*
226	Cuphea platycentra	hhA	1	scarlet	Jy to Oc	6	Useful bedding plant.
227	Cyanus minor, mixed	hA	2	various	Jy to Sp	3	Showy hardy annual.
228	Cyclamen Persicum	hhP	½	,,	Fe to Ap	1 0	Saved from a fine collection.
229	,, **James' Prize, sweet scented** ...	,,	,,	,,	,,	1 6	From Mr. James' celebrated strain.
	Daisy. See Bellis perennis.						
230	***Dahlia, finest double mixed** ...	hhP	4-5	,,	Jy to Oc	1 0	Carefully saved from a splendid collection of named flowers.
231	* ,, ,, ,, sm. pkt.	,,	,,	,,	,,	6	
232	Datura Huberiana fl. pl.	hhA	3	,,	Ju to Sp	6	Handsome sweet-scented annual.
233	***Delphinium formosum** ...	hP	3	deep blue	Jy & Au	3	Splendid plants for large beds or borders. D. formosum is a well-known fine variety, having rich coloured blooms of dark blue.
234	* ,, **cœlestinum** ...	,,	,,	sky blue	,,	4	
235	* ,, **nudicaule**	hB	1½	scarlet	,,	6	
236	* ,, **pumila alba** ...	hP	1	white	,,	3	
237	***Dianthus Heddewigi** ...	hB	,,	various	Jy to Sp	4	Fine varieties of Indian Pink from Japan, flowers very large and of brilliant colours.
238	* ,, ,, fl. pl. alba ...	,,	,,	white	,,	4	
239	,, diadematus, fl. pl. ...	,,	1	various	,,	6	Free flowering and brilliant varieties, should be in every garden.
240	,, latifolius splendens ...	,,	,,	,,	,,	6	

Aug. 28th, 1875. From Mr. THOMAS LANE, Easton Wells, Somerset.

"I feel great pleasure in telling you that all your Seeds have turned out first-class."

Sutton's Flower Seeds—Complete List for 1895—continued.

CINERARIA.

Greenhouse annual. Height 1 foot.

CINERARIAS,
SUTTON'S SUPERB SINGLE.

Per packet, 5s. and 2s. 6d. (See below.)

Sutton's Superb Single. We have, as usual, received a great number of letters from our customers, expressing astonishment at the immense size, rich and varied colouring, symmetrical form, and profusion of flowers borne by plants of our Superb strain. A few brief extracts are given below. (*Spray of flowers illustrated above.*) Mixed colours ... ... per packet, 5*s.* and 2*s.* 6*d.*

'**For variety of colour, fine branching habit of the plants, and immense** size of the blooms, your Superb Cineraria is the best strain I have seen during my twenty years' experience.'—Mr. W. HOPKINS, *Gardener to* Mrs. GRAVES.

'**Mr. Ingram wishes me to state that the Cineraria seed produced** splendid specimens of all shades of colour; in fact, I have never grown such a fine strain before.'—Mr. W. H. BARNETT, *Gardener to* F. W. INGRAM, Esq.

'**I have the grandest lot of Cinerarias I ever saw. The plants are** dwarf, the foliage good, colours clear, and large heads of charming flowers. My friends call them single Dahlias.'—Mr. H. F. RICHARDSON, *Gardener to* W. E. HUBBARD, Esq.

'**Your Cinerarias are a picture. Out of 102 plants no two are alike,** and some of the flowers measure 3½ inches across.'—Mr. J. MURRANT, *Gardener to* T. W. HARVEY, Esq.

Sutton's White. A lovely single pure white flower, with fine broad petals ... ... per packet, 5*s.*

Sutton's Blue. A charming contrast to the single White; flowers very rich in colour ... ... per packet, 5*s.*

Sutton's Red-edged. One of the most highly prized colours in the single Cineraria. The centre of each flower is white, surrounded by a distinctly defined red ring ... per pkt. 5*s.*

James's Exhibition (Single). This strain has been awarded Certificates both at the Royal Horticultural and Royal Botanic Societies' Shows. We have, as usual, received from Mr. James seed saved from his show plants ... ... per packet, 2*s.* 6*d.*

Covent Garden strain, single, mixed ... ... ,, 1*s.* 6*d.*
,, ,, ,, ,, collection of six colours, separate, 10*s.* 6*d.*
This strain is popular with many growers. The flowers, though small, are produced in great profusion on compact plants, and the variety of colour is charming.

Sutton's Superb Double, mixed. A splendid strain, saved exclusively from the most double flowers. Although a good proportion of the plants produce beautiful double blossoms, some of them revert to the original type ... per packet, 5*s.* and 2*s.* 6*d.*

CULTURE.—In some gardens seed is sown in April for producing flowers at Christmas, and again in May and June for succession. Where only one sowing must suffice, May should be preferred. Cinerarias grow so freely that the seedlings may go straight from the seed-pans to thumb-pots. After the transfer place the pots in a close frame and shade until they start. Gradually diminish the heat, and manage them by almost hardy treatment. When the pots become full of roots shift on till the flowering size is reached. Details as to soil, the treatment of pests, and other particulars, are given in Sutton's Book on Gardening. Price 5*s.*

SUTTON & SONS, Seed Growers and Merchants, READING, ENGLAND.

104

Sutton's Flower Seeds—Complete List for 1895—continued.

GAILLARDIAS, SUTTON'S LARGE-FLOWERED. *Per packet, 1s. 6d.* (*See below.*)

FUCHSIA.

Half-hardy perennial.

Seedling Fuchsias are robust in habit, and bloom profusely in the summer from sowings made at the beginning of the year. Height about 2 feet.

Sutton's Superb, mixed, carefully saved from the finest single and double varieties ... ... per packet, 2*s.* 6*d.* and 1*s.*

'**I had splendid Fuchsia plants from your seed, and they are still in** bloom (December 2).'—Mr. P. STAUNTON, *Gardener to* M. J. KELLY, Esq.

'**What grand Fuchsias I had from your seed! When I saw the** illustration in your Catalogue I thought it was impossible to grow them so large in so short a time, but I have some quite as good. From seed sown in March I had, in the second week of August, a plant 2 feet high and 14 inches through, literally covered with bloom.'—Mr. CHAS. WARD, *Gardener to* A. E. WENHAM, Esq.

'**My Fuchsias are two feet high and more than a foot through, nice** pyramids; some have been in bloom since September (Nov. 13).'—Mr. F. BARTLEY, *Gardener to* the Rev. G. BLISSETT.

'**The Fuchsia plants from your seed are of a good habit and free** bloomers.'—Colonel COURTENAY, Millbrook House.

CULTURE.—Seed may be sown at any time of the year. If a start be made in January or February, it must be in heat, and the plants will bloom in July or August. The soil should be firm and good, including plenty of decayed cow-manure. Prick off the seedlings early, and subsequently pot singly, affording shade and moisture after each transfer. Flowering will not commence so long as increased pot-room is given.

GENTIANA ACAULIS.

Useful hardy perennial for edgings; rich ultramarine blue trumpet-shaped flowers. Height 3 inches ... ... per packet, 6*d.*

GAILLARDIA.

With the exception of G. amblyodon the following varieties are all half-hardy perennials, which deserve to be extensively grown. The long blooming period and splendid colours will eventually make these flowers great favourites. The Picta varieties are 18 inches in height.

Sutton's Large-flowered. An exceedingly showy and effective strain of this popular plant, producing throughout the summer and autumn months large handsome flowers of various colours, including clear golden-yellow selfs, brilliant crimson-edged blossoms and others banded with gold. Height 3 feet. (*Illustrated above*) ... ... per packet, 1*s.* 6*d.*

Picta Lorenziana, double, mixed. Large heads of bright yellow and red flowers, very double, with quilled petals, suitable for bouquets ..per packet, 6*d.*

Picta Lorenziana, double yellow. Very showy ... ,, 6*d.*

Amblyodon. A strong-growing half-hardy annual. Flowers deep red. Height 2 feet ... ... per packet, 3*d.*

Picta. Favourite bedding plant producing throughout the summer numerous yellow and scarlet flowers ... ... per packet, 3*d.*

Picta marginata. Showy crimson flowers with yellow margin. ,, 3*d.*

Picta fistulosa. Beautiful yellow and red flowers with quilled petals ,, 3*d.*

Sutton's Special Mixture ... ... ,, 1*s.*

GESNERA.

Zebrina discolor. A valuable conservatory perennial. The stout leaves have a surface like velvet; colour deep claret, marked with still deeper veins, and mottled with vivid green. Flowers bright orange and scarlet. A beautiful table plant. Height 2 feet ... ... per packet, 2*s.* 6*d.*

Titia. Bright scarlet, very free-flowering; comes true from seed. Height 2 feet. ... Per packet, 2*s.* 6*d.* **Novelty.**

Gesnera Bulbs *are offered on page* 152.

CULTURE.—Sow in January in very rich soil. A warm and even temperature and plenty of water are requisite to promote luxuriant growth. The culture advised for Gloxinias will exactly suit the Gesnera.

SUTTON & SONS, READING, Seedsmen by Royal Warrant to Her Majesty the Queen.

Webbs' General List of Flower Seeds—*Continued.*

EUTOCA.

Per packet. s. d.

413. **Eutoca viscida,** a bright-coloured and free-flowering hardy annual; blue, 1 ft., ... 3

FENZLIA.

414. **Fenzlia dianthiflora,** a charming little half-hardy annual; valuable for pots; rosy-lilac, 4 in., . . 6

FERDINANDIA.

415. **Ferdinandia eminens,** a stately ornamental-foliaged plant; 10 ft., *greenhouse shrub,* 6

FERNS.

These well-known plants require no recommendation.

416. **Ferns, greenhouse varieties,** ornamental foliage, various height, *greenhouse perennial,* . 1 0
417. ,, **hardy varieties,** ornamental foliage, various height, *hardy perennial,* 1 0

FORGET-ME-NOT *See* Myosotis, page 83.

FOXGLOVE. *See* Digitalis, page 77.

FRAXINELLA.

418. **Fraxinella,** a sweet-scented herbaceous plant: mixed, 2 ft., *hardy perennial,* 3

FRENCH HONEYSUCKLE.

419. **French Honeysuckle,** a showy hardy perennial, with fragrant flowers; mixed, 2 ft., ... 3

LADY ALBEMARLE GODETIA.
444. *3d. per packet. See page 79.*

FUCHSIA.

Per packet. s. d.

420. **Fuchsia,** saved from the best varieties; choice mixed, *half-hardy perennial,* 1 6

GAILLARDIA.

Beautiful half-hardy perennials, with large showy flower-heads, suitable for beds and borders.

421. **Gaillardia Josephus,** yellow and scarlet, 1 ft., . . 3
422. ,, **picta,** scarlet and yellow, 1 ft., . . . 3
423. ,, ,, **Lorenziana,** mixed, 1 ft., . . . 6

GAZANIA.

424. **Gazania splendens,** a handsome and valuable bedding plant; yellow, 6 in., *half-hardy perennial,* . 1 0

GENTIANA.

425. **Gentiana acaulis** (SEE ILLUSTRATION below), prized for its large tubular flowers; dark blue, 4 in., *hardy perennial.* 6

GENTIANA ACAULIS.
425. *6d. per packet. See above.*

GERANIUM. *See* Pelargonium, page 86.

GEUM.

Per packet. s. d.

426. **Geum coccineum,** a free-blooming hardy perennial; scarlet, 1½ ft., ... 3

GILIA.

Pretty and free-flowering; suitable for patches on mixed beds or borders; *hardy annuals.*

427. **Gilia tricolor,** variegated, 1½ ft., ... 3
428. ,, ,, **alba,** white, 1½ ft., ... 3

GLOXINIA.

A magnificent strain of this exquisite stove plant; its decorative qualities render it invaluable; *tender perennial.*

429. **Gloxinia, Webbs' Excelsior, mixed** (SEE ILLUSTRATION, page 60), **6 in.,** 2 6
430. ,, ,, ,, **smaller packet,** . 1 6
431. ,, ,, ,, **extra large packet,** 5 0
432. ,, ,, ,, **drooping varieties, mixed, 6 in.,** . 2 6
433. ,, ,, ,, **larger packet,** . 5 0
434. ,, ,, ,, **erect varieties, mixed, 6 in.,** . 2 6
435. ,, ,, ,, **larger packet,** . 5 0

From W. H. LEY, Esq., Sunnyside.

"I am anxious that you should see a few flowers from the Fuchsia Seed you sent me early this year. I have 120 good bushy plants, and they are mostly very free-blooming. I am very much pleased with the result. My Zinnias, Asters, Phlox, Petunias, and Primulas have been much admired this summer."

Webbs' General List of Flower Seeds—*Continued.*

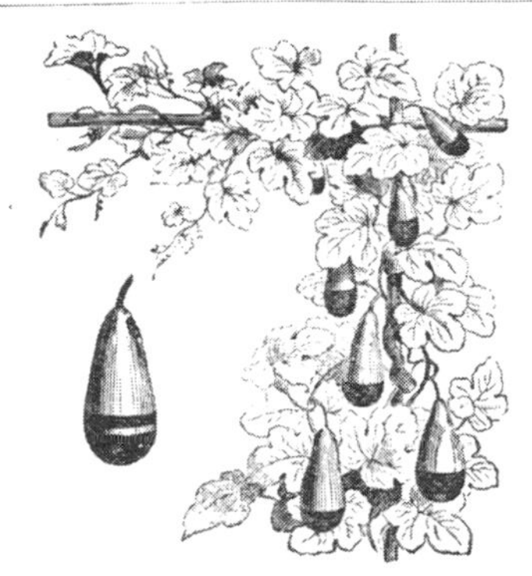

ORNAMENTAL GOURDS. 436. *6d. per packet.* *See below.*

GOURD.

Per packet. s. d.

436. **Gourd, ornamental** (See Illustrations above), a climbing or trailing plant, bearing curiously-shaped and prettily-coloured fruit; mixed, *half-hardy annual*, ... 6
437. **24 choice varieties**, separate, ... 3s. 6d.
438. **12** ,, ,, ... 2s. 0d.
439. **6** ,, ,, ... 1s. 0d.

GNAPHALIUM.

Handsome everlasting flowers, useful for bouquets, wreaths, etc.; *hardy perennials.*

440. **Gnaphalium decurrens,** white, 1½ ft., ... 6
441. ,, **fœtidum,** yellow, 1½ ft., ... 3
442. ,, **leontopodium** ("**Edelweiss**"), a charming Alpine plant; white, 6 in., ... 1 0

GODETIA.

A brilliant and profuse-flowering class of annuals, which are extremely hardy and easy of cultivation; should be grown in every garden; *hardy annuals.*

443. **Godetia, Duchess of Albany,** satiny white, 1½ ft., . 6
444. ,, **Lady Albemarle** (See Illustration, page 78), crimson, 1½ ft., ... 3
445. ,, **Lindleyana,** rosy-purple, 1½ ft., . . . 3
446. ,, **Bijou,** white and rose, 6 in., . . . 3
447. ,, **rosea alba,** rose and white, 1 ft., . . . 3
448. ,, **rubicunda,** purple, 1½ ft., . . . 3
449. ,, **The Bride,** white and crimson, 2 ft., . . 3
450. ,, **Whitneyi,** purple and crimson, 1 ft., . . 3

GOLDEN FEATHER. *See* Pyrethrum, page 89.

GRAMMANTHES.

451. **Grammanthes gentianoides,** a neat-growing plant, suitable for pots; scarlet, 6 in., *half-hardy annual*, . 6

GRASSES, ORNAMENTAL. *See* page 96.

GREVILLEA.

452. **Grevillea robusta,** an ornamental-foliaged plant of graceful habit; 10 ft., *greenhouse shrub*, . . . 6

GUNNERA.

453. **Gunnera scabra,** a half-hardy perennial, suitable for sub-tropical gardens; ornamental foliage, 3 ft., . 6

GYPSOPHYLLA.

Per packet. s. d.

Free-blooming, and very attractive plants for the edgings of beds; *hardy annuals.*

454. **Gypsophylla elegans,** white and rose, 6 in., . . . 3
455. ,, **muralis,** pink, 6 in., ... 3

HABROTHAMNUS.

456. **Habrothamnus elegans,** a strong-growing plant, continuing in bloom for a great length of time; crimson, *greenhouse climber*, ... 1 0

HELICHRYSUM.
468. *6d. per packet.* 469. *Smaller packet, 3d.*
See page 80.

HAWKWEED.

Per packet. s. d.

Showy and useful; growing freely in any soil or situation; *hardy annuals.*

457. **Hawkweed, red,** 1½ ft., ... 3
458. ,, **white,** 1½ ft., ... 3
459. ,, **yellow,** 1½ ft., ... 3

From Mr. J. LONGWORTH, Great Lever.
"The Seeds I have had from you previously have been good both in quality and quantity. I was foolish last season to try a German House and was duped. It has taught me the value of dealing with a respectable firm, where I have been well used."

From Mr. A. HIPKINS, Bloomfield Road.
"I beg to thank you for the trouble you have taken, also for the courteous and business-like manner in which you treated my little order. You certainly offer every encouragement to all who wish to cultivate a taste for flowers."

BELLIS

Perennis fl. pl. (Double Daisy.) A hardy perennial, which is indispensable for spring gardening; flowers of various colours. Height 3 inches. Per packet, 1*s*.

Perennis alba fl. pl. Pure white Double Daisy; makes a very distinct edging to a flower bed or border. Height 3 inches ... per packet, 1*s*.

BRACHYCOME

Iberidifolia. Brilliant free-flowering hardy annual, suitable for beds or borders; Cineraria-shaped blue flowers. Height 9 inches per packet, 3*d*.

BROWALLIA

Elata. Elegant half-hardy annual about 18 inches in height; foliage glossy green.
Blue ... ... per packet, 3*d*. | **White** ... ... per packet, 3*d*.

CACALIA

Coccinea. Dense heads of scarlet flowers borne on long foot-stalks. Hardy annual. Height 18 inches ... ... per packet, 3*d*.

CALANDRINIA

Grandiflora. Hardy annual, especially adapted for sunny positions; leaves thick and fleshy; flowers rose-coloured. Height 18 inches. Per packet, 3*d*.

Speciosa. Thrives in open sunny places; magenta-coloured flowers. Height 9 inches ... ... per packet, 3*d*.

Umbellata. Hardy perennial of trailing habit, producing brilliant crimson flowers. Succeeds admirably if sown among stones ... per packet, 6*d*.

CALENDULA OFFICINALIS FL. PL., ORANGE KING.
Per packet, 1s. (See below.)

CALENDULA

Officinalis fl. pl. (Double Pot Marigold.) Large orange or yellow flowers; remains in bloom until quite late in autumn. Hardy annual. Height 18 inches ... ... per packet, 3*d*.

Officinalis fl. pl., Meteor. Flowers of a beautiful lemon colour, striped with white. Hardy annual. Height 18 inches ... ... per packet, 6*d*.

Officinalis fl. pl., Orange King. A grand variety with enormous rich orange flowers, perfectly double and beautifully formed. Hardy annual. Height 1 foot. (*See illustration above*) ... ... per packet, 1*s*.

Officinalis fl. pl., Prince of Orange. Rich orange flowers slightly striped with white. Hardy annual. Height 18 inches ... per packet, 6*d*.

Pluvialis. (Cape Marigold.) White and purple flowers, somewhat resembling a Marguerite. Hardy annual. Height 18 inches ... per packet, 3*d*.

CALLIOPSIS.

See Coreopsis, page 87.

CALLIRHOE

Digitata. A hardy annual which blooms late in summer; flowers crimson. Height 2 feet ... ... per packet, 3*d*.

CAMPANULA.

All the Campanulas can be grown with the greatest ease in ordinary gardens, and the plants are exceedingly beautiful when in flower. The dwarf varieties succeed well as rock plants. Hardy perennials unless otherwise stated.

Macrostyla. Curiously veined upright purple flower, with protruding style of extraordinary length. Half-hardy annual. Height 18 inches. Per packet, 1*s*.

Turbinata. Large bright blue flowers. Height only 6 inches ,, 6*d*

Fragilis. Light blue flowers. Habit trailing and therefore valuable for suspended baskets. Half-hardy perennial ... ... per packet, 1*s*.

Pyramidalis. (The Chimney Campanula.) Flowers blue. Makes an elegant pot plant. Height 4 feet ... ... per packet, 6*d*.

Pyramidalis alba. Flowers white ... ... ,, 6*d*.

Calycanthema. A Canterbury Bell producing large blue semi-double flowers, each resembling a cup and saucer. Height 3 feet per packet, 6*d*.

Calycanthema alba. Similar to the preceding, but the flowers are white ... ... per packet, 6*d*.

Carpatica cærulea. Bell-shaped blue flowers; very free-flowering; makes a brilliant display in mixed borders. Height 1 foot per packet, 3*d*.

Carpatica alba. White flowers; otherwise resembling the preceding variety ... ... per packet, 3*d*.

Carpatica, mixed ... ... ,, 3*d*.

Attica. Blooms profusely and remains in flower for a long period; colour violet. Hardy annual. Height 6 inches ... ... per packet, 6*d*.

Attica alba. Pure white flowers, which contrast admirably with the preceding. Hardy annual. Height 6 inches ... ... per packet, 6*d*.

Loreyi. Free blooming and of a light purple colour. Hardy annual. Height 1 foot ... ... per packet, 3*d*.

CAMPION.

See Agrostemma, page 72.

CANARY CREEPER.

See Tropæolum canariense, page 100.

CANDYTUFT.

One of the most useful classes of hardy annuals. The following varieties are worthy of a place in every garden.

Sutton's Improved Tom Thumb. Produces much larger pure white flowers than the ordinary variety. Height 6 inches ... per packet, 1*s*.

Dwarf carmine. Attractive bright carmine flowers; habit dwarf and compact. Height 9 inches ... ... per packet, 6*d*.

Dwarf hybrid, mixed. Including the best large-flowering dwarf varieties ... ... per packet, 6*d*.

Dark crimson. Exceedingly showy and effective. Height of this and the following four varieties 1 foot ... ... per ounce, 1*s*.; per packet, 3*d*.

Lilac. Pale lilac or purple flowers ... ... ,, 9*d*.; ,, 3*d*.

White rocket. Large pure white rocket-shaped flowers. Per ounce, 9*d*.; ,, 3*d*.

White spiral. Long spiral spikes of white flowers ... ,, 6*d*.

Sweet-scented. Slightly scented small white flowers; foliage distinct. Per packet, 3*d*.

Mixed. A combination of the 5 preceding varieties. Per ounce, 9*d*.; per packet, 3*d*.

Collection of 6 varieties in separate colours ... ... 1*s*. 6*d*.

Sutton's Flower Seeds—Complete List for 1892 continued.

HELICHRYSUMS. (*See below.*)

HELICHRYSUM.

This hardy annual produces the well-known everlasting flower in many different colours. It is an ornament to the garden when growing, and everywhere prized for the winter decoration of vases, and for durable bouquets.

Sutton's Golden Globe. A beautiful strain, producing an abundance of large handsome globular flowers of a clear golden yellow. Valuable for winter bouquets ... ... per packet, 6*d.*

Sutton's Silver Globe. A companion to the preceding, the chaste silvery-white flowers being very double and perfect in form per packet, 6*d.*

Sutton's Fireball. Showy deep scarlet-crimson flowers ,, 6*d.*

Monstrosum, 6 varieties in separate colours. Large handsome double flowers. Height 3 feet ... ... 1*s.* 6*d.*

Monstrosum, mixed. The preceding colours in mixture, per packet, 6*d.*

Mixed. Including the finest colours ... ... ,, 3*d.*

Bracteatum. Showy bright yellow flowers. Height 3 feet ,, 3*d.*

,, **album.** Pure white flowers, much prized for decorative purposes in winter. Height 3 feet ... ... per packet, 3*d.*

Macranthum. Pretty flowers of various shades of rose ... ,, 3*d.*

Dwarf crimson. Valuable for its dwarf compact habit and deep crimson flowers. Height 2 feet ... ... per packet, 3*d.*

Dwarf yellow. Similar to the preceding, except that the flowers are a bright yellow ... ... per packet, 3*d.*

Dwarf white. Pure white flowers... ... ... ,, 3*d.*

Procumbens, double. A dwarf variety, with red flowers of various tints. Height 1 foot ... ... per packet, 6*d.*

HONESTY.

Early-flowering hardy perennial, which will grow under trees. Chiefly prized for its shining silvery seed-pods. Height about 2 feet.

Purple. Bright purple flowers ... ... per packet, 3*d.*

White. Flowers white ... ... ,, 3*d.*

HOLLYHOCK, DOUBLE.

Hardy perennial.

Hollyhocks may now be grown and flowered as annuals with great ease. Seedlings are far more robust than plants grown from cuttings, so that this stately flower may now adorn our gardens without the trouble of wintering plants. Height 6 feet.

Sutton's Prize. Saved from a magnificent collection of fine named sorts.
Ten varieties ... separate, 6*s.* | **Six varieties** ... separate, 3*s.* 6*d.*
Mixed ... ... per packet, 2*s.* 6*d.*

'The Hollyhocks from your seed are the best I ever saw.'—S. WILLSON, Esq., Peterborough.

'The Hollyhocks turned out all double and were very handsome.'—Professor LAURIE, Nairne Lodge.

Ordinary mixed ... ... per packet, 1*s.* and 6*d.*

CULTURE.—Sow in January in well-drained pots or in seed-pans filled with rich soil freely mixed with sand, and cover the seed with a slight dusting of fine earth. Place in a temperature of 65° or 70°, and in about a fortnight the plants will be an inch high, ready to be pricked off round the edges of 4½-inch pots, filled with a good porous compost. Re-pot so that the first leaves just touch the surface. At the beginning of March, transfer singly to thumb pots, and immediately the roots take hold, remove to pits or frames, where they can be exposed to genial showers, and be gradually hardened. Defer planting out until the weather is quite warm and settled.

HUMULUS

Japonicus. (Annual Hop.) Grows rapidly; valuable for covering verandahs, &c. Height 10 feet ... ... per packet, 1*s.*

HYACINTHUS

Candicans. Long spikes of graceful bell-shaped white flowers. Hardy perennial. Height 3 feet ... ... per packet, 6*d.*

Roots are offered on page 121.

IBERIS

Sempervirens. Early-blooming hardy perennial with white flowers, valuable for spring gardening or rockeries. Height 6 inches ... per packet, 6*d.*

Pruiti. Beautiful white flower. Habit dwarf and compact; an admirable free-blooming spring plant ... ... per packet, 1*s.*

ICE PLANT

Large. The foliage of this trailing half-hardy annual is covered with white icy-looking protuberances; valuable for garnishing, per packet, 6*d.* and 3*d.*

IMPATIENS SULTANI.

Tender perennial. Height 3 feet.

One of the most useful plants of recent introduction. Its brilliant rosy-scarlet flowers are produced in great profusion, and it remains in bloom for a long period. As a decorative plant for the conservatory or dinner table, it will be found invaluable ... ... per packet, 2*s.* 6*d.* and 1*s.*

A Correspondent of the GARDENERS' CHRONICLE made the following remarks concerning this flower :—'There is such a charm about the erect prominent flowers, in colour rosy-magenta, that I am sure all will like them. It is at this time of the year (September) far more decorative than are the best of double Balsams, and more easily grown.'

CULTURE.—We do not advise a start before March, and not then unless a steady heat of 60° or 65° can be relied on. Sow in well-drained pots, filled with soil composed of two parts of turfy loam and one part of leaf soil, with very little sand added. The seedlings are exceedingly brittle at the outset, and re-potting should not be attempted until they are about an inch high. Even then they need delicate handling, and after the task is accomplished they should be promptly placed in a warm frame or propagating pit for a few days. In June or July the plants should reach 48-sized pots, but they must not be transferred to the conservatory without careful hardening, or the whole of the flowers will fall.

INDIAN PINK.

See Dianthus chinensis, page 89.

INDIAN SHOT.

See Canna, page 83.

IPOMŒA.

See under Convolvulus, page 87.

JAPAN PINK.

See Dianthus Heddewigii, page 89.

MISCELLANEOUS CHOICE FLOWER SEEDS IN COLLECTIONS

No.		s.	d.
32	**Antirrhinum Majus,** in 12 brilliant varieties	2	0
	Mixed seed ... per packet, 3d.		
33	**Auricula,** in 12 splendid varieties 50 seeds each	6	0
	Mixed seed ... per packet, 6d. and 1s.		
34	**Balsam,** Rose-flowered, in 8 splendid varieties, 50 seeds each	2	6
	Mixed seed ... per packet, 6d.		
35	**Balsam,** Camellia-flowered, in 8 splendid varieties, 50 seeds each	2	6
	Mixed seed ... per packet, 1s.		
	Carnation and Picotee. These are of unrivalled excellence, and guaranteed to produce 80 per cent. of fine double flowers.		
36	An assortment of 25 var. (named), 10 seeds ea.	6	0
37	,, 12 ,, ,,	3	0
	Mixed seed per packet, 1s. and 2s. 6d.		
38	**Convolvulus Major,** in 12 beautiful colours	2	0
	Mixed seed ... per packet, 3d.		
39	**Everlasting Flowers,** in 12 varieties	2	6
40	**Grasses** (ornamental), in 12 varieties ...	2	0
41	**Gourds** (ornamental), 12 varieties ...	2	0
	Mixed seed ... per packet, 6d.		
42	**Helichrysum** (everlastings), very fine, 12 varieties	2	0
	Mixed seed ... per packet, 3d.		
43	**Hollyhocks,** Prize English, 12 splendid varieties, of each colour 20 seeds ...	4	0
	Mixed seed ... per packet, 6d. and 1s.		
44	**Larkspur,** Hyacinth-flowered, in 12 varieties	2	0
	Mixed seed ... per packet, 3d.		
45	**Marigold, African and French,** in 8 varieties	1	6
46	**Pansies,** 12 choice varieties ...	2	6
	Mixed seed ... per packet, 6d. and 1s.		
47	**Petunia,** 8 choice varieties	2	6
	Mixed seed ... per packet, 6d. and 1s.		
48	**Portulacca,** splendid double, in 6 varieties	1	6
49	,, ,, 4 ,,	1	0
	Mixed seed ... per packet, 6d.		
50	**Primula Sinensis Fimbriata,** in 6 varieties	4	6
	Mixed seed per packet, 6d., 1s., and 2s. 6d.		
51	**Pink, Chinese or Indian, Double,** 12 varieties	2	0
	Mixed seed ... per packet, 4d.		
52	**Phlox Drummondi,** in 12 splendid var.	2	6
53	,, ,, 8 ,,	2	0
	Mixed seed ... per packet, 6d,		
54	**Salpiglossis,** in 12 fine varieties ...	2	0
	Mixed seed ... per packet, 4d.		
55	**Tropæolum Lobbianum&Hybrids** in 12 splendid varieties	2	6
56	**Wallflowers,** double German, in 12 choice varieties, extra double	3	6
57	**Wallflowers,** double German, in 6 choice varieties, extra double	2	0
	Mixed seed ... per packet, 6d.		
58	**Zinnia Elegans, new double,** in 12 splendid varieties	2	6
59	**Ditto,** in 6 splendid varieties ...	1	6
	Mixed seed ... per packet, 4d.		

SEEDS OF CHOICE PLANTS FOR BEDDING OUT, SUB-TROPICAL GARDENING, &c.

	per pkt. s.	d.
Ageratum Imperial, dwarf blue ...	0	4
Ageratum Imperial, dwarf white ...	0	4
Amaranthus melancholicus ...	0	4
Amaranthus salicifolius	0	4
Aralia Japonica	0	6
Begonia Sedeni Victoria	1	0
Beet, dwarf dark-leaved	0	6
Beet Chilian, variegated foliage	0	6
Canna Indica coccinea	0	6
Canna Nepalensis	0	6
Centaurea candidissima	1	0
Centaurea Clementei	1	0
Cerastium Biebersteini	0	4
Chamœpuce diacantha	0	4
Echeveria metallica	1	0
Eucalyptus globosus	1	0
Gazania splendens	0	6
Heliotrope, choice mixed	0	4
Lantana, choice mixed	0	6
Lobelia erinus speciosa	0	6
Marigold, Orange African ...	0	3
Marigold Aurea floribunda ...	0	6
Marigold signata pumila	0	3
Mimulus cupreus	0	6
Nasturtium, King of Tom Thumbs ...	0	4
Petunia hybrida, choice mixed ...	1	0
Petunia hydrida, choice crimson ...	0	6
Phlox Drummondi grandiflora ...	1	0
Phlox Drummondi, brilliant scarlet ...	0	6
Portulacca, finest double	0	6
Pyrethrum, golden feather	0	4
Ricinus major sanguineus	0	3
Solanum hæmatocarpum	0	6
Solanum Warscewiczioides ...	0	6
Tobacco, giant	0	3
Verbena hybrida, choice mixed ...	1	0
Verbena hybrida, scarlet	0	6
Wigandia caracassana	0	6

From Mr. BLANCHARD, Down Cottage, Petworth.

"I have taken First Prize two consecutive years at our Flower Show with your Victoria Asters, and also with Improved Pæony-flowered last year."

EVERLASTING FLOWERS

FOR WINTER BOUQUETS, VASES, &c.

Rhodanthe maculata. No. 602.

Helichrysums. No. 595.

The popularity of Everlasting Flowers has been wonderfully on the increase during the past few years, and not without reason, for their culture is very easy and simple, and their flowers, if carefully gathered, dried and preserved, will retain their beauty for years. Their bright and pleasing colours will be found of great service in the decoration of the Church or the home in Winter, when other flowers are scarce. Many of the light varieties may be dyed of various brilliant colours; and made up into bouquets with some of the Ornamental Grasses, are truly charming. Everlasting flowers for preserving should be cut just as the blooms are beginning to expand, or when they are not more than half open, and tied up in bunches and hung up in a cool place to dry, with the flowers downwards. Small bunches are preferable for drying, as large bunches are apt to mould and spoil.

The Helichrysums are perhaps the most useful, and produce a great variety of brilliant and beautiful colours. Rhodanthe maculata and Rhodanthe maculata alba are two charming and elegant varieties of fine dwarf habit; these and Helichrysums are not unfrequently introduced in the trimming of ladies' bonnets. Rhodanthe manglesi fl. pl. is a fine new double-flowered variety of great merit.

No.	Name.	Hard Dur.	Ht in feet.	Colour.	Months of Flowering	Per Pkt.	Observations.
						s. d.	
589	Acroclinium roseum	hhA	2	rose	Jy to Sp	3	Free-flowering varieties, excel-
590	,, ,, album ...	,,	,,	white	,,	3	lent for light soil.
591	Amaranthus, Globe, mixed ...	tA	,,	various	Ju to Sp	3	Useful greenhouse pot plant.
592	*Ammobium alatum	hP	,,	white	My to Au	3	Winged sand-flower.
593	*Catananche bicolor	,,	,,	white & blue	Jy to Oc	3	Showy hardy perennial.
594	Gnaphalium fœtidum	hA	1½	yellow	Jy to Sp	3	Useful variety.
595	**Helichrysum, finest mixed** ...	,,	2½	various	,,	3	A handsome and valuable class,
596	,, **scarlet**	,,	,,	scarlet	,,	3	continuing in bloom from
597	,, **yellow**	,,	,,	yellow	,,	3	the end of June until killed
598	,, **purple**	,,	,,	purple	,,	3	by the frost. Indispensable
599	,, **rose**	,,	,,	rose	,,	3	as a Winter flower for bou-
600	,, **white**	,,	,,	white	,,	3	quets, &c.
601	Helipterum Sandfordi	hhA	1	yellow	,,	3	A handsome variety.
602	**Rhodanthe maculata**	,,	,,	rose & crim.	,,	4	Charmingly beautiful & elegant
603	,, ,, **alba** ...	,,	,,	white	,,	4	varieties. R. maculata alba
604	,, **manglesi fl. pl.** ...	,,	,,	rose	,,	1 6	is the most beautiful white Everlasting known.
605	Statice spicata	hA	,,	pink	,,	6	Fine new dwarf variety.
606	**Waitzia aurea grandiflora** ...	hhA	,,	various	,,	6	Fine and valuable varieties.
607	,, corymbosa	,,	,,	yellow	,,	6	
608	**Xeranthemum, golden** ...	hA	,,	golden yell.	,,	3	A pretty and useful class, will
609	,, ,, **purple** ...	,,	,,	purple	,,	3	thrive in any good garden
610	,, ,, **white** ...	,,	,,	white	,,	3	soil.

One packet of each of the above 22 varieties, post free ... ... 6s. 0d.
Twelve fine varieties, our own selection from the above, post free ... ... 2s. 6d.

June 9th, 1875. From the Rev. W. R. DAVIES, Portlock, near Minehead.
"The Helichrysums I had from you last year were the finest I ever saw."

The Flower Garden—its present position.

WE have seen within the past few years many most useful applications of the principles as well as the work of the florists to the general decoration of the English garden, much to the advantage of all interests, for a collective effect may be worthy of analysis when it is found to be as meritorious in detail as it is satisfactory in the general view. Our commonest garden flowers have partaken of the improvement, of which the most striking lessons are afforded by such flowers as the Aster, the Stock, the Phlox, and the Begonia; and we have but to look through the picture-books of thirty or forty years to become convinced that a splendid revolution has been accomplished.

What is called fashion is of some account in the history of the garden. Probably fashion is generally founded in sense, however extravagant its manifestations may be. Those who rail against summer bedding make a fanciful entity called Fashion responsible for what they deem a low-toned folly; but we may conclude, without violence to reason, that the prevalence of summer bedding indicates its usefulness as a sort of visible antidote to the gloom we are so often involved in by our very peculiar climate. In countries where open-air exercise can be taken at all seasons, there is less need than here of the brilliant though brief display that so deeply interests all classes. The contrast without and the reaction within are requisites of human nature, and the business of the garden artist is to provide these by the surest and cheapest means at his command. It is singular that those who perceive in the prevalence of bedding evidences of the decadence of art, and even of the dissolution of society, are equally alarmed and incensed at the prosperity of floriculture, the objects of which are so widely divergent from those of the promoters of bedding. The florists may derive some amusement from the eccentric criticisms to which they are subjected, but they cannot be much moved thereby to change their course. Their object is not to realise large ideas in chromatic planting, but to develope the perfections of flowers in detail. In the broad view of things, it is easy to perceive where and how these apparent opposites are brought into juxtaposition, so that the florist labouring for refined particulars readily plays into the hands of the man who looks only for a general and collective effect. The truth of the whole case is to be found in the many-sidedness of human nature. As there are diversities of gifts, so there must be differences of tastes, and Nature is generous in providing materials for all.

It is not the less interesting to note that while the florists are concentrating their attention on certain subjects—as, for example, the Auricula, the Carnation, the Pelargonium, and the Gladiolus—they are abandoning some of their old favourites, or at all events altering their ways in accordance with their altered views in respect of them. It is not long since immense pains were taken to perpetuate named varieties of Primulas, Cinerarias, Antirrhinums, Gloxinias, Pansies, Lobelias, Verbenas, and other subjects that gave trouble out of proportion to results. To be sure, these and kindred subjects are still grown to name and prized for quality, as we hope and believe they ever will be, for the standards of quality must be maintained and advanced. But for the general work of the world a better method has been developed, and the need for an abundance of beautiful flowers is, in respect of many of the subjects, readily met by the simple process of growing them from seeds instead of the laborious and precarious mode of perpetuation by cuttings. In no one department of our trade has there been accomplished a more remarkable advance, or one tending more directly to the public advantage, than in the improvement of the strains and races and stocks of the seeds of florists' flowers. For all the ordinary and for the highest of the ordinary purposes of the horticulturist, the raising of these plants from seed is sufficient, provided always that the seed is produced and saved with the aid of all the knowledge that science has brought to bear upon the business. Why should the man who has to decorate a conservatory and a set of flower-beds be subjected to the worry of working up a stock of soft-textured plants from offsets and cuttings, when the sowing of a pinch of seed will ensure to him all he can desire at a tenth part of the trouble and with a greater degree of certainty? Why go far away round the country to reach a place to which there is a short cut by a comfortable new road? Why encumber pits and frames and houses with stores of troublesome plants that might be thrown away with advantage, leaving the glass at liberty to produce winter Cucumbers, and Kidney Beans, and Mushrooms, or to shelter the nobler forms of permanent vegetation and encourage plant beauty of the highest interest? The growth of florists' and decorative flowers from seed is a gain every way to the community, for the process liberates glass and garden room, and labour, and time, and money for better work than the perpetuation of named varieties, the beauty of which can, for all practical purposes, be equalled by stock raised from seed. The recognition of these truths explains the more important of the recent expansions of the seed trade; but the return to old methods will soon be made whenever it shall be found that the seed stocks have degenerated. To prevent this, and indeed to accomplish further advances, is in the power of the seed producers, and having succeeded thus far in proving the possibility of providing seed which will produce Begonias, Calceolarias, Primulas, Cinerarias, Cyclamens, and Gloxinias, equal to any named varieties, we see before us an unlimited opportunity, through careful crossing and selection, for still further advances.

As the true florist is the best friend of the floral decorator, so he is the real right-hand man of the producer of flower-seeds of high quality. It is to him we must look for maintaining in all their integrity the true canons of floral perfection, and to these canons our stocks and strains must conform less or more, and the more the better; and beyond this the florists are our friends. By their severe rules of criticism they assist us subjectively, and by the actual results of their agreeable labours they bring objective aid, their finest flowers serving not only as our types but as the actual stud to breed from. Thus the decline of floriculture implies the deterioration of flowers, and, on the other hand, the prosperity of floriculture is concurrently reflected in the improved and improving quality of flowers of all kinds, including such as the florists have never taken any special notice of. They constitute the school in which the public taste is formed, and they provide the ideas and the materials which aid in the gratification and advancement of the taste which finds in flowers an intellectual as well as a sensuous exercise. Let us not, therefore, be unmindful of the importance of the study of technical details and hereditary characters and the requirements of the artistic instinct in the flower garden, but reverently bear in mind that the least things in nature display the goodness no less than the wisdom and power of the Eternal Mind whence all things have proceeded; while the greatest object that can attract our attention is but an aggregation of atoms, every one of which is in its proper place as a contributory to the compactness of the whole. The study of a flower may help us to a knowledge of the world, and we may see cause to thank the florist who has detected beauties before unknown to us, and who has proved his capability of perpetuating those beauties by means within the embrace of all.

WEBBS'
SPRING
CATALOGUE
FOR
1888
WEBB & SONS, WORDSLEY, STOURBRIDGE.

WEBB & SONS, THE QUEEN'S SEEDSMEN, WORDSLEY, STOURBRIDGE; & LONDON.
WEBBS' PERFECTION CYCLAMEN.
Red, 2s. 6d. and 5s. per packet; White, 2s. 6d. and 5s. per packet; Mixed colours, 1s. 6d., 2s. 6d., and 5s. per packet.

In horto Webb ad nat del
G. Severeyns, Chromolith. London and Brussels
Webbs' New Dwarf Mignonette, 1s. per packet. Webbs' New Giant Mignonette, 1s. per packet.
Webbs' New Myosotis - "Blue King", 1s. per packet. Webbs' New Prize Hollyhock, 6d. and 1s. per packet.
Webbs' New Double Wallflower, 1s. per packet. Webbs' New Champion Dianthus, 1s. per packet.

Issued with "Sutton's Amateur's Guide in Horticulture."

CONVOLVULUS MINOR, NEW CRIMSON VIOLET.

SUTTON'S
NEW AND CHOICE
RADISHES.
ISSUED WITH
SUTTON'S
AMATEUR'S GUIDE.
THE
SUTTON
RADISH.
SUTTON'S
FERN-LEAVED
RADISH.
SUTTON'S
LONG WHITE
RADISH.
SUTTON'S
WHITE OLIVE
RADISH.
SUTTON'S
CRIMSON OLIVE
RADISH.
SUTTON'S GEM WHITE-TIPPED RADISH.
SUTTON'S EARLIEST OF ALL RADISH
SUTTON'S SCARLET GLOBE RADISH.

THE SUTTON GLOBE ONION.
SEE SUTTON'S AMATEUR'S GUIDE IN HORTICULTURE.
ALF COOKE LEEDS

WEBBS' TUBEROUS-ROOTED BEGONIA, 1s. 6d. AND 2s. 6d. PER PACKET.
In horto. Webb. ad. nat. del.
G. Severeyns. Chromolith. Brussels
WEBB & SONS, THE QUEEN'S SEEDSMEN, WORDSLEY, STOURBRIDGE.

GROUP OF GLADIOLI.
1, Horace Vernet. 2, Shakespeare. 3, Le Vesuve. 4, Pactole.

SUTTON'S
AMATEUR'S GUIDE
1881
IN HORTICULTURE
SUTTON & SONS, the Queen's Seedsmen, READIN

A SUGGESTION FOR A WINTER GARDEN IN "TREILLAGE"

BOULTON & PAUL, Ltd., Manufacturers, NORWICH.

WINTER GARDENS

WINTER GARDEN SURROUNDED BY A PERGOLA

Designs to suit any style of Architecture

BOULTON & PAUL, Ltd., Manufacturers, NORWICH.

WINTER GARDENS

Our own Architect will call on intending purchasers to give advice and will be pleased to prepare schemes to meet all requirements

WEBBS' PRIZE SELECTED SEED CORN.
DIEU ET MON DROIT
AWARDED THE GOLD MEDAL OF FRANCE 1882 FOR CEREALS'
WEBBS' "CHALLENG
WHITE WHEA
WEBBS' SELECTED
OUGHCHAFF WHEA
G. Severeyns. Chromolith. Brussels

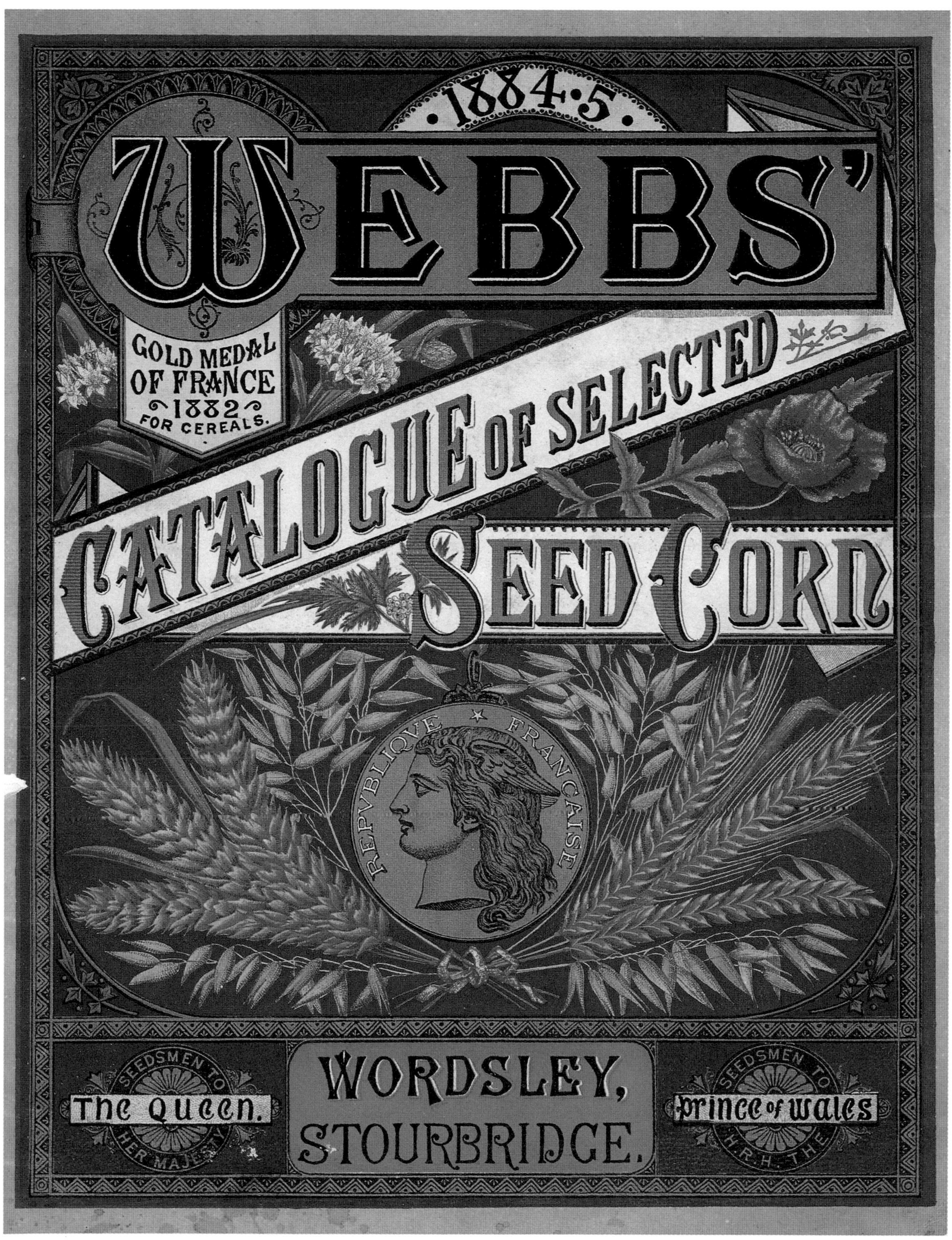
1884·5
WEBBS'
GOLD MEDAL OF FRANCE 1882 FOR CEREALS.
CATALOGUE OF SELECTED
SEED CORN
REPVBLIQVE ★ FRANCAISE
SEEDSMEN TO HER MAJESTY
The Queen.
WORDSLEY,
STOURBRIDGE.
SEEDSMEN TO H.R.H. THE
Prince of Wales

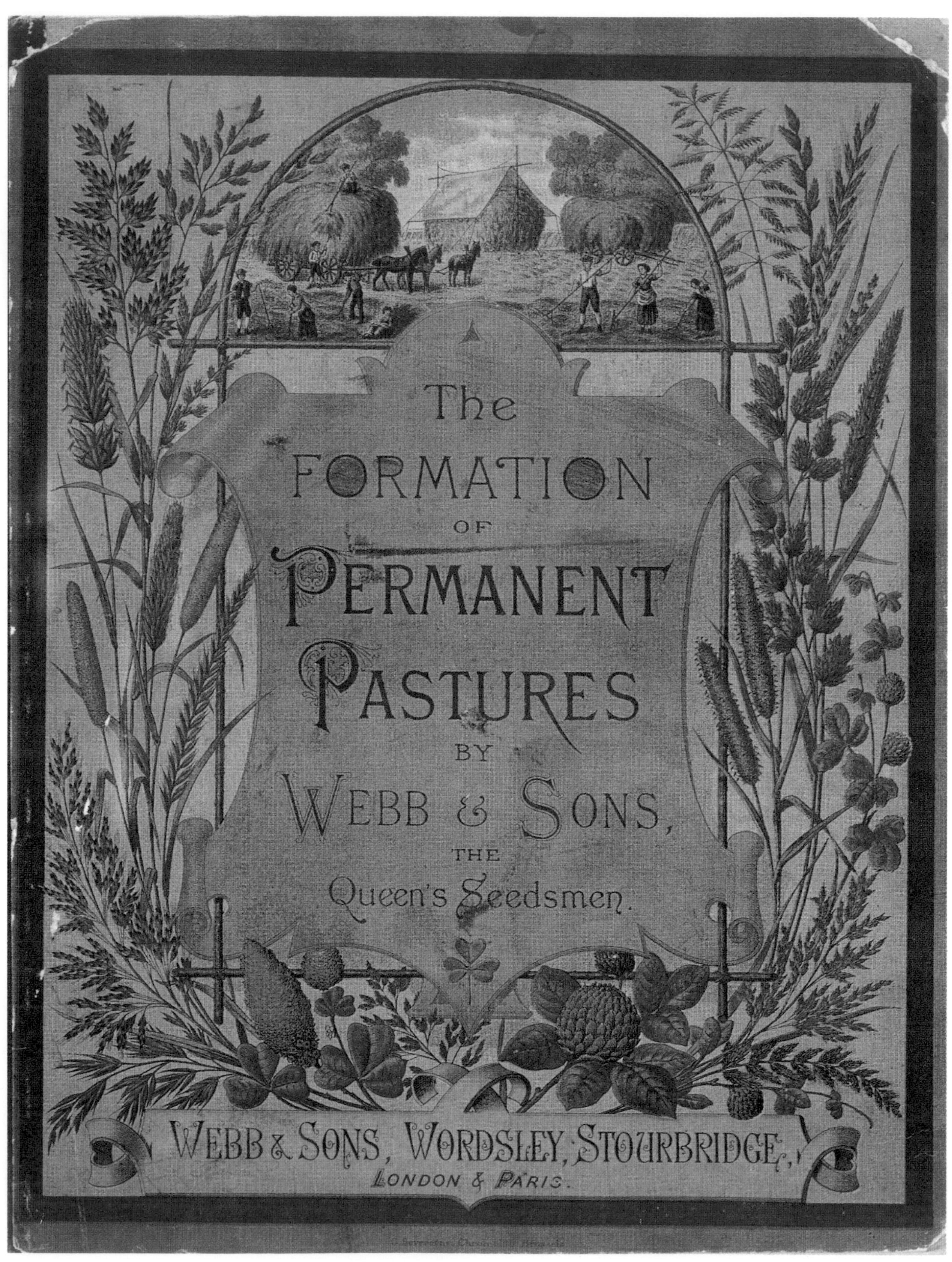
The
FORMATION
OF
PERMANENT
PASTURES
BY
WEBB & SONS,
THE
Queen's Seedsmen.
WEBB & SONS, WORDSLEY, STOURBRIDGE,
LONDON & PARIS.

All Flower Seeds are sent free by Post or Rail.

FLOWER SEEDS.

Important Novelties for 1881.

Primula, 'Sutton's Reading Pink.' This charming novelty will, without doubt, become a great favourite. In habit the plant somewhat resembles 'Sutton's Ruby King,' but the flowers are of a rich salmon-pink colour. The yellow eye is clearly defined, and is surrounded with a narrow band of carmine. The entire stock of this beautiful Primula is in our hands, and has not before been offered to the public .. .. per packet, 5*s*.

Primula, Fern-leaved, 'Sutton's Rosy Queen.' This splendid novelty is now offered for the first time. It is a great improvement on other Fern-leaved Primulas, as its leaves are shorter and the habit more compact. The colour of the flowers is a delicate salmon rose ... ... per packet, 5*s*.

White Primula, 'Sutton's Pearl.' This beautiful variety was introduced by us last year. It has been selected from a great number of seedlings raised by ourselves. The flowers are larger than those of our Superb White Primula, and even more beautifully fringed ; and the habit of the plant is the most perfect of any white Primula yet introduced ... ... per packet, 5*s*.

Primula, Sutton's Double Lilac. This is a new colour in Double Primulas, and we now offer it for the first time. It will be found valuable, as forming a pleasing contrast to the other double varieties ... ... per packet, 5*s*.

Tuberous Begonia, 'Sutton's Reading Beauty.' A most beautiful and entirely new variety. The flowers are very large and of a fine creamy lemon colour, passing into white as they become developed. The leaves are exquisitely marked, like those of B. Pearcei—dark marbled green above, with crimson markings on the lower surface. 'Sutton's Reading Beauty' is quite distinct from all others, and from the colour and size of blooms must become a great favourite. The habit is dwarf and compact, very free-flowering, and continues in bloom all the summer ... ... per packet, 5*s*. and 2*s*. 6*d*.

Ageratum, 'Little Dorrit.' A beautiful dwarf variety not exceeding 6 inches in height. It possesses a robust constitution, and is very free-blooming, the plants being literally covered with bright lavender-blue flowers during the whole summer and autumn. Valuable for ribbon borders or bedding purposes per pkt., 1*s*. 6*d*.

Begonia robusta perfecta rosea. A splendid variety, of robust habit, and with succulent dark green foliage. The flowers are large in size, and of a fine delicate rose colour. Their firm texture renders them less liable to drop off than many other varieties ... ... per packet, 5*s*.

Begonia Schmidti (Fibrous-rooted). An excellent autumn and winter flowering variety, with small pink flowers, which are produced in abundance, and are very valuable for cutting ... ... per packet, 2*s*. 6*d*.

Lobelia, Sutton's 'Best of All.' This variety, which we now offer for the first time, will be found invaluable for bedding purposes. It is compact in habit, with dark green foliage, and is covered during the entire summer with flowers of the most intense ultramarine blue ... ... per packet, 2*s*. 6*d*.

Marigolds, Sutton's Selected Striped French. These have been carefully selected by us from the most beautifully striped flowers in our seed-grounds, and may be depended on for producing a variety of finely striped flowers of perfect form and large size.

Tall Striped ... ... per packet 1*s*. 0*d*.
Dwarf ... ... ,, 1*s*. 6*d*.

Mignonette, Golden Queen. An attractive and distinct variety, of dense pyramidal habit. It throws up very numerous flower-stalks terminated by spikes of golden yellow blossoms, with which the bright green foliage of the plant forms a pleasing contrast ... ... per packet, 2*s*. 6*d*.

Myosotis alpestris nana. The three varieties of dwarf Myosotis here offered are valuable additions to the favourite class of Forget-me-nots, being compact in habit, and very free-flowering.

Alba ... ... per packet 1*s*. 0*d*.
Cærulea ... ... ,, 1*s*. 0*d*.
Rosea ... ... ,, 1*s*. 6*d*.

Petunia grandiflora robusta fl. pl. This is the most robust race of Petunias yet introduced. The plants are of very compact and symmetrical growth, about 1 foot in height and 15 inches in diameter, with large double flowers of the finest shades of colour. It is so robust in habit as to render any support from sticks needless, and is thus especially valuable for bedding or pot culture ... ... per packet, 2*s*. 6*d*.

Phlox Drummondii nana compacta, 'Sunrise.' A valuable acquisition to this beautiful race of Phloxes. It is of the same dwarf habit as the older varieties. The deep salmon-red flowers are very striking and attractive. Per packet, 2*s*. 6*d*.

Phlox Drummondii nana compacta cinnabarina. This is a charming companion to the above, differing from it only in the colour of its flowers, which are of a brilliant cinnabar red ... ... per packet, 2*s*. 6*d*.

Primula fimbriata alba magnifica. A new White Primula of exquisite form and substance, and a great improvement on the old varieties. The plants are of compact habit, and freely produce fine trusses of pure white flowers, with a large yellow eye, each petal being deeply and beautifully fringed ... ... per packet, 5*s*.

Pyrethrum aureum selaginoides. An entirely new and distinct form of Pyrethrum, of very compact habit, with flat foliage resembling two fronds of Selaginella overlaying each other. Its great recommendation, however, is the fact that it does not flower the first year, thereby saving the time and attention in pinching back &c. required by the old variety. Per packet, 1*s*. 6*d*.

Scabious, Dwarf Golden. This novelty forms a compact globular bush of about one foot high ; is richly branched, and the foliage is of a beautiful golden yellow, equal in brightness and effect to 'Golden Feather.' It surpasses the latter, however, in the brilliancy of its numerous dark and blackish purple and red flowers, which form a pleasing contrast in itself. Suitable for bedding out with other ornamental foliaged plants per packet, 1*s*.

Senecio speciosus. A very free-flowering half-hardy perennial, introduced from South Africa. The flowers are a bright magenta colour, about an inch and a half in diameter. In the open ground it blooms during the *entire* summer and autumn, or in a cool greenhouse it continues to flower throughout the *entire* year ... ... per packet, 2*s*. 6*d*.

'The Flower Seeds had from you far exceeded my most sanguine expectations.'—Mr. Thos. M. Edwards, *Gravesend.*

47

SUTTON'S NOVELTIES in FLOWERS—LIST for 1892.

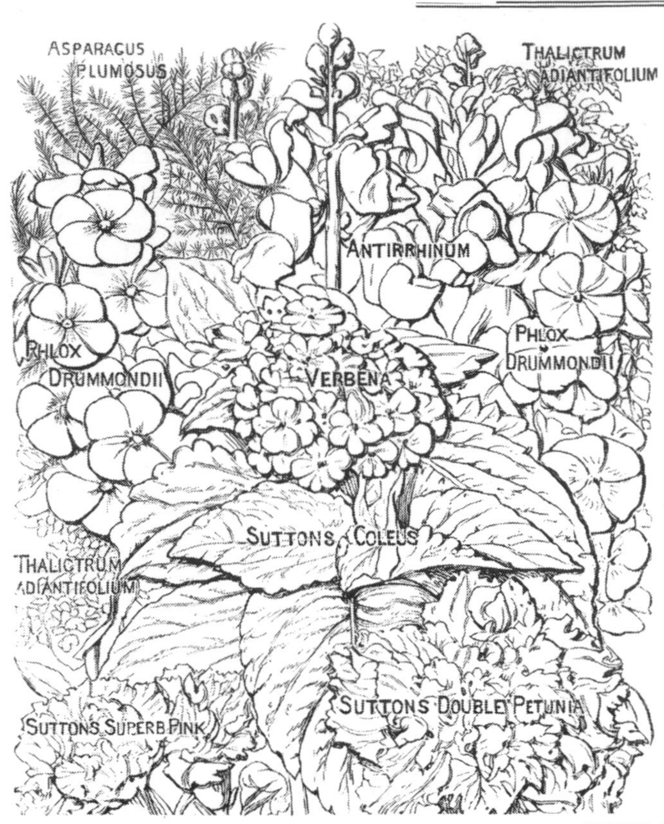

KEY TO COLOURED ILLUSTRATION *facing this page.* COPYRIGHT S. & S.

Asparagus plumosus. We feel a special pleasure in being able to offer seed of this conspicuously beautiful plant. Either in the conservatory or on the table it invariably commands attention, and its finely cut feathery foliage is unrivalled for bouquets. (*See illustration on coloured plate facing this page, to which a key is given above*) ... per packet of 12 seeds, 2*s.* 6*d.*

Aster, The Bride. An exceedingly beautiful Aster. The pure white flowers are as faultless in shape as a Pompone Dahlia. Valuable for pot culture, the plants being compact in habit, producing deep, almost globular flowers composed of short reflexed petals, in great profusion ... per packet, 2*s.* 6*d.*

Aubrietia Leichtlinii is a new and charming variety, the cushion-like plants being covered with beautiful large rosy carmine flowers. Invaluable for spring bedding, edgings, and rock-work ... ... per packet, 1*s.* 6*d.*

Begonia, Sutton's Reading Gem. A most interesting break in Tuberous Begonias. The flowers have glistening white centres which gradually merge into delicate rose-pink, deepening into rich carmine at the edges of the four petals. They are well formed, have plenty of substance, and are very freely produced. Beautiful as all the finest strains of Begonia undoubtedly are, the exceptional loveliness of this variety will ensure for it admission into every high-class collection, and it will be indispensable for the exhibition stage... per packet, 5*s.*

Begonia, Sutton's Prince of Orange. Quite a new shade of colour in this beautiful class of flowers. The plants are perfect in habit and produce a profusion of large well-formed blossoms of a glowing orange scarlet which appear to be almost luminous... ... ... per packet, 5*s.*

Begonia semperflorens, Sutton's Duchess of Edinburgh. An exceedingly beautiful and profuse flowering Fibrous-rooted Begonia, obtained from a cross made in our own seed houses. The plant is robust and well-proportioned in habit, and it has proved to be almost a continuous bloomer. Flowers white suffused with pink, and twice the size of the ordinary Begonia semperflorens. An admirable companion to the Reading Snowflake sent out by us a few years ago.
Per packet, 2*s.* 6*d.*

Begonia semperflorens atropurpurea. A magnificent Fibrous-rooted variety with brilliant red flowers, which are strikingly relieved by the bright yellow stamens of the male blossoms. The foliage is of a fine glossy green colour, broadly margined with bronze and purple ... ... per packet, 2*s.* 6*d.*

Centaurea Cyanus nana compacta Victoria. A dwarf variety of the popular Blue Cornflower, neat and compact in habit, carrying a profusion of beautiful azure-blue flowers. Admirably adapted for pot culture, and for borders
Per packet, 1*s.* 6*d.*

Chrysanthemum, Annual, Double mixed. Seed of double forms of this useful annual, producing a diversity of colours, including many new shades of bronzy yellow, edged and pencilled with crimson, lilac, rose, &c. Other flowers are pure white, yellow and crimson selfs, all equally charming, either in the border or as cut flowers ... ... per packet, 1*s.* 6*d.*

Helichrysum, Sutton's Golden Globe. A beautiful strain producing an abundance of large, handsome globular flowers of a clear golden yellow. Valuable for winter bouquets.
Per packet, 6*d.*

Helichrysum, Sutton's Silver Globe. A companion to the preceding, the chaste silvery-white flowers being very double and perfect in form ... ... per packet, 6*d.*

Lavatera rosea splendens. Handsome variety of Lavatera, the plants being profusely covered with beautiful large flowers of a rich deep pink. Very desirable for borders or for cutting ... ... per packet, 1*s.*

Pansy, Meteor. A novel and attractive Pansy, the flowers being of a bright reddish brown or mahogany colour. Most effective for groups or bedding... ... per packet, 2*s.* 6*d.*

Pansy, Victoria. A very effective variety with rich velvet-like petals of a bright claret colour. Flowers good in shape and substance with a well-defined eye ... per packet, 2*s.* 6*d.*

Silene, Sutton's Golden Bedder. Very ornamental dwarf compact variety; leaves of a golden yellow colour; flowers delicate rose. Well suited for carpet or spring bedding.
Per packet, 1*s.* 6*d.*

Sweet Pea, Apple-blossom. A superb variety with bright rose standards and blush wings, flowers very large, borne three or four on a stem, and remain in perfection for a long period.
Per packet, 1*s.* 6*d.*

Thalictrum adiantifolium (Hardy Maidenhair). Singularly graceful plant with elegant foliage resembling that of the Maidenhair Fern. Admirable for bouquets, as the leaves retain their form for a long time when cut. (*See illustration on coloured plate facing this page, to which a key is given above.*)
Per packet, 1*s.* 6*d.*

Wallflower, Single, Sutton's Flower of Spring. A magnificent strain of Single German Wallflower, the result of many years' selection. The plants are dwarf and compact, but throw up immense heads of very large sweetly scented flowers, including a number of distinct and effective colours.
Per packet, 1*s.* 6*d.*

The above Novelties are, in our Order List, offered under their own classes.

SUTTON & SONS, Seedsmen by Royal Warrant to Her Majesty the Queen.

69

BULBOUS and other FLOWER ROOTS.

For full instructions on the Culture of Bulbous Flowers, see Sutton's Book on Gardening. Particulars on pages 127 and 128.

AMARYLLIS (*drawn to a reduced scale*). COPYRIGHT S. & S.

AMARYLLIS.

The following are beautiful varieties for the conservatory or drawing-room, where their large and brilliant flowers are very effective.

Formosissima (Jacobea Lily), crimson ...	each, 6*d.*
Johnsonii, scarlet and white ...	each, 4*s.* 0*d.*
Longiflora alba, fine white, hardy ...	,, 1*s.* 0*d.*
Prince of Orange, large orange ...	,, 3*s.* 6*d.*
Vittata, white, striped with purple ...	,, 3*s.* 6*d.*
,, **seedlings,** various shades ...	,, 2*s.* 0*d.*

ACHIMENES.

Sutton's Rosy Queen. First-class Certificate awarded April 1890. Strong, robust growth, flowers of great substance and large size, freely produced; colour beautiful soft rose, with white throat. This variety, raised by ourselves, will prove a valuable acquisition to this class of decorative plants... ... ... strong bulbs, each, 1*s.* 6*d.*; per dozen, 15*s.*

'An extremely distinct and handsome variety, with large flowers, the corolla broad, bright clear rose, white in the throat.'—JOURNAL OF HORTICULTURE.

OLDER VARIETIES.

Admiration, reddish purple.
Alba maxima, large pure white.
Ambroise Verschaffelt, white, dark starry centre.
Celestial, pale mauve.
Cherita, deep blue.
Coccinea, scarlet.
Harry Williams, rosy magenta.
Lady Lyttleton, orange scarlet.
Longiflora major, large blue.
Margaretta, pure white.
Masterpiece, rosy purple, white throat.
Rosea magnifica, rose.
Scarlet Perfection, scarlet.
Sir Treherne Thomas, purple.
Splendens, scarlet.

The above varieties, by name, per doz. 7*s.* 6*d.*; in mixture, per doz. 4*s.*

BEGONIAS.

TUBEROUS-ROOTED.

DOUBLE VARIETIES.

Our selected Double strain is of good dwarf habit, producing an abundance of large perfectly double flowers. We offer strong flowering bulbs as under :—

Pure white and cream ...	each, 5*s.*;	per dozen, 55*s.*
Rose ...	,, 5*s.*;	,, 55*s.*
Salmon ...	,, 5*s.*;	,, 55*s.*
Scarlet ...	,, 5*s.*;	,, 55*s.*
Mixed ...	,, 4*s.*;	,, 42*s.*

SINGLE VARIETIES.

Sutton's Reading Beauty Strain.

We continue to improve this valuable strain, and the bulbs offered below produced a remarkably fine display of bloom in our greenhouses during the past summer. The plants are dwarf and sturdy in habit, and the flowers have been larger and of greater substance than in any previous year. We can supply the following distinct colours :—

Crimson ...	each, 1*s.* 6*d.*;	per dozen, 15*s.*
Scarlet ...	,, 1*s.* 6*d.*;	,, 15*s.*
Pure white ...	,, 2*s.* 6*d.*;	,, 25*s.*
Creamy white ...	,, 1*s.* 6*d.*;	,, 15*s.*
Rose and carmine ...	,, 1*s.* 6*d.*;	,, 15*s.*
Blush ...	,, 1*s.* 6*d.*;	,, 15*s.*
Citron and primrose ...	,, 1*s.* 6*d.*;	,, 15*s.*

In addition to the above we still offer

Sutton's Prize Begonias in various colours.

These are now so well known that little need be said about them. It may be sufficient to mention that many of the shades of colour above enumerated are included in this mixture. For general decorative purposes no better Begonias can be obtained ... ... each, 1*s.*; per dozen, 10*s.* 6*d.*

Bedding Begonias.

Specially selected for dwarf habit and showy flowers, per doz. 7*s.* 6*d.*; 100, 50*s.*

FIBROUS-ROOTED AND SHRUBBY BEGONIAS.

Sutton's Reading Snowflake. Beautiful pure white flowers, at least twice the size of Semperflorens, from which it is a seedling. This Begonia continues in bloom throughout the year, and is very useful for producing flowers for cutting during the winter each, 1*s.* 6*d.*; per dozen, 15*s.*

Semperflorens rosea. Similar to Reading Snowflake, except that the flowers are of a delicate rose colour and smaller each, 1*s.* 6*d.*; per dozen, 15*s.*

Sutton's Bedding Begonia, Princess Beatrice. A most useful variety for summer bedding in the open ground, where it flowers profusely, and the same plants if potted in the autumn will bloom through the winter under glass ... ... each, 1*s.*; per dozen, 10*s.* 6*d.*

Sutton's Bedding Begonia, After-glow. Awarded a First-class Certificate at Bath Horticultural Show. This is of similar habit to the preceding, but the flowers, which are more drooping, are produced at every point; the outside of the petals is a glowing crimson, the inside a pale blush. A small bed in our Trial Grounds attracted the attention of all visitors. Each, 1*s.* 6*d.*; per dozen, 15*s.*

'**The Begonia recently introduced by Messrs. Sutton & Sons, under** the designation of "After-glow," is a most excellent companion to that popular bedding variety Princess Beatrice, distributed about four years since. The variety has a dense bushy habit, and attains a height ranging from nine to fourteen inches, according to the character of the soil and other conditions. It is remarkably free in blooming, the flowers being produced at every point. They are more pendulous than are those of Princess Beatrice, and the petals are glowing crimson outside and of a pale blush colour inside. After-glow was employed here during the past season for filling match beds to Princess Beatrice, and was greatly admired.—THOMAS WEAVER, *Oakley Hall Gardens.*'—GARDENERS' MAGAZINE.

SUTTON & SONS, Seed Growers and Merchants, READING, ENGLAND.

Webbs' General List of Flower Seeds—*Continued.*

PEA, SWEET.

Per packet. s. d.

Well-known climbers, exceedingly fragrant; adapted for screens or trellis-work, and very useful to cut from; *hardy annuals.*

No.	Variety	s.	d.
669.	**Pea, Sweet, Butterfly,** blue and white,		6
670.	,, ,, **Crown Princess of Prussia,** lilac,		6
671.	,, ,, **Fairy Queen,** rose,		6
672.	,, ,, **Imperial purple,**		3
673.	,, ,, **lilacina splendens,** purple,		3
674.	,, ,, **Painted Lady,** rose and white,		3

PELARGONIUM.

Per packet. s. d.

Beautiful large-flowering and fancy varieties; *greenhouse shrubs.*

No.	Variety	s.	d.
681.	**Pelargonium, Webbs' Fancy,** mixed, $1\frac{1}{2}$ ft.,	2	6
682.	,, ,, ,, **smaller packet,**	1	6
683.	,, ,, **Large-flowering,** mixed, 2 ft.,	2	6
684.	,, ,, ,, **smaller packet,**	1	6
685.	,, **zonale,** saved from choice named varieties; finest mixed, 1 ft., *half-hardy perennial,*	1	0

PETUNIA.

These admirable bedding plants contrast effectively with Scarlet Geraniums, Calceolarias, and Verbenas; and as pot-plants they are very effective for greenhouse and conservatory decoration; *half-hardy perennials.*

No.	Variety	s.	d.
686.	**Petunia, Webbs' Brilliant** (SEE ILLUSTRATION), mixed, $1\frac{1}{2}$ ft.,	2	6
687.	**Smaller packet,**	1	6
688.	**Petunia, Webbs' Choice Fringed,** mixed, $1\frac{1}{2}$ ft.,	2	6
689.	**Smaller packet,**	1	6
690.	**Petunia, Webbs' Miniature, double,** mixed, 8 in.,	2	6
691.	**Petunia, Webbs' Miniature, single,** mixed, 8 in.,	1	6
692.	**Petunia, Webbs' Prize Double** (SEE ILLUSTRATION, page 95), mixed, $1\frac{1}{2}$ ft.,	2	6
693.	**Petunia, Countess of Ellesmere,** rose, 2 ft.,		6
694.	**Petunia, nyctaginiflora,** white, 2 ft.,		6
695.	**Petunia, purpurea,** purple, 2 ft.,		6
696.	**Petunia, yellow-throated,** mixed, 2 ft.,	1	6
697.	**Petunia, single,** finest mixed, 2 ft.,		6
698.	**12 choice varieties,** separate, **3s. 0d.**		
699.	**6 choice varieties,** separate, **1s. 6d.**		
700.	**Petunia, double,** finest mixed, 2 ft.,	1	6
701.	**12 choice varieties,** separate, **3s. 6d.**		
702.	**6 choice varieties,** separate, **2s. 0d.**		

WEBBS' BRILLIANT PETUNIA.

686. 2*s.* 6*d. per packet.* 687. *Smaller packet,* 1*s.* 6*d.* *See above, and page* 64.

PEA, SWEET—*Continued.*

No.	Variety	s.	d.
675.	**Pea, Sweet, Princess Beatrice,** carmine-rose,		6
676.	,, ,, **Scarlet Invincible,**		3
677.	,, ,, **scarlet-striped,**		3
678.	,, ,, **white,**		3
679.	,, ,, **mixed,**		3
680.	,, ,, **10 distinct varieties,** separate, 2s. 6d.		

PEA, EVERLASTING. *See* **Lathyrus,** page 81.

PASSIFLORA ("Passion Flower").

Elegant climbers for either outdoor or greenhouse cultivation, producing showy flowers in profusion; *hardy perennials.*

No.	Variety	s.	d.
703.	**Passiflora alba,** white,		6
704.	,, **cærulea,** blue,		6

PENTSTEMON.

No.	Variety	s.	d.
705.	**Pentstemon,** a showy herbaceous plant; finest mixed, 2 ft., *hardy perennial,*		6

From W. REYNOLDS, Esq., Odsey Lodge.
"Your Brilliant Petunia is truly named; it was admired by all who saw it."

From Mr. JOHN CLARK, Gardener to the Most Noble the Marquis of Ripon.
"I have some very fine varieties out of Webbs' (Prize Double) Petunia Seed."

WEBBS' SUPERB STRAINS OF FLORISTS' AND OTHER FLOWER SEEDS—*Continued.*

Webbs' New Golden Cloud Chrysanthemum.

289. **1s. per packet.** (SEE ILLUSTRATION ANNEXED.)

An exceedingly handsome strain of the annual Chrysanthemum, valuable for any purpose where cut flowers are in demand, or for bed and border decoration. It produces its large and bright golden-coloured flowers freely under ordinary cultivation.

From Mr. HENRY JIPSON, Vicarage Cottage.
"The Golden Cloud Chrysanthemum Seed supplied by you came up in great abundance, and the flowers have been considered very fine and lasting."

From Mr. W. W. MAIN, Marwood.
"The Seeds I had of you last year answered admirably."

Webbs' New Challenge Antirrhinum.

90. **1s. per packet.** (SEE ILLUSTRATION, page 68.)

Few flowers are more easily grown, and fewer still deserve to be more extensively cultivated than the Snapdragon. The brilliancy of colour and free-flowering qualities of this splendid strain should ensure it a position in every herbaceous border.

From Mr. J. T. IRELAND, Worsley.
"Webbs' New Challenge Antirrhinum was greatly admired. I have seen some very good ones, but I can truly say this is the best."

From Mr. R. BURTON, Radcliffe Bridge.
"The Antirrhinum Seed, you supplied me with last spring, produced a most beautiful show all through the summer, and were admired by all who saw them; without doubt they were the best I ever grew."

From Mr. W. PLANT, Boothen.
"The Antirrhinums, raised from your Seed, are the finest that I have ever grown; and I have grown Antirrhinums for many years."

Webbs' New Spotted Digitalis.

384. **6d. per packet.**

A very ornamental and handsome variety of Foxglove, having large spikes of pure white flowers, which are beautifully spotted with purple. It is specially adapted for back lines in the hardy herbaceous border, and for shrubberies.

WEBBS' NEW GOLDEN CLOUD CHRYSANTHEMUM.

Webbs' Brilliant Petunia.

686. **2s. 6d. per packet.** 687. **Smaller packet, 1s. 6d.**

(SEE ILLUSTRATION, page 86.)

The flowers produced from this remarkably fine strain are of very brilliant colours, large size, and beautiful shape. We have received the most flattering accounts of the excellence of this Petunia, which, for bedding purposes, is unequalled.

From Mr. A. HOSSACK, Gardener to the Most Noble the Marquis of Hertford.
"Webbs' Brilliant Petunia contains some of the brightest forms of Petunias I ever grew."

From T. L. SEATON, Esq., Cross House.
"Webbs' Brilliant Petunia Seed sent to my brother in Hull has produced the greatest variety of colours that I have ever seen."

From Mr. S. MORTON, Owston.
"Your Brilliant Petunia is really beautiful."

From Mr. J. McKINLAY, Gardener to the Right Hon. Lord Foley.
"Your Brilliant Petunia has been admired by every one that has seen it."

Webbs' Choice Carnation.

256. **2s. 6d. per packet.** 257. **Smaller packet, 1s. 6d.**

(SEE ILLUSTRATION, page 73.)

Webbs' Choice Picotee.

711. **2s. 6d. per packet.** 712. **Smaller packet, 1s. 6d.**

Carnations and Picotees are invaluable in all gardens for simplicity of culture and delicious perfume. Our strains are remarkable for dwarf and compact habit of growth, and for their large and choice assortment of richly coloured and superbly marked flowers, which are produced in the greatest profusion.

From Mrs. C. PUFFET, Lower Onslow.
"I had a splendid bed of Carnations last year from your Seed. I never saw such a mass of bloom."

From Mr. H. PALMER, Duck End.
"Your Carnation and Picotee Seed gave me great satisfaction; I have one and a half dozen of fine plants."

Complete List of Webbs' Flower Seeds, 1897—*continued.*

SWEET PEA.

Well-known climbers, exceedingly fragrant; adapted for screens or trellis-work, and very useful to cut from; ***hardy annuals.***

From Mr. H. LANCASTER, Lea.

"Webbs' Seeds have come wonderfully well; my neighbours asked where I got them from."

From D. PROSSER, Esq., Bryn Derwen.

"I have had Webbs' Seeds for many years, and always found them excellent."

		Per packet. *s.*	*d.*
925.	**Sweet Pea, New Cupid.** The foliage is very dark green; blossoms pure waxy-white, and fully as large as the ordinary climbing varieties. The entire height of the plant is about 6 inches, and seldom more than 12 to 15 inches in diameter. The flower-stems are about 4 inches long, each bearing two or three blossoms. It is a wonderfully free bloomer, beginning to flower as early as May and continuing until November.—(See ILLUSTRATION below),	1	0
926.	**Sweet Pea, New Cupid, smaller packet,**		6
927.	**Sweet Pea, Blanche Burpee,** pure white,	1	
928.	„ „ **Butterfly,** blue and white,		3
929.	„ „ **Countess of Radnor,** pale blue,		6
930.	„ „ **Crown Princess of Prussia,** lilac,		6
931.	„ „ **Dorothy Tennant,** rosy mauve,		6
932.	„ „ **Emily Henderson,** a new pure white variety, with extra large flowers,		6
933.	„ „ **Fairy Queen,** rose,		6
934.	„ „ **Her Majesty,** bright rose,	1	0
935.	„ „ **Imperial purple,**		3
936.	„ „ **Mrs. Sankey,** white, changing to rose,		6
937.	„ „ **Orange Prince,** orange-pink,		6
938.	„ „ **Painted Lady,** rose and white,		3
939.	„ „ **Primrose Queen,** pale primrose,		6
940.	„ „ **Princess Beatrice,** carmine-rose,		6
941.	„ „ **Princess May,** a beautiful and distinct new variety, of most pleasing colour. It is throughout of a delicate shade of pale heliotrope or lavender,	1	0
942.	„ „ **Scarlet Invincible,**		3
943.	„ „ **Senator,** bronzy purple,		6
944.	„ „ **Stanley,** dark red,	1	0
945.	„ „ **Venus,** creamy white,	1	0
946.	„ „ **scarlet-striped,**		3
947.	„ „ **white,**		3
948.	„ „ **mixed,**		3
949.	„ „ **10 distinct varieties,** separate,	2s. 6d.	

WEBBS' SELECTED LARGE-FLOWERING SWEET PEA.

For Price and Description, see below.

950. Sweet Pea, Webbs' Selected Large-flowering (see ILLUSTRATION above), a very fine selection, producing large and beautiful flowers in great profusion, many of which are both new and novel in colour; mixed, **6d.** *per packet.*

951.	**White,**	*per packet*	**6d.**
952.	**Crimson,**	„	**6d.**
953.	**Rose,**	„	**6d.**
954.	**Canary Yellow,**	„	**6d.**
955.	**Purple-striped,**	„	**6d.**
956.	**Mauve,**	„	**6d.**
957.	**Pink,**	„	**6d.**
958.	**Blue and White,**	„	**6d.**
959.	**Purple,**	„	**6d.**
960.	**Scarlet and White,**	„	**6d.**
961.	**Collection of 10 varieties,** separate,		**5s.**

From Mr. R. W. WALKER, Little Stukeley.

"The Seeds I bought of you were pure and good."

88

NEW DWARF SWEET PEA—"CUPID." 925. 1*s. per packet.* 926. *Smaller packet,* 6*d.* *See above.*

Webbs' Choice Bulbs for Spring planting—*continued.*

LILIUMS. (See ILLUSTRATIONS below.)

	Each. s. d.	s. d.	s. d.
Auratum (*Golden-rayed Japan Lily*); excellent flowering bulbs,	1 0	1 6 and	2 6
„ (*Golden-rayed Japan Lily*) extra large bulbs (*very fine*)	.	.	3 6
Browni, white, tinged with brown,	.	1 6 and	2 6

Candidum (*White Garden Lily*), 3d. *each.*
Chalcedonicum (*Scarlet Martagon Lily*), ... 1s. 6d. *each.*
Croceum (*Orange Lily*), 4d. *each.*
Excelsum, cream colour, 1s. *and* 1s. 6d. *each.*
Giganteum, a gigantic Lily, 8 to 10 feet high, with white flowers striped reddish-violet, and of the most powerful fragrance, 3s. 6d. to 10s. 6d. *each.*

	Each. s. d.	s. d.
Lancifolium album, pure white,	6 and	1 0
„ **roseum,** white and rose,	6 ,,	1 0
„ **rubrum,** white, with red spots,	6 ,,	1 0
Longiflorum, white,	.	4
„ **Harrisi** (*Bermuda Lily*), white,	6 and	1 0

Thunbergianum grandiflorum, blood red; a very choice variety, 6d. *each.*
Tigrinum (*Tiger Lily*), 3d. *each.*
„ **flore pleno** (*Double Tiger Lily*), ... 4d. *each.*
Umbellatum, orange scarlet, 4d. *each.*
„ **erectum,** orange scarlet, ... 4d. *each.*

LILIUM CANDIDUM.—*See above.*

LILIUM AURATUM.—*See above.*

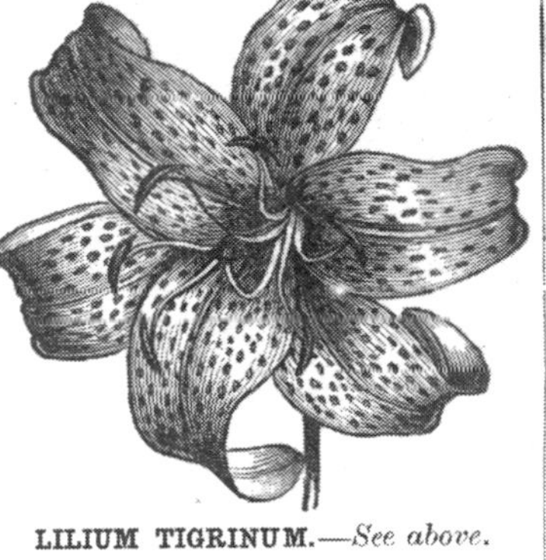

LILIUM TIGRINUM.—*See above.*

RANUNCULUS.

	Per doz. s. d.	Per 100. s. d.
Persian varieties, mixed colours,	4	2 6
Turban varieties, mixed colours,	4	2 0
French varieties, mixed colours,	6	3 6

SCHIZOSTYLIS COCCINEA.

1s. *per dozen.*

TIGRIDIAS.

	Each. s. d.	Per doz. s. d.
Canariensis, yellow, deep scarlet spots,	3	2 0
Conchiflora, yellow and red, spotted scarlet,	3	2 0
Grandiflora alba, creamy white, very beautiful,	3	2 0
Pavonia, scarlet and orange yellow,	3	1 6
Speciosa, yellow, spotted crimson,	3	2 0

TROPÆOLUMS.

	Each. s. d.
Jarratti, scarlet and yellow,	6
Pentaphyllum, yellow and orange,	1 0
Polyphyllum, pale yellow,	6
Tuberosum, red and yellow, hardy,	4

TUBEROSES.

(See ILLUSTRATION, page 97.)

Imported Italian Roots, 3s. *per doz.*; 21s. *per* 100.
Imported American Roots, 3s. 6d. *per doz.*; 25s. *per* 100.
Imported African Roots, 2s. 6d. *per doz.*; 17s. 6d. *per* 100.

From Mr. W. COATES, Hurcott.
"The Liliums surpassed all I have ever seen."

From ALFRED E. BICKHAM, Esq., Manchester.
"All the Bulbs I had from Messrs. Webb for my friends this year did well."

From Mr. W. BRENNAND, West Bromwich.
"The Bulbous Flower Roots gave every satisfaction."

☛ *Webbs' Illustrated Annual Catalogue of Hyacinths, Crocus, Tulips, and other Bulbs, is published in August; gratis and post free.*

From Mr. A. HUGHES, Gardener to W. L. Hodgkinson, Esq., Norwood House.
"The Bulbs supplied last autumn gave every satisfaction; the bedding Tulips were very fine, also the pot Hyacinths and other Bulbs."

From Mr. W. WOOD, Gardener to Rev. H. E. Hulton, Great Waltham Vicarage.
"I beg to say that the Bulbs you supplied to the Rev. H. E. Hulton were very satisfactory."

From Mr. R. BONIFACE, Gardener to J. T. Firbank, Esq., M.P., Coopers.
"The Bulbs received from you for several years past have proved of the highest quality, giving us the greatest satisfaction."

From Mr. J. DUNKLEY, Gardener to T. A. Howland, Esq., Rushymead.
"The Bulbous Flower Roots were very successful."

Webbs' Seeds of Ornamental Grasses.

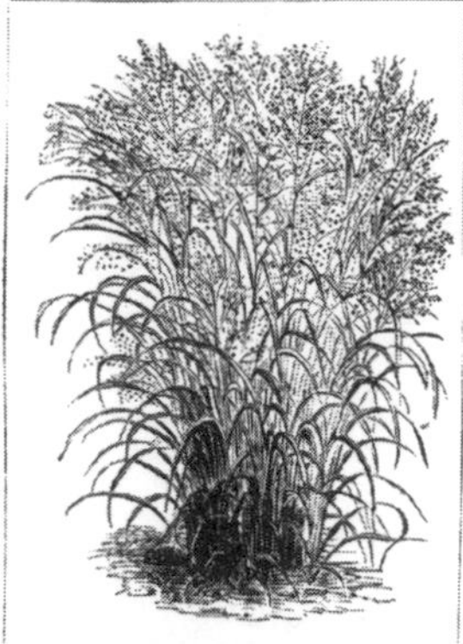

PANICUM ALTISSIMUM.
1120. 6d. *per packet. See below.*

HORDIUM JUBATUM.
1116. 3d. *per packet. See below.*

STIPA PENNATA.
1125. 6d. *per packet. See below.*

ERIANTHUS RAVENNÆ.
1112. 3d. *per packet. See below.*

☞ *Explanations of Abbreviations used below.*

h. a. Hardy Annual. | **h. h. a.** Half-hardy Annual. | **h. p.** Hardy Perennial. | **h. h. p.** Half-hardy Perennial.

NAME	REMARKS.	*Price per packet.*	*Hardiness and duration.*	*Height.*
		s. d.		
1090. **Agrostis nebulosa,**		3	h. a.	1½ ft.
1091. " **plumosa,**	Very ornamental, and of graceful habit; suitable for bouquets and	3	h. a.	1½ ft.
1092. " **pulchella,**	mixing with flowers in vases,	3	h. a.	6 in.
1093. " **Steveni,**		6	h. a.	1 ft.
1094. **Anthoxanthum gracile,**	An elegant variety,	3	h. a.	9 in.
1095. **Arundo conspicua,**	Exceedingly ornamental, producing elegant silvery plumes of large	6	h. p.	6 ft.
1096. " **Donax,**	size. They require plenty of water in summer,	6	h. p.	8 ft.
1097. **Avena sterilis,**	"*Animated Oats.*" Very graceful,	3	h. a.	3 ft.
1098. **Briza geniculata,**		3	h. a.	1 ft.
1099. " **gracilis,**	"*Quaking Grass.*" These beautiful varieties are some of the best of	3	h. a.	1 ft.
1100. " **maxima,**	the ornamental grasses,	3	h. a.	1 ft.
1101. " **spicata,**		1 0	h. a.	1 ft.
1102. **Brizopyrum siculum,**	Used for edgings and bouquets,	3	h. a.	9 in.
1103. **Bromus brizæformis,**	A choice and valuable variety,	3	h. a.	1 ft.
1104. **Chloris barbata,**	These varieties produce elegant spikes, which are arranged in a	3	h. a.	1½ ft.
1105. " **elegans,**	singularly radiated manner,	3	h. a.	1 ft.
1106. **Chrysurus cynosuroides,**	A pretty golden-spiked tufted grass,	3	h. a.	6 in.
1107. **Coix lachryma,**	"*Job's Tears.*" Very effective,	3	h. h. a.	1½ ft.
1108. **Elymus caput-medusæ,**	An elegant sort; useful for borders,	3	h. p.	1 ft.
1109. **Eragrostis cylindriflora,**		3	h. a.	2 ft.
1110. " **elegans,**	"*Love Grass.*" Very ornamental, and suitable for bouquets,	3	h. a.	1 ft.
1111. " **maxima,**		6	h. a.	1½ ft.
1112. **Erianthus Ravennæ,**	Fine handsome grasses, having exquisite silvery plumes,	3	h. p.	5 ft.
1113. " **violascens,**		6	h. p.	5 ft.
1114. **Gynerium argenteum,**	The stately "*Pampas Grass.*" *G. variegatum* is very beautiful,	6	h. p.	10 ft.
1115. " **variegatum,**		1 0	h. p.	10 ft.
1116. **Hordium jubatum,**	The handsome plumes of this variety look well in bouquets,	3	h. a.	1½ ft.
1117. **Isolepsis gracilis,**	An excellent variety for growing in jardinettes on window-sills,	6	h. h. p.	6 in.
1118. **Lagurus ovatus,**	"*Hare's Tail Grass.*" Indispensable for bouquets,	3	h. a.	1½ ft.
1119. **Leptochloa gracilis,**	Hardy and graceful,	6	h. a.	2 ft.
1120. **Panicum altissimum,**	An effective class. *P. altissimum* is of fine habit, presenting a most	6	h. p.	4 ft.
1121. " **capillare,**	striking appearance,	3	h. a.	2 ft.
1122. " **sulcatum,**		3	h. h. p.	1½ ft.
1123. **Pennisetum villosum,**	A beautiful variety,	3	h. a.	2 ft.
1124. **Stipa elegantissima,**	"*Feather Grass.*" These popular grasses present a most attractive	6	h. p.	2 ft.
1125. " **pennata,**	appearance in borders, and when cut are elegant in bouquets,	6	h. p.	2 ft.
1126. **Zea gracillina,**	"*Miniature Maize.*" Valuable for the greenhouse and sub-	3	h. h. a.	2 ft.
1127. " **japonica variegata,**	"*Striped Japanese Maize.*" tropical garden,	3	h. h. a.	4 ft.

For Webbs' "Kinver" Collections of Ornamental Grass Seeds, see page 99.

From **LADY MARGARET CECIL**, London.
"The Seeds have given satisfaction, and Lady Margaret is much pleased."

From **Mr. R. W. WALKER**, Little Stukeley.
"The Seeds I bought of you were pure and good."

Webbs' New Princess Aster.

FOR PRICE, DESCRIPTION, AND ILLUSTRATION, *see page* 69.

Webbs' New Golden Cloud Chrysanthemum.

FOR PRICE, DESCRIPTION, AND ILLUSTRATION, *see page* 64.

Webbs' New Champion Dianthus.

FOR PRICE AND DESCRIPTION, *see page* 76, AND FOR COLOURED PLATE, *see facing page* 80.

Webbs' New Double Wallflower.

FOR PRICE AND DESCRIPTION, *see page* 94, AND FOR COLOURED PLATE, *see facing page* 80.

1128. Webbs' New Aster—"Scarlet King."

1s. 6d. *per packet.*

An entirely distinct Aster, of dwarf habit of growth, specially adapted for massing or bedding purposes; growing about 8 inches high, and each plant bearing from 20 to 30 large and perfectly formed blooms of deep scarlet colour.

1129. Aster—"Comet."—1s. 6d. *per packet.*

This new Aster deviates from all other varieties in cultivation, the flower resembling very closely a large-flowered Japanese Chrysanthemum. The petals are long, and twisted or curled from the centre of the flower in such a regular manner as to form a loose, but still dense, semi-globe. The colour of the flower is a lovely delicate pink, bordered with white.

1130. Lupinus Albo-coccineus Nanus.

1s. 6d. *per packet.*

A new variety of this splendid genus of ornamental and free-flowering annuals, which is of very dwarf growth, forming handsome compact bushes of about 1 foot in height and breadth. The flower-spikes are from 3 to 5 inches in length, of a rich rosy-crimson colour half up the spike—from thence to the apex pure white, and of delicious fragrance.

1131. Myosotis Alpestris, Victoria.—1s. *per packet.*

This new Forget-me-not is remarkable for its stout and bushy habit of growth, and umbels of large, bright, azure-blue flowers. The plant attains a height of from 5 to 7 inches, and when fully grown is quite globular in shape, and perfectly covered with flowers. Not alone for carpet bedding, edgings, and masses, but also for growing in pots for market, as well as for cut blooms, it may be safely pronounced a novelty of the first order.

Webbs' New Primula—"Modesty."

FOR PRICE, DESCRIPTION, AND ILLUSTRATION, *see page* 61.

Webbs' New Primula—"Purity."

FOR PRICE, DESCRIPTION, AND ILLUSTRATION, *see page* 61.

Webbs' New Primula—"Scarlet Emperor."

FOR PRICE, DESCRIPTION, & ILLUSTRATION, *see pages* 61 *and* 88.

Webbs' New Primula—"Rosy Morn."

FOR PRICE AND DESCRIPTION, *see page* 61.

598. Webbs' New Myosotis—"Blue King."

1s. *per packet.* (*See also page* 83, *and* COLOURED PLATE *facing page* 80.)

1132. Webbs' New Myosotis—"White Queen."

1s. 6d. *per packet.*

These handsome new varieties of Forget-me-not, will be found exceedingly valuable for spring bedding. The plants are of neat and bushy appearance, and produce their large and beautifully-coloured flowers in great abundance.

1133. Delphinium, Zalil.—2s. 6d. *per packet.*

A new and handsome hardy perennial, being the only known yellow-flowering variety of this species in cultivation. Its dark green and finely laciniated leaves cover the lower part of the main stem, each branch of which bears a spike of bloom 8 to 16 inches in length. The flowers are of the finest shade of sulphur-yellow, and as they expand almost simultaneously from the base to the summit of the spike, the beauty of this attractive plant is seen to full advantage. The seed should be sown in the open ground in April for flowering in the following summer.

1134. Mina Lobata.—1s. 6d. *per packet.*

A charming half-hardy climber, useful for covering arbours, trellises, etc. The flowers appear on long racemes, and in colour they are both singular and attractive; the buds being at first of vivid red, but they turn to orange-yellow before opening, and when fully expanded are creamy-white. The plant, which attains a height of from 18 to 20 feet, is strikingly beautiful, and produces flowers from the base to the summit. It requires the same treatment as other half-hardy annuals, but should be planted in a sheltered situation.

ROSES:—HYBRID PERPETUAL.

This magnificent and beautiful class of Roses, is better than any other, adapted for exhibition and pot culture. They continue in flower from the early part of June to the end of October, and are the most desirable for general cultivation.

We have much pleasure in offering the following liberal collections, which are carefully made up to insure a fine variety, and the plants being particularly fine and healthy, Customers ordering may depend on their giving the most unqualified satisfaction.

From Mr. THOMAS E. HAY, Killingworth, Newcastle-on-Tyne.
Nov. 1st, 1875.

"I received the Roses in excellent condition, and am very much obliged for your liberal collection. They are the best lot I ever saw."

From Mrs. R. BUSTON, Buston, Lesbury, Northumberland.
Aug. 18th, 1875

"Mrs. R. Buston is much pleased with the Roses she got in April, they have all flowered well and look healthy."

HYBRID PERPETUAL ROSES IN COLLECTIONS.

The selection left to ourselves. In ordering please state the nature of soil to be grown on, and purposes for which intended.

These Collections are Carriage Free to any Railway Station in England or Wales.

N.B.—In ordering from the general list, please give a few supplementary names in case of our being sold out of sorts first named.

	Standards and Half-Standards. £ s. d.	Dwarfs. £ s. d.
12 plants in 12 of the most select varieties	1 1 0	0 12 6
12 „ 12 good and popular varieties	0 18 0	0 10 6
25 „ 25 of the most select varieties	2 0 0	1 1 0
25 „ 25 good and popular varieties	1 15 0	0 18 0
50 „ 50 of the most select varieties	3 15 0	1 15 0
50 „ 50 good and popular varieties	3 3 0	1 10 0
100 „ not less than 50 of the most select varieties ...	7 0 0	3 3 0
100 „ not less than 50 good and popular varieties ...	6 0 0	2 12 0
1000 plants in not less than 100 of most select varieties ...	65 0 0	30 0 0
1000 plants in not less than 100 good and popular varieties ...	55 0 0	25 0 0
Collections containing 500 plants and upwards will be charged at the rate per 1000.		
Mixed dwarfs for borders and Shrubberies per 100		1 10 0

N.B.—The above prices, being strictly for cash, no order for these collections can be attended to unless accompanied by a remittance.

From JOHN AIREY, Esq., Myrtle Hill, Ramsey, Isle of Man
Autumn, 1875.

"You may send me a dozen good **Roses**; what I had from you in the Spring were very good."

ROSE TRAINERS FOR CLIMBING ROSES, Etc.

DESIGNED BY MR. H. INIGO TRIGGS.

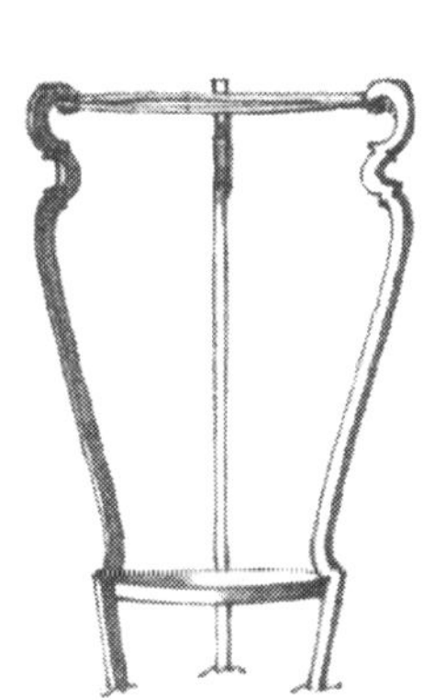

No. 2. Price 23/6.

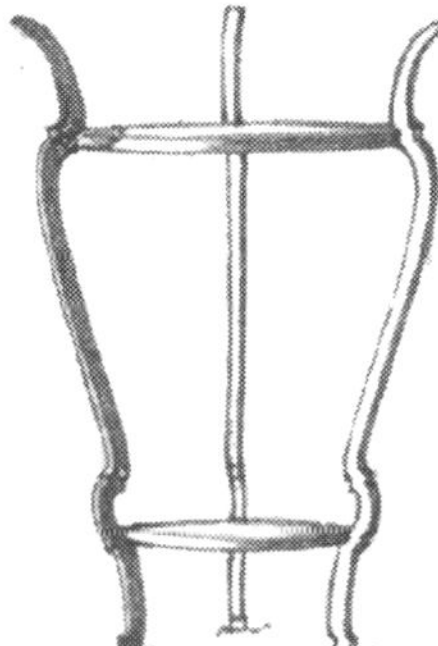

No. 3. Price 21/-.

These standards are easily movable, and are suitable for ramblers, sweet peas and other plants of a similar nature.

Far preferable to ordinary pea-sticks or bamboo rods, as they are never unsightly, even when the plants are growing or when the foliage begins to disappear.

No. 1. Price 23/6.

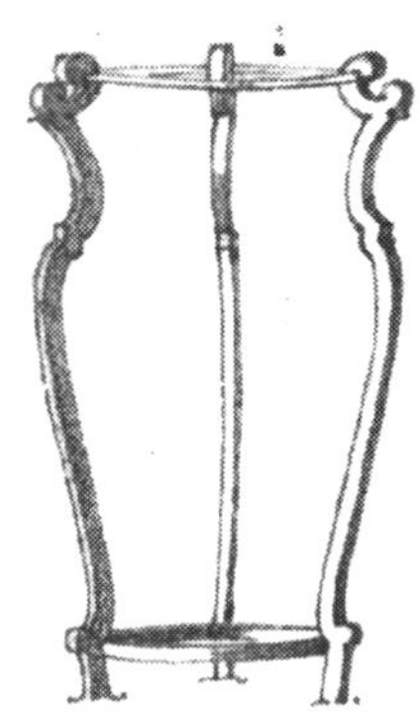

No. 4. Price 23/6.

Sketch shewing rose trainer in use, with suggestion for random stone surround.

The shaped standards are in sawn oak, left natural colour, and the rings are in wrought iron.

Total height 5 ft. 6 in. out of ground.
Posts ... 1 ft. 6 in. in ground.

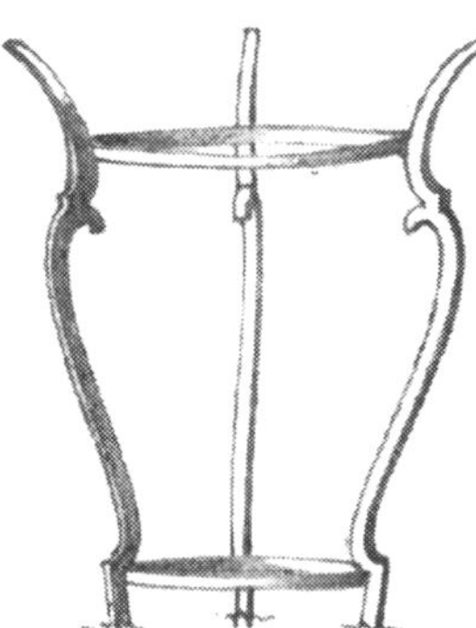

No. 5. Price 21/6.

FLOWER, ROSE, SWEET PEA, &c. TRAINERS.

No. 658. Umbrella Trainer, with Single Stem.

Height out of Ground.	Diameter across Top.	Price.
3 ft. 0 in.	2 ft. 0 in.	**6/8** each.
4 ft. 0 in.	2 ft. 6 in.	**8/8** ,,
5 ft. 0 in.	2 ft. 9 in.	**12/-** ,,
6 ft. 0 in.	3 ft. 0 in.	**14/-** ,,
7 ft. 0 in.	3 ft. 6 in.	**16/-** ,,

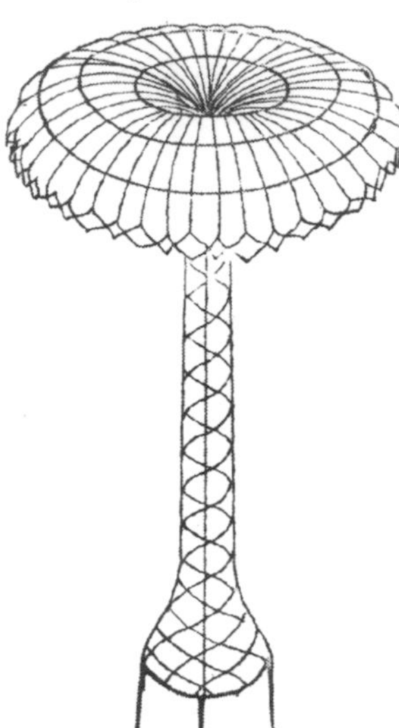

No. 660. Umbrella Trainer, with Spiral Stem.

Height out of Ground.	Diameter across Top.	Price.
3 ft. 0 in.	2 ft. 0 in.	**10/6** each.
4 ft. 0in.	2 ft. 6 in.	**14/-** ,,
5 ft. 0 in.	2 ft. 9 in.	**16/8** ,,
6 ft. 0 in.	3 ft. 0 in.	**20/8** ,,
7 ft. 0 in.	3 ft. 6 in.	**24/-** ,,

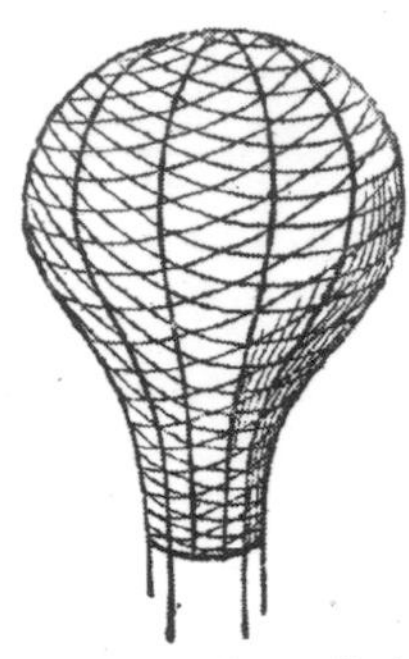

No. 664. Balloon Trainer.

6 to 8 in. diam. at Bottom.

12 in. high	..	**2/4** each.
15 ,,	..	**2/8** ,,
18 ,,	..	**3/-** ,,
21 ,,	..	**3/8** ,,
24 ,,	..	**4/8** ,,
27 ,,	..	**5/4** ,,
30 ,,	..	**6/4** ,,
36 ,,	..	**8/-** ,,
42 ,,	..	**10/4** ,,

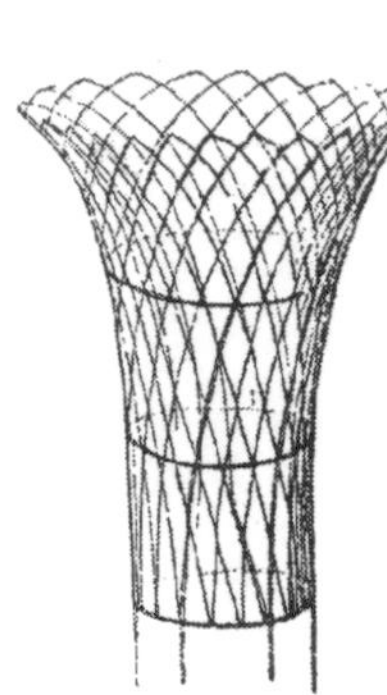

No. 659. Bell Trainer.

8 to 11 in. diam. at Bottom.

18 in. high	..	**2/8** each.
21 ,,	..	**3/4** ,,
24 ,,	..	**4/-** ,,
27 ,,	..	**4/8** ,,
30 ,,	..	**6/-** ,,
36 ,,	..	**7/4** ,,

The No. 664 Trainer is now made in halves for convenience of transit.

Special Trainers of every size, shape or design, made to order at short notice.

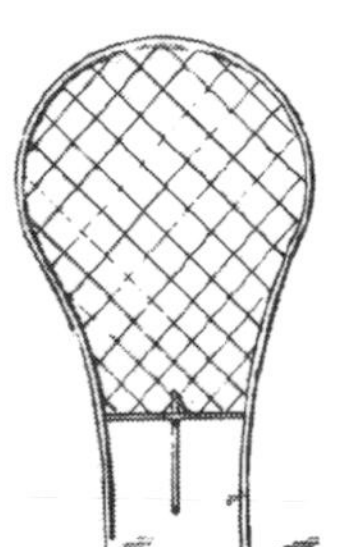

No. 650. Flat Trainer.

8 in. high,	**4d.** each.
10 ,,	**6d.** ,,
12 ,,	**7d.** ,,
15 ,,	**8d.** ,,
18 ,,	**1/-** ,,
24 ,,	**1/8** ,,
27 ,,	**2/-** ,,
30 ,,	**2/8** ,,
33 ,,	**3/4** ,,
36 ,,	**4/-** ,,

No. 657. Sweet Pea Trainer.

2 ft. diam.
3 ft. high, **7/-** each.
2 ft. 3 in. diam.
4 ft. high, **10/-** each.
2 ft. 6 in. diam.
5 ft. high, **13/6** each.

Can be made any size to order.

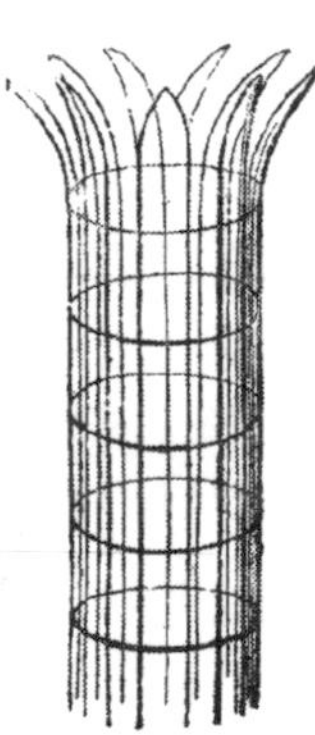

No. 662. Sweet Pea Trainer.

9 in. diam. at Bottom.

18 in. high,	**2/-** each.
21 ,,	**2/8** ,,
24 ,,	**2/9** ,,
27 ,,	**4/-** ,,
30 ,,	**4/8** ,,
36 ,,	**5/4** ,,

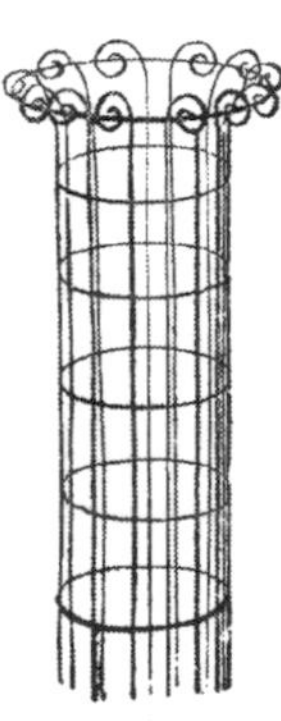

No. 665. Sweet Pea Trainer.

4 in. to 9 in. diam. at Bottom.

18 in. high,	**2/-** each.
21 ,,	**2/8** ,,
24 ,,	**3/8** ,,
27 ,,	**4/-** ,,
30 ,,	**4/8** ,,
36 ,,	**5/4** ,,

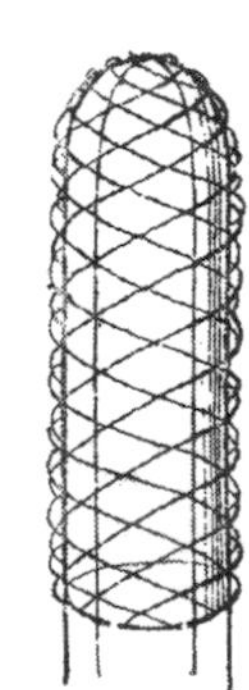

No. 666. Sweet Pea Trainer.

9 in. to 12 in. diam. at Bottom.

18 in. high,	**2/-** each.
21 ,,	**2/8** ,,
24 ,,	**3/8** ,,
27 ,,	**4/-** ,,
30 ,,	**4/8** ,,
36 ,,	**5/4** ,,

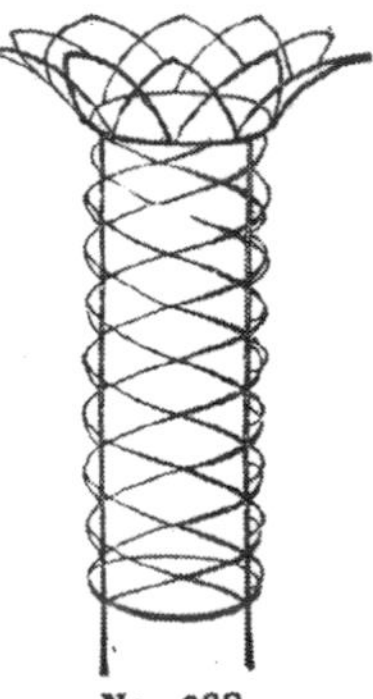

No. 668. Sweet Pea Trainer.

8 in. to 11 in. diam. at Bottom.

18 in. high,	**2/-** each.
21 ,,	**2/8** ,,
24 ,,	**3/8** ,,
27 ,,	**4/-** ,,
30 ,,	**4/8** ,,
36 ,,	**5/4** ,,

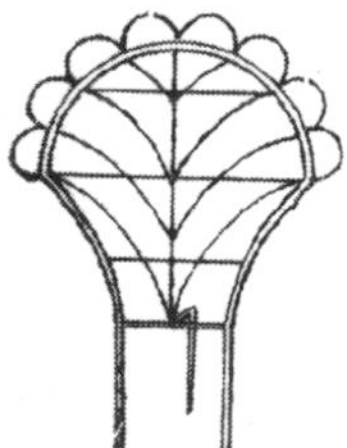

No. 654. Pot Trainer.

12 in. high,	**10d.** each.
18 ,,	**1/8** ,,
24 ,,	**3/-** ,,
30 ,,	**3/8** ,,

No. 656. Pink Trainer.

7 in. diam. at btm.
12 ,, at top.
1/4 each.

Can be made any size to order.

FLOWER POT TRAINERS.

Japanned Green or Galvanized.

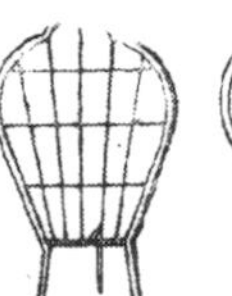

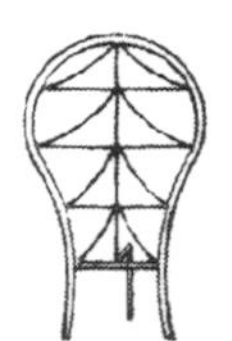

No. 646. No. 648. No. 647. No. 649. No. 653. No. 651.

Sizes and Prices of above six patterns—

12in.	18in.	24in.	30 in. high.
8d.	**1/3**	**2/-**	**3/-** each.

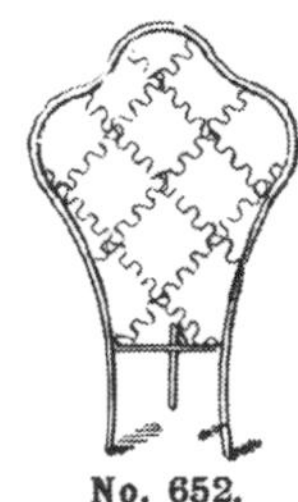

No. 652. Pot Trainer.

Made in spiral wire.

12 in. high,	**10d.** each.
18 ,,	**1/8** ,,
24 ,,	**3/-** ,,
30 ,,	**3/8** ,,

TREILLAGE PILLARS FOR CLIMBING ROSES, ETC.

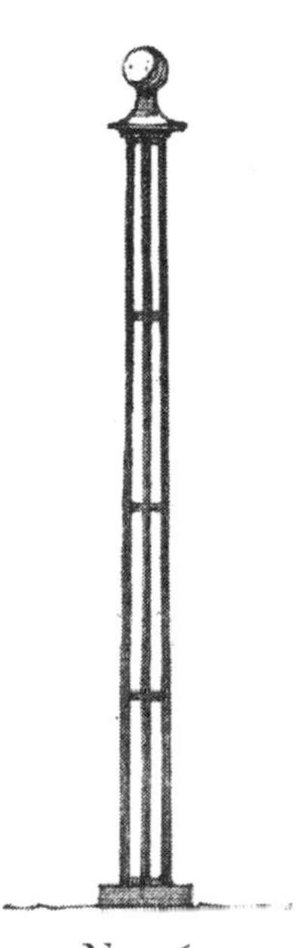

No. 6.

Square. Height 8 ft. 0 in.

Oak ...	... £1	3	6
Deal ...	... £1	1	6

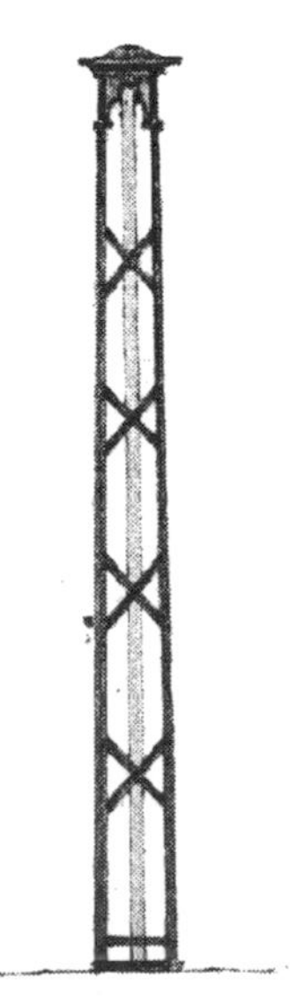

No. 7.

Square. Height 8 ft. 0 in.

Oak ...	... £1	10	0
Deal ...	... £1	7	6

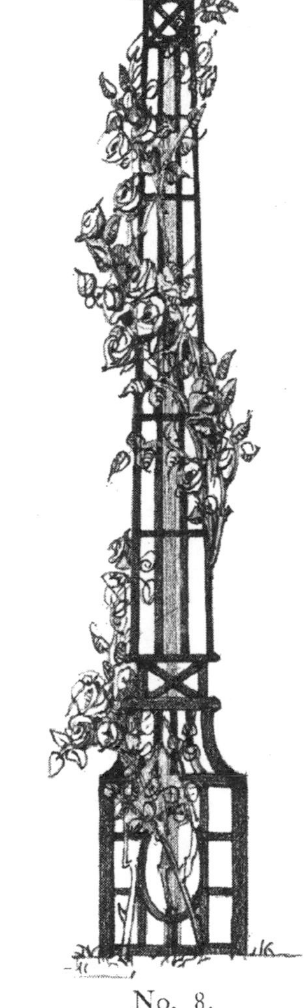

No. 8.

Square. Height 10 ft. 0 in.

Oak	... £3	10	0
Deal	... £3	0	0

Made in sawn oak left plain, or deal painted.

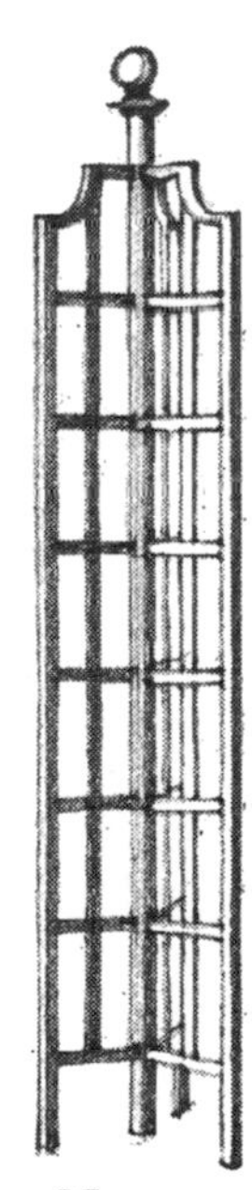

No. 9.

Height ... ... 8 ft. 0 in.

Oak ...	... £1	7	6
Deal ...	... £1	5	0

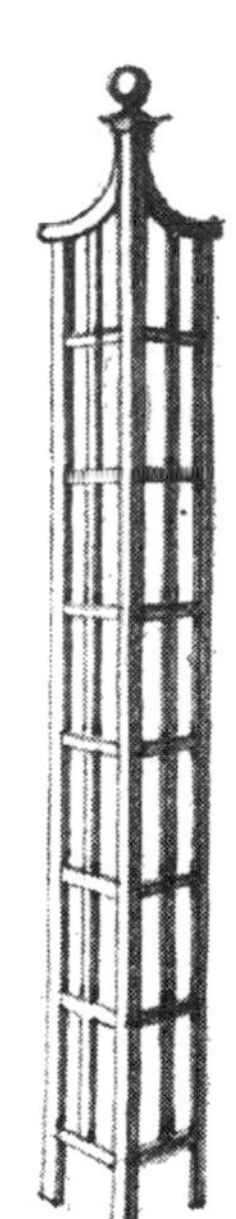

No. 10.

Triangular. Height 8 ft. 0 in.

Oak ...	... £1	12	6
Deal ...	... £1	9	0

ORNAMENTAL GAME-PROOF HURDLES.

For Pleasure Grounds, Enclosing Flower Beds, Shrubberies, Ornamental Waters, &c.

Nos. 23 and 24. Hurdles in 6 ft. lengths (straight or curved), 3 ft. 6 in. high. ¼-in. round vertical bars, 1½ in. apart, about 2 ft. from ground, 3 in. apart above. Frames 1 in. by ¼ in. Painted one coat. Shorter lengths to order.

FOR PRICES SEE INTERLEAF.

Hand Gate to match, 15/- each. Cast Posts, will self-fixing bases, 30/- per pair.

ORNAMENTAL GARDEN BORDERING.

Made in 6 ft. lengths, and from 1 ft. in height. Vertical bars, ¼ in. round, about 3 in. apart. Painted one coat. May be curved to any given radius.

FOR PRICES SEE INTERLEAF.

GALVANIZED HARD WIRE GARDEN BORDERINGS.

Galvanized after manufacture. Can be fixed or removed instantly. Reduced prices, including the necessary spikes for fixing.

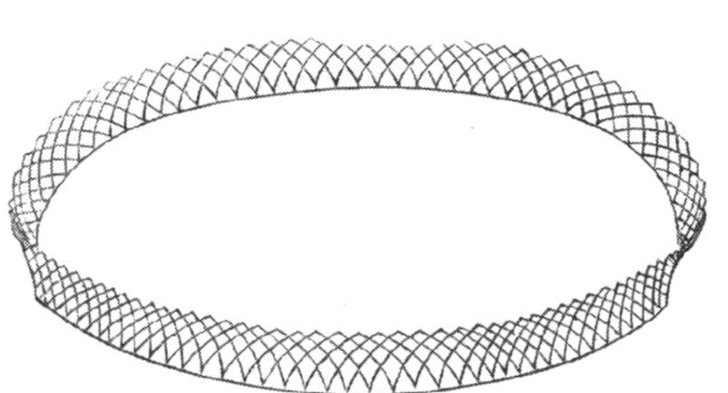

No. 581. CIRCULAR BORDERS FOR FLOWER BEDS.

8 in. high, per foot run .. .. .. 10d.
10 ,, ,, ... 1/-
12 ,, ,, ... 1/2

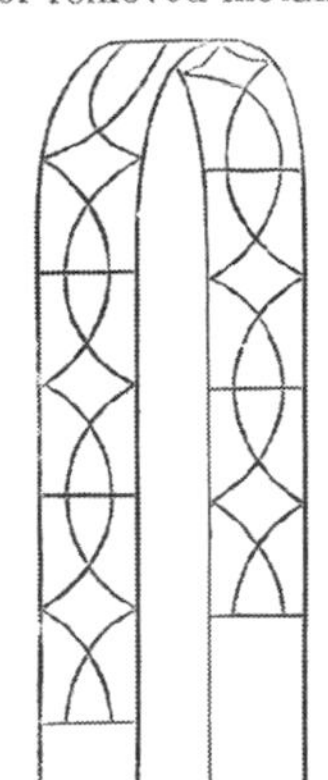

No. 585. HANDLES FOR THE CIRCULAR BORDERS.

6 in. wide, per foot run, **8d.**

9 in. wide, per foot run, **10½d.**

12 in. wide, per foot run, **1/1½.**

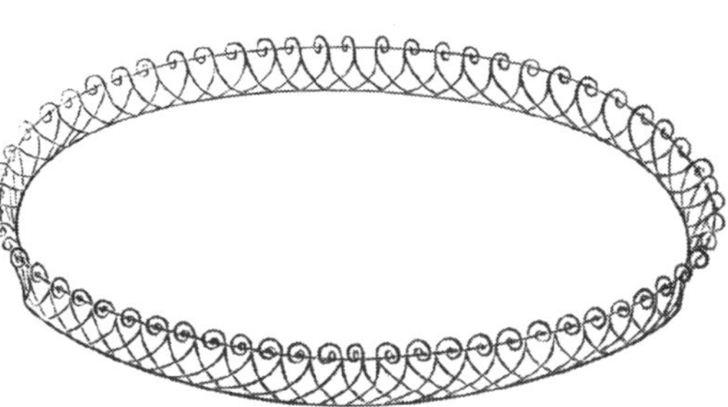

No. 584. CIRCULAR BORDERS FOR FLOWER BEDS.

8 in. high, per foot run 1/-
10 ,, ,, ... 1/2
12 ,, ,, ... 1/4

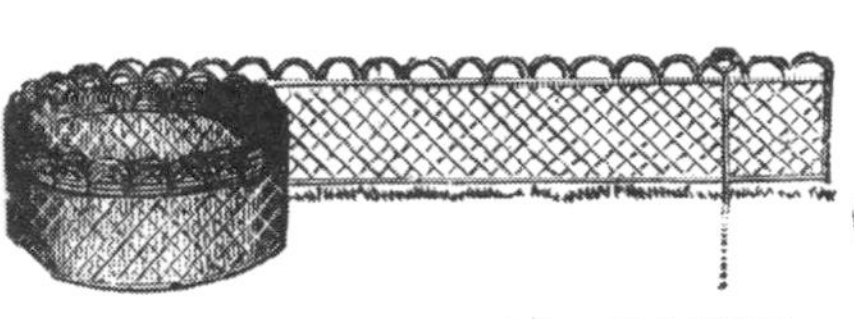

No. 300. LIGHT WIRE CROQUET BORDERING.

Made in 3 ft. lengths and 50 yd. rolls.

	6	9	12	15 in. high.
In 50 yd. rolls,	**8d.**	**10d.**	**11d.**	**1/3** per yd.
In 3ft. lengths,	**9d.**	**11d.**	**1/-**	**1/4** ea. lgth.

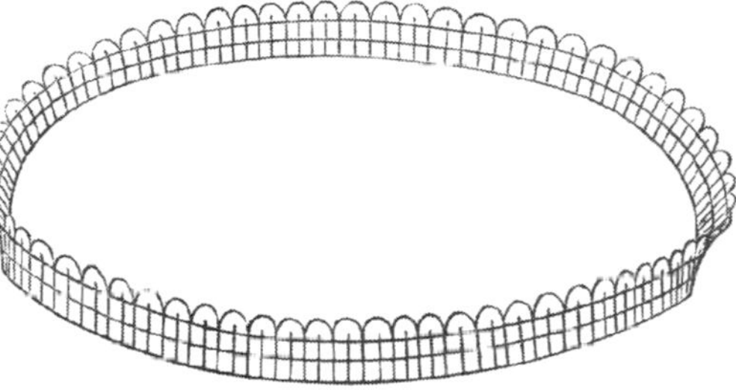

No. 588. CIRCULAR BORDERS FOR FLOWER BEDS

8 in. high, per foot run .. .. .. 10d.
10 ,, ,, ... 1/-
12 ,, ,, ... 1/2

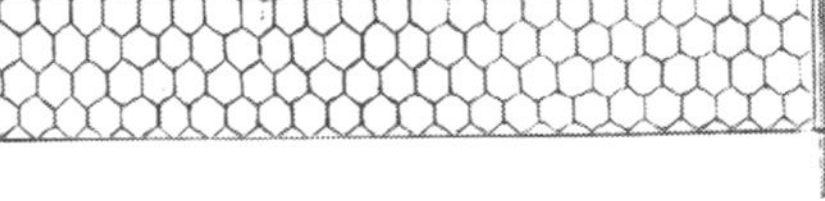

No. 582. CHEAP WIRE CROQUET BORDERING.

Made of galvanized wire netting. Made in 3 ft. lengths and 50 yd. rolls.

	6	9	12	in. high.
In 50 yd. rolls,	**3½d.**	**4½d.**	**6d.**	per yd.
In 3 ft. lengths,	**4½d.**	**6d.**	**7½d.**	ea. lgth.

LIGHT WIRE CROQUET BORDERINGS. Made in 3 ft. lengths.

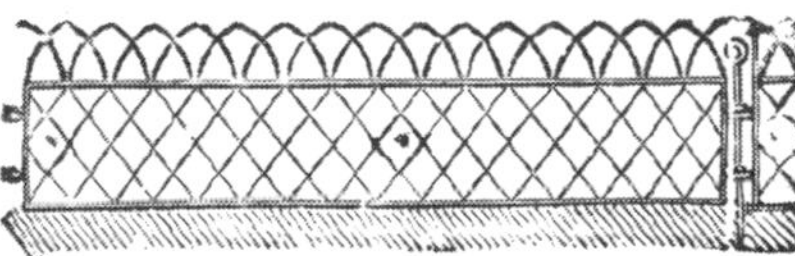

No. 301.

6	9	12	15	in. high.
9½d.	**11½d.**	**1/1½**	**1/6**	each length.

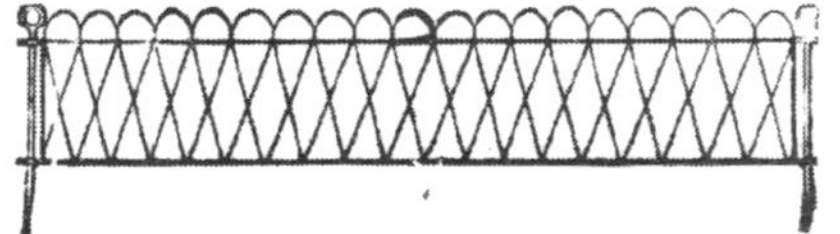

No. 54.

6	9	12	15	in. high.
10d.	**1/0½**	**1/2½**	**1/8**	each length.

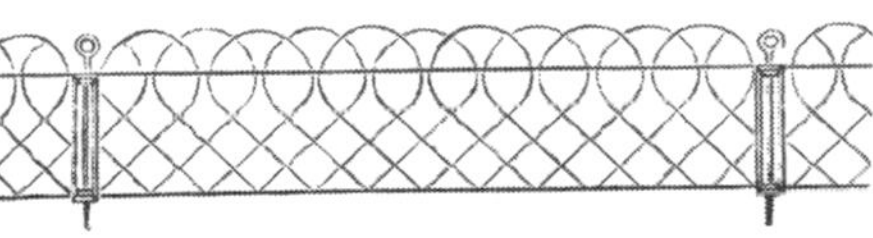

No. 583.

6	9	12	15	in. high.
11½d.	**1/1½**	**1/4**	**1/9**	each length.

GALVANIZED IRON SPIRAL AND PLAIN BORDERING.

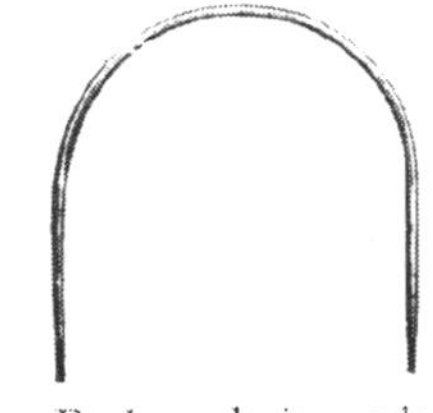

No. 586. Each arch is made of plain round rod, and forms a very durable, cheap, and handy border.

9	12	15 in. wide.
2/4	**3/-**	**3/4** per doz. arches.

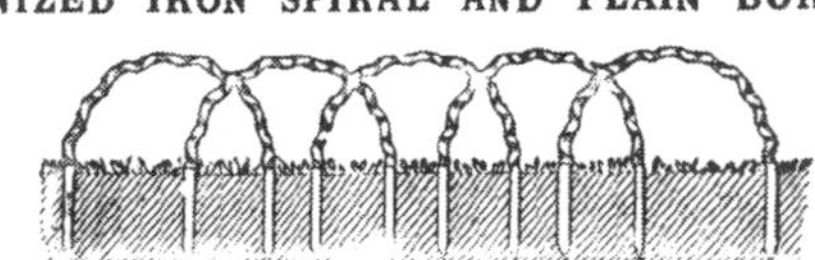

No. 55. Each arch is made of flat iron, and twisted, and is easily fixed to any shaped lawn or flower bed.

9	12	15 in. wide.
2/8	**3/4**	**4/-** per doz. arches.

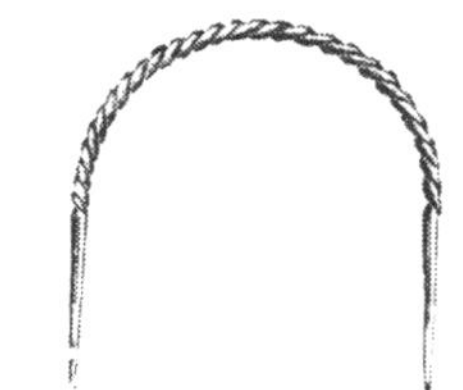

No. 587. Each arch is made of square rod and twisted, and forms a very durable and handsome bordering.

9	12	15 in. wide.
3/-	**3/8**	**4/4** per doz arches.

EXTRA STRONG ORNAMENTAL BORDERINGS FOR FLOWER BEDS. Prices per **running foot,** pieces less than 6 feet charged extra.

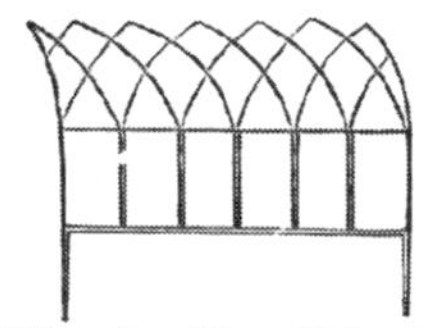

No. 589. 8 10 12 in. high.
8½d. 11d. 1/1½ per ft.

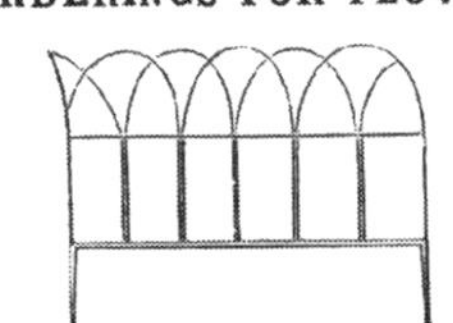

No. 593. 8 10 12 in. high.
8½d. 11d. 1/1½ per ft.

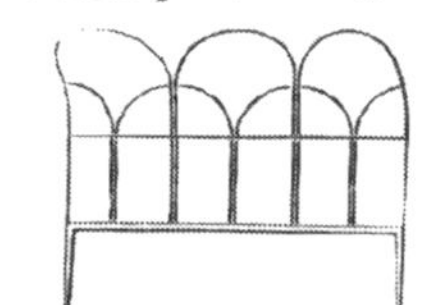

No. 595. 8 10 12 in. high.
8½d. 11d. 1/1½ per ft.

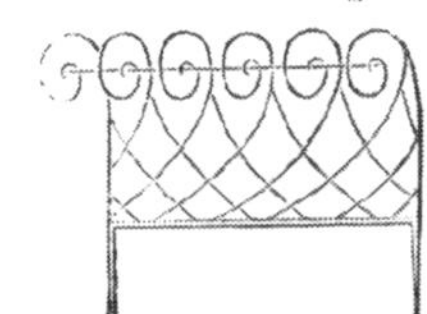

No. 590. 8 10 12 in. high.
1/- 1/2 1/4 per ft.

These extra strong Borders for Gardens can be had with an iron band round base 2 in. deep to prevent mould coming through, at an advance of 2d. per running foot on each pattern.

THE LEYDEN TRELLIS.

This design is adapted from an old Dutch XVIIth Century design.

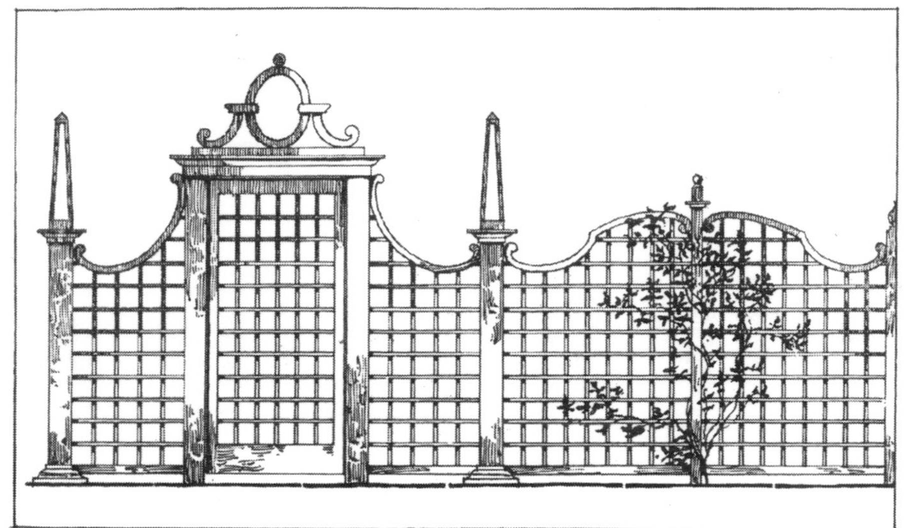

Height ... 6 ft. 0 in.

PRICES PER YARD:

Deal, painted ... 18/6

„ left from the saw and stained carbolineum 16/-

Oak, do. do. 24/-

„ left from the saw, plain 23/-

„ wrought, fumed and oiled... ... ... 30/-

For every gate and arch add 50/- extra in Deal and 70/- in Oak.

THE DELFT TRELLIS.

A modified version of the Leyden design above.

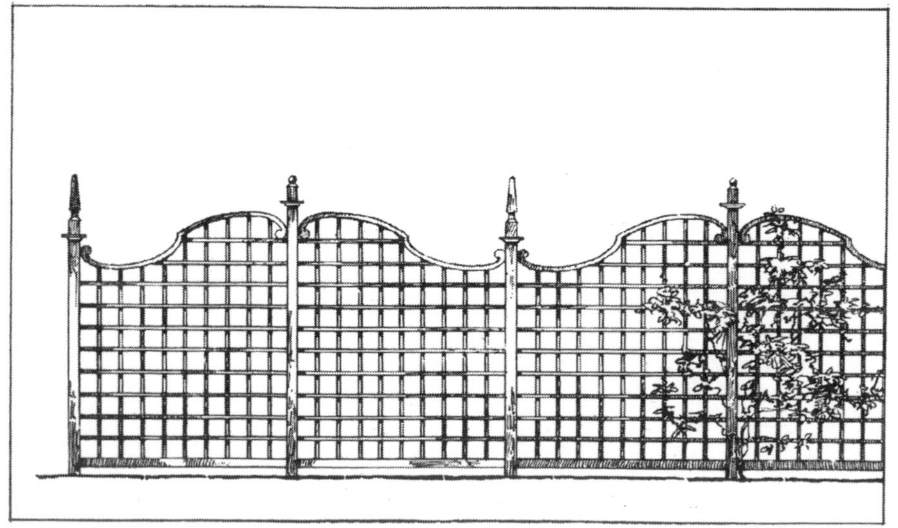

Height ... 6 ft. 0 in.

PRICES PER YARD:

Deal, painted ... 15/6

„ left from the saw and stained carbolineum 14/-

Oak, do. do. 19/-

„ left from the saw, plain 18/-

„ wrought, fumed and oiled... .. ... 25/-

THE ARDINGLEY TRELLIS.

A simple, strongly framed and inexpensive Treillage Screen.

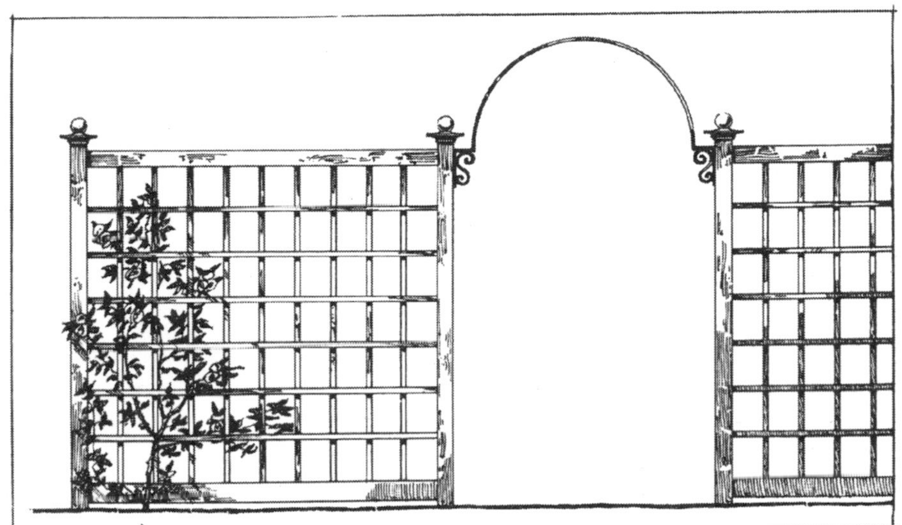

Height ... 6 ft. 0 in.

PRICES PER YARD:

Deal, painted ... 6/9

„ left from the saw and stained carbolineum 5/-

Oak, do. do. 8/-

„ left from the saw, plain 7/6

„ wrought, fumed and oiled... ... ... 10/-

Wrought iron arch and scrolls 10/6

THE BALCOMBE TRELLIS.

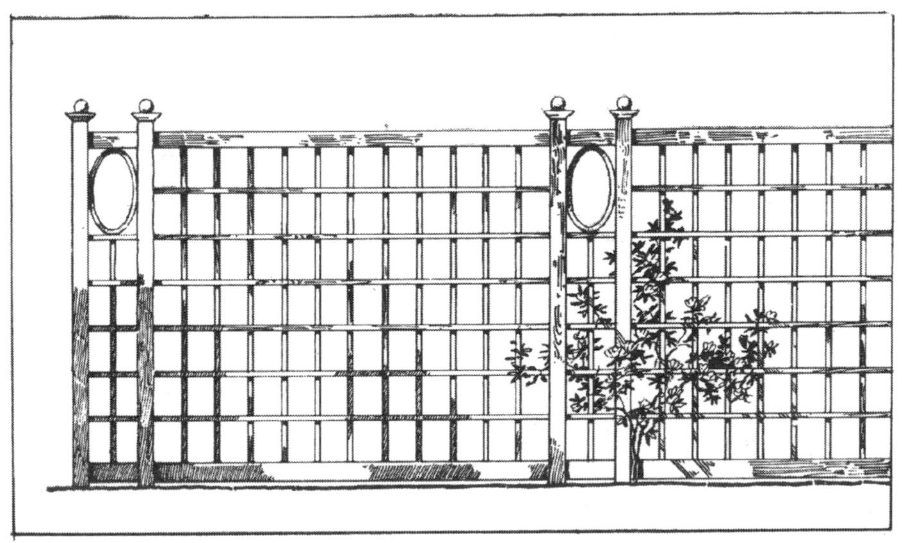

Height ... 6 ft. 0 in.

PRICES PER YARD:

Deal, painted ... 8/-

„ left from the saw and stained carbolineum 6/6

Oak, do. do. 10/-

„ left from the saw, plain 9/6

„ wrought, fumed and oiled... ... ... 12/6

Wrought-iron Palisading for Cottages and Gardens.

Special Estimates on application.

No. 291. No. 291. No. 180. No. 290. No. 290.

Enlarged Head. *Enlarged Head.*

No. 297. No. 300.

Wrought Head. *Wrought Head.*

No. 290. ½-in. rods, 3 in. apart, 3 ft. high. No. 291. ½-in. rods, 3 in. apart, 3 ft. high.
No. 290. ½-in. ,, 3 in. ,, 3 ft. 6 in. high. No. 291. ½-in. ,, 3 in. ,, 3 ft. 6 in. high.
No. 180. Hand Gate for Nos. 290 and 291 Palisading, ½-in. rods, 16/6

No. 293. No. 105. No. 292.

No. 293. No. 292.

Enlarged Head. *Enlarged Head.*

No. 298. No. 301.

No. 292. 3 ft. high, ½-in. rods, 3 in. apart. ... Cast-iron Posts 30/- per pair.
No. 292. 3 ft. ,, ⅝-in. ,, 3½ in. ,, ... Wrought-iron Standards 8/6 pair.
No. 293. 3 ft. ,, ⅝-in. ,, 3½ in. ,, ... Cast Coping for 4½ in. Walls, 2/6 yd.

Wrought Head. *Wrought Head.*

No. 294. No. 295.

No. 299. No. 295.

Wrought Head. *Wrought Head.*

No. 294. For fixing into soil, 3 ft. 6 in. high, 1 in. by ¼ in. vertical bars.
No. 295. For fixing on wall, 3 ft. high, 1 in. by ¼ in. vertical bars.
Hand Gate for Nos. 292, 293, 294, and 295 palisading; ½-in. rods, 19/- each; ⅝-in. rods, 25/- each; 1 by ¼-in. flat bars, 20/- each.

FOR PRICES SEE INTERLEAF.

ORNAMENTAL GARDEN AND PARK HURDLES.

Special Estimates on Application.

No. 19.

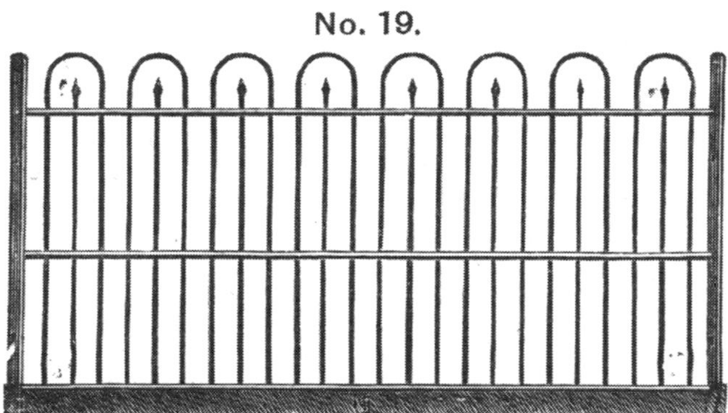

2 ft. 6 in. high, vertical rods $\frac{1}{4}$-in. round iron, placed $1\frac{1}{4}$ in. apart.
3 ft. high, with $\frac{3}{8}$-in. round vertical bars, $1\frac{1}{2}$ in. apart.
Hand Gate to match, with wrought-iron standard each 22/6.

No. 20.

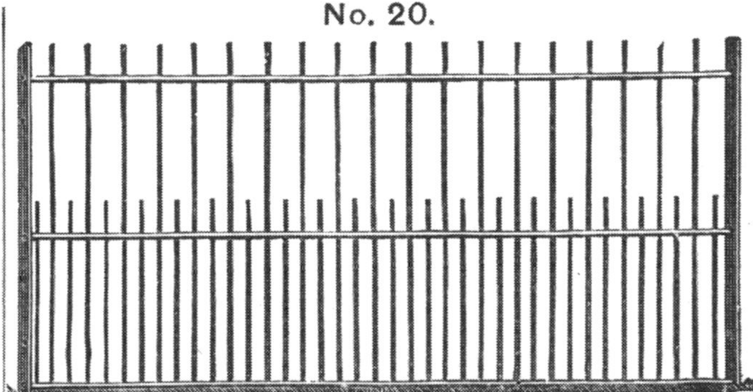

2 ft. 6 in. high, vertical rods $\frac{1}{4}$-in round iron, placed $1\frac{1}{4}$ in. apart.
3 ft. high, with $\frac{3}{8}$-in round vertical rods placed 2 in. apart.
Hand Gate to match, with wrought-iron standard, each 22/6.

No. 22.

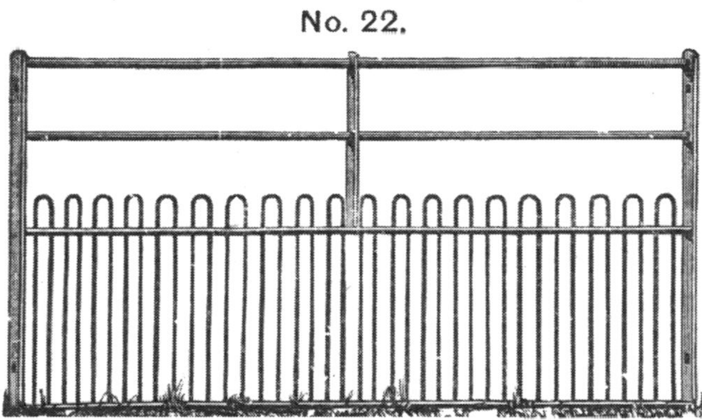

6 ft. long, 3 ft. 6 in. high, $\frac{1}{4}$-in. vertical wires.
Hand Gate to match, with wrought-iron standard each 20/-

No. 25.

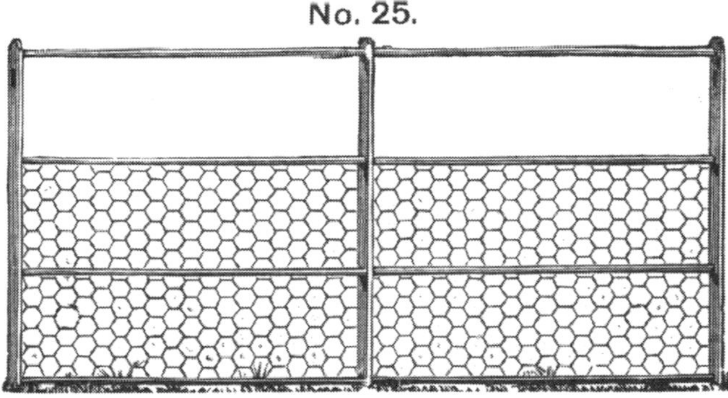

6 ft. long, 3 ft. high, covered to second bar with $1\frac{1}{2}$ in. netting.
Hand Gate to match, with wrought-iron standard each 20/-

No. 18.

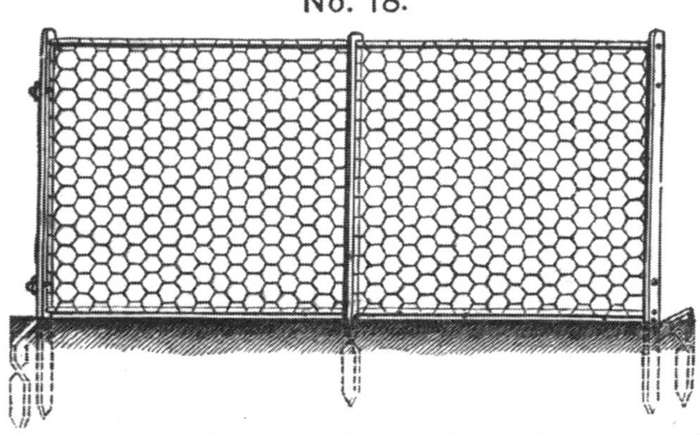

CHEAP Game-proof Hurdle, upright bars 1 in. by $\frac{1}{4}$ in., galvanized horizontal bars $\frac{3}{8}$-in. diameter, covered with $1\frac{1}{2}$-in. mesh netting. Frame varnished black.
2 ft. 6 in. high ... ...
3 ft. high, with 3 horizontal bars ... ...

No. 8.

CHEAP Rabbit and Game-proof Fence, 2 ft. 6 in. high, for surrounding flower gardens, pleasure grounds, &c. including stout galvanized wire top and bottom, galvanized netting, $1\frac{1}{2}$-in. mesh, No. 18 gauge, with standards two yards apart.

Wrought-iron straining pillars, extra.

FOR PRICES SEE INTERLEAF.

IMPROVED WROUGHT-IRON TREE GUARDS.

Special Estimates on application.

No. 400.

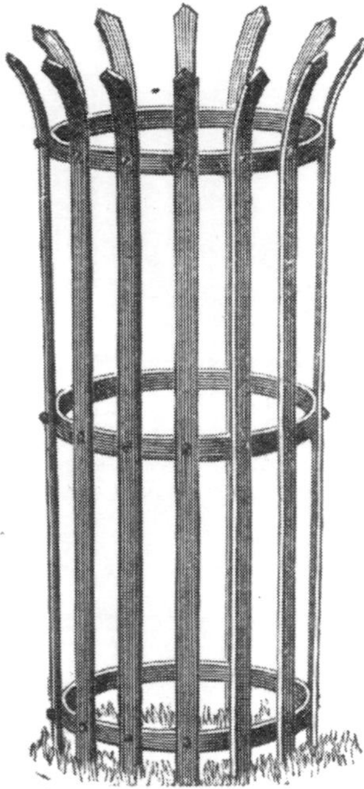

6 ft. high, 2 ft. 0 in. diameter.
6 ft. ,, 2 ft. 3 in. ,,
4 Vertical Bars, 1¼ in. by ¼ in., others 1 in. by ¼ in.

No. 405.

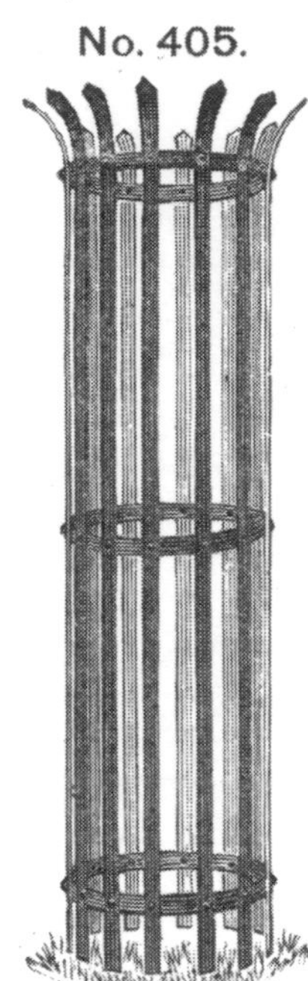

6 ft. high, 12 in. diameter, 4 Vertical Bars, 1 in. by ¼ in., others ¾ in. by ¼ in.

No. 406.

6 ft. high, 12 in. diameter, 4 Vertical Bars. 1 in. by ¼ in., others ¾ in. by ¼ in.

No. 407.

6 ft. high, 12 in. diameter at top, 16 in. diameter at bottom, 4 Vertical Bars, 1 in. by ¼ in., others ¾ in. by ¼ in.

All these Guards are supplied with plate feet, but pronged feet can be had if preferred.

FOR PRICES SEE INTERLEAF.

No. 408.

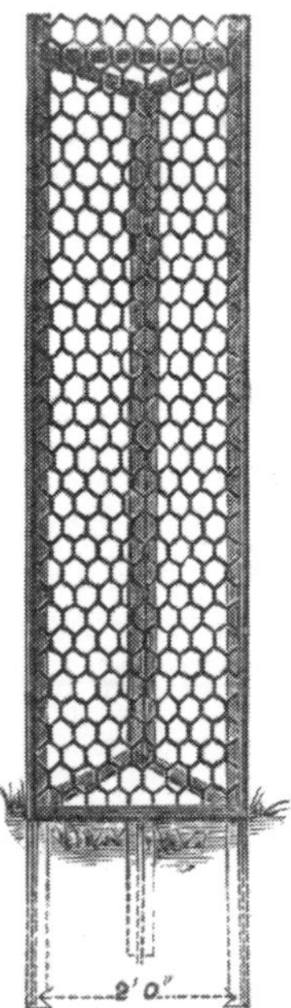

T Iron Uprights covered with 1½-in. strong Galvanized Netting.
5 ft. high, 18 in. diameter.
6 ft. ,, 18 in. ,,

No. 402.

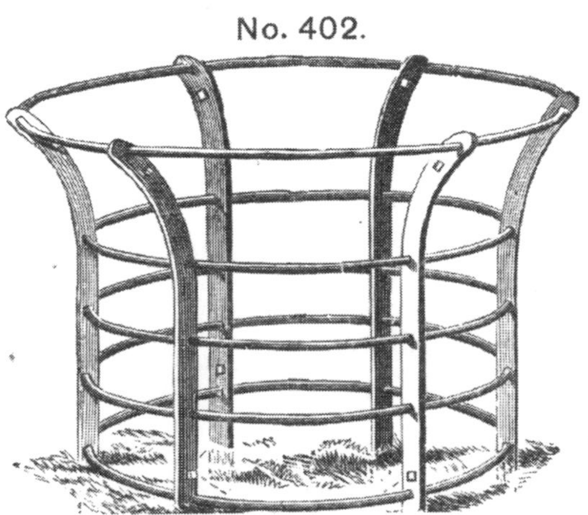

THIS Guard is specially suited for low-growing and any bushy trees or for clumps. Very effective and strong against cattle.
4 ft. high. 4 ft. diameter, 5 rings, top one ⅝ in., others ½ in.
4 ft. 6 in. high, 4 ft. diameter, 5 rings, top one ⅝ in., others ½ in.

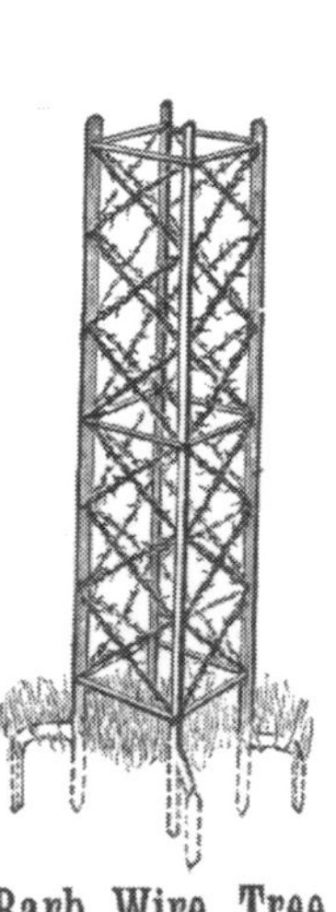

Barb Wire Tree Guard.

6 ft. high, 12 in. square.

No. 409.

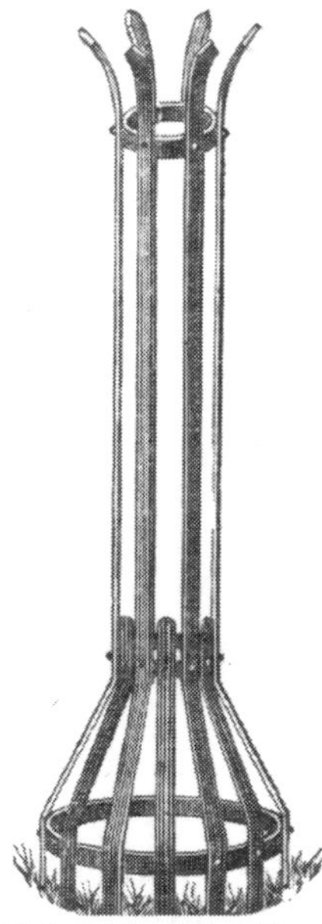

6 ft. high, 6 in. diam. at top. 18 in. diam. at bottom. 2 Vertical Bars, 1 in. by ¼ in., others ¾ in. by ¼ in.

NATURAL GRASS SEEDS FOR PERMANENT PASTURE
AND
ALTERNATE HUSBANDRY;
ALSO FOR
FINE GARDEN LAWNS AND PARKS.

The following Sorts may be had *separate* or *mixed*, at the lowest market prices. **The Seeds of each sort may be seen in large quantities in our Warehouses, and growing Specimens of most of them in our Sample Grounds.** All the best and most suitable of them are contained in our Mixtures for the several purposes described in next page.

Alopecurus pratensis.
Anthoxanthumodoratum
Agrostis stolonifera.
Avena flavescens.
Achillea Millefolium.
Avena pratensis.
Cynosurus cristatus.
Dactylis glomerata.
Festuca duriuscula.
Festuca elatior.
Festuca gigantea.
Festuca heterophylla.
Festuca pratensis.
Festuca ovina.
Festuca rubra.
Festuca tenuifolia.
Festuca hordeiformis.
Glyceria fluitans.
Glyceria aquatica.
Holcus lanatus.
Holcus avenaceus.
Hordeum bulbosum.
Lolium Italicum.
Lolium perenne tenue.
Lolium perenne Stickneyanum.
Lolium perenne Paceyanum.
Lolium perenne sempervirens.
Lotus corniculatus.
Lotus corniculatus major.
Medicago sativa.
Medicago lupulina.
Phleum pratense major.
Phleum pratense minor.
Poa pratensis.
Poa trivialis.
Poa nemoralis.
Poa angustifolia.
Poa fertilis.
Poa sempervirens.
Petroselinum sativum.
Trifolium repens.
Trifolium pratense perenne.
Trifolium minus.
Trifolium hybridum.

And several others.

As some Agriculturists feel a pleasure in making their own selection of Grass Seeds, the above List is presented, but the greatest economy and certainty of success will be obtained by procuring our Mixtures, which are specially adapted for various soils.

We have had the honour of supplying our Grass Seeds to the

ROYAL FARMS near WINDSOR and at OSBORNE, ISLE OF WIGHT;
ALSO TO THE
CRYSTAL PALACE COMPANY,
the Grass Seeds by which so many acres of arable land have been converted into the **Beautiful Park and Lawns now so much admired at SYDENHAM;**
ALSO TO THE
HORTICULTURAL SOCIETY OF LONDON, FOR THE GARDENS AT TURNHAM GREEN;
And to most of the Public Parks, Gardens, Asylums, &c. in the Kingdom.

THE PEOPLE'S PARK, HALIFAX.

This magnificent Park, presented to the town of Halifax by Frank Crossley, Esq., M.P., was laid down with our permanent Grass Seeds, and, at the inaugural meeting held last summer, had already become a beautiful sward. (See ILLUSTRATED LONDON NEWS, *August* 22*nd*, 1857.) We have since been honoured with further orders for Seeds to extend the Pleasure Ground.

THE ALDERSHOT CAMP.

By the skill of the Engineers' Corps, and with a supply of our Grass Seeds especially adapted to the soil and situation, there are now some very perfect swards formed on these bleak hills, especially those at the stations of LORD PANMURE and THE COMMANDER'S, GENERAL KNOLLYS, forming a pleasing contrast to the surrounding barren waste.

FORMATION OF GRASS LAWNS FROM SEED.

It will be admitted by all that good velvety turf is one of the most ornamental objects of which dressed ground can boast; therefore any hint in the way of improving a lawn not very good is at all times acceptable, especially as there is much unsightly turf to be seen in various places, some of which might be improved by a little judicious outlay.

In the first place, let us suppose that a sort of hungry gravel has to be covered with lawn turf. Here the predominance of stones is a great drawback, as the earth recedes from them, and leaves them standing in bold relief when the seed is sown, for we presume the case will not admit of turf being imported into it. From a soil of this sort it is prudent to rake off all the stones that can be had from the surface, and if a covering of about an inch of good earth can be had, so much the better. On this let the grass seeds be sown at any time when it is ready, and the ground very well rolled; nature will usually do the rest. The object in removing the stones is to keep them away from the scythe, and the more fine earth placed at the top the better the quality of the grass lawn, and the less likelihood of its burning in hot summers.

A shallow soil resting on chalk is almost as unmanageable as the last, not so much from the presence of stones as from a disposition it has to produce plants inimical to a nice close-bottomed turf, the Plantain being the most annoying. Prepare for sowing as directed above. Mow as often as possible, and when Plantain and other weeds assume an unbecoming growth, let boys be directed to go over the lawn, and cut each one up singly about an inch below the surface, not deeper, and put about a teaspoonful of salt on the cut part. This will not in all cases exterminate these pests, but it kills many. The evils of these plants are the naked, raw spots seen in the lawn in winter, as they die down then. May is, perhaps, the best time to kill them. Dandelions may be subjected to a like fate, and, if necessary, Yarrow or Milfoil, Sainfoin, Chicory, and some other weeds might be extirpated in the same way.

A rich garden soil for a lawn is as bad as any to manage; not but that the grasses grow well on it, and their general luxuriance checks the production of Daisies, but then the richness of the soil encourages worms, which are very troublesome in autumn and in mild winters. The only remedy for this is to give a good coating of ashes or chalk an inch or so below the surface. A partial remedy for the time being is to give the lawn a good watering with lime water; but, as may be expected, this is not lasting in its effects.

A dry, black, peaty soil sometimes produces a nice agreeable surface, moss being predominant, and, to those who like this kind of surface, black peat earth might be added to other soils when it can be obtained; but the grasses it produces are hard and wiry, and were it not for the presence of moss its surface would not be agreeable.

A loose, running sand is also bad for producing a good sward, though it may be done with time and patience; but the grasses on this soil are not deep rooted, and are easily affected by dry weather, and also easily damaged by any one running or stamping about. It is, however, free from worms, and sometimes becomes mossy.

Perhaps the best description of soil for a lawn is the stiff loam or clayey soils which predominate in so many districts. This ought not to be by any means rich, as a rapid growth is not wanted in the grasses of a lawn; but, in preparing it for laying down, let the surface be as much alike in quality as possible, and do not stint the quantity of seed. A very stiff clay is no better than a very dry sand for resisting drought, as it is, in a measure, sealed up against the insertion of roots, and the surface contracting by the withdrawal of moisture, it is liable to crack, &c., to a great depth. Nevertheless, a stiff soil usually makes the best lawn.

Sowing seed is the general way of establishing a lawn. Much depends on the season and condition of the ground at the time of sowing, and still more on the absence of small birds, who are very fond of grass and clover seeds, and destroy more than is generally supposed. A very slight raking in will protect the seeds much, or a sowing of wood-ashes will render them distasteful. Rolling, however, is at all times indispensable, and it is a good practice to sow a very thin scattering of barley amongst the grass seeds, which, coming up quickly, tends to shade and protect the tender grass.

The best time to sow grass seeds is either in April or about the beginning of September. If at the latter time, the seeds ought to have been the produce of the same season. Sowing plenty of them is also advised, as the little extra expense for a good lawn ought not to be denied.

One important thing should not be forgotten in the preparation of the ground: let it all have a surface of about six inches alike, for nothing looks worse than to see a lawn grow all in patches. One exception, however, may be mentioned, and that is, if there be any steep slopes facing the south or other exposed places, let the earth on them be better than in the ground level, for the aspect and other causes render such places liable to burn with less sun than level places. They ought, therefore, to be of better material, and turf ought to be provided to lay there if accuracy be expected.

It is only proper here to observe that no lawn can be maintained long in good order without successive rollings, unless it be well used in walking on. Mowing alone will not secure a good bottom without that compression which the roller or foot of the pedestrian alike tend to give.

From the JOURNAL OF HORTICULTURE.

ST. PAUL'S CHURCHYARD, LONDON.

As a striking instance of the possibility of producing a good green sward under the most unfavourable circumstances, we may instance St. Paul's Churchyard, London. The remarkable transformation which has been effected in this Churchyard, in the centre of the great Metropolis, by sowing grass seeds specially prepared by us last Spring, has surprised all who remember its former bare and untidy appearance. The Cricket Ground of Christ Church, Oxford, also sown at the same time, is now as perfect a piece of turf as can be desired.

MR. MARTIN SUTTON'S ESSAY ON LAYING DOWN LAND TO PERMANENT PASTURE.

This Essay, which appeared in Vol. XXII. Part II. of the "Journal of the Royal Agricultural Society," and has been pronounced by high authority to be one of the most practical articles on the subject yet published, will be supplied gratis to any of our customers who may be pleased to apply for it.

TENNIS LAWNS from SUTTON'S SEEDS

Are far more enduring, of finer quality, and less costly than lawns made from laid turf. We prepare the several prescriptions named below from the best seeds produced by the last harvest, proved by reliable tests to be strong in germinating power.

Sutton's Pamphlet on the Formation and Improvement of Lawns and Tennis and Cricket Grounds, gratis and post free.

Sutton's Fine Grasses only, for Tennis Grounds and Bowling Greens.

Sow from 3 to 4 bushels per acre to form new grounds, or 1 bushel per acre to improve the sward.

Per gallon, **3s. 6d.**; *per bushel,* **25s.**

'My Tennis Lawn which was sown with your seed in April was played on nearly all the season from the end of June and has been most satisfactory.'—G. J. EADY, Esq., M.D., Roslin.

'The Grass seed you supplied for a new Tennis Court has made a splendid sward—far better than if laid down with turf.'—Mr. H. HOWARD, *Gardener to* A. E. STUDD, Esq.

'Our Tennis Court is indeed a success. It has not a weed, and there is not a better court in England.'—The Rev. G. R. ROBERTS, Fulmodestone Rectory.

'The Tennis Lawn sown with your seeds has turned out a complete success. It has been a great surprise to many friends living near who quite laughed at my idea of raising a lawn from seed to play on the same season.'—W. B. BILLINGHURST, Esq., Woodlands.

Sutton's Fine Grasses and Clovers for Garden Lawns.

Sow from 3 to 4 bushels per acre for making a new lawn, or 1 bushel per acre for improving the sward.

Per gallon, **3s. 6d.**; *per bushel,* **25s.**

'The velvet lawns produced from Sutton's fine Lawn Grass Seeds were so exquisitely close, fine, and green, that they might have been growing many months, but as a matter of fact were only the production of a few weeks.'—*From the Report of the Windsor Agricultural Meeting in the* 'JOURNAL OF THE ROYAL AGRICULTURAL SOCIETY OF ENGLAND.'

Sutton's Fine Grasses and Clovers for Shaded Lawns.

Per gallon, **3s. 6d.**; *per bushel,* **25s.**

'The Lawn Grass Seeds had from you for the last three years for sowing under trees, where it is very difficult to grow in London, have given great satisfaction.'—Mr. W. SWEETING, *Gardener to* H. BONHAM CARTER, Esq.

'The Lawn from your Seeds looks such a beautiful green, quite a contrast to the other part of the Lawn surrounding it. The Lawn is quite shaded by large trees.'—Mr. H. M. BUTCHER, *Gardener to* W. CHADWICK, Esq.

Sutton's Fine Grasses and Clovers for Cricket Grounds.

Sow 3 bushels per acre to form a new ground, or 1 bushel per acre to improve the sward.

Per gallon, **3s. 6d.**; *per bushel,* **25s.**

'The Committee desire me to say that they have every reason to be satisfied with the Grass Seeds you have supplied for this ground (Kennington Oval) during the last few years.'—C. W. ALCOCK, Esq., Secretary to the Surrey County Cricket Club.

'Your Grass Seed for our Cricket Ground makes a good lawn, the grass being so fine in the blade. I cannot say too much respecting the quality of its germinating power, and it is also perfectly clean.'—Mr. W. WHITAKER, *Gardener to* the Rev. F. F. BRACKENBURY.

Sutton's Grasses and Clovers, specially adapted for Recreation Grounds.

Sow 3 bushels per acre to form a new ground, or 1 bushel per acre to improve the sward.

Per bushel, **17s. 6d.**

Sutton's Grasses and Clovers for Golf Links and Putting Greens.

For Golf Links, per bushel, **17s. 6d.**; *and for Putting Greens, per bushel,* **25s.**

The Sutton Lawn Mower ... ... *For sizes, prices, and other particulars see preceding page.*

SUTTON & SONS, Seed Growers and Merchants, READING, ENGLAND.

68

Sutton's Amateur's Guide and Spring Catalogue for 1881.

SUTTON'S PRIZE GRASS SEEDS.

Prize Medal, Paris 1878.

FOR LAWN TENNIS, GARDEN LAWNS, AND CRICKET GROUNDS,

IN SPECIALLY PREPARED

MIXTURES OF THE FINEST GRASSES AND CLOVERS.

		Price of Seed.
For Garden Lawns AND Croquet Grounds.	Sutton's 'Prize' Mixture of Fine Lawn Grasses and Clovers, as supplied to the Principal International Exhibitions, the Royal Palaces, and many of the largest Estates in Europe ... ... *Sow 3 bushels (or about 60 lbs.) per acre for making a New Lawn, or 20 to 30 lbs. per acre for improving the sward.*	Per lb., 1s. 3d. Per bushel, 25s.
For Lawn Tennis Grounds AND Bowling Greens.	Sutton's 'Lawn Tennis' Mixture of Fine Grasses only, as supplied to the principal grounds in the country ... ... *Sow 3 bushels per acre to form new grounds, or 30 lbs. per acre to improve.*	Per lb., 1s. Per bushel, 22s. 6d.
For Cricket Grounds.	Sutton's Cricket Ground Mixture of Fine Grasses and Clovers, as supplied to the Principal Cricket Grounds in England, also to Gibraltar, Malta, and other parts ... ... This Mixture has been used for many years at the Kennington Oval. The turf produced from it was greatly admired at the recent Intercolonial Cricket Match. *Sow 3 bushels per acre to form a new ground, or 30 lbs. per acre to improve an old one.*	Per lb., 1s. Per bushel, 20s.

Sutton's Mixture for Shady Places on Lawns, &c. ... ... per lb., 1s. 3d.; per bushel, 25s.

SUTTON & SONS, SEEDSMEN TO H.I.M. THE GERMAN EMPEROR.

32

Fine Grass and Clover Seeds specially prepared for Lawns.

USEFUL HINTS ON LAWNS.

Making new or Improving old Garden Lawns, Lawn Tennis and Cricket Grounds, Croquet Grounds, and Bowling Greens.

IT will be admitted that a good, close, velvety turf is not only one of the most ornamental features in connection with a residence, but that it is of especial value in such enjoyable pastimes as Lawn Tennis, Cricket, and other games practised in the open air during the summer months.

It is quite an erroneous idea to suppose that a good close turf can only be obtained from turves; on the contrary, we have no hesitation in saying that the best Lawns and Tennis Grounds are those which have been produced from seed. By this means (supposing at all times that *pure* and suitable Grass seeds are sown) weeds, which are almost invariably found in turves, are avoided. But a little patience is necessary to avoid using the ground before the young plants are thoroughly established. If the spot proposed to be made into a Lawn or Tennis Ground is thoroughly cleaned, levelled, &c. by August, and the seed sown either in that month or in September, the turf will be ready for use during the following summer, provided proper attention has been paid to mowing, rolling, &c. Grounds sown in the spring will, with good management, produce greensward in a few weeks, and a turf in a few months. We have in our minds a Lawn sown on April 16, which by the beginning of August was a close turf fit for playing Lawn Tennis; but we need scarcely say that it is not desirable to commence playing too early on newly-made Lawns.

There are four principal points to be remembered in making a Lawn:—

1. **The preparation.**
2. **The sowing.**
3. **The after management.**
4. **The best means of improving after constant use.**

These points we will briefly refer to in the order named.

1. In the first place, careful preparation of the ground proposed to be laid down to turf is necessary. This should be commenced by draining, if found requisite, and digging to the depth of 6 to 12 inches, according to the nature of the soil. The land should then be levelled and made firm with a heavy iron roller, and subsequently raked, to remove stones, &c. Where the natural soil is too stony, a supply of good mould should be spread over it, to the depth of 2 or 3 inches. If the land is poor, some well-rotted stable dung will be very beneficial; but where this cannot be obtained, the best dressing of artificial manure is 2 cwt. of superphosphate of lime, 1 cwt. of Peruvian guano, and 1 cwt. of ground bones per acre. After the ground has been made thoroughly fine and clean, a heavy iron roller should again be used to make it perfectly level, and as the subsequent appearance of the Lawn depends in a great measure on this part of the preparation, we cannot too strongly urge the importance of its being well done. The ground should then be evenly raked and the seed sown.

From the middle of March to the end of April, and from the middle of August to the middle of September, are the best periods to sow seeds for making New Lawns; but a handful of seed can with advantage be scattered on bare spots at any time except in the severe winter months.

2. The sowing is a most important feature to be observed. Not only should the seeds be new and pure, but it is essential that suitable varieties be chosen, or there cannot be a satisfactory result. From long practical experience we recommend the following sorts as most suitable for producing a close, velvety Garden Lawn:—

Cynosurus cristatus, *Crested Dogstail.*
Festuca ovina, *Sheep's Fescue.*
Festuca tenuifolia, *Fine-leaved Fescue.*
Lolium perenne Suttonii, *Sutton's Dwarf Perennial Rye Grass.*
Poa pratensis, *Smooth-stalked Meadow Grass.*
Poa sempervirens, *Evergreen Meadow Grass.*
Poa nemoralis, *Woodside Meadow Grass.*
Medicago lupulina, *Yellow Trefoil.*
Lotus corniculatus, *Birdsfoot Trefoil.*
Trifolium repens perenne, *Perennial White Clover.*
Trifolium minus, *Yellow Suckling.*

These we mix in their proper proportions, and they should be sown at the rate of 3 bushels or 60 lbs. per statute acre, or 1 gallon to 6 rods or perches. Birds are very fond of Grass seeds, and care should be taken to keep them off until the seeds are well up. For Lawn Tennis grounds we advise the sowing of fine Grasses only, because Clover plants do not wear so well as grass, and they retain moisture longer.

3. After the sowing has been accomplished, the ground should again be rolled, and as soon as the young plants have attained the height of 2 or 3 inches, the whole plot should be carefully gone over with a sharp scythe. From April to October it should be mown at least every ten days, and more often if the weather be showery and a quick growth produced. **Frequent mowing and rolling are indispensable to maintain the turf in good order.** A close green sward will thus be obtained in nearly as short a time as a Lawn produced by turves, while it will be far more permanent, and at much less expense. Mowing Machines are excellent after a comparatively close turf is established; but for the first six months after sowing we recommend the scythe to be used in preference to the machine.

It will sometimes happen that annual weeds come up; these can easily be checked, if not destroyed, by mowing them off *as soon as they make their appearance.* Plantains, dandelions, and daisies, too, being indigenous to the soil, will often appear, and these must be taken up, each one singly, about an inch below the surface (not deeper), and a little salt dropped over the cut part.

4. For Lawns requiring improvement, it is only necessary to sow seed, at the rate of about 20 lbs. per acre, either in the spring or autumn. Before doing this well rake the ground with a small-tooth rake, then sow, and carefully roll the plot.

On Lawn Tennis or Cricket Grounds, where the turf has become bare through constant use, we advise a thick sowing of seeds on the bare spots in September, or early in March, rolling subsequently, and mowing as soon afterwards as practicable. A slight dressing of manure over the whole playing square during the winter will often be found beneficial in encouraging the growth of finer kinds of Grasses, and help to produce a close-growing turf. We should not omit to mention that here, as in fine Garden Lawns, mowing alone will not ensure a good bottom without that compression which a roller only can give.

Moss in Lawns is generally a sign of poorness in the soil, or a want of drainage; to remove the moss, rake off as much as possible, apply a top-dressing of quick-lime mixed with rich compost in the winter, and sow more seed in the spring; or a top-dressing of soot will, by encouraging the growth of grass, destroy the moss. This should be applied in the spring, at the rate of about 16 bushels per acre.

'The Lawn sown with your Seed last September has far exceeded my most sanguine expectations.'
A. E. SEYMOUR, Esq., *Teddington.*

100 Webbs' Spring Catalogue for 1888.

WEBBS' PRIZE LAWN GRASS SEEDS.

Either with Clovers, without Clovers, or to Renovate Lawns, etc.

PARIS, 1878.

FOR LAWNS.

WEBBS' BEST MIXTURES.

1s. 3d. *per pound,*
24s. *per bushel.*

WEBBS' ORDINARY MIXTURES.

1s. *per pound,*
20s. *per bushel.*

LIVERPOOL, 1886.

FOR LAWNS.

From GEO. ROWE, Esq., Hale. 30th March.
"A Lawn was laid down here with your Seeds in September last, and although the weather was anything but favourable the result is most satisfactory, it now being well covered and looking very green. I shou'd never think of using other Seeds after trying yours."

From THOMAS YATES, Esq., Padgate.
"Webbs' Lawn Grass Seeds, had in 1883, rapidly produced a most splendid Lawn, and its luxuriant appearance is admired by every one that sees it. I am so much pleased with its fine texture and compact growth that I purpose extending it next year."

From Mr. ROBERT CROSS, Gardener to H. C. Beddoes, Esq.
"I am pleased to tell you that the Lawn Grass Seeds you supplied for the Hereford Ladies' College have given great satisfaction, and are looking remarkably well."

WEBBS' PRIZE LAWN GRASS SEEDS ARE THE BEST FOR GARDEN LAWNS, TENNIS, CROQUET & CRICKET GROUNDS, BOWLING GREENS, ETC.

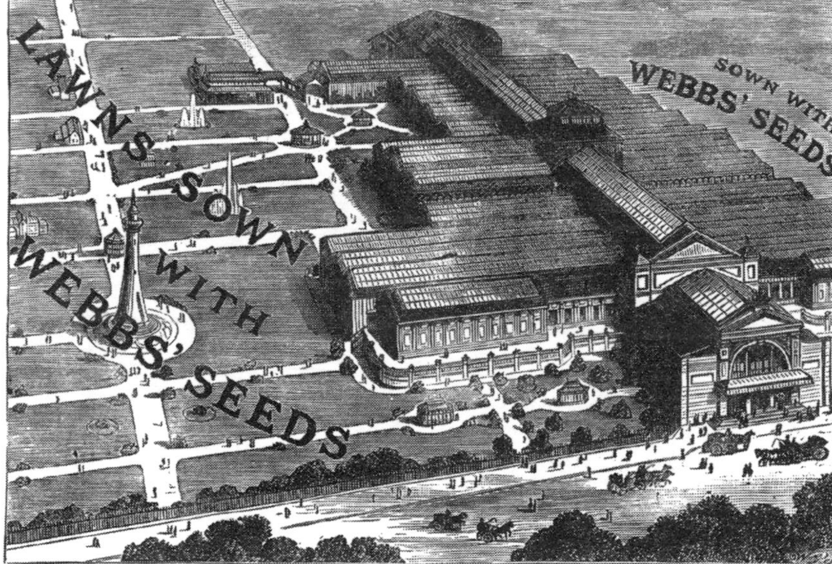

BIRD'S-EYE VIEW OF THE LIVERPOOL INTERNATIONAL EXHIBITION, 1886,
where Webbs' Prize Lawn Grass Seeds produced the magnificent Lawns in a marvellously short time.

FOR INSTRUCTIONS ON MAKING AND RENOVATING A LAWN, ALSO ON MAKING A LAWN TENNIS GROUND, SEE NEXT PAGE.

From "THE LIVERPOOL DAILY POST," May 26, 1886.
"LIVERPOOL INTERNATIONAL EXHIBITION.—*The plots sown by Messrs. Webb, of Stourbridge, who are elsewhere exhibitors, are doing their part nobly, and fairly disproving the theory that green Lawns can be more quickly formed out of sods than well-conditioned Grass Seeds. In this instance, at all events, the very opposite is the case, Messrs. Webbs' sowings looking beautifully fresh and green, while many portions of the ground which had a start of them by being carefully sodded among the first operations on the plateau are looking bare and brown, and only beginning to sprout. Contrasting the appearance of these plots with that of the eastern portion of the ground makes one long for an extension of this excellent system to that still benighted part.*"

From HARRY HEATON, Jr., Esq., Deanhurst.
"The 'Special Lawn Tennis Grass and Clover Seeds' with which you supplied me last year have given great satisfaction."

From Mr. RICHARD SANDFORD, Gardener to Sir John Willoughby, Bart., Baldon House.
"The Grass Seeds you supplied for our new Lawn (about 2 acres) last June have given great satisfaction. About one-half was sown then, and the other half as late as August, and considering the short time (now January) it is making a very fine thick turf."

From W. H. READ, Esq., Swindon.
"The Grass Seeds you supplied for the New Cemetery have come remarkably well, and have given me great satisfaction."

☛ "Fairy Rings on Lawns and their Eradication," see Webbs' Pamphlet, *gratis and post free.*

See pages 48 and 49 for Webbs' original article—"Historical Notes on Vegetables."

Making and Renovating Lawns.

UNQUESTIONABLY one of the most important adjuncts to the modern garden, whether of large or small dimensions, is a good Lawn, and to provide this no expense should be spared in the first instance, for as with many other things, if the work be thoroughly and efficiently done, much after expense and trouble are avoided. In too many cases, however, especially as regards the villa gardens in the suburbs of large towns, Lawns are a constant source of anxiety to the proprietors or occupiers, as not only is considerable outlay incurred in their formation, but the frequent renovation required to preserve them in satisfactory condition very quickly renders them the most expensive, and at the same time the least pleasing, portion of the garden. In a great measure this is due to the employment of turf, concerning which there is an erroneous impression amongst amateurs to the effect that a good Lawn can be more quickly produced by turfing than by sowing seeds It is true there are some positions in which turf is preferable, namely for very steep slopes; but in the majority of cases, where the Lawn is to be level or only slightly sloped, good grass seeds are far more suitable, as all who have had much experience in Lawn-making can testify. It is not easy to procure thoroughly good turf, and where it has to be purchased or conveyed long distances it becomes extremely expensive; moreover, there is always the danger that it may contain a number of weeds, which would cause much trouble to eradicate during the ensuing year; further still, often when every care has been taken, the turf will fail to 'take' to the soil, and die, leaving bare patches. With seed-sowing, however, there is no such difficulty if due attention be given to the proper preparation of the ground and thoroughly good seeds are procured; but if otherwise, disastrous results may be anticipated. It may be further observed that, when ordering grass seeds, the character of the soil and subsoil, situation, whether sheltered or exposed, should be stated, as mixtures suitable to the particular soil and locality can then be provided; much trouble and dissatisfaction both to vendor and purchaser being prevented by attention to these matters.

The respective merits of seeds and turf for Lawn-making have been thus compared, chiefly with a view to correct the too prevalent idea that the latter is the best; and if any one who still doubts the facts will take the trouble to compare the expenditure incurred and the results achieved in a few typical instances of each, the decision will be undoubtedly in favour of the seeds.

PREPARING THE GROUND.—When a site has been chosen for the Lawn, the first point needing attention is the nature of the soil and subsoil, upon which will depend much of the labour required. If the soil be of a good medium texture, neither very heavy nor excessively light, with sufficient drainage below in the shape of a porous subsoil, the proprietor is fortunate, as he has all the preliminary requirements to ensure success in his undertaking. This is, however, seldom the case, for the soil usually needs special preparation, and in some instances it is even necessary to thoroughly drain it; but before undertaking the latter operation, it should be carefully considered if some more favourable position could be selected. With good natural drainage, all that is essential is well-digging the ground a spit or more in depth, thoroughly pulverising it to ensure its subsequent firmness and regular sinking. If it be too heavy, some lighter vegetable soil must be freely incorporated with it; if too light a little moderately heavy turfy loam will improve it, and if there be any doubt as regards its fertility, **our Special Grass Manure** should be dug in liberally. The next point of importance is levelling the surface, which must be well and repeatedly raked, all large stones being removed, and any hardened pieces of earth which cannot be readily broken. As portions sink, the hollows should be firmly filled, ample time being allowed for the thorough settling of the soil, which is greatly aided by a few heavy showers of rain, and at the best time for Lawn-making—March or April—these are usually sufficiently abundant. Preparing the ground should never be attempted when it is very dry, as it takes much longer to settle satisfactorily when dug at that time, and if it be urgent to proceed with the work under such conditions, the soil must be well watered and allowed to remain undisturbed for a short time. All being in readiness, the next operation will be—

SOWING THE SEEDS.—Having ascertained that the soil is firm, level, and suitably moist, preparation must be made for sowing the seeds. Here it may be remarked, in the interest of those forming Lawns, that it is unwise to be too economical in the quantity of seeds used, if the best results are desired, and the slight additional outlay needed to procure an adequate quantity will yield ample satisfaction in the success achieved. To ensure a thick and even sward, **3 to 4 bushels (or 60 to 80 lbs.) of our best Mixture of Prize Lawn Grass Seeds, per acre,** will be required,—some of the finest Lawns we have ever seen having been sown with seeds at the last-mentioned rate. The selection of suitable mixtures is best left to the seedsman, whose reputation will be the purchaser's safeguard. The seeds should be sown broadcast and as evenly as possible, then lightly rake the soil and roll it, also watering it if necessary, repeating the latter, if the weather be dry, until the seeds germinate. In a fortnight to three weeks or a month, according to the season and locality, the grass will be ready for the first cutting, which should be done with a scythe, care being taken not to cut it too closely. If good progress is made, and it is seen that the grass is strong, the machine may be run over it lightly in a week's time from the first cutting, continuing this treatment until the grass is well-established, when it must be frequently rolled and cut as required. It is sometimes advisable to form the verges with turves if a good sample can be obtained, as a firm neat edge is then secured at once, which adds greatly to the beauty of a Lawn.

RENOVATING LAWNS.—To preserve a Lawn in good condition, an annual dressing of manure is needed, and if this be regularly and judiciously performed, little will be required in the way of renovation, as if a few seeds be sown each year when the dressing is applied, wherever the turf shows a tendency to become bare, a fresh even verdure will be maintained. Unfortunately, neglect for a few years often renders elaborate measures indispensable to its preservation, or rather renewal. When this is the case, well-decomposed horse or cow manure—the latter being very good—or **our Special Grass Manure** may be applied **at the rate of 5 to 6 cwt. per acre.** The first-named should be spread on, about an inch or so in thickness, the bare surface having been first raked and sown with **our mixture of Seeds, at the rate of 1 bushel (or 20 lbs.) per acre,** while, if the Lawn appears to want substance, **10 to 12 lbs. per acre of Trifolium repens** may be sown over the whole. Renovation, however, is only advisable where the Lawn has been thoroughly made, as if it is uneven or insufficiently drained it would be far better to make a new one.

Our specially-prepared Compound Manure has proved very successful when applied as a dressing for Lawns, either annually to preserve their beauty or to renovate those that have been neglected. This manure should be mixed with about twice its weight of fine soil, and thinly strewn over the surface **at the rate of 3 to 4 cwt. per acre.** As a liquid manure it may be employed if well mixed with water in the proportion of 5 to 6 ounces to a gallon of water, and applied by means of a can with a coarse rose.

Making a Lawn Tennis Ground.

THE particulars given above, in reference to forming Lawns generally, are equally applicable to a Lawn Tennis Ground as regards the preparation of the soil; but, if possible, greater attention must be given to draining the site, especially if the soil is at all inclined to be heavy. The position should, however, be very carefully selected, as on a light soil, if the drainage be suitable, the turf is soon in good condition after a shower; and play is better on such a Lawn. The correct size of a Lawn Tennis Ground may not be generally known: the regulation court for four players is a space 26 yards long, by 12 yards wide, but a considerable margin should be allowed on all sides, the total space being about 35 yards in length, by 20 yards in width. The majority of such grounds, which are now almost as indispensable in the garden as the Lawn itself, are made perfectly level, but some players contend that this is not so satisfactory as when the ground is raised to the centre slightly, say 4 to 6 inches. **Our best Mixture of Prize Lawn Grass Seeds** should be used, and liberally, as it is important to procure a dense even turf, which, if frequently rolled and cut with a machine, and watered in hot and dry weather, will ultimately become as soft as velvet. It is advisable to have the Ground surrounded by a light wire fence, which should be constructed as neatly as possible, and painted green, so that it is not too conspicuous. The height at the ends may be 5 to 6 feet, and at the sides 3 feet. If it is desired to form a Tennis Ground on a portion of a Lawn already existing, it is a good plan to raise the turf and spread a layer of fine coal ashes upon the soil before re-laying it.

From S. H. FACEY, Esq., Abergavenny.
"I cannot speak too highly of the Lawn Grass Seeds supplied by you in March last. I have a splendid Lawn."

From J. SCRIVEN, Esq., The Hirst.
"The Lawn Seeds have produced a perfect Lawn in every respect; it is now quite equal to any old grass."

Celery.

(*Apium graveolens.*) FRENCH, *Céleri.* ☞ For Cultivation, see page 52.

Webbs' Mammoth Red Celery.

The best Red Celery. 6d. and 1s. per packet.

This is a very large, quick-growing variety ; solid, crisp, and possessing an excellent nutty flavour. It is the hardiest Celery in commerce—grown successfully everywhere, and consequently very popular. Awarded **First Prizes** at the leading Shows.

From Mr. J. MOORE, Close Cottage.

"I decidedly prefer the Mammoth Celery for a first crop, as it is quick in growth, and will cut a larger heart than Celery twice as thick."

From Mr. JAMES OWEN, Springfield Cottage.

"I gained 1st and 2nd Prizes with your Mammoth Red Celery at our Show. It was grown side by side with other kinds, and is the best in cultivation."

Webbs' New Pearl White Celery.

The best White Celery. 1s. 6d. and 2s. 6d. per packet.

A splendid new variety of very strong constitution, and one extremely valuable for exhibition purposes. The heads, which remain fit for use a long time, are large, solid, exceedingly crisp, and fine-flavoured.

From W. SAUL, Esq., Lancaster.

"The 'New Pearl White' Celery is exceedingly crisp, of very good flavour, and easily cultivated ; it has been praised by all who have either seen or tried it. I shall grow it in preference to any other kind."

From Mr. JOHN GUYER, Aden Cottage.

"The quality of your New Pearl White Celery was very good ; the best I have ever tasted."

Per packet.	s.	d.
Webbs' Solid White.—A large, handsome variety, with dwarf habit of growth ; very solid, crisp, and of the finest flavour, . *6d. and*	1	0
Major Clarke's Red.—Very solid and crisp ; keeps well, ... *6d. and*	1	0
Sandringham White.—A splendid variety ; dwarf habit, ... *6d. and*	1	0
White Plume.—Firm, large, and of fine flavour,	1	0
Perfection.—A superior white sort, . *6d. and*	1	0

Per packet.	s.	d.
Webbs' Improved Leicester Red.—A distinct variety ; very crisp, *6d. and*	1	0
Wright's Grove White.—An excellent sort for early use, ... *6d. and*	1	0
Wright's Grove Red.—A large variety of fine flavour, ... *6d. and*	1	0
Celeriac, or Turnip-rooted.—Principally used for soups, ... *6d. and*	1	0
Celery Seed, for Soups, *3d. per oz., 2s. 6d. per lb.*		

We can also supply the following superior varieties at 6d. and 1s. per packet:—

Williams' Matchless White. | Cole's Crystal White. | Ivery's Nonsuch. | Sulham Prize Pink.
Williams' Matchless Red. | Cole's Superb Red. | Manchester Red. | Seymour's Champion White.

THE KITCHEN GARDEN AND ORCHARD

In the 1990s, with its advanced methods of food preservation, chilled, fast distribution and an unlimited supply of out-of-season crops through imports and deep freezing, the kitchen garden has ceased to have the significance it had in the Victorian era, when it played a vital part in supplying the householder with a year-round balanced diet. Whether vegetables were produced by the cottager in the plot around his home, or on a grander scale in the sheltered, walled areas of larger houses, it was essential that a constant and balanced supply was obtained in order to prevent the malnourishment so often encountered in poorer areas where access to such necessities was limited.

The Victorian gentry could afford to have an appetite for out-of-season vegetables and fruit, and home production necessitated complex glasshouse cultivation and forcing techniques. It is easy to see why the numbers of vegetables in modern seed lists have dwindled so significantly since the Victorian era, and why flower seeds now occupy the lion's share of catalogues. What is worth noting, however, is with all the plant breeding and research of the intervening years, some varieties popular with Victorians, such as 'Musselburgh' leeks, 'Tom Thumb' and 'All the Year Round' lettuces, 'The Student' parsnips, 'Early Scarlet Horn' carrots and 'Victoria' rhubarb remain household names.

Whilst a well-stocked vegetable garden or plot is still the pride of many a modern gardener, with land at a premium, gardening staff an unusual luxury and the convenience of a well-stocked local supermarket, it is now more difficult, despite new root-stocks and trained varieties, for the average householder to be self-supporting in fresh fruit. The Victorian interest in producing a range of staple and exotic fruits is reflected in full lithographic glory in the catalogues of the day.

CULTIVATION OF ONION.

These require deep, strong, rich soil; therefore select ground which has been trenched two feet deep and heavily manured. Sow for the main crop as early in March as the ground can be found in a fit state. Mark out the ground into beds four feet wide, with alleys one foot wide between. If the ground is light, tread the beds firmly; after throwing a little out of the alleys and levelling them, rake the surface. Draw lines nine inches apart, sow thinly, and cover about a quarter of an inch thick with fine soil. Thin out when strong enough to proper distances, and keep the surface of the ground clean. If very large bulbs are desired, water liberally during dry weather, in summer with manure water. If the crop shows a tendency to grow too much to top and produce what is termed thick necks, press the tops down with the hand at the back of a wooden rake, and repeat this as may be necessary. Pull as soon as the tops decay; thoroughly dry, and house in a dry cool place. The silver-skin should be sown thickly upon poor hard ground in May to produce small bulbs for pickling and cooking, and a sowing should be made the second week in August for spring and summer use.

PARSLEY.

	Ounce. *s.*	*d.*
Dunnett's Garnishing	0	6
Hardy Winter Matchless	0	6
Myatt's Garnishing	0	6
Fine Double Curled	0	4

CULTIVATION.

Sow early in March for summer use in lines one foot apart, and thin out the plants to nine inches or one foot in the lines. For winter use sow the beginning of June, and transplant early in August to where slight protection can be afforded against severe weather. A turf pit covered with hurdles thatched with straw will answer. To secure fine large leaves the ground must be deep and full of manure, and a sprinkling of soot spread between the lines occasionally during showery weather will greatly increase the vigour of the plants. Hamburgh parsley is grown for its roots, and requires similar treatment to carrots, only that the plants need not be quite as far apart.

PARSNEP.

(Cheaper by the pound or half-pound.)

	Packet. *s.*	*d.*	Ounce. *s.*	*d.*
"The Student," a New Parsnep of delicious flavour, introduced by Professor Buckman, of the Royal Agricultural College, Cirencester. Gained First Prize at the Royal Horticultural Society's International Show . . . . . *In packets 2s. 6d., 1s., and*	0	6		
Hollow Crown, a well-known sort			0	4
True Jersey Marrow, imported direct from Jersey			0	6

Any spare piece of land sown with Parsnep will produce valuable feed for Cows and Pigs, if not required for the table.

The Parsnep a good substitute for the Potato.

An English resident in Jersey, writing to the Editor of *The Times*, recommends the Parsnep as a substitute for the Potato. He says:—"In Jersey and Guernsey many thousand tons of parsneps are grown annually, and without his dish of parsneps a real Jerseyman would scarcely think he had dined; a pig's foot, boiled or stewed with parsneps, forms the sole dinner of many a poor family. Jersey pork, the best in the world, is fed entirely on parsneps; the rich and delicious flavour of the Jersey butter in the winter time, when most other butters are rank and tasteless, is produced by the use of the parsnep in feeding cows."

CULTIVATION.

Sow in February or early in March in drills one foot or fifteen inches apart, covering the seed thinly. Thin out early to about nine inches apart, and keep the surface of the ground open and free from weeds. Store for winter use in a cool dry shed in sand or fine rich soil. These require a deep soil, and as fresh manure tends to cause the roots to branch, this should not be used; but land that has been very heavily manured the previous season, and trenched two feet deep in autumn and ridged up, should be selected; and if manure must be added, let this be kept eighteen inches below the surface.

THE STUDENT PARSNEP.

This was originated, or rather "ennobled," by Professor Buckman, of the Royal Agricultural College, Cirencester, from the wild Parsnep, a native of Britain.

Among his numerous experiments in the Botanical Gardens of the College, Professor Buckman has for successive years carried on the process of "ennobling" some of our native plants, from which he has gradually produced several valuable culinary vegetables of very superior flavour to the varieties in general cultivation.

The Student Parsnep is one of these, and will be found a great acquisition to the public when it is brought into general cultivation.

Having been favoured with the original stock of seed of this valuable plant three years since, and having had sufficient opportunities of testing its "fixedness" of character, as well as its superior flavour, we have this season raised a sufficient crop of seed to enable us to offer it in limited quantities to the public.

"From the Cheltenham Examiner," Oct. 30, 1862.

"THE STUDENT PARSNEP.—From the fact that this variety of parsnep took the first prize at the International Root and Fruit Show the first time that it has been exhibited, a few notes upon its production may be interesting to our readers. In 1847 was collected some wild parsnep seed, growing among some bushes on the top of the Cotteswolds, where this is one of the most frequent of weeds. The seed, after having been carefully kept through the winter, was sown in a prepared bed in the spring of 1848, in drills about eighteen inches apart. As the plants grew, they were duly thinned, leaving for the crop, as far as could be done, such specimens as had the broadest and smoothest leaves.

"The wild root is long, woody, and forked. The first crop from the wild seed presented great diversities in shape, being for the most part even more forked than the originals, but still with a decided tendency to fleshiness. Of these the best shaped were reserved for seeding, and having been kept the greater part of the winter in sand, some six of the best were planted in another plot for seed. The seed, then, of 1849 was sown in the spring of 1850 in a freshly prepared bed, the plant being treated as before; and so, following out the same plan one generation after another, a perfect root of a new shape, more delicate skin, freedom from disease, and a much better flavour, has been added to our list of garden esculents.

"The seed of this new variety is in the possession of the Messrs. Sutton, of Reading, it having been consigned to them, not only to insure a healthful condition from change of air and soil, but in order to its distribution over the country."

PEAS.

A Quart of Peas weighs rather less than 2 lbs.

N.B.—We have divided the best sorts of Peas into Five Sections, in accordance with their time of coming to maturity, &c., which will enable purchasers to select such as will succeed each other throughout the season, by taking one or more kinds from each Division. The leading kinds, marked thus (*), will be supplied by the peck at considerably reduced rates.

FIRST DIVISION—FOR THE VERY EARLIEST CROP.

To be sown in November, December, or January, for gathering in May and June.	Height in feet.	Quart. *s.*	*d.*
***Sutton's Early Champion**	3	1	0
This pea is worth a much higher price, being the forwardest pea known.			
*Early Emperor	3	0	9
***Daniel O'Rourke,** a popular variety, considered by some the forwardest pea	3	1	0
Sangster's No. 1, very similar to Daniel O'Rourke	3	1	0
Tom Thumb, very early, good for forcing, or for small gardens	1	1	6
Beck's Early Gem, very early and very dwarf	1	1	6

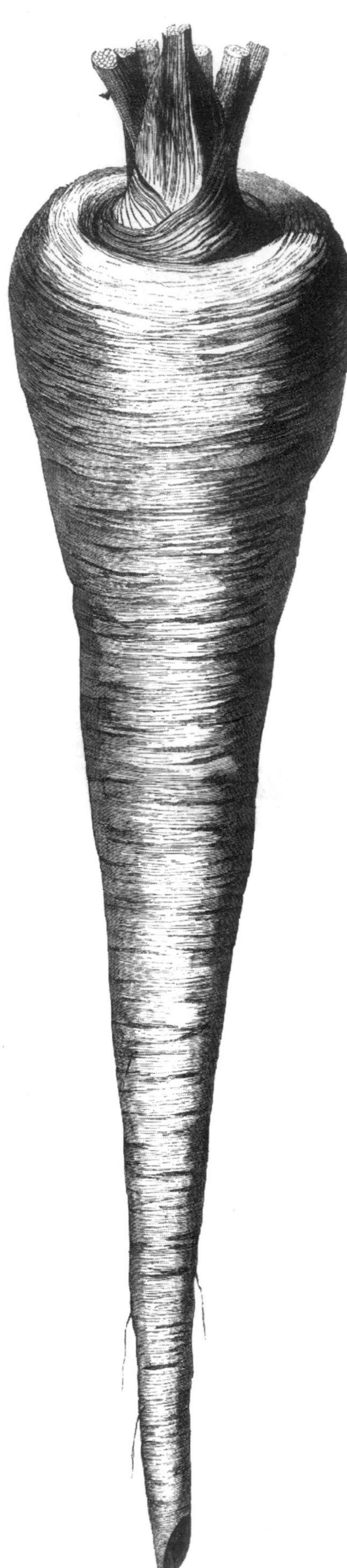

26 *Sutton's Spring Catalogue and Amateur's Guide for* 1863.

SCORZONERA, per ounce 9d.

CULTIVATION.

This requires exactly similar treatment as Salsafy, only it occupies rather more space; the lines should be eighteen inches apart, and the plants from nine to twelve inches.

STRAWBERRY SEED.

True French Alpine, British Queen, Princess Royal, and other choice sorts, each per packet, 6*d.*

The French Alpine Strawberry is easily raised from seed, and produces a succession of delicate fruit throughout the Summer and Autumn.

CULTIVATION.

Many cultivators consider that raising seedling plants is the best way of propagating the Alpine; for the plants from seed are vigorous, and produce finer fruit than those propagated by runners; and seedling plants of these, when properly managed, furnish fruit in autumn after the latest varieties are over. Sow early in March on a gentle hot-bed, either in boxes or on a bed of rich light soil, six to nine inches deep, placed on the fermenting materials, covering the seed very lightly with fine soil, and watering carefully until the plants appear. Then give air freely on fine days, and moderately when the weather is not frosty, and if the plants are too thick, thin them to about three inches each way, and aim at obtaining stout stocky plants, keeping them close to the glass. In June they should be fit for planting out, which should be done as soon as they are strong enough. Plant four lines in a five-foot bed, seven inches from plant to plant, and allow an eighteen-inch alley between the beds, and carefully attend to watering, until they get established, and during dry weather. If seedlings are to be raised with the view of obtaining new or improved sorts, the seeds may be sown in April on a bed of nicely prepared soil, on an open border, covering the seed very lightly with fine soil, and thinning out the plants as soon as strong enough, and keeping the surface of the ground clear of weeds, and open and watering during dry weather. Transplant early in August to where they are to stand to fruit, placing the plants one foot apart each way; and the Alpine, if not wanted to fruit the first autumn, may be raised and treated in the same way, and by picking off the blossoms as they appear until July, they will furnish a late crop the following season. For preparation of soil, see STRAWBERRY PLANTS.

SPINACH.

	Quart. s.	d.	Pint. s.	d.	Ounce. s.	d.
Round, *for summer use*	1	3	0	9	0	2
Prickly, *for winter and spring use*	1	3	0	9	0	2
					Packet.	
Perpetual Spinach, or Spinach Beet, excellent			2	6	0	6
New Zealand, *to be sown in heat, and transplanted*			2	6	0	6
Orache, or Mountain Spinach, very productive			2	6	0	6

CULTIVATION.

Sow the round-seeded early in March, and at intervals of three weeks, and for crops to furnish a supply during hot weather, sow every ten days. Sow the prickly-seeded the first or second week in August on rich but light well-drained soil, such as is not retentive of moisture, in lines one foot apart, thinning out the plants to eight inches in the line. Keep the surface of the ground clear of weeds, &c., by frequent stirrings with the hoe. The summer crop should be sown in lines the same distance apart, or between lines of peas or celery, &c., but if sown thinly, it need not be thinned out. For this spring or summer sowing, the ground cannot be too rich or too retentive of moisture, and it should be liberally supplied with water during dry hot weather, and sowings made when the ground is in a very dry state will vegetate sooner if the lines are well watered before the seeds are put in. The perennial spinach or white beet furnishes an excellent substitute for spinach during the summer, and as a vegetable is fully equal to the ordinary spinach, but is perhaps not as useful for greening in cookery. This requires the same treatment as beet, and a small breadth will yield a large supply. The New Zealand spinach requires to be treated like a half-hardy annual, raising it in gentle heat in March, and planting out from the middle of May to the beginning of June on rich, light, warm soil, and as the plants grow freely they should be placed about three feet apart each way. A dozen plants will furnish a supply for a moderate-sized garden.

Sutton's Spring Catalogue and Amateur's Guide for 1863. 27

TOMATO, OR LOVE APPLE.

Per Packet, 6d.

Large Red | Red Cherry
Large Yellow | Powell's New Early
New Upright, or Tomato de Láye

TURNIP.

	Pint. s.	d.	Ounce. s.	d.
Sutton's Early Short-top, *quite new, the quickest turnip known, a very superior turnip for general use*			0	6
Sutton's Improved White Globe	1	6	0	3
Polley's Nonsuch	1	6	0	3
Orange Jelly, good for late sowing	1	6	0	3
Red-top White Mousetail, *a remarkably sweet and mild turnip*	1	6	0	3
Early White Six Weeks Stone, a very early sort	1	6	0	3
Green-top Six Weeks, a delicious turnip for late use	1	6	0	3
Early Strap-leaved, very quick	2	6	0	6
Jersey Navet, an oblong white turnip of sweet mild flavour, good for late sowing to stand the winter			0	6
Chirk Castle Black Stone, keeps till late in spring, a white turnip with black skin			0	6
Smart's Mousetail Globe, large and solid, fine shape	1	6	0	3
New Long French (exhibited at the International Show)			0	6

The following at 3d. per ounce:—

White Dutch | Snowball | Pomeranian (large)
Finland Yellow | | American Red Stone

CULTIVATION.

Sow an early variety on a warm sheltered border, from the beginning to the middle of March, again early in April, and, at intervals of three weeks, until the middle of July. For winter use, sow the Orange Jelly, or some approved hardy variety, from the beginning to the middle of August. Sow in lines from one foot to fifteen inches apart, and thin out early to nine inches in the lines, selecting good, deep, rich soil especially for the summer crops, and before sowing in dry weather, well water the drills. If fly is troublesome on the young plants, which is frequently the case during dry hot weather, dust the plants early in the morning, when the foliage is wet with dew, with quick-lime, one or two dressings of which will eradicate this pest.

COMPLETE COLLECTIONS OF KITCHEN GARDEN SEEDS FOR ONE YEAR'S SUPPLY.

Gentlemen who do not keep a professional gardener, and who are not themselves acquainted with the sorts and quantities of Seeds required for the Kitchen Garden, can be supplied economically, as under; the extent of garden being given, and the sorts of Seeds being left to us:—

		£	s.	d.
For one year's supply	for a full-sized garden	£3	0	0
ditto	for a medium-sized garden	2	0	0
ditto	for a smaller garden	1	0	0
ditto	ditto	0	10	6
Collection for an extra large garden		5	0	0

The above Collections do not include Potatoes.

28 *Sutton's Spring Catalogue and Amateur's Guide for* 1863.

POTATOES FOR PLANTING.

PRICES PER TON MAY BE HAD ON APPLICATION.

☞ We have other sorts, but these are most worthy of recommendation.

*** *The sorts marked* (K) *are kidney-shaped.*

PRESENT PRICES.	Per pk. or stone of 14lbs. s.	d.	Per bushel of 56lbs. s.	d.	Per sack of 1½ cwt.
Sutton's Early Racehorse (K), earlier than any other potato known	5	0	18	0	Prices per sack will be given on application.
Hudson's Nonsuch (K), forwarder than the Early Ashleaf	5	0	18	0	
Hudson's Early May (K), quite new; one of the best potatoes for the main crop; it comes early, bears enormously, and keeps well	4	0	14	0	
Daintree's First Early, new sort, highly spoken of	2	6	9	0	
Carter's Champion, early forcing	5	0	18	0	
Early Ashleaf (K), a well-known early sort	3	0	10	0	
Myatt's Early Ashleaf (K), more productive than the preceding	3	0	10	0	
Early Walnutleaf (K), somewhat similar to Ashleaf, but shorter haulm, rather earlier, and fuller flavour	3	0	10	0	
Handsworth Early, one of the forwardest and best for forcing; very short in the haulm	3	6	12	0	
Early China, quite new, second early	4	0	14	0	
Soden's Early Oxford, one of the best early round potatoes	3	0	10	0	
Improved Early Shaw, a favourite potato with the London Market Gardeners	3	0	10	0	
Webb's Imperial (K), new large, very fine	3	6	12	0	
Fluke (K), fine productive and popular sort	2	0	7	0	
Dalmahoy, fine second early, and good for main crop	2	6	9	0	
Wellington, pink-eyed, round, strongly recommended	2	0	7	0	
Bracken (K), a fine mealy potato, red skin, delicious flavour	2	6	9	0	
Golden Ball or Red Regent, large, well-shaped, and fine-flavoured. (This sort gained a First Prize at the International Show, 1862, where it attracted much attention)	2	6	9	0	
Red Ashleaf (K), mealy, and keeps well	3	6	12	0	
Skerry Blue, very large and productive, new from Ireland	2	6	9	0	
Dawe's Matchless (K), prolific, large, fine flavour and shape	3	6	12	0	
The King (K). This may be fairly described as the finest potato in cultivation; gained a First Prize at the Royal Horticultural Society's International Show, and at Birmingham	5	0	18	0	
Mr. HUDSON, one of the most experienced potato growers in the kingdom, writes us:—"In all my fields of potatoes, the 'King' and 'Early May' are free from disease, though other sorts have it worse than usual. These two potatoes are about the finest and most productive of all I have ever grown, and to Market Gardeners will prove invaluable."					
The Queen (K), a very fine late sort, keeps well. (This was exhibited by Mr. Choyce, at the International Show, with "The King," to which the Prize was awarded)	5	0	18	0	
Flour Ball, the true sort, strongly recommended	2	0	7	0	
York Regent. (Cheaper in large quantities)	1	9	6	0	
Fortyfold, very productive, mealy, and fine flavour	2	0	7	0	

Early Frame | Snowball | Prince of Wales | Lemon Kidney
Birmingham Prizetaker | Fortyfold | Glory of England | Goldfinder
Alstone Kidney | Lapstone Kidney | Arrowsmith Seedling | British Queen

FOR FIELD CULTURE IN LARGE QUANTITIES, WE CAN SUPPLY GOOD SORTS OF POTATOES AT MUCH LOWER RATES.

N.B.—We deliver Potatoes, as well as Seeds, carriage free.

Sutton's Spring Catalogue and Amateur's Guide for 1863. 29

CULTIVATION OF THE POTATO.

For this crop select deep, rather light, sandy or loamy soil, well drained and of a rather dry nature, and, to avoid the necessity of applying fresh manure, choose ground that has been heavily manured for some exhausting green crop the previous season; the ground for spring planting should also be trenched, and ridged up as early in autumn as possible. Plant an early sort the beginning of January, as soon as the ground can be found in working condition, or if the soil is light and not retentive of moisture, in November, in lines eighteen inches apart, and eight inches between the sets, using for sets medium-sized whole tubers. Have the ground neatly levelled, and dig it over lightly, planting the sets in the opening at the proper distances, and covering with from four to six inches of soil. Early crops are also obtained by planting upon very slight hot-beds, and protecting by a garden-frame or mats stretched upon hoops; the main crops should be planted as early in March as possible, and the drills for sorts that produce much top should be two feet apart in the sets, in the lines from nine to twelve inches. When the plants appear above ground carefully draw up the soil about them, especially while there is any danger of frost, and until the haulm covers the ground, keep the surface deeply stirred by frequent hoeing, &c., and free from weeds. A sprinkling of charred vegetable refuse or wood-ashes, thrown over the sets in planting, will be useful as a manure, and may be of some service in preventing disease, and on strong retentive soil decayed tan used freely will be highly beneficial to the crop. But early planting is the most certain method of escaping the disease.

SEEDS FOR DISTRIBUTION TO COTTAGERS.

These are supplied at a reduction of about one-fourth from the Catalogue prices, with the view of assisting Clergymen and others who desire to encourage their Cottagers in the cultivation of their gardens. For this purpose we send the most useful kinds of Seeds only.

Should any of our customers who desire to distribute Seeds among Cottagers not find it convenient to purchase them, we shall be glad to hear from them, in case we have any to spare free of charge.

SUNDRY GARDEN REQUISITES.

Shaw's Tiffany, a light and durable material for protecting from sun or frost (20 yards long, 3 feet wide), 6s. per piece.

Ditto, the same size mineralised, 7s. per piece.

Ditto, 18 yards long, much stouter, 10s. per piece.

Gishurst Compound for destroying blight, mealy bug, scale, &c., in boxes, 1s., 3s., and 10s. 6d. each.

Netting for Fruit Trees in different sizes.

Cuba Bast for tying, 2s. 6d. per pound.

Ditto in packets, 6d., 1s., and 1s. 6d. each.

Largest Garden Mats.

Appleby's Tobacco Paper for fumigating, in 4lb. packets for 5s.

Neal's Patent Aphis Pastils, a cheap and convenient substitute for Tobacco Paper, 2s. per packet.

Wolff's Patent Pencils for marking wooden labels, 3d. and 6d. each.

Parmenter's Preparation for destroying mildew on vines and cleansing greenhouse plants, in jars, 2s., 3s. 6d., and 10s. 6d. each.

Garden Gloves, 1s. 6d. per pair.

CLIMBING or RUNNER BEANS—continued.

CLIMBING FRENCH BEAN. SUTTON'S TENDER AND TRUE.
Per pint, 2s. (See accompanying description.)

Climbing French Bean, Sutton's Tender and True ... ...per pint, *2s.*

Although a true Runner, this new type of Bean does not usually climb higher than four to six feet; the long, straight pods possess the characteristics of the Dwarf class; and the crop is ready quite as early in the season as Canadian Wonder. The handsome pods are produced in great profusion, and in 1891 the Royal Horticultural Society acknowledged its merits by the award of a First-class Certificate. In the second year's trial at Chiswick the Committee were so impressed with its value that they again gave it the highest possible award, viz. three crosses (XXX). (*The habit of growth is shown in the accompanying illustration, and a cluster of pods is illustrated on page* 10.)

FIRST-CLASS CERTIFICATE, ROYAL HORTICULTURAL SOCIETY.

'TENDER AND TRUE RUNNER BEAN.—**The public ought to be greatly** indebted to Messrs. Sutton & Sons for the introduction of this splendid novelty. The seed resembles the ordinary French Bean. Canadian Wonder sown at the same time is all over. Tender and True is covered to a height of 4 feet with well shaped pods about the size of those of Canadian Wonder, and is likely to continue cropping until frost cuts it down. This Bean is likely to be much heard of in the near future.—R.'—JOURNAL OF HORTICULTURE.

'**Royal Horticultural Society's Show.—Messrs. Sutton & Sons sent** samples of their new climbing Bean, Tender and True. The pods were straight, stout, and brittle, somewhat resembling fine examples of Canadian Wonder, but thicker, and they were borne in extraordinary profusion on plants that were sent to show the productiveness of the variety.'—JOURNAL OF HORTICULTURE.

'RUNNER BEAN—TENDER AND TRUE.—**This is very distinct and free-**cropping and has a pod like that of one of the dwarf varieties. It reaches a height of six feet or so, and crops profusely all the way along the twining shoots. The pods are large, long, and symmetrical, and it promises to make a good exhibition variety.—R. DEAN.'—GARDENERS' MAGAZINE.

'**Royal Horticultural Society, Chiswick, September 3.—Scarlet and** other Runner Beans. Forty-four lots. These were found to be scarcely in condition for examination, with few exceptions. A First-class Certificate was awarded to Sutton's Tender and True—a Runner Bean of the dwarf kidney section, with fine, long, straight pods.'—GARDENING WORLD.

Sutton's A 1.

We introduced this fine Scarlet Runner in 1891, and it has now an established reputation as a successful competitor on the exhibition stage. The series of exhaustive comparative trials made in our Experimental Grounds justifies our statement that it is the largest-podded and heaviest cropping Scarlet Runner Bean yet raised. In growth it can easily be distinguished from other varieties by the darker colour of its leaves and flowers. The deep green pods, which hang in great clusters, are perfectly straight, fleshy, and, notwithstanding their enormous size, they are tender and of splendid quality, showing no tendency to the coarseness which appears to be inherent in some large Beans of recent introduction ... per pint, *1s. 6d.*

'**Sutton's A 1 Runner has this season confirmed the high opinion I** formed of it last year. The pods are straighter and more fleshy than any other Bean I know.'—Mr. W. MACKIE, *Gardener to* Mrs. RUDDLE.

'**I had a splendid crop of your A 1 Runner Bean. I began picking the** first week in July, some of the pods being 11½ inches long. I never saw such beans.'—Mr. J. COPPER, *Gardener to* C. F. HUTH, Esq.

'**The heaviest cropper I have ever grown, enormous in size, 14 to** 16 inches long, and 1½ inch wide; flavour excellent.'—Mr. S. TIDEY, *Gardener to* J. G. COVELL, Esq.

'**Your A 1 Runner Bean is the best I have ever grown. I began** picking in July, and am picking now from the same rows (Oct. 27).'—Mr. G. W. BATEMAN, *Gardener to* A. DEED, Esq.

'**A magnificent Runner Bean, pods very straight and broad, and** borne in clusters of from 8 to 12 beautiful dark green beans of excellent flavour. The very best Runner Bean I ever saw.'—Mr. S. COLBERT, *Gardener to* G. W. EWEN, Esq.

'**I planted your Sutton's A 1 Runner Bean by the side of Champion.** The difference was very marked, A 1 being more productive and ten days earlier, although sown on the same day and under the same treatment.'—Mr. A. H. HARYETH, *Gardener to* J. S. PROCKTER, Esq.

Runner Beans continued on page 10.

Sutton's Vegetable Seeds—Complete List for 1895—continued.

1. EAST INDIA CAYENNE CHILI. 2. MAMMOTH LONG RED CAPSICUM.
3. SUTTON'S MAMMOTH LONG RED CHILI. 4. SUTTON'S ERECT-FRUITING CAPSICUM.
5. SUTTON'S CORAL RED CHILI. 6. GOLDEN DAWN CAPSICUM.

Engraved from a photograph. (*See accompanying descriptions.*)

CAPSICUM.

(*Capsicum annuum.*) German, Spanischer Pfeffer.—French, *Piment.*

Sutton's Erect-fruiting. A novel, decorative plant. Fruit brilliant glossy deep red, upright in growth. (*See accompanying illustration, figure* 4) ... ... per packet, 1*s.*

Prince of Wales ... ... per packet, 6*d.* and 1*s.*

'An extremely pretty variety, the fruits being about the size of large cobnuts, bright canary yellow and shining, and these contrasted with the deep green foliage produce a charming effect.'—THE GARDEN.

Mammoth Long Red. (*See accompanying illustration, figure* 2.) Per packet, 6*d.* and 1*s.*

Golden Dawn. A large yellow-fruited Capsicum of mild flavour. Very ornamental. (*See accompanying illustration, figure* 6) per packet, 6*d.* and 1*s.*

Little Gem. A small fruiting scarlet variety; dwarf habit. Per packet, 6*d.* and 1*s.*

Long Red. Bright red conical fruit, 2 to 3 inches long ... per packet, 6*d.*

Long Yellow. Rather larger than the Long Red, and unusually hot in flavour ... ... per packet, 6*d.*

Bell (or Bull's Nose). Fruit red, about 2 inches in length, and the same in diameter. Flavour mild ... ... per packet, 6*d.*

Red Tomato-shaped. Fruit corrugated, medium size, of mild flavour. Per packet, 6*d.*

Yellow Tomato-shaped. Similar in form to the red variety, but yellow. Per packet, 6*d.*

Red Cherry. Cherry-shaped and extremely hot ... ,, 6*d.*

Red Giant. Very large, irregular conical fruit of a deep rich red when ripe. Flavour mild, and valuable for use in the green state per packet, 6*d.*

Mixed Capsicum ... ... ,, 6*d.*

CULTURE.—Capsicums are grown both for use and ornament, and for the latter purpose are worth more attention. Sow on a hotbed in February or March, and pot on the young plants until fully grown, when they may go to the conservatory until the pods are gathered for use.

CHILI.

(*Capsicum baccatum.*) German, Spanischer Pfeffer.—French, *Piment.*

Sutton's Crimson Bouquet. An exceedingly attractive plant, very dwarf and compact. The bright scarlet fruits are from 1 to 1½ inch in length, and in artificial light they gleam like jewels among the foliage. Per packet, 1*s.* and 1*s.* 6*d.*

'The most prolific Chili I have grown; pods of medium size, excellent in shape. Apart from its usefulness for culinary purposes, it makes a handsome decorative plant.'—Mr. H. C. PRINSEP, The Gardens, Buxted Park.

Sutton's Coral Red. A singularly beautiful miniature plant, appropriate as an ornament for the dinner table, and suitable for general decorative purposes. Habit compact; height only about eight or nine inches. The deep scarlet berries are borne erect and in great profusion. Award of Merit, R. H. Society. (*See accompanying illustration, figure* 5.) Per packet, 1*s.*

Sutton's Black Prince. Totally unlike any other variety, being of a purplish-black colour; a pleasing contrast to the scarlet and yellow fruiting kinds. Fruit, 3 to 4 inches long, and tapering ... per packet, 1*s.*

Sutton's Tom Thumb. A beautiful variety, adapted for ornamental purposes; dwarf, compact, and abundantly covered with bright scarlet pods; flavour very pungent ... ... per packet, 6*d.* and 1*s.*

Sutton's Mammoth Long Red. Seed saved from large handsome brilliant red fruit, 6 to 8 inches long; flavour full. (*See accompanying illustration, figure* 3) ... ... per packet, 1*s.*

Long Red. Fruits slender, often attaining 3 to 4 inches in length ,, 6*d.*

East India Cayenne. (*See accompanying illustration, figure* 1) ,, 6*d.*

Mixed Chili ... ... ,, 6*d.*

CULTURE.—Chili is a tender annual, and must be raised in heat. Sow about the end of March, and nurse the plants until June, when they will do well at the foot of a south wall.

CARDOON.

(*Cynara Cardunculus.*) German, Spanische Artischocke.—French, *Cardon.*

Large Solid ... ... per ounce, 1*s.*

CULTURE.—Sow towards the end of April in rows four feet apart, putting the seeds in groups at intervals of 18 inches in the rows. Thin to one plant at each station. In August or September commence blanching by gathering the leaves together, wrapping them round with a band of hay, and earthing up. As the plants develop continue the process, which requires from eight to ten weeks. A retentive moist soil is essential to fine growth. On dry soils grow in trenches.

SUTTON'S
AMATEUR'S GUIDE AND SPRING CATALOGUE
FOR 1881.

READING GIANT ASPARAGUS.
Per ounce, 4d. See page 5.

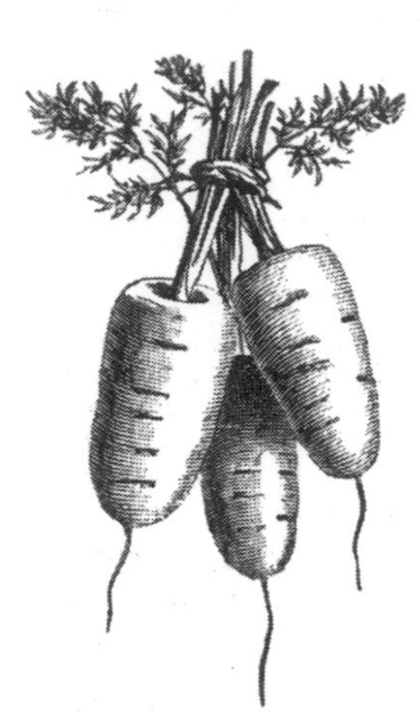

SUTTON'S CHAMPION SCARLET SHORT HORN CARROT.
Per ounce, 1s. See page 16.

SUTTON'S EXTRA CURLED SCOTCH KALE.
Per ounce, 1s. See page 10.

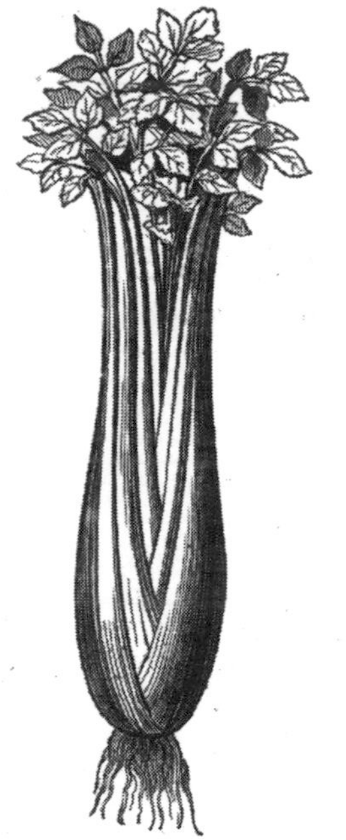

SUTTON'S SULHAM PRIZE CELERY.
Per packet, 1s. 6d. See page 11.

SUTTON'S 'KING OF THE RIDGE' CUCUMBER.
(Showing habit of Plant.)

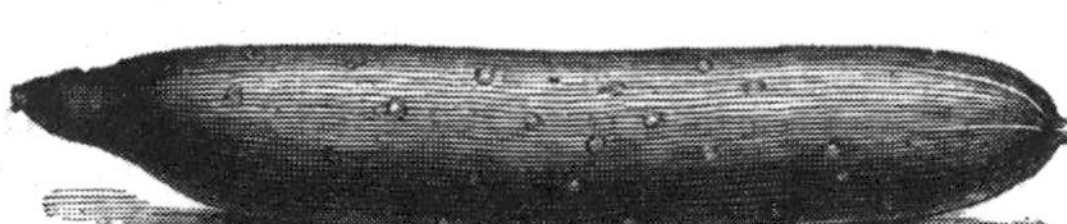

SUTTON'S KING OF THE RIDGE' CUCUMBER.
(Showing type of Fruit.)
Per packet, 1s. 6d. See page 16.

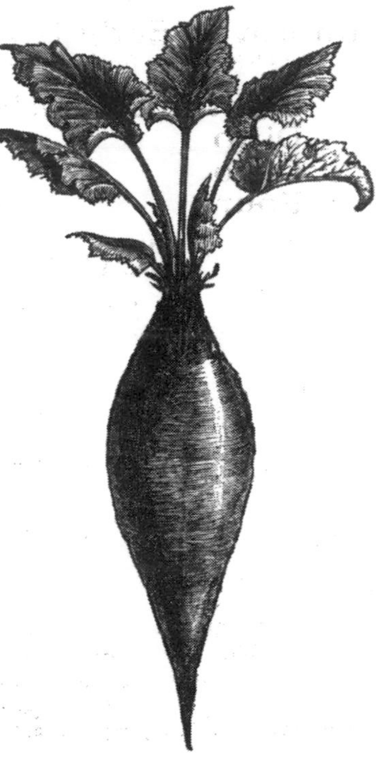

SUTTON'S IMPROVED DARK RED BEET
Per ounce, 1s. 6d. See page 10.

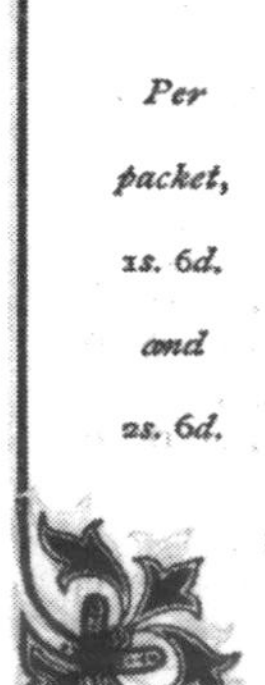

Per packet, 1s. 6d. and 2s. 6d.

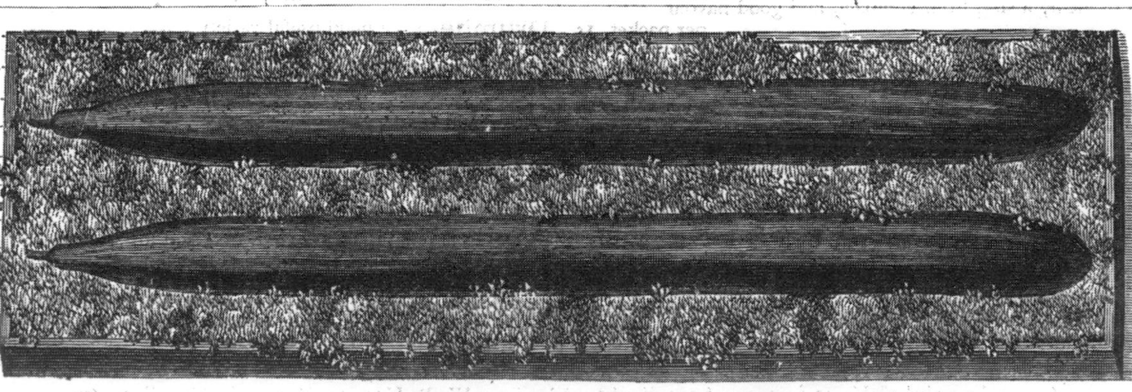

See description page 15.

SUTTON'S DUKE OF CONNAUGHT CUCUMBER.

14

A Discount of 5 per cent. (1s. in the £) allowed for Cash Payments.

Frame Cucumber.

(*Cucumis sativus.*) German, Gurke.—French, *Concombre.*—Russian, Огурецъ.

Packet. *s. d.*

Sutton's Duke of Connaught.

This remarkably handsome Cucumber, of our own introduction, is the finest white-spined variety known. It is perfectly level, from 22 to 26 inches in length, with a bright green skin, well covered with bloom, spine scarcely discernible, and the fruit very little ribbed. Its great recommendation, however, is its wonderfully small handle, not more than ¾ to 1 inch in length. This gives it a beauty of form not possessed by any other Cucumber, and shows its decided superiority for exhibition and table purposes. It is remarkably productive and of superior flavour. (*See illustration, page* 14.) ... ... 1*s.* 6*d.* and 2 6

From SHIRLEY HIBBERD, Esq.

'The Cucumber "Duke of Connaught" is of even width from the handle to the nose, as straight as an arrow, with glossy green skin, and distinct, though not conspicuous, white spines. It is quite tender, and deliciously flavoured. For beauty and quality I am quite sure it cannot be surpassed.'

From Mr. W. TILLERY, Gardener to His Grace the Duke of Portland.

'"Duke of Connaught" is a first-rate white-spined Cucumber, of good length and shape for exhibition. It is also of very good flavour, and with little waste.'

'CUCUMBER, DUKE OF CONNAUGHT.—This is one of the best of Cucumbers, either for exhibition or for general use. It is indeed most prolific, producing frequently three fruit at a joint, very symmetrical in shape, and averaging 24 in. in length.'—F. D., *from* GARDENING, *February* 21, 1880.

From Mr. G. ABBEY, Gardener to Sir C. M. Palmer, Bart.

'Your "Duke of Connaught" Cucumber is very handsome and free-bearing. The plants have a good constitution, and it is the best Cucumber in every respect that has come under my observation.'

From the 'GARDENERS' MAGAZINE, Feb. 1, 1879.

'Sutton's "Duke of Connaught" is a model in point of form, attains an average length of 24 inches; the flavour is remarkably good, and the plant is comparatively hardy and a free bearer. It is a capital variety both for exhibition and general culture.'

Sutton's Marquis of Lorne.

This splendid Cucumber was originally introduced by us, and is the longest variety grown. It has a white spine, short neck, is very straight and prolific, with a remarkable absence of seed, and when not allowed to grow too old is of delicious flavour. It has been awarded First Prizes at many of the great Horticultural Shows in England and on the Continent 1 6

Tender and True, a fine variety, from 24 to 30 inches in length; handsome in shape and colour, very small handle, and of excellent flavour. Awarded a First-Class Certificate by the R.H.S. 1 6

Cuthbert's Perfection, a splendid Cucumber, free bearing, and of strong constitution; length 20 to 25 inches; recommended for exhibition, market, and general purposes 1 6

The London Market.

This fine variety has been placed in our hands by one of the leading growers for the London market, and we can with confidence recommend it. It is a black-spine, very smooth, fine form, dark green skin with a rich covering of bloom, and exceedingly productive 1 6

From Mr. A. Ingram, Gardener to His Grace the Duke of NORTHUMBERLAND, Alnwick Castle, Aug. 25, 1879.

'Your new frame Cucumber has been in bearing all the summer; I have still a lot of fruit on it. I find it to be an excellent variety, and the best I know for frame work. It is black spine, sweet, and crisp; a strong grower and a free setter. I consider it just the Cucumber for amateurs.'

Packet *s. d.*

Sutton's Berkshire Champion.

One of the best and most prolific Cucumbers for ordinary frame cultivation, of good form, from 18 to 24 inches in length, and of excellent flavour ... ... 1*s.* and 1 6

From the 'GARDENERS' MAGAZINE.'

'For productiveness and high quality I have not met with a Cucumber that can equal Sutton's Berkshire Champion. On the 1st of March four seeds were sown. They were ready for planting in about three weeks, and were put in a two-light cold pit with a small quantity of fermenting materials underneath. In five weeks after I began to cut well developed fruit. From that time (the beginning of May) until the early part of November, the plants yielded a continuous and abundant supply of fruit ranging in length from 20 to 22 inches. Six hundred good Cucumbers were cut, being at the rate of one hundred and fifty to each plant. From first to last they were perfectly free from disease.'—RILEY SCOTT, Gardener to J. R. Campbell, Esq., Oakover, Ticehurst.

Sutton's Improved Telegraph.

This improved strain has been grown by us for the past two years, but we have hitherto failed to secure sufficient seed to offer it to the public. It is without exception the finest type of Telegraph Cucumber yet offered; handsome in shape, very small neck, and remarkably prolific. 2 6

Sir Garnet Wolseley. A remarkably handsome variety, very prolific and of excellent flavour. It grows to a great length, and is very useful for exhibition purposes ... 2 6

Hamilton's Goliath, very fine 1 6

Hamilton's Needle Gun, Hamilton's British Volunteer, Hamilton's Invincible, and **Hamilton's British Challenge.** All splendid varieties... ... each 1 6

All the Year Round. One of the best for winter use. Fine shape and flavour, and an abundant cropper, answering equally well in the forcing house or cold frame... 1 0

Blue Gown. Grows to a good size, uniform in shape, and of excellent flavour 1 6

Dean's Early Prolific, a valuable Cucumber, perfect in form, and very solid; prolific and of good flavour; grows 14 to 16 inches in length 1 6

Berkshire Challenge. Excellent white-spine... 1 6

Model. Very handsome and prolific, suitable for exhibition purposes 2 6

	Packet. *s.*	*d.*
Cuthill's Black Spine	1	0
Crystal Palace Pet	1	6
Duke of Edinburgh (Munro's)...	1	6
Improved Sion House...	1	0
Kirkstall Abbey ...	1	6
Lord Kenyon's Favourite	1	0
Market Favourite, Improved	1	0
Masters's Prolific ...	1	6
Star of the West ...	1	0
Sooly Qua (Chinese) ...	1	6
Telegraph (Rollison's)	2	6
Ditto (small packet) ...	1	6

Ornamental Cucumber, 10 varieties... ... 3 6

ditto ditto mixed, packets, 6*d.* and 1 0

The above List comprises all the best varieties in cultivation, but other advertised sorts can be supplied at the usual prices.

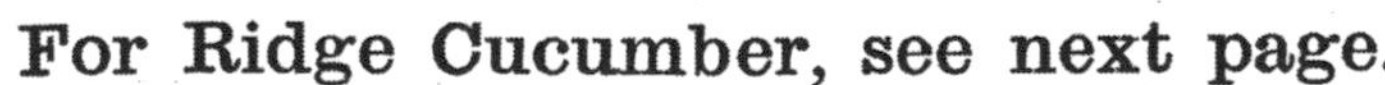

For Ridge Cucumber, see next page.

'I have cut Cucumbers from your Berks Champion three weeks earlier than any of my neighbours.'
The Rev. J. R. BARLOW, *Pertenhall, Kimbolton.*

15

KITCHEN GARDEN CALENDAR,

WRITTEN EXPRESSLY FOR

THE ILLUSTRATED GUIDE FOR AMATEUR GARDENERS.

CALENDARS are, probably, as old as the art of writing and the spread of learning. They are at once landmarks of time, and timemarks of practice. A collection of Garden Calendars from the beginning, were such possible, would be one of the most trustworthy records of horticultural doings and progress. Hardly has any one succeeded in doing anything as well or better than his fellows than he proceeds to make a note of it for his own gratification and use, or the instruction of others. In this way the knowledge of the wisest has become the property of all.

We have not yet out-grown, and it is doubtful whether we ever shall out-grow, the use of Calendars. Times and Seasons of sowing and planting; modes of treatment; selections of varieties, are all of essential moment to successful results. What so useful as a Calendar to remind us of the one, point out the other, and select only the best varieties ready to our hand? It is this threefold service we purpose rendering to our readers; and we hope that our Calendar will not be without use to Professional Gardeners, and prove a trustworthy Guide to Amateurs.

JANUARY.

All vacant ground should be deeply trenched and heavily manured; without attention to these foundation matters, vegetables, however carefully selected and skilfully cultivated, cannot be of the highest quality. A deep tilth and rich is the secret of success. If water is stagnant at three or five feet from the surface, see that it is drained off at once, for though vegetables are greedy of moisture, they will not thrive in sour soil, nor with their roots in stagnant water. In digging and trenching vacant ground at this season, the surface cannot be left too rough. The more angles presented to sun, air, and wind, the better, and the more thorough the work of comminution and atmospheric enrichment. The cropping in January must wait on the weather. If frost hinder other operations, it facilitates the wheeling of manures and composts to where they will be needed by and by.

Beans.—Mazagan, or Broad Beans may be planted, choosing a warm sheltered border for these early crops. Attend also to those planted in November; draw a portion of earth to the stems, and scatter a little barley chaff over their crowns and along their sides, to baffle the precocious black slugs that are ever ready to pounce upon such early morsels of green.

Peas.—Make a second sowing of Dillestone's First Early, the earliest Pea grown—or Early Emperor, Sangster's No. 1, Emerald Gem, Kentish Invieta, or that fine early new Pea, William the First, almost equal in quality to Ne plus ultra. It is often possible to find a warmer place for a dwarf than a tall Pea, as at the foot of a south wall. In such a position, McLean's Blue Peter will do well, and prove itself of higher quality than any of the other dwarf varieties.

Cauliflowers.—Attend to those in frames and under handlights; give plenty of air to prevent their drawing. Should the plants look weakly, or show any symptoms of running, sow a few seeds of the Early London White, or the Walcheren, under a handlight, to succeed the Autumnal sowings.

Cabbages.—Fill up blanks from nursery beds, and consolidate any thrown out by the frosts.

Carrots.—Sow a small frame of the Early Forcing Horn, and Early Scarlet Horn; and also at the same time a few on a warm raised bank or under a south wall.

Radishes.—Sow Wood's Early Frame and Olive-shaped Scarlet on a slight hotbed, also in a cold frame, and in the open air. The three sowings will afford a useful succession if they succeed, and if not, sow again under glass next month.

Autumn-sown Onions.—Look through, keep clean, and consolidate if raised by the frosts or sudden thaws.

Flanders Spinach.—Run a hoe through in dry weather.

Broccolis; Walcheren and White Cape, or other early varieties; look over weekly in open weather, and tie the leaves of any forward ones over head to protect from frost; also cut as soon as fit, or take up by the roots, and store in pits or open sheds till wanted.

Lettuces and Endive.—Attend to the protection of the former, under glass or in the open; also to the tying and blanching of the latter. As soon as it is nearly full-grown, Endive may be taken up and stored in a cellar, or any dark place, where it will keep, and blanch into tenderness at the same time.

Asparagus, Rhubarb, Sea Kale.—Force either with fermenting material or other means of heating on the ground, or take up the roots in batches as wanted and force growth in a temperature of 60 to 65 degrees, in a pit, house, mushroom shed, or cellar. Sea Kale must be kept in the dark. Rhubarb may or may not, there is no perceptible difference in the flavour either way. Asparagus is decidedly best in flavour, and can only be had green when grown in the light. Where Chicory is in demand for salads, bring in a box or two of roots once a week or fortnight, and grow in the dark.

Celery.—A small patch of Sandringham Dwarf may be sown in heat, 65 degrees or so for furnishing very early plants.

Cucumbers and Melons.—Prepare fermenting materials for forming a seed-bed, or a bed for growing, raising Melon, Cucumber, plants, &c. The two should not be iden-

tical, else the best part of the bed will be spent before the plants are ready. For early work, if no Winter Cucumbers are grown, sow Daniels' Improved Telegraph, Monro's Duke of Edinburgh, and Abbott's Early Prolific. The longer sorts may be sown towards the end of the month, such as Daniels' Duke of Edinburgh, Manchester Prize, and Blue Gown.

Melons should also be reared during this month, though they will do but little good on dung beds till February. Sow about the middle of January, Cox's Golden Gem, Turner's Scarlet Gem, Veitch's Golden Perfection, Monro's Little Heath, &c. Keep near the glass, and pot off in single pots as soon as they show the rough leaf, wind the stems round the edges of the pots up to the leaf, and plunge the pots to their rims in a bottom heat of 75 to 80 degrees.

FEBRUARY.

See that all arrears of draining, trenching, manuring, digging, &c., are brought up this month, for March will prove the busiest month in the year to the kitchen gardener. What October is to the farmer, March is to the gardener, and no arrears of work must stand over from February.

Beans.—Attend to those planted in November or January, and guard them against mice, slugs, and birds. Make a fresh planting of successional and superior varieties, such as Seville Longpod, Harlington Windsor, Green Nonpareil, Green Longpod, and Johnson's Wonderful. Sometimes during "February fillditch," the black slugs make an end of the Winter and even Spring-sown Beans. The mischief may be remedied by planting a boxful or two in light rich soil, or a spare frame, urging them up as fast as may be in a temperature not exceeding 50 to 60 degrees, giving abundance of air as soon as fairly above ground, and planting out in mild weather on rich sweet ground. In this way Beans may be gathered about as early—sometimes earlier—than if planted in November.

Peas.—Early Peas may be treated in the same way, and are worth the further trouble of being sown on strips of inverted turf, about three inches wide and two deep. Cut a small furrow in the middle to prevent the Peas rolling off. Sow early varieties; cover with light earth, and stand in heat, or under the shelter of glass till quite through the soil; then keep close to the glass, and give abundance of air to hinder them from drawing. Plant out when about three inches high; earth and stake at the same time, leaving only an inch of the Peas out of the ground. Plant them half way up the south side of ridges about a foot high. With the heat thus procured and the protection and drawing power of the stakes, Peas treated thus are often a fortnight earlier than those sown in November. Sow also a boxful or two of Peas thickly, in heat, to furnish green pea-stems to be rubbed through a sieve, to convert preserved peas into real green pea-soup, alike in colour and flavour. Sow twice during the month in quantities, proportionate to ground or demand, on good rich soil; such as Prizetaker, Blue Scimitar, Kentish Invicta, Auvergne, Harrison's Glory, Woodford's Green Marrow, Champion of England, Laxton's Alpha, Supreme, Advancer, and Ne plus ultra, less or more, at each sowing, from now till June. Burbridge's Eclipse is one of the best semidwarf Peas, and McLean's Little Gem is a gem for pots, borders, or orchard-houses, or the foot of south walls. Those who value Sugar Peas, to be cooked and eaten like French Beans, should sow a row of the Tamarind Sugar, the tender pods of which make an excellent dish.

Onions.—Early sowing, in rich, deep, moderately hard tilths, doubtless command success in the culture of this important crop. A good deal depends on varieties, but far more on thorough preparation and early sowing. The general extension of the Autumn cultivation of the Onion has led some to look on the Spring crop as of less importance; but an excess of Onions is almost an impossibility in most establishments, and it is therefore wise to grow a good breadth alike of Spring and Autumn-sown. The drill system is preferable where any quantity is grown, and the ground that has grown early celery is generally in good heart, with another coat of manure, for a crop of Onions. Prepare and manure as soon as vacant, lay up to the weather as roughly as possible, rake down fine as early as found dry. Top dress with burnt wood ashes, lime, and soot, to add more manurial strength, and give a short shrift to slugs, worms, &c., if the ashes can be applied hot, all the better. Tread or roll the surface firm, run a fine rake over, draw drills or marks less than a quarter, and more than an eighth of an inch deep, sow the seeds rather thickly, but not too thick, as this is a source of weakness; stamp in carefully with the foot, level all with rake or light roller, and the seeds will be sure to vegetate well. Deep sowing in a loose surface proves the grave of thousands of Onions, and should they ever come out of it they are heaved out bodily by the first frost, and become the prey of birds.

As to varieties sow the Queen, an excellent Onion, nearly two months earlier than any other, and one that may be harvested with the Autumn-sown varieties. The following are among the more useful for general crop:—White Spanish, James' Keeping, White Globe, Early White Naples, Strasburg, Blood Red, Danver's Yellow and Santa Anna.

Parsnips.—Sow Guernsey, or Hollow-crowned, on deep soil, in drills from eighteen inches to two feet apart.

Potatoes.—Plant some of the earlier varieties that have been greened in Autumn and stored in single file during Winter; these should be planted in drills a foot deep, on dry warm borders, without breaking off or disturbing the strong green shoots or started eyes. Where the subsoil is cold it is good practice to place the earliest potatoes on the surface, cover the tubers with burnt earth or wood ashes, and heap the most mellow surface soil over them, to a depth of eight or ten inches.

Among the best varieties for these early plantings are Snowflake, Rivers' Royal Ashleaf, Fenn's Early White Kidney, True Ashleaf Kidney, and the American Early Rose, earlier than either of the others treated as above. Among round Potatoes, Fenn's Early Market, Table King, Early Oxford, Early Shaw, Early Edinboro', and Robson's Challenge, may be planted now. The main crop will be time enough next month. Watch Autumn planted varieties, and draw a little earth to the stems as soon as fairly through the soil, to shield them from the frost.

Cabbages.—Plant out of nursery beds as thick again as wanted for final cabbaging, and as soon as they are fit to eat pull up every alternate one, to make room for the others.

Cauliflowers.—Air with care under handlights, sprinkle with soot and lime, to destroy slugs; sow a pinch of seed under glass, and prick off those sown last month.

Celery.—Sow under glass, prick off those sown last

month; earth up late crop; protect the crown from excessive wet; take up and store for a week's supply at one time, during frosty weather, and store in sand or earth in a frost-proof shed.

Carrots.—Sow successive crops of Horn varieties; also Radishes, Round Spinage, and Parsley.

Rhubarb, Sea Kale, and **Asparagus.**—Renew fermenting material to keep up supply, or take up roots and place in heat. Make fresh plantations of the first, and prepare ground, by deep trenching and rich manuring, for fresh sowings or plantings of Asparagus.

Hot-beds. — Prepare fermenting materials — dung, leaves, tan, cocoa-nut fibre refuse, chips, shavings, sawdust, anything and everything that will heat—for the formation of hot-beds for raising seeds, growing Cucumbers and Melons, &c. Main crops of the two latter should be planted out on hot dung or other beds, at least four feet in depth; on hills of loam or other good soil from a foot to eighteen inches in depth. Plant on hills in the centre of the beds to allow the heat to pass more freely through the surface; and also that the roots may be fed with fresh additions of soil as they grow.

Lettuces.—Under glass protectors, cut when fit for use, plant more from nursery beds, fill up vacant space in frames or in the orchard-houses; sow under glass and in a sheltered place, out of doors, All the Year Round, Tom Thumb, Cabbage varieties, Black Seeded Cos. and Paris White.

Small Saladings.—Sow weekly, in heat, in pots or boxes, according to demand.

Broccolis.—Attend to protecting, and cut the moment they are fit for table.

MARCH.

Potatoes.—Proceed with the planting of the main crop. If the ground was well manured, trenched, or deeply dug up in the Autumn, it will now be in the best possible order for the planting of the main crop. There are few better methods of proceeding than placing the line at two feet, thirty inches, or a yard apart, and drawing out the drills with a hoe, or toss them out with the cut of a spade along the line, to about a depth of ten inches or a foot; the potatoes should then be planted whole, or in sets, along the bottom of the trench, and the earth returned on to the sets. It was common before the disease to set the Potatoes on dung, or place some over them; but since then the best cultivators prefer to have the ground in good condition, and apply little or no manure direct to the crop. Some also plant the whole crop on the surface, as recommended for early varieties last month, thus providing them with warmer quarters and more perfect drainage.

Among the surest and best proved croppers are Mona's Pride, Prince of Wales Kidney, Excelsior Kidney, Fluke, Willard Kidney, American Early and Late Rose. Among the rounds—Climax, Breese's Prolific, Breese's Peerless, Milky White, Edinburgh Early, Paterson's Victoria, York Regent, and Red-skinned Flour Ball, a magnificent Potato and tremendous grower, that ought to be planted from four to six feet apart Of the new introductions—Rector of Woodstock; the American varieties, Snowflake, Vermont Beauty, Eureka, and Extra Early Vermont are among the best.

Beans.—Sow the main crop in good strong soil. A good many cultivators drop a few Beans among the Potatoes at long intervals; a few do little harm, and some think them an antidote to disease. Possibly if the spores of the Potato fungus (*Peronospora infestans*) were about when the Beans were in bloom the strong odour might be potential enough to ward them off, or neutralize their power.

Peas.—Repeat the sowing of all the varieties recommended last month, adding Veitch's Perfection, and not omitting Ne plus ultra. Sow some at wide intervals among other crops all over the garden, thus making them contribute shelter and shade; while the wide distance, by affording light and air all round, develops their productive powers to the utmost. The tops of Celery ridges may also be furnished with Peas. Make the trenches at once, from eighteen inches to two feet wide, and from four to six feet apart. Manure the spaces heavily where the centre of the ridge will be; dig out the trench, place the earth over the manure, and sow a row on each, of such as Laxton's Alpha, Advancer, Prizetaker, Blue Scimitar, or any other variety that does not grow above a yard high. These, if sown now, will help the Celery by their shade when first planted, and be cleared off before the soil is needed to earth it up.

Dwarf, French, and **Runner Beans.**—Plant in pots, pits, or boxes, in moderate heat, to spring up and prepare for planting out-of-doors under temporary shelter early in May. By this simple process the season of these universal favourites in the open air is anticipated by a month or more. Williams' Early Prolific, Osborn's Early Forcing, Sion House, Robin's Egg, Fulmer's Early Forcing, and Early Prince Albert, are among the best dwarfs for this purpose, and the Scarlet, Champion, and Painted Lady Runners.

Asparagus.—Sow and plant on rich deep soil of light texture. The ground should have been prepared in the Autumn. But if not, prepare it now, by trenching four feet deep, and adding a third part of farmyard manure, and a sixth of sand. To have it fine, plant or sow in rows two or three feet apart, and the plants from eighteen to thirty inches from each other. The roots should not be kept out of the ground nor exposed to the air one moment more than is necessary. Plant with care. Connover's Colossal is not only different, but better than the Giant, though the latter, well-grown, deserves its name. Take up more plants for forcing, or apply heat and glass, so as to subject the plants in the ground to a temperature of fifty-five to sixty degrees.

Sea Kale and **Rhubarb.**—Take up and force, or apply fermenting material to them in the ground. Cut as required, and beware of exposing either to sharp March winds, as it takes the flavour out of both, as well as forced Asparagus.

Divide and plant Globe Artichokes. Part of these should be replanted every year, as the fresh planted ones continue to throw up their useful crowns for months after the older plants have finished flowering, thus prolonging the season. Plant in rows five feet apart, and three feet from plant to plant, in light, rich, deep soil, such as Asparagus delights in. Plant Jerusalem Artichokes, if not done in the Autumn, in rows six feet apart, and two feet from set to set.

Shallots, Potatoe-Onions.—Plant, Sow Leeks and the main crop of Onions if not already done, and make another sowing for green Onions for salading. Sow also thickly on a poor piece of ground the silver-skinned Onion for pickling. Dust the beds over with soot or lime in mild

weather to finish small slugs and worms, the latter often draw the young plants out to their destruction.

Carrots.—Make another sowing of Horn, and in the north the main sowing of James's Scarlet, Red Surrey, Long Orange, and Altringham. Deep, sweet soil, not over rich, is most suitable to the crop,

Cauliflowers.—Sow again under glass if any failures have occurred. Plant out in warm places towards the end of the month. Water those under handlights, &c., with sewage.

Cabbages.—Make up blanks; earth up; sow a pinch of seed.

Savoys.—Sow Green Curled, or other choice varieties; also Kales, green and variegated; and a pinch of Brussels Sprouts for early work.

Celery.—Sow in heat, also on warm border outside. Prick off early plants under glass.

Lettuces.—Sow the best Cabbage and Cos varieties. Attend to those in frames. Cut as fit, and fill up with strongest plants from nursery beds in the open air.

Tomatoes.—Sow in heat; also Chilies and Capsicums.

Cucumbers and **Melons.**—Sow, pot off, plant out: keep up heat by lining, fire, and coverings, from 70 to 75 degrees. Water and air with caution, and see that the searching winds of March do not touch them.

Small Saladings.—Make sowings of these, such as Mustard and Cress, &c., once a fortnight; also another sowing of Spinach.

Radishes.—Sow on light warm soil.

Turnips.—Sow White Dutch, and Daniels' Snowball.

Keep down all weeds, and preserve the surface among all growing crops sweet and clean.

APRIL.

Potatoes.—Finish planting late Crop. If Potatoes were stored in single file in a cool place, many of them will keep till now without growing much. Some hold that late planting is an antidote to disease. It is certain that late planting is a sure mode of prolonging the season of new potatoes, which are in great demand in many families. Some keep old potatoes in a dry place, behind a north wall, and keep picking them over till the end of May, and then plant, so as to extend the season of new Potatoes till and through September. Such cultural expedients are useful in extending and altering seasons, and thus suiting the tastes of possessors of gardens. Earth-up liberally this month, to protect their stems from Spring frosts. Should the tops be frozen, the future of the crop is greatly dependent on the amount of Stem left uninjured, and that is safe in fickle Springs only so far as it is hidden in the earth.

Beans.—Plant successive crops of Seville Longpod, Harlington Windsor, Johnson's Wonderful, Windsor Green, or Nonpareil, or other approved sorts. Top the Early Mazagan, to hasten their flowering and finishing: earth up successive crops.

Dwarf Kidney, or **French** and **Runner Beans.**—Plant the former in rows two feet apart. Buff, Negro, Early Prince Albert, Black Speckled, &c., are fine useful varieties. Runners may be planted as wide apart as Peas, wherever a screen of beauty or utility is wanted. Treated thus, nothing can exceed them in fertility; and the amount of sweet nourishing food they yield is beyond all calculation and belief. On rich land they should have stakes from six to eight feet high. On poor soil many grow them without stakes, as they would dwarf varieties, only further apart.

Peas.—Sow for succession Laxton's Omega, Premier, Kentish Invicta, Fillbasket, Champion of Scotland, and British Queen, McLeans' Best of All, James's Prolific Marrow, Prince of Wales, Veitch's Perfection, Ne plus ultra, in single rows if possible, and if not, in breadths by themselves, from four to eight feet apart. Stake advancing crops; earth up, and water with sewage the earlier varieties coming into flower.

Carrots.—Sow main crop in shallow drills, from fifteen to eighteen inches or two feet apart.

Beet.—Sow the main crop in drills two feet apart. Among the best varieties are Dell's Black, Pine Apple, Perfection Salad, Nutting's Dwarf Red, Egyptian Turnip. Where ground is scarce these may generally be grown on the flowerbeds or borders, as the foliage of most of them is equal to Perilla or Iresine as decorative foliage plants. The Egyptian Turnip-rooted, resembling in form the Snowball Turnip, whilst of the deepest blood red colour, makes a nice variety of form of slice in the salad bowl; while the tender stalks of Beck's improved Sea Kale Beet, are almost equal—some say superior—to Sea Kale cooked, and served in the same manner. It can also be had in perfection when Sea Kale is wholly out of season. The leaves of this variety are not only fit for eating, grown in the open ground in Summer, but if the roots are placed in heat early in the Autumn, the leaves and stalks may be forced faster than Sea Kale.

Sow Salsafy and Scorzonera in drills, fifteen inches apart; also Chicory, where such is in demand for Winter salading. Sow Cauliflower: prick out previous crops. Plant out from under glass; top dress those under handlights with manure.

Broccolis.—Sow such splendid varieties as Daniels' King of the Broccolis, Daniels' Latest White, Cooling's Matchless and Leamington, for use this time next year. Also Lee's White Sprouting, Osborn's Winter White, Early White Malta, and Early Purple Sprouting. It is also a good rule to make a sowing of Walcheren, with all other Broccolis, as it is sure to come in useful, and yield sweet heads, equal to Cauliflower, that can never be out of season.

Cauliflowers.—This is in every respect the flower of the season. In purity of blanched whiteness; in beauty of form; in contrast of leaf with flower, and in sweetness, it has no rival among vegetables, and not many equals among flowers. To have Cauliflowers nearly all the year round, seeds should be sown each month, from February to August. A considerable sowing should be made in April of the King of the Cauliflowers, Veitch's Autumn Giant, Walcheren, Early London White, Erfurt's Dwarf Mammoth. Prick out early sowings as soon as they will bear handling. Plant out advancing crops. Deluge with manure water in dry weather.

Lettuces.—Plant out. Sow once a fortnight till the end of August, of such varieties as Daniels' Bros. Giant Cos, Goldring's Black-seeded Cos, Kingsholm Cos, Alexandra Cos, Paris White, Bath Brown. Of Cabbage Lettuces, Wheeler's Tom Thumb, Black-seeded Texter, Brown Dutch. Drumhead, Malta, Naples, and Blood Red.

Endive.—When the curled leaves of this are preferred to the finest Lettuce, to add variety of appearance as well as of flavour to the salad bowl, make small sowings of Digswell Prize, White or Green Curled, or Moss varieties.

Savoys, Kales, Brussels Sprouts—Make final sowings for the season.

Turnips, Spinach, Parsley, and **Small Saladings**—Sow for succession.

Sow Cucumbers, Gourds, and Vegetable Marrows, for ridging out in the open air in May. Pot off Tomatoes, Chilies, Capsicums, and bring on in heat ready for planting in the open air, towards the end of May.

Radishes—Sow once a fortnight throughout the season—French Breakfast, Scarlet Short Top, Long White, Olive-shaped, and Scarlet and White Turnip; also Raphanus Caudatus, or Rat Tail, to those fond of novelties in appearance and flavour, the pods only of which are edible.

Celery—Sow, prick off.

Cucumbers and **Melons**—Sow, pot off, plant out, earth up, cut as fit. Keep up a brisk heat of 75 to 80 degrees.

Herbs.—Sow Summer Savory, Sweet or Bush Basil, Borage, Chervil, Pot Marigold, Sweet Marjoram, Golden Purslane, Rampion, Thyme, &c. Divide, renew, or plant afresh such herbs as Angelica, Mint, Burnet, Fennel, Tarragon, Hyssop, Lemon Thyme, Pennyroyal, Sage Winter Savoury, Winter Marjoram, Lavender, Peppermint. Few things add more to the pleasure of eating than a good supply of Herbs, and April is the best month in the year for refurbishing or refurnishing the Herb Garden.

MAY.

Peas.—Continue to sow such Fine sorts as "G. F. Wilson," Best of All, James's Prolific Marrow, Veitch's Perfection, Ne plus ultra, Fillbasket, Dr Hogg. Often during the Summer, and, indeed, at all seasons, mice and rats devour seed Peas, and Beans, in the ground. A capital preventive is to wet the Peas, and sprinkle them with red lead, until all are coated. The lead either protects the Peas, or destroys the vermin, and either way the seed is safe. The lead dressing also proves a panoply of safety to seeds of all sorts, and is specially valuable for protecting Turnip, Cauliflower, Cabbage, Kale, Broccoli, &c. How often the seedsman is blamed for what the birds have feasted on, and the latter have waxed fat and sung over lost trade and lowered reputations. Earth up; stake and water advancing crops of Peas; gather all the produce young, as the surest means of making the plants yield a continuous supply.

Beans.—Make another planting of Broad, Kidney, and Runner Beans. Plant out of doors those raised under glass; earth up in the planting, and stake at once.

Potatoes.—Earth up as they grow, and keep the earth constantly stirred among them.

Rhubarb.—The early varieties will now be pushing forth without forcing; and the forcing of Sea Kale may also be discontinued at the end of the month, as also Asparagus.

Cauliflowers.—Encourage to grow as freely as possible; prick out young plants, and transplant into final quarters.

Broccoli.—Sow another batch of such sorts as White and Purple Cape, Snow's Winter White, Cooling's Matchless, King of the Broccolis, Daniels' Latest White, Late White, Wilcove's White. Prick out those sown earlier as soon as fit to handle, in beds of rich earth, about three inches apart. Prick out Savoys, Brussels Sprouts, Kales, &c., in the same way. None of the Brassica tribe should go from the seed-bed to the open quarter.

Parsnips, Early Carrots, Onions, &c.—Thin out, and hoe between.

Leeks.—Plant out in trenches, manured and prepared as for Celery.

Celery.—Sow seed, prick off plants on a rich basis of dung and soil, about six inches in depth. Transplant early plants from such a basis, or out of pots or pits into their final quarters; if a piece of soil two or three inches square can be transferred with each plant into the trench all the better; water thoroughly, to consolidate the earth and moisten the trench right through its mass.

Turnips, Spinach, Lettuces.—Sow. Plant out Lettuces from seed beds once a fortnight.

Tomatoes.—Plant out on sloping banks or against walls; sow or put in cuttings for succession crops. Tomato all the year round has now become a necessity to many people. To ensure this, they are grown in houses, on trellises or walls, in pits, frames, in pots, and cultivated with as much and more care than Melons and Cucumbers. Those who only grow one or two crops should plant them out now. There is, perhaps, no better varieties than New Early Dwarf, Sims' Mammoth, and Hathaway's Excelsior. The Trophy is one of enormous size, and Carter's Greengage is of unusual quality.

Chilies and **Capsicums.**—Plant out against walls or warm borders.

Ridge Cucumbers, Vegetable Marrows.—Plant out on a ridge of earth from four to six feet wide, with a yard of fermenting material underneath and a foot of good loam on the top; place a handlight over the plants until thoroughly established. No vegetable is more useful, none more in demand than Vegetable Marrow. The Custard and the Long Green and White are among the sweetest. They should be eaten young, about four inches long, to have them in perfection. Gourds may be grown in the same way and planted against dwarf or other walls.

Sow Radishes of sorts in a shady situation once a fortnight; also small salading every week.

JUNE.

Beans.—Plant a final and last crop of Seville Longpod and Green Windsor, and a good width of Kidney Beans for succession.

Peas.—Sow British Queen, Ne plus ultra, Dwarf Mammoth, and Veitch's Perfection. It is well to sow these late crops in trenches, so that they may be deluged with water in dry weather, as drought, rather than cold or damp, is the promoter of mildew on Autumn Peas.

Potatoes.—Earth up, keep clean.

Onions.—Thin to four or six inches, unless for large bulbs, then a foot, stir the surface, top dress with soot and guano and a dust of salt.

Parsnip.—Thin to fifteen inches in the rows.

Carrots.—Thin to nine inches.

Beet.—Thin to a foot.

Salsafy and **Scorzonera** to six or nine inches.

Parsley.—Thin to a foot or more asunder, if fine leaves are desired for garnishing.

Brussels Sprouts and **Broccoli.**—Plant out in final

quarters, in showery weather if possible. If space cannot be now had for these crops plant them out between the rows of Early Potatoes. When those are lifted the plants will be earthed up, having been previously established. Harvest Autumn-sown Onions as soon as ripe. Plant out Cauliflowers, prick off young plants from seed-beds in a shady situation, sow another pinch of seed. Attend to those coming in, and if too many come at once, pull a quantity up before the flowers open, and hang them, head downwards, in an ice-house or cold cellar, or lay them in by the heels on a north border, earthed up to the leaves, and well watered in. Plant out a few Cabbages for Autumn use.

Celery.—Water, plant out in trenches. and make a final sowing of seed for standing through the Winter. Prick off plants from previous sowings. The secret of a good supply of Celery from August to April is successive sowings and plantings. Sow a row of Cardoons, if they are relished, in rich ground, either in a trench like Celery, or on the level ground; in any case where they are to remain, as transplanting is ruinous to the plant.

Artichokes.—Cut all the flowers in bud, about half grown, and allow none to open or run to seed, unless wanted for bottoms for preserving. Top dress Asparagus beds with salt and guano, and allow all grass to run from this time, late cutting one year means weak grass the next. Sow Turnips, Lettuce, Endive, small Salading, or Spinach once or twice a month. Plant out New Zealand Spinach on rich ground; it should have been sown under glass in April. This, when it is liked, ensures a good supply of Spinach throughout the Summer and Autumn months, as it does not run to seed. It is not all families that will eat it, the flavour being different, and inferior to common Spinach.

Cucumbers and **Melons.**—Dress, stop, set, &c., once a week at least; sow seeds for late crop of Melons; give abundance of air night and day, during hot weather; raise ripening Melons off the ground, and expose them fully to the light and heat of the sun.

JULY.

Kidney Beans.—Make a final sowing in the open air of some of the earliest varieties. Earth up advancing crops; gather the pods young, and leave none for seed, if you would gather long and plentifully from the same plants. Stake Runner Beans, feed them with manure water in dry weather.

Peas.—Make a final sowing of any of the early varieties, such as Kentish Invicta, Emerald Gem, and on a raised southern bank, Blue Peter. Earth up and water copiously advancing crops; gather young and gather all, if you would gather long and plentifully.

Broccoli, Borecole, Brussels Sprouts, Cauliflower, Cabbage.—Plant out in their final quarters; prick out from seed beds; sow a pinch of Walcheren Broccoli and Cauliflower. Sow about the middle of the month for the early crop of Cabbages for next Summer; this will prove too early in some districts, but is well adapted for others. The Early Battersea, Ewing's No. 1, Little Pixie, Enfield Market, Nonpareil, Shilling's Queen, Cocoa-Nut, and Red Dutch, the latter for pickling, will be found good varieties.

Endive.—Sow a good breadth of the latter, the White Batavian, Moss, Green Curled, or other varieties.

Leeks.—Make another plantation on rich ground.

Small Salads, Radishes, Spinach.—Sow once or twice a month. During dry weather it is best to sow Lettuces and Endive where they are to remain, otherwise they are apt to bolt into seed-bearing instead of plumping out for the salad bowl.

Celery.—Plant out, water; earth up the earliest crop; remove all suckers and useless leaves, examine the roots, and if dry, soak them and the trench through, leave them for a few days, then choose a dry time and earth up all at once.

Onions.—Finish thinning, and also Carrots, Parsnips, Beet, &c. Scarify the surface among growing crops. Earth up advancing crops of Peas, Broccoli, Cauliflower, Potato, &c. Attend to the training of Tomatoes, Ridge Cucumbers, Gourds, and Vegetable Marrows; water liberally during dry weather; keep Tomato shoots thin, and stop beyond the first show of fruit, if wanted early. Cut herbs for drying when in full flower, as then their aromatic properties are fully developed; dry off quickly, in the sun or in a slow oven, rub down the leaves to powder, and preserve in closely corked and sealed bottles.

Parsley.—This is a good time for preparing a good supply of young Parsley, that often stands the Winter better than older plants. The soil for sowing Parsley in March can hardly be too rich and deep. Sow now on sweet dryish not over rich soil; and sow Covent Garden Garnishing or Extra Fine Curled, in rows ten inches or a foot apart. It is a good practice to cut down part of the old Parsley this month, dry and preserve as with sweet or other herbs, and the beheaded Parsley stands the Winter better, and yields more gatherings than that which has not been cut, and is also admirably adapted for potting or filling a frame with, for use in Winter.

Harvest Shallots, Garlic, Autumn-sown Onions, and plant the ground with Salading, late Cauliflowers, Walcheren, or other Broccoli; also harvest early Potatoes, clear off early Peas and Beans, and fill the ground with late grown Savoys, Broccoli, or Celery.

Cucumbers, late Tomatoes, and Melons in frames, require attention. Sow early varieties of Cucumbers for Winter use, and get the plants strongly established for planting out.

AUGUST.

Cabbages.—This is the month for sowing the main crop of Cabbages, to stand the Winter and come in through the next Spring and Summer. From the middle of July to the middle of August may be said to be the set time all over the country for this purpose; also for the sowing of Cauliflowers, to Winter under glass, or in sheltered situations, and furnish the first, and in many gardens, the best crops next year. Choose a nice open, rather firm bit of ground, and sow rather thinly, and either red-lead the seeds over or net the birds out. Sow also at the same time or afterwards, Cos and Cabbage Lettuces, to come in during, and stand through the Winter. It is difficult to find better varieties for this sowing than the Hardy Hammersmith Cabbage and Black Seeded Brown Cos, Goldring's Black Seeded Bath Cos, &c.

Onions.—In many gardens the Autumn-sown prove by far the best and heaviest croppers, a larger breadth of these are being sown year by year. Improved varieties have also stimulated Autumnal cultivation. The Giant Rocca has proved a magnificent Onion, alike for Autumn or Spring sowing; the Santa Anna and large Globe

Tripoli are also modern additions to the old Red and White Tripoli. There are two general modes of cultivation, the sowing of the seeds on beds rather thinly, to be transplanted into new ground in March; or sowing early in August in drills a foot apart, on the ground that they are to swell and finish on. Splendid bulbs may be obtained by either method. The ground should be rich, deep, and firm for Autumn varieties, and the seed should not be sown too thickly, as that will cause a weakly growth. With proper care and liberal dressings of soot, guano, &c., during the Spring and Summer, and soakings of sewage during dry weather, Autumn-sown Onions may be grown in many parts of England equal in size and quality to Spanish. Over a pound each has frequently been attained. Autumn-sown Onions mostly escape the Onion grub.

Potatoes.—Earth up, keep clean, harvest early.

Celery.—Plant out, earth up, and use as required, Clear off early Peas from the top of ridges, and plant Walcheren Broccoli, Lettuce or Endive, between the ridges as the Celery is earthed up.

Spinach.—Sow a good breadth of the Flanders, for standing the Winter, also of White Stone Turnips.

Radishes.—Sow Black Spanish and Chinese Rose for Winter use.

Endive—Plant out, blanch for use by turning a flower-pot or pan, or laying a slate over.

Lettuces.—Continue to plant out.

Walcheren Broccoli.—Every inch of vacant ground should be filled up with these.

Tomatoes.—Attend to thinning, training, stopping.

Chilies and **Capsicums.**—Gather as they ripen.

Cucumbers and **Vegetable Marrows.** — Cut for pickling or use.

Gourds.—Thin the fruit, leaving on the large varieties only a few, to swell to full size,

Cucumbers.—Plant Telegraph, Sion House, or Monro's Duke of Edinburgh, in pits or houses, to fruit through the Winter. Plant out the last crop of Little Heath or other hardy Melons. Keep up the top and bottom heat of both, and cover during cold nights. Water from this time, in the morning, and use water five degrees in advance of the temperature of the air.

SEPTEMBER.

Clear off all crops that are exhausted or their produce gathered, and thus gain all the space possible for almost the final plantings, for the season, of Cauliflowers, Broccoli, Greens, Savoys, Celery, Coleworts. Good clearances of Peas, Potatoes, Broad and Kidney Beans, Onions, Cauliflowers, Spinach, Turnips, Early Cabbages, &c., may now be made, and the ground finally refilled with the crops already named; or Lettuces, Endive Turnips, and Spinach, all of which may yet be either sown or planted in quantity.

Late Broccoli and Cauliflower prove invaluable, and hundreds of these may yet be grown into a sweetness, though not size, almost rivalling those of any other season of the year. Attend to the earthing up and encouragement of all Cauliflower and Broccoli intended to come in during the Autumn. Prick out and kindly nurse the plants sown last month, and also the Cabbages, or plant the latter into their final quarters as soon as large enough. The Onion ground, when cleared and heavily manured, does well for the main crop of Autumn Cabbages. Stake and water late Peas and Kidney Beans. Water and earth up Celery as it requires it. Attend to the gathering of Tomatoes, as soon as ripe; keep the shoots and leaves thin, and fully expose the fruit to the sun. Gather ridge Cucumbers and Gherkins for pickling; also Kidney Beans, Cauliflowers, Red Cabbages, Onions, Chilies, Capsicums, Nasturtiums. Encourage Cardoons to grow vigorously, by liberal applications of manure water, and wind a hay-band round their stems a week or two before earthing them up.

Cucumbers and **Melons.**—Remove dead leaves; cut the fruit of the former young, and of the latter a few days before it is fully ripe, and lay it up in a dry place to finish.

OCTOBER.

Potatoes.—This is more of a storing than a growing month. The main Summer crops of the garden are now either over or fit to harvest. The storing of Potatoes is one of the most important operations of the month; it should be set about with care, and all sorted and carefully stored as lifted, each variety by itself, correctly named; and each variety further sorted into two or three lots, as bests, seconds and smalls. Seed Potatoes should likewise receive a special treatment, and be stored differently from others. First, green them by exposure to light and air, and then store till wanted for planting, on latticed shelves, in single file if possible. This treatment adds immensely to the vigour of the eyes and the strength of the shoots, and also enables the seed to withstand the disease with more energy than those not so treated. Those for eating should be stored in earth rather than pitted under it. Layers of Potatoes and earth, say six inches, or a foot in depth at most, should alternate. Thus stored they can hardly be rotted by contact, and they will be found to retain that sweet nutty flavour which the best only have when they are newly harvested.

Harvest Beet without breaking a fibre if you want a blood red slice in your salad bowl. Everyone should grow Beet. It takes four hours to boil. Sliced, and with vinegar, it is an excellent, wholesome, and nutritious condiment with cold meat and even bread. Take up Carrots, Parsnips, Salsafy, Scorzonera, and Chicory, and store in sand till wanted for use. Plant Cauliflowers under glass, or at the foot of south walls; also Lettuces, Endive, and Cabbages to stand through the Winter. Store Walcheren or other Autumn Cauliflowers as fast as they show flower, in pits or frost-proof sheds, or lay them in closely together, out of doors, where they may be readily protected from the frost. Heel over or in-lay Broccoli; also furnish the floors of Orchard-houses with Lettuce, Endive, and Parsley, for Winter use, and lay Endive in thickly at the foot of walls.

Mushrooms.—Prepare manure for Mushroom beds. Droppings only, from corn-fed horses, is the best material. Let this lie in a shed, a foot or eighteen inches in thickness, for ten days or a fortnight, to heat slightly and sweat out the rank steam. Turn upside down every other day; then form into a ridge-bed, out of doors, six feet wide at the base, and of ridge or semi-circular form, about four feet high. Leave it for a few days to test the heat, and when that remains steady at 65 degrees spawn the bed, by inserting small pieces all over it, at distances

of about six inches and three inches deep. Leave it for ten days or more, for the spawn to run, covering when the weather is cold, and finally case the bed with three or four inches of loam, and cover, if outside, with a foot of litter. If the beds are formed inside a house, eighteen inches or two feet in depth of dung will suffice, and the surface covering of the bed may be dispensed with. From six weeks to two months from the time of spawning the Mushrooms will be in, that is if the air around the bed and its mass is kept at a temperature of 60 to 65 degrees. Hasten late crops of Melons, by a high and dry temperature of 70 to 75 degrees. Keep Cucumbers close to the glass, and growing briskly, in a temperature of 70 degrees.

NOVEMBER.

Finish storing all late Potatoes, and clearing the ground of all dead or dying crops. Clear the dead leaves and stems of Asparagus, Sea Kale, and Rhubarb, and commence forcing all these, either on the ground where they grow, or by taking up the roots, as advised in January. A very simple mode of forcing Sea Kale consists in planting it in double rows, about five feet asunder. Proceed now to dig a trench in the middle of the intervals between the rows, a yard deep, and about the same width ; heap the excavated earth over the crowns, placing a stake to each to show where it is. Then fill the trench with hot dung, and scatter also a little over the earth that covers the crowns. The whole ground looks like a heap of dung, and in about three or four weeks the Kale will be fit to cut ; and some prefer such Kale to that grown in pots or in dark hot-houses or pits in the ordinary way. Asparagus and Rhubarb are often forced by a trench of hot dung in the same way, only pots or glass cases are placed over their tops.

Rhubarb may be planted this month. The ground can hardly be too rich, deep, and heavy for the crop. For early work and high colour few varieties are finer than Scarlet Defiance, New Crimson, Myatt's Crimson Perfection, and the old Linnæus, if it can be had. These are not very strong growers, and a yard apart in rows, and two feet from plant to plant will suit them. Myatt's Victoria is perhaps the best of all for a main crop and for forcing. To do it justice, the rows should not be closer than six feet, nor the plants than three feet. Fresh plantations of Sea Kale may also be made : a light, rich, sandy soil is best for this valuable vegetable.

Horse Radish.—Make fresh plantations. It is a good plan to take up a Winter supply now, and store in sand, reserving all the nice, straight, small pieces and the crowns for fresh plantations. The ground should be deep and rich ; the pieces from two to three feet long being let in with a crowbar or strong stake, and the holes filled up with sand ; or the crowns can be dropped into deep holes, or better still, planted on the surface of suitable soil, from six to nine inches apart, and two feet between the rows.

Peas.—Sow the first crop of early varieties, rolling the seed in red lead, and filling the drills half full over the Peas with chopped furze or barley chaff. Sow dwarf Peas in pots. Plant Mazagan Beans, and treat in the same way. Plant Kidney Beans in pots for forcing, to succeed those planted in pits and frames in many gardens in August and September. Place these in a temperature of 60 degrees. Continue to blanch and store Endives and Lettuces in sheds, orchard-houses, and in sheltered places, easily protected out of doors. Plant Lettuce in frames, &c., for growing into usefulness in Winter. Place cloches over them in the open air.

Cauliflowers.—Attend to those under handlights, &c. Protect from severe weather. Watch Walcheren and other Broccolis in the open, and place them in safe quarters almost before they are fit for use. Run a hoe through all growing crops, such as Spinach, Cabbages, Onions, Lettuces, &c., as a loose surface is not only distasteful to slugs, worms, &c., but a preventive to the penetrating power of the frost.

DECEMBER.

Continue to take up and lay in roots of Asparagus, Sea Kale, and Rhubarb, for forcing in succession. A fresh batch once a fortnight will yield a continuous supply. Thousands of roots are grown and offered at cheap rates for these purposes, and a supply can be kept up by bought roots at less cost than that of the labour and material for producing them in the ground at home. Where the latter plan is adopted, fresh dung and leaves must be applied about once a fortnight, and great care must be taken to shelter the produce from the cold when cutting it in frosty weather, and also against chills of cold and excessive heat.

Peas and Broad Beans.—Protect from mice and birds, and see that black slugs are not preying upon them underground.

Kidney Beans.—Sow another batch, William's Early Prolific, or Osborn's Early Forcing, only filling the pots one-third full of earth, the other to be added as a top-dressing as the plants grow. When a constant succession is required all the year round, sow in pots every three weeks, up to next April.

Celery.—Earth up to the leaves, and spread a little litter over the crowns of the ridges during severe frost. Litter the crowns of Globe Artichokes, and store Cardoons in sand till required for use. Introduce two or three boxes of Chicory into the Mushroom house, or other dark place, once a fortnight or so, all Winter, according to the demand. The blanched leaves are much prized as a vegetable, as well as for salad. Protect Cauliflowers under glass, and see that all late Broccolis are cut or stored before the frost bites their crowns. Make up a small hot-bed for the planting of early Potatoes, the sowing of Horn Carrots, and Radishes, in a gentle heat ; also a seed-bed for Cucumbers, &c. Remove Lettuces from the open air to the inside, as space becomes vacant. Remove pots or boxes of Parsley and Mint under glass, to secure garnishing in all weathers, and provide Mint sauce for early lambs ; also a few pots of Tarragon, Fennel, and Chervil, for salading and sauces. All ground work, such as draining, levelling, carting, or wheeling new soil, composts, or manures, trenching, digging, &c., should now be pushed forward ; and all manner of rubbish, scraped, mixed, fermented, decomposed, or charred, to add to the bulk and richness of the manure heap ; for though it is true that a constant supply of sweet, crisp, succulent vegetables is largely dependent on good seeds, sown at the right time, and in the best manner, and the skill thrown into their cultivation, yet it is manure only that can make them grow well, or carry their products to perfection.

Cabbage Lettuce—*Continued.*

	Per ounce. s.	d.
American Gathering.—Of exceedingly fine flavour; may be used from spring until late in the autumn, . . *6d. and 1s. per packet.*		
All the Year Round.—Very solid, crisp, and hardy. May be used all the year round if sown at different times, ... *6d. per packet,*	1	3
Tom Thumb, or Tennis Ball.—Small firm heads, white and crisp; stands the winter well, *6d. per packet,*	1	3
Brown Dutch.—For autumn sowing, *6d. & 1s. per pkt.,*	1	6
Commodore Nutt.—Small and remarkably early; of dark green colour, compact habit, and splendid flavour, . . . *1s. per packet,*	2	6
Drumhead, or Malta.—Large and crisp; one of the best for summer use, . *6d. per packet,*	.	9
Grand Admiral.—For winter use, *6d. per packet,*	1	0
Hammersmith Hardy Green.—A well-known compact winter kind, . . . *6d. per packet,*	.	9
Neapolitan.—Hearts well, . . *6d. per packet,*	1	0
Victoria, or Red-edged, . . *6d. per packet,*	.	9

WEBBS' COLLECTIONS OF CABBAGE LETTUCE.

	s.	d.
The best six sorts for succession (*our selection*), one packet of each, ...	2	9
The best three sorts for succession (*our selection*), one packet of each, ...	1	6

Leek.

(*Allium; porrum.*) FRENCH, *Poireau.* ☞ For Cultivation, see page 53.

Webbs' New Colossal Leek.

The best Leek. 1s. 6d. per packet. (SEE ILLUSTRATION.)

A new and very choice variety of this useful vegetable; rapid in growth, and extremely hardy. It is of splendid quality, and being of immense size and superior shape is specially suitable for exhibition purposes.

From R. RATCLIFFE, Esq., The Poplars.
"*Your Colossal Leeks were the finest I ever had, and the admiration of all who saw them.*"

From Mr. HENRY RAMSDALE, Chew Moor.
"*Please forward two packets of your New Colossal Leek Seed, as the last I had gave great satisfaction.*"

From Mr. THOMAS MINKS, Victoria Garesfield.
"*Please send one packet of your Colossal Leek. I had one last year from which I grew splendid specimens; they are the best I ever had—they do not belie their name.*"

From Mr. HENRY WILLS, Bedworth.
"*I was very successful with your Seeds, and had some splendid produce. I took four First Prizes with your Celery, and two with your Leeks. I also had the pleasure of winning your First Prize at Nuneaton.*"

WEBBS' NEW COLOSSAL LEEK.

	Per ounce. s.	d.
Henry's Prize.—A large and splendid variety, . . *6d. per packet,*	1	3
Musselburgh.—A very hardy variety of large size, *6d. and 1s. per packet,*	1	6
The Lyon.—A fine variety for exhibition, ... *1s. per packet.*		
Ayton Castle Giant.—Very large, ... *6d. per packet,*	1	0
Large Rouen.—Leaves broad; stem very thick, . . . *6d. per packet,*	1	0
London Flag.—A well-known sort, ...		6

Mustard.

(*Sinapis alba* and *Sinapis nigra.*) FRENCH, *Moutarde.* ☞ For Cultivation, see page 54.

	Per ounce. s.	d.
White.—Used generally for salads, *2s. per quart, 1s. 3d. per pint,*	.	2
Chinese.—Very distinct, black-seeded, fine pungent flavour, ...		3

From Mr. J. MUIR, Gardener to C. R. M. Talbot, Esq., M.P., Margam Park.
"*The Vegetables shown at the Cardiff Exhibition on August 11th formed the most extensive and best display I have ever seen in South Wales. There were 13 lots competing in the class for a Collection of 9 dishes. I succeeded in securing the First Prize, and the whole of my dishes, with the exception of one, were the produce of 'Webbs'' Seeds. I also had First Prize for your Banbury Onion, First for your Red Globe Onion, and First for your Colossal Leek.*"

From Mr. E. WOOD, Winshill.
"*The Seeds arrived safely—I hope to do as well with them as I did last year, viz., a total of 73 Prizes from your Seeds. Cucumbers, Turnips, and Carrots very fine—taking 11 First Prizes.*"

From Mr. A. CLARK, Matlock Bath.
"*You will be glad to know that for the last 4 years I have taken the whole of the First Prizes for the following Vegetables—Longpod Bean, Windsor Bean, and Cos Lettuce—at our Show, and that they were grown from Seeds supplied by you.*"

Melon.

(*Cucumis Melo.*) FRENCH, *Melon.* ☞ For Cultivation, see page 53.

THE BEST SCARLET-FLESHED MELON.

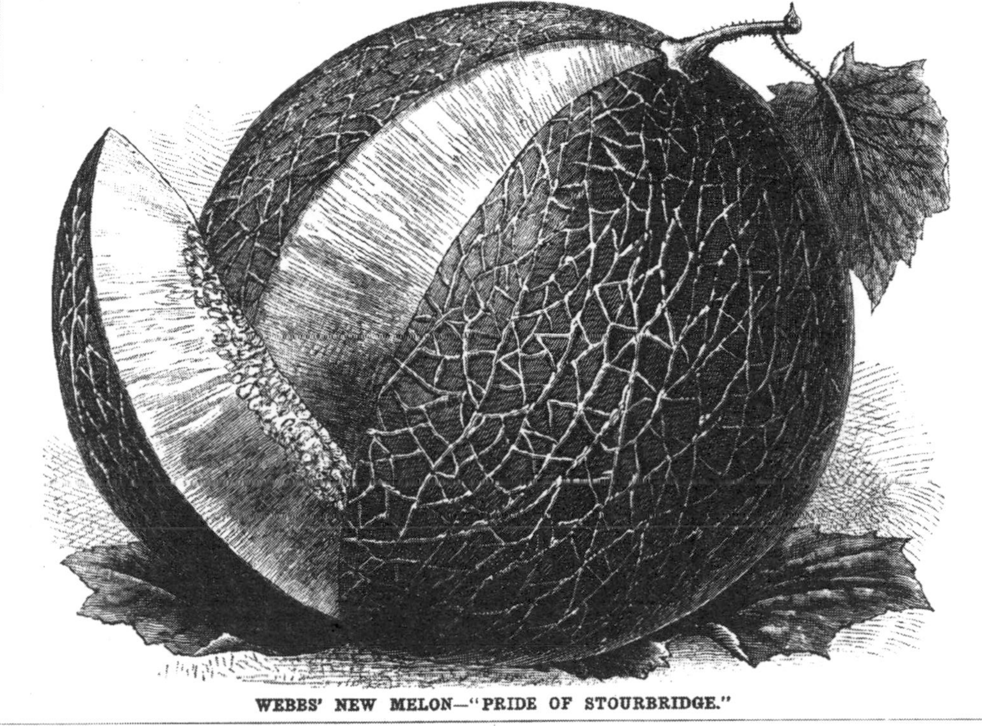

VALUABLE FOR EXHIBITION PURPOSES.

WEBBS' NEW MELON—"PRIDE OF STOURBRIDGE."

Webbs' New Melon— "Pride of Stourbridge."

1s. 6d. and 2s. 6d. per packet. (SEE ILLUSTRATION.)

This magnificent Melon has become an exceedingly popular variety, as it is distinct from, and superior to, all other scarlet-fleshed varieties in cultivation. The fruit is regularly and beautifully netted, and the flesh is of great depth, exceedingly tender, melting, and of the richest flavour. It is a remarkably free setter, of robust constitution, very productive, and unequalled for its handsome form and splendid quality. It is specially adapted for exhibition purposes, and has gained First Honours at important Meetings.

From Mr. W. FINCH, Gardener to J. Marriott, Esq., Queen's Road.

"I was awarded a First-class Certificate at the Birmingham Show for your Melon—'Pride of Stourbridge.' I consider it an excellent variety, and the best-flavoured Scarlet-fleshed Melon I know; I have more than a dozen sorts growing here now."

Webbs' New Melon— "Queen Victoria."

2s. 6d. per packet.

This splendid new variety has a strong and vigorous constitution; it sets its fruit freely, and is an abundant bearer. The fruit is nearly round, of large size and remarkably handsome appearance, having a lightish-yellow and very thin skin, which is regularly netted. Its dark-green flesh is of great depth, very solid, sweet, and luscious. For exhibition purposes this variety is strongly recommended.

From Mr. R. D. PAGE, Hollydene.

"I have much pleasure in stating that your New Melon 'Queen Victoria' gave me extreme satisfaction. It is handsome in form, and of delicious flavour; certainly one of the best I have grown."

From Mr. J. WILKES, Gardener to Geo. Meakin, Esq., Cresswell Hall.

"'Queen Victoria' Melon grows well and sets its fruit very freely, which are very handsome, averaging 5 lbs. in weight. It keeps well after being cut, and is valuable on that account."

Webbs' Woodfield Melon.

1s. 6d. and 2s. 6d. per packet.

From the time of its introduction in 1877 this exquisite and popular green-fleshed Melon has given universal satisfaction, being rich, melting, juicy, and of delicious flavour; remarkable for its beautiful netting and handsome shape. It is a distinct variety of good growth, a free setter, and of strong and robust constitution; it has a firm and very thin skin, and is all that can be desired for the table. It is also specially adapted for pot-culture, and valuable as an exhibition Melon, having been awarded numerous First Prizes at the principal Shows.

☞ *For List of Special Prizes offered by Webb & Sons at Horticultural Shows in 1888, see pages 4 and 5.*

Historical Notes on Vegetables.

THE majority of cultivated vegetables date from very early times, but it is only within the present century that much advance has been made in the production of improved varieties. The following notes are intended to show the origin of the principal Kitchen Garden crops, and in another part of this Catalogue will be found descriptions and illustrations of the best modern forms, the results of hybridisation and many years' careful selection and trials.

ARTICHOKE.

THE Globe Artichoke, *Cynara Scolymus*, was used by the Greeks and Romans, and so much esteemed that it is said "the common people" were not allowed to eat it. The supplies were principally obtained from the African coast, according to some writers, though it is probable that it was also cultivated in Europe, especially if the surmises of some botanists be correct, namely, that the Artichoke is derived from the wild Cardoon, *Cynara cardunculus*. It is believed, however, that it was first introduced to Florence from Naples in 1466, and the first recorded instance of the cultivation of the Artichoke in Britain occurs in 1548. The plant is included amongst those mentioned by Gerard in his 'Herbal,' and ever since then it has held a place in British gardens. The Jerusalem Artichoke, *Helianthus tuberosus*, is a native of North America, which seems to have been first cultivated in this country in 1616, and, as the plant is very readily increased, it rapidly spread.

ASPARAGUS.

ASPARAGUS, *Asparagus officinalis*, has been a favourite vegetable for over 2000 years, and, though we are familiar with Giant Asparagus, the Romans seem to have surpassed us in this respect, for Pliny relates that in his time it was obtained of such a size that three heads weighed a pound, and were sold for a sum equivalent to three farthings English. The plant is a native of the sea-shores in this country, and is mentioned by Gerard as a cultivated plant, though it does not appear to have been forced until some years later; the first forced Asparagus sent into the London markets is said to have been in 1670.

BEANS.

THE Broad Bean, *Faba vulgaris*, or *Vicia Faba*, is believed to have been cultivated in Europe in prehistoric times; at least, it is known to have been used by the Athenians at certain feasts, and by the Romans at the festival Fabaria. Some have thought that the Bean was cultivated in China more than 2000 years before the Christian era; but there is good evidence that this ancient plant was *Dolichos Soja*, as the Bean does not appear to have been introduced to China until the year 100 B.C. Modern botanists incline to the view that the Broad Bean has really been derived by culture from *Vicia narbonensis*, a common wild plant in the Mediterranean region. The Kidney Bean, *Phaseolus vulgaris*, has been cultivated for a considerable time, but there is an uncertainty as to whether it was known in Europe before the discovery of America, where the genus is strongly represented. The Scarlet Runner, *Phaseolus multiflorus*, is a Mexican plant, and was first cultivated in England in 1633, since which time it has become one of the most important and extensively cultivated members of the family.

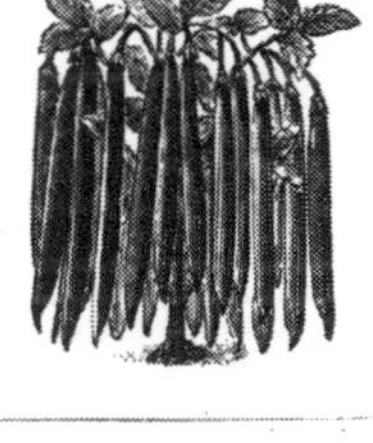

BEET.

BEET, *Beta vulgaris*, is another ancient vegetable, the cultivation of which can be traced back to the fourth century B.C. It is a native of South Europe, and the red and white varieties were known to the early cultivators. Some doubt exists as to when it was first grown here, 1548 being assigned as the date by certain writers, while others give it as nearly one hundred years later; but the former is probably correct, as the Cicla Beet was introduced from Portugal in 1570.

CABBAGE.

AN historical account of the Cabbage, and the numerous other varieties derived from *Brassica oleracea*, would fill a volume; but we can only glance at a few points. The Greeks and Romans knew and appreciated the Cabbage, and there is a fable to the effect that the latter people, at an early period, expelled all their physicians for several hundred years, preserving their health by a free use of this vegetable. In later times, when the people had become more 'civilised,' it is related that Cabbage was commonly eaten uncooked to correct the effects of excessive indulgence in intoxicating liquors. Whether the cultivation of the plant was introduced to England by the Romans is uncertain, but in the 15th and 16th centuries it was well known, the red, white, curled, and 'Savoie' varieties being then grown.

CARROT.

THE Carrot, *Daucus carota*, is a biennial umbelliferous plant, a native of this country, but, like so many other vegetables, we owe its first culture to the inhabitants of Eastern and Southern Europe. Pliny states that in his time the best Carrots were obtained from Candia, but it was also grown on the mainland. The culture was commenced here in the 16th century, at Sandwich, and it is believed that the Flemings were the introducers. Philip Miller tried some interesting experiments with the wild Carrot, endeavouring to improve it by cultivation, but did not succeed, probably because insufficient time was devoted to it to effect the desired change.

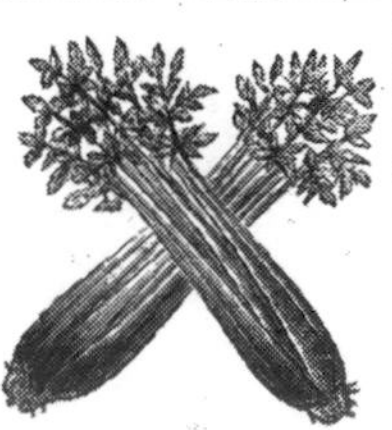

CELERY.

CELERY, *Apium graveolens*, is very widely distributed as a wild plant, being found in Britain and several other European countries, extending into Asia. It was known to the ancients, and is mentioned by Homer, Theophrastus, Dioscorides, and Pliny. It was cultivated on the European continent for centuries before it came into favour here, and it is uncertain when it first attracted general attention in Britain. Celeriac, the Turnip-rooted Celery, is a variety much more commonly grown on the Continent at the present time than it is here, though it is esteemed in some gardens.

HISTORICAL NOTES ON VEGETABLES—*Continued.*

LETTUCE.

LETTUCE, *Lactuca Scariola var. sativa*, is one of our oldest cultivated salad plants, for it is said to have been a favourite with the Persian kings 500 years before the Christian era, and we certainly know that it was much valued by the Romans. Three kinds were known to the ancients, and in Gerard's time, when it came into use in England, eight varieties were in cultivation; how many there are now it would be impossible to say, but not less than fifty have been named and catalogued.

ONION.

THE Onion, *Allium Cepa*, ranks amongst the oldest and most valued of vegetables, the ancient Greeks Romans, and Egyptians having grown it extensively; indeed, it has now been so long in cultivation that its native country is unknown, but it is supposed to have been widely distributed in Western Asia. It was grown in Britain at the time of the earliest herbalists, but we have no record respecting its first introduction. The Leek, *Allium ampeloprasum var. porrum*, is also not known in a wild state, though the species from which it is thought to be derived is found in Eastern Central Europe. Leeks have been cultivated from very early times, and it is related that Nero used to eat them for several days in each month to clear his voice.

PARSLEY.

PARSLEY, *Petroselinum sativum*, or *Apium petroselinum*, is found wild in South Europe, and was employed by the Romans, but does not seem to have been cultivated by them, as Pliny only speaks of it as a wild plant. It was, however, grown in Charlemagne's time, and is especially commended by him. In England it was grown in 1548, that being the earliest record we have of its production here.

PARSNIP.

THE Parsnip, *Pastinaca sativa*, is found in a natural state in several districts of Britain, and has been cultivated for a considerable period. It was known to the Romans, but their chief supplies are doubtfully recorded as being obtained from Germany by the orders of the Emperor Tiberius.

PEA.

THE Pea, *Pisum sativum*. Researches amongst the remains of the Swiss lake-dwellings, dating from the bronze age, have revealed samples of seeds that are considered to have been similar to cultivated peas of the present day, or at least of the same origin. *Pisum sativum* itself is not found wild now, but West Asia is pointed out as its most probable home, and its culture, therefore, must date from extremely early times. Peas appear to have been grown in England in Henry VIII.'s reign, but they were not abundant even in Queen Elizabeth's time, and some were then imported from Holland. They were much cultivated around Fulham for some years after they became a regular crop here, and the 'Fulham Pease,' which are said to have come originally from France, were quite famed.

POTATO.

THE Potato, *Solanum tuberosum*, has occasioned much writing and many disputes as to its first introduction and its true origin, and it would be impossible in these notes to even briefly review all that has been recorded respecting it. There is no doubt, however, that it is an American plant, and that it had been cultivated by the Peruvians or Chilians long before Europeans visited their country. It was introduced to Ireland about 1586 by Sir Walter Raleigh, or more probably by Thomas Heriot, one of his companions, in returning from an expedition to Virginia, but it is believed to have been sent to Europe by the Spaniards before that date. Gerard describes and figures the plant in 1597, and states that he had it from Virginia. It is not, however, a native of that region, being confined to the western side of South America, and it was most likely obtained from some of the Spanish ships.

RADISH.

THE Radish is perhaps entitled to the leading place amongst cultivated vegetables as regards its antiquity, for it has been grown from the earliest historical times throughout Asia and Europe. It is a native of the temperate regions of the Old World, and was long regarded as a distinct species under the name of *Raphanus sativus*. Some extremely interesting experiments, conducted several years ago by M. Carrière of Paris, have, however, conclusively proved that it is really a cultivated variety of *R. Raphanistrum*, with a non-articulated seed-vessel, and an enlarged root. It does not appear to have been grown in England before 1548, but it rapidly extended when once known, and now scarcely a garden in Britain could be found without it.

SPINACH.

SPINACH, *Spinacea oleracea*, belongs to comparatively modern times, as it did not make its debut in England until 1568. It was probably first known to the Persians, and is thought to have extended into Europe during the fifteenth century. It is not found in a wild state, the nearest species being *S. tetrandra*, which resembles the prickly variety, and is a native of Turkestan and Persia. The New Zealand Spinach, *Tetragonia expansa*, was found in Captain Cook's voyage to the South Seas, and introduced by Sir Joseph Banks.

TURNIP.

THE Turnip, *Brassica rapa*, or *B. rapa depressa*, has long been cultivated in Europe and Asia, but was not introduced to England until 1550, when it is said to have come from Holland. Gerard says: 'The small Turnip groweth by a village neare London (called Hackney), in a sandie ground, and they are brought to the cross in Cheapside by the women of that village to be sold, and are the best we ever tasted.' The plant is not known in a wild state, but seems to have been originally a native of temperate Europe.

D

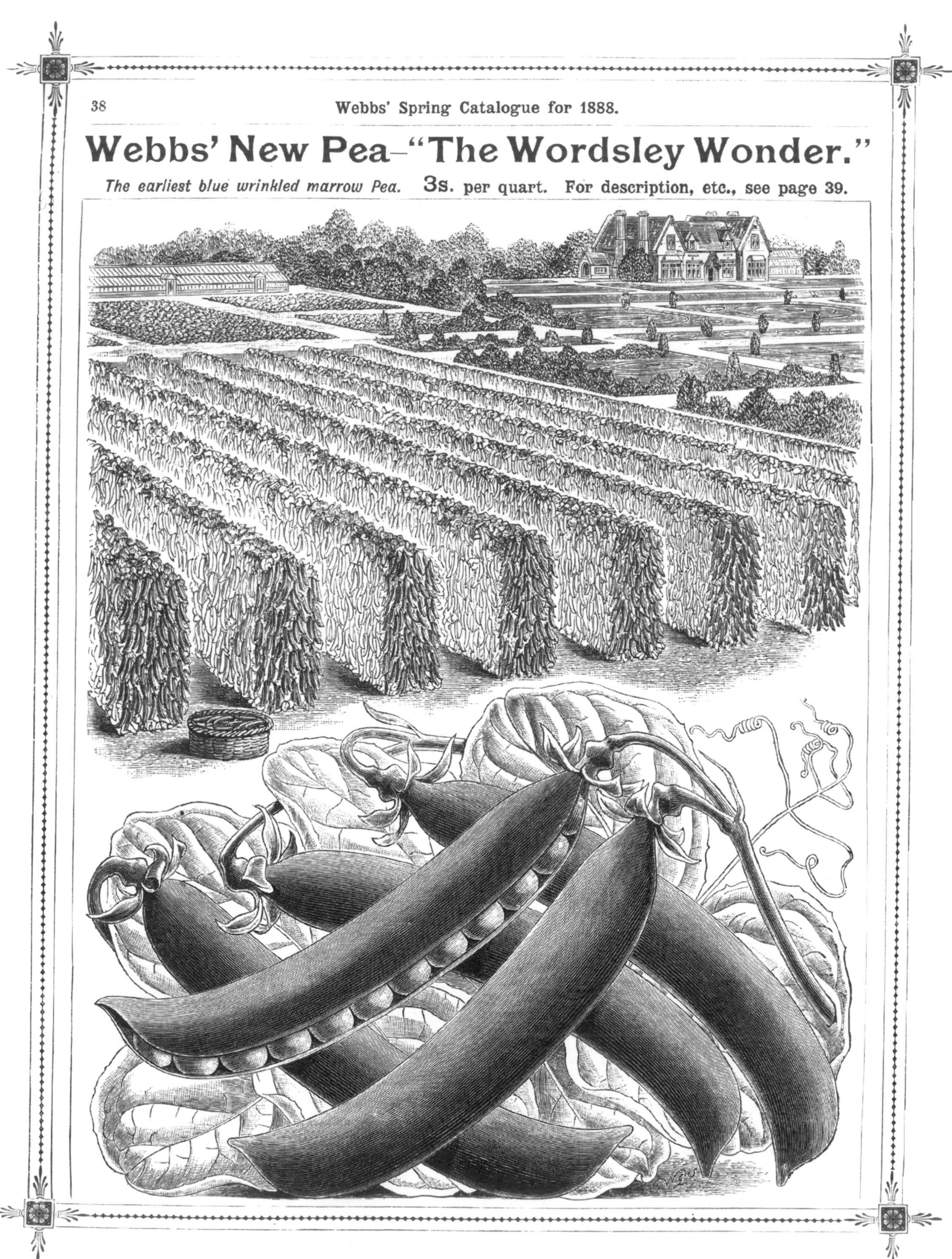
38
Webbs' Spring Catalogue for 1888.
Webbs' New Pea–"The Wordsley Wonder."
The earliest blue wrinkled marrow Pea. 3s. per quart. For description, etc., see page 39.

See pages 4 and 5 for List of Prizes offered by Webb & Sons in 1888.

Webbs' New Pea—"The Wordsley Wonder."

The earliest blue wrinkled marrow Pea. 3s. *per quart.* (SEE ILLUSTRATION, *page* 38.)

The unparalleled qualities of our New Pea—"The Wordsley Wonder," are verified by the numerous testimonials we have received in its favour, and by the number of Prizes awarded to it. This wonderful Pea is the result of crosses between Advancer, Little Gem, and Prizetaker, and whilst possessing all the good qualities of the two former varieties, it has both the constitution and productiveness of the latter. It is a blue wrinkled marrow, growing 2½ feet high, of strong and vigorous habit, and is the earliest Pea of the kind in cultivation, as it comes into use but a few days after Sangster's No. 1, and Kentish Invicta. The pods—produced in pairs at every joint—are of medium size, slightly curved, and each pod is literally packed with from 10 to 12 large peas, which are exceedingly sweet, of beautiful colour, and the finest flavour. As a first early Pea for large gardens, it is unequalled, and its convenient height and cropping properties render it indispensable to the amateur.

Proofs of Superiority.

From WM. HY. MORTON, Esq., Shepton Mallet.

"Your Seeds have given me every satisfaction, more especially 'Wordsley Wonder' Pea. I have had in many cases pods with 13 Peas in a pod, and (in one instance only) the, to me, unparalleled number of 14 in a pod. It does not come in quite so early as some others, but I am content to wait a day or two, and contentment in this case brings great gain."

From Mr. HENRY ELLIOTT, Gardener to the Most Noble the Marquis of Normanby, Mulgrave Castle.

"I find your Pea, 'The Wordsley Wonder,' to be of first-rate quality and colour, and a good cropper."

From Mr. OWEN THOMAS, Gardener to His Grace the Duke of Devonshire, Chatsworth.

"'Wordsley Wonder' Pea I think highly of. It is a good grower, and has a hardy constitution, having withstood the recent dry weather better than most other Peas in the garden. It is a prolific bearer, the pods being long, rather thin, and filled almost to bursting with Peas—nine and ten and sometimes eleven in a pod."

From Mr. W. PRATT, Gardener to the Most Noble the Marquis of Bath, Longleat.

"I can speak in the highest terms of your 'Wordsley Wonder' Pea. The pods are wonderfully well-filled, and the Pea is one of the very best croppers I know of. The flavour is excellent."

From Mr. JAMES BONE, Gardener to the Right Hon. Lord Chesham, Latimer.

"I can again speak very favourably of your 'Wordsley Wonder;' having sown it much earlier, it again turned out first-class, the pods being well filled and the Peas of excellent flavour."

From Mr. E. GILMAN, Gardener to the Right Hon. the Earl of Shrewsbury and Talbot, Ingestre Hall.

"Your 'Wordsley Wonder' Pea is a blue wrinkled marrow, of strong and vigorous habit. It is a grand Pea, and I intend to grow it largely another year."

From Mr. C. DENNING, Gardener to the Right Hon. the Earl of Chesterfield, Holme Lacy.

"I consider your 'Wordsley Wonder' Pea a most useful one—it is a great cropper, of good flavour, and the length of time it keeps on bearing is surprising."

From Mr. WILLIAM DAVIES, Gardener to the Right Hon. Lord Dormer, Grove Park.

"I think your New Pea, 'Wordsley Wonder,' a first-class variety, its merits being large pods, and excellence in colour and flavour. I consider it one of the best Peas I have grown."

From G. BEVAN, Esq., Sudbury.

"Send me one quart of Wordsley Wonder Pea; it is by far the best that I have ever grown."

From Mr. ROBERT SQUIBBS, Gardener to the Most Noble the Marquis of Bristol, Ickworth Park.

"I found the 'Wordsley Wonder' Pea a very excellent variety, of robust habit, with fairly long well-filled pods, produced in abundance, and I think perhaps the best Pea I ever tasted for quality and flavour."

From Mr. EDWARD WARD, Gardener to the Right Hon. Lord Windsor, Hewell Grange.

"I consider your 'Wordsley Wonder' Pea a great acquisition to the early class, it being of first-rate flavour, and a free bearer, with well-filled pods."

From "THE GARDENERS' MAGAZINE," Sept. 11th.

"NEW PEAS.—*Amongst the Peas of recent introduction, Webbs' 'Wordsley Wonder' and 'Chancellor' are two excellent varieties, as they produce enormous crops, and are of high quality.*—H. W. WARD, Longford Castle, Salisbury."

From Mr. J. IRVINE, Gardener to the Right Hon. the Earl of Suffolk and Berkshire, Charlton Park.

"Your New Pea 'Wordsley Wonder' is one of the best that has come under my notice; haulm covered from top to bottom with handsome pods, which are remarkably well filled, each containing nine to eleven Peas of first-rate quality. My employer says the flavour of your New Pea is excellent."

From Mr. A. PETTIGREW, Gardener to the Most Noble the Marquis of Bute, Cardiff Castle.

"I have grown your New Pea, 'Wordsley Wonder,' for two years, and I consider it a most excellent variety; it is a great bearer, podding close to the ground. It fills its pods well, and when cooked the flavour is all that could be desired."

From Mr. D. SNELLING, Gardener to the Right Hon. Earl Lucan, Laleham House.

"Your 'Wordsley Wonder' Pea has well-filled pods, with from seven to ten Peas in each, of deep-green colour, and marrow-like flavour—I shall cultivate it freely."

From Mr. J. TAYLOR, Gardener to the Right Hon. Earl Ferrers, Chartley Castle.

"Your 'Wordsley Wonder' Pea is a free-bearing sort, producing medium-sized pods, well filled with Peas of excellent quality, and fine flavour."

From Mr. GEORGE BRUNT, Gardener to the Right Hon. the Countess of Chesterfield, Bretby Park.

"I think the 'Wordsley Wonder' a first class Pea both for cropping and eating—in fact I hope to grow it next year on a larger scale; the pods were well filled, having from nine to eleven Peas in each."

From "THE GARDEN," August 23.

"WORDSLEY WONDER PEA.—*This Pea merits all that can be said in its favour.*—J. MUIR."

From Mr. W. H. HARRIS, Redditch.

"The Wordsley Wonder Peas were most beautiful, and admired by every one that saw them."

From Mr. O. OWENS, Gardener to the Most Noble the Marquis of Anglesey, Hageley Hall.

"Your New Pea, 'The Wordsley Wonder,' is of extra good quality, with large and well-filled pods, and a most abundant bearer. I have recommended it to all my friends, as I think no one should be without such a Pea."

From Mr. J. BEST, Gardener to His Grace the Duke of Hamilton, Easton Park.

"I was very pleased with the 'Wordsley Wonder' Pea. I must say that it is a grand Pea, a very prolific bearer, and of excellent flavour."

From Mr. G. M. BREESE, Gardener to the Right Hon. Lord Leconfield, Petworth Park.

"I have never yet met with a Pea to yield so much per gallon pods as the 'Wordsley Wonder'—it has such a very thin shell and is so full of Peas, which are of excellent colour and fine flavour. I think it one of the best I have tried for some time as a dwarf Pea."

From "THE JOURNAL OF HORTICULTURE," July 31.

"Messrs. Webb and Sons, Wordsley, Stourbridge, send us samples of their New Pea, 'Wordsley Wonder,' which they describe as 'the earliest blue wrinkled Marrow Pea.' It is a very prolific and useful variety, with pods of medium size, mostly in pairs, and extremely well filled, the pods containing from eight to twelve Peas, the majority containing ten. Some very handsome samples of this variety were exhibited at Kensington, and attracted much attention from the experienced vegetable growers present. The height is about 2½ feet, and the flavour of the Peas is very satisfactory."

IMPORTANT NOTICE.—*Webbs' Seeds can only be obtained direct from Wordsley. Orders may be sent either by post, or through our representatives.*

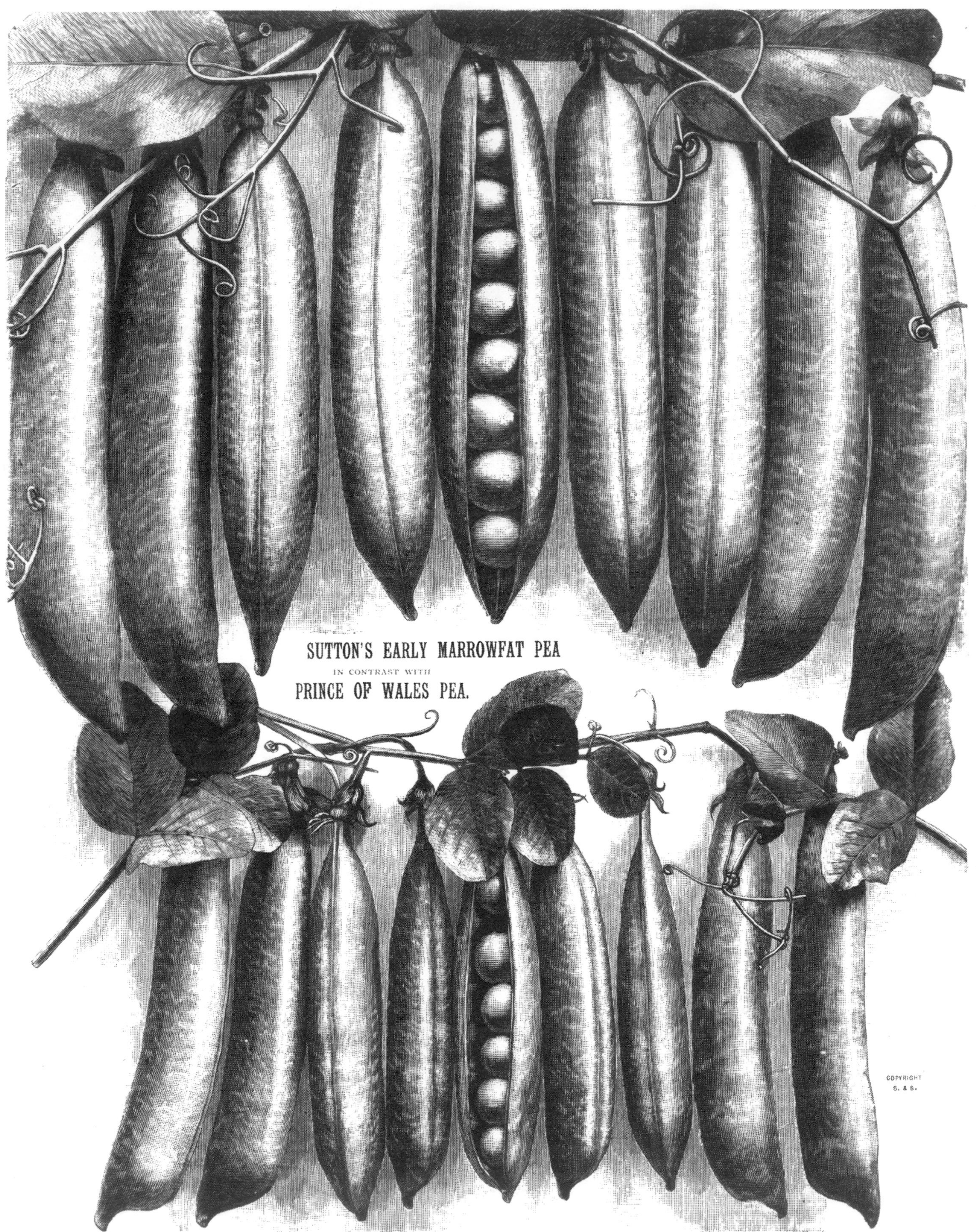

38 *Engraved from a Photograph of the two Peas taken together. See particulars on next page.*

Sutton's Vegetable Seeds—Complete List for 1892 continued.

GARDEN PEAS—continued.

SECOND DIVISION: FOR SECOND EARLY CROPS.

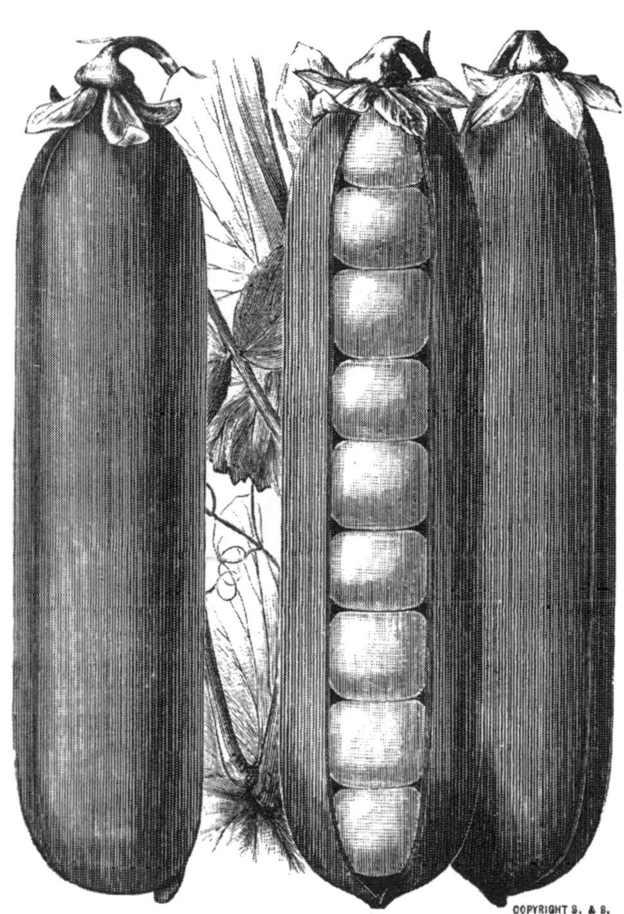

SUTTON'S PERFECT GEM PEA.
Per quart, 3s. 6d.

Sutton's Perfect Gem. This remarkably handsome dwarf wrinkled Pea was introduced by us in 1889, and has proved to be a most valuable acquisition to the second early class. The haulm only attains a height of 18 to 24 inches, and is almost hidden beneath a crowd of perfectly straight, handsome pods, well filled with large peas of superior flavour. Many letters have reached us testifying to its great merits. (*See illustration above*) ... ... per quart, 3*s.* 6*d.*

'**Sutton's Perfect Gem is another first-class variety, only attaining** the height of two feet, so that it is well adapted for a small garden. The straight well-filled pods are produced in abundance almost close to the ground. —KITCHEN GARDENER.'—AMATEUR GARDENING, *March* 21, 1891.

'**Your Perfect Gem Pea is one of the best dwarfs I have ever had,** producing a good crop of large pods filled with delicious peas.'—Mrs. COOKE, St. John's Wood.

'**Just the kind that is wanted for small gardens where space is limited** and good crops of delicious peas are desired.'—AMATEUR GARDENING.

'**Your Perfect Gem is an excellent dwarf second early Pea, heavy** cropper, with large well-filled pods of splendid flavour—the very best dwarf I have ever grown.'—Mr. J. W. BUNN, *Gardener to* E. M. PRICE, Esq.

Sutton's Early Marrowfat was introduced by us in 1890 as the finest wrinkled Pea of the second early class, and our customers' experience has fully confirmed our own opinion of its merits. The long pods are produced in great abundance, and they are literally packed with large peas of exceptional sweetness. On the preceding page we give an illustration, engraved direct from a photograph, of pods grown under ordinary field cultivation at our Experimental Grounds, in comparison with pods of Prince of Wales, fairly picked from a row grown under garden culture. Height 2 feet.

Per packet, 1*s.* 6*d.* and 2*s.* 6*d.*

'**Sutton's Early Marrow is a new variety sent out by the firm from** whom it takes its name. The seed was sown on April 7, and it proved a first-class variety. It grows about two feet in height, is of robust constitution, and produces well-filled pods of good flavoured peas.—KITCHEN GARDENER.'—AMATEUR GARDENING, *March* 21, 1891.

'PEAS AT CHISWICK.—**A good sort is Sutton's Early Marrowfat, with** broad, light, glaucous green pods, 3 to 4 inches long, and containing 6 to 8 large, tender, and sweetly flavoured peas.'—GARDENING WORLD, *August* 1, 1891.

'**A first-rate cropper, pods very broad. Haulm thick, and heavily** laden with large handsome pods, each containing from 9 to 12 peas of extraordinary size, most beautiful green colour, and excellent flavour.'—Mr. S. COLBERT, The Lodge Gardens.

'**A grand variety, strong grower, very productive, and stands the** drought well.'—Mr. W. CLARKE, The Gardens, Bessborough.

'**A grand second early, growing about 2½ feet high, with an abundance** of large massive pods, well filled and of a beautiful dark green colour. Sown on south border March 1, ready to gather June 25.'—Mr. T. LOCKIE, The Gardens, Oakley Court.

'**Large well-filled pods, averaging 9 peas in a pod. Strong sturdy** grower, good cropper, and fine flavour.'—Mr. JAMES TEGG, The Gardens, Bearwood.

Sutton's Plentiful. This fine Pea was originally selected from Early Sunrise, but altogether surpasses that variety in productiveness, the haulm being literally crowded with good-sized pods. It will be prized by those who appreciate blue-seeded varieties. We recommend our customers who have not yet grown this Pea to give it a trial, and we are confident they will not be disappointed either with the crop or the quality when cooked. Height 2½ feet ... ... per quart, 2*s.* 6*d.*

Sutton's Prolific. A very fine round-seeded Pea, as productive as Market Favourite, but earlier. Habit bushy, and haulm covered with pods; peas very sweet. Admirably suited for market work. Height 4 feet ... per quart, 2*s.* 6*d.*

Nelson's Vanguard was introduced by us some years ago, and it is still one of the very best second early wrinkled varieties. The haulm is bushy and profusely covered with pods; flavour excellent. Height 2½ feet. Per quart, 2*s.* 6*d.*

Advancer. Well-filled pods, delicious flavour, very prolific. Our stock has been carefully selected, and we can strongly recommend this Pea for the second early crop. Height 2½ feet ... ... per quart, 1*s.* 9*d.*

Early Paragon. Awarded First-class Certificate by the R.H.S. An excellent second early wrinkled Pea; large pods. Height 4 feet...per quart, 2*s.*

Early Sunrise. Early, hardy and robust in constitution; abundant cropper; fine flavour; recommended for autumn sowing. Height 2½ feet...per quart, 1*s.*

Fillbasket. A greatly improved stock, strongly recommended for growing on a large scale. Height 3 feet ... ... per quart, 1*s.* 3*d.*

Taber's Market Favourite. Excellent and productive; a very fine market variety. Height 4 feet... ... ... per quart, 1*s.*

Prince of Wales. A heavy cropping Pea, which has long been popular with amateurs and cottagers. Height 3 feet ... ... per quart, 1*s.* 6*d.*

Sutton's Amateur's Guide and Spring Catalogue for 1881.
THE EARLIEST WRINKLED PEA FOR FORCING.
GOOD SEEDS Suttons&Sons CARRIAGE FREE TRADE MARK REGISTERED
As early as SUTTON'S RINGLEADER, which is the forwardest Round White Pea.
Haulm only 10 inches high, thickly covered with fine pods, each containing from 7 to 9 peas of delicious flavour.
THE ILLUSTRATION IS FROM A PHOTOGRAPH, AND SHOWS THE HABIT OF GROWTH.
FOR DESCRIPTION OF THIS NEW PEA SEE REMARKS ON NEXT PAGE.
INVALUABLE FOR EARLY FORCING.
UNSURPASSED FOR SMALL GARDENS.
AMERICAN WONDER PEA.
SIZE OF POD.
SIZE OF POD.
CAUTION.—Sutton & Sons are the only English House to whom a consignment of this new Pea has been sent for sale by the raisers, Messrs. B. K. Bliss & Son, of New York.
Every package will bear Messrs. Sutton's Registered Trade Mark.
24

Highest Distinction.—'THE LEGION OF HONOUR.' Paris, 1878.

SPECIAL AWARD—GOLD MEDAL, PARIS, 1878

'FOR PEAS AND BEANS.'

SEE OFFICIAL LIST OF AWARDS.

GOLD MEDAL. GOLD MEDAL.

AMERICAN WONDER PEA.

NEW EARLY DWARF WRINKLED VARIETY.

We have the pleasure of introducing to the English public this new and perfectly distinct Wrinkled Pea, feeling convinced, after a most careful trial, that it is not only the earliest Dwarf Wrinkled Pea, but that for quickness of growth, productiveness, and flavour it is unequalled by any other early variety. It is the result of a cross between those two popular varieties, Little Gem and Champion of England, and is superior in flavour to the Champion of England, and in productiveness to Little Gem. It grows from eight to ten inches in height, comes ready for table very quickly, and is invaluable for forcing under glass or for early sowings in the garden. The great want hitherto has been a Wrinkled Pea which will occupy but little space, and come in as quickly as the first early round white varieties. This Pea remedies that want, and it has only to be tried to ensure general cultivation. It was introduced in America two years ago by Messrs. B. K. Bliss & Son, the eminent seedsmen of New York, from whom we have purchased the entire stock which will be sent by them to England this season. Every packet will bear our Registered Trade Mark. (*See illustration, page* 24.) Per ¼-pint, 1*s.* 6*d.*; per ½-pint, 2*s.* 6*d.*; per quart, 8*s.* 6*d.*

NEW SOUTH WALES, *May 21st*, 1879.

'I exhibited at the late Intercolonial Exhibition in Sydney, Bliss's American Wonder Pea, and they received a special diploma, being highly esteemed on account of their quality and earliness, so that they have quite eclipsed the best English varieties tested against them; and the product of the Seed is grand in size and quality. A. A. DUNNICLIFF.'

In alluding to the above the *Sydney Morning Herald* remarked that:—'Among vegetables specially worthy of notice was Bliss's American Wonder Pea, shown for the first time. It is remarkable for the rapidity of its growth, as it is ordinarily ready for the table in thirty-three days from the time of planting. Mr. Dunnicliff had three crops since September last.'

Sutton's Emerald Gem Pea.

This valuable and distinct first early Pea is still the best for first gathering. It is perfectly distinct from every other early Pea; the haulm, foliage, and pods being of a bright green colour, similar to our Giant Emerald Marrow. It comes in at the same time as our Ringleader, which was previously the forwardest Pea in cultivation. It is more prolific and has larger pods than any other early variety, and the peas possess a delicious marrow-like flavour.

The habit of growth is very robust, from 3 to 3½ feet in height; the pods are produced in pairs, well filled, and contain from seven to ten peas. (*See illustration, page* 26.) Per quart, 2*s.* 6*d.*

From Mr. A. INGRAM, Gardener to His Grace the Duke of Northumberland.

'I find your "Emerald Gem" a first-class early Pea in every respect. In every sowing Emerald Gem and Ringleader came into flower at the same time. If any difference in earliness, Emerald Gem had it. It is an excellent cropper. In cooking it keeps its colour, and is of good flavour.'

Day's Early Sunrise Pea.

A new and distinct first early variety which we strongly recommend. The peas are slightly wrinkled—very large for an early Pea, and of fine flavour. It has a very hardy and robust constitution, is exceedingly prolific; useful alike for autumn or for spring sowing. First-class for market-gardening purposes. Height, 3 feet. (*See illustration, page* 26.) Per quart, 3*s.* 6*d.*

From Mr. J. FORD, Gardener to H.R.H. the Duke of Edinburgh, K.G.

'"Early Sunrise" is of splendid quality, robust and quick in growth.'

From Mr. J. HOSSACK, Gardener to the Right Hon. the Marquis of Conyngham.

'"Early Sunrise" is a strong grower and great bearer, coming in with our very earliest sorts; a great acquisition.'

From Mr. J. COLLARD, Hardacre Farm.

'"Early Sunrise" far surpasses anything I have ever seen or grown as a first Early Pea.'

Sutton's Duchess of Edinburgh Pea.

For productiveness and fine flavour, this variety (originally sent out by us) is acknowledged by the most eminent connoisseurs to be one of the best Peas in cultivation. We cannot recommend it too highly. The pods are long and broad, with a beautiful show of bloom, which renders them exceedingly handsome and suitable for exhibition; and they contain from ten to twelve fine peas. The flavour is unequalled, and even when the peas are quite old they are tender and sweet. It withstands the drought well, and is a continuous bearer, commencing at the end of June, and good peas can be gathered up to the third week in July. Height, 5 feet. (*See illustration, page* 26.) Per quart, 2*s.* 6*d.*

From Mr. ROBERT COCKS, Gardener to Lord Auckland.

'"Duchess of Edinburgh" is, without exception, the best Pea I have ever seen: it is a wonderful bearer, the pods are all well filled, and the flavour is most delicious. It has been admired by all who have seen it.'

From W. P. HARRIS, Esq., Braunton.

'The quantity on the three rows of your "Duchess of Edinburgh" Peas surpasses anything I ever saw, and the flavour is superior to that of any other sort.'

From Mr. JOHN BAKER, Bampton.

'I have yet (October 22nd) some of your "Duchess of Edinburgh" Peas growing splendidly. I could gather a dish of fine pods, clean and of good colour. I find them the best late Peas I have ever tried.'

Sutton's Royal Berks Marrow Pea.

This vigorous-growing and productive Pea was introduced by us in 1879, and has given great satisfaction. In haulm, pod, and seed, this is distinct from any other sort. It grows from 5 to 6 feet high, and is a wonderful cropper, producing pods, each containing from eight to ten peas, in great profusion from bottom to top. The pods grow in pairs, and are so closely filled that the peas are quite angular in shape. The flavour is delicate, and is retained for a considerable time. When dished, the colour is a beautiful deep green. (*See illustration, page* 26.) Per quart, 3*s.* 6*d.*

From Mr. E. Y. YEATMAN, Gardener to the Rev. E. C. INCE, Sunbury House, Watford.

'Your Royal Berks Marrow Pea has done remarkably well with me. It is the finest Pea that has ever been seen here. When cooked it is of a beautiful dark green, invaluable for the table. It was included in the first prize collection of vegetables at the Watford Horticultural Show.'

'I took four first prizes with Duchess of Edinburgh Pea.'—Mr. R. KIDD, *Hawsker, Whitby.*

25

A Discount of 5 per cent. (1s. in the £) allowed for Cash Payments.

The English Vegetable Garden in 1881.

WHEN the progress of art and science in the present century becomes the subject of discourse by an historian of the comprehensive school, the work of this generation in the Vegetable Garden will doubtless prove rich in entertainment and instruction. We appear to be passing through an era of excessive activity in gardening, and the many and great advances accomplished within the past few years do certainly hint that the near future has much in store for us. Every horticulturist of experience can count up a number of great events that have occurred in his own time, and can see foreshadowings of events of equal or greater importance that appear to be near at hand. This generation has witnessed not only the recognition of the necessity for public parks and gardens, and a complete revolution in the delightful art of floriculture, but the very birth of the Seed Business as altogether distinct from the Plant or Nursery Trade. And, amid the puerilities common to every age and every pursuit, there can be no question that this generation's work in the Vegetable Garden has accomplished much substantial improvement in the means and ways of life, and has caused corresponding progress in the acquisition and advancement of the higher kinds of knowledge. It has certainly distinguished itself in the roll of the ages by its ever-increasing demand for reality, and to that we may charge some of its failings, while we, at the same time, indulge in feelings of pride for the better tone of thought and work that increased sincerity has secured to us.

Horticulture has not only shared in all this as fully as any of the arts, but more fully than some, because of its intimate association with the domestic life of the people. Whatever is accomplished in this region 'comes home to us,' and we judge immediately of results and are but rarely mistaken. A comparison of the state of things in any department of the vegetable garden with that which prevailed one hundred or even fifty years ago, will show that the general growth of knowledge and the improvement of the public taste are most strikingly and pleasingly reflected there. All our esculents, and more especially Potatoes, Peas, and Melons, have undergone immense improvement. When Parkinson directed his readers to prepare Melons for eating by mixing with the pulp 'salt and pepper and good store of wine,' he must have had in mind a very different class of fruit from the magnificent variety which we offer this year as 'Hero of Lockinge.' When the Charlton was the best of the early Peas, as it was in the days of men who are scarcely old as yet, there appeared no distinct prospect of the production of the American Wonder, a delicious wrinkled variety, only 10 inches high, bearing pods as large and as numerous as those produced by the Champion of England; for it seemed, at that day, impossible that any Pea of first-class quality should ever be gathered without the aid of a ladder. The Potato in its improved forms, which are the result of systematic selection and hybridisation, has contributed in a wonderful degree to the reformation of the national dietary, so that, while the masses are better fed, so they are less familiar with scrofula and scurvy, and as for 'plagues and pestilences' of the older sort, they appear to be banished out of civil society, and the average length of life of the whole population appears to increase from year to year. Towards this happy end the garden has contributed largely, and thus we are in a great degree compensated for the growth of towns, although we are bound to keep in mind that the system is unsound which permits increase of houses without a corresponding multiplication of gardens.

The weather of the past summer has been for the most part highly favourable to vegetation, though often unfavourable to the gathering in of the crops, more particularly of Peas, Onion, Lettuce, Carrot, &c. But the almost complete loss of some particular races and varieties in the vegetable garden that occurred in 1879 has been partially retrieved during 1880, and we now see many things re-established that we feared had gone for ever. The favourable sowing time of the past year contributed greatly towards this agreeable result.

The seed crop of 1879 was a poor one, and when all had been done that it was in the power of man to do, it was feared that the germinating power of many things would be low, and that the growth would be unsatisfactory. But when, after a good sowing time, the rain came, there was healthy growth, and kindly Nature brought us through our trouble, so that we begin the seed season of 1881 with good stocks of new seeds of most varieties. There have, however, been some serious failures. Broccoli, for instance, put out for seed in 1879 was almost decimated by the following winter. Large breadths estimated to produce cwts. of seed were completely destroyed. What escaped is invaluable, and has been secured in fine condition, the harvest time proving all that could be desired.

Onion has collapsed in a most unexpected, and, we might almost say, unprecedented manner, just as the harvest was coming on. Some plantations from which a ton of seed was expected have yielded scarcely 1 cwt.

In 1879 certain kinds of Lettuce were entire failures. Not an ounce of seed was saved. Although unable to offer these sorts to the public last year, happily a supply of pedigree stock seed to grow from remained in our store, or the summer of 1879 might have resulted in the total loss of some of the varieties that are most highly prized. To replace these would have required years of patient work, and even then the task might have proved impossible. Again, the crop of Lettuce is very short indeed. These are examples of difficulties which a disastrous season increases and intensifies. But difficulties in a minor degree have attended every harvest we have ever known: for each year is unfavourable to some one variety or other, and every autumn we find it necessary to omit from our Catalogue certain good sorts which the weather has spoiled.

When the produce of the past year is fairly reviewed, it will be found, with some exceptions, to be average in bulk and good in quality; and, although some crops of great importance have failed, we may hope the tide has turned. One of our weather prophets has gravely hinted at the probability that the winter of 1880–1 will be one of the mildest, and the summer that follows one of the brightest. But as no one knows what will happen in a day or an hour, so the forecast of a season is but a summary of probabilities, and often attaches more strongly to our hope than our faith.

The future of horticulture is in many ways foreshadowed by things that are seen and by events that are in progress. It cannot be doubted that we have entered upon an era of advance and improvement in every branch of art, but more especially in those branches that need the help of the seed trade. Even the improvement of our Vegetable Garden depends much on the results of travel in foreign lands, and one of our partners is constantly travelling for this purpose, collecting every novelty worthy of trial, while others are at home carefully testing, noting, and comparing the new sorts thus brought under our notice. The improvement of Vegetables and Flowers has been for fifty years the study and aim of our business life, and we are determined that no effort on our part shall be wanting to ensure for our customers the opportunity of growing every really improved variety of Vegetable, Flower, or Potato that the coming, or any future, season may produce.

'From your beautiful and valuable Amateur's Guide, I have made a common labouring lad into a most excellent practical Gardener. I do not see anywhere nicer work or so good things as he grows, and all his education has been from one of your Guides.'—MRS. PARSONS, *The Castle, Buttevant, co. Cork.*

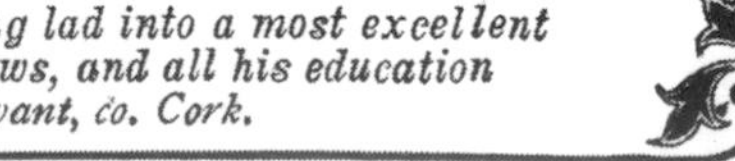

A 2 3

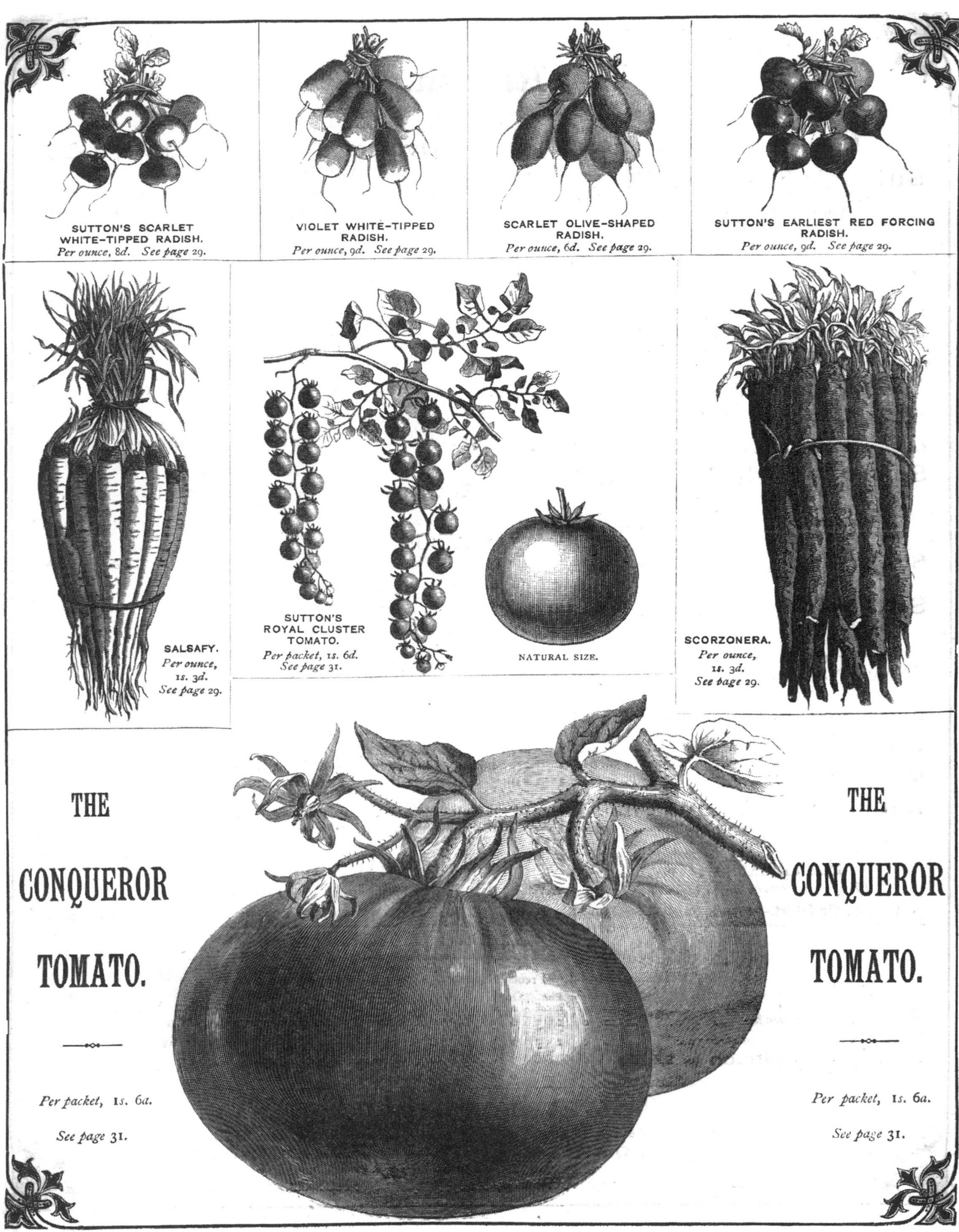
SUTTON'S SCARLET WHITE-TIPPED RADISH.
Per ounce, 8d. See page 29.
VIOLET WHITE-TIPPED RADISH.
Per ounce, 9d. See page 29.
SCARLET OLIVE-SHAPED RADISH.
Per ounce, 6d. See page 29.
SUTTON'S EARLIEST RED FORCING RADISH.
Per ounce, 9d. See page 29.
SALSAFY.
Per ounce, 1s. 3d.
See page 29.
SUTTON'S ROYAL CLUSTER TOMATO.
Per packet, 1s. 6d.
See page 31.
NATURAL SIZE.
SCORZONERA.
Per ounce, 1s. 3d.
See page 29.
THE CONQUEROR TOMATO.
Per packet, 1s. 6d.
See page 31.
THE CONQUEROR TOMATO.
Per packet, 1s. 6d.
See page 31.
30

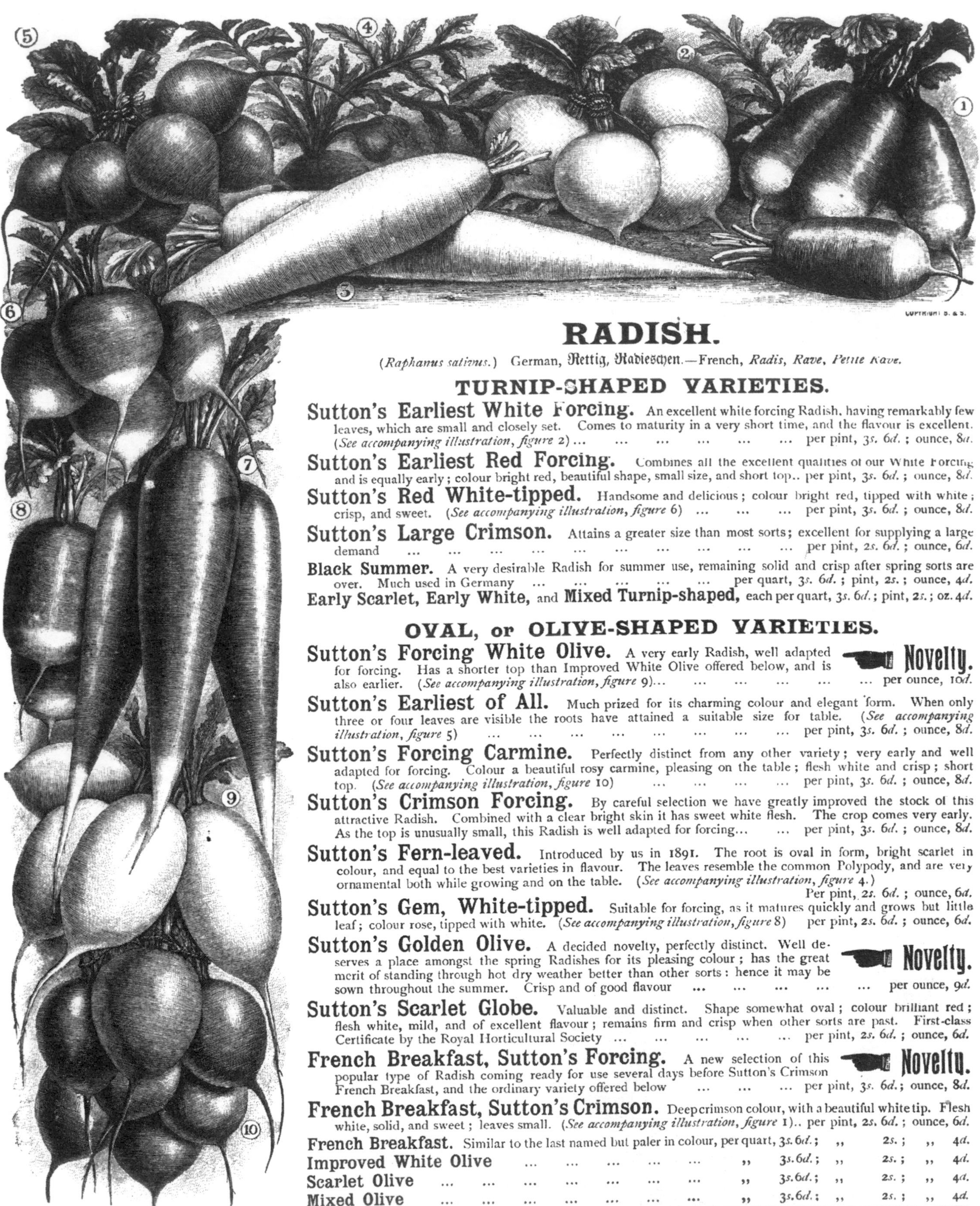

RADISH.

(*Raphanus sativus.*) German, Rettig, Radieschen.—French, *Radis, Rave, Petite Rave.*

TURNIP-SHAPED VARIETIES.

Sutton's Earliest White Forcing. An excellent white forcing Radish, having remarkably few leaves, which are small and closely set. Comes to maturity in a very short time, and the flavour is excellent. (*See accompanying illustration, figure* 2) ... ... per pint, 3*s.* 6*d.*; ounce, 8*d.*

Sutton's Earliest Red Forcing. Combines all the excellent qualities of our White Forcing and is equally early; colour bright red, beautiful shape, small size, and short top.. per pint, 3*s.* 6*d.*; ounce, 8*d.*

Sutton's Red White-tipped. Handsome and delicious; colour bright red, tipped with white; crisp, and sweet. (*See accompanying illustration, figure* 6) ... ... per pint, 3*s.* 6*d.*; ounce, 8*d.*

Sutton's Large Crimson. Attains a greater size than most sorts; excellent for supplying a large demand ... ... per pint, 2*s.* 6*d.*; ounce, 6*d.*

Black Summer. A very desirable Radish for summer use, remaining solid and crisp after spring sorts are over. Much used in Germany ... ... per quart, 3*s.* 6*d.*; pint, 2*s.*; ounce, 4*d.*

Early Scarlet, Early White, and **Mixed Turnip-shaped,** each per quart, 3*s.* 6*d.*; pint, 2*s.*; oz. 4*d.*

OVAL, or OLIVE-SHAPED VARIETIES.

Sutton's Forcing White Olive. A very early Radish, well adapted for forcing. Has a shorter top than Improved White Olive offered below, and is also earlier. (*See accompanying illustration, figure* 9)... ... ... per ounce, 10*d.* **Novelty.**

Sutton's Earliest of All. Much prized for its charming colour and elegant form. When only three or four leaves are visible the roots have attained a suitable size for table. (*See accompanying illustration, figure* 5) ... ... per pint, 3*s.* 6*d.*; ounce, 8*d.*

Sutton's Forcing Carmine. Perfectly distinct from any other variety; very early and well adapted for forcing. Colour a beautiful rosy carmine, pleasing on the table; flesh white and crisp; short top. (*See accompanying illustration, figure* 10) ... ... per pint, 3*s.* 6*d.*; ounce, 8*d.*

Sutton's Crimson Forcing. By careful selection we have greatly improved the stock of this attractive Radish. Combined with a clear bright skin it has sweet white flesh. The crop comes very early. As the top is unusually small, this Radish is well adapted for forcing... ... per pint, 3*s.* 6*d.*; ounce, 8*d.*

Sutton's Fern-leaved. Introduced by us in 1891. The root is oval in form, bright scarlet in colour, and equal to the best varieties in flavour. The leaves resemble the common Polypody, and are very ornamental both while growing and on the table. (*See accompanying illustration, figure* 4.) Per pint, 2*s.* 6*d.*; ounce, 6*d.*

Sutton's Gem, White-tipped. Suitable for forcing, as it matures quickly and grows but little leaf; colour rose, tipped with white. (*See accompanying illustration, figure* 8) per pint, 2*s.* 6*d.*; ounce, 6*d.*

Sutton's Golden Olive. A decided novelty, perfectly distinct. Well deserves a place amongst the spring Radishes for its pleasing colour; has the great merit of standing through hot dry weather better than other sorts: hence it may be sown throughout the summer. Crisp and of good flavour ... ... per ounce, 9*d.* **Novelty.**

Sutton's Scarlet Globe. Valuable and distinct. Shape somewhat oval; colour brilliant red; flesh white, mild, and of excellent flavour; remains firm and crisp when other sorts are past. First-class Certificate by the Royal Horticultural Society ... ... per pint, 2*s.* 6*d.*; ounce, 6*d.*

French Breakfast, Sutton's Forcing. A new selection of this popular type of Radish coming ready for use several days before Sutton's Crimson French Breakfast, and the ordinary variety offered below ... ... per pint, 3*s.* 6*d.*; ounce, 8*d.* **Novelty.**

French Breakfast, Sutton's Crimson. Deep crimson colour, with a beautiful white tip. Flesh white, solid, and sweet; leaves small. (*See accompanying illustration, figure* 1).. per pint, 2*s.* 6*d.*; ounce, 6*d.*

French Breakfast. Similar to the last named but paler in colour, per quart, 3*s.* 6*d.*; ,, 2*s.*; ,, 4*d.*
Improved White Olive ... ... ,, 3*s.* 6*d.*; ,, 2*s.*; ,, 4*d.*
Scarlet Olive ... ... ,, 3*s.* 6*d.*; ,, 2*s.*; ,, 4*d.*
Mixed Olive ... ... ,, 3*s.* 6*d.*; ,, 2*s.*; ,, 4*d.*

For List of Long Radishes and Winter varieties see next page.

54 SUTTON & SONS, Seed Growers and Merchants, READING, ENGLAND.

TOMATO.
SUTTON'S DESSERT.
Engraved from a photograph.
Per packet, 1s. 6d. and 2s. 6d.

COPYRIGHT. S & S.

TOMATO—continued.

RED VARIETIES—continued.

Sutton's Dessert.

FIRST-CLASS CERTIFICATE, ROYAL HORTICULTURAL SOCIETY.

A singularly beautiful Tomato, producing long elegant racemes, each carrying from eight to fifteen fruits symmetrical in form, and about the size of a small plum. The delicious flavour justifies the name, and those who are fond of Tomatoes in a natural state will especially appreciate the size and quality of the fruit. As a decorative variety it has become popular. (*See accompanying illustration*) ... ... per packet, 1*s.* 6*d.* and 2*s.* 6*d.*

'Messrs. Sutton & Sons, Reading, sent dishes of their Golden Nugget and red Dessert Tomatoes, small and highly attractive fruits in huge clusters. These varieties having won Three Marks of Merit in the Chiswick Trials were now awarded First-class Certificates.'—JOURNAL OF HORTICULTURE, *August* 16, 1894.

Sutton's A 1.

A free-bearing Tomato, deep in form, very rich in colour and of superb flavour. The fruits are produced in bunches. This recent introduction of ours has gained for itself a very high reputation. Per packet, 1*s.* 6*d.* and 2*s.* 6*d.*

'Sutton's A 1 with me has repeatedly proved a distinct improvement on Ham Green. A 1 possesses a stronger constitution (this being most apparent in either poor soil or in the open), is equally productive, the later-formed fruit not falling off much in size—colour rich red. A 1 was also good in the open when other varieties failed badly.—W. IGGULDEN.'—THE GARDEN.

'Your A 1 Tomato has more than borne out its name. I have had as many as 8 bunches on one plant, with 6 on a bunch, all perfect fruit, fit to show.'—Mr. E. E. HAZELDEN, *Gardener to* Mrs. BLORE.

Sutton's Perfection.

FIRST-CLASS CERTIFICATE, ROYAL HORTICULTURAL SOCIETY.

A superb Tomato, combining great productiveness with excellence of form, high quality, and large size. Fruit round and perfectly smooth; colour rich bright crimson; flesh solid, almost free from seeds, and of an agreeable piquant flavour. Undoubtedly the finest Tomato for exhibition, and for general indoor cultivation. In favourable seasons enormous crops may be grown out of doors ... ... per packet, 1*s.* 6*d.* and 2*s.* 6*d.*

'Perfection Tomato is a grand variety, perfect in shape and colour.' Mr. D. WINCHESTER, *Gardener to* the Rev. W. T. B. HAYTER.

'I have never had such fine Tomatoes as this year from Perfection grown out of doors. I have gathered bushels, and such a fine shape.'—Mr. SAML. SITCH, *Gardener to* Mrs. CONYBEARE.

Sutton's Abundance.

A productive Tomato, either under glass or out of doors. Fruit round, medium in size, produced in clusters, bright crimson in colour, early, and of excellent flavour. A favourite variety for market ... ... per packet, 1*s.* 6*d.*

Sutton's Cluster. Distinct and handsome, producing long racemes of small round fruit, agreeable in flavour. Fruit larger and the plant more productive than the old Cluster Tomato ... per packet, 1*s.* and 1*s.* 6*d.*

Sutton's Chiswick Red. One of the most productive Tomatoes in cultivation. Fruit bright red, oval, of medium size, and perfectly smooth, growing in large heavy clusters, each cluster having from ten to twenty-five fruits, and every plant bearing several clusters per packet, 1*s.* and 1*s.* 6*d.*

Frogmore Selected. (Veitch.) A new variety from the Royal Gardens, Windsor ... ... per packet, 2*s.* 6*d.*

Sutton's Miniature Pear-shaped. A very ornamental variety. Useful for dessert and decorative purposes, per pkt., 1*s.* and 1*s.* 6*d.*

Early Ruby. An American Tomato. Exceedingly productive, whether grown indoors or in the open ground ... ... per packet, 6*d.* and 1*s.*

The Peach. This variety has a velvety surface resembling that of a Peach. Fruit about the size of a small Peach, borne in clusters. Per packet, 6*d.* and 1*s.*

Conference. Free bearer, fine flavour. Fruit medium size. Per packet, 1*s.* 6*d.*

Ham Green Favourite. Produces a heavy crop of handsome fruit. Per packet, 1*s.* 6*d.*

Hathaway's Excelsior. Handsome and prolific ... ,, 1*s.*

Ifield Gem. An early variety of great merit ... per packet, 1*s.* and 2*s.* 6*d.*

The Mikado. An American Tomato of deep crimson colour, per pkt. 1*s.* 6*d.*

Hackwood Park Prolific ... ... ,, 1*s.*

The Trophy. Large fruit ... ... ,, 1*s.*

Vick's Criterion ... ... ,, 1*s.*

Dedham Favourite ... ... ,, 1*s.* 6*d.*

Early Large Red ... ... per packet, 6*d.* and 1*s.*

Mixed ... ... ,, 6*d.* ,, 1*s.*

CULTURE.—Under glass Tomatoes are now produced almost the year through, and in warm seasons and favourable districts tons of fruit are ripened in the open air. It will therefore be obvious that there are no formidable difficulties in the culture of this delicacy. But the necessary details require more space than we can here spare. Full particulars will be found in our book on **'The Culture of Vegetables and Flowers,' price 5*s*.**

59

Sutton's Vegetable Seeds—Complete List for 1895—continued.

GARDEN TURNIP.

(*Brassica Rapa.*) German, Speise-Rübe.—French, *Navet à potage.*

COPYRIGHT S. & S.

TURNIP, SUTTON'S EARLY SNOWBALL. *Engraved from a photograph.*
Per pint, 2s. 6d.; per ounce, 6d. (*See below.*)

Sutton's Early Snowball.

The earliest and most perfectly formed round white Turnip for garden use. Our stock has been continuously selected for many years, resulting in a beautiful shape, with short top, and a single tap root. Flesh snowy white, solid, and mild in flavour. This Turnip has been awarded First Prizes at the Royal Horticultural Society's and other leading meetings, and the numerous awards of the past year prove that Snowball is still unequalled for the exhibition table. (*Illustrated above.*)

SILVER-GILT KNIGHTIAN MEDAL for COLLECTION OF VEGETABLES, including SUTTON'S EARLY SNOWBALL TURNIP, R. H. SOCIETY, Oct. 24, 1893.

Per pint, 2*s.* 6*d.*; ounce, 6*d.*

'**I took First Prize for Turnips at the Shrewsbury Flower Show** in the Open Class with your Snowball. At Oakengates Flower Show I again took First Prize with it. Undoubtedly this Turnip is superior to all other varieties that have ever been sent out.'—Mr. G. H. C. SHORTING, Broseley.

'**We took First Prize with your Turnip at the Bath September** Show. There was a great competition.'—Mr. JNO. RIDDICK, *Gardener to* Mrs. PINDER.

'**In the last few years I have grown a large number of varieties of** white Turnip, but I have not yet met with one to beat Sutton's Snowball. I consider it as near perfection as it is possible to get.'—Mr. R. LYE, Sydmonton Court Gardens.

Sutton's Scarlet Perfection.

A remarkable Turnip of great merit. In shape and general characteristics it is a counterpart of our Yellow Perfection, but the skin is of a crimson-scarlet colour, and on the exhibition table it presents a most attractive appearance. The flesh is white, close, and when cooked the flavour is delicious. Strongly recommended ... ... per ounce, 8*d.*

'**I consider Scarlet Perfection to be a grand Turnip, far superior in** quality to the Six-weeks. It keeps crisp and tender a long time.'—Mr. J. RICHARDSON, Leake.

'**Scarlet Perfection Turnip is quick in growth, with small top and** very handsome; firm and good in flavour.'—Mr. F. AKERS, *Gardener to* W. NEWTON, Esq., jun.

'**Scarlet Perfection Turnip is a very handsome variety, delicious in** flavour.'—Mr. E. KELLAND, *Gardener to* Sir J. B. PHEAR.

Sutton's Yellow Perfection.

We can with confidence recommend this fine Yellow Turnip for its delicious flavour. The shape is rather flat with very short top; colour golden yellow; certainly one of the handsomest Turnips we have grown in all our long experience. It also possesses the great advantage of maturing very quickly. Per pint, 2*s.* 6*d.*; ounce, 6*d.*

'**Your Yellow Perfection Turnip is quite a model. The shape is** beautiful. It was admired by everybody; comes early, and has only one straight tap root.'—Mr. S. COLBERT, The Lodge Gardens.

Sutton's Early Red Milan.

The earliest Turnip in cultivation; bulb flat, of medium size, quite smooth, with a bright crimson top. Flesh white, and flavour excellent. Can be strongly recommended for the early border, or for growing under glass ... ... per ounce, 10*d.*

Sutton's Early White Milan.

A counterpart of the preceding except in colour ... ... per ounce, 10*d.*

Sutton's Improved Orange Jelly. Superior to the ordinary stock. Rich colour ... ... per pint, 2*s.* 6*d.*; ounce, 6*d.*

Dobbie's Model. A good early Turnip, resembling Snowball. Per pint, 2*s.* 6*d.*; ounce, 6*d.*

Purple-top Munich. A very handsome Turnip, having flesh of snowy whiteness, delicious in flavour. Although not a strap-leaved variety, in other respects it resembles the Early Milan, and comes in almost as early as that favourite Turnip ... ... per pint, 2*s.* 6*d.*; ounce, 6*d.*

Red-top Mousetail, or Red Strap-leaved. A sweet and mild Turnip ... ... per pint, 1*s.* 9*d.*; ounce, 4*d.*

French Forcing or Jersey Navet. An oblong white Turnip, of sweet mild flavour, withstands drought; one of the best for forcing and early use ... ... per pint, 2*s.* 6*d.*; ounce, 6*d.*

Sutton's Early White Strap-leaved. Quick-growing, suitable for forcing and early use ... ... per pint, 2*s.* 6*d.*; ounce, 6*d.*

Sutton's All the Year Round. Valuable and distinct, pale yellow flesh, green top. Delicate in flavour, and remains solid when others are past. Should not be sown too early ... per pint, 1*s.* 9*d.*; ounce, 4*d.*

Sutton's Early Six-weeks. A well-known and excellent variety; white flesh ... ... per pint, 1*s.* 9*d.*; ounce, 4*d.*

Sutton's Green-top White. Many of our customers appreciate this valuable Turnip for its shape. It attains a good size, and is therefore useful for large establishments ... ... per pint, 1*s.* 9*d.*; ounce, 4*d.*

Veitch's Red Globe. Large and distinct, white flesh, pint, 2*s.* 6*d.*; ,, 6*d.*

Chirk Castle Black Stone. Keeps well ... ,, 2*s.* 6*d.*; ,, 6*d.*

White Dutch. Flat shape; early ... ... ,, 1*s.* 9*d.*; ,, 4*d.*

Green-top Six-weeks. An early Turnip. Roots somewhat flat, with green top. White flesh ... ... per pint, 1*s.* 6*d.*; ounce, 3*d.*

Sutton's Garden Swede ... per pint, 1*s.* 9*d.*; ounce, 4*d.*

CULTURE.—Early crops may be raised in frames, and successional sowings in the open ground should follow in accordance with requirements up to the beginning of September. Always sow in drills twelve to fifteen inches apart. Thin early and boldly until the plants stand at intervals of six inches or a foot according to the size required. Our Book on Gardening contains instructions on the best means of battling with the foes of Turnip crops.

SUTTON & SONS, Seed Growers and Merchants, READING, ENGLAND.

Sutton's Vegetable Seeds—Complete List for 1895—continued.

VEGETABLE MARROW.

(*Cucurbita Pepo ovifera.*) German, Kleiner Kürbiß.—French, *Courge à la moelle.*

VEGETABLE MARROW, SUTTON'S LONG WHITE. COPYRIGHT S. & S.
Per packet, 1s. and 1s. 6d. (*See below.*)

VEGETABLE MARROW, SUTTON'S LONG GREEN. COPYRIGHT S. & S.
Per packet, 6d. and 1s. (*See below.*)

Sutton's Long White. We strongly recommend this as the best form of Long White Marrow. Fruit of immense size, very handsome, and of excellent quality. One of the most productive Marrows in cultivation. (*Illustrated above.*)
Per packet, 1*s.* and 1*s.* 6*d.*

'**The best White Marrow ever sent out. I have been cutting fine** tender Marrows of this kind ever since April (August 4).'—Mr. W. C. LEACH, *Gardener to* His Grace the DUKE OF NORTHUMBERLAND.

Sutton's Vegetable Marrow. Repeated trials in our Experimental Grounds prove that this variety possesses all the qualities which are prized in this vegetable. Cream-coloured oval fruit, of medium size and first-rate quality. The plant is unusually prolific, and has the additional advantage of coming very early ... ... per packet, 1*s.* and 1*s.* 6*d.*

'**An early, excellent and long continued bearer, in size it is just what** a Marrow should be, neither too large or small, and in quality it is first-class.'—Mr. J. OLIVER, Eslington Park Gardens.

Sutton's White Bush. In habit the plant resembles the Green Bush, but the fruits are of a beautiful creamy white; exceedingly productive, and the flavour will please every lover of this vegetable ... ... per packet, 6*d.* and 1*s.*

'**Your White Bush is the Vegetable Marrow of the future. Planted a** yard apart they have been most prolific.'—Mr. E. BURGESS, *Gardener to* H. B. DEARE, Esq.

Sutton's Long Green may be justly described as an ideal type of this favourite form of Vegetable Marrow. It has been carefully selected, is very prolific and far superior to the stock generally grown as Long Green. (*Illustrated above.*)
Per packet, 6*d.* and 1*s.*

'**The finest of any of the Green Marrows I have ever met with. It is** a splendid companion to your Long White. I have been exceedingly pleased with it.'—Mr. T. TURTON, The Gardens, Maiden Erlegh.

Sutton's Long Cream. An excellent variety, which can be thoroughly recommended. Fruit of pale cream colour, almost white, and very long ... ... per packet, 6*d.* and 1*s.*

Pen-y-byd. Of extraordinary productiveness; fruit almost globular in form, creamy white in colour, with thick firm flesh of delicate flavour. Awarded First-class Certificate by the R. H. Society...per packet, 6*d.* and 1*s.*

Improved Custard. This Vegetable Marrow has a trailing and very prolific habit. The fruits are exceedingly ornamental while growing. When cut quite young, they are delicious eating ... per packet, 6*d.* and 1*s.*

Improved Green Bush. Very pretty green-veined fruit, produced in great abundance ... ... per packet, 6*d.* and 1*s.*

Moore's Cream. Oval cream-coloured fruit of medium size; quality excellent; sets freely ... ... per packet, 6*d.* and 1*s.*

Large Cream ... ... ,, 3*d.* ,, 6*d.*
Long Yellow ... ... ,, 3*d.* ,, 6*d.*
Finest Mixed ... ... ,, 3*d.* ,, 6*d.*

CULTURE.—Where very early Marrows are in demand frame culture is a necessity. For full instructions see Sutton's Book on Gardening. In the open Marrows are grown on mounds, ridges, and also on the flat, singly or in long rows, with the aid of manure. Plants are raised under glass in pots, and seeds are sown where they are to stand. Protection in the early stage is afforded by hand-lights, oiled paper, and other cheap contrivances. The plants must have plenty of room to ramble, and abundance of water if necessary. Cut the fruit young, even if not wanted, and the plants will continue in bearing.

SUTTON & SONS, READING, Seedsmen by Royal Warrant to Her Majesty the Queen. 61

SUTTON'S SEED POTATOES for 1892—cont.

Division 3.—MID-SEASON VARIETIES.

NEW POTATO, SUTTON'S PERFECTION. (*Engraved from a Photograph.*) COPYRIGHT S. & S.

New Potato, Sutton's Perfection. With great satisfaction we now introduce a new White Kidney which we have had under trial for several years. It was raised by the late Mr. Clark, the raiser of our Magnum Bonum, Abundance, and other heavy cropping varieties, and combines the high quality of Victoria in its best days with the productiveness of White Elephant. The haulm is strong and erect in growth with distinct broad leaves. Tubers kidney-shaped, inclining to the pebble form, almost uniform in size, of unsurpassed table quality, and the yield has astonished the experienced growers to whom we sent small parcels for trial, only a few of whose reports we have space to quote. (*See illustration above*) ... per 7 lbs. 3s. 6d.; per 14 lbs. 6s.

'Crop immense, all good sized tubers, and quite free from disease. Altogether a very fine Potato.'—Mr. JAMES TEGG, The Gardens, Bearwood.

'Crop excellent, each tuber a fac-simile of the other; quality quite first-rate.'—Mr. C. ILOTT, The Gardens, Wokefield Park.

'A splendid cropper. The cooking qualities are of the very best, like a ball of flour.'—Mr. G. TRINDER, The Gardens, Dogmersfield Park.

'From 3 lbs. of seed I lifted 90 lbs., all good sound tubers.'—Mr. W. COX, The Gardens, Calcot Park.

'Crop six gallons of tubers from 3 lbs. Free from disease, very clean. Splendid quality when cooked.'—Mr. A. MAXIM, Heckfield Place.

'A heavy crop of clean beautiful tubers. Cooks dry and floury without falling to pieces, good flavour. Mr. W. POPE, The Gardens, Highclere Castle.

Sutton's Matchless. Obtained from a cross between Fox's Seedling and Beauty of Hebron, and it reveals characteristics of both parents in haulm and tubers. Haulm moderate in quantity, dark green in colour, broad and glossy. Tubers produced in great abundance, very free from disease; flesh white, and of superb quality when cooked. Not only excellent for general crop, but keeps well for winter use ... ... per 14 lbs. 4s.; per ½ cwt. 14s.

'We had an excellent crop of your Matchless Potato, handsome tubers, free from disease, and cooking quality all that one could wish for.'—Mr. R. PENNINGTON, *Gardener to* E. BANNER, Esq.

'The heaviest crop of all the kinds I had this, or perhaps any other year; tubers very fine, and quite free from disease. When cooked it was pronounced to be really good.'—Mr. C. ILOTT, The Gardens, Wokefield Park.

'Good crop of medium-sized tubers, very like "Schoolmaster," but a decided improvement on that variety. Quite free from disease; excellent flavour and quality when cooked.'—Mr. R. LYE, The Gardens, Sydmonton Court.

'Beautiful, bright even tubers quite free from disease, and when cooked of splendid quality.'—Mr. T. JONES, The Gardens, Elvetham.

Sutton's Nonsuch. The result of a cross between those two fine Potatoes, Sutton's Reading Hero and Sutton's Early Regent. The broad dark green haulm is moderate in height, showing distinct traces of the Hero parentage, and this is also evident in the white flattish round tubers, which occasionally show some tendency to become kidney-shaped. Sutton's Nonsuch is a heavy-cropping mid-season Potato of first-class quality, and offers the additional advantage of cooking well until quite late in the season ... ... per 14 lbs. 4s.; per ½ cwt. 14s.

Sutton's Reading Russet. For beauty and quality combined this Potato is without a rival. Shape flattish round with a red russeted skin and lemon-white flesh. Habit strong and robust; foliage dark green; flowers white. The crop may be lifted in July and August, and will keep until June of the following year. A great prize winner. Per 14 lbs. 3s.; per ½ cwt. 10s. 6d.

Sutton's Lady Truscott. Varies in shape between round and oblong. A heavy cropper, keeps well; excellent for exhibiting, and the table quality is first-rate. Robust in growth, and ripens about a week later than the Early Regent. Very free from disease. Per 14 lbs. 3s. 6d.; per ½ cwt. 12s.

Schoolmaster (Turner). Robust habit; tubers large; flesh white; a heavy cropper ... ... per 14 lbs. 3s.; per ½ cwt. 10s. 6d

Sutton's Fiftyfold. A heavy cropper of high quality which may be lifted during July and August; tubers mostly round, but some few are elongated; flesh firm and white. The special merits of this Potato are great productiveness, remarkable power of withstanding disease, splendid cooking quality, and excellence for late keeping. Per 14 lbs. 3s.; per ½ cwt. 10s. 6d.

White Elephant. Large; resembles Beauty of Hebron in shape and colour. Flesh white, boils floury ... ... per 14 lbs. 2s.; per ½ cwt. 7s.

Late Rose. White-fleshed and fine grained; heavy cropper; keeping quality excellent ... ... per 14 lbs. 3s. 6d.; per ½ cwt. 12s

Covent Garden Perfection. Excellent for medium crop; prolific, and good quality ... ... per 14 lbs. 3s. 6d.; per ½ cwt. 12s.

SUTTON & SONS, Seedsmen by Royal Warrant to Her Majesty the Queen.

57

SUTTON'S SEED POTATOES for 1892—cont.

Division 4.—MAIN CROP and LATE VARIETIES.

NEW MAIN-CROP POTATO, SUTTON'S TRIUMPH. *(Engraved from a Photograph.)*

New Main-crop Potato, Sutton's Triumph. We have the gratification of introducing a new Main-crop Potato, raised by ourselves, from our renowned Magnum Bonum. The seed was sown in March 1886, and a single plant put out in the following June produced the amazing crop of 6 lbs. 9½ ozs. The two heaviest tubers weighed respectively 15¾ ozs. and 14¾ ozs. It was therefore obvious that we were in possession of a seedling of no ordinary productiveness. From such a parentage the haulm is naturally strong and upright; the foliage rather pointed and of good substance. This, however, is only important as an indication of cropping power, and in this respect we are able to speak with confidence, and in the highest terms.

The tubers are white, with a rough skin, rather pebble-shaped, some of them very much resembling the old Fluke, and in cooking quality they have no superior among the finest Potatoes in cultivation. The most conspicuous merit, however, is the enormous produce obtained from it year after year. That there might be no doubt, on this point we have for two successive seasons distributed small parcels for trial to experts, from whose reports we quote the following brief extracts. *(See illustration above)* ... ... **per 7 lbs., 3s. 6d.; per 14 lbs., 6s.**

'**A very handsome white Potato. Crop heavy, fine even sized tubers,** clean and good. Cooks well. No disease.'—Mr. J. TEGG, The Gardens, Bearwood.

'**From 4 lbs. I raised a crop of 124 lbs. of beautiful Potatoes, all** sound and quite free from disease. Table qualities most excellent, indeed it is one of the best flavoured Potatoes I ever tasted.'—Mr. W. COX, The Gardens, Calcot Park.

'**Very heavy crop, tubers handsome, cooking dry and floury, flavour** excellent.'—Mr. W. POPE, The Gardens, Highclere Castle.

'**Very heavy cropper, shape flattish round, eyes quite level with the** surface; haulm compact; perfectly free from disease. Cooking quality all that can be desired. Splendid for exhibition purposes.'—Mr. S. COLBERT, The Lodge Gardens, Farnboro'.

'**Of fine form, no disease, splendid when cooked.**'—Mr. GEO. HARRIS, Castle Gardens, Alnwick.

'**A heavy crop of handsome tubers of good size and first-class** quality.'—Mr. R. LYE, The Gardens, Sydmonton Court.

Sutton's Best of All. This Potato has proved to be excellent in every respect. As a cropper it has few equals. Tubers handsome and even in size, and we have received many reports speaking highly of its freedom from disease. Shape full flattish round; flesh white, firm and excellent when cooked ... ... **per 14 lbs. 4s.; per ½ cwt. 14s.**

'**Your Best of All has given an abundant crop, and proved excellent in** cooking quality.'—Mr. C. LAMBLE, *Gardener to* H. B. BAKER, Esq.

'**Your Best of All Potato has not got its name for nothing, and, like all** your seeds, is first-rate.'—The Rev. GEO. H. WOODCOCK, Ratcliffe-on-Wreake.

Sutton's Masterpiece. One of the finest main crop Potatoes we have ever offered. Tubers round and heavy, with a rough skin; flesh firm, white, and of first-rate cooking quality. Haulm erect, carrying broad leaves of a deep green colour. The crop grows in a cluster close to the stem. For its great productiveness it has given immense satisfaction, and even during the disastrous season of 1891 splendid crops of sound tubers have been grown, confirming previous experience of its comparative freedom from disease. Very handsome for the exhibition table... ... **per 14 lbs. 3s. 6d.; per ½ cwt. 12s.**

'**Your Masterpiece far surpasses my expectations. After I and my** bailiff had weighed the crop and measured the land I was quite convinced that the yield would be 12 tons per acre, if not more.'—E. LUCAS, Esq., Baginton.

'**The produce of 2 lbs. of your Potato Masterpiece was 83 lbs.,** some of the tubers weighing 1½ lb., good and sound.'—Mr. J. BIGNELL, *Gardener to* the Rev. J. UWINS, Cainscross.

'**Crop excellent; round, even-sized tubers; 7½ bushels from 14 lbs.** No disease. A very fine Potato. Cooking qualities good.'—Mr. J. TEGG, The Gardens, Bearwood.

'**Very strong growth, large tubers, sound and good. First-rate in** quality; the best of the Potatoes I have tried this year.'—Mr. W. LEES, The Wilderness Gardens.

SUTTON & SONS, Seed Potato Growers and Merchants, READING, ENGLAND.

58

MISCELLANEOUS FRUIT TREES, &c.

All well grown, strong, and healthy plants, including all the best varieties in cultivation.

NEW APPLE, LADY HENNIKER.

A splendid variety, raised by Mr. John Perkins, The Gardens, Thornham Hall, Eye. A first-rate Apple, chiefly valuable as a cooking variety, but also very useful in the dessert. The fruit are large and handsome, and the tree is very healthy, and a great bearer. Sir Saml. W. Baker says:—"The best Apple when baked that I have tasted."

Lady Cotterell says:—"I think it most excellent."

Strong Maidens, 7s. 6d. each. Three ditto, 20s. Scions can be sent post free for 6d. each. Six ditto for 2s. 6d. Twelve ditto, 4s. 6d. Twenty-five ditto, 7s. 6d.

APPLES.

		each s.	d.
Standards		1	6
Pyramids	1s. 6d. to	3	6
Dwarfs		1	0
,, Fan Trained	2s. 6d. to	3	6
,, Horizontal Trained		3	6
,, ,, Cordon Trained	1s. to	2	6

APRICOTS.

Dwarf Maidens		2	0
,, Trained		5	0
Standard Trained	7s. 6d. to	10	6
Orchard-house Trees, in pots, with fruit buds	5s. to	7	6

CHERRIES.

Dwarf Maidens		2	0
,, Trained		3	6
Standards		2	0
,, Trained		5	0
Pyramids	1s. 6d. to	3	6
Orchard-house Trees, in pots, with fruit buds	3s 6d. to	5	0

MULBERRIES.

Standards ..	7s. 6d. to	10	6
Dwarfs	2s. 6d. to	5	0

NUTS AND FILBERTS.

Dwarf Bushes	per doz. 6s. to	9	0
Standards, 3 ft. to 5 ft. stems	each	2	0

NECTARINES.

Dwarf Maidens		2	0
,, Trained		5	0
Standard Trained	7s. 6d. to	10	6
Orchard-house Trees, in pots, with fruit buds		5	0

PEACHES.

Dwarf Maidens		2	0
,, Trained		5	0
Standard Trained	7s. 6d. to	10	6
Orchard-house Trees, in pots, with fruit buds		5	0

CHESTNUTS, SPANISH.

Standards		2	0

Banks' Prolific | Common

CRABS.

Standards		1	6

Red Siberian | Common

CURRANTS AND GOOSEBERRIES.

A good collection of the best varieties, strong bushes, 3s. to 6s. per dozen.

FIGS.

Strong Plants, in pots	1s. 6d. to	3	0
Fruiting, ditto	3s. 6d. to	5	0
Dwarf Trained, for walls	3s. 6d. to	5	0

GRAPES.

Strong Planting Canes, in pots	3s. 6d. to	5	0
Fruiting Canes	7s. 6d. to	10	6

MEDLARS.

		each s.	d.
Standards	1s. 6d. to	2	0
Pyramids	1s. 6d. to	3	6

PEARS.

Dwarf Maidens		1	6
,, Trained		3	0
Standards		2	6
,, Trained		5	0
Pyramids on Pear or Quince stock	1s. 6d. to	3	0
Orchard-house Trees, in pots, with fruit buds	3s. 6d. to	5	0

PLUMS.

Dwarfs		1	0
,, Trained		3	6
Standards		2	0
,, Trained		5	0
Pyramids	1s. 6d. to	3	6
Orchard-house Trees, in pots, with fruit buds	3s. 6d. to	5	0

QUINCES.

Standards	1s. 6d. to	2	6

RASPBERRIES.

Fine Strong Canes	per doz. 3s. to	4	0

WALNUTS.

4 feet to 6 feet, 1s. Standards, 2s. 6d. to 5s. each.

Ornamental Trees and Shrubs, Hardy Evergreens, Coniferous Plants, Hardy Climbers, Transplanted Forest Trees, &c., in great variety.

Special Prices on application.

PLANTS FOR FENCING.

Beech, 1½ to 2 feet—per 100, 5s.—per 1000, 40s.
,, 2 to 3 feet—per 100, 6s.—per 1000, 50s.
Box, 1½ to 2 feet—per dozen, 4s. 6d.—each, 6d.
Holly, 1 to 1½ feet—per dozen, 6s.—each, 9d.
,, 2 to 3 feet—per dozen, 12s.—each, 1s. 6d.
Hornbeam, 2 to 3 feet—5s. per 100—per 1000, 40s.
Laurel, 1½ to 2 feet—per 100, 18s.—per doz., 2s. 6d.
,, 3 to 4 feet—per 100, 30s. to 40s.—per dozen, 6s. to 9s.
Myrobella, one of the best materials in existence for making new or mending old fences—per 100, 4s. 6d.—per 1000, 35s.
,, extra strong plants—per 100, 6s.—per 1000, 50s.
Privet, good stuff—4s. 6d. and 8s. per 100
White Thorn, Seedling—per 1000, 10s.
,, Transplanted—per 1000, 15s. to 20s.
Yew, Common, 1 to 1½ feet—per doz. 6s.—each, 9d.
,, 2 to 3 feet—per doz., 15s.—each, 1s. 6d.
,, 4 to 5 feet—each, 3s. 6d.

An excellent Collection of Azalea Indica, Camellias with flower buds, Stove and Greenhouse Plants, Ferns, &c.

WILLIAM COOPER, 755, Old Kent Road, London, S.E.
HORTICULTURAL PROVIDER.

Glazed Cover for Fruit Walls.

Invaluable to those who value their fruit, and are desirous of protecting it, thus securing a heavier crop.

No. 26.

This illustration shows a Cover, with sloping front, which allows for a narrow walk and for fruit trees in pots near the glass. It can be adapted to walls of different heights, and is also made in three widths.

SPECIFICATION.—Framework substantially constructed of red deal; the whole of sides, and 2ft. 6in. of ends, boarded with well-seasoned tongued and grooved matchboards. Half-glass door, complete with rim lock and brass fittings, in one end; glass 16oz. throughout, English cut. Ventilators supplied, according to size, and stays necessary for opening same; stages for plants entire length of Cover. All woodwork painted one coat of good oil paint, and the whole structure securely packed and placed on rail (being carefully marked in readiness for erection), or delivered, erected, and glazed, within 20 miles of London Bridge, at the following respective prices:—

For Walls 10ft. High.				For Walls 12ft. High.			
Length.	Width.	On rail.	Erected complete.	Length.	Width.	On rail.	Erected complete.
20ft.	6ft.	£12	£15	20ft.	6ft.	£13	£16
40ft.	6ft.	20	26	40ft.	6ft.	22	28
60ft.	7ft.	30	40	60ft.	7ft.	34	44
100ft.	8ft.	50	65	100ft.	8ft.	56	70

Other sizes at proportionate prices.

Erection Price includes an extra Coat of Paint at Works.

A cheaper style of Wall Cover with Straight Front can be supplied. Prices on application.

47

WILLIAM COOPER, 755, Old Kent Road, London, S.E.
HORTICULTURAL PROVIDER.

Glazed Cover for Fruit Walls.

No. 27.

ADVANTAGES.

Complete Protection of trees from frost. Perfect Ventilation. Cheapness—will repay its cost in a few seasons. Simple in Construction—can be fixed by any handy man. Proper Ripening of the wood is secured. Ventilation is gained by means of the front sashes, all of which slide, thus also enabling the whole of the foliage to be syringed.

CONSTRUCTION.

The sashes slide in runners, and are entirely removable, the roof lights are supported on strong iron brackets bolted to wall. The framing is of the best well-seasoned red deal, painted two coats best oil colour, carried on iron supports. Glass 21oz. throughout, English cut. All parts carefully marked before leaving Works, and can be fixed by any handy man.

The Cover—with Front Lights, Iron Supports, Roof Lights, and Brackets for a Wall 10ft. high—costs 9s. per foot run; Ends extra, 30s. each.
Securely packed on rail.

Improved Wall Fruit Protector.

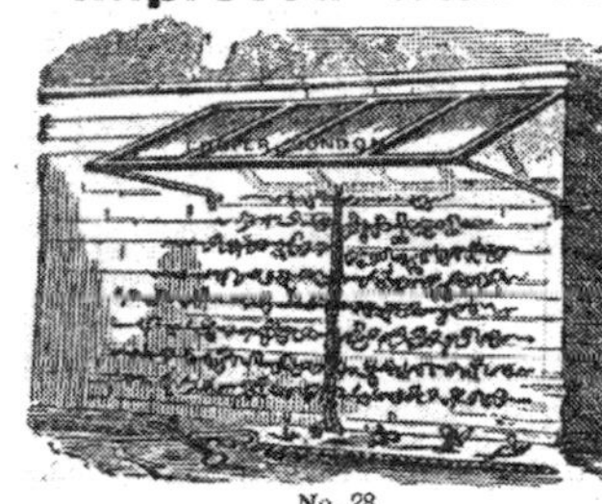

No. 28.

This form of Wall Fruit Protector will be found most convenient, it being easily detached or attached at will. It is also the cheapest form introduced, and it is strongly recommended. The price includes the wall fittings, 21oz. glass, and the necessary lights; painted one coat.

PRICE,
1s. 9d. per foot run.

48

WILLIAM COOPER, 755, Old Kent Road, London, S.E.
HORTICULTURAL PROVIDER.

Wall Cover.

No. 20.

This Cover is made in sashes in lengths of 10ft. of good, sound, well-seasoned red deal; the stiles, which are 2in. by 3in., being well mortised and pinned to tenoned rails, properly rabbeted for the glass, and fitted with 2in. sash-bars. Complete with glass 16oz. throughout, English cut; and strong cast iron bracket necessary for fixing same. All woodwork painted one coat of good oil paint; the whole securely packed and placed on rail (being carefully marked in readiness for erection) at the following respective prices:—

Lengths.	Width.	Prices.	Lengths.	Width.	Prices.
10ft.	2ft.	£1 5 0	10ft.	2ft. 6in.	£1 10 0
20ft.	2ft.	2 0 0	20ft.	2ft. 6in.	2 10 0
30ft.	2ft.	3 0 0	30ft.	2ft. 6in.	3 15 0
40ft.	2ft.	4 0 0	40ft.	2ft. 6in.	5 0 0
50ft.	2ft.	5 0 0	50ft.	2ft. 6in.	6 5 0
60ft.	2ft.	6 0 0	60ft.	2ft. 6in.	7 10 0

From the eaves of the glass coping, tiffany or other protecting materials may be suspended.

Gardeners' Plant Barrow.

No. 30.

Well and strongly made, and painted three coats best oil colour.
Price .. .. 12s. 6d.

49

WILLIAM COOPER, 755, Old Kent Road, London, S.E.
HORTICULTURAL PROVIDER.

Fruit Tree Labels.

No. 691.

Full size 24in. by 1¾in., 1s. 6d. per dozen.

Rose Tree Labels.

No. 692.

Full size 1¾in. by 12in., 1s. per dozen.

1500 Names in Stock.

No extra charge for names not in stock.

333

CONTINUOUS ARCH ESPALIERS.

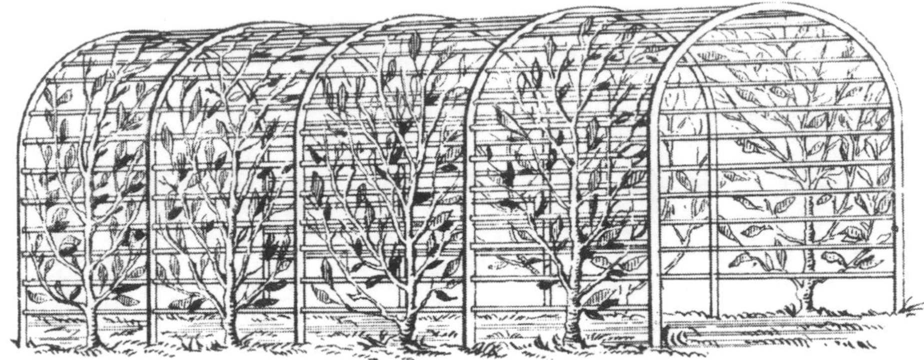

No 960. CONTINUOUS COVERED WAY, PORTABLE, ARCHED, TRAINING ESPALIER.

For training creepers, fruit trees, &c., very strong and substantially made entirely of wrought-iron, in 6 feet lengths joined in the centre and fitted together with nuts and bolts, which are included. Easily fixed or removed by any inexperienced labourer

	7 ft. high × 4 ft. span		7 ft. 6 in. high × 4 ft. 6 in. span		8 ft. high × 5 ft. span out of ground.
Price, Painted,	**14/-** per yard run	.. ..	**15/4** per yard run	.. ..	**16/8** per yard run.
,, Galvanized,	**20/6** ,, ,,	.. ..	**22/-** ,, ,,	.. ..	**26/-** ,, ,,

A lighter description of espalier archway can be made if a cheaper article is required, but it is not recommended. Any size can be made to order. Estimates given.. Lengths under 2 yards charged *ad valorem*.

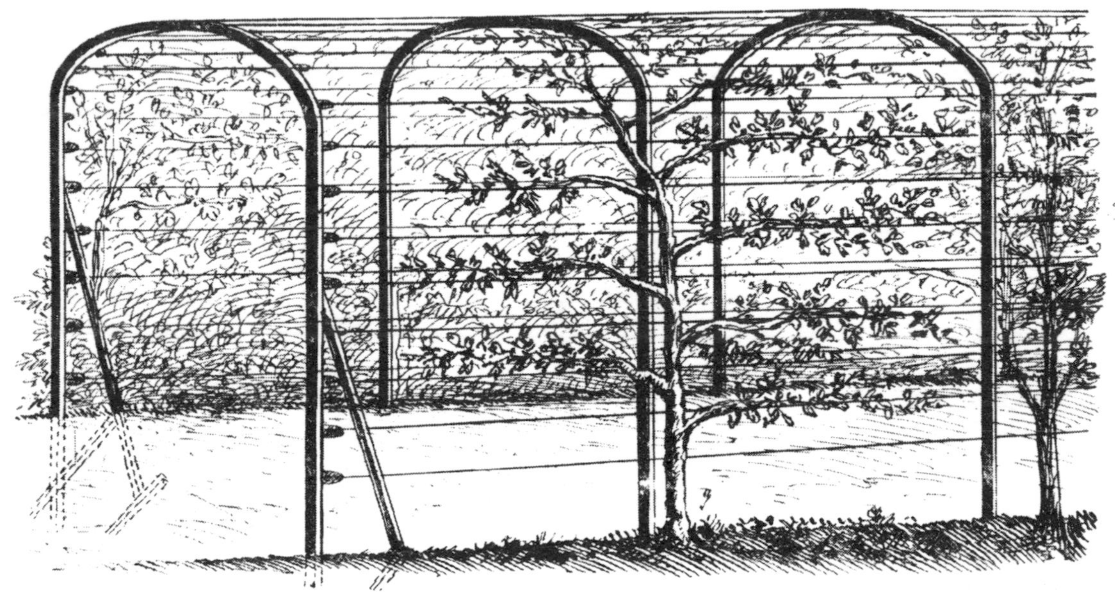

No. 960a. NEW DESIGN, STRAINED WIRE CONTINUOUS ARCH ESPALIER.

Especially suited for long lengths. We have supplied many lengths of this strained wire espalier and it invariably gives entire satisfaction. It is absolutely effectual, very strong and durable, and in view of the long lengths which can be strained from the end straining pillars, it is the **cheapest method known**! It can be supplied any size to order, but below we give sample of price of a good generally useful size.

SIZES AND PRICES (Out of Ground).

8 feet high by 5 feet wide, flat iron, intermediate arches, usually spaced about 10 feet apart, and No. 13 W.G. galvanized wires, spaced about 10 inches apart.

Price, **4/8** per yard run.

Strong T iron terminal straining arches, fitted with raiddisseurs for straining the wires and with earth plates, stays, &c., complete. Price, **53/-** each.

Estimates supplied for any size on receipt of specification.

The above strained wire espalier can be adapted to any position or requirement. Arches can also be made to suit cross paths if required. Price on application.

IMPROVED IRON & WIRE ESPALIER FENCINGS.

FOR TRAINING FRUIT TREES.

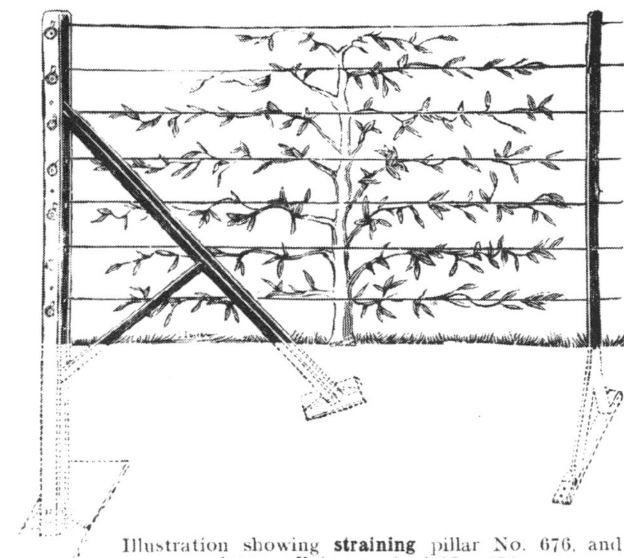

Illustration showing **straining** pillar No. 676, and **intermediate** standard No. 678.

No. 676. TERMINAL STRAINING POSTS.

With double stay, as illustrated, and fitted with **raiddisseurs** for winding the wires, not ratchets as shown.

	4 ft. For 6 Wires.	5 ft. For 8 Wires.	6 ft. high. For 10 Wires.
Painted	**14/-**	**16/8**	**20/8** each.
Galvanized	**22/-**	**25/-**	**31/4** ,,

No. 678. INTERMEDIATE STANDARDS, as shown.

Of 1 in. by ¼ in. iron, usually spaced about 10 ft. apart.

	4 ft.	5 ft.	6 ft. high.
Painted	**2/-**	**2/4**	**2/8** each.
Galvanized	**3/-**	**3/8**	**4/8** ,,

NOTE.—A pillar without raiddisseurs may be used for one end of each length, and can be supplied at 20 per cent. less than No. 676, but it is recommended to use a winding pillar at **each** end of **each** length, as giving much more satisfactory results.

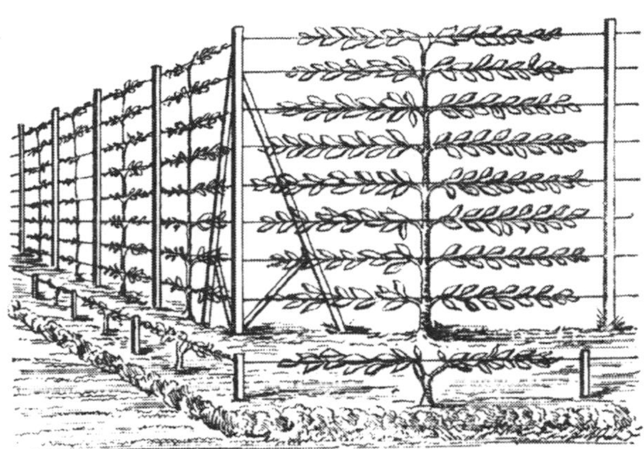

Illustration showing **Angle** of Espalier Fencing, with *Single Cordon Edging* in front as border.

No. 677. WROUGHT IRON ESPALIER ANGLE POSTS.

With double stays, as illustrated, and fitted with two rows of raiddisseurs for winding the wires.

	4 ft.	5 ft.	6 ft. high.
Painted	**22/-**	**25/4**	**30/-** each.
Galvanized	**31/4**	**39/4**	**44/-** ,,

SINGLE CORDON FOR TRAINING FRUIT TREES, as shown above.

No. 679. TERMINAL POSTS, 12 in. above ground. Price, Painted, **6/-**; Galvanized, **8/8** each.

No. 680. INTERMEDIATE STANDARDS, with plate feet. Price, Painted, **8d.**; Galvanized, **1/-** each.

BEST QUALITY GALVANIZED WIRE.

SPECIALLY PREPARED FOR ESPALIER USE.

Gauge.	1 cwt. contains about	per cwt.	per 7 lbs.
No. 12 ..	1,333 yards ..	**31/-**	**2/2**
No. 13 ..	1,723 ,, ..	**32/-**	**2/3**
No. 14 ..	2,240 ,, ..	**34/-**	**2/5**

For enlarged view of RAIDDISSEURS, see page 55.

No. 13 GAUGE WIRE is generally used for Espalier Fencing and should **stouter** wire be used, much stronger straining posts will be required. Prices on application.

TANNED GARDEN NETTING.

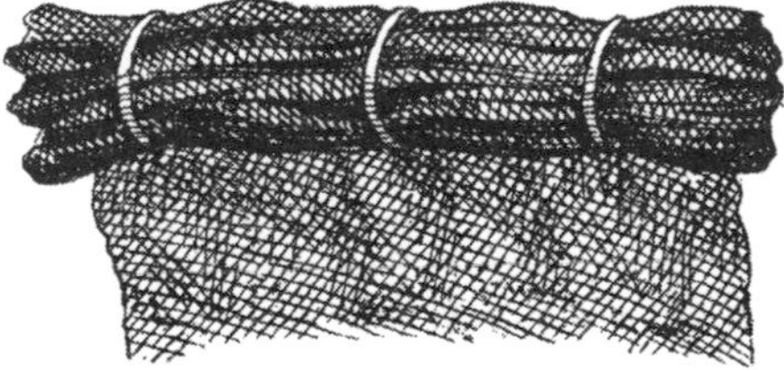

No. 1638. This is now very largely used everywhere for **protecting wall or Espalier Fruit Trees,** strawberries, currant bushes, etc. from birds and frosts, surrounding lawn tennis lawns, etc., and is very useful in the garden. It is not absolutely new material, being made from repaired fishing nets, but it is of very good quality and well tanned.

For spring protection against frosts, it cannot be equalled. If attached to the top of walls or espaliers with a few forked sticks, it will break the force of all storms and keep out any ordinary frost, at the same time allowing plenty of light and air to get to the trees. The blooms that are so often destroyed in the early spring will thus be protected and the fruit saved.

50 yards long to stretch 4 yards in width	**12/-** per bundle.
50 ,, ,, ,, 2 ,, ,, ...	**6/-** ,, ,,
50 ,, ,, ,, 1 ,, ,, ...	**3/4** ,, ,,

Sizes given are measured on the stretch and exact size is not guaranteed.

The above being a diamond mesh, a third more should always be allowed than the surface measurement, as the netting shrinks one third of its stretched length on being opened to the specified width, and this rule applies to all diamond mesh netting, *e.g.*, a net 50 yards long, only covers about 33 yards when opened to its correct width.

Subject to the fluctuations of the market, and supply uncertain and not guaranteed.

IRON SUPPORTS SUITABLE FOR SUPPORTING THIS NETTING ROUND TENNIS COURTS, see page 57.

No. 100. Improved Espalier Fencing and Wall Trainers.

For Training Fruit Trees on the French System.

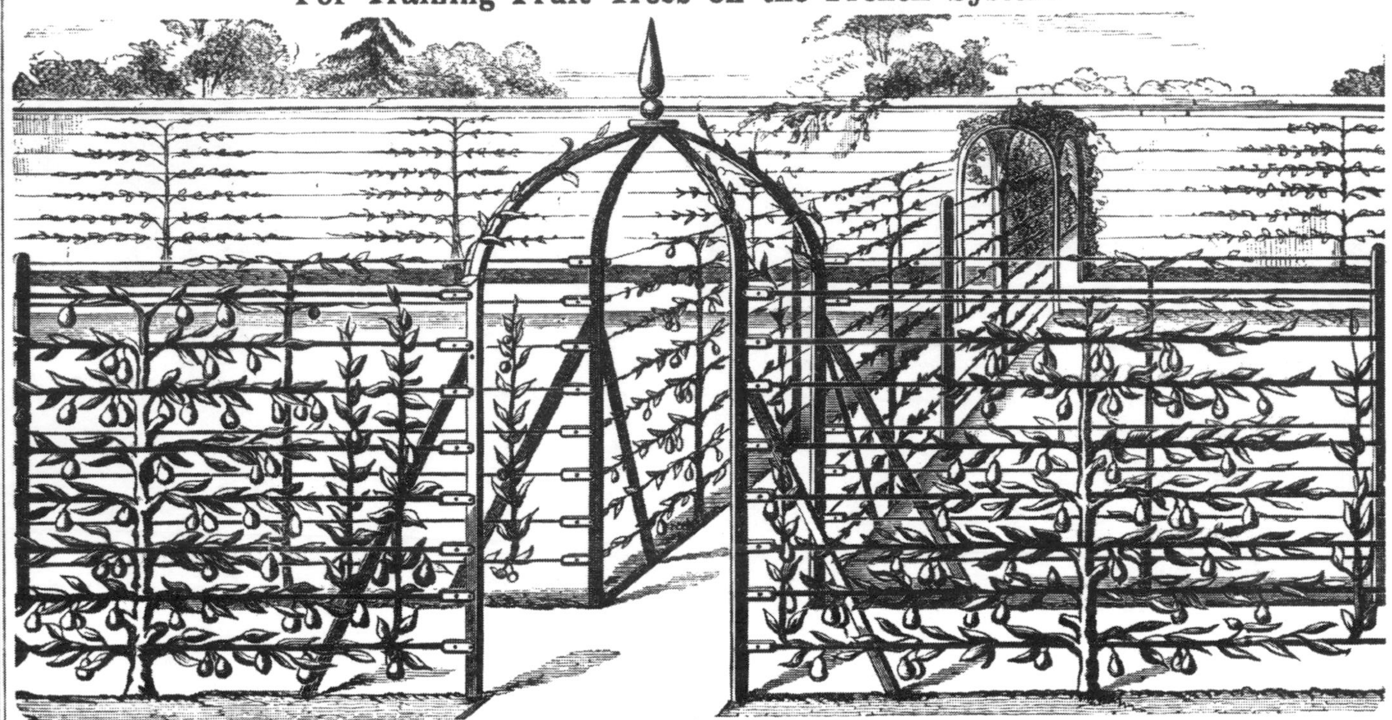

Prices.

For Pears, Apples, etc. 4 ft. high, with standards 10 ft. apart, and 6 lines of galvanized wire	per yard	6d.
Terminal Posts, with Raidisseurs	each	9/-
For Pears, Apples, etc. 5 ft. high, with standards 10 ft. apart, and 8 lines of galvanized wire	per yard	7d.
Terminal Posts, with Raidisseurs	each	12/6
For Pears, Apples, etc. 6 ft. high, with standards 10 ft. apart, and 9 lines of galvanized wire	per yard	9d.
Terminal Posts, with Raidisseurs	each	13/9
For Raspberries, Gooseberries, or Currants, with standards 4 ft. high, with 4 lines of wire ...	per yard	4d.
Terminal Posts, with Raidisseurs	each	8/6

Materials Required.

No. 104. T Iron Terminal or Angle Posts.

WITH self-fixing bases. Two required for each length.

Prices.

	Painted.		Galvd.
4 ft. high, each	7/6	...	12/6
5 ft. „ „	10/-	...	15/-
6 ft. „ „	11/6	...	16/-

No. 105. Intermediate Standards.

WITH anchor feet. Generally placed 10 ft. apart.

Prices.

	Painted.		Galvd.
4 ft. high, each	1/1	...	2/-
5 ft. „ „	1/3	...	2/6
6 ft. „ „	1/6	...	3/-

No. 106. Double Straining Post for Corners.

Prices.

	Painted.		Galvd.
4 ft. high, each	12/9	...	16/9
5 ft. „ „	14/-	...	18/-
6 ft. „ „	15/6	...	22/9

Galvanized Raidisseurs,

For Straining the Wires.

One required for each Wire.

Price 3/- per doz.

Stronger pattern per doz. 7/6

Ex. strong for heavy wire per doz. 10/-

Wrought-iron Key for ditto ... 6d.

Best Galvanized Wire.

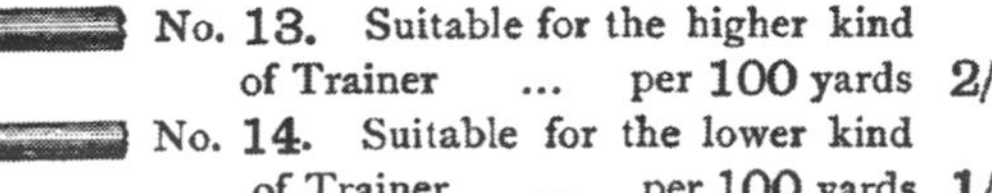

No. 13. Suitable for the higher kind of Trainer ... per 100 yards 2/-

No. 14. Suitable for the lower kind of Trainer ... per 100 yards 1/6

Estimates given for any quantity on receipt of particulars. Carriage Paid on orders of 40/- value and upwards.

43

NEW METHOD OF WIRING IN FRUIT TREES.

FOR protecting buds and bloom from frost and birds, seed in the ground, and fruit whilst ripening. By a simple method of straining wires an enclosure of any size can be wired in with bird-proof netting, wire netting on the sides, and string netting on top.

Enquirers should send plan showing measurements and shape of space to be enclosed, with positions of doorways required.

Special Estimates given.

No. 102. CONTINUOUS WROUGHT-IRON ESPALIER.

THIS Fencing is complete in itself, requiring no stone blocks; it is readily fixed by a handy labourer, and can be adapted to any line.

Prices.

4 feet high with 5 bars, standards 3 feet apart	...	per yard 3/-
5 feet ,, 7 ,, ...	...	,, 3/6
6 feet ,, 8 ,, ...	...	,, 4/-

Cast-iron Terminal Pillars extra.

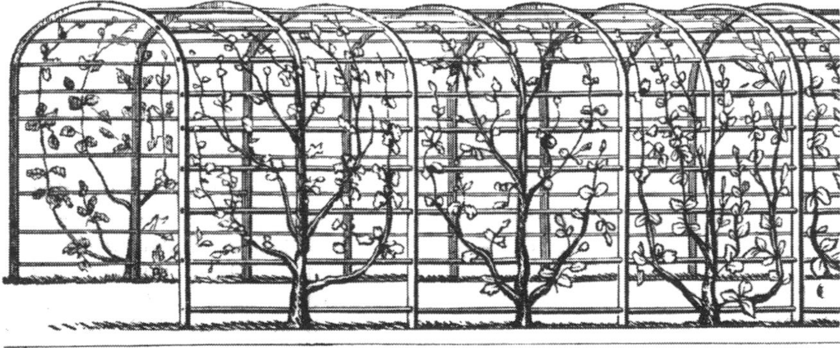

No. 103. CONTINUOUS COVERED-WAY ESPALIER.

FOR training fruit trees or climbing plants, 8 feet high, 5 feet wide. Painted green or any colour.

Price 9/6 per yard run.

Made in 6 feet lengths, with plate feet, jointed in the centre and fitted together with small bolts and nuts.

Estimates given for any work of this kind upon receipt of specification, giving length, width, and height of arch.

No. 1. Garden Arch.

COVERED with Galvanized Wire Netting.

7 ft. high, 4 ft. span, 2 ft. wide.

Price 8/6. painted Frames.

No. 3. Garden Arch.

All wrought-iron.

7 ft. high, 4 ft. span, 1 ft. 6 in. wide.

Price 11/- painted.

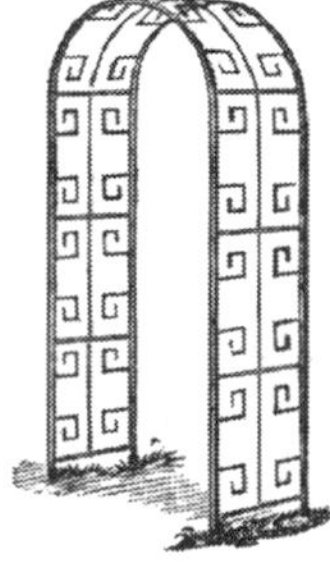

No. 4. Garden Arch.

All wrought-iron.

7 ft. high, 4 ft. span, 1 ft. 6 in. wide.

Price 13/- painted.

Carriage Paid on orders of 40/- value and upwards.

WIRING GARDEN WALLS.

THE arrangement is so simple, that it can be applied to any walls by inexperienced hands, and in very much less time than the old system.

All the Fittings are Galvanized.

Glass Lights and Brackets can be supplied as illustrated. Estimates on application.

Materials Required.

Galvanized Wrought-iron Eyes.

For Guiding the Wires on the Wall.

Spaced about 10 ft. apart.

No. 110. 4 in. long ... 5d. per doz.

No. 112. 2 in. long ... 5d. per doz.
3½ in. ,, ... 9d. ,,

No. 111. Straining Bolt and Holdfast.

All Galvanized.

THIS Strainer is preferred by some as neater than the French Raidisseur.

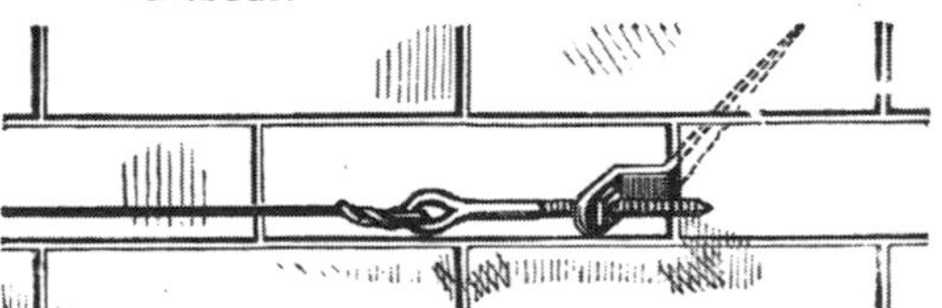

Price, including Holdfast, 4/- per doz.

One required for each Wire.

Keys for turning the nuts, 4d. each.

Best Quality Galvanized Wire.

No. 11 ... 3/- per 100 yards.
No. 12 ... 2/6 ,, ,,
*No. 13 ... 2/- ,, ,,
*No. 14 ... 1/6 ,, ,,

* THESE SIZES ARE RECOMMENDED AS THE BEST FOR WALLS.

No. 108. Galvanized Raidisseurs.

For Straining the Wires.

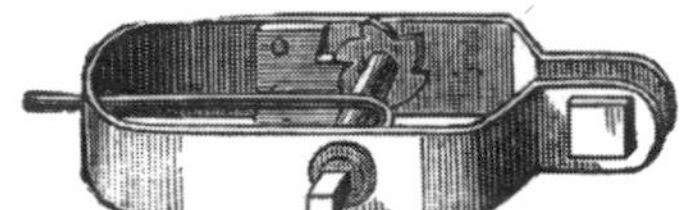

One required for each Wire.

Price 3/- per doz., used for wire up to No. 12 gauge.
Larger size, 7/6 per doz., for wire up to No. 10 gauge.
Extra large size, 10/- per doz., for wire up to No. 8 gauge.
Keys for ditto, 6d. each.

No. 109. Galvanized Terminal Holdfasts.

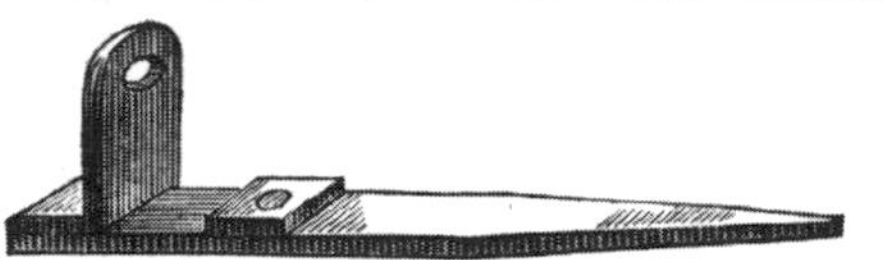

Two required for each wire. **Price** 2/- per doz.

No. 1. No. 2.

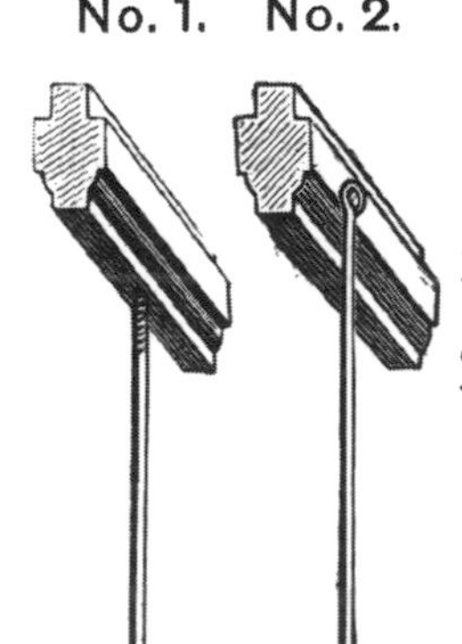

Galvanized Wrought-iron Training Hooks and Eyes.

4 in. long ... 1/4 per doz.
6 in. ,, ... 1/6 ,,
9 in. ,, ... 1/8 ,,
12 in. ,, ... 2/- ,,

Wrought-iron Plates & Eyes for Straining Wire in Vineries, &c.

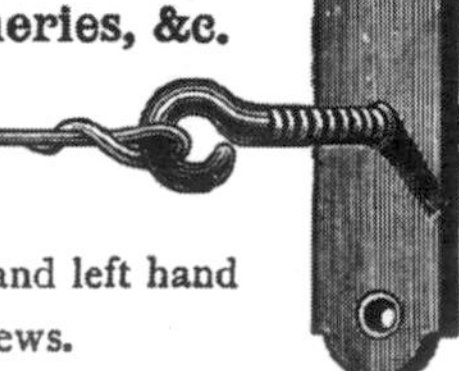

Price 3/6 per doz.

Made right and left hand Screws.

Carriage Paid on Orders of 40/- and upwards.

Diamond Wood Trellis for Screens, Fencing Training Plants.

CAN be made in sizes to suit any purpose, either for fixing on walls, or for fastening to posts to train creepers to form light fences. The splines are **1** inch by ¼ inch, unpainted.

Stock sizes, when open, **4** feet by **12** feet, and **6** feet by **12** feet.

Price 1½d.
per square foot.

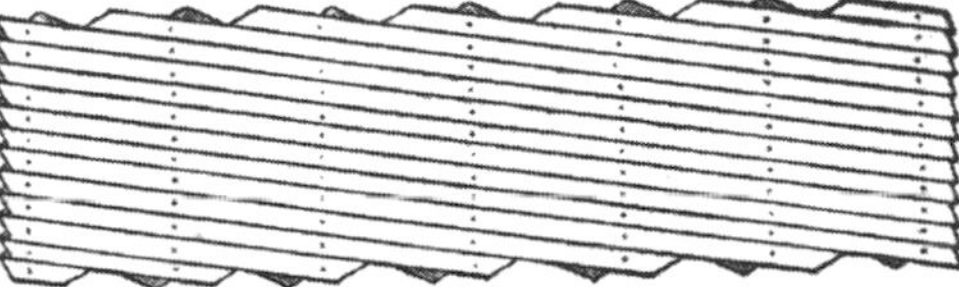

CLOSED FOR PACKING.

Special Estimates given for quantities.

Diamond Wire Trellis for Training Plants.

No. 1.

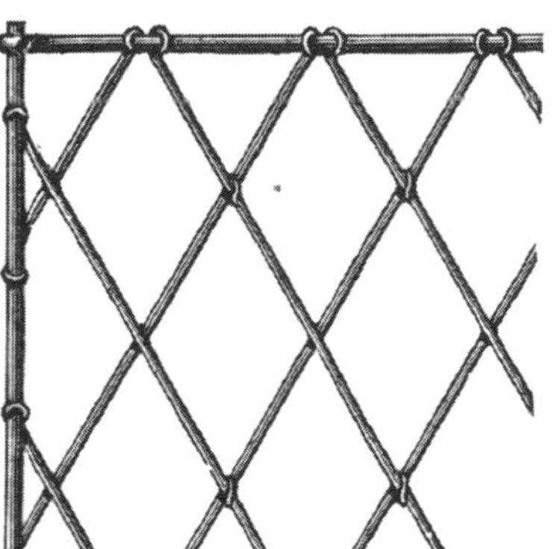

Prices.

Stock sizes—5 in. Mesh, Light Quality.

6 ft. by 3 ft. ... each	2/6	6 ft. by 5 ft. ... each	4/6
6 ft. ,, 4 ft. ... ,,	3/6	6 ft. ,, 6 ft. .. ,,	5/6

Made any size to order at the following prices per square foot.

Mesh.	ADAPTED FOR	Light Quality. Gauge.		Medium Quality. Gauge.		Strong Quality. Gauge.	
1½ in.	Protecting Windows.	15	6d.	14	7d.	13	7½d.
2 in.		14	4½d.	13	5½d.	12	6d.
4 in.	Plants in Conservatories, on House Walls, etc.	12	3d.	11	4d.	10	4½d.
5 in.		12	3d.	11	4d.	10	4½d.
6 in.		12	2½d.	11	3½d.	9	4d.

Prices of other Meshes on application.

Straight Wire Lattice for Protecting Windows & Skylights.

No. 2.

Prices.

No. 2. Prices of Straight Wire Lattice per square foot.

Mesh.	ADAPTED FOR	Light Quality. Gauge.		Medium Quality. Gauge.		Strong Quality. Gauge.	
⅜ in.	Protecting Church and other Windows, Skylights, Aviaries, etc.	15	5d.	14	6d.	13	7d.
½ in.		15	4½d.	14	5d.	13	6d.
1 in.		14	4d.	13	4½d.	12	5d.
1½ in.	Training Plants on Walls in Conservatories, etc.	13	3½d.	12	4d.	11	5d.

Prices of other Meshes on application.

Carriage Paid on Orders of 40/- *value and upwards.*

GALVANIZED STRAWBERRY PROTECTORS.

Nº 74.

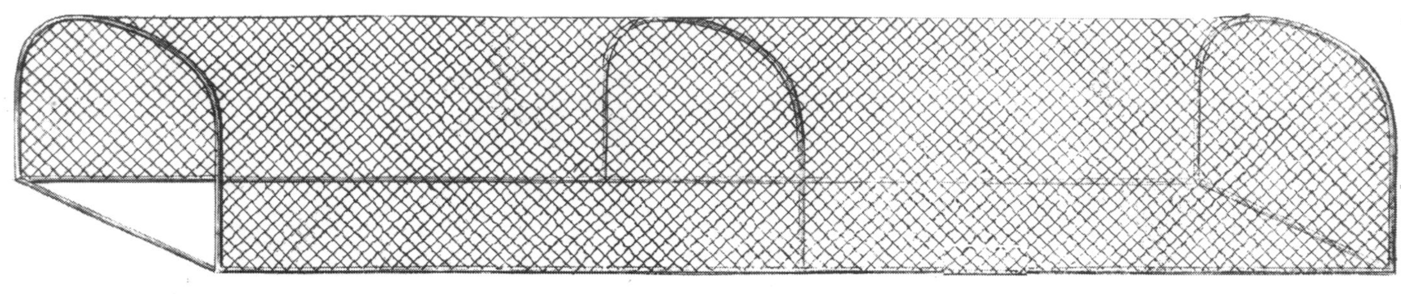

Nº 75

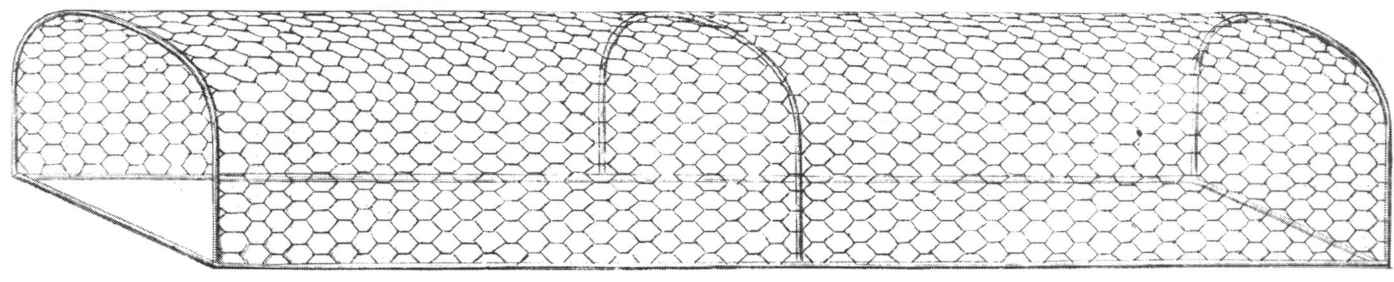

6 FEET LONG 18 IN WIDE 12 IN HIGH

	5/6	5/-	4/6 each
Nos 74 & 75	7/8	1	1¼ in Mesh

GALVANIZED PEA & SEED PROTECTORS

Nº 70.

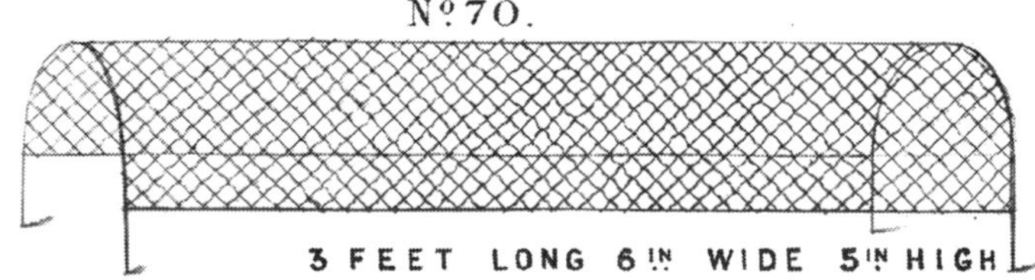

Nº 72.

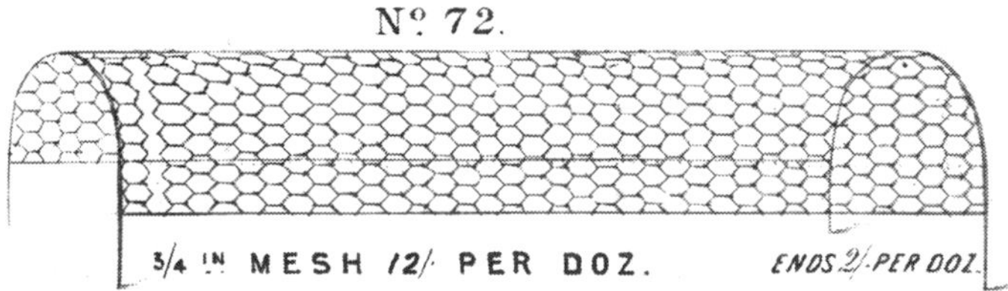

GALVANIZED PEA TRAINERS 6 FT LONG

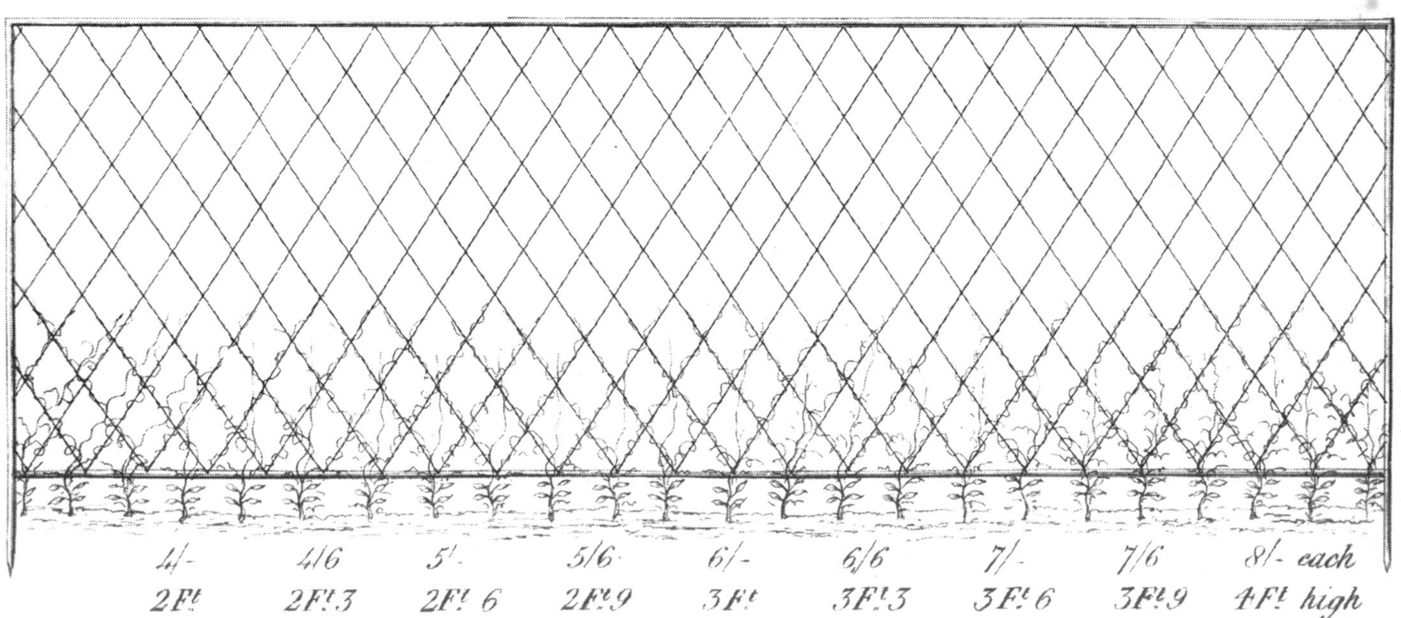

Cucumber or Melon Frame.

These Frames are constructed of well-seasoned red Deal, 1¼ in. thick, screwed together at angles, making them portable. Lights 2 in. thick, glazed with 21 oz. sheet glass, and sent out complete ready for use.

1 Light	...	4 ft. x 6 ft.	...	£1	16	9
2 "	...	8 ft. x 6 ft.	...	£2	17	6
3 "	...	12 ft. x 6 ft.	...	£3	17	6
4 "	...	16 ft. x 6 ft.	...	£4	18	0
5 "	...	22 ft. x 6 ft.	...	£5	18	0

Three-quarter Span Plant Frame.

These Frames are an improvement on the ordinary frame, as they give greater height at back. The Lights are hung with the latest improved hinges. Painted and glazed complete.

2 Lights	...	4 ft. x 6 ft.	...	£3	3	0
4 "	...	8 ft. x 6 ft.	...	£4	12	6
6 "	...	12 ft. x 6 ft.	...	£6	10	0

Span Plant Frame.

These Frames are most useful in a variety of garden operations. Being span roof, they get all sun. The Lights are hung with improved joints, which enables them to be turned right over. Thoroughly well made of best materials. Complete.

6 ft. x 3 ft.	...	...	...	£1	15	6
6 ft. x 4 ft.	...	...	...	£2	5	0
6 ft. x 5 ft.	...	...	...	£3	5	0

Border or Violet Frame.

These Frames will be found most useful for protecting plants on borders, or for violets. They are strongly made, the Frames being 1 in. thick, and the Lights 1½ in. Made for sliding, or hinged as shown. Painted 3 coats and glazed with 21 oz. glass.

1 Light	...	4 ft. x 3 ft.	...	£1	2	0
1 "	...	4 ft. x 4 ft.	...	£1	6	0
2 "	...	8 ft. x 3 ft.	...	£2	0	0
2 "	...	8 ft. x 4 ft.	...	£2	7	6

Single Light.

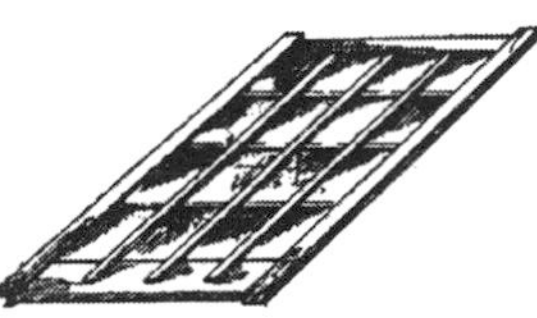

These Lights are made from red Deal, well mortised together, and finished in the best possible manner. Styles and top Rail, 2 in. x 3 in.; bottom Rail, 4 in. x 1¼ in.; Bars, 2 in. x 1½ in, Strengthened with iron rod through centre.

6 ft. x 4 ft., unglazed and unpainted	£0	5	0
6 ft. x 4 ft., glazed and painted 3 coats	£0	14	6

Special quotation for quantity.

Pit Frame.

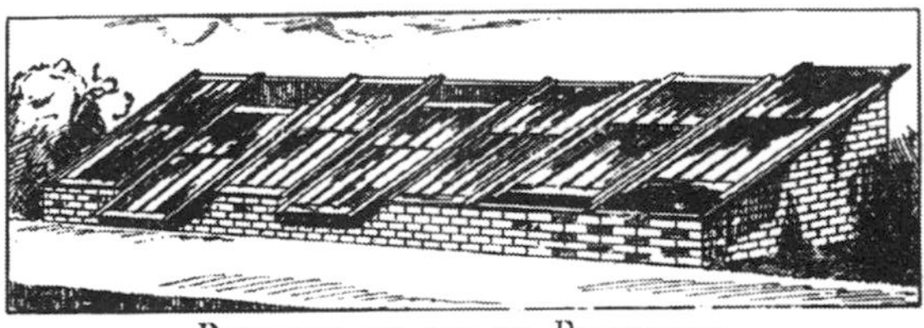

Prepared to set on Brickwork.

Woodwork of well-seasoned red Deal. Sills, 4½ in. x 3 in.; Runners, 3½ in. x 3 in.; Lights, 2 in. Glazed with 21 oz. sheet glass. Painted 3 coats. Complete on rail.

2 Lights	..	..	8 ft. x 6 ft.	.. ..	£2	7	0
3 "	..	..	12 ft. x 6 ft.	.. ..	£3	5	0
4 "	..	..	16 ft. x 6 ft.	.. ..	£4	2	0
5 "	..	..	20 ft. x 6 ft.	.. ..	£5	2	0
6 "	..	..	24 ft. x 6 ft.	.. ..	£6	2	0
7 "	..	..	28 ft. x 6 ft.	.. ..	£7	2	0
8 "	..	..	32 ft. x 6 ft.	.. ..	£7	19	0
9 "	..	..	36 ft. x 6 ft.	.. ..	£8	16	6

NEW PATENT GREENHOUSES,

Specially adapted for Amateurs and others.

SPECIAL NOTICE! We wish it to be distinctly understood that these Houses are constructed upon a New Patent Principal, and are complete, so that upon arrival they can be erected **without the aid of either Carpenter, Glazier, Painter, or Bricklayer.** Each House, before leaving the Works, is carefully fitted together with all the necessary Iron-work, Gutters, Down Pipes, Set-opes for Ventilation, Lock, Bolts, Screws, &c. Painted three coats, glazed with twenty-one oz. best Horticultural Glass, packed and delivered Carriage Free to any Station in England.

Purchasers will find them no more trouble to fix than the well-known Portable Plant Preservers, which any gardener can put together. Every part is numbered. Anyone thinking of erecting a Greenhouse, can, by means of this list, tell the exact cost of a really well-make and durable House, delivered Carriage Paid. Although the prices are very low complete provision is made for thorough ventilation.

PATENT PORTABLE LEAN-TO GREENHOUSES.

To place against an existing Wall.

* Tenant's Fixture, requiring no Brickwork at Front or Ends.
† If prepared to build on Brickwork, 2 ft. 6 in. high at Front and Ends.

Length.		Width.	* Tenant's Fixture.			† Brickwork.			Stages.			Foot Path.		
ft.		ft.	£	s.	d.	£	s.	d.	£	s.	d.	£	s.	d.
10	by	8	17	0	0	15	5	0	2	8	0	1	3	0
12	,,	8	19	0	0	17	0	0	2	16	0	1	8	0
15	,,	8	22	10	0	18	17	0	3	3	0	1	14	6
18	,,	8	25	10	0	21	10	0	3	15	0	2	0	0
20	,,	8	27	0	0	23	12	0	4	3	0	2	6	0
24	,,	8	31	0	0	26	15	0	5	0	0	2	16	0
30	,,	8	36	15	0	31	0	0	6	5	0	3	10	0
12	,,	10	22	0	0	18	10	0	4	4	0	1	8	0
15	,,	10	25	5	0	21	10	0	5	5	0	1	14	6
18	,,	10	28	15	0	24	15	0	6	6	0	2	0	0
20	,,	10	31	10	0	26	15	0	7	0	0	2	6	0
24	,,	10	35	15	0	29	15	0	8	8	0	2	16	0
30	,,	10	41	10	0	35	15	0	10	0	0	3	10	0
15	,,	12	29	15	0	26	15	0	6	0	0	1	14	6
18	,,	12	34	5	0	29	15	0	7	7	0	2	0	0
20	,,	12	36	10	0	32	5	0	8	0	0	2	6	0
24	,,	12	41	5	0	36	15	0	9	12	0	2	16	0
30	,,	12	48	15	0	43	15	0	12	0	0	3	10	0
36	,,	12	56	15	0	49	10	0	14	10	0	4	4	0
42	,,	12	63	0	0	52	10	0	16	10	0	4	18	0

PATENT PORTABLE SPAN-ROOF GREENHOUSES.

* Tenant's Fixture, requiring no Brickwork.
† If prepared to Build on Brickwork, 2 ft. 6 in. high.

Length.		Width.	* Tenant's Fixture.			† Brickwork.			Stages.			Foot Path.		
ft.		ft.	£	s.	d.	£	s.	d.	£	s.	d.	£	s.	d.
10	by	8	23	10	0	16	10	0	2	10	0	1	3	0
12	,,	8	26	10	0	18	10	0	2	18	0	1	8	0
15	,,	8	30	10	0	20	18	0	3	6	0	1	14	6
18	,,	8	34	10	0	23	15	0	3	18	0	2	0	0
20	,,	8	37	10	0	25	10	0	4	7	6	2	6	0
24	,,	8	42	18	0	30	0	0	5	5	0	2	16	0
30	,,	8	50	10	0	36	10	0	6	10	0	3	10	0
12	,,	10	28	10	0	20	15	0	4	6	0	1	8	0
15	,,	10	33	0	0	24	10	0	5	10	0	1	14	6
18	,,	10	37	10	0	28	5	0	6	10	0	2	0	0
20	,,	10	40	17	0	30	10	0	7	10	0	2	6	6
24	,,	10	45	0	0	35	5	0	8	18	0	2	16	0
30	,,	10	52	10	0	41	15	0	10	7	0	3	10	0
36	,,	10	60	0	0	46	15	0	12	0	0	4	4	0
15	,,	12	35	5	0	27	10	0	6	6	0	1	14	6
20	,,	12	42	5	0	33	10	0	8	0	0	2	6	0
24	,,	12	48	10	0	39	0	0	9	12	0	2	16	0
30	,,	12	54	10	0	45	15	0	12	0	0	3	10	0
36	,,	12	62	15	0	51	15	0	14	10	0	4	4	0
42	,,	12	70	10	0	58	0	0	16	10	0	4	18	0

Since the introduction of improved steam-power machinery for working wood, we are enabled to supply first-class Horticultural Buildings of every description at very low prices. Only the best materials used. Houses designed to suit any situation. Estimates given Free. Gentlemen are respectfully invited to have price from us before ordering elsewhere. Ladies and Gentlemen requiring advice as to the situation, style, dimensions, &c., of proposed Horticultural Buildings, waited upon in any part of England, Ireland or Scotland.

Carriage paid to all the Principal Stations and Ports in England when orders amount to 60s.

PLANT PRESERVERS AND CUCUMBER AND MELON FRAMES.

THE UNIVERSAL PLANT PRESERVERS.

Awarded the only PRIZE MEDAL at the Royal Horticultural Society's Great Meeting held at Birmingham, 1872, for Plant Preserving and Ground Vineries.

PRICES AND SIZES.

They are made in the following sizes. One pair of ends is sufficient for any number of lengths, set in a continuous row. In ordering, state the number of ends required. Carriage paid to any station in England on orders amounting to 60s. and upwards.

Size	£ s. d.		s. d.	Size	£ s. d.		s. d.
6 ft. by 2 ft.	1 5 0	Ends	5 0	6 ft. by 4 ft.	2 6 0	Ends	8 6
12 ,, 2 ,,	2 10 0	per	5 0	12 ,, 4 ,,	4 4 0	per	8 6
6 ,, 3 ,,	1 15 0	pair	7 0	12 ,, 5 ,,	5 10 0	pair	10 6
12 ,, 3 ,,	3 5 0	extra	7 0	12 ,, 6 ,,	7 0 0	extra	12 0

Small Illustration of Three-light Melon Frame, 12 ft. by 6 ft. £4 17s. 6d.

Cash Prices, painted three times, glazed with twenty-one oz. glass. Carriage paid to any Railway Station in England on orders amounting to 60s.

		£ s. d.			£ s. d.
1-Light Frame,	4 ft. by 6 ft.	£1 17 6	4-Light Frame,	16 ft. by 6 ft.	£6 7 6
2 ,, ,,	8 ft. ,,	3 5 0	5 ,, ,,	20 ft. ,,	7 17 6
3 ,, ,,	12 ft. ,,	4 17 6	6 ,, ,,	24 ft. ,,	9 7 6

These Frames or Boxes, and Lights, are made in the best manner, with the best red deal, 1¼ in. thick, 24 in. high at the back, 13 in. high at the front, made to screw together at the angles, with runners and parting pieces between each Light. The Lights are made 2 in. thick, and glazed with best twenty-one oz. glass, 10 in. wide and 12 in. long, not in odd pieces (as is usual, from Glazier's waste); each pane of glass is firmly nailed in and bedded in good oil-putty. The same applies to the Plant Preservers.

UNIVERSAL PLANT PRESERVERS, LAWN CONSERVATORIES, OR GROUND VINERIES,

(PATENTED,) WITH GLASS SIDES AND ENDS.

Complete, with two ends, 12 ft. long, 4 ft. wide, 18 in. high at sides, 2 ft. 6 in. high inside of ridge... ... ... £7 5 0
,, ,, 12 ,, 5 ,, 18 ,, ,, 3 ,, 0 ,, ,, ... 8 15 0
,, ,, 12 ,, 6 ,, 18 ,, ,, 3 ,, 3 ,, ,, ... 10 0 0

The above Plant Preservers and Frames are invaluable for the use of Amateurs in the forwarding of Hyacinths and other flowering bulbs in pots, the rearing of various seeds, the growth of Cucumbers, Melons, &c. The Universal Plant Preserver answers admirably as a miniature or ground vinery.

From Mrs. HAMMOND, Manor House, Swaffham, Norfolk.

Oct. 30th, 1874.
"Mrs. Hammond begs to enclose cheque for the Plant Preserver, which gives her much satisfaction."

Lean-to Forcing House.

No. 21.

The above Illustration will convince all practical minds of the importance and utility of this class of House for Gentlemen, Nurserymen, Market Gardeners, and, in fact, all those who require a cheap, strong House for Forcing, or growing Cucumbers, Tomatoes, Melons, &c., &c.

SPECIFICATION.—Built for brickwork 3ft. high; framework throughout 3½in. by 2in. well-seasoned red deal, door complete, with rim lock and brass furniture at one end; roof ventilation according to size, necessary ironwork for opening same, and good 21oz. glass throughout.

House painted one coat good oil colour, carefully marked, packed, and put on rail at the following prices:—

	9ft. wide.	12ft. wide.	14ft. wide.
	£ s. d.	£ s. d.	£ s. d.
20ft.	7 10 0	9 10 0	12 10 0
30ft.	10 5 0	13 5 0	17 15 0
40ft.	14 0 0	18 0 0	21 10 0
60ft.	20 10 0	25 10 0	30 10 0
100ft.	35 0 0	40 0 0	47 0 0

Estimates for Stages, Footpaths, and Heating Apparatus (see Section V.), also for erecting Forcing Houses in any part of the country, sent free on application.

Braehead, Kirkcaldy.

"Mrs. Hutchison begs to inform Mr. W. Cooper that the Forcing House arrived safely; it has been put up, and is very satisfactory."

Fairholme, Sunbury.

MR. W. COOPER, 751, Old Kent Road, S.E.

"DEAR SIR,—I am pleased to say the Span-roof Greenhouse I had from you in 1891 gives me every satisfaction.—Yours faithfully, J. S. SKIDMORE."

WILLIAM COOPER, 755, Old Kent Road, London, S.E.
HORTICULTURAL PROVIDER.

Span-roof Forcing House.

No. 22.

The above Illustration will convince all practical minds of the importance and utility of this class of House for Gentlemen, Nurserymen, Market Gardeners, and, in fact, all those who require a cheap, strong House for Forcing, or growing Cucumbers, Tomatoes, Melons, &c., &c.

SPECIFICATION.—Built for brickwork 3ft. high; framework throughout 3½in. by 2in. well-seasoned red deal, door complete, with rim lock and brass furniture at one end; roof ventilation according to size, necessary ironwork for opening same, and good 21oz. glass throughout.

House painted one coat good oil colour, carefully marked, packed, and put on rail at the following prices:—

	9ft. wide.	12ft. wide.	14ft. wide.
	£ s. d.	£ s. d.	£ s. d.
20ft.	8 0 0	10 0 0	13 0 0
30ft.	11 0 0	14 0 0	18 10 0
40ft.	15 0 0	19 0 0	22 10 0
60ft.	22 0 0	27 0 0	32 0 0
100ft.	35 0 0	42 0 0	50 0 0

Partition, with extra door	£1 15 0 each.
Ventilating Boxes, side walls	0 5 9 "
Door at both ends, add	0 15 0 "

Estimates for Stages, Footpaths, and Heating Apparatus (see Section V.) also for erecting Forcing Houses in any part of the country, sent free on application.

Longton, Staffs.

"The Forcing Pit arrived safely and gives entire satisfaction. It is a very good and suitable one. I gave your address to a gentleman, and shall be pleased to give it to others whom I know to be requiring anything in your way. Believe me, yours faithfully, W. J. BARKER."

Drill House.

"DEAR SIR,—I have had Greenhouse erected; am very pleased with it.—Yours respectfully, W. READ."

WILLIAM COOPER, 755, Old Kent Road, London, S.E.
HORTICULTURAL PROVIDER.

Three-Quarter Span-Roof Greenhouse.

TENANT'S FIXTURE.

No. 23.

This is a very useful form for Plant-houses or Vineries, more especially where the back wall is not high enough for a Lean-to; as by adding extra cost for brickwork to the price of latter, it will then at once be perceived to be in favour of the Three-quarter Span; moreover, plants will grow much better, the House being thoroughly lighted.

This House is made of the best materials, well and substantially built, and so constructed that any handy man can put it together, and is artistically finished with diagonal panels and barge boards. The whole of framework consists of good sound 3½in. by 2in. red deal, the lower part doubly lined with tongued and grooved matchboards, roof in complete sashes. The House is supplied with English-cut 16oz. glass throughout, half-glass door, rim lock, key, and brass fittings for same, two plant stages the length of both sides, and footpath for centre. Ventilators given according to size, and necessary Ironwork for opening same, also gutters and downpipes. Woodwork is painted two coats good oil colour. Houses are securely packed and put on rail (all parts being carefully marked); or delivered, erected, and glazed (with an extra coat of good oil paint after glazing) within 20, 50, or 100 miles of London Bridge at the following respective prices:—

Long.	Wide.	High.	To eaves.	Packed on rail.	Erected within 20 miles.	Erected within 50 miles.	Erected within 100 miles.
				£ s. d.	£ s. d.	£ s. d.	£ s. d.
7	5	7 0	4 0	4 10 0	6 0 0	7 0 0	8 10 0
8	5	7 0	4 0	5 10 0	7 10 0	8 15 0	10 10 0
9	6	7 6	4 6	6 10 0	9 0 0	10 10 0	12 10 0
10	7	8 0	5 0	7 10 0	10 0 0	11 15 0	13 15 0
12	8	8 6	5 6	9 0 0	12 0 0	14 10 0	17 0 0
15	10	9 0	6 0	11 0 0	15 10 0	18 0 0	21 0 0
20	10	9 0	6 0	16 0 0	22 0 0	25 0 0	29 0 0
25	10	9 0	6 0	21 0 0	28 0 0	32 0 0	37 0 0
50	10	9 0	6 0	40 0 0	55 0 0	60 0 0	65 0 0
100	10	9 0	6 0	70 0 0	90 0 0	100 0 0	110 0 0

21oz. glass for roof 5 per cent. extra. Deduct 12½ per cent. if for brickwork.

If all Top and Side Ventilators are required to open as shown, 10 per cent. extra. When ordering, it should be stated at which end the door is to be inserted (when facing front of House from outside); if required, it can be placed in front.

For Heating Apparatus suitable to above Houses, see Section V.

WILLIAM COOPER, 755, Old Kent Road, London, S.E.
HORTICULTURAL PROVIDER.

Three-Quarter Span Garden Frame.

No. 24.

This illustration shows a Frame similar to my No. 34, adapted for building on brick walls, making the most useful Frame that can be had for general purposes. Owing to plenty of light and air, plants grow quickly and healthy. The framework is made of the best seasoned red deal, and a plate is formed to rest on the wall. The Lights are very strong, the hinges, which are malleable iron, form a strong square to strengthen the corners. Two glazed ends are included. Set-opes to each light. Painted three times and glazed with 21-oz. English glass. Any length or width made.

CASH PRICES.

Lgth. of Frame.	Price, 5ft. Wide.	Price, 6ft. Wide.	Price, 7ft. Wide.
	£ s. d.	£ s. d.	£ s. d.
10ft.	3 5 0	3 10 0	3 15 0
15ft.	4 8 0	5 0 0	5 10 0
20ft.	5 10 0	6 10 0	7 0 0
25ft.	7 0 0	8 0 0	8 10 0
30ft.	8 10 0	9 10 0	10 0 0
40ft.	11 10 0	12 10 0	13 10 0
50ft.	14 0 0	15 0 0	15 10 0
60ft.	16 10 0	18 0 0	18 10 0

Packing free for Cash with Order.

Heating Apparatus (see Section V.), with my Invincible Boilers, plans and estimates free: 20ft. by 7ft., with 4-inch single pipes, flow and return the entire length, £5 5s. complete.

Plans for brickwork, and estimates for any size free on application

The Gardens, Telcourt, East Grinstead.

"SIR,—Mr. Penfold has received Amateur Span-roof Greenhouse quite safe, and is much pleased with it."

WILLIAM COOPER, 755, Old Kent Road, London, S.E.
HORTICULTURAL PROVIDER.

Span-Roof Garden Frame.

No. 33.

These Improved Garden Frames can be strongly recommended for storing plants, and growing cucumbers, melons, &c., being much more convenient than the lean-to. The illustration shows a six-light frame, 12ft. by 6ft., height at sides 11in., and ridge 24in. These frames are composed of 1in. thoroughly well seasoned, red deal boards Painted three coats best oil colour. The lights are glazed with good 21oz. glass, bedded in superior oil putty, and are fitted with stays, which safely support them for ventilation.

Securely packed and put on rail at the following prices:

Size.	Price.	Size.	Price.
4ft. by 4ft.	£1 8 0	12ft. by 6ft.	£4 3 0
4ft. by 6ft.	1 19 0	16ft. by 6ft.	5 10 0
8ft. by 6ft.	3 5 0	20ft. by 6ft.	7 0 0

24ft. by 6ft. £8 10 0

Estimates given for larger sizes free on application.

17 & 18, Basinghall Street, E.C.

"I have much pleasure in enclosing my cheque to balance my account; kindly own safe receipt. I must compliment you upon the way in which the work has been done.—Yours very faithfully, J. R. CLAYPOLE."

WILLIAM COOPER, ESQ.,
751, Old Kent Road, S.E.

The Gardens, Leonards Lee, Horsham, Sussex.

"Sir,—The Span-Roof Plant Frame and Bars came safely. I am very pleased with the Frame. With thanks, I am, Sir, yours truly, SYDNEY FORD, F.R.H.S."

51

WILLIAM COOPER, 755, Old Kent Road, London, S.E.
HORTICULTURAL PROVIDER.

Melon and Cucumber Frames.

No. 47.—SINGLE LIGHT AND FRAME.

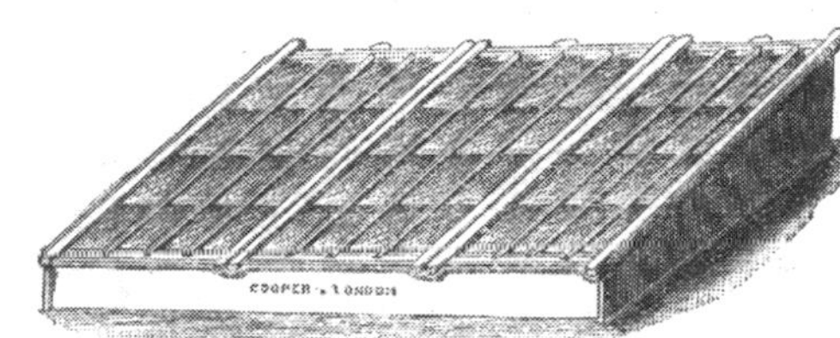

No. 48.—THREE LIGHTS AND FRAME.

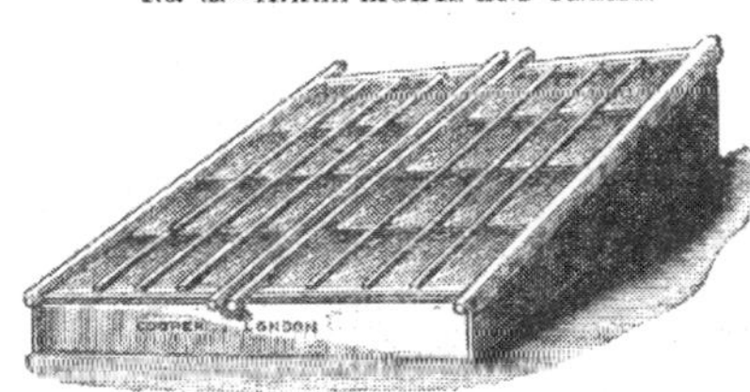

No. 49. TWO LIGHTS AND FRAME.

These are very useful Frames, being suitable for the storage of plants in winter, and well adapted for the cultivation of Melons, Cucumbers, &c., in summer. (The illustrations show One, Two, and Three Light Frames, height at front 11in., and height at back 22in.)

60

WILLIAM COOPER, 755, Old Kent Road, London, S.E.
HORTICULTURAL PROVIDER.

Melon and Cucumber Frames.—

They are composed of 1¼in., thoroughly deal boards, have necessary Parting Pieces, and runners for lights which are 2in. thick, and which are glazed with good 21oz. glass, nailed and bedded in oiled putty, and fitted with an iron handle. All parts painted three coats of good oil paint, and securely packed and put on rail at the following prices:—

One Light Frames	4ft. by 3ft.	... ...	£0 17 0
,, ,,	4ft. ,, 4ft.	... ...	1 1 0
,, ,,	5ft. ,, 4ft.	... ...	1 3 0
,, ,,	6ft. ,, 4ft.	... ...	1 8 0
Two Light ,,	6ft. ,, 4ft.	... ...	1 10 0
,, ,,	8ft. ,, 4ft.	... ...	1 16 0
,, ,,	8ft. ,, 6ft.	... ...	2 10 0
Three Light ,,	10ft. ,, 6ft.	... ...	3 0 0
,, ,,	12ft. ,, 6ft.	... ...	3 10 0
Four Light ,,	16ft. ,, 6ft.	... ...	5 10 0
Five Light ,,	20ft. ,, 6ft.	... ...	5 15 0
Six Light ,,	24ft. ,, 6ft.	... ...	6 10 0

Estimates submitted for Special Sizes, Free.

The "Amateur" Plant Frame.

No. 50.

No. 51.

No. 52.

Made of 1in. thoroughly well-seasoned red deal boards. Lights are 2in. thick, hinged at back, and are glazed with good 21oz. glass, nailed and bedded in oiled putty, and fitted with iron set to open for ventilation, &c. Painted three coats best oil paint, and securely packed and put on rail.

4ft. by 3ft.	... ...	**£0 18 0**
5ft. by 3ft.	... ...	**1 4 0**

61

WILLIAM COOPER, 755, Old Kent Road, London, S.E.
HORTICULTURAL PROVIDER.

Lean-to Potting Shed.
FOR PLACING AGAINST A WALL.

No. 31.

Constructed with wood framework, painted, and covered with galvanized corrugated iron, unlined and without floor. Woodwork painted one coat. Made in sections, and fitted ready for purchaser to erect. Two ends and one door hung and fitted with lock. Glass cut to sizes. Carefully packed on rail.

CASH PRICE—12ft. by 8ft., 6ft. high at eaves, 8ft. at back .... £5 10s.

Complete Heating Apparatus for Small Greenhouses, *see Section V.*

Garden Lights.

These lights are substantially constructed of good, sound, well-seasoned red deal; the stiles, which are 2in. thick, being well mortised and pinned to tenoned rails properly rabbeted for the glass, and fitted with 2in. sash bars. The Glazed Lights are painted two coats of good oil paint, and the glass in same nailed and bedded in superior oil putty.

Packed securely on rail at the following respective prices:—

No. 32.

Unglazed Lights.		Lights Glazed with 21oz.	
6ft. by 4ft.	3s. 6d. each.	6ft. by 4ft.	9s. 0d. each.
4ft. by 3ft.	2s. 9d. ,,	4ft. by 3ft.	6s. 6d. ,,
3ft. by 2ft.	2s. 3d. ,,	3ft. by 2ft.	5s. 0d. ,,

Special Quotations for Large Quantities.

Prices given, by return of post, for all kinds of Sashes and Doors, Glazed and Painted.

50

THREE-QUARTER SPAN VINERY. No. 9.

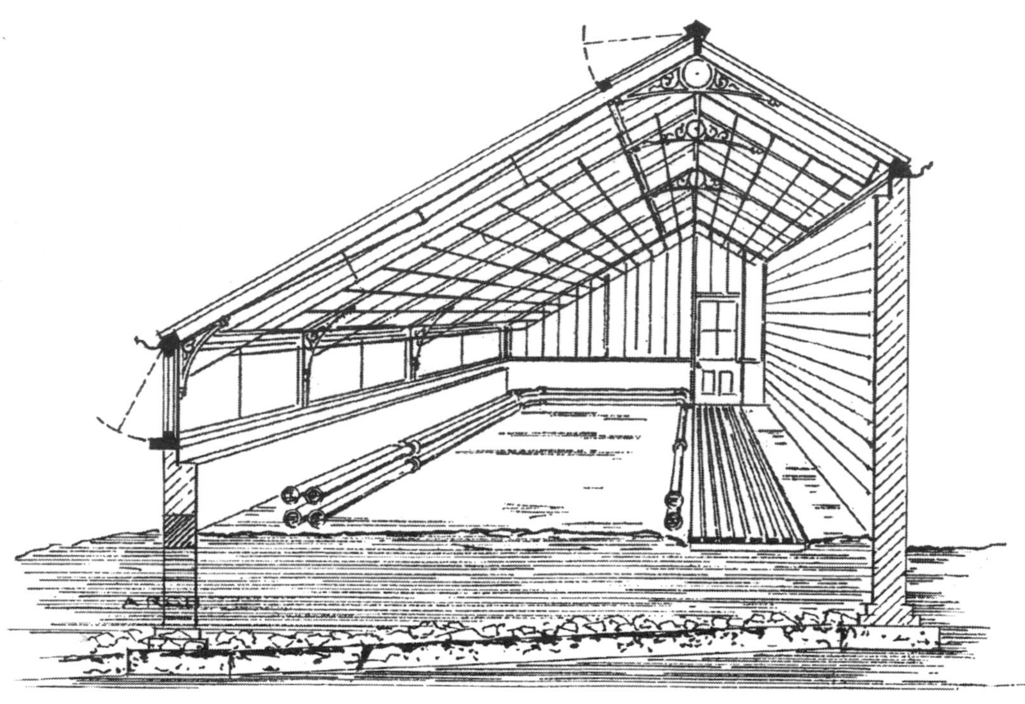

About 16 ft. 9 in. wide and 4 ft. 6 in. from path to eaves, including 2 ft. 0 in. of brickwork, and requiring a back wall 8 ft. 6 in. high. The front brickwork is built on arches and the bottom of border concreted. The front sashes are hung at top, and abundant ventilation is provided in roof by continuous lifting light; all the opening lights are fitted with screw gearing for opening them in sets. The front rafters are trussed with a light wrought iron truss rod, and spandril brackets are fixed at apex and foot of each rafter. The roof is wired on an improved principle for training vines, and so arranged that the wires may be moved for cleaning purposes. A stout wood trellis or cast iron grating path is provided through the house. The back wall is also wired for climbers. The heating provided is by four rows of piping along front about 2 ft. 0 in. from wall, two pipes along ends and two pipes along edge of path, the whole being controlled by screw-down valves, so that the heat may be shut off or regulated at pleasure.

THREE-QUARTER SPAN PEACH HOUSE. No. 10.

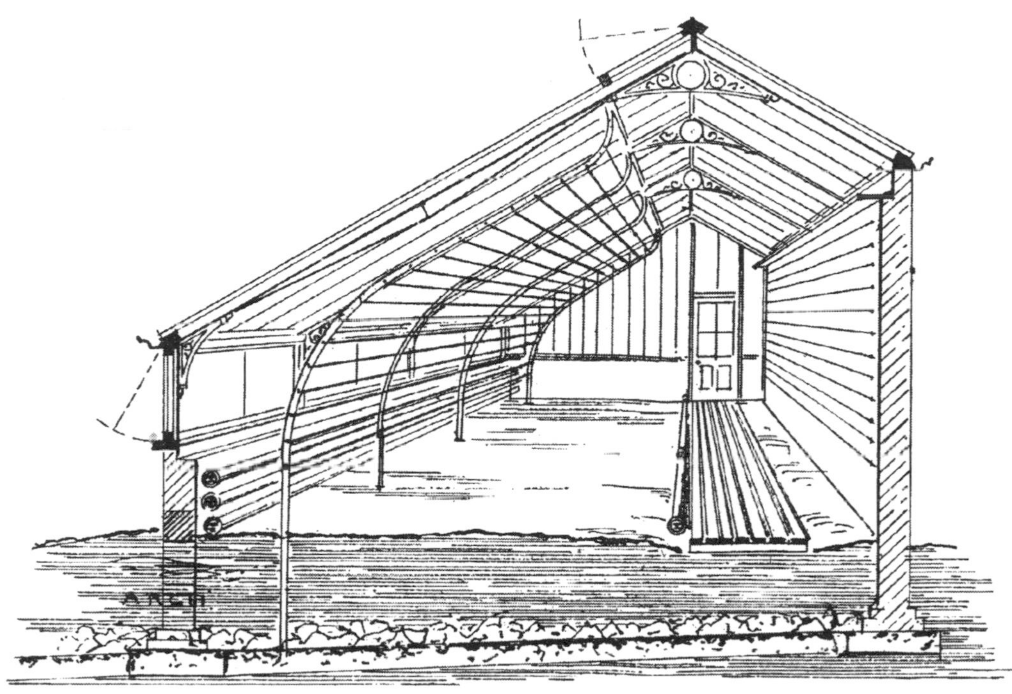

About 16 ft. 9 in. wide, 4 ft. 6 in. from path to eaves, and requiring a back wall 8 ft. 6 in. high, the brickwork along front is built on arches, and the bottom of peach border concreted over for inside and outside border. The whole of the front sashes are hung at top to open well for ventilation, and the roof is freely ventilated by a continuous lifting light on one side, improved screw gearing being fitted to all. The rafters to front of roof are trussed with light wrought iron truss rods, and cast iron spandril brackets are fixed at apex and foot of each rafter. A curved peach trellis is provided along front of house, with a wrought iron standard under and secured to each rafter, and light wrought iron training rods running through same from end to end, an opening being left for access to the outside of the trellis along front. A solid grooved shelf is fitted along back wall close to the glass, and a stout wood trellis or iron grating path runs from end to end of the house. The back wall may be wired for training peaches if desired. The heating comprises three pipes along front wall and one along edge of path.

A DESIGN FOR SMALL CONSERVATORY.

Architecture, Furniture and Garden Ornament

The conservatory, the grandest of garden buildings, reached its apotheosis in the Victorian age, against the backdrop of travel to new and exotic areas of the world, and an interest in collecting and cultivating new and unimagined species, in defiance of the inhospitable climate of the British Isles. Reflecting this enthusiasm for bringing plants not only into the country but into the home, garden catalogues abounded with conservatories and their trappings, peach houses and vineries of all kinds, to suit virtually every situation, architectural style and requirement. The most opulent of these structures provided a vast and lofty area for plants, furniture and other accessories such as palm boxes for specimen plants, flowerpot stands and hanging baskets.

The fashion for fanciful garden buildings extended beyond the conservatory and its utilitarian counterpart, the greenhouse. To add a romantic finishing touch to the home and grounds and complement the stock of plants, ready-made verandas, porches, summer houses, temples, arches, arbours, bowers, pergolas, screens, trellises, niches, seats, tables and outdoor benches in sawn and rustic timber, wrought iron and wire were available for prompt delivery by rail to the local station.

Just as the Victorians extended their gardens into the home, so they took their indoor 'garniture' outside, with lead and iron urns, terracotta containers, stone vases of fruit and flowers, classical statuary and marble fountains of every description. The plethora of modern-day conservatory and garden furniture companies testifies to this lucrative and expanding market for such goods, and the nostalgic, notably Victorian style of many of their products is evidence of the continuing appeal of nineteenth century design.

WILLIAM COOPER, 755, Old Kent Road, London, S.E.
HORTICULTURAL PROVIDER.

Span-Roof Conservatory.

TENANT'S FIXTURE.

No. 8.

This Conservatory is well and substantially constructed on the most approved principle, of the very best materials, and is artistically finished with circular lights. All the framework is made of well-seasoned 2in. by 3½in. red deal; the panels are diagonal, made of tongued and grooved boards, double lined. Lattice staging for plants the entire length of house, on both sides; footpath; rim lock, with brass fittings and key for door; gutters, down-pipes, and all necessary ironwork and fittings provided.

The whole of woodwork is painted two coats of good oil paint. Ventilation given according to size. 21oz. glass cut to size, packed (no charge for packing). Each house is erected at my Works, carefully numbered, and can be easily fixed by any handy man in a few hours. Securely packed on rail, or delivered, erected and glazed (with extra coat of good oil paint after glazing) within 20, 50, or 100 miles of London Bridge, at the following respective prices :—

	On Rail.	Erected within 20 miles.	Erected within 50 miles.	Erected within 100 miles.
7ft. long, 5ft. wide, 7ft. high, 4ft. to eaves	£6 0 0	£8 0 0	£9 0 0	£11 0 0
8ft. long, 5ft. wide, 7ft. high, 4ft. ,,	7 0 0	10 0 0	12 0 0	14 0 0
9ft. long, 6ft. wide, 7ft. high, 4ft. 6 ,,	8 0 0	11 0 0	13 0 0	15 0 0
10ft. long, 7ft. wide, 7ft. 6 high, 4ft. 6 ,,	9 0 0	12 0 0	14 0 0	16 10 0
10ft. long, 8ft. wide, 7ft. 6 high, 4ft. 9 ,,	10 10 0	14 0 0	16 0 0	19 0 0
12ft. long, 8ft. wide, 8ft. high, 5ft. ,,	12 10 0	16 10 0	19 10 0	23 0 0
15ft. long, 10ft. wide, 8ft. 6 high, 5ft. 3 ,,	18 0 0	23 0 0	27 0 0	30 0 0
18ft. long, 10ft. wide, 9ft. 6 high, 5ft. 6 ,,	21 0 0	26 0 0	30 0 0	35 0 0

If required for Brickwork, deduct 12½ per cent.

For Heating Apparatus suitable for above Houses, see Section V.

Estimates given for larger sizes free on application; also for all kinds of Centre-Dome Conservatories, Ranges of Houses, &c.

29

WILLIAM COOPER, 755, Old Kent Road, London, S.E.
HORTICULTURAL PROVIDER.

Lean-to Conservatory.

No. 11.

Designed especially to suit Modern Built Houses, it can be adapted to almost any size, and put up at small cost. The upper lights over door are filled in with tinted glass.

SPECIFICATION.—Constructed of the very best materials, and are well, substantially, and handsomely built, all woodwork consisting of good well-seasoned red deal; ventilators at top and front, with casement irons for opening same; 21oz. glass throughout; half-glass door, complete with lock, brass fittings, and key; stages, footpath, iron O.G. gutters and downpipes, &c. All woodwork painted two coats of good oil colour. Carefully packed on rail with every part marked ready for fixing at the following respective prices:

CASH PRICES, EXCLUSIVE OF BRICKWORK:

Length.	Width.	Price of House.
15ft.	9ft.	£25
20ft.	12ft.	42
25ft.	14ft.	65
30ft.	15ft.	80
40ft.	16ft.	100

Proportionate prices for other sizes.

Estimates for erection in any part of the country, also for Heating Apparatus, free on application. Plan for Brickwork supplied free on receipt of Order.

For Heating Apparatus suitable for above House, see Section V.

32

WILLIAM COOPER, 755, Old Kent Road, London, S.E.
HORTICULTURAL PROVIDER.

Lantern Roof Conservatory.

No. 16.

This Design can be made detached if desired. Prices on application. The upper side lights are filled in with tinted glass.

SPECIFICATION.—Constructed of the very best materials, and are well, substantially, and handsomely built, all woodwork consisting of good well-seasoned red deal; ventilators at top and front, with casement irons for opening same; 21oz. glass throughout; half-glass doors, complete with lock, brass fittings, and keys; stages, footpath, iron O.G. gutters and downpipes, &c. All woodwork painted two coats of good oil colour. Carefully packed on rail with every part marked ready for fixing at the following (exclusive of brickwork) prices:

Length.	Width.	Price of House.
15ft.	9ft.	£25
20ft.	12ft.	42
25ft.	14ft.	65
30ft.	15ft.	80
40ft.	16ft.	100

Proportionate prices for other sizes.

Estimates for erecting in any part of the country, also for Heating Apparatus, free on application.

Ivy Cottage, Sharrow Street, Sheffield.

"Greenhouse arrived yesterday. I am delighted with it, and don't know how you can produce them for the money. They are a marvel of cheapness.

"G. HIBBERD."

The Rectory, Castle Eden, Durham.

"The Greenhouse that Mr. Cooper sent the Rev. J. Robinson has now been put up. It looks very well, and has been much admired."

37

WILLIAM COOPER, 755, Old Kent Road, London, S.E.
HORTICULTURAL PROVIDER.

Hipped-roof Conservatory with Lantern.

No. 13.

An ornamental Conservatory of a design adapted to secure the maximum of light with thorough ventilation.

HEATING APPARATUS.—This consists of an Invincible Hot-water Apparatus (see Section V.), complete with syphon, flue-pipe, and a double row of 4in. pipe along one side of the houses under 12ft. wide, one side and one end of houses 12ft. to 16ft. wide, and both sides and one end of houses above this width.

SPECIFICATION.—Constructed of the very best materials, and are well, substantially, and handsomely built, all woodwork consisting of good well-seasoned red deal; ventilators at top and front, with casement irons for opening same; 21oz. glass throughout, half-glass door, complete with lock, brass fittings, and key; stages, footpath, iron O.G. gutters, and downpipes, &c. All woodwork painted two coats of good oil colour. Carefully packed on rail with every part marked ready for fixing at the following respective prices:

CASH PRICES, EXCLUSIVE OF BRICKWORK:

Length.	Width.	Price of House, with circular-headed glass in sashes as engraving.	Heating Apparatus.	Division with Door.	Extra door at end.
15ft.	10ft.	£30 0 0	£4 5 0	—	£1 1 0
20ft.	12ft.	40 0 0	6 6 0	£5 10 0	1 1 0
25ft.	14ft.	55 0 0	7 10 0	6 10 0	1 1 0
30ft.	16ft.	70 0 0	10 10 0	8 0 0	1 1 0
35ft.	18ft.	90 0 0	15 10 0	9 0 0	1 1 0
40ft.	20ft.	120 0 0	18 0 0	11 0 0	1 1 0

Proportionate prices for other sizes. Estimates for erecting in any part of the country free on application.

39

FOLLOWS & BATE Limited,

GARDEN & SUMMER-HOUSE TABLES.

ROUND TOP OPEN.

SQUARE TOP FOLDED.

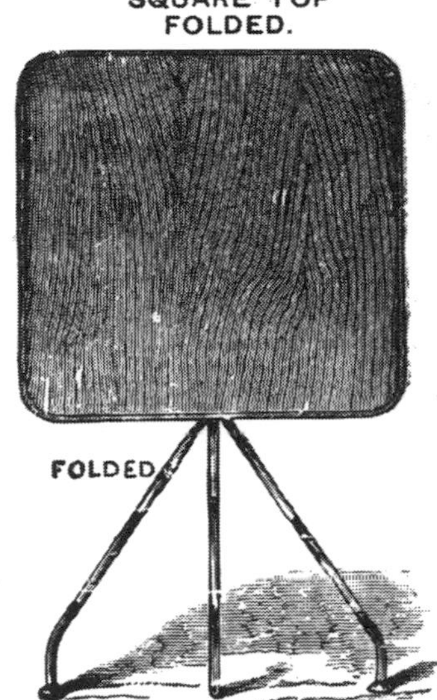

IMPROVED WROUGHT-IRON

FOLDING TABLES.

Legs Japanned Bamboo, and Tops Grained Oak.

Prices.

Round Top.		Square Top.	
21in. diameter	**8/6** each.	21in.	**10/-** each.
24in. ,, ...	**10/-** ,,	24in.	**10/6** ,,

ORNAMENTAL TABLES.

SUITABLE FOR RESTAURANTS, COFFEE PALACES, WAITING ROOMS, CAFÉS, CONSERVATORIES, &c.

"BRITANNIA" TABLE.

Fine Cast Legs, Painted and Bronzed.

Fitted with Polished Bay-wood Top, 25in. diameter, O. G. edge	**£1 7 6**
Fitted with Sicilian Marble Top, 24in., with round edge	**1 10 0**

OBLONG TABLE.

Fine Cast Standards, with Two Brackets and One Tie Rod for 36in. Table, Painted and Bronzed.

Fitted with Polished Mahogany Top, 36in. by 18in., round edge ..	**£1 5 6**
,, ,, Sicilian Marble Top, 36in. by 18in., round edge	**1 12 6**
Cast-iron Bearing Frame for Marble Top, extra	**0 3 0**

GORTON, MANCHESTER.

WROUGHT-IRON PORTABLE FLOWER STANDS & GREENHOUSE STAGING.

Strongly constructed, japanned green, for Greenhouses, Conservatories, &c.

Being made of wrought-iron throughout they are stronger than those made of wire or wood. They harbour no insects, are easily taken apart and put together again by any labourer in a few minutes, and pack quite flat for transit by ship or rail, or for storing away when not wanted, 12 stands only occupying the room of one ordinary stand, and can be made any size to order. They are fitted together with nuts and bolts, which are included in the prices.

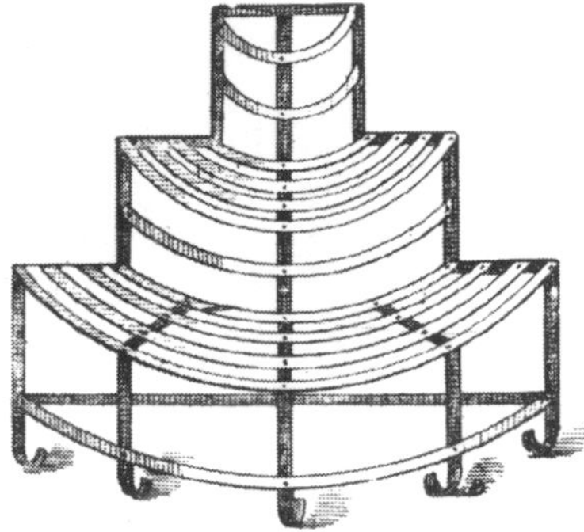

No. 1708. HALF CIRCLE.
3 ft. 9 in. wide, 3 ft. high.
Price **42**/- each.

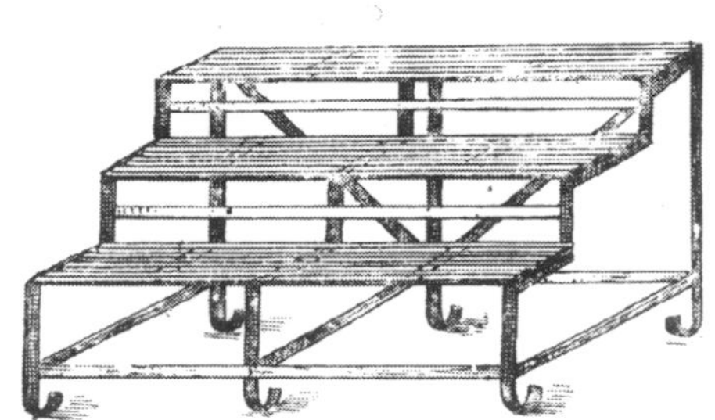

No. 1709. THREE-TIER STAND.
4 ft. wide, 3 ft. high.
Price **44**/- each.

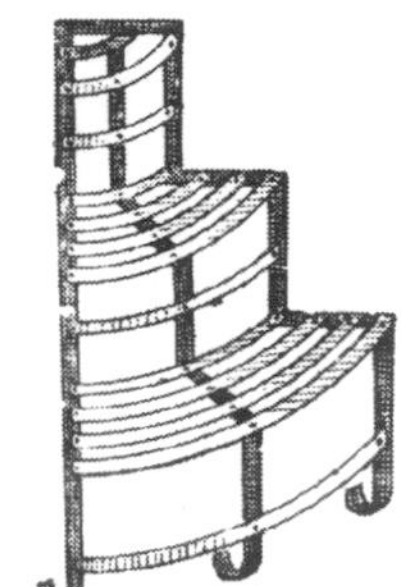

No. 1710. CORNER STAND.
2 ft. 3 in. wide, 3 ft. high.
Price **40**/- each.

NOTE.—The above pack absolutely flat for shipment.

No. 1711. CHEAP USEFUL STAND OR GREENHOUSE STAGING.

Made of wrought-iron and rivetted together, and japanned green.

Sizes.	3 Stages.	4 Stages.	5 Stages.	6 Stages.
Height A-B	1ft. 10in.	2ft. 6in.	3ft. 2in.	3ft. 10in. high.
Width A-D	1ft. 9in.	2ft. 3in.	2ft. 10in.	3ft. 6in. wide.
Length B-C	£ s. d.	£ s. d.	£ s. d.	£ s. d.
3 ft.	**1 8 0**	**1 14 8**	**2 2 6**	**2 10 6**
4 ft.	**1 11 6**	**2 2 6**	**2 14 6**	**3 2 8**
5 ft.	**1 18 6**	**2 8 6**	**2 18 6**	**3 9 0**
6 ft.	**2 2 6**	**2 13 6**	**3 4 0**	**3 16 0**

When required for shipment they can be made to pack nearly flat by removal of the cross stay.

A cheaper Staging than above, round bars, can also be had. Prices on application.

ORNAMENTAL WIRE FLOWER STANDS.

No. 1712. Japanned green.
3ft. wide, 3ft. high **26/6**
3ft. 6in. wide, 3ft. 6in. high, **29/6**
4ft. ,, 3ft. 6in. ,, **33/-**

No. 1713. Japanned green.
3 ft. wide by 4 ft. high. Price **40**/- each.

No. 1714. Japanned green.
3 ft. 9 in. long, 2 ft. 9 in. high.
Price **32**/- each.

Any of the above three Flower Stands can be had japanned in two colours at an advance of **1/6** to **2/-** each. If galvanized **2/-** to **3/-** each extra.

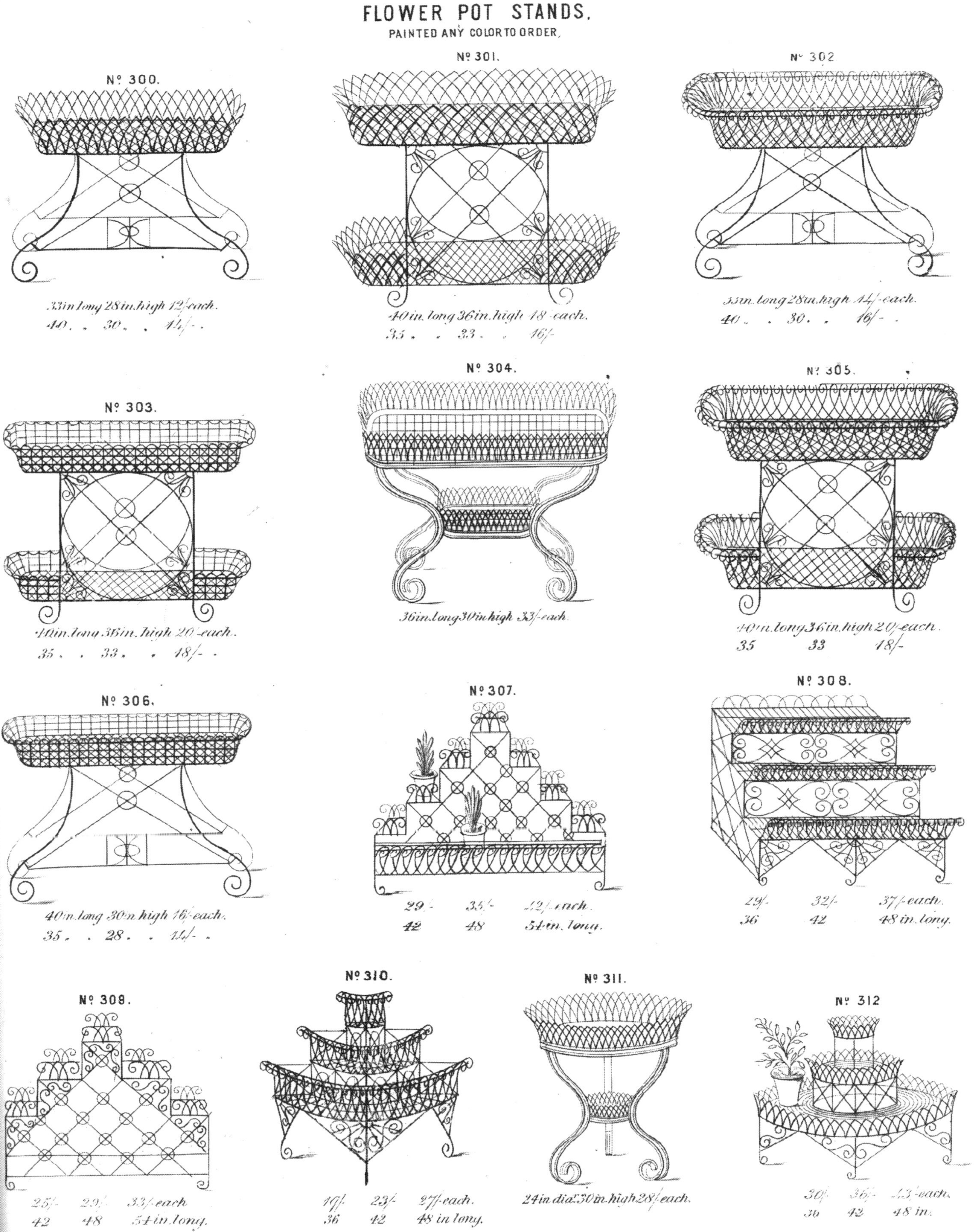
FLOWER POT STANDS.
PAINTED ANY COLOR TO ORDER.
Nº 300.
33 in long 28 in high 12/- each.
40 „ 30 „ 14/- „
Nº 301.
40 in long 36 in high 18/- each.
35 „ 33 „ 16/-
Nº 302
33 in long 28 in high 14/- each.
40 „ 30 „ 16/- „
Nº 303.
40 in long 36 in high 20/- each.
35 „ 33 „ 18/- „
Nº 304.
36 in long 30 in high 33/- each.
Nº 305.
40 in long 36 in high 20/- each.
35 33 18/-
Nº 306.
40 in long 30 in high 16/- each.
35 „ 28 „ 14/- „
Nº 307.
29/- 35/- 42/- each.
42 48 54 in long.
Nº 308.
29/- 32/- 37/- each.
36 42 48 in long.
Nº 308.
25/- 29/- 33/- each
42 48 54 in long.
Nº 310.
16/- 23/- 27/- each.
36 42 48 in long.
Nº 311.
24 in dia. 30 in high 28/- each.
Nº 312
30/- 36/- 43/- each.
36 42 48 in.

FLOWER STANDS.—Continued.

No. 183.

Japanned Green.
Size, 24 in. by 48 in.
16/- each.

No. 184.

Japanned Green.
Size, 24 in. by 33 in. 11/- each.

No 185.

Japanned Green.
Size 20 in. by 33 in.
18/- each.

No. 186.

Japanned Green.
Size, 30 in. by 36 in. 15/6 each.

No. 187.

Japanned Green.
Size, 36 in. by 48 in.
22/- each.

No. 189.

Japanned Green.
4/6 each.

No. 188.

Japanned Green.
Size 38 in. by 48 in.
36/- each.

40

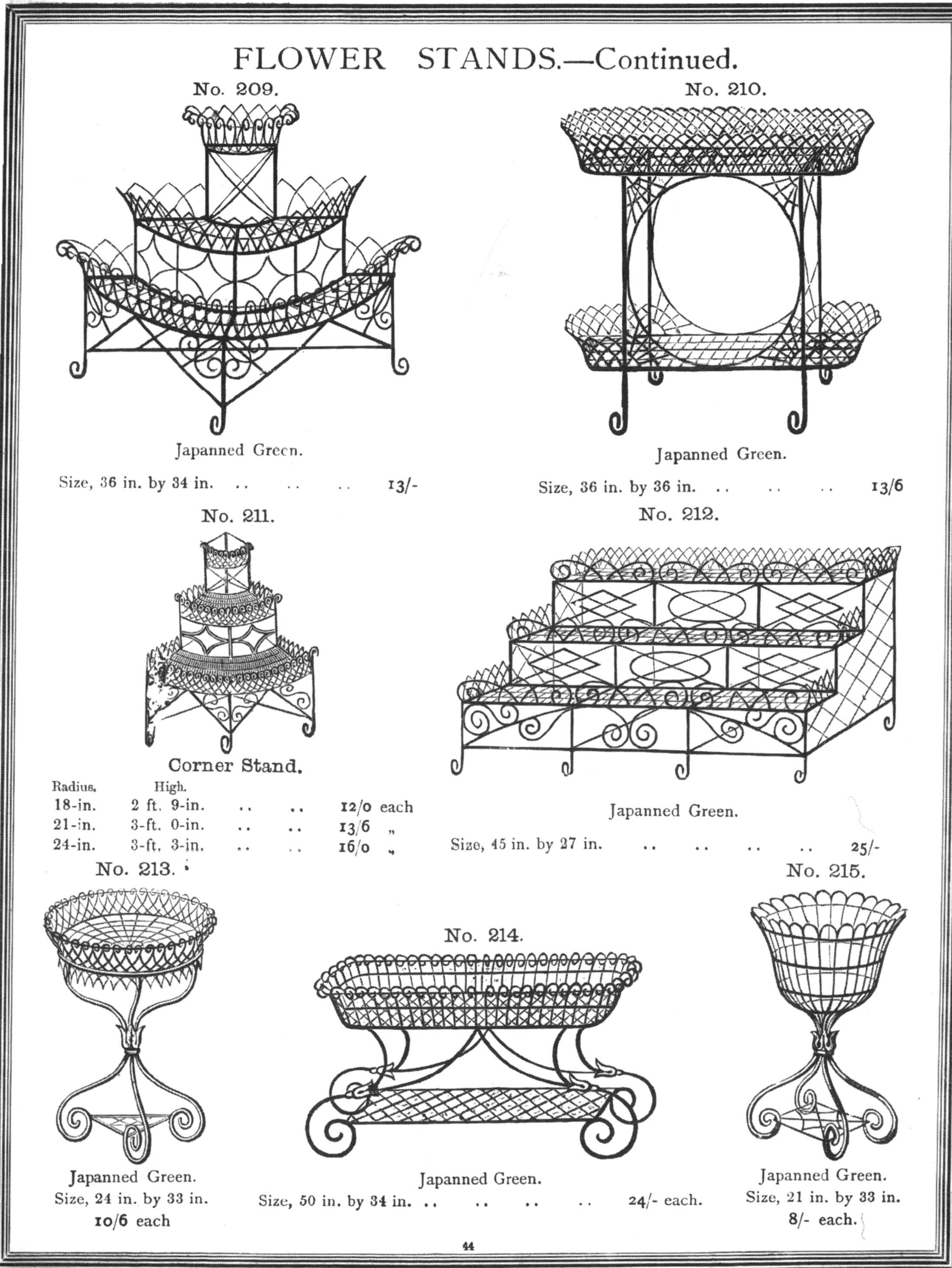

FLOWER STANDS.—Continued.

No. 209.

Japanned Green.

Size, 36 in. by 34 in. 13/-

No. 210.

Japanned Green.

Size, 36 in. by 36 in. 13/6

No. 211.

Corner Stand.

Radius.	High.			
18-in.	2 ft. 9-in.	..	..	12/0 each
21-in.	3-ft. 0-in.	..	..	13/6 „
24-in.	3-ft. 3-in.	..	..	16/0 „

No. 212.

Japanned Green.

Size, 45 in. by 27 in. 25/-

No. 213.

Japanned Green.
Size, 24 in. by 33 in.
10/6 each

No. 214.

Japanned Green.
Size, 50 in. by 34 in. .. .. 24/- each.

No. 215.

Japanned Green.
Size, 21 in. by 33 in.
8/- each.

44

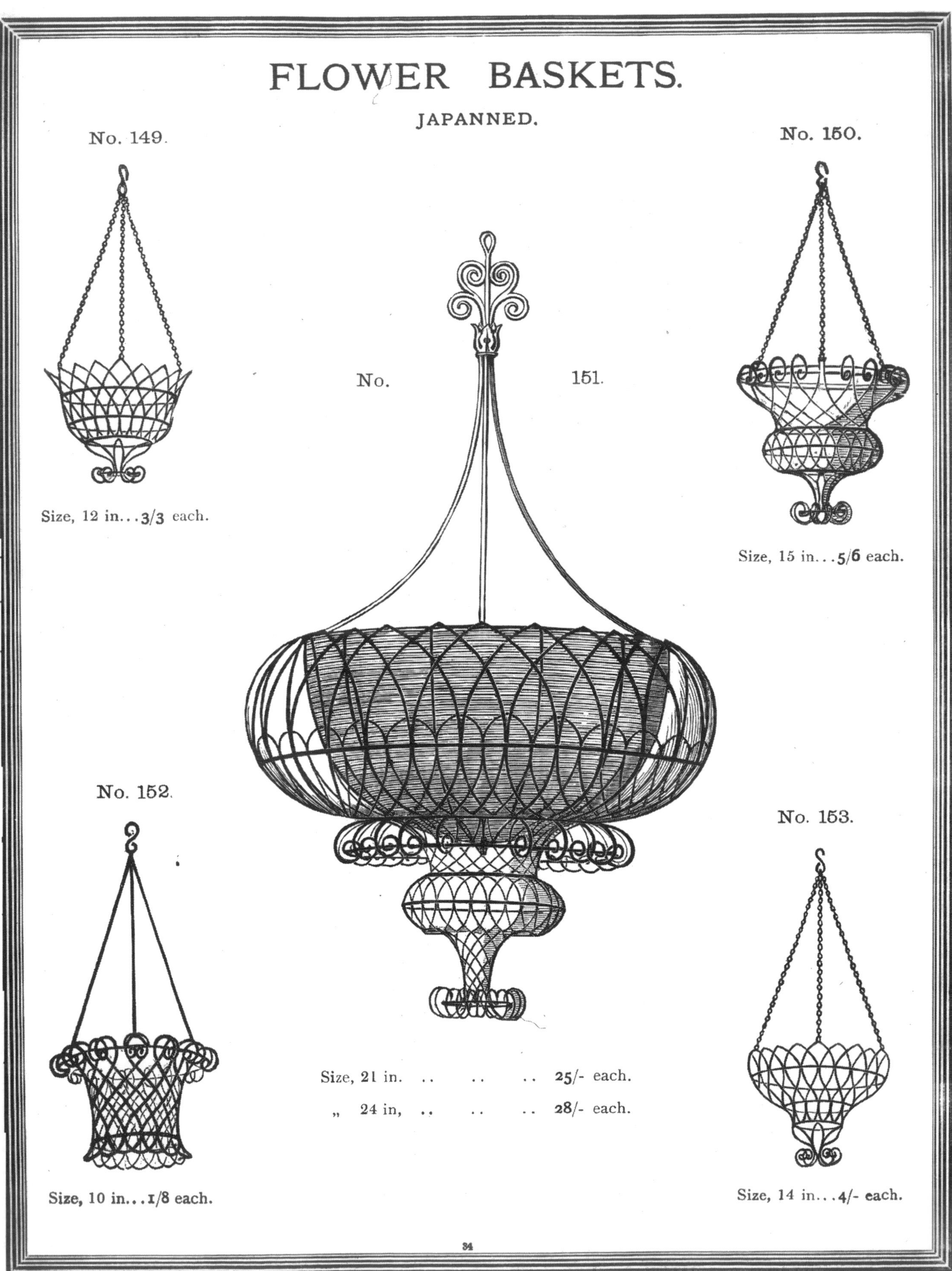

FLOWER BASKETS.

JAPANNED.

No. 149.

Size, 12 in. . . 3/3 each.

No. 150.

Size, 15 in. . . 5/6 each.

No. 151.

Size, 21 in. .. .. .. 25/- each.
„ 24 in, ... 28/- each.

No. 152.

Size, 10 in. . . 1/8 each.

No. 153.

Size, 14 in. . . 4/- each.

34

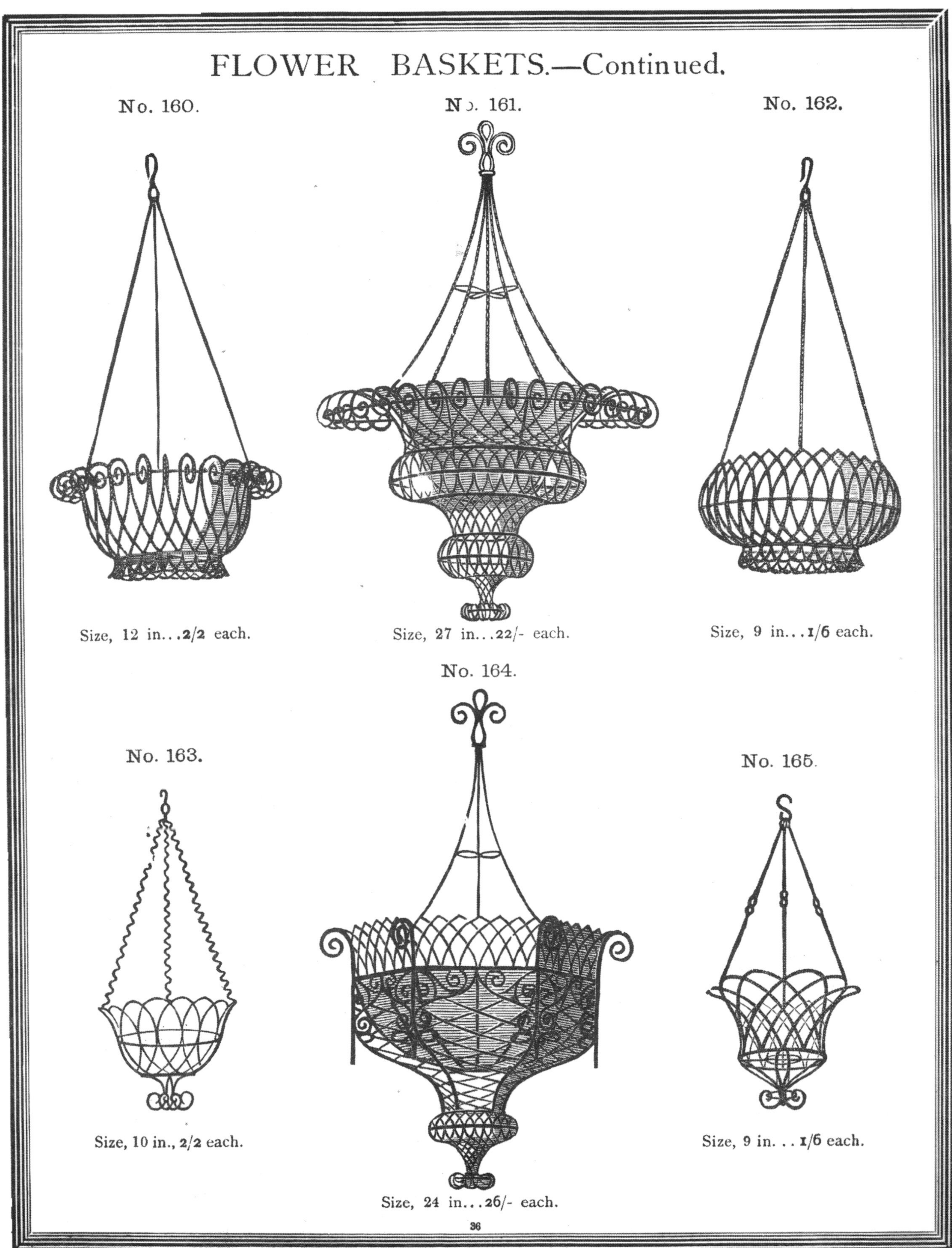
FLOWER BASKETS.—Continued.
No. 160.
No. 161.
No. 162.
Size, 12 in...2/2 each.
Size, 27 in...22/- each.
Size, 9 in...1/6 each.
No. 164.
No. 163.
No. 165.
Size, 10 in., 2/2 each.
Size, 9 in. . . 1/6 each.
Size, 24 in...26/- each.
36

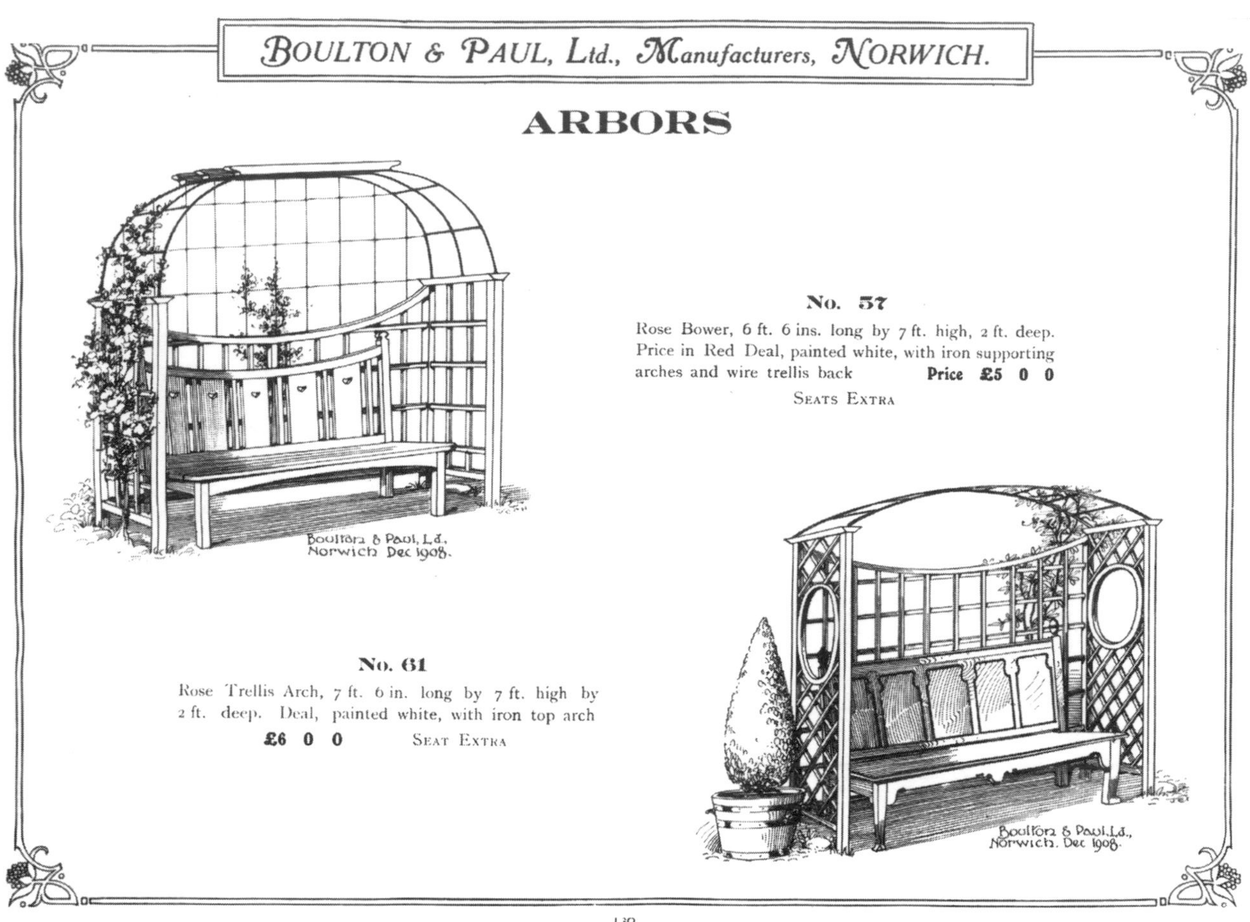

BOULTON & PAUL, Ltd., Manufacturers, NORWICH.

ARBORS

No. 57

Rose Bower, 6 ft. 6 ins. long by 7 ft. high, 2 ft. deep. Price in Red Deal, painted white, with iron supporting arches and wire trellis back **Price £5 0 0**

SEATS EXTRA

No. 61

Rose Trellis Arch, 7 ft. 6 in. long by 7 ft. high by 2 ft. deep. Deal, painted white, with iron top arch

£6 0 0 SEAT EXTRA

130

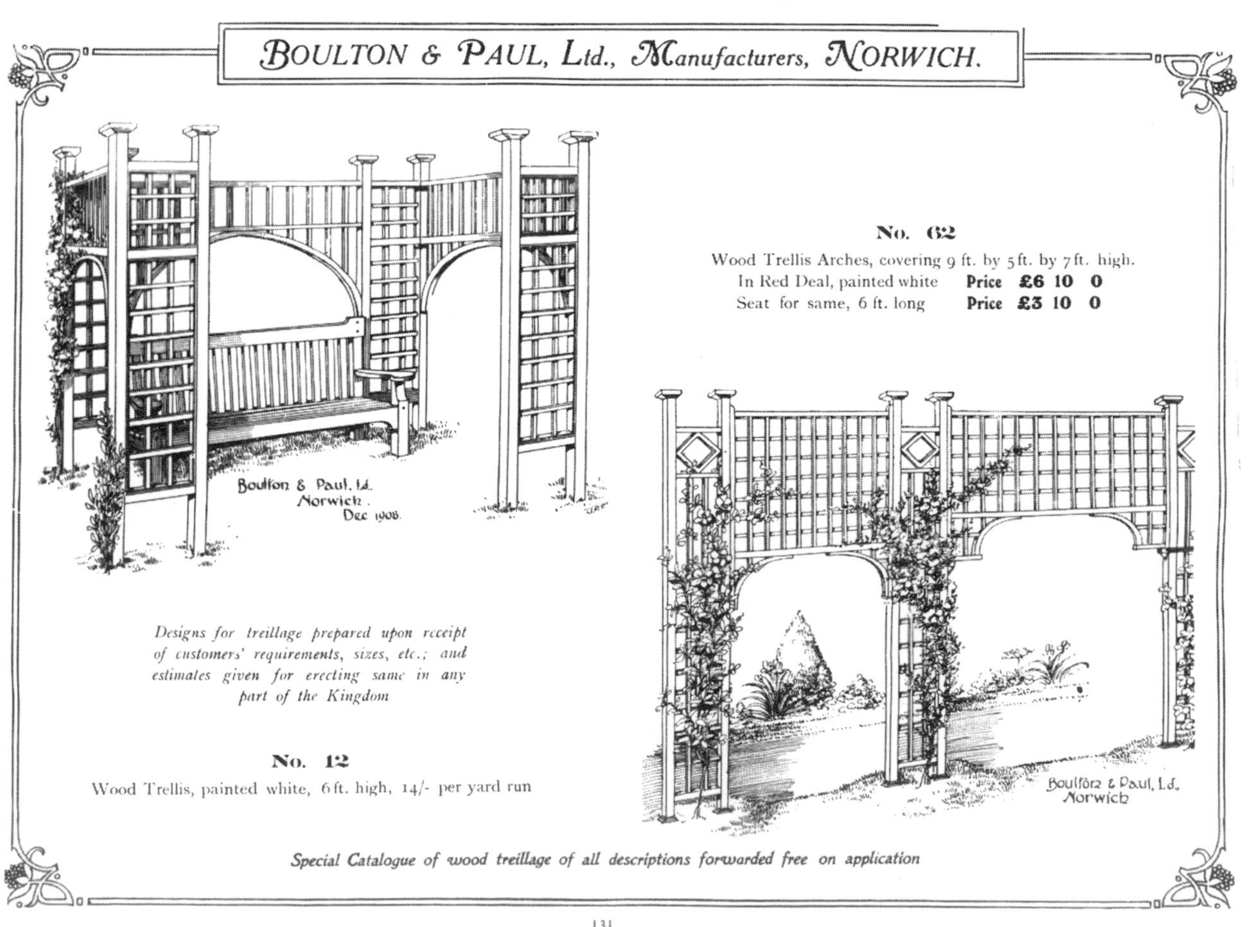

BOULTON & PAUL, Ltd., Manufacturers, NORWICH.

No. 62

Wood Trellis Arches, covering 9 ft. by 5 ft. by 7 ft. high.
In Red Deal, painted white **Price £6 10 0**
Seat for same, 6 ft. long **Price £3 10 0**

Designs for treillage prepared upon receipt of customers' requirements, sizes, etc.; and estimates given for erecting same in any part of the Kingdom

No. 12

Wood Trellis, painted white, 6 ft. high, 14/- per yard run

Special Catalogue of wood treillage of all descriptions forwarded free on application

131

Design No. 1.

3 ft. 0 in. High. 2 ft. 0 in. Wide.

Teak, oiled	£4 10 0
Oak, varnished	£4 0 0
Deal, painted	£2 17 6

With zinc lining fitted with 2 handles to lift out, 10/- extra.

Design No. 2.

2 ft. 6 in. High. 1 ft. 9 in. Wide.

This box can be taken to pieces if required.

Teak, oiled	£3 18 6
Oak, varnished	£3 10 0
Deal, painted	£2 12 6

With zinc lining fitted with 2 handles to lift out, 10/- extra.

Design No. 8 (Octagonal).

2 ft. 6 in. High. 2 ft. 9 in. Wide.

Teak, oiled	£4 18 6
Oak, varnished	£4 8 6
Deal, painted	£3 4 6

With zinc lining fitted with 2 handles to lift out, 15/- extra.

Design No. 9 (Square).

2 ft. 6 in. High. 2 ft. 9 in. Wide.

Teak, oiled	£4 10 0
Oak, varnished	£3 17 6
Deal, painted	£2 18 6

With zinc lining fitted with 2 handles to lift out, 12/- extra.

A MARBLE FOUNTAIN.

No. 3110.

Total Height ... ... 7 ft. 0 in.

Price in best hard Carrara Marble £63 0 0

Price does not include circular marble rim, for which price will be quoted according to dimensions required.

A MARBLE FOUNTAIN.

No. 8108.

Total Height	6 ft. 2 in.
Diameter of Basin	3 ft. 0 in.
Price in best hard Carrara Marble	£75 0 0

Price does not include circular marble rim, for which price will be quoted according to dimensions required.

VASES FOR TERRACES, STEPS, Etc.

ALL FINELY CARVED IN VICENZA STONE.

No. 650.
Height ... 1 ft. 6 in.
Price ... £4 4 0

No. 310.
Height ... 1 ft. 8 in.
Price .. £3 3 0

No. 110.
Height ... 1 ft. 8 in.
Price ... £3 3 0

No. 830.
Height ... 1 ft. 8 in.
Price ... £4 2 6

No. 160.
Height ... 1 ft. 6 ft.
Price ... £4 0 0

No. 730.
Height ... 1 ft. 6 in.
Price ... £3 18 6

WILLIAM COOPER, 755, Old Kent Road, London, S.E.
HORTICULTURAL PROVIDER.

Stone Fountains, Vases, Statuary, &c., &c.

This Stone has been manufactured for over 30 years, and being indurated by a special process, renders it in every respect equal in colour and durability to carved Portland Stone. It has for years stood the test of all weather without any sign of vegetation or decay. The illustrations given are from photographs of the actual article. I can strongly recommend this stone as being far superior in every way to Terra-cotta and Fireclay goods.

No. 524.
TRIPOD TAZZA FOUNTAIN.
Height, 6ft. 6in. Price £7.

No. 525.
TAZZA FOUNTAIN WITH OCTAGON BLOCK,
Height, 2ft. 6in. Plinth, 2ft.
Price, £5.

A Variety of other Designs kept in Stock in addition to those illustrated.

282

WILLIAM COOPER, 755, Old Kent Road, London, S.E.
HORTICULTURAL PROVIDER.

Stone Fountains, Vases, Statuary, &c.—*continued.*

No. 526.
BASKET BOY.
Height, 3ft. 3in.
Plinth, 12in.
Price £2 2s.

No. 527.
PANDORA.
Height, 3ft. 11in
Plinth, 12in.
Price, £3 5s.

No. 528.
HERON AND SHELL FOUNTAIN.
Height, 5ft. 6in. Price, £10 10s.

No. 529.
LARGE ACANTHUS VASE AND PEDESTAL.
Total Height, 3ft. 5in. Price £1 15s.

A Variety of other Designs kept in Stock in addition to those illustrated.

283

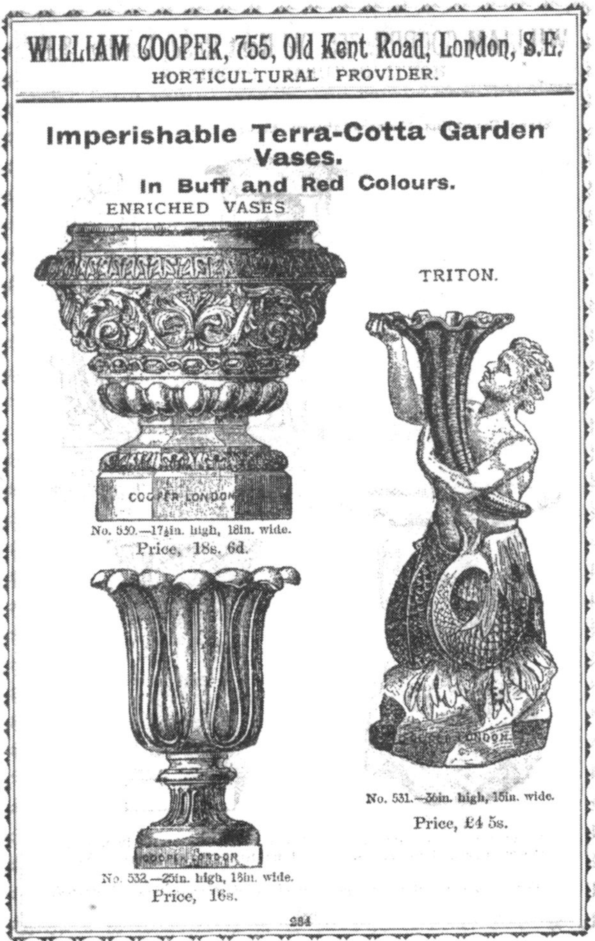

WILLIAM COOPER, 755, Old Kent Road, London, S.E.
HORTICULTURAL PROVIDER.

Imperishable Terra-Cotta Garden Vases.

In Buff and Red Colours.

ENRICHED VASES.

No. 530.—17½in. high, 18in. wide.
Price, 18s. 6d.

TRITON.

No. 531.—36in. high, 15in. wide.
Price, £4 5s.

No. 532.—25in. high, 18in. wide.
Price, 16s.

284

WILLIAM COOPER, 755, Old Kent Road, London, S.E.
HORTICULTURAL PROVIDER.

Imperishable Terra-Cotta Garden Vases—*continued.*

LION'S HEAD BOWL.

No. 533.—23½in. high, 30in. wide.
Price, £2.

LOTUS LEAF VASE.

No. 534.—17in. high, 20in. wide.
Price, 15s.

A large variety of other Designs, also Pedestals, kept in Stock.

285

Vase & Pedestal No. 9
36"
Tazza Pattern.
Width at Top 15½ ins. at Base 7¾ ins. and 10½ ins. high.
No. 10.
13 ins
10 ins
Bust Bracket.
7 ins
PLATE 312

VASES.

No. 17.

Size of Vase. 25 ins. diar. × 19 ins. high
" " Pedestal 19 " square × 26½ " "

No. 18.

Sizes of Vase. 25 ins. diar. × 19 ins. high.
" " Pedestal 19 " square × 26½ " "

PLATE 312A.

THE CLOVELLY DIAL.

Height ... ... 3 ft. 6 in.

Price complete including engraved brass dial and gnomon.

(A) with ordinary dial ... £8 10 0

(B) with special dial ... £10 10 0

If supplied without the base stone in two halves, 20/- less in each case.

THE BIDEFORD DIAL.

Height ... ... 3 ft. 8 in.
Diameter of base ... ... 3 ft. 0 in.

Price complete in Portland stone, including 12 in. Globe dial in best English gilt, specially made to suit locality £15 15 0

If with ordinary horizontal brass dial and gnomon £10 10 0

With special horizontal brass dial and gnomon £12 12 0

DESIGN NO. 5.

Similar in design to No. 1, but for 12 pairs only.
Height ... ... 15 ft. 0 in.
Made in Deal painted, post green, cote white, roof stained carbolineum, with strong underground supports.
Price £9 12 6

DESIGN NO. 6.

Similar in design to No. 3, but for 12 pairs only.

Made in Deal painted, post green, cote white, roof stained carbolineum, with strong underground supports.

Price £6 17 6

DESIGN NO. 7.

The cote is made from a strong Oak barrel, and roofed with oak shingles.
Total Height ... ... 15 ft. 0 in.
With base formed to bolt down to concrete bed.
Price, painted complete £9 9 0

DESIGN NO. 8.

To hold 8 pairs.

Post Deal, painted green, with strong framed supports, cote white, roof covered with lead.

Price £5 18 6

TREILLAGE (as is sufficiently obvious) is of French origin, and is, broadly speaking, an elaboration of the Trellis motif of which the illustrations herewith will give a far better notion than many words.

Treillage was in use as far back as the days of Pompeii, as some of the frescoes on the excavated walls had clear indications of Treillage in use as a garden decoration. In France the art of the Treillageur has long flourished, and much beautiful work of this description can be seen in that country. In Holland this form of decoration for gardens was much in vogue during the XVIIth and XVIIIth Centuries, and in a curious Dutch gardening book, "Der Netherlandtsen Hovenier," published in 1670, are many quaint illustrations of the Dutch Treillage of that day. Two examples from this book are illustrated herewith.

In England, Treillage was in vogue from the XVIth to the end of the XVIIIth Century. In 1761 Horace Walpole visited a friend of his "and drank tea in the arbour of treillage," which seems to have impressed him, as, some time after, he writes with reference to a Garden Bower he proposes to erect: "I have decided that the outside shall be of a treillage, which, however, I shall not commence till I have again seen some of old Louis' old-fashioned galanteries at Versailles."

Up to the last decade, very little attention was paid to Treillage in this country, except that from time to time travellers of taste and discrimination imported it into England, but the expense has been almost prohibitive, as the material itself is very fragile and difficult to pack, and, beyond this, it is advisable, although perhaps not absolutely necessary, that workmen who understand the work should accompany it for the erection and completion.

During the last few years, with the growing demand for this form of garden decoration, my resources for the designing and economical manufacture and erection of Treillage have enormously increased, and I am now able to carry out this work in all its branches, whether for outdoor or indoor use, much more economically than any Continental firms under equal conditions.

Treillage, as we may gather from the accompanying illustrations, is by no means a stock article—sold in lengths—such as the expanding trellis one obtains from an ironmonger's shop, but must be specially designed and made in each case to fill with character and distinction the spaces to be treated.

A DUTCH TREILLAGE ARBOUR
(from an old book published 1670).

The different ways in which Treillage may be used to advantage are almost too numerous to mention, but a few of the various forms are as follows :

As a Covering to Blank Walls where creepers are inadvisable or impossible.

As a Screen in the Garden to divide one part from another.

For Garden Temples, Pergolas, Arches, Roseries, Arbours, etc.

For the interior Decoration of Conservatories, Winter Gardens, Loggias, Verandahs, Balconies, etc., and a variety of other purposes.

EXAMPLES OF DUTCH TREILLAGE
(from an old book published 1670).

It is, of course, impossible to issue a comprehensive catalogue and price list of this work, and the examples here shown are merely to illustrate what has been and may be done, and are, for the most part, of work which I have carried out in various parts of the country.

In nearly every case where a scheme of Treillage is under consideration, it is advisable that the site should be inspected, and a design prepared to fill the needs of the case, and for this purpose I am always willing to send representatives to all parts of the country, and to prepare special designs free of charge.

TREILLAGE VERANDAHS.

No. 1. With glass roof and treillage parapet above eaves.

No. 2. With zinc, copper, lead or Willesden canvas roof.

Illustrations of various types of treillage verandahs, for which special quotations will be given according to width, length and material required.

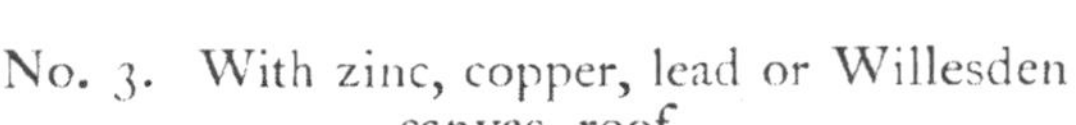

No. 3. With zinc, copper, lead or Willesden canvas roof.

No. 4. With wood shingle roof.

The roofs of any of these designs can be of glass, wood shingles, lead, zinc, copper or Willesden canvas, painted.

ARCHITECTURAL GARDEN TREILLAGE.

A GARDEN ENTRANCE IN TREILLAGE.

TREILLAGE SCREEN AND NICHE FOR STATUE.

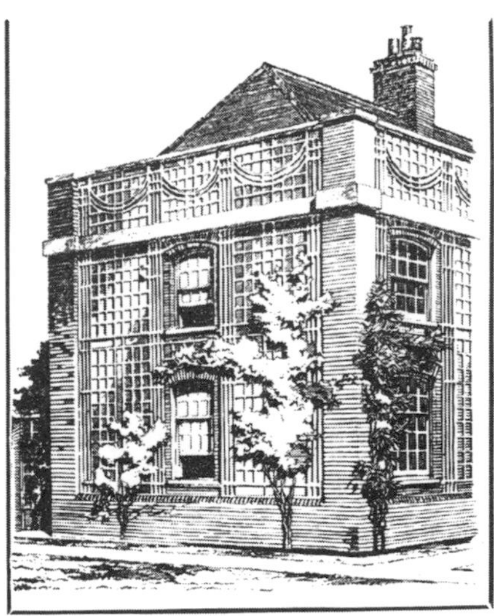

TREILLAGE ON BLANK WALLS OF HOUSE.

TREILLAGE RECESS FOR SEAT, WITH DOMED ROOF.

ORNAMENTAL WIRE PORCHES, &c.

No. 36a.

Very magnificent Column Arch, of very imposing appearance, painted or galvanized.

SIZES AND PRICES.

Inside measure out of ground.

High.	Span.	Price.
7 ft. 0 in.	4 ft. 0 in.	**80/-** each.
7 ft. 6 in.	4 ft. 6 in.	**87/-** ,,
8 ft. 0 in.	5 ft. 0 in.	**95/-** ,,

Wire Summer Houses are far preferable to wooden ones, as they harbour no insects.

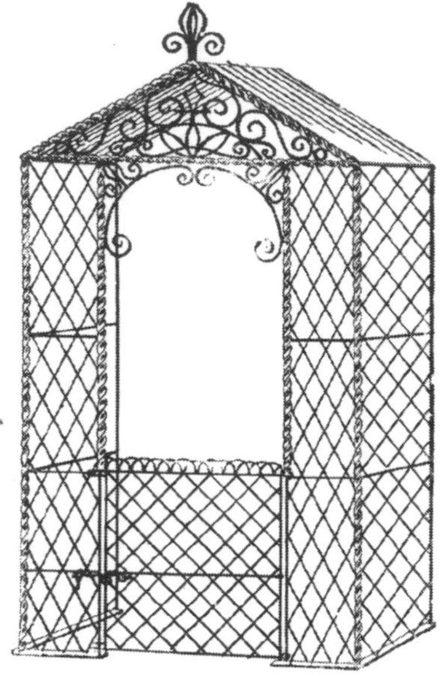

No. 612. **No. 615.**

These Ornamental Porticoes for Doorways are now much approved. When covered with creeping plants they present a very handsome appearance, and are a great addition to the front of a house. Being covered with *zinc at top* they effectually prevent rain, &c., beating into the hall during wet weather, and form an agreeable shelter.

SIZES AND PRICES.

FLAT ZINC TOP.

At Sides High	At Back Span.	Wide.	Painted Green.	Galvanized.
7ft. 6in.	4ft. 6in.	2ft. 0in.	**56/-**	**60/-** each.
8ft. 0in.	5ft. 0in.	2ft. 6in.	**66/-**	**72/-** ,,
8ft. 6in.	5ft. 6in.	3ft. 0in.	**80/-**	**86/-** ,,

SIZES AND PRICES.

SLOPE ZINC TOP, WITHOUT GATE.

At Sides High	At Back Span.	Wide.	Painted Green.	Galvanized.
7ft. 6in.	4ft. 6in.	2ft. 0in.	**58/-**	**62/-** each.
8ft. 0in.	5ft. 0in.	2ft. 6in.	**68/-**	**74/-** ,,
8ft. 6in.	5ft. 6in.	3ft. 0in.	**82/-**	**89/-** ,,

Wicket gate can be fixed to either of the above patterns at an advance of **7/6** on each. See illustration, No. 615. The width of all the front panels in both patterns is 9 inches.

Patterns No. 612 and 615 also make magnificent Summer Houses at an extremely low price. Either pattern can be had without zinc top, at a reduction of **4/-** each, but will be sent with zinc top in all cases, unless ordered otherwise.

No. 611.

No. 614.

No. 616.

Ornamental patterns, suitable for windows or porches, or, if placed against a wall, for summer houses. Both patterns are made at the same price.

Very ornamental pattern, suitable for window or porch, or, if placed against a wall, for a summer house.

At Back High.	Span.	Depth of Trellis.	Nos. 611 and 614. Painted.	Nos. 611 and 614. Galvanized.	No. 616. Painted.	No. 616. Galvanized.
7 ft. 0 in.	4 ft. 0 in.	1 ft. 0 in.	**30/-**	**36/-**	**44/-**	**50/-** each.
7 ft. 6 in.	4 ft. 6 in.	1 ft. 6 in.	**36/6**	**44/6**	**54/-**	**64/6** ,,
8 ft. 0 in.	4 ft. 6 in.	2 ft. 0 in.	**43/-**	**53/-**	**65/-**	**74/6** ,,

Zinc or Galvanized Iron Roofs can be fitted to these if required. Prices on application. Made in parts for convenience of transit, and easily fitted together.

ORNAMENTAL ROSE TEMPLES, GARDEN ARCHES, Etc.

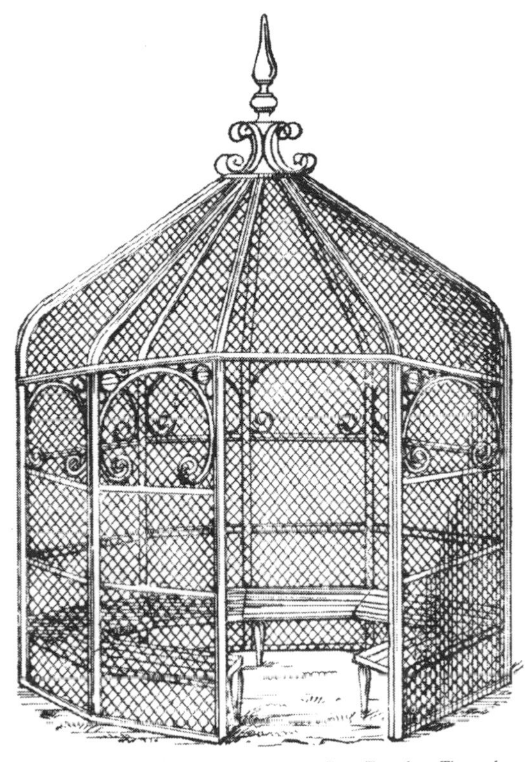

No. 35. Octagon Garden Bower, Summer-house or Rose Temple. These elegant bowers are a great acquisition to gardens, not only as summer-houses, but as temples for training roses or any kind of creeper. They have eight sides, which take to pieces in segments, rendering them very portable for transit and easy to remove or put together. They are not affected by weather, the wrought-iron frame work being painted and the wirework of strong diagonal mesh, made of hard wire and galvanized after made. They are far preferable to wooden houses, as the plants climb more easily and they harbour no insects. Seats extra, according to requirements.

SIZES AND PRICES.

8 ft. 6 in. high,	6 ft. 0 in. diam.	.. ..	**£12 12 0** each.
9 ft. 6 in. ,,	7 ft. 0 in. ,,	.. ..	**15 5 0** ,,
11 ft. 6 in. ,,	8 ft. 6 in. ,,	.. ..	**18 12 0** ,,

Any size can be made to order.

N.B.—The above can readily be adapted for an OUT-DOOR AVIARY at moderate cost, by the addition of zinc roof and finer mesh wirework—either diagonal or straight mesh pattern: or cheaper still, with wire netting—mesh according to the size of birds it is intended for. We shall be pleased to quote prices, including door with lock and key, perches, feeding troughs, &c., complete, on receipt of particulars giving sizes, &c.

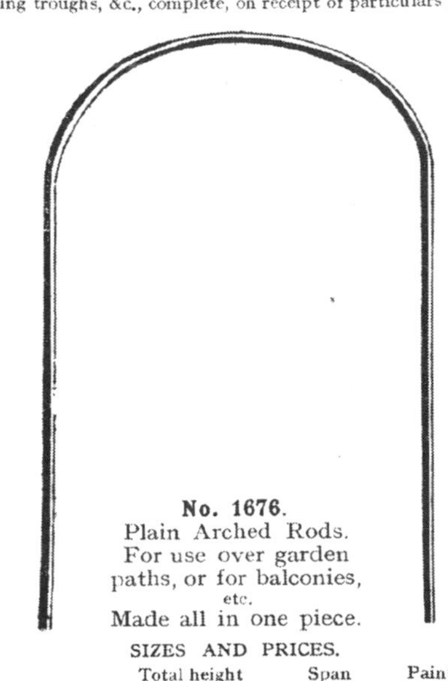

No. 1676.
Plain Arched Rods.
For use over garden paths, or for balconies, etc.
Made all in one piece.

SIZES AND PRICES.

	Total height	Span	Painted	Galvanized
Three-eighth inch rod	8 ft. 0 in.	4 ft. 0 in.	**3/-**	**4/8** each.
,, ,, ,,	8 ft. 6 in.	4 ft. 6 in.	**3/8**	**5/8** ,,
Half-inch rod ..	8 ft. 0 in.	4 ft. 0 in.	**4/4**	**6/4** ,,
,, ,, ..	9 ft. 0 in.	5 ft. 0 in.	**5/4**	**7/8** ,,

No. 963. Ornamental Rosary. The above engraving represents a series of continuous arches, forming an elegant Rosary. They can be adapted to any shape required, either along a winding path, in a straight line, or in a circle as shown. They are made of strong wrought-iron, and fitted with strong double-pronged feet for fixing securely in the ground, and fitted together with nuts and bolts, which are included. Can be fixed by any inexperienced labourer.

SIZES AND PRICES—Painted or Galvanized. For not less than six arches at a time, without baskets.

Height inside out of ground	Span	Each arch	Height inside out of ground	Span	Each arch
7 ft. 0 in.	4 ft. 0 in.	**£1 11 0**	8 ft. 0 in.	5 ft. 0 in.	**£2 2 0**
7 ft. 6 in.	4 ft. 6 in.	**1 15 0**	8 ft. 6 in.	5 ft. 6 in.	**2 10 0**

If a cheaper article is required, arches can be supplied made on the same plan, but filled in with plain corrugated diagonal wire lattice instead of ornamental wirework, at about 25 per cent. less in cost.

For Patterns and Prices of our Wire Baskets, see pages 87 91.

No. 1672. Very Ornamental Porch, Garden Arch, or Summer-house. It is made in parts for convenience of transit, and is easily fixed or removed by any inexperienced labourer. If used as a summer-house, the back can be fitted with corrugated diagonal mesh wire lattice at an advance of **20/-**, **27/-**, and **34/-** each, according to size.

SIZES AND PRICES.

Height at back	Span at back	Depth back to front.	Painted	Galvanized
7 ft. 6 in.	4 ft. 6 in.	2 ft. 0 in.	**£4 4 0**	**£4 13 0**
8 ft. 0 in.	5 ft. 0 in.	3 ft. 0 in.	**5 3 0**	**5 16 0**
8 ft. 6 in.	5 ft. 6 in.	4 ft. 0 in.	**6 6 0**	**7 3 0**

Zinc or galvanized iron roof can be fitted if required at small extra charge.

THE KNOTTING ARCH.

Consisting of two square posts with moulded caps, connected by wrought iron arch bar.

	Deal painted.	Oak oiled.
4 ft. 0 in. between posts	25/-	35/-
5 ft. 0 in. ,, ,,	27/6	37/6
6 ft. 0 in. ,, ,,	28/6	38 6
8 ft. 0 in. ,, ,,	29/6	40/-

THE HARROLD ARCH.

Consisting of two square posts connected by a wrought iron arch bar, with scroll brackets.

	Deal painted.	Oak oiled.
4 ft. 0 in. between posts	38/-	48/-
5 ft. 0 in. ,, ,,	40/-	50/-
6 ft. 0 in. ,, ,,	42/-	52/-
8 ft. 0 in. ,, ,,	45/-	55/-

THE STREATLEY ARCH.

Consisting of two posts with moulded caps, connected with a double wrought iron arch.

	Deal.	Oak.
4 ft. 0 in. between posts	55/-	65/-
5 ft. 0 in. ,, ,,	56/-	66/-
6 ft. 0 in. ,, ,,	57/6	67/6
8 ft. 0 in. ,, ,,	60/-	70/-

THE ICKWELL ARCH.

Consisting of four posts connected with wrought iron arch and ornamental scroll brackets.

	Deal.	Oak.
4 ft. 0 in. between posts	90/-	110/-
5 ft. 0 in. ,, ,,	95/-	115/-
6 ft. 0 in. ,, ,,	100/-	120/-
8 ft. 0 in. ,, ,,	105/-	125/-

ROSE TEMPLES, ARCHES FOR BALCONIES, GARDEN PATHS, &c.

No. 961. OCTAGONAL ROSE TEMPLE OR SUMMER-HOUSE.

These Temples, when set up, present an elegant appearance, and no garden is complete without them. They are made in sections, but are so simply constructed that they can be easily taken to pieces and put together again by any ordinary labourer. The wrought-iron framework is painted and covered with strong diagonal mesh wire trellis, galvanized. The creeping plants climb very quickly through the wire trellis and when covered with foliage they form a very grateful retreat in summer, while they harbour no insects as do wooden houses. Seats and tables extra, according to requirements.

SIZES AND PRICES.

8 ft. 6 in. high, 6 ft. diam., **£14 0 0** 11 ft. 6 in. high, 8 ft. 6 in. diam., **£20 14 0**
9 ft. 6 in. „ 7 ft. „ **16 12 0** 13 ft. 6 in. „ 10 ft. „ **24 12 0**

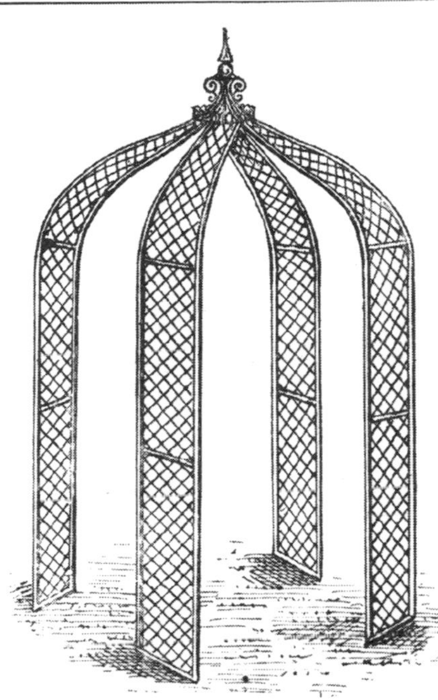

No. 1674. DOUBLE ARCHWAY, SPECIALLY ADAPTED FOR CROSS PATHS.

The above style of garden arch, when erected over cross paths or in the centre of a lawn, will be found a great addition to the garden. When covered with creeping plants or roses it offers a very striking and most unique appearance, and is greatly admired. They are very strong and portable, and easily fitted together by any inexperienced labourer in a few moments.

Sizes and Prices. Galvanized or painted green.

7 ft. high, above ground, 5 ft. span, **40/-** 8 ft. high, above ground, 6 ft. span, **50/-**
9 ft. high, above ground, 7 ft. span, **65/-**

The widths of trellis is 12 ins., 12 ins. and 15 ins. respectively at base.

No. 1675. CONTINUOUS FLAT ARCHES FOR BALCONIES.

Galvanized or painted any plain colour.

Sizes and Prices of **each arch** when three or more are supplied, as shown above.

4 ft. 6 in. high inside, 3 ft. span inside, **24/-** 6 ft. high inside, 4 ft. span inside, **30/-**
5 ft. „ 3 ft. 6 in. „ **26/6** 7 ft. „ 4 ft. 6 in. „ **33/6**

No. 1676. CONTINUOUS FLAT ARCHES FOR BALCONIES.

Galvanized or painted any plain colour.

Sizes and Prices of **each arch**, when three or more are supplied, as shown above.

4 ft. 6 in. high, inside, 3 ft. span, inside, **18/-** 6 ft. high, inside, 4 ft. span, inside, **24/-**
5 ft. „ 3 ft. 6 in. „ **20/6** 7 ft. „ 4 ft. 6 in. „ **28/-**

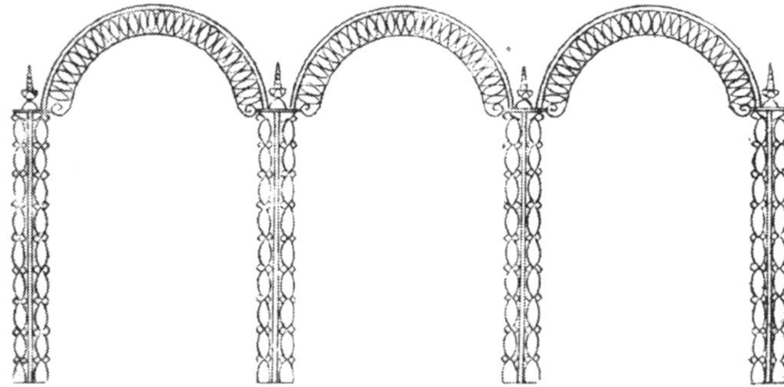

No. 1677. CONTINUOUS FLAT-ARCHES FOR BALCONIES.

Galvanized or painted any plain colour.

Sizes and Prices of **each arch**, when three or more are ordered, as shown above.

4 ft. 6 in. high inside, 3 ft. span inside, **14/-** 6 ft. high inside, 4 ft. span inside, **18/8**
5 ft. „ 3 ft. 6 in. „ **16/-** 7 ft. „ 4 ft. 6 in. „ **21/6**

No. 1678. CONTINUOUS IRON ROD ARCHES.

Sizes and Prices of **each arch**, when three or more, as shown above, are supplied.

		Painted	Galvanized
4 ft. 6 in. high,	3 ft. 0 in. span,	**9/6**	**11/-**
5 ft. „	3 ft. 6 in. „	**10/-**	**12/-**
6 ft. „	4 ft. 0 in. „	**11/6**	**14/-**
7 ft. „	4 ft. 6 in. „	**13/-**	**15/6**

All the above Balcony Arches are made in parts and fitted together with nuts and bolts which are sent for the purpose. Single arches are charged 20 per cent. extra. Baskets extra according to patterns. See FLOWER BASKETS Section.

GARDEN ARCHES, GALVANIZED OR PAINTED.

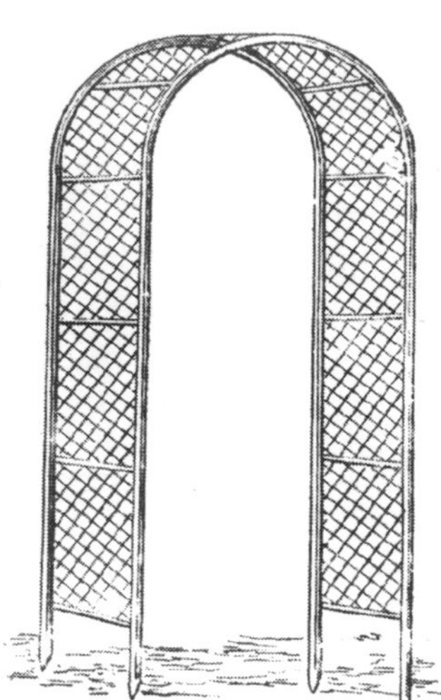

No. 49. A plain, useful arch, made with plain iron frame, fitted with diamond lattice.

Out of Ground High	Span	Wide	Common Each	Strong Each	Extra Strong Each
7ft. 0in.	4ft. 0in.	1ft. 0in.	**6/8**	**9/-**	**12/8**
7ft. 0in.	4ft. 0in.	1ft. 3in.	**7/6**	**11/-**	**15/-**
7ft. 0in.	4ft. 0in.	1ft. 6in.	**9/2**	**13/2**	**17/4**
7ft. 0in.	4ft. 0in.	2ft. 0in.	**13/-**	**19/4**	**24/6**
7ft. 6in.	4ft. 6in.	1ft. 0in.	—	**11/6**	**16/-**
7ft. 6in.	4ft. 6in.	1ft. 6in.	—	**14/-**	**18/6**
7ft. 6in.	4ft. 6in.	2ft. 0in.	—	**20/6**	**26/6**
8ft. 0in.	5ft. 0in.	1ft. 0in.	—	**11/4**	**16/-**
8ft. 0in.	5ft. 0in.	1ft. 6in.	—	**16/6**	**23/4**
8ft. 0in.	5ft. 0in.	2ft. 0in.	—	**22/-**	**31/4**

No. 49a. A lighter and commoner Arch, 7 ft. × 4 ft. × 1 ft. Price **5/2** each.

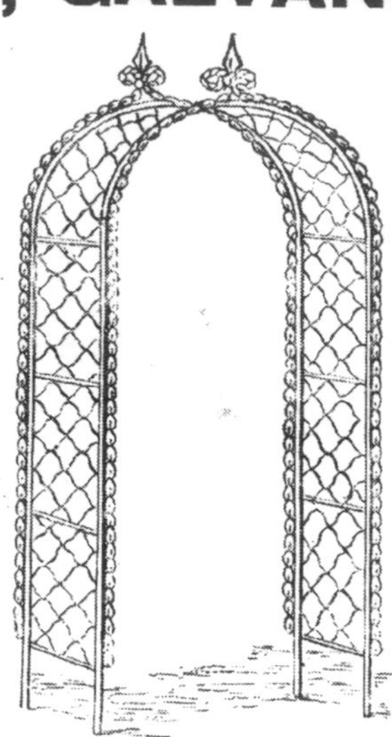

No. 63. A useful ornamental Arch, filled in with diamond lattice, and fitted with spiral iron border.

Out of Ground High	Span	Wide	Common Each	Strong Each	Extra Strong Each
7ft. 0in.	4ft. 0in.	1ft. 0in.	**8/8**	**11/-**	**15/8**
7ft. 0in.	4ft. 0in.	1ft. 3in.	**9/6**	**13/-**	**18/6**
7ft. 0in.	4ft. 0in.	1ft. 6in.	**11/2**	**15/4**	**21/-**
7ft. 0in.	4ft. 0in.	2ft. 0in.	**15/6**	**20/-**	**28/-**
7ft. 6in.	4ft. 6in.	1ft. 0in.	—	**13/8**	**19/-**
7ft. 6in.	4ft. 6in.	1ft. 6in.	—	**16/6**	**21/6**
7ft. 6in.	4ft. 6in.	2ft. 0in.	—	**22/8**	**30/-**
8ft. 0in.	5ft. 0in.	1ft. 0in.	—	**14/6**	**21/-**
8ft. 0in.	5ft. 0in.	1ft. 6in.	—	**19/8**	**28/-**
8ft. 0in.	5ft. 0in.	2ft. 0in.	—	**26/-**	**38/-**

No. 63a. A lighter and commoner Arch, 7 ft. × 4 ft. × 1 ft. Price **7/2** each.

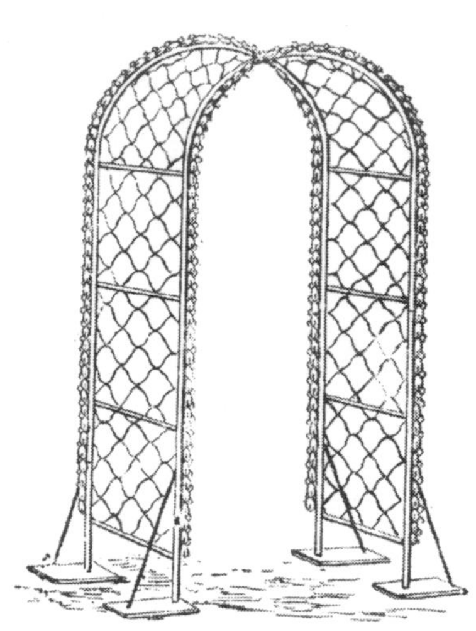

No. 600. Extra strong and substantial Archways, with plate feet bases, a great advantage, having a much firmer hold in the ground than the ordinary straight pronged feet.

Out of Ground High	Span	Wide	Strong Each	Extra Strong Each
7 ft. 0 in.	4 ft. 0 in.	1 ft. 0 in.	**16/6**	**26/6**
7 ft. 0 in.	4 ft. 0 in.	1 ft. 6 in.	**25/-**	**34/6**
7 ft. 0 in.	4 ft. 0 in.	2 ft. 0 in.	**30/-**	**43/-**
7 ft. 6 in.	4 ft. 6 in.	1 ft. 6 in.	**26/-**	**37/-**
7 ft. 6 in.	4 ft. 6 in.	2 ft. 0 in.	**36/6**	**46/6**
8 ft. 0 in.	5 ft. 0 in.	1 ft. 6 in.	**32/6**	**41/-**
8 ft. 0 in.	5 ft. 0 in.	2 ft. 0 in.	**40/-**	**53/-**
8 ft. 0 in.	5 ft. 0 in.	3 ft. 0 in.	**58/-**	**73/-**

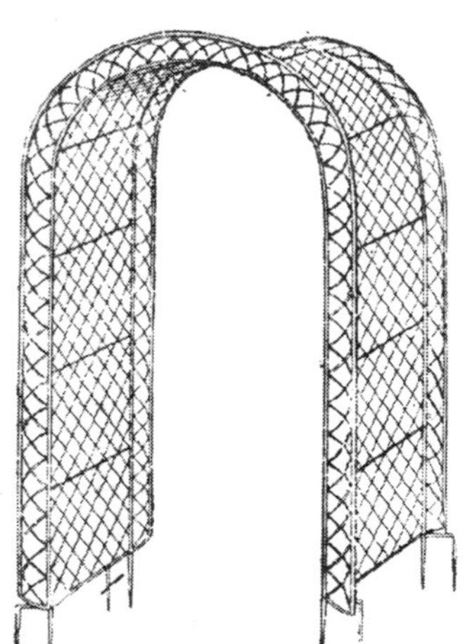

No. 302. Ornamental Arch, with double front.

Sizes and Prices—Extra strong.

Out of Ground High	Inside Measure. Span	Wide	Each
7 ft. 0 in.	4 ft. 0 in.	1 ft. 0 in.	**20/-**
7 ft. 0 in.	4 ft. 0 in.	1 ft. 6 in.	**33/6**
7 ft. 0 in.	4 ft. 0 in.	2 ft. 0 in.	**40/-**
7 ft. 0 in.	4 ft. 0 in.	3 ft. 0 in.	**56/-**
7 ft. 6 in.	4 ft. 6 in.	1 ft. 6 in.	**37/6**
7 ft. 6 in.	4 ft. 6 in.	2 ft. 0 in.	**48/-**
7 ft. 6 in.	4 ft. 6 in.	3 ft. 0 in.	**67/-**
8 ft. 0 in.	5 ft. 0 in.	1 ft. 6 in.	**43/-**
8 ft. 0 in.	5 ft. 0 in.	2 ft. 0 in.	**53/6**
8 ft. 0 in.	5 ft. 0 in.	3 ft. 0 in.	**73/6**

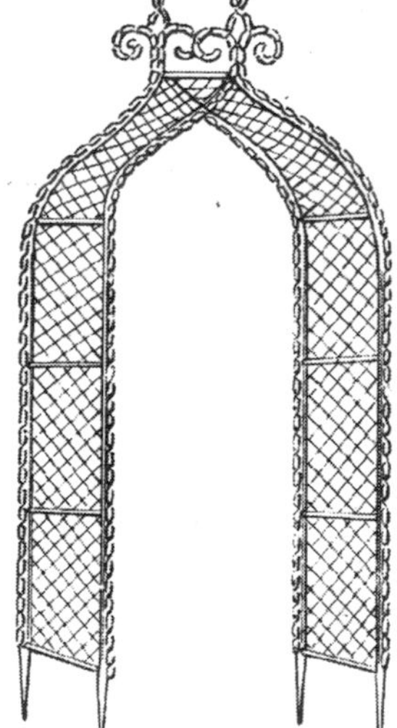

No. 601. Gothic Arch, with ornamental spiral iron all round.

Out of Ground High	Span	Wide	Strong Each	Extra Strong Each
7 ft. 6 in.	4 ft. 0 in.	1 ft. 0 in.	**14/8**	**20/6**
7 ft. 6 in.	4 ft. 0 in.	1 ft. 6 in.	**22/-**	**26/-**
7 ft. 6 in.	4 ft. 0 in.	2 ft. 0 in.	**28/6**	**33/-**
8 ft. 0 in.	4 ft. 6 in.	1 ft. 0 in.	**18/6**	**22/6**
8 ft. 0 in.	4 ft. 6 in.	1 ft. 6 in.	**23/6**	**28/-**
8 ft. 0 in.	4 ft. 6 in.	2 ft. 0 in.	**30/6**	**35/-**
8 ft. 6 in.	5 ft. 0 in.	1 ft. 0 in.	**20/6**	**24/6**
8 ft. 6 in.	5 ft. 0 in.	1 ft. 6 in.	**27/-**	**31/-**
8 ft. 6 in.	5 ft. 0 in.	2 ft. 0 in.	**36/-**	**40/6**

No. 606. Ornamental Gothic Arch, with double front.

Sizes and Prices—Extra strong.

Out of Ground High	Inside Measure. Span	Wide	Each
7 ft. 6 in.	4 ft. 0 in.	1 ft. 6 in.	**37/-**
7 ft. 6 in.	4 ft. 0 in.	2 ft. 0 in.	**45/-**
7 ft. 6 in.	4 ft. 0 in.	3 ft. 0 in.	**62/-**
8 ft. 0 in.	4 ft. 6 in.	1 ft. 6 in.	**42/6**
8 ft. 0 in.	4 ft. 6 in.	2 ft. 0 in.	**52/-**
8 ft. 0 in.	4 ft. 6 in.	3 ft. 0 in.	**72/-**
8 ft. 6 in.	5 ft. 0 in.	1 ft. 6 in.	**46/-**
8 ft. 6 in.	5 ft. 0 in.	2 ft. 0 in.	**60/-**
8 ft. 6 in.	5 ft. 0 in.	3 ft. 0 in.	**80/-**

All patterns of Arches can be made other sizes as required. For convenience of transit all the above Arches are made in halves, and fitted together with nuts and bolts, which are included.

ORNAMENTAL ARCHWAYS, GALVANIZED OR PAINTED.

No. 604. Ornamental Column Arch.

Sizes and prices—Inside measure.

Out of Ground High	Span		
7 ft. 0 in.	4 ft. 0 in.	..	**43/-** each.
7 ft. 6 in.	4 ft. 6 in.	..	**50/-** ,,
8 ft. 0 in.	5 ft. 0 in.	..	**63/-** ,,

No. 608. Extra Strong Wrought-iron Garden Arch.

This Arch is much recommended for hard wear, as, being made of very strong material all through, there are no small wires that can become bent or misplaced, while the price will be found extremely low.

Out of Ground High	Span	Wide	Painted Green Each	Galvanized Each
7 ft. 0 in.	4 ft. 0 in.	1 ft. 0 in.	**14/6**	**18/-**
7 ft. 6 in.	4 ft. 6 in.	1 ft. 6 in.	**16/8**	**22/-**
8 ft. 0 in.	5 ft. 0 in.	2 ft. 0 in.	**24/8**	**30/-**

No. 613. Flat Archways.

To fix against the wall to train flowers round windows, over doorways, etc.

Out of Ground High	Span		
7 ft. 0 in.	3 ft. 6 in.	..	**26/-** each.
7 ft. 6 in.	4 ft. 0 in.	..	**29/-** ,,
8 ft. 0 in.	4 ft. 6 in.	..	**33/4** ,,

The panels of arches are 9 inches wide.

No. 609. Extra Strong Garden Arch or Porch.

To stand over doorway, with ornamental front projecting outwards.

Inside Measures

Out of Ground High	Span	Wide	Each
7 ft. 0 in.	4 ft. 0 in.	1 ft. 6 in.	**40/-**
7 ft. 0 in.	4 ft. 0 in.	2 ft. 0 in.	**45/-**
7 ft. 0 in.	4 ft. 0 in.	3 ft. 0 in.	**56/-**
7 ft. 3 in.	4 ft. 6 in.	1 ft. 6 in.	**44/-**
7 ft. 3 in.	4 ft. 6 in.	2 ft. 0 in.	**48/-**
7 ft. 3 in.	4 ft. 6 in.	3 ft. 0 in.	**60/-**
7 ft. 6 in.	5 ft. 0 in.	1 ft. 6 in.	**52/-**
7 ft. 6 in.	5 ft. 0 in.	2 ft. 0 in.	**56/-**
7 ft. 6 in.	5 ft. 0 in.	3 ft. 0 in.	**66/6**

No. 36. Ornamental Column Arch.

Sizes and prices—Inside measure.

Out of Ground	Span		
7 ft. 0 in.	4 ft. 0 in.	..	**50/-** each.
7 ft. 6 in.	4 ft. 6 in.	..	**53/6** ,,
8 ft. 0 in.	5 ft. 0 in.	..	**57/-** ,,

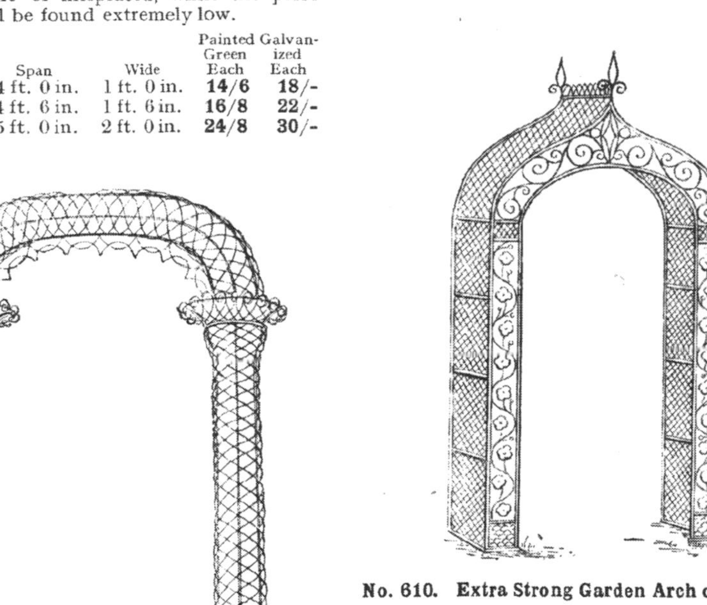

No. 610. Extra Strong Garden Arch or Porch.

To stand over doorway, made with twisted or spiral iron and wire.

Sizes and prices—Inside measure at back.

Out of Ground High	Span	Wide	Each
7 ft. 0 in.	4 ft. 0 in.	1 ft. 6 in.	**60/-**
7 ft. 0 in.	4 ft. 0 in.	2 ft. 0 in.	**70/-**
7 ft. 0 in.	4 ft. 0 in.	3 ft. 0 in.	**84/-**
7 ft. 3 in.	4 ft. 6 in.	1 ft. 6 in.	**64/-**
7 ft. 3 in.	4 ft. 6 in.	2 ft. 0 in.	**73/6**
7 ft. 3 in.	4 ft. 6 in.	3 ft. 0 in.	**90/-**
7 ft. 6 in.	5 ft. 0 in.	1 ft. 6 in.	**68/-**
7 ft. 6 in.	5 ft. 0 in.	2 ft. 0 in.	**76/6**
7 ft. 6 in.	5 ft. 0 in.	3 ft. 0 in.	**94/-**

All patterns of Arches can be made any sizes required. For convenience of transit all Arches are made in parts and fitted together with nuts and bolts, which are included in above prices.

LATEST DESIGNS IN RUSTIC WORK.

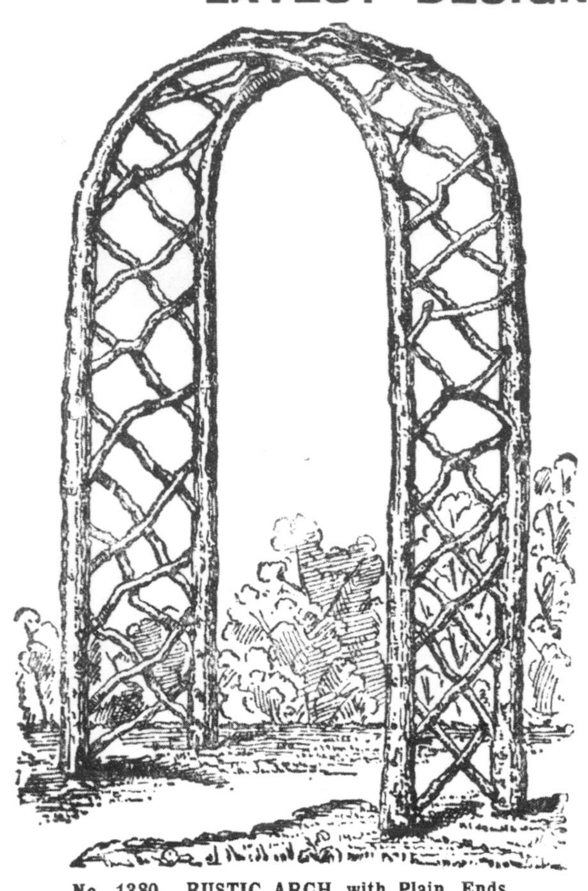

No. 1380. RUSTIC ARCH with Plain Ends.
Stained with best oil stain and varnished two coats. 8 ft. high, 4 ft. span, 12 in. deep. Price **30/-** each. Larger sizes—for every additional 3 in. across path, **1/-**, and for every additional 3 in. in depth, **6/-** extra.

No. 1381. RUSTIC ARCH, with Ornamental Ends.
Stained best oil stain and varnished two coats. 8 ft. high, 4 ft. span, 12 in. deep. Price **40/-** each. Larger sizes—for every additional 3 in. across path, **1/-**, and for every additional 3 in depth, **6/-** extra.

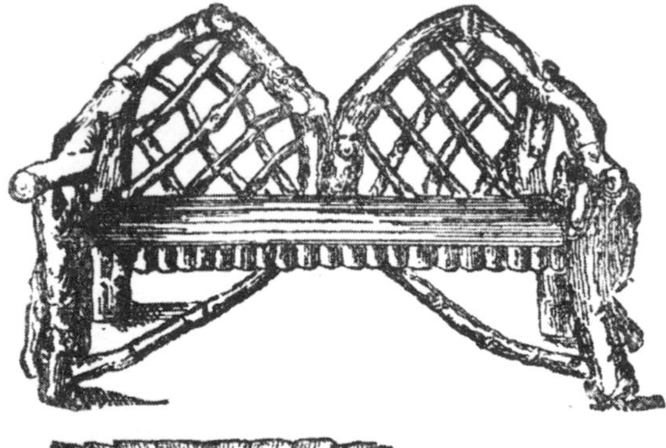

No. 1382.
RUSTIC GARDEN SEAT.
Stained best oil stain and varnished two coats. 5 ft. long, hollow bottom, strong and comfortable. Best yellow deal laths and oak rustic wood, **9/-** per ft. Superior ditto, hard wood, pitch pine laths, **11/-** per ft. run.

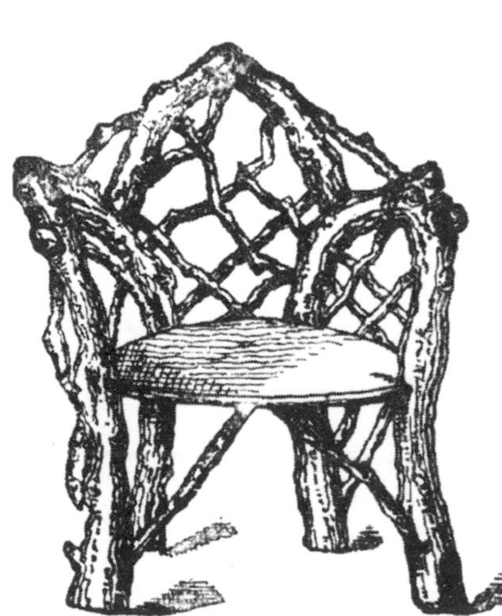

No. 1383. RUSTIC ARM CHAIR.
Elm bottom, very comfortable. In oak rustic wood, **28/-**. In hard rustic wood, **32/-**. Without arms, No. 1384, strongly made, **15/6**

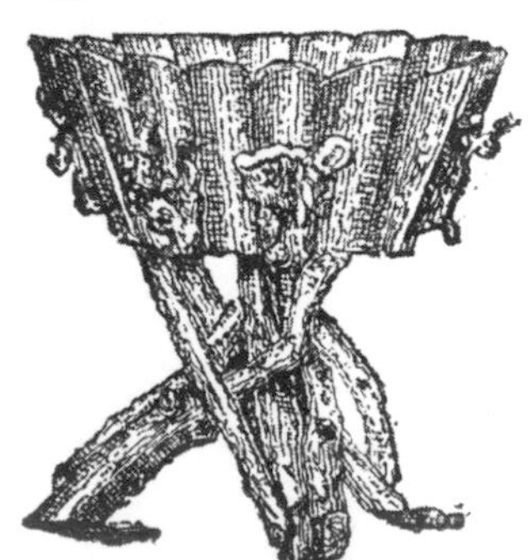

No. 1385. RUSTIC VASE.
10 in. diameter, price **13/-** each. Other sizes, **1/8** per inch.

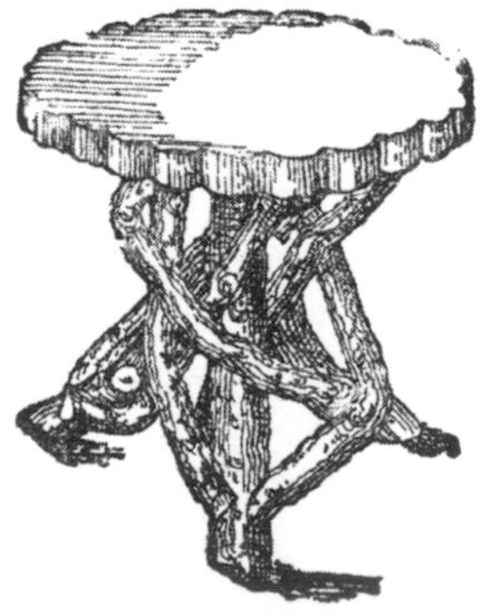

No. 1386. RUSTIC TABLE.
Elm top, any shape, 15 in. diameter, **13/-** each. Other sizes, **2/-** per inch.

...SIGNS IN RUSTIC WORK.

...MMER-HOUSE.

...y are exceedingly ...l value, and are ... worth attention ...othing better has ... been offered at ... the price.

No. 1378a. RUSTIC FLOWER STAND.

This stand is an entirely new article, very strongly made, and well varnished and finished.

3 steps, 3 ft. long, price **15/4** each.

No. 1379. RUSTIC TREE SEAT.

This is a very ornamental seat, and a very great addition to park or pleasure grounds. It is stained best oil stain, and varnished two coats.

Price **10/-** per foot run, measuring the front of seat.

Footboard to match, **1/4** per foot run.

SIZES AND PRICES. Inside dimensions.

From angle to angle.	From back to front.	Height under eaves.	PRICE. £	s.	d.
6 ft. 0 in.	5 ft. 6 in.	6 ft. 0 in.	16	0	0
6 ft. 6 in.	5 ft. 11 in.	6 ft. 0 in.	19	0	0
7 ft. 0 in.	6 ft. 5 in.	6 ft. 6 in.	22	0	0

No. 1377. SPECIAL PORTABLE OBLONG SUMMER-HOUSE.

Size 5 ft. by 3 ft., inside measurement, stained and varnished. Specially recommended for small gardens.

Can be put together in half-an-hour.

Price **£9 0 0**

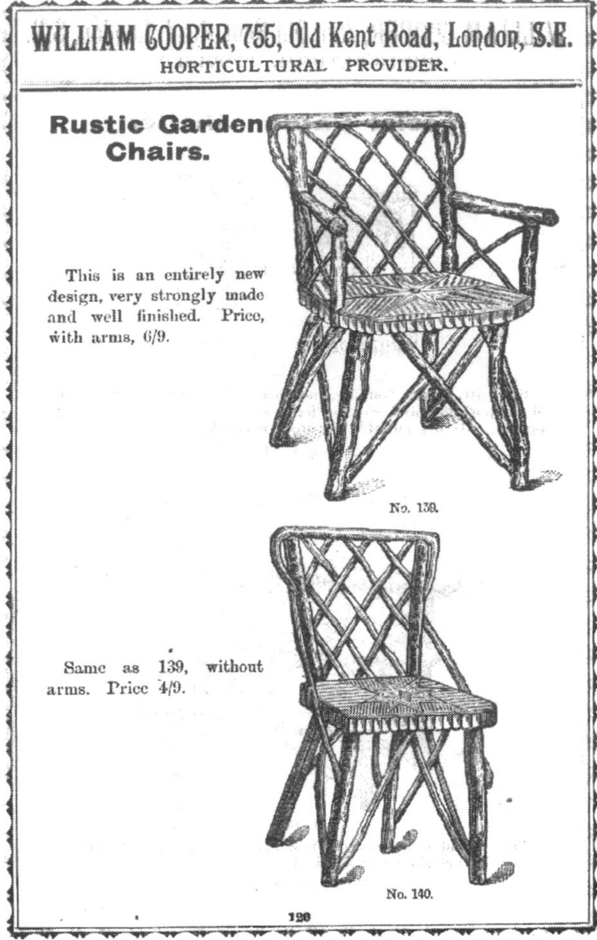

WILLIAM COOPER, 755, Old Kent Road, London, S.E.
HORTICULTURAL PROVIDER.

Rustic Garden Chairs.

This is an entirely new design, very strongly made and well finished. Price, with arms, 6/9.

No. 139.

Same as 139, without arms. Price 4/9.

No. 140.

120

WILLIAM COOPER, 755, Old Kent Road, London, S.E.
HORTICULTURAL PROVIDER.

Rustic Garden Chairs.

With arms, stained and varnished. Strongly made. Price 9/6.

No. 141.

Without arms, stained and varnished. Strongly made. Price 7/6.

No. 142.

121

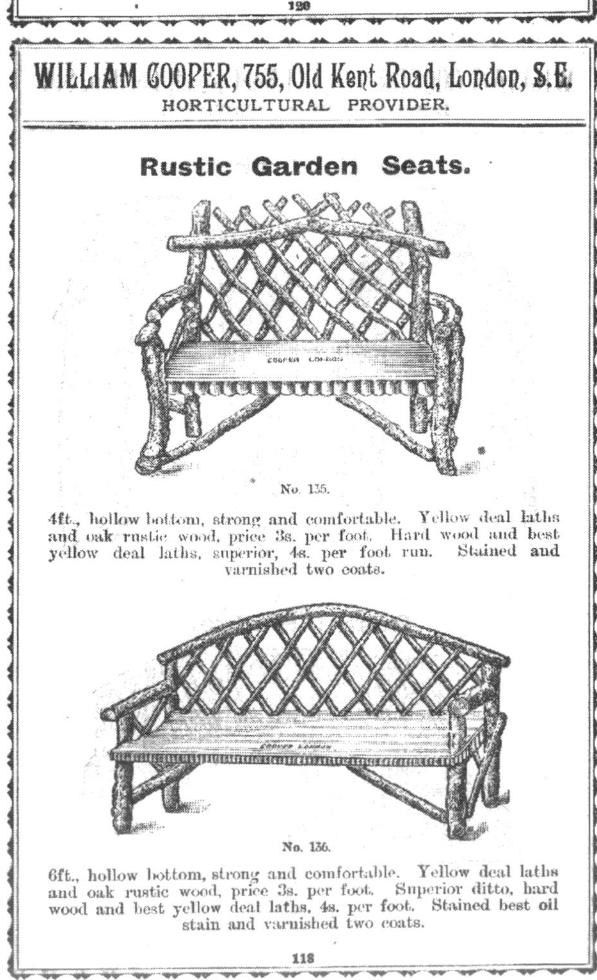

WILLIAM COOPER, 755, Old Kent Road, London, S.E.
HORTICULTURAL PROVIDER.

Rustic Garden Seats.

No. 135.

4ft., hollow bottom, strong and comfortable. Yellow deal laths and oak rustic wood, price 3s. per foot. Hard wood and best yellow deal laths, superior, 4s. per foot run. Stained and varnished two coats.

No. 136.

6ft., hollow bottom, strong and comfortable. Yellow deal laths and oak rustic wood, price 3s. per foot. Superior ditto, hard wood and best yellow deal laths, 4s. per foot. Stained best oil stain and varnished two coats.

118

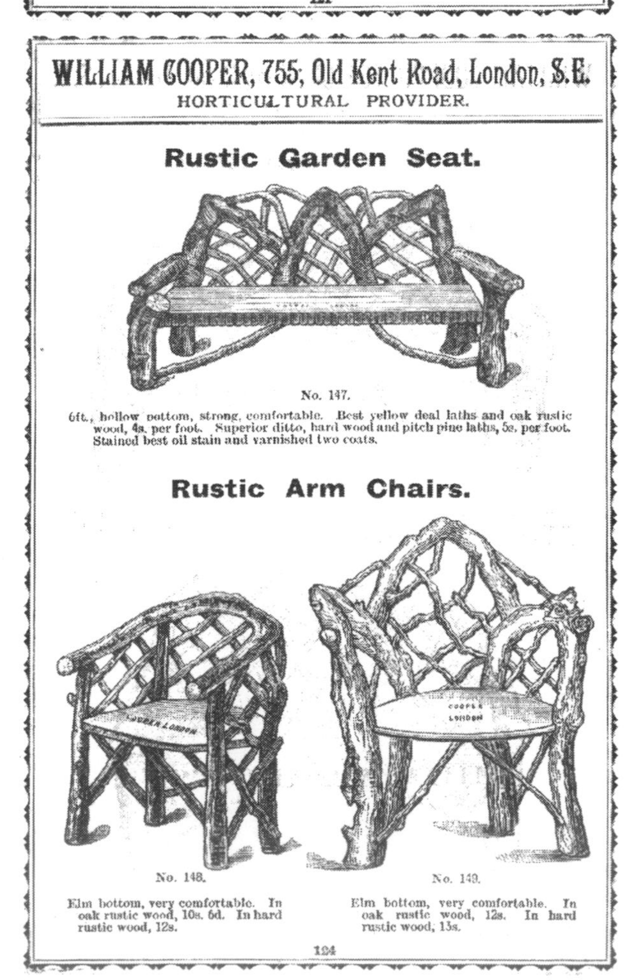

WILLIAM COOPER, 755, Old Kent Road, London, S.E.
HORTICULTURAL PROVIDER.

Rustic Garden Seat.

No. 147.

6ft., hollow bottom, strong, comfortable. Best yellow deal laths and oak rustic wood, 4s. per foot. Superior ditto, hard wood and pitch pine laths, 5s. per foot. Stained best oil stain and varnished two coats.

Rustic Arm Chairs.

No. 148.

Elm bottom, very comfortable. In oak rustic wood, 10s. 6d. In hard rustic wood, 12s.

No. 149.

Elm bottom, very comfortable. In oak rustic wood, 12s. In hard rustic wood, 13s.

124

WILLIAM COOPER, 755, Old Kent Road, London, S.E.
HORTICULTURAL PROVIDER.

Special Cheap House.

Well and strongly made in seasoned timber, cleats over all joints. Highly recommended for small gardens as it is easily taken to pieces and removed from one garden to another, and can be erected in twenty minutes. Hundreds of these have been sold. Size, 5ft. by 3ft. 6in. (outside measurement).

ANY SIZE MADE

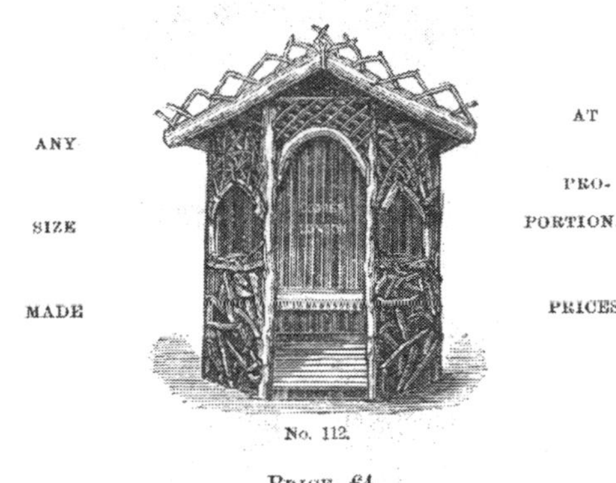

AT PRO-PORTIONATE PRICES.

No. 112.

PRICE £4.

Carefully Packed on Rail.

5, Coop Street, Blackpool.
"DEAR SIR,—Received the Heating Apparatus all right last night: I have fixed it to-day. I am well pleased with it, and it gives me every satisfaction. I can highly recommend it for its simplicity in erection.—I am, yours truly,
MR. COOPER. W. C. PATRICK."

Elliott Street, Ipswich.
"DEAR SIR,—The Invincible Heating Apparatus arrived all right. I consider it an excellent principle; being water-jacked at top is a great improvement on the Loughborough Boilers I have fixed, and I think the price is very reasonable.—Yours faithfully, W. H. HUDSON, JUN."

Buckhaven.
"DEAR SIR,—The case of glass arrived, and I am well pleased with it.—Yours, ROBERT DUNVIRE."

102

WILLIAM COOPER, 755, Old Kent Road, London, S.E.
HORTICULTURAL PROVIDER.

Rustic Lawn Tennis House.

No. 109.

Tenant's fixture. This house is made in sections, and can easily be put together, or taken down and removed. Price complete, carefully packed on rail, £10. Size, outside measurement, 10ft. long, 5ft. from back to front. Stained and varnished.

Rustic Summer Houses.

No. 110.

Price complete, carefully packed on rail, £3 5s. Seat at back only, Size, outside measurement, 5ft. long, 3ft. 6in. back to front. Stained and varnished. Made in sections and easily put together by a handy man in an hour.

No. 111.

Price complete, carefully packed on rail, £9. Size, outside measurement, 6ft. long, 5ft. 6in. back to front. Made in best materials only, well-seasoned, and in sections. Can easily be fixed by any handy man. Stained and varnished.

101

WILLIAM COOPER, 755, Old Kent Road, London, S.E.
HORTICULTURAL PROVIDER.

Summer Houses.

No. 106.—£4.
5ft. wide by 3ft. 6in. deep.

No. 107.—£7.
6ft. wide by 5ft. 6in. deep.

Carefully Packed on Rail.

Made in Sections, and easily put together by a handy man in one hour.

No. 108.

£4 15s., with Table.
5ft. wide by 3ft. 6in. deep.

100

WILLIAM COOPER, 755, Old Kent Road, London, S.E.
HORTICULTURAL PROVIDER.

Portable Rustic Summer Houses.

No. 128.

Double boarded and felted roof, cleated over joints. Size, 12ft. by 5ft. by 7ft. to doorway.
PRICE £28. *Carefully Packed on Rail.*

No. 129.

Can be put together easily in two or three hours.

Special Lawn Tennis House; double boarded roof, felted between boards, thoroughly waterproof. Size, 12ft. by 7ft.

PRICE £20. *Carefully Packed on Rail.*

114

THE STONDON DESIGN.

Made in Deal, painted white, roof covered with shingles, stained with carbolineum.

Size inside ...	...	7 ft. 9 in. x 4 ft. 9 in.
Total Height	... ...	... 10 ft. 0 in.
Price, as above	... ...	... £22 10 0

Price includes comfortable seat and deal floor.

Can be painted any colour desired. Estimates will be given for fixing complete.

THE GIRTFORD DESIGN.

Made in deal, painted white, roof covered with shingles, stained with carbolineum.

Size inside ...	...	8 ft. 0 in. x 6 ft. 0 in.
Total Height ...	... ...	10 ft. 0 in.
Price, as above	... ...	£29 15 0

Price includes comfortable seat and deal floor.

Can be painted any colour desired. Estimates will be given for fixing complete.

THE FARNDISH DESIGN.

Made in Deal, painted white, roof covered with shingles, stained with carbolineum.

Size inside	... ...	8 ft. 0 in. x 8 ft. 0 in.
Total Height	... ...	12 ft. 0 in.
Price ...	... ...	£48 10 0

Price includes comfortable seat and deal floor.

Can be painted any colour desired. Estimates will be given for fixing complete.

THE EATON DESIGN.

Made in Deal, painted white, roof covered with shingles, stained with carbolineum.

Size inside ...	...	8 ft. 0 in. x 5 ft. 6in.
Total Height	... ...	11 ft. 6in.
Price ...	... ...	£35 10 0

Price includes comfortable seat and deal floor.

Can be painted any colour desired. Estimates will be given for fixing complete.

THE EVESHAM SUMMERHOUSE.

This Summerhouse is designed so that seating room may be obtained facing three different aspects, so that whichever way the wind may be blowing shelter can always be obtained.

This is a very convenient shelter for Tennis Courts, Bowling Greens, etc.

Centre portion, 8 ft. 0 in. x 6 ft. 0 in. inside. Side Wings, 6 ft. 0 in. x 2 ft. 6 in. inside.

Made in deal, painted green or white or any colour to customer's choice, with wide comfortable seats in each part. Roof covered with wood shingles stained with carbolineum, and with deal floor. Sent in parts ready for fixing £43 15 0

Fixed complete, within 150 mile radius, (longer distances more in proportion) and painted one coat after fixing £51 10 0

Black and white tiled floor in lieu of deal, as shewn in illustration, extra £4 10 0

THE WESTMEATH PERGOLA.

A very inexpensive Pergola, formed of trellis pilasters with shaped brackets, connected by strong rafters with shaped ends, and longitudinal ribs.

Height inside ... ... 7 ft. 6 in. Width inside ... ... 8 ft. 0 in.

Sawn Deal, stained carbolineum	7/6	per lineal foot.
„ Oak, „ „	11/6	„
Deal, painted any colour	10/6	„
Wrought Oak, oiled	13/6	„

BOULTON & PAUL, Ltd., Manufacturers, NORWICH.

PERGOLAS

No. 109

A Pergola in the "Queen Anne" Style, a particularly effective pattern to employ on an entrance path from gate to house, the woodwork painted white and floor laid in old square red pantiles; with blue brick borders. Prices according to span and length

No. 110

Italian Style Pergola, with handsome fluted columns, with carved Corinthian Caps. Such a structure is particularly suitable for gardens in proximity to towns, where the climbers are not over luxuriant, and an effective architectural feature is desired

126

BOULTON & PAUL, Ltd., Manufacturers, NORWICH.

PERGOLAS

No. 111

Japanese Pergola. This style is particularly appropriate for garden work, and a delightful scheme can be arranged by using purely Japanese plants upon and in close proximity to such a structure. Price upon application

No. 112

Quaint Style Pergola, with stout square cut tapered columns and treillage sides. This Pergola can be made for any width of path and any height or length desired. Estimates will be given including fixing this or any preceding patterns, and cost of carriage, to any part of the Kingdom

127

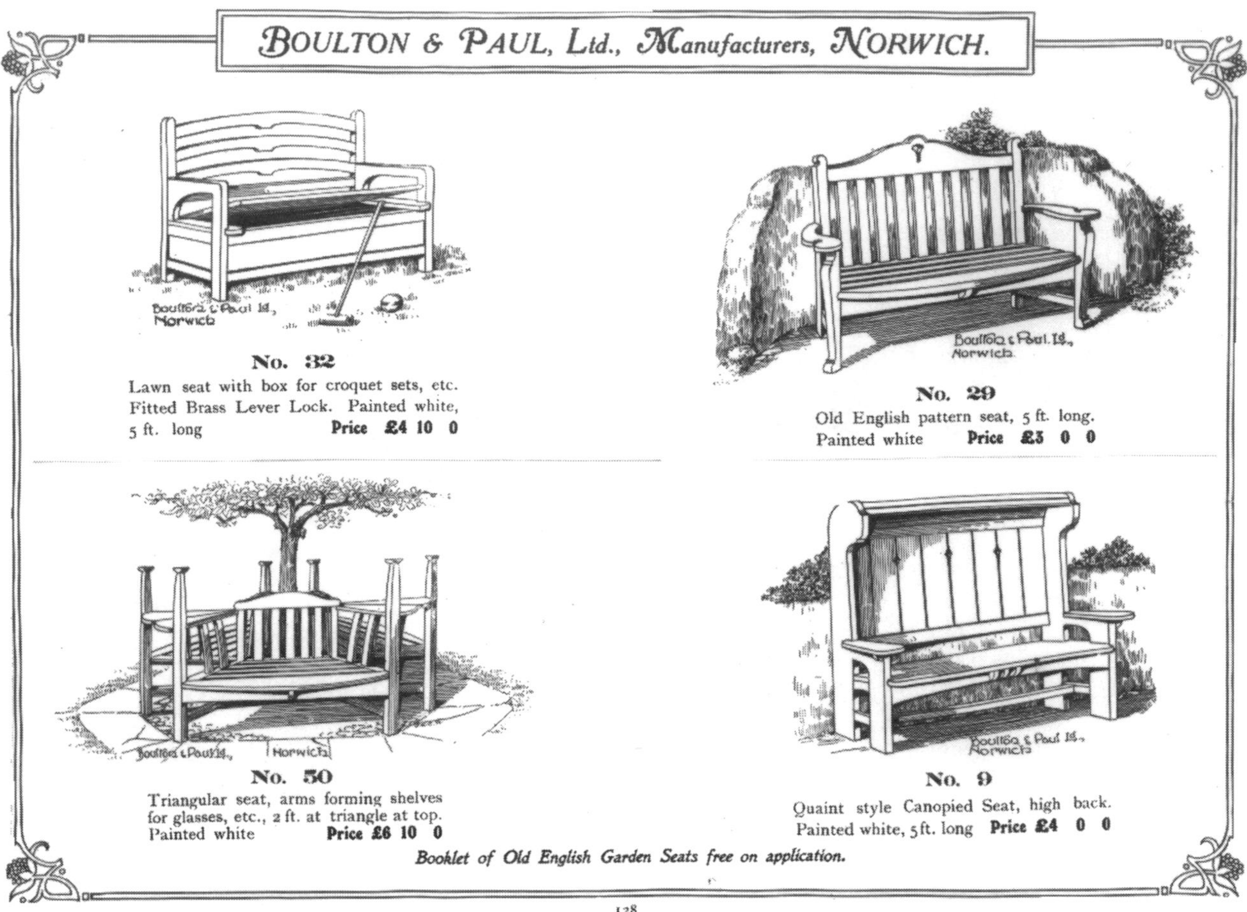

BOULTON & PAUL, Ltd., Manufacturers, NORWICH.

No. 32
Lawn seat with box for croquet sets, etc. Fitted Brass Lever Lock. Painted white, 5 ft. long **Price £4 10 0**

No. 29
Old English pattern seat, 5 ft. long. Painted white **Price £3 0 0**

No. 50
Triangular seat, arms forming shelves for glasses, etc., 2 ft. at triangle at top. Painted white **Price £6 10 0**

No. 9
Quaint style Canopied Seat, high back. Painted white, 5ft. long **Price £4 0 0**

Booklet of Old English Garden Seats free on application.

128

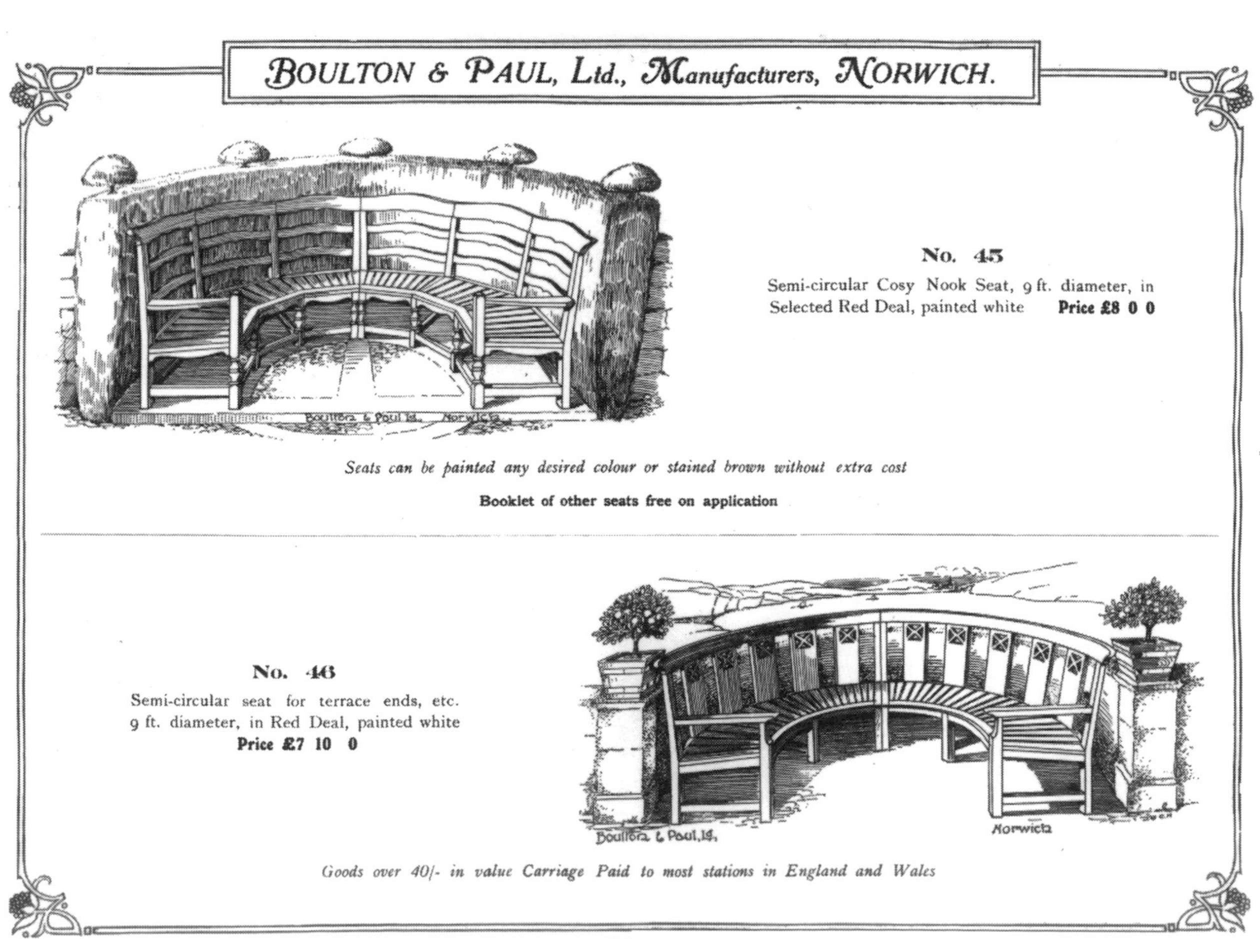

BOULTON & PAUL, Ltd., Manufacturers, NORWICH.

No. 45
Semi-circular Cosy Nook Seat, 9 ft. diameter, in Selected Red Deal, painted white **Price £8 0 0**

Seats can be painted any desired colour or stained brown without extra cost

Booklet of other seats free on application

No. 46
Semi-circular seat for terrace ends, etc. 9 ft. diameter, in Red Deal, painted white
Price £7 10 0

Goods over 40/- in value Carriage Paid to most stations in England and Wales

129

THE BEDFORD DESIGN.

TO FIT ANY TREE NOT EXCEEDING THREE FEET IN DIAMETER.

Width of seat	1 ft.	6 in.
Height of back (to top of centre ornament)	2 ft.	8 in.
Length at front	6 ft.	0 in.

Footboards can be supplied for this seat (see page 22).

Deal, painted green or white	£13	0	0
Dark Oak, varnished	£19	10	0
Teak, oiled	£21	10	0

For every additional foot, or part of foot in diameter of tree, above 3 feet, add : deal, 40/- ; oak, 60/- ; teak, 67/6.

This seat is made in four sections, which can be fitted together at the angles, by the thumbscrews provided, and which will be found attached to the rails under seat.

Of course, a much larger tree would be equally as suitable for this seat as the small tree shewn above.

Garden Seats
No. 4.
No. 3.
PLATE 304A
Sizes 4, 5, 6 Feet, can be made other sizes if required

Garden Seats
Nº 15.
Sizes 4. 5. 6 ft long. Other sizes if required.

Nº 16
Sizes 4. 5. 6 ft long. Other sizes if required.

No. 30. Rustic Garden Chair.

THIS Seat is specially designed for the **Park** and **Public Pleasure Grounds.** The iron-work is painted in imitation of oak branches when peeled, and is grained.

Prices.

Pitch Pine, varnished 6 ft. long	... ...	£1 15 0
Red Deal, stained oak	... ...	1 12 6

No. 16. The Paris Garden Seat.

THIS handsome Seat, with cast-iron rustic supports, is very comfortable and strong, and is suitable for Balconies, Porticos, Terraces, Promenades, Lawns, or any situation where a Garden Seat is required.

Prices.

Pitch Pine, varnished, 6 ft. 6 in. long	...	£2 7 6
Red Deal, stained oak	... .	2 5 0
If fitted with Awning	... ... extra	2 0 0

No. 22. Improved Wrought-iron Garden Chair.

THE above is made entirely of wrought-iron, and recommended for strength, comfort, and lightness. Can be packed in a small compass for shipment.

Prices.

	Length—5 ft.	6 ft.	7 ft.
Japanned Green, or any plain colour...	20/9	23/6	26/9

Longer lengths can be had at proportionate prices.

No: 7. Wrought-iron Tree Seat.

THIS illustration represents a seat 4½ feet in diameter, to fix round a tree 18 inches in diameter, back 3 feet high from the ground, made in halves, and fitted with bolts and nuts.

Prices.

As illustrated, painted green	£3 0 0
Without elbows and back	2 5 0
Circular foot rest ...	1 10 0

Any size made to order.

No. 7. Rustic Table.

CAST-IRON legs and wood top, 24 inches in diameter; legs painted in imitation of birch; top grained oak or stained.

Price 17/6.

Carriage Paid on Orders of 40/- net value and upwards.

No. 36. Tennis Chair.

Prices.

Pitch Pine, varnished ... 6/-
Red Deal, stained oak ... 5/6

Iron-work Japanned Green.

No. 42. The Lady's Lounge.

Prices.

Pitch Pine, varnished ... 9/6
Red Deal, stained oak ... 8/9

Iron-work Japanned Green.

No. 50. Single Chair.

Prices.

Pitch Pine, varnished ... 8/9
Red Deal, stained oak ... 8/-

Iron-work Japanned Green.

Iron Tables.

WILL fold and pack in a very small space when not in use. Grained oak and varnished, or japanned green.

Prices.

No. 1. 21 in. diameter ... 7/-
No. 2. 25 in. ,, extra strong 8/9

Grained oak and varnished, or japanned green.

Prices.

No. 8. 21 in. diameter ... 7/-
No. 8a. 25 in. ,, ... 8/9

Fancy Colours extra.

Finished in superior style.

Wrought-iron Foot Rest.

For use in connection with small Garden Chairs.

Price.

Japanned green 2/-

No. 38. Tennis Arm Chair.

Prices.

Pitch Pine, varnished ... 8/-
Red Deal, stained oak ... 7/6

Iron-work Japanned Green.

No. 35. Folding Chair.

Prices.

Pitch Pine, varnished ... 6/-
Red Deal, stained oak ... 5/6

Iron-work Japanned Green.

No. 51. Single Chair.

Prices.

Pitch Pine, varnished ... 10/-
Red Deal, stained oak ... 9/6

Iron-work Japanned Green.

Carriage Paid on Orders of 40/- net value and upwards.

OPEN.

THE "DUPLEX" FOLDING SEAT,

With Arms.

An extra strong and beautifully finished Seat, made of selected pitch pine; put together with brass screws.

Price.

3½ft. long, with 3 legs .. .. **13/6** each.

FOLDED.

"EASY" GARDEN CHAIR.

Prices.

With Awning Painted Green,

20/-

Grained Oak and Varnished,

22/-

Without Awning Painted Green,

15/-

Grained Oak and Varnished,

17/-

Thousands of these Chairs have been supplied; it is one of the easiest, and is fitted with stays and much improved in design; is suitable for large Gardens, Parks, &c., but yet light enough to be portable.

"TENNIS" CHAIR.

Prices.

Painted Green, **7/6.**

Grained Oak and Varnished, **9/6.**

A Light Folding Chair, made entirely of wrought-iron, very comfortable and without doubt the best and cheapest of its kind.

THE "CROQUET" CHAIR.

A comfortable Seat for use on the Lawn, Tennis Grounds, &c.

Prices.

Without Arms.		With Arms, 3in. wider.
6/-	Pitch Pine, Varnished	**8/-** each
5/6	Plain Green, ,,	**7/6** ,,
6/-	Green with lines, or Painted Oak, and Varnished.	**8/-** ,,

Foot Rests for above, Painted to match Chairs **2/9** *each.*

GORTON, MANCHESTER.

No. 7. INDEPENDENT AWNING.

This Awning is for use in connection with any garden chair not exceeding 6 feet in length. It is portable, and easily fixed into the ground. The Awning is of strong striped ticking; it can be instantly rolled up, and protected from the weather by a zinc cover.

Prices, Carriage Paid.

6 ft. wide, neatly japanned, including box (not returnable), for packing Awning and zinc cover; useful for stowing away in winter £2 10 0

Zinc cover to protect Awning when rolled up 7/6 extra.

No. 48. GARDEN SEAT.

This Seat is very light and comfortable. The wood splines are bolted to the iron-work. Can be put together in a few minutes. Iron-work japanned green.

Prices.

Pitch Pine, varnished, 5 ft. long 15/9
Red Deal, stained oak 14/9

Carriage Paid on Orders of 40/- net value and upwards.

GARDEN SWING.

By using the new lever arrangement, the swing can be kept in motion by the occupants of the chair, or independently outside.

Price, Carriage Paid, £5 0 0

PATENT

"SPEEDWELL" LAWN MOWER.

"A Marvel of Cheapness and Good Withal!"

Simple, well-made, and cuts like a rasor!

THOUSANDS IN USE.

The very best value on the Market.

☞ The Cutters in the Cylinder and the Bottom Blades are of the highest quality, and all tempered and unbreakable.

FOR PRICES, SEE NEXT PAGE.

Tools and Sundry Horticultural Requisites

Modern seed and garden catalogues often contain essential horticultural sundries, but the range is usually limited and mainly for the instant convenience of the customer, who can usually find a much larger selection at the local garden centre or hardware shop. The Victorian garden catalogue had to carry a much wider range of gardening commodities, and it was possible to order from home every conceivable horticultural requirement from pest and disease controls and specially formulated compound manures, to a complete range of hand and mechanical gardening tools, plant labels, tying and training materials and hyacinth glasses.

Sadly, while many small hand tools sold in the late 1800s are still available, albeit in many cases through specialist horticultural suppliers, it is unlikely that any single company would now be in a position to offer, for instance, around twenty pruning knives and a dozen budding knives, as did Sutton's in 1881.

In the 'nothing new under the sun' category, it is worth noting that Follows and Bate Limited of Manchester were producing a water-ballast garden roller before the turn of the century, which worked on exactly the same principle as today's counterpart — using a refillable drum which could be emptied after use to make it more manoeuvrable. And any notion that environmentally-friendly coir, or coconut fibre, is a recent growing substitute for peat, is dispelled by the discovery that 'coconut refuse' was offered in Daniels Brothers' catalogue of 1876, at 2 shillings, 6d. per bushel.

We can, at least, be thankful that we no longer need to worry about fitting the horse, the Victorian equivalent of our stripe-producing, grass-collecting lawn mower, with 'mowing boots' — an essential 1800s procedure when venturing out to cut the grass.

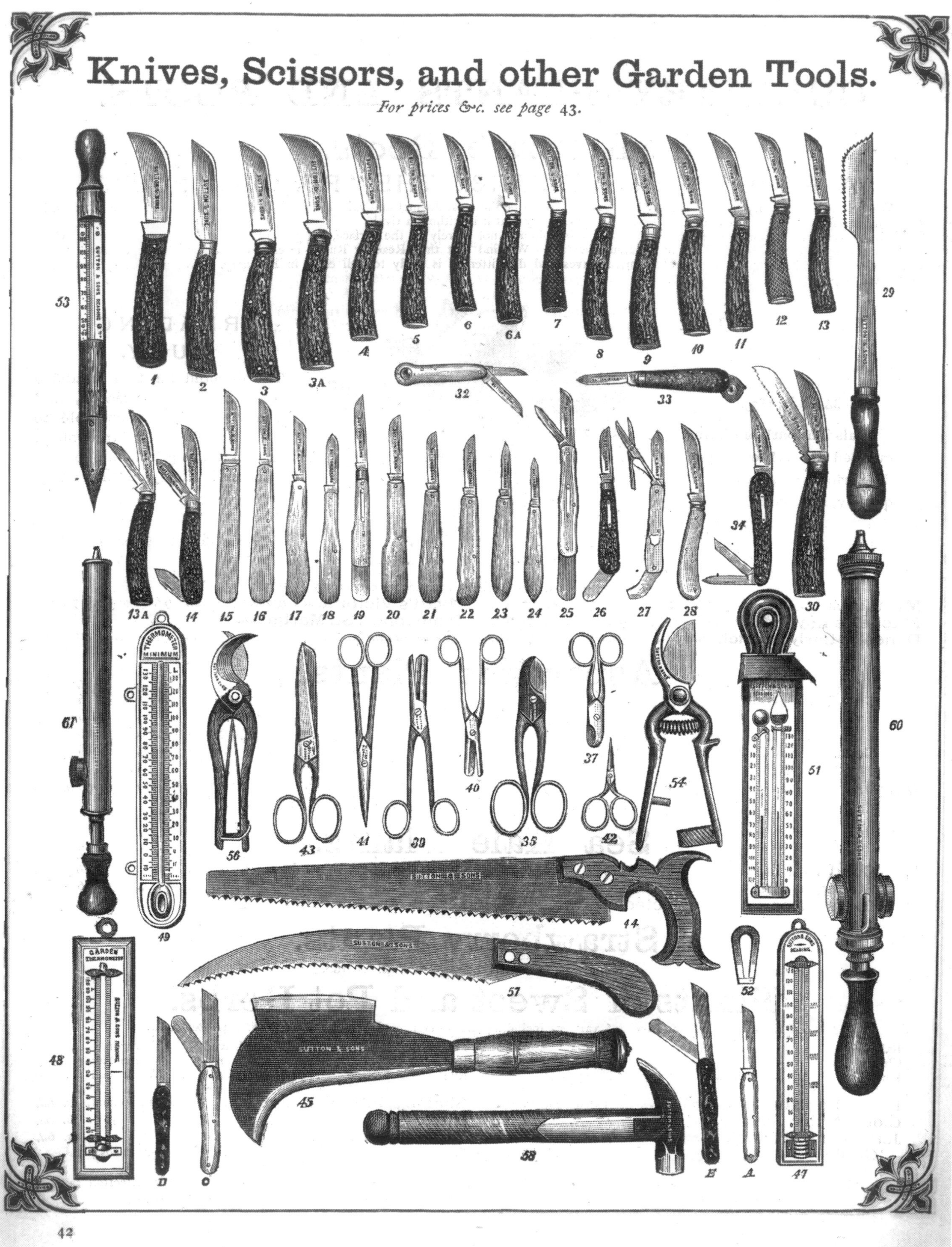

Knives, Scissors, and other Garden Tools.
For prices &c. see page 43.
SUTTON & SONS
1 2 3 3A 4 5 6 6A 7 8 9 10 11 12 13
13A 14 15 16 17 18 19 20 21 22 23 24 25 26 27 28 29 30
32 33 34
37 38 39 40 41 42 43 44 45 47 48 49 51 52 53 54 56 57 58 60 61
A B C D E
THERMOMETER MINIMUM
GARDEN THERMOMETER
42

We carefully test all Seeds before sending them out.

Knives, Scissors, and other Garden Tools.

No.	Article	Each s.	d.
No. 1	Sheath Pruning Knife, large size ...	2	0
,, 2	Ditto small size (superior)	2	3
,, 3	Pruning Knife, largest size	3	6
,, 3A	Ditto large size ..	3	3
,, 4	Ditto medium size	3	0
,, 5	Ditto medium size (composition handle)	2	3
,, 6	Ditto small size ...	3	0
,, 6A	Ditto medium size	3	0
,, 7	Ditto medium size (composition handle)	2	0
,, 8	Ditto medium size (superior)	4	0
,, 9	Ditto large size ...	3	6
,, 10	Ditto medium size	3	0
,, 11	Ditto medium size	3	6
,, 12	Ditto small size (composition handle)...	1	9
,, 13	Ditto small size ...	3	0
,, 13A	Ditto 2 blades ...	4	6
,, 14	Pruning and Budding Knife combined	4	6
,, 15	Sheath Budding Knife, large size	3	0
,, 16	Budding Knife, large size...	3	3
,, 17	Ditto medium size	3	0
,, 18	Ditto small size...	2	9
,, 19	Ditto medium size	3	6
,, 20	Ditto medium size	3	3
,, 21	Ditto small size...	3	0
,, 22	Ditto small size...	3	0
,, 23	Ditto small size...	3	0
,, 24	Ditto small size...	2	0
,, 25	Ditto 2 blades ...	4	6
,, 26	Ladies' Budding Knife	3	6
,, 27	Ditto with Scissors (superior)...	7	6
,, 28	Pruning Knife, white handle	1	9
,, 29	Asparagus Knife ...	3	6
,, 30	Pruning Knife and Saw (superior)	5	6
,, 31	Ditto ditto	3	6
,, 32	Knife with two blades and botanical lens	5	0
,, 33	Ditto one blade and ditto	4	0
,, 34	Gentleman's Pocket Knife, three blades (superior)	5	0
,, 35	Pruning Scissors, large size	3	3
,, 36	Ditto large size, japanned handles ...	3	9
,, 37	Ditto small size	2	6
,, 38	Ditto small size, japanned handles	3	0

No.	Article	Each s.	d.
No. 39	Flower Gatherer, large size	4	0
,, 40	Ditto small size	2	9
,, 41	Vine Scissors	3	0
,, 42	Propagating Scissors	2	6
,, 43	Shred Scissors	2	3
,, 44	Pruning Saw, 14-inch	3	0
,, 45	Garden Bill	3	0
,, 46	Pruning Saw and Hook ...	5	0
,, 47	Boxwood Thermometer, 8-inch ...	1	3
,, 48	Ditto single degrees, minimum registering	2	6
,, 49	Metal Thermometer, minimum registering	4	0
,, 50	Porcelain Thermometer, minimum registering	5	0
,, 51	Thermometer, maximum and minimum registering, japanned case, boxwood scale (superior)	8	6
,, 52	Magnet for ditto ...	1	0
,, 53	Plunging Thermometer, oak frame, 12-inch	5	0
,, 54	Pruning Shears. Extremely powerful ...	5	0
,, 55	Sécateurs, or French Pruning Shears, 7-inch	4	6
,, 56	Ditto ditto 8-inch	5	0
,, 57	Grecian Pruning Saw	2	6
,, 58	Garden Hammer, large size	2	6
,, 59	Ditto small size	2	0
,, 60	Syringe, Ladies' Garden, 2 roses and 1 jet, 12 inches	7	6
,, 61	Ditto, ditto Greenhouse, 1 rose and 1 jet	2	6
,, 62	Ditto, Reid's Patent Ball Valve, 2 roses and 1 jet, 18 in. × 1½ in.	17	6
,, 63	Syringe, Reid's Patent Ball Valve, 2 roses and 1 jet, 20 in. × 1¾ in.	21	0
,, 64	Aphis Brushes ...	1	9

Ivory Fruit Knives.

These are made with ivory springs, which are not liable to rust like knives fitted with steel springs.

	Article	s.	d.
A.	Ivory handle, 3-inch, single blade ...	1	0
B.	Ditto 3½ ,, blade and scoop	2	3
C.	Ditto 4 ,, ditto	3	0
D.	Tortoiseshell handle, 3½-inch, single blade ...	2	6
E.	Ditto 4 ,, blade and scoop (superior) ...	4	6
F.	Ornamental inlaid handle, 3½-inch, ditto ditto	2	6

The Willesden Insoluble Metallic Card Labels

FOR ROSE TREES, FRUIT TREES, SHRUBS, &c.

NO SPECIAL INK REQUIRED.

These Labels are insoluble in water of any temperature; can be readily written upon with ORDINARY INK, and such writing, even after years of exposure, will be perfectly legible.

These Labels may have the names of Roses, &c., printed upon them. The Registered 'Combination' Labels, in sizes 9, 10, and 11, can be used for suspending purposes or for insertion in the soil. Copying or Fancy Inks are unsuitable.

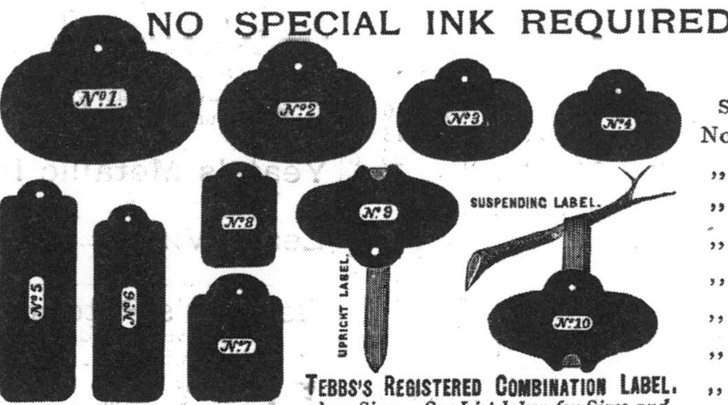

TEBBS'S REGISTERED COMBINATION LABEL.
In 3 Sizes. See List below for Sizes and Prices.

Size	Inches	Per box of 100. s.	d.	Per box of 50. s.	d.
No. 1,	2¾ × 2⅛ ...	3	6	2	0
,, 2,	2¼ × 1⅜ ...	3	0	1	9
,, 3,	2 × 1½ ...	2	6	1	6
,, 4,	1⅝ × 1¼ ...	2	0	1	3
,, 5,	3¼ × 1 ...	2	6	1	6
,, 6,	2¾ × 1 ...	2	0	1	3
,, 7,	1⅞ × 1⅜ ...	2	6	1	6
,, 8,	1⅜ × 1¼ ...	2	0	1	3

Waterproof Twine

For using with the Metallic Card Labels.

		s.	d.		s.	d.
Thin	100 lengths	1	0	50 lengths	0	6
Thick	,,	1	3	,,	0	8

Tebbs's Registered Combination Label.

No.	Size		s.	d.
No. 9,	3⅜ × 2¼	Per box of 50	3	6
,, 10,	3 × 1⅞	,,	3	0
,, 11,	2½ × 1⅝	,,	2s. 6d.	

'Your Le Floral is the most remarkable stuff I ever came across. Its effects on pot plants and flowers are really magical.'—Sergeant-Major J. BINNS, *Pachmarhi, Central Provinces, East India.*

43

HORTICULTURAL REQUISITES—continued.

HORTICULTURAL MANURES.

s. d.

Sutton's A 1 Garden Manure. The best artificial manure yet offered for garden use ... ... Tins, each, 1*s*., 2*s*. 6*d*., and 4 6
Kegs, 28 lbs., 10*s*. 6*d*.; 50 lbs., 16*s*.; 112 lbs. 28 6

Sutton's A 1 Lawn Manure. Equal in all respects to our Garden Manure, but specially adapted for Lawns.
Tins, each, 1*s*., 2*s*. 6*d*., and 4 6
Kegs, 28 lbs., 10*s*. 6*d*.; 50 lbs., 16*s*.; 112 lbs. 28 6

Nitrate of Soda ... ...Tins, each, 9*d*., 1*s*. 3*d*., 1*s*. 9*d*., 3*s*. 6*d*., and 5 0
Guano, highest quality ... ... Tins, each, 9*d*., 1*s*. 6*d*., 3*s*., ,, 5 0
Standen's Manure ... ... Tins, each, 1*s*., 2*s*. 6*d*., ,, 5 6
,, ,, ... Kegs, 28 lbs. 10 6
Thomson's Vine and Plant Manure ... Tins, each, 1*s*., 2*s*., and 3 6
,, ,, ,, ,, Bags, 28 lbs., 6*s*.: 50 lbs. 9 0
Manure or Plant Food, McDougall's ... ... 2 lbs., 1*s*.; 7 lbs. 2 6
,, ,, ,, ,, 14 lbs., 5*s*.; 28 lbs., 7*s*. 6*d*.; 50 lbs. 11 6
Clay's Fertiliser ... ... Packets, each 1 0
,, ,, Bags, 7 lbs., 2*s*. 6*d*.; 14 lbs. ; 28 4*s*. 6*d*. lbs. 7*s*. 6*d*.; 50 lbs. 11 6
Flor Vita ... ... Bottles, each, 1*s*. and 2 6

We shall be pleased to procure other Manures for customers at the usual prices.

PROTECTING & SHADING MATERIALS.

Garden Mats, Largest New Archangel.
A splendid sample ... ... per dozen 24 0
Floral Shading, pieces 30 yards long and about 4 feet wide.
White, stout ... ... per piece 15 0
,, thin ... ... ,, 10 0
Tiffany, 20 yards long, 38 inches wide ... ... ,, 5 0
Frigi Domo, 2, 3, and 4 yards wide ... ... per square yard 1 0
Scrim, 34 in. wide, per yard, 6*d*.; 54 in. wide ... ... per yard 0 9
,, 72 in. wide ... ... ,, 1 0
Marpedo Sunshade, Green. For shading glass houses in summer.
Tins, each, 1*s*., 1*s*. 6*d*., and 2 6
Summer Cloud Shading, Elliott's, green ... ... per packet 1 0
Summer Shading, Caiger's, white or green ... packets, 1*s*. and 2 0

TYING and GRAFTING MATERIALS.

Raffia Grass (best) ... ... per packet, 6*d*.; per pound 1 3
Cuba Bast ... ... ,, 6*d*.; ,, 1 3
Russian Fibre ... ... ,, 1 0
Floral Cement, or Gum ... ... Bottles, each, 1*s*. and 2 0
Bouquet Wire. In packets of 500 9-in. lengths ... per packet 0 6
,, ,, Fine, for binding, $\frac{1}{4}$-lb. reels ... ... each 0 9
,, ,, For Camellias, in 7-in. lengths ... per pound 1 6
,, ,, Stout, for stems, in 7-in. lengths ... ,, 1 0
Budding Cotton ... ... ,, 2 0
Grafting Wax ... ... Tins, each, 1*s*., 2*s*., and 4 0

SHREDS, NAILS, and NAIL BAGS.

Shreds, Waterproof ... ... $\frac{1}{2}$ in. wide, 3 in. long, per 100 0 9
,, ,, ... $\frac{3}{4}$,, 4 ,, ,, 1 0
,, ,, ... $\frac{7}{8}$,, 5 ,, ,, 1 3
,, ,, ... $\frac{7}{8}$,, 6 ,, ,, 1 6
,, **Cloth** ... ... per pound 0 6
Wall Nails, Cast ... ...Boxes, 2 lbs., 9*d*.; 4 lbs., 1*s*. 4*d*.; 7 lbs. 2 0
,, ,, Wrought, Jucke's diamond-pointed ... ... 3 lbs. 0 9
,, ,, ,, ,, ,, 7 lbs., 1*s*. 9*d*.; 14 lbs. 3 6
,, ,, Chandler's Patent. No shreds required when this nail is used. Boxes of 100, $1\frac{1}{4}$ in., 1*s*. 4*d*.; $1\frac{3}{8}$ in., 1*s*. 6*d*.; $1\frac{1}{2}$ in. 1 8
2 in., 2*s*.; $2\frac{1}{2}$ in., 2*s*. 4*d*.; 3 in. 2 8
Nail Bags, Leather, with compartments ... ... each 6 0

GARDEN GLOVES.

s. d.

Lampreil's Patent Waterproof.
Ladies', superior quality ... ... per pair 3 0
Gentlemen's, ditto ... ... ,, 3 6
Ladies' ... ... ,, 2 6
Gentlemen's, superior ... ... ,, 3 0
Men's Hedgers ... ... ,, 1 6
,, **Oxford** ... ... ,, 2 3
,, **Drummond's Button** ... ... ,, 2 6
,, **Harvest Tan** ... ... ,, 2 0

LABELS, &c.

Wood Labels, Painted.
3 inches long ... per 100 6*d*. | 6 inches long ... ...per 100 1 0
4 ,, ,, ... ,, 8*d*. | 9 ,, ,, ... ,, 1 9
5 ,, ,, ... ,, 10*d*. | 12 ,, ,, per 50, 1*s* 6*d*. ,, 2 9
With holes for suspending, 4 inches long ... ... ,, 1 0
,, ,, ,, ,, 6 ,, ,, ... ,, 1 3

Yeats's Zinc Labels.

	Size in inches.	100, with box & ink. *s. d.*	100, without box & ink. *s. d.*
1. The 'Veitch' conservatory and border label ...	$4\frac{3}{4}$ by $3\frac{1}{2}$	5 0	4 0
2. The 'Drummond' pot and border label ...	4 ,, $2\frac{3}{4}$	4 0	3 0
3. The 'Paxton' pot and border label ...	4 ,, 3	4 6	3 6
4. The 'Dickson' pot label	5 ,, 1	4 0	3 0
5. The 'Dr. Hogg' fruit tree, 2-hole suspending label ...	$3\frac{1}{2}$,, $2\frac{1}{2}$	4 6	3 6
6. The 'Paul' Rose label	2 ,, $2\frac{1}{4}$	3 6	2 6
7. The 'Barron' trial ground label ...	$2\frac{3}{4}$,, $\frac{7}{8}$	3 0	2 0
13. The 'Sutton' Rose label	$2\frac{5}{8}$,, $1\frac{1}{4}$	3 0	2 0
14. The 'Rivers' nursery label	$1\frac{1}{2}$,, $1\frac{1}{4}$	2 0	1 3
15. The 'Erfurt' potting label	$4\frac{1}{4}$,, $\frac{3}{4}$	2 6	1 6

Metallic Ink, for zinc labels ... ... Bottles, each, 6*d*. and 1 0
Lead Wire, for suspending labels, &c. ... ... per pound 1 3
Waterproof Twine, for labels, per bundle of 50, fine 6*d*., stout ... 0 8

SUNDRY GARDEN REQUISITES.

The Martin Flower Rack (Patent). For displaying cut flowers to advantage. $1\frac{1}{2}$ in. diameter, doz. 6*s*.; 2 in., doz. 8*s*.; $2\frac{1}{2}$ in., doz. 10*s*. 6*d*.; 3 in., doz. 13*s*. 6*d*.; $3\frac{1}{2}$ in., doz. 16*s*.; 6 in. (for large bowls), doz. 20*s*.; 6 in., with perpendicular spring to regulate height ... . doz. 24*s*.

Beckett's Exhibition Flower Tube, for Chrysanthemums, Roses, &c.

Shallow Cup.		Deep Cup.	
No. 1 ...	diameter $2\frac{3}{4}$ inches.	No. 3 ...	diameter $2\frac{1}{4}$ inches.
,, 2 ...	,, $2\frac{1}{2}$,,	,, 4 ...	,, 2 ,,
,, 5 ...	,, $1\frac{3}{4}$,,	,, 6 ...	,, $1\frac{1}{2}$,,

Prices.—ZINC OUTER TUBE AND CUP, with brass spiral raising tube and new clip: all sizes, 9*s*. per dozen.
BRASS OUTER TUBE AND CUP, lacquered, with spiral raising and extra extension tube: all sizes, 13*s*. per dozen.
When ordering please state the size and shape of cup required. *s. d.*

Bamboo Flower Sticks, about 4 feet long ... ... per 100 5 0
Belt, for carrying Scythe Rubber ... ... each 2 6
Chrysanthemum Tweezers, Bray ... ... per pair 2 6
Coir Scrubbers, for cleaning flower pots ... ... each 0 6
Crock, Porter's Patent. A useful invention for plant pots per 100, 3*s*.; per 1,000 25 0
Garden Lines, 30 yards long, 1*s*. 6*d*.; 60 yards long ... each 2 9
Garden Pencils, Wolff's ... ... 7 in. long, each, 3*d*. and 0 4
,, ,, ,, 5 in. long, Black, Red, or Blue, with point protector ... ... each 0 3
Gardeners' Aprons, best shalloon ... ... each, 4*s*. and 4 6
Sutton's Waterproof Dubbing. A superior preparation for gardeners' or sportsmen's boots ... ... Tins, each, 6*d*. and 1 0
Gishurstine. For gardeners' boots, &c. ... ,, ,, 6*d*. ,, 1 0
Sutton's Mowing Machine Oil. Tins, each, 1*s*., 1*s*. 6*d*., 2*s*. 6*d*., and 4 0
Styptic for Vines, Thomson's ... ... Bottles, each 3 0
Tam o' Shanter Hone, for sharpening knives ... ... ,, 1 0
,, ,, ,, in polished wood case, superior ... ,, 2 0
Verbena Pins ... ... per gross 1 3

SUTTON & SONS, Seed Growers and Merchants, READING, ENGLAND.

86

SUTTON'S LIST OF GARDEN IMPLEMENTS.

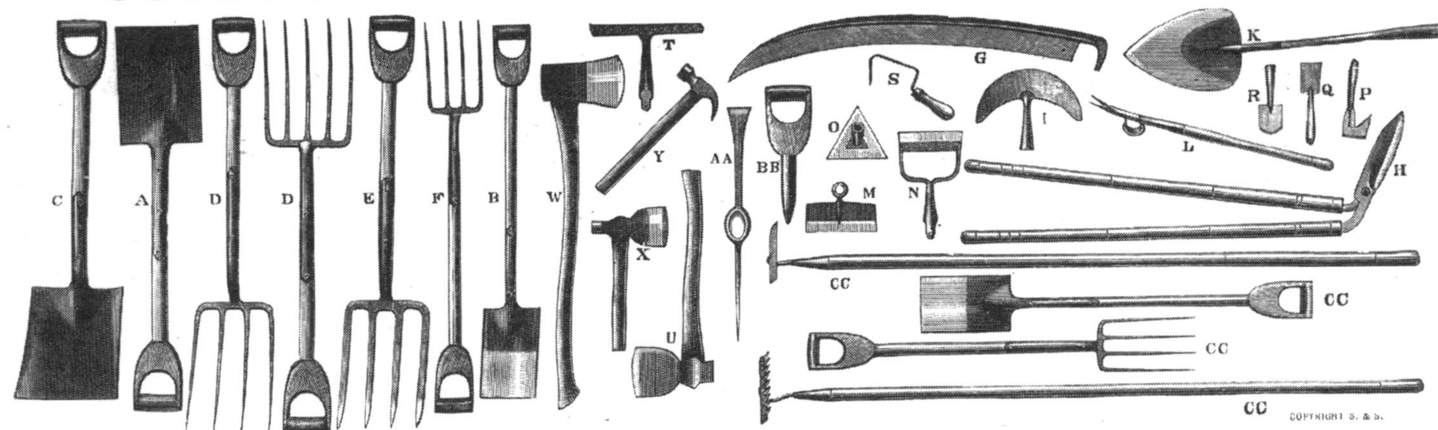

The letters which precede the articles offered below will facilitate reference to the above illustrations.

		s.	d.
A	**Spades,** best London treaded, solid steel.		
	No. 1. 7½ inches × 11½ inches ... ... each,	3	6
	,, 2. 7¾ ,, × 12 ,, ... ,,	3	9
	,, 3. 8¼ ,, × 12½ ,, ... ,,	4	0
	Bright steel, each 6*d.* extra.		
	Spades, best London treaded, cast-steel-faced.		
	No. 1. 7½ inches × 11½ inches ... ... ,,	4	0
	,, 2. 7¾ ,, × 12 ,, ... ,,	4	6
	,, 3. 8¼ ,, × 12½ ,, ... ,,	5	6
	Bright steel, each 6*d.* extra.		
B.	**Border Spade** ... ... ,,	3	6
C.	**Shovels,** steel, London.		
	No. 1. 12 inches × 9 inches ... ... ,,	4	0
	,, 2. 12½ ,, × 9½ ,, ... ,,	4	6
D.	**Digging Forks,** strapped steel.		
	Four-prong ... ... ,,	3	6
	Five-prong ... ... ,,	4	0
	Digging Forks, best closed socket.		
	Four-prong ... ... ,,	4	6
	Five-prong ... ... ,,	5	0
E.	**Potato Fork,** flat prongs.		
	Four-prong ... ... ,,	4	6
	Bright steel, 6*d.* extra.		
F.	**Border Fork** ... ... ,,	3	6
G.	**Scythe,** for short grass.		
	36 inch. riveted back ... ... ,,	4	0
	Scythe Stone ... ... ,,	0	6
H.	**Grass Edging Shears.**		
	8 inch ... ... each, 6*s.* | 9 inch ... ... ,,	7	9
	8½ ,, ... ,, 7*s.* | 9½ ,, ... ,,	8	6
I.	**Edging Irons.**		
	8 inch ... ...each, 2*s.* 6*d.* | 10 inch ... ... ,,	3	6
	9 ,, ... ,, 3*s.* | 11 ,, ... ,,	4	0
K.	**Turfing Irons** each, No. 1, 7*s.*; No. 2, 8*s.* 6*d.*; No. 3,	10	0
L.	**Daisy Drawer** ... ... each,	2	0

		s.	d.
M.	**Hoes,** cast steel garden.		
	4 inch ... ... each, 10*d.* | 7 inch ... ... each,	1	4
	5 ,, ... ,, 1*s.* | 8 ,, ... ,,	1	6
	6 ,, ... ,, 1*s.* 2*d.* | 9 ,, ... ,,	1	9
	10 ,, ... ,,	2	0
N.	**Dutch Hoes.**		
	4 inch ... ...each, 1*s.* 2*d.* | 7 inch ... ... ,,	2	0
	5 ,, ... ,, 1*s.* 6*d.* | 8 ,, ... ,,	2	6
	6 ,, ... ,, 1*s.* 9*d.* | 9 ,, ... ,,	3	0
O.	**Triangular Hoes.**		
	4 inch ... ...each, 1*s* | 6 inch ... ... ,,	2	0
	5 ,, ... ,, 1*s.* 9*d.* | 7 ,, ... ,,	2	3
	8 ,, ... ,,	2	6
P.	**Spud** ... ... ,,	1	3
Q.	,, ... ,,	1	3
R.	,, ... ,,	1	6
S.	**Eradicating Weeder** ... ... ,,	2	0
T.	**Rakes,** best garden, steel teeth.		
	4 teeth, each, 9*d.* | 8 teeth, each, 1*s.* 3*d.* | 12 teeth, each, 1*s.* 9*d.*		
	5 ,, ,, 10*d.* | 9 ,, ,, 1*s.* 4*d.* | 13 ,, ,, 1*s.* 10*d.*		
	6 ,, ,, 1*s.* | 10 ,, ,, 1*s.* 6*d.* | 14 ,, ,, 2*s.*		
	7 ,, ,, 1*s.* 2*d.* | 11 ,, ,, 1*s.* 8*d.* | 15 ,, ,, 2*s.* 3*d.*		
	16 ,, ,, 2*s.* 6*d.*		
	Rakes, socket, solid steel, bright.		
	8 teeth, each, 1*s.* 9*d.* | 12 teeth, each, 2*s.* 3*d.* | 16 teeth, each, 3*s.*		
	10 ,, ,, 2*s.* | 14 ,, ,, 2*s.* 6*d.*		
		s.	*d.*
U.	**Hatchet** ... ... each,	3	0
W.	**Felling Axe** ... ... ,,	5	0
X.	**Hatchet and Hammer combined** ... ... ,,	3	6
Y.	**Fence and Rail Hammer** ... ... ,,	3	0
AA.	**Mattock** ... ... ,,	3	6
	Pickaxe ... ... ,,	3	6
BB.	**Dibber,** steel-pointed ... ... ,,	1	6
CC.	**Special Set of Garden Tools,** comprising Hoe, Rake, Spade, and Fork.		
	Lady's size ... ... ,,	13	6
	Children's size ... ... ,,	8	6

Stott's Specialities in Gardening Implements. Descriptive List post free on application.

PATENT ROLLERS.

Made with double cylinders; outer edges rounded; well finished.

		£	s.	d.
Diameter 16 in., width 17 in.	... Carriage Free	£2	5	0
,, 20 in., ,, 22 in.	,,	3	5	0
,, 24 in., ,, 26 in.	,,	4	10	0
,, 26 in., ,, 28 in.	,,	6	0	0
,, 30 in., ,, 32 in.	,,	7	10	0

WATER BARROWS.

Strong wrought iron, with galvanised tub, painted within and without; fitted with Martin's patent tipping arrangement.

		£	s.	d.
To hold 20 gallons, with wheels 13 inches high	... Carriage Free	£3	7	6
,, 30 ,, ,, 19 ,, ...	,,	4	1	0
,, 38 ,, ,, 24 ,, ...	,,	5	3	0

With lip and guard, 8s. extra.

IMPROVED GARDEN ENGINES.

		£	s.	d.
Galvanised and painted iron tub to hold 12 gallons	... Carriage Free	£3	14	6
,, ,, ,, ,, 16 ,, ...	,,	4	8	0
,, ,, ,, ,, 24 ,, ...	,,	5	10	0
,, ,, ,, ,, 30 ,, ...	,,	6	12	0
Cock and Spreader for watering Lawns, extra		1	9	0

SMALL GARDEN ENGINE.

To hold 6 gallons; light, portable, and easily worked by a lady or child ... ... Carriage Free £2 16 0

AMERICAN SINGLE-WHEEL HOE, CULTIVATOR AND PLOUGH, COMBINED.

This implement does excellent work and effects a great saving of labour.

With the attachments ... ... Carriage Free £1 6 6

AMERICAN DOUBLE-WHEEL HOE, CULTIVATOR, RAKE AND PLOUGH COMBINED.

A powerful implement for garden use, easily adapted to various purposes.

		£	s.	d.
Without the attachments	... Carriage Free	£1	5	0
With ,, ,, ...	,,	2	2	0

AMERICAN SEED DRILL.

Specially designed for garden use. A simple but thoroughly efficient Drill.

		£	s.	d.
Without the attachments	... Carriage Free	£2	5	0
With ,, ,, ...	,,	3	3	0

An illustrated Catalogue of the above American implements will be forwarded on application.

SUTTON & SONS, READING, Seedsmen by Royal Warrant to H.R.H. the Prince of Wales.

87

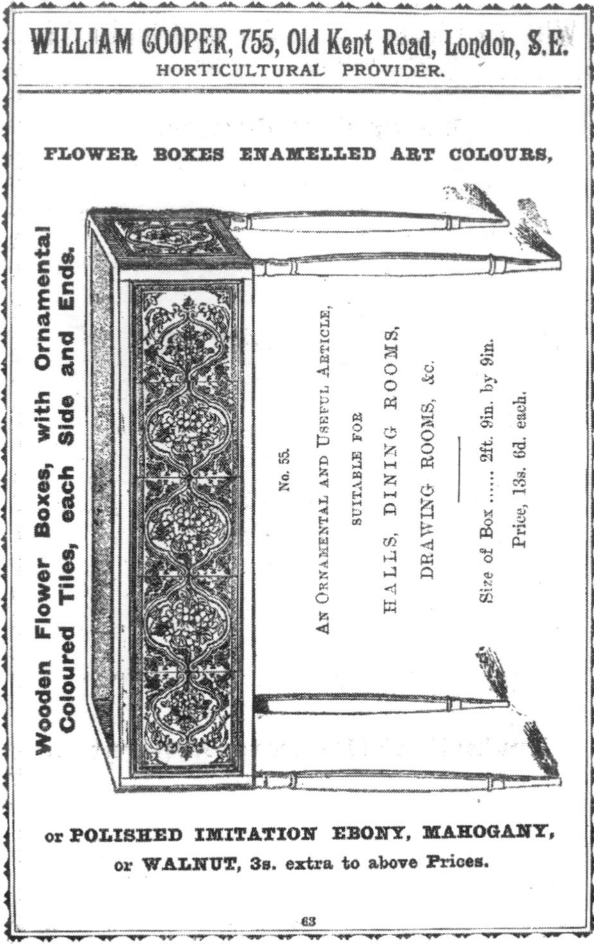

WILLIAM COOPER, 755, Old Kent Road, London, S.E.
HORTICULTURAL PROVIDER.

FLOWER BOXES ENAMELLED ART COLOURS,

Wooden Flower Boxes, with Ornamental Coloured Tiles, each Side and Ends.

No. 55.

AN ORNAMENTAL AND USEFUL ARTICLE, SUITABLE FOR HALLS, DINING ROOMS, DRAWING ROOMS, &c.

Size of Box ...... 2ft. 9in. by 9in.
Price, 13s. 6d. each.

or POLISHED IMITATION EBONY, MAHOGANY, or WALNUT, 3s. extra to above Prices.

63

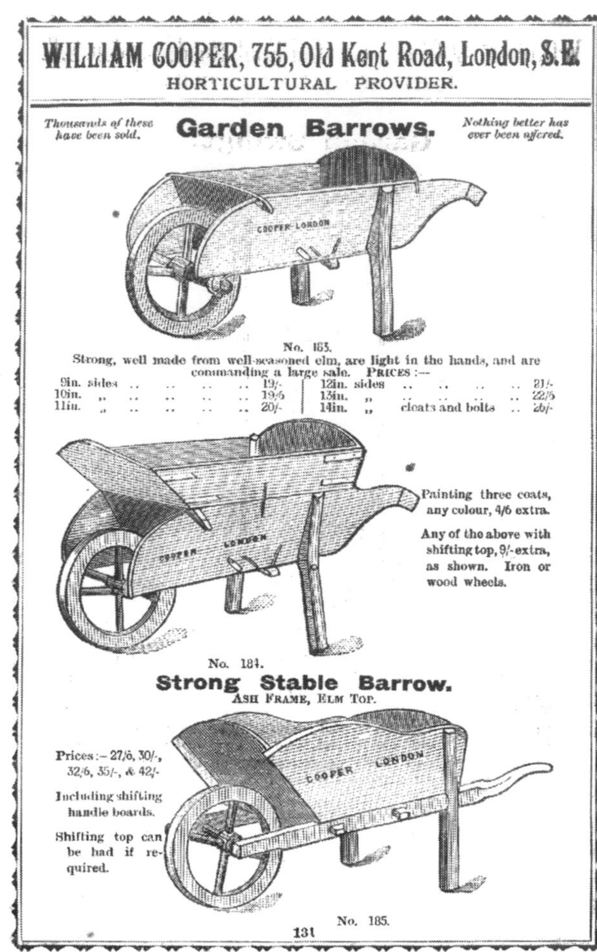

WILLIAM COOPER, 755, Old Kent Road, London, S.E.
HORTICULTURAL PROVIDER.

Thousands of these have been sold. **Garden Barrows.** *Nothing better has ever been offered.*

No. 183.

Strong, well made from well-seasoned elm, are light in the hands, and are commanding a large sale. PRICES :—

9in. sides	19/-	12in. sides	21/-
10in. ,,	19/6	13in. ,,	22/6
11in. ,,	20/-	14in. ,, cleats and bolts	26/-

Painting three coats, any colour, 4/6 extra.

Any of the above with shifting top, 9/- extra, as shown. Iron or wood wheels.

No. 184.

Strong Stable Barrow.
ASH FRAME, ELM TOP.

Prices:—27/6, 30/-, 32/6, 35/-, & 42/-

Including shifting handle boards.

Shifting top can be had if required.

No. 185.

131

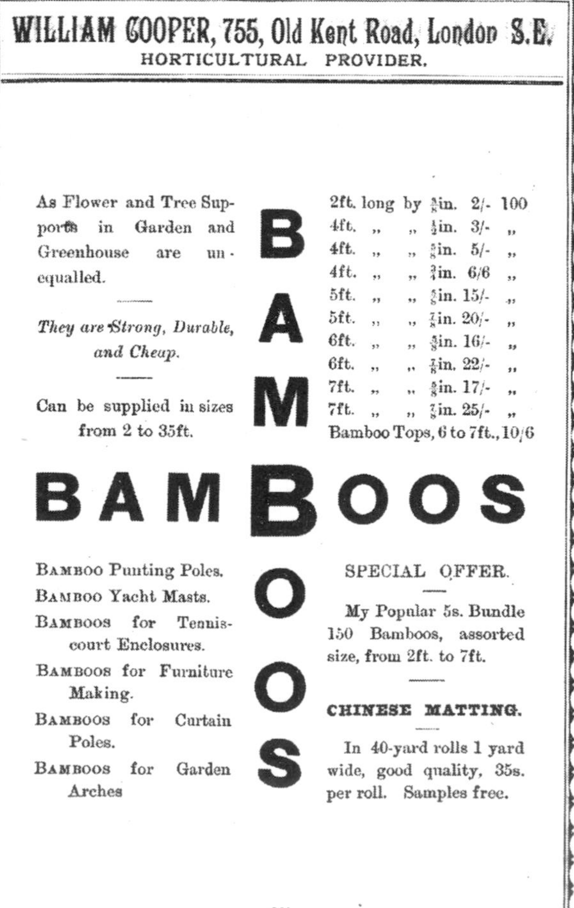

WILLIAM COOPER, 755, Old Kent Road, London S.E.
HORTICULTURAL PROVIDER.

As Flower and Tree Supports in Garden and Greenhouse are unequalled.

They are Strong, Durable, and Cheap.

Can be supplied in sizes from 2 to 35ft.

BAMBOOS

2ft. long by ⅜in. 2/- 100
4ft. ,, ,, ½in. 3/- ,,
4ft. ,, ,, ⅝in. 5/- ,,
4ft. ,, ,, ¾in. 6/6 ,,
5ft. ,, ,, ⅝in. 15/- ,,
5ft. ,, ,, ⅞in. 20/- ,,
6ft. ,, ,, ⅝in. 16/- ,,
6ft. ,, ,, ⅞in. 22/- ,,
7ft. ,, ,, ⅝in. 17/- ,,
7ft. ,, ,, ⅞in. 25/- ,,
Bamboo Tops, 6 to 7ft., 10/6

BAMBOOS

BAMBOO Punting Poles.
BAMBOO Yacht Masts.
BAMBOOS for Tennis-court Enclosures.
BAMBOOS for Furniture Making.
BAMBOOS for Curtain Poles.
BAMBOOS for Garden Arches

SPECIAL OFFER.

My Popular 5s. Bundle 150 Bamboos, assorted size, from 2ft. to 7ft.

CHINESE MATTING.

In 40-yard rolls 1 yard wide, good quality, 35s. per roll. Samples free.

246

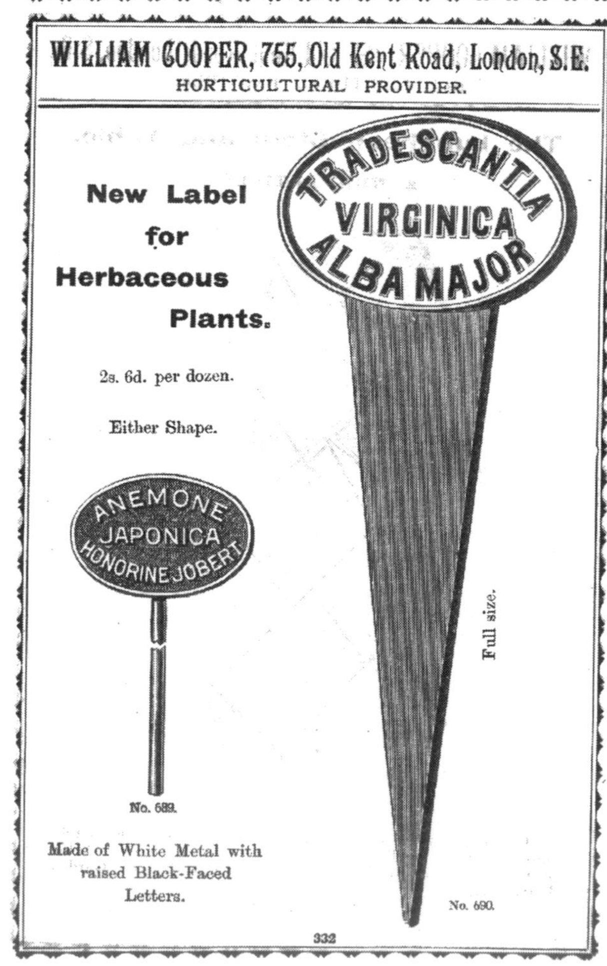

WILLIAM COOPER, 755, Old Kent Road, London, S.E.
HORTICULTURAL PROVIDER.

New Label for Herbaceous Plants.

2s. 6d. per dozen.

Either Shape.

Full size.

No. 689.

Made of White Metal with raised Black-Faced Letters.

No. 690.

332

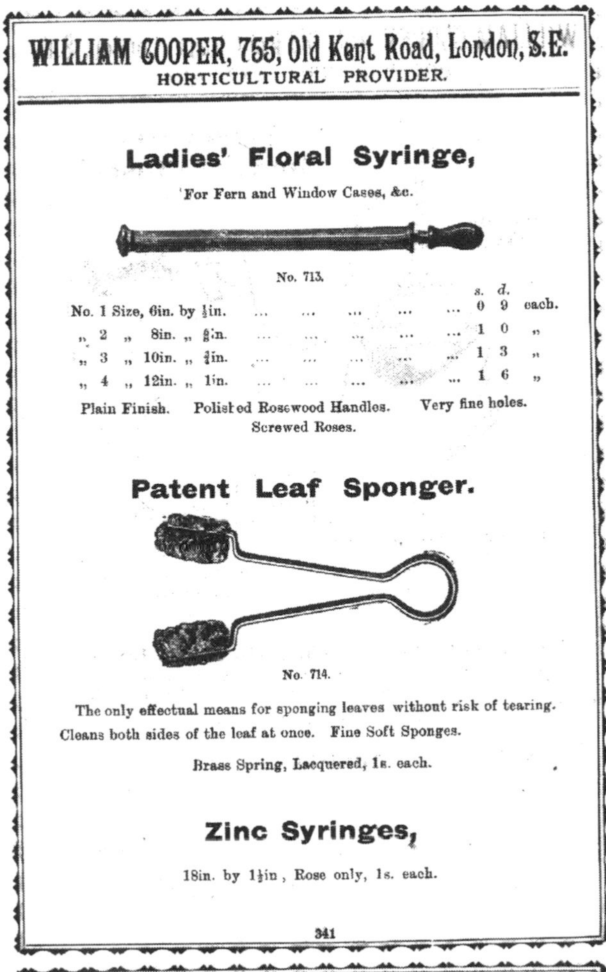

WILLIAM COOPER, 755, Old Kent Road, London, S.E.
HORTICULTURAL PROVIDER.

Ladies' Floral Syringe,

For Fern and Window Cases, &c.

No. 713.

		s.	d.	
No. 1 Size, 6in. by ½in.	...	0	9	each.
„ 2 „ 8in. „ ⅝in.	...	1	0	„
„ 3 „ 10in. „ ¾in.	...	1	3	„
„ 4 „ 12in. „ 1in.	...	1	6	„

Plain Finish. Polished Rosewood Handles. Very fine holes.
Screwed Roses.

Patent Leaf Sponger.

No. 714.

The only effectual means for sponging leaves without risk of tearing. Cleans both sides of the leaf at once. Fine Soft Sponges.

Brass Spring, Lacquered, 1s. each.

Zinc Syringes,

18in. by 1½in., Rose only, 1s. each.

341

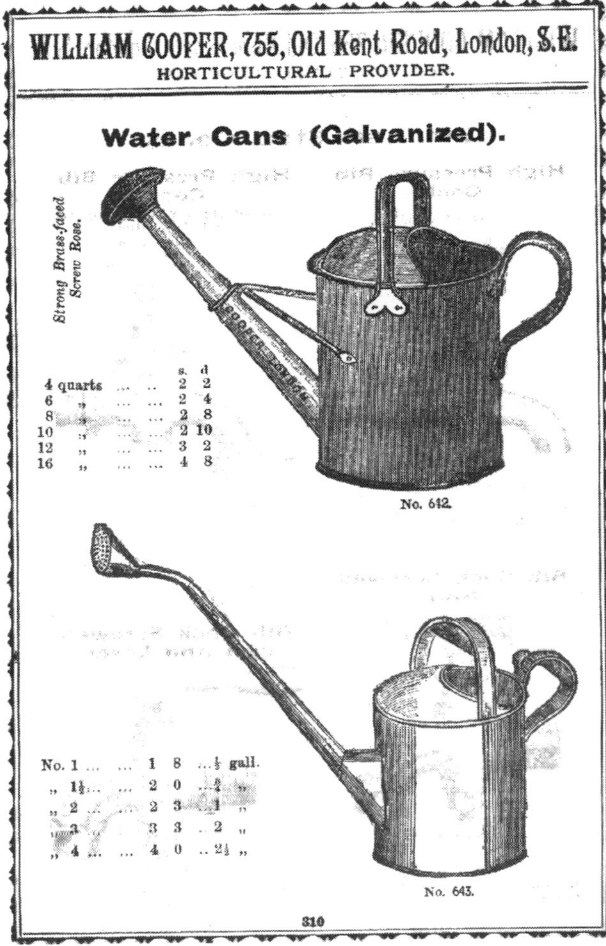

WILLIAM COOPER, 755, Old Kent Road, London, S.E.
HORTICULTURAL PROVIDER.

Water Cans (Galvanized).

Strong Brass-faced Screw Rose.

		s.	d
4 quarts	...	2	2
6 „	...	2	4
8 „	...	2	8
10 „	...	2	10
12 „	...	3	2
16 „	...	4	8

No. 642.

No. 1 ...	1	8	... ½ gall.
„ 1½ ...	2	0	... ¾ „
„ 2 ...	2	3	... 1 „
„ 3 ...	3	3	.. 2 „
„ 4 ...	4	0	.. 2½ „

No. 643.

310

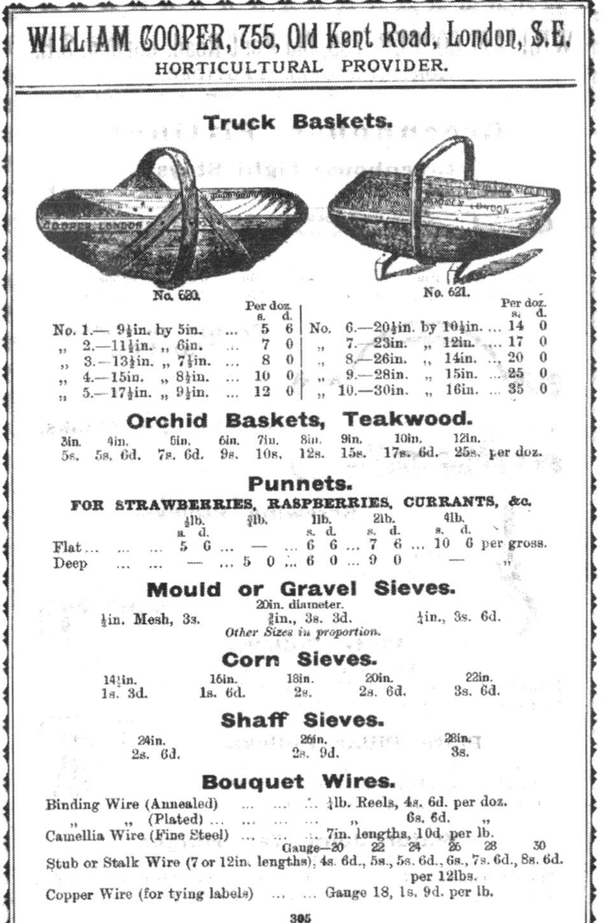

WILLIAM COOPER, 755, Old Kent Road, London, S.E.
HORTICULTURAL PROVIDER.

Truck Baskets.

No. 620. No. 621.

	Per doz. s.	d.		Per doz. s.	d.
No. 1.—9½in. by 5in. ...	5	6	No. 6.—20½in. by 10½in. ...	14	0
„ 2.—11½in. „ 6in. ...	7	0	„ 7.—23in. „ 12in. ...	17	0
„ 3.—13½in. „ 7½in. ...	8	0	„ 8.—26in. „ 14in. ...	20	0
„ 4.—15in. „ 8½in. ...	10	0	„ 9.—28in. „ 15in. ...	25	0
„ 5.—17½in. „ 9½in. ...	12	0	„ 10.—30in. „ 16in. ...	35	0

Orchid Baskets, Teakwood.

3in.	4in.	5in.	6in.	7in.	8in.	9in.	10in.	12in.
5s.	5s. 6d.	7s. 6d.	9s.	10s.	12s.	15s.	17s. 6d.	25s. per doz.

Punnets.

FOR STRAWBERRIES, RASPBERRIES, CURRANTS, &c.

	½lb. s. d.	¾lb.	1lb. s. d.	2lb. s. d.	4lb. s. d.	
Flat ...	5 6	—	6 6	7 6	10 6	per gross.
Deep ...	—	5 0	6 0	9 0	—	„

Mould or Gravel Sieves.

20in. diameter.

⅛in. Mesh, 3s. ⅜in., 3s. 3d. ¼in., 3s. 6d.

Other Sizes in proportion.

Corn Sieves.

14½in.	16in.	18in.	20in.	22in.
1s. 3d.	1s. 6d.	2s.	2s. 6d.	3s. 6d.

Shaff Sieves.

24in.	26in.	28in.
2s. 6d.	2s. 9d.	3s.

Bouquet Wires.

Binding Wire (Annealed) ... ¼lb. Reels, 4s. 6d. per doz.
„ „ (Plated) ... „ 6s. 6d. „
Camellia Wire (Fine Steel) ... 7in. lengths, 10d. per lb.
Gauge—20 22 24 26 28 30
Stub or Stalk Wire (7 or 12in. lengths), 4s. 6d., 5s., 5s. 6d., 6s., 7s. 6d., 8s. 6d. per 12lbs.
Copper Wire (for tying labels) ... Gauge 18, 1s. 9d. per lb.

305

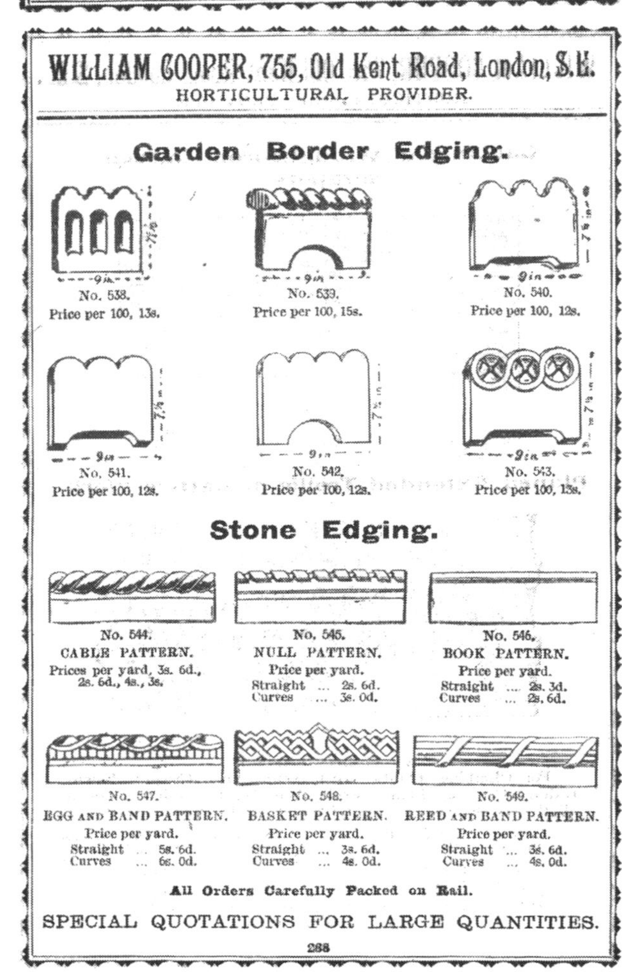

WILLIAM COOPER, 755, Old Kent Road, London, S.E.
HORTICULTURAL PROVIDER.

Garden Border Edging.

No. 538. Price per 100, 13s.
No. 539. Price per 100, 15s.
No. 540. Price per 100, 12s.
No. 541. Price per 100, 12s.
No. 542. Price per 100, 12s.
No. 543. Price per 100, 13s.

Stone Edging.

No. 544. CABLE PATTERN. Prices per yard, 3s. 6d., 2s. 6d., 4s., 3s.

No. 545. NULL PATTERN. Price per yard. Straight ... 2s. 6d. Curves ... 3s. 0d.

No. 546. BOOK PATTERN. Price per yard. Straight ... 2s. 3d. Curves ... 2s. 6d.

No. 547. EGG AND BAND PATTERN. Price per yard. Straight ... 5s. 6d. Curves ... 6s. 0d.

No. 548. BASKET PATTERN. Price per yard. Straight ... 3s. 6d. Curves ... 4s. 0d.

No. 549. REED AND BAND PATTERN. Price per yard. Straight ... 3s. 6d. Curves ... 4s. 0d.

All Orders Carefully Packed on Rail.

SPECIAL QUOTATIONS FOR LARGE QUANTITIES.

268

GALVANIZED CROQUET BORDERING,

COMPLETE WITH 25 STAKES TO 50 YARDS.

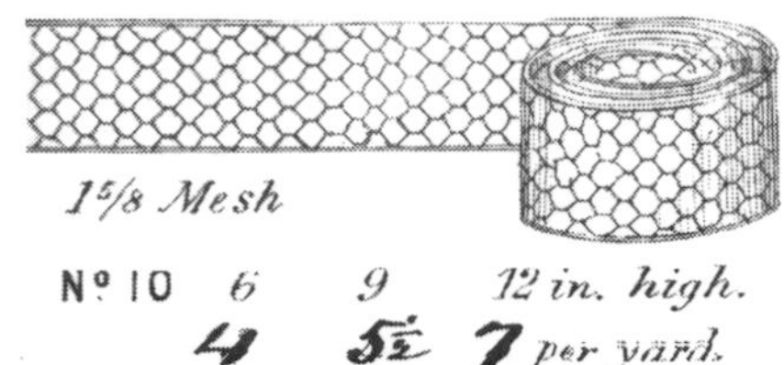

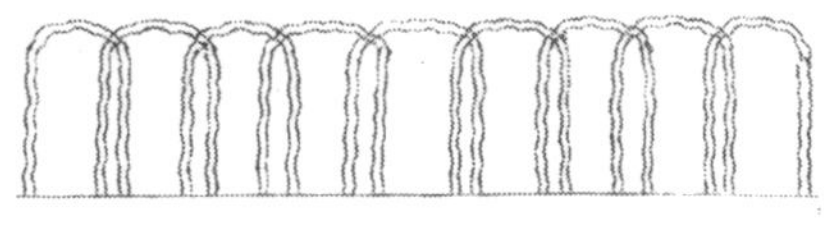

1⅝ Mesh

Nº 10 6 9 12 in. high.
4 5½ 7 per yard.

Nº 11 12 in. high 4/- per doz.

1⅝ Mesh

Nº 12 6 9 12 in. high.
6 8 10 per yard.

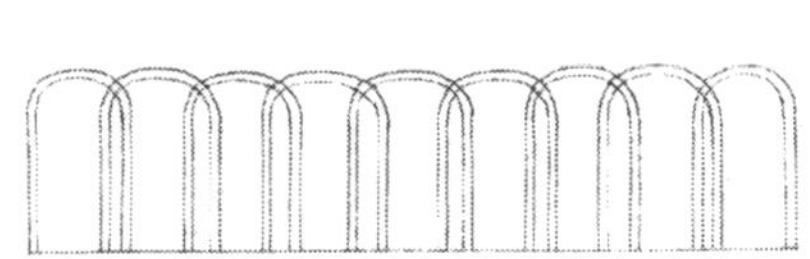

Nº 13 6 9 12 in. high
1/ 1/4 1/8 per yard.

Nº 14 12 in. high 3/6 per doz.

Nº 15 6 9 12 in. high.
1/- 1/4 1/8 per yard.

GALVANIZED GARDEN BORDERING,

9 IN. HIGH PER LINEAL FEET.

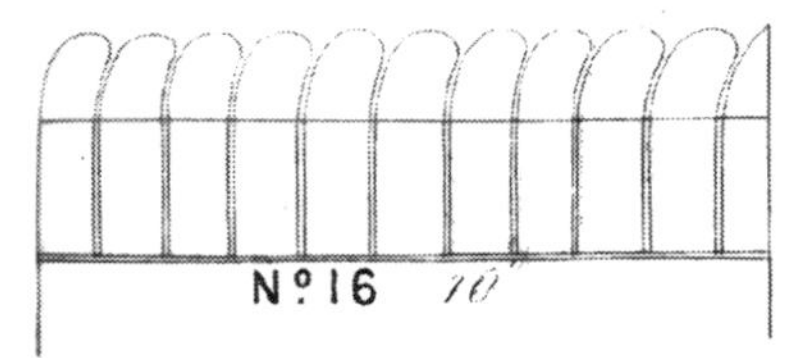

Nº 16 10

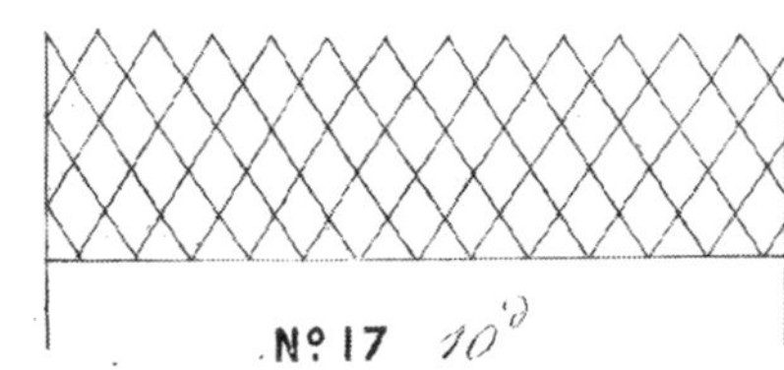

Nº 17 10d

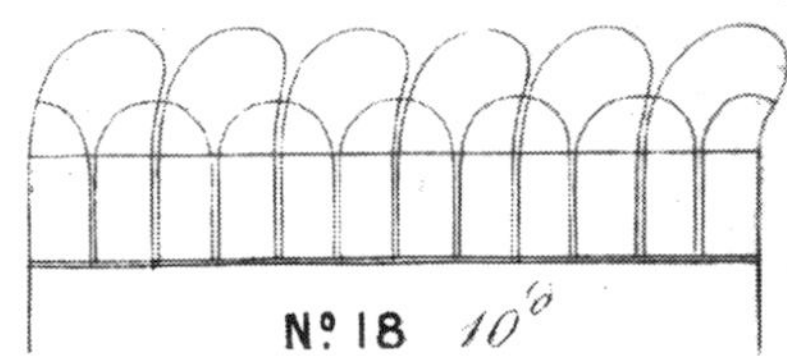

Nº 18 10d

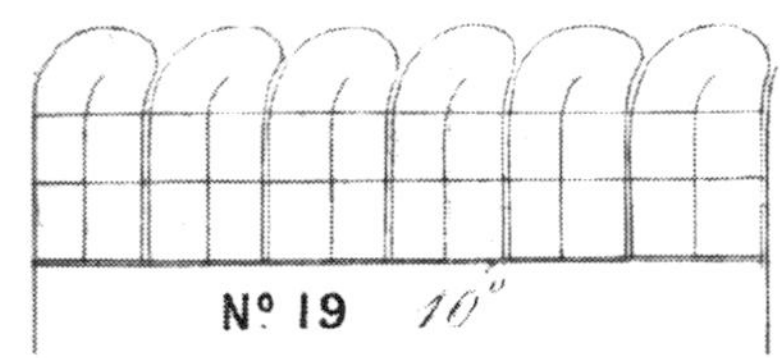

Nº 19 10d

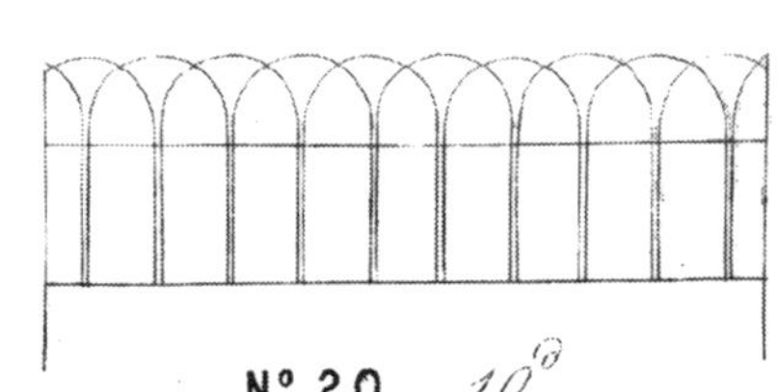

Nº 20 10d

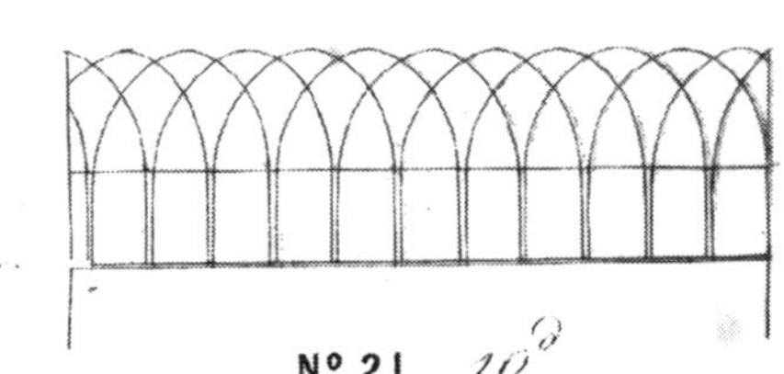

Nº 21 10d

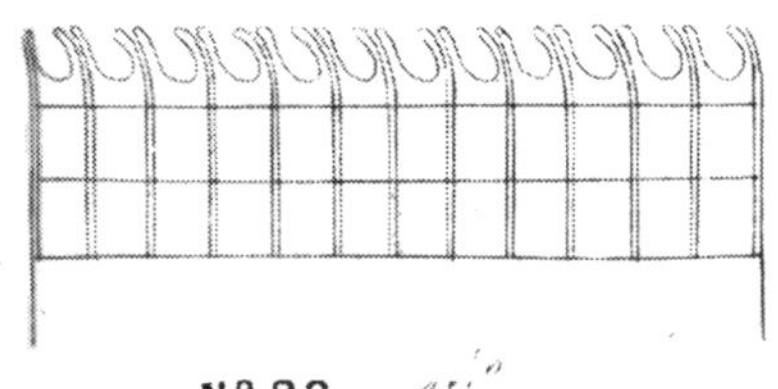

Nº 22 10d

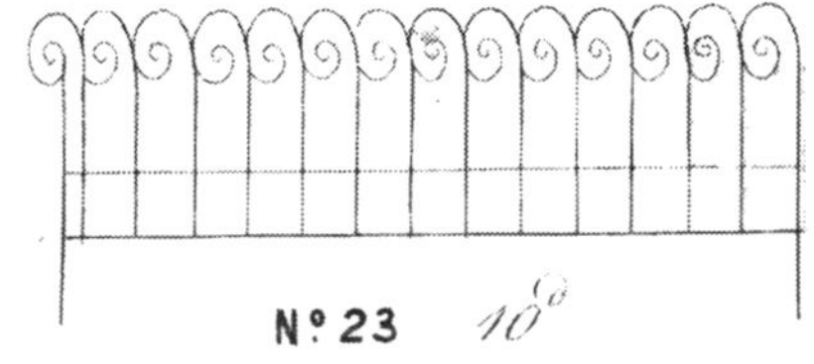

Nº 23 10d

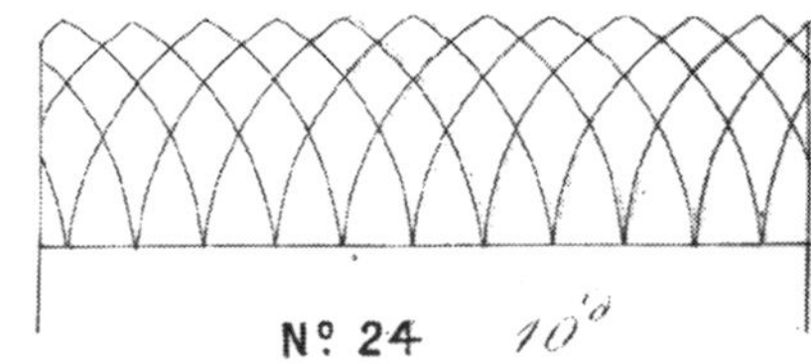

Nº 24 10d

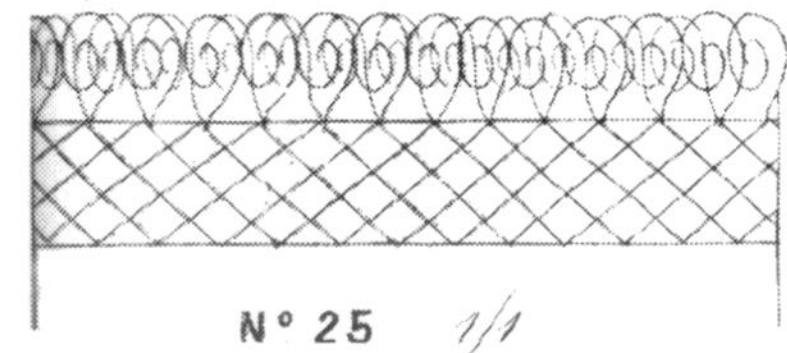

Nº 25 1/1

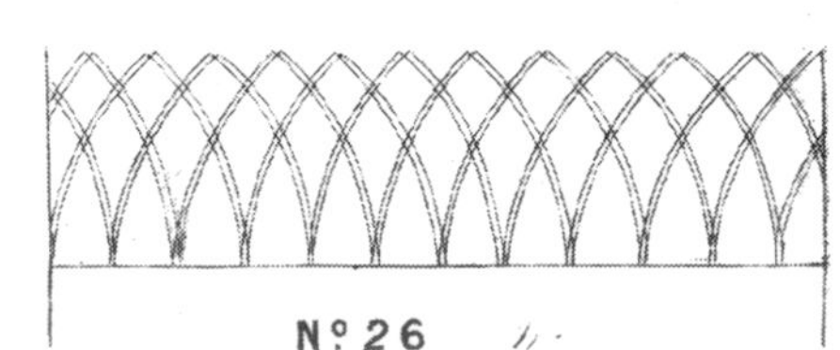

Nº 26 1/-

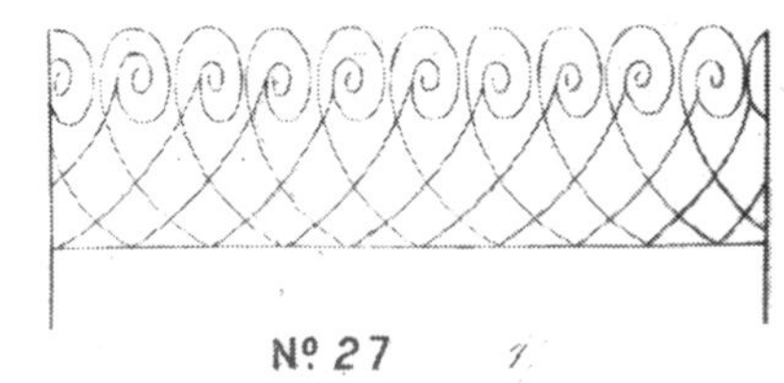

Nº 27 1/

DIRECTION PLATES & POSTS FOR GARDEN & PARK.

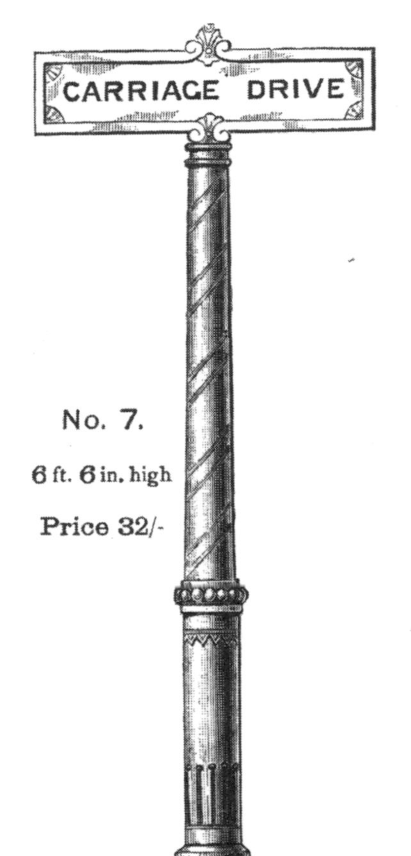

No. 7.

6 ft. 6 in. high

Price 32/-

No. 6.

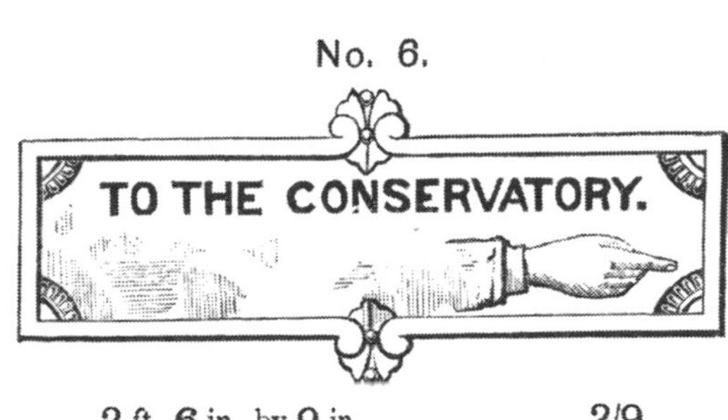

2 ft. 6 in. by 9 in. 2/9

No. 13.

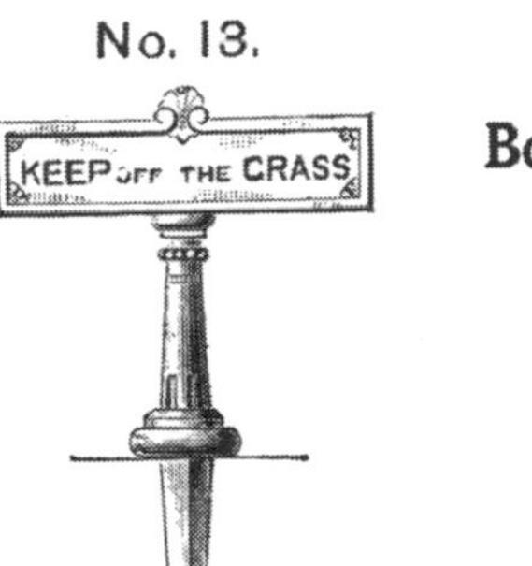

18 in. long ... 3/6

Botanical Tablets.

No. 4.

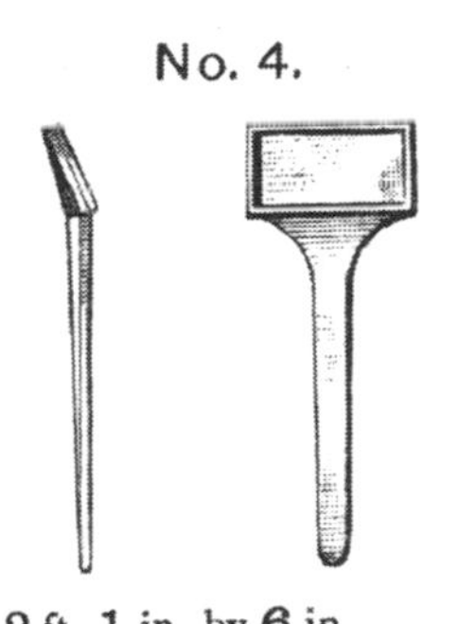

2 ft. 1 in. by 6 in. ... 2/6

Line Reel.

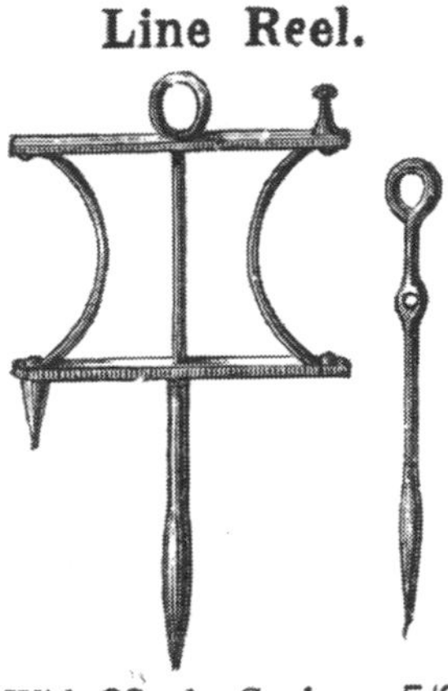

With 60 yds. Cord ... 5/6

No. 12.

16 in. high ... 4/-

GARDEN BORDERINGS.

No. 5.

Wrought-iron Spiral Bordering.

Prices.

9 in. wide, galvanized	...	per doz.	2/3
12 in. ,,	,,	...	,,	2/9
15 in. ,,	,,	...	,,	3/6

No. 7.

Galvanized Wire Garden Borderings.

No. 6.

Made any length or shape required.

No. 6.	12 in. high	...	per yard	9d.
No. 7.	15 in. ,,	...	,,	10d.
No. 8.	18 in. ,,	...	,,	1/-

No. 4.

Cast-iron Garden Bordering.

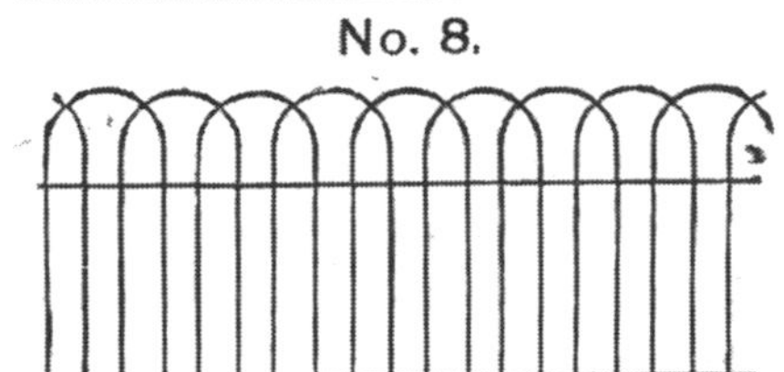

Price.

1 ft. lengths, painted ... per ft. 5d.

No. 8.

Carriage Paid on Orders of 40/- net value and upwards.

IMPROVED GARDEN ROLLERS.

These Rollers are thoroughly well made, and have rounded edges and balanced handles.

Prices.

SINGLE CYLINDER.

Width and Diameter. Inches.	Approximate Weights. Cwt. qr. lb.		£ s. d.
16 by 16	2 0 7	..	**1 19 0**
18 ,, 18	2 2 0	..	**2 11 0**
20 ,, 20	2 3 10	..	**2 17 0**
22 ,, 22	3 2 24	..	**3 9 0**
24 ,, 24	4 0 16	..	**4 8 0**

DOUBLE CYLINDER.

Width and Diameter. Inches.	Approximate Weights. Cwt. qr. lb.		£ s. d.
18 by 16	2 1 7	..	**2 7 0**
20 ,, 18	2 2 14	..	**2 17 0**
22 ,, 20	2 3 20	..	**3 7 6**
24 ,, 22	3 3 0	..	**4 5 0**
26 ,, 24	3 3 16	..	**4 18 6**
30 ,, 26	6 3 10	..	**7 0 0**

PATENT

WATER-BALLAST GARDEN & ASPHALT ROLLERS.

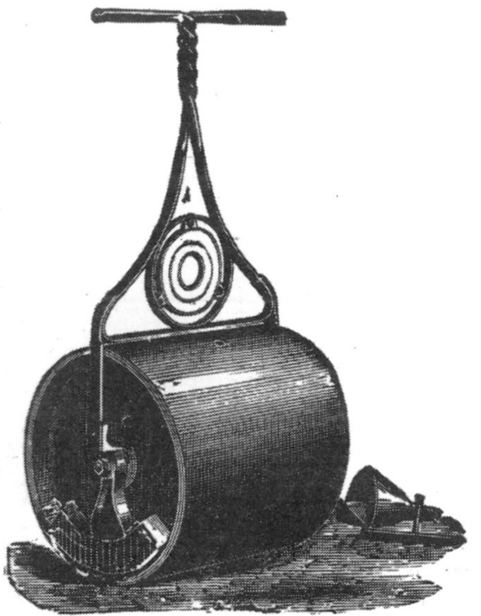

Prices.

SINGLE CYLINDER.

Width and Diameter. Inches.	Approximate Weight. Empty. Cwt. qr. lb.	Approximate Weight. Full. Cwt. qr. lb.		£ s. d.
18 by 18	2 2 4	3 3 7	..	**3 3 0**
21 ,, 21	3 1 0	5 1 4	..	**3 19 0**
24 ,, 24	4 1 0	7 0 14	..	**5 1 0**
27 ,, 27	6 2 14	10 0 4	..	**6 15 0**
30 ,, 30	8 2 0	13 2 14	..	[illegible]

DOUBLE CYLINDER.

Width and Diameter. Inches.	Approximate Weight. Empty. Cwt. qr. lb.	Approximate Weight. Full. Cwt. qr. lb.		£ s. d.
20 by 20	4 0 24	6 0 7	..	**6 0 0**
24 ,, 24	5 3 4	7 2 7	..	**7 10 0**
26 ,, 26	6 2 10	9 1 7	..	**9 0 0**
28 ,, 28	8 1 7	11 1 0	..	**10 15 0**
30 ,, 30	9 2 7	13 0 14	..	**12 0 0**

Pony Shafts can be fitted to the 28in. and 30in. sizes in place of handles at—28in., **21/-**; and 30in., **22/6** extra.

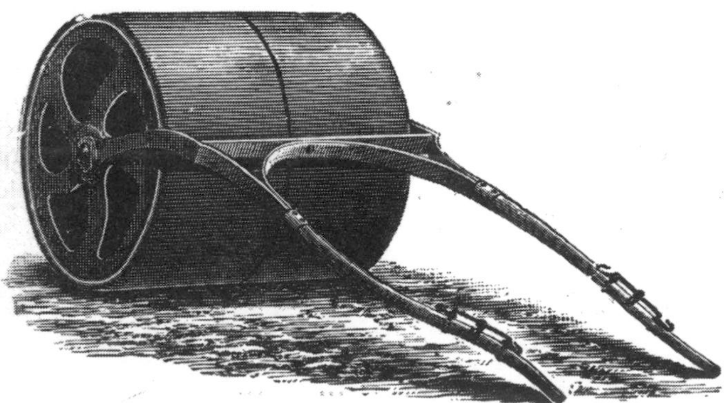

PONY

GARDEN ROLLERS

Adapted for Public Grounds, Lawns, Cricket Grounds, Golf Links, Gravel Walks, &c.

Prices and particulars on application.

GORTON, MANCHESTER.

WROUGHT-IRON WHEELBARROWS.

No. 2. GARDEN BARROW.

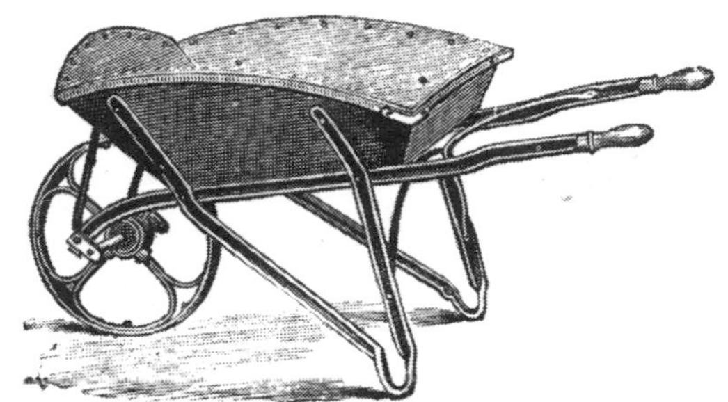

Extra strong Barrow, with large body. For Garden and Stable use.

Price.

Painted		23/6
Body galvanized	extra	5/6

No. 5. Wrought-Iron Fodder Barrow.

Made entirely of wrought-iron. Suited for carrying leaves, and for carting and conveying food for cattle.
Size of Body—2 ft. 6 in. long, 1 ft. 10 in. wide, 1 ft. 2 in. deep.

Price.

Painted		38/6
Body Galvanized	extra	5/6

No. 6. WROUGHT-IRON ASHES OR OFFAL BARROW.

Garden Barrow and Cinder Sifter Combined.

The top can be taken off, making an Excellent Leaf and Garden Barrow.

Size of B dy—2 ft. 7 in. long, 2 ft. wide, 1 ft. 5 in. deep.

Price.

Painted		30/-
Body galvanized	extra	7/6
If fitted with Registered Cinder Sifter ...	,,	5/-

Registered, No. 7,655.

NEW CINDER SIFTER.

Registered, No. 120,537.

Can be used in connection with any ordinary Wheelbarrow, Offal Barrow, or Ash Pit. No fixing required. Any one can use it.

Price 5/- each, net.

Wrought-iron Greasing Jack.

For Carriages, etc.

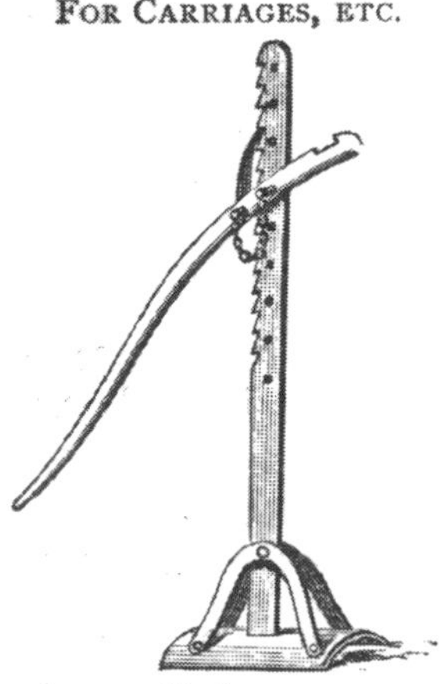

Price.

No. 1, 5/6; No. 2, 6/6; No. 3, 7/6

No. 4. STRONG GARDEN WHEELBARROW.

Ash frame, deal body, wrought-iron wheel, painted.

Price £1 10 0

Shifting boards for carrying leaves, &c., fitted to barrow, 12/- extra.

Carriage Paid on Orders of 40/- net value and upwards.

Wrought-iron Hand Sack Barrow.

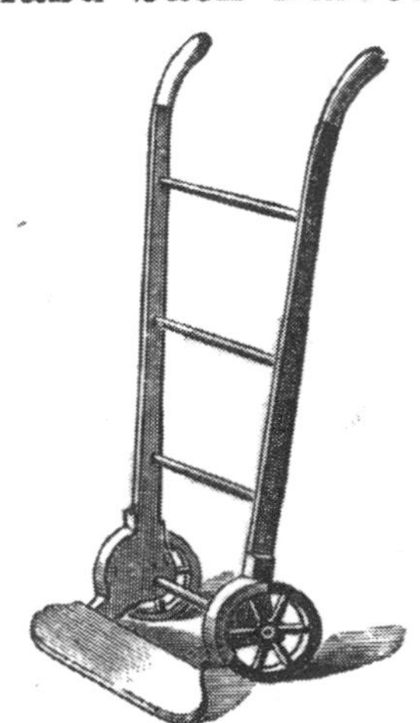

Price 10/- each.

GARDEN SHEARS.

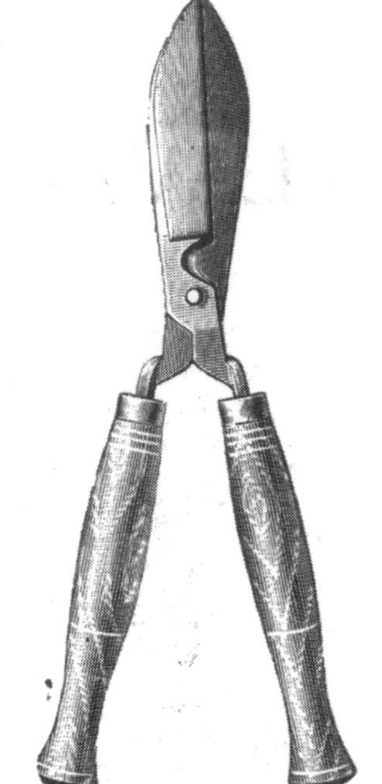

LADIES' GARDEN SHEARS.

No. 1	2	3	4
3/6	**3/6**	**3/6**	**4/0** each.

No. 100—WITH BRIGHT HOOPS. No. 101—WITH PRUNING NOTCH.

	7½	8	8½	9	9½	10	10½	11	11½	12	12½ inches.
No. 100—	***3/2**	***3/3**	***3/6**	***4/0**	***4/6**	***4/9**	**5/0**	**5/6**	**6/3**	**7/3**	**8/9** per pair.
„ 101—	**3/8**	***3/9**	***4/0**	***4/6**	***5/0**	***5/3**	**5/6**	**6/0**	**6/9**	**7/9**	**9/3** „

GRASS AND BORDER SHEARS.

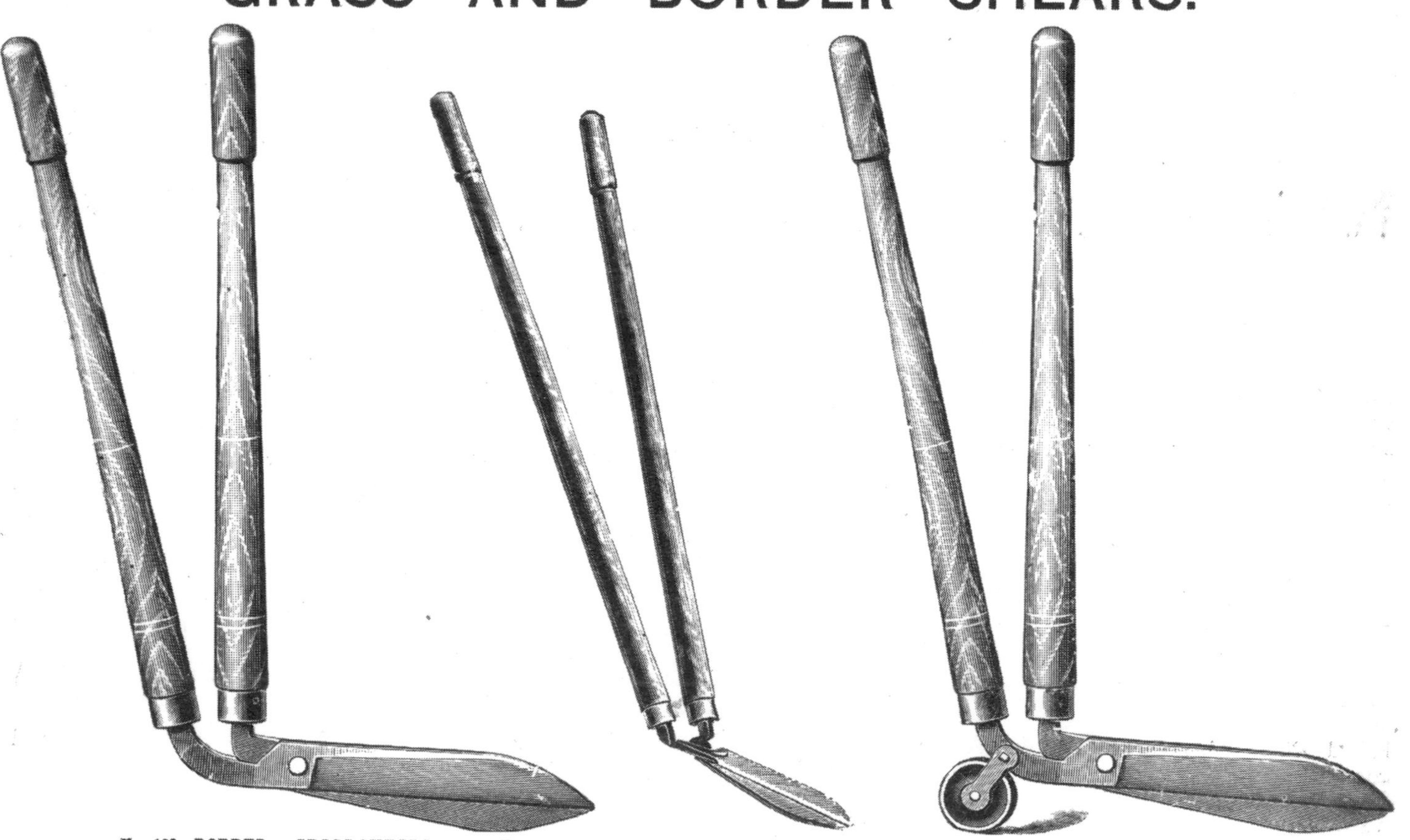

No. 103—BORDER or GRASS SHEARS. No. 105—GRASS LAWN SHEARS. No. 104—BORDER or GRASS SHEARS, with Wheel.

	8	8½	9	9½	10	10½	11 inches.
No. 103—	***5/0**	***5/6**	***6/0**	***6/6**	***7/0**	**7/6**	**8/0** per pair.
No. 104—	**6/0**	**6/6**	***7/0**	***7/6**	***8/0**	**8/6**	**9/0** „
No. 105—	**5/0**	***5/6**	***6/0**	***6/6**	***7/0**	***7/6**	***8/0** „

......If with two wheels, **2/0** per pair extra.

N.B.—Those marked with an asterisk are the most saleable sizes.

GORTON, MANCHESTER.

PATENT SQUARE HAND GLASSES.

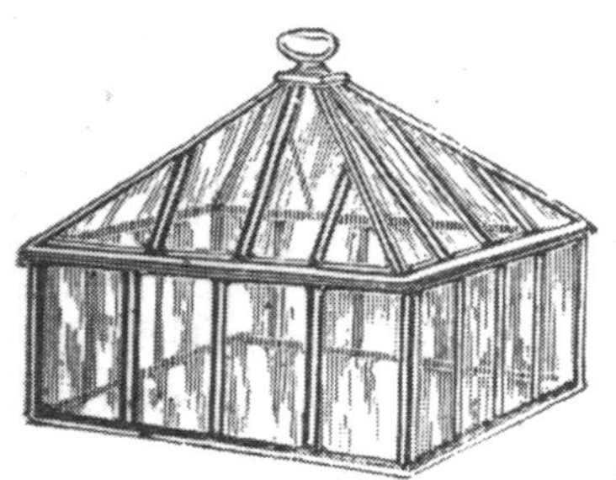

Zinc Frame.

ADVANTAGES.

STRENGTH.—No putty required. Every frame alike in size and shape. No glazier needed for repairing.

DURABILITY.—Will retain its original shape and strength should all the glass be broken and be re-glazed by any inexperienced person.

The frames are made of strong corrugated zinc and glazed with zinc clips, no putty or solder being required; the operation of glazing is simple and can be performed by anybody.

The glass can be removed instantly from one frame and fixed to another without damage; all the glass is interchangeable and every frame alike.

Prices.

12	14	16	18	20	24 inch.
5/6	**7/-**	**9/-**	**10/6**	**12/6**	**20/-** each.

The four smaller sizes nest into the 20in. and pack securely into crate, charged 1/6. The same crate is required for single ones.

PATENT CAP GLASSES.

The Cheapest and Best Plant Protector in the Market. Extensively used by Market Gardeners.

Zinc Frame.

Prices.

20in., **2/6** each; 21in., **3/0** each; 21in., extra strong, **4/0** each.

A nest of one dozen Cap Glasses, pack into a crate, charged 1/6 extra.

Testimonial from the late SHIRLEY HIBBERD, Esq., F.R.H.S.

"Stoke Newington, London, W.

"I like your Square and Cap Glasses immensely; with a reasonable stock a gardener may easily make himself safe during winter respecting cauliflowers, lettuces, and Christmas roses.

"Yours truly,

"SHIRLEY HIBBERD."

HAND SEED DRILL.

WITH IMPROVED HARROW OR RAKE, BROAD RUN WHEEL, AND DOUBLE SPRING.

This small drill is of great utility on the Farm for filling up blank places in rows of Mangold Wurzel or Turnips, and also in the garden for drilling almost every kind of garden seeds; in fact, it would be a valuable implement for every farmer and gardener to possess. Its utility may be judged of from the fact that several thousands have already been sold.

This simple but useful little Drill is the invention of a working man, has found its way to the colonies in large numbers, and no gardener—market or otherwise—should be without one, [illegible] he [illegible] is desirous to economise in the sowing of his seed; and the Drill is so simple in its construction that it is scarcely possible for it to get out of order. The seed is deposited in the hopper and by simply pushing the Drill along the ground the travelling wheel gives a motion to a slide at the bottom of the hopper and the seed falls through a tube situated behind the coulter and drops into the soil. The seed on the other hand ceases to run through the moment the Drill is lifted off the ground. A boy is capable of working it with ease and it will drill as fast as he can walk. On the farm it is found of considerable advantage in filling up blank places left by the larger drills which have passed over the ground. By simply turning a thumb-screw it can be adjusted with ease for sowing mangolds, barley, wheat, sainfoin, tares, onions, cabbage, flax, cauliflower, and brocoli seeds.

ADMIRABLY ADAPTED FOR EMIGRANTS.

Prices.

No. 1.—One Row Drill as illustrated	**10/6** each.
" " fitted with two adjustable wheels for different widths	**14/-** "
No. 2.—One Row Drill same as No. 1 but larger	**14/-** "
" " fitted with two adjustable wheels for different widths	**16/6** "

GORTON, MANCHESTER.

PATENT

"RUNAWAY" LAWN MOWER.

Collecting the Grass

(When the plate in the foreground is in position behind the cylinder).

Box & Plate removed,

As used for cutting long wet grass on uneven ground or distributing short cuttings behind.

Turned Completely Over,

For Wheeling away, out of gear, with cylinder raised off the ground.
Safe on the roughest road.

Special attention is invited to this high-class machine. It will be found superior to any of its rivals, and although only introduced in 1893 many thousands are now in use, and the universal opinion is that the "Runaway" is by far the best lawn mower of its class—a strong boy can work the largest size without assistance. It can be used for mowing long or short grass, wet or dry, is easy to work on uneven ground, and will keep a lawn in the perfection of order, imparting to it an even, velvety appearance.

The facility of transport from the tool house to the lawn is unique. By simply turning the handle over (see engraving), the cutting cylinder is raised from the ground and at the same time thrown out of gear so that the machine can be wheeled away in perfect safety on the roughest road. For **Golf Links, Tennis and Croquet Grounds,** the large sizes are specially recommended.

When so ordered, the driving wheels are surrounded with broad, thick India-rubber Tyres of best quality, which afford considerable protection to the adjustments of the machine whenever roughly handled by careless persons.

The whole machine is thoroughly well made and durable. The Cutting Cylinder is of the latest and most approved construction, running in gun metal bushes; it makes a clean, even cut, without ribbing, and throws all the cut grass into the box provided.

Prices and Sizes.

Without India-rubber Tyres:—

9in. **38/6** 11in. **45/-** 13in. **57/6** 15in. **67/6** 17in. **84/-** 19in. **105/-** 21in. **120/-**

With India-rubber Tyres:—

9in. **46/-** 11in. **52/6** 13in. **65/-** 15in. **75/-** 17in. **92/6** 19in. **115/-** 21in. **130/-**

Grass Collecting Boxes and Delivery Plates Complete, extra:—

9in. **5/-** 11in. **5/-** 13in. **7/6** 15in. **7/6** 17in. **10/-** 19in. **10/-** 21in. **10/-**

N.B.—When fitted with wheels, encircled with thick India-rubber Tyres, the Machine is absolutely noiseless in operation, and is highly recommended.

GORTON, MANCHESTER.

PATENT "ANGLO-AMERICAN" PONY LAWN MOWERS.

These machines are simple in construction, easy to work, inexpensive to keep in good repair, splendid mowers whether on level or undulating ground, and are fitted with the best tipping arrangement yet introduced.

The Cylinders and Driving Shafts are made of solid steel, the Cutters are toughened by a new process and are not liable to snap, and all the various parts are constructed to ensure great durability.

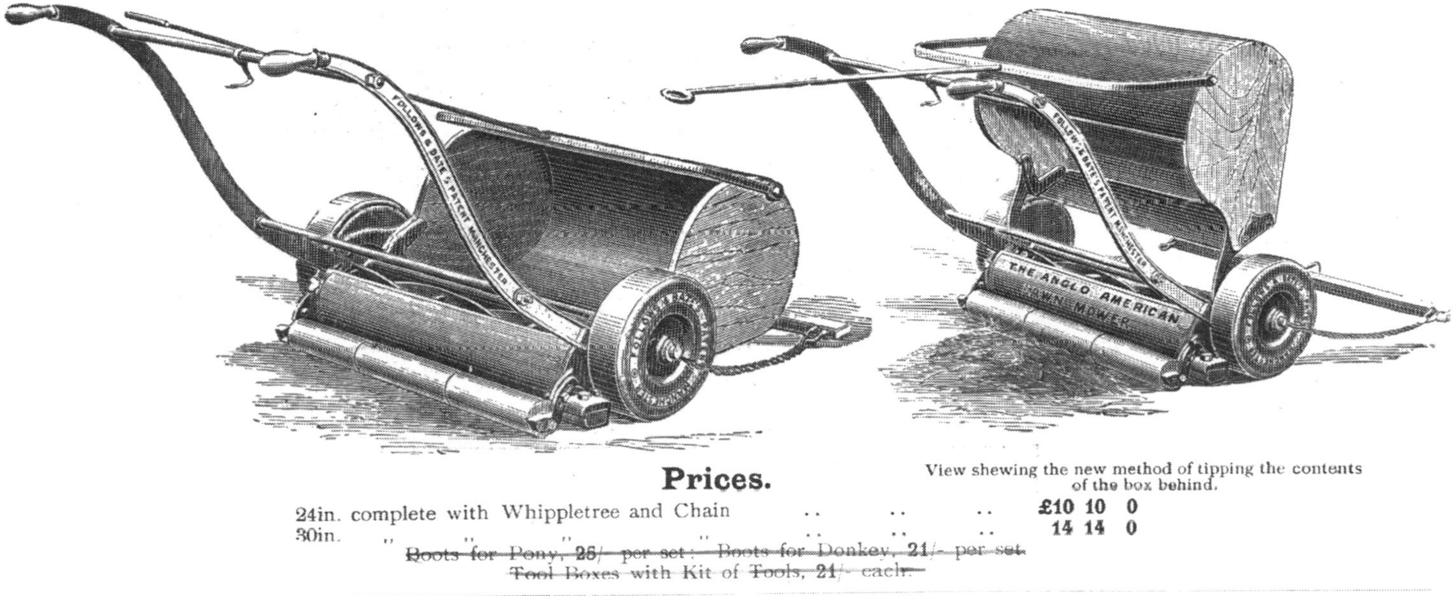

View shewing the new method of tipping the contents of the box behind.

Prices.

24in. complete with Whippletree and Chain	£10 10 0
30in. " " "	14 14 0

~~Boots for Pony, 25/- per set; Boots for Donkey, 21/- per set.~~

~~Tool Boxes with Kit of Tools, 21/- each.~~

HORSE AND PONY POWER "ROLLER" MACHINES.

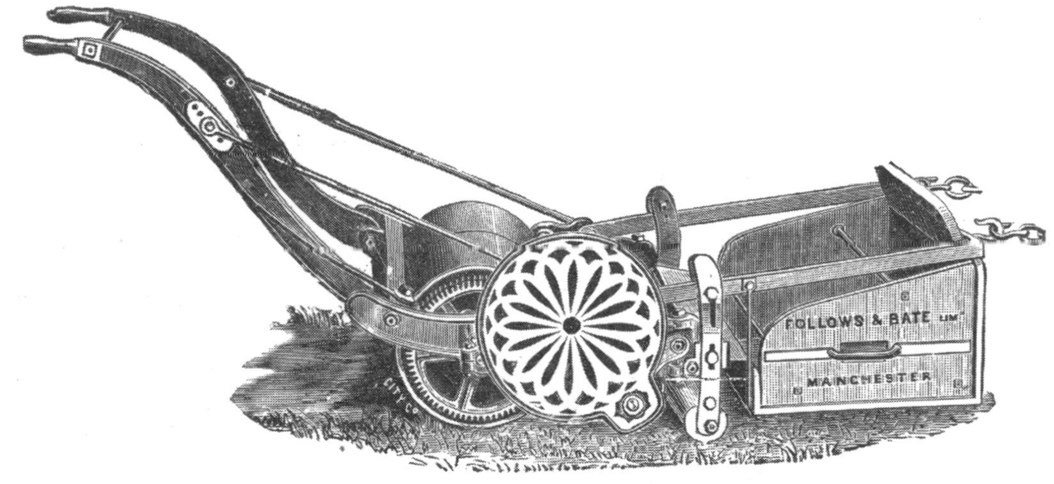

These newly-designed Horse Power Lawn Mowers are of unusual strength, and will be found to surpass anything of the kind before offered. They are suitable for large Lawns and Pleasure Grounds, Cricket Grounds, Bowling Greens, Lawn Tennis Grounds, Golf Links, Parks, &c., &c.

They are fitted with adjustable handles, an improved form of Grass Collecting Box, and Side Delivery.

The Cutters are made by a new process, and are so tough that they will perform the heaviest work without risk of injury, the method of setting and adjusting them is also exceedingly simple.

Prices.

Pony Machines, 26in. ..				£14 10 0
" " 30in. ..				18 0 0
	30in.	36in.	42in.	48in.
Horse Machines,	£20	£24	£28	£32

Leather Boots, see page 22.

GORTON, MANCHESTER.

PATENT "EVERLASTING" SOLID

LAWN MOWING HORSE BOOTS.

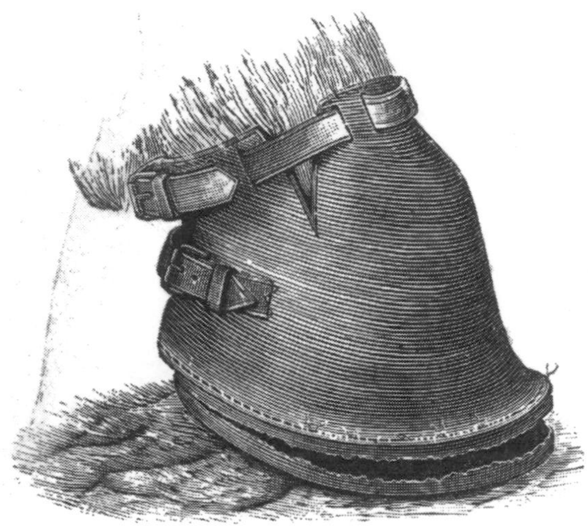

This illustrates the **OLD STYLE.**
Lawn cut up and the boot ripped and done for.

THESE Boots being blocked, sole and upper in one piece, fit better, are more compact and comfortable, and much more durable than any others in use. They retain their shape, and having no sharp edges cannot cut up or mark the lawn and are far superior in every way to the ordinary boot. The Vamp is secured by patent rivets.

Price, per Set of Four.

Horse	**35/-**
Cob	**30/-**
Pony	**25/-**

Extra size, extra price.

This illustrates the **NEW STYLE.**
Lawn perfect and the boot sound.

FOLLOWS & BATE'S

NEW LAWN MOWER TOOL CHEST.

To all users of Lawn Mowing Machines, whether professional gardeners, or amateurs, the **Lawn Mower Tool Chest** will be found most useful, indeed almost indispensable. It contains precisely such a set of Tools as is used by a skilled workman for taking to pieces, sharpening, and adjusting these machines.

The Box is well and strongly made of best Polished Pine, with separate compartments for the various Tools and Fittings, of which a list is given.

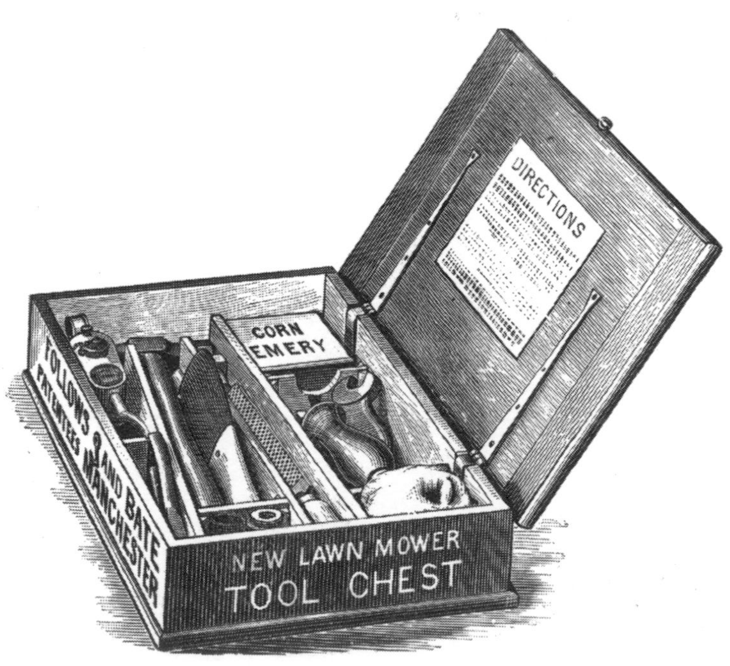

CONTENTS OF TOOL CHEST.

Box of prepared Corn Emery, and Leather Pad with Handle, for sharpening cylinder; pair of strong Flat Nose Plyers; one dozen Taper and Eye Pins for Wheels; four Ratchet Keys; Coil of Soft Iron Wire and Drift Punch, for fastening a loose Cutter; two Wrenches, for various sizes of Nuts; one Sharpening Handle; Sponge Cloth; Patent Spring Valve Oiler; File and Handle; Hammer; assortment of Iron Washers, &c.

Price complete, 12/6.

GORTON, MANCHESTER.

PORTABLE GARDEN HOSE REEL.

No. 99.

This Reel will carry 120 feet of $\frac{1}{2}$inch, or 100 feet of $\frac{3}{4}$inch Hose, or can be fitted to carry larger quantities at a little extra cost.

The Water passing from the Standpipe direct through the centre of the Reel, as well as through the Hose, enables the user to water with a part of, or all the Hose on the Reel, or out at the full length of the Hose.

Price .... £2. 15s. 0d.

IMPROVED BRASS GARDEN SYRINGES.

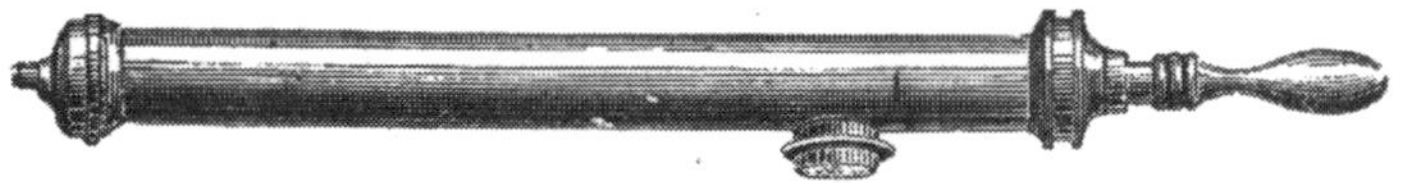

Sizes and Prices.

	Best Quality. 2 Roses and 1 Jet.	Second Quality. 1 Rose and 1 Jet.
$1\frac{1}{4}$in. diameter by 14in.	**8/-** each	.. **3/6** each.
$1\frac{1}{4}$in. diameter by 16in.	**9/-** ,,	.. **4/-** ,,
$1\frac{1}{4}$in. diameter by 18in.	**12/-** each	.. **4/6** each.
$1\frac{1}{2}$in. diameter by 20in.	**15/-** ,,	.. **6/6** ,,

IMPROVED HOSE REEL

No. 100.

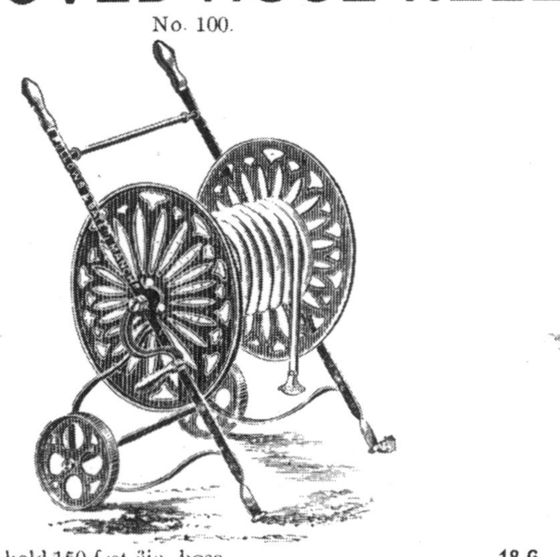

No. 1.—16in. to hold 150 feet $\frac{3}{4}$in. hose 18/6
No. 2.—20in. to hold 200 feet $\frac{3}{4}$in. hose 27/6
No. 3. 24in. to hold 250 feet $\frac{3}{4}$in. hose 32/6

CHEAP HOSE REEL.

No. 101.

To hold 90 feet $\frac{1}{2}$in. Hose.

For Small Gardens.

Price 10/6 each.

GORTON, MANCHESTER.

See pages 4 and 5 for List of Prizes offered by Webb & Sons in 1888.

WEBBS' COMPOUND MANURE.

THE BEST FERTILISER FOR HORTICULTURAL AND FLORICULTURAL PURPOSES.

Tin Cases containing 1 lb., 1s.; 3 lbs., 2s. 6d.; 7 lbs., 5s.; and Bags of a quarter-cwt., 13s.; or half-cwt., 24s. (☞ *Directions for use accompany each package.*)

WE have the greatest confidence in recommending our Compound Manure as being the best fertiliser for Horticultural and Floricultural purposes ever offered, the most extraordinary results having been obtained from its use. It contains a high percentage of Phosphates, Ammonia, and other ingredients calculated to greatly assist the growth of Vegetables, and to increase the bloom and brilliancy of Flowers. It is admirably adapted for Lawns, and Vine-borders; and may be used with great advantage for Pot-plants in Conservatories, Frames, Greenhouses, etc.

☞ OPINIONS OF OUR CUSTOMERS, TAKEN FROM HUNDREDS OF A SIMILAR CHARACTER:—

From Mr. JOHN BLADON, Gardener to F. Ratcliffe, Esq., Cliff House.
"*I have found the greatest benefit from the use of your Compound Manure. I have used it on Camellias, Azaleas, Fuchsias, Pelargoniums, Zonal Geraniums, Chrysanthemums, etc., with the very best results.*"

From Mr. A. OVERTON, Astley.
"*I consider your Compound Manure very good for Vegetables and Flowers. I obtained thirteen Prizes at the last Horticultural Show at Stourport for specimens grown from your Seeds, and with the aid of your Manure.*"

"**Mrs. GIBBONS (Athol House)** *has much pleasure in saying that she considers Messrs. Webb and Sons' Compound Manure very good for Flowers and Shrubs.*"

From Mr. A. PRINCE, Kingsland.
"*Webbs' Compound Manure is a real treasure to the amateur.*"

From Mr. GEORGE MOYLE, Gardener to C. B. James, Esq., Oakland Villa.
"*Webbs' Compound Manure is the best Manure I have ever used.*"

From Mr. T. HAWKESFORD, Gardener to Sir V. Corbet.
"*I used your Compound Manure to my Azaleas and Camellias, and it has given great satisfaction.*"

From Mr. E. J. STACEY, Norton.
"*I have used your Compound Manure for my Flowers during the past season with most satisfactory results.*"

From Mr. E. WILLIAMS, Jun., Trevallyn.
"*Your Compound Manure gave me great satisfaction. The Flowers to which it was applied, such as the Asters and Stocks, bloomed beautifully.*"

From Mr. THOS. RAWLINGS, Gardener to J. W. Yates, Esq., Glenthorne.
"*I have used your Compound Manure for Cucumbers, Melons, Vines, and all kinds of Pot-plants with the best results. Many of the Gloxinias were 2 feet 6 inches across them, and stout in foliage, with very fine blooms; the colours were all that could be desired. The blooms measured 3½ to 4 inches across, and were greatly admired by all who saw them.*"

From Mr. CHARLES PRATT, Gardener to the Rev. A. E. Robinson, Wootton Rectory.
"*The Compound Manure I had last spring has answered very well indeed. I used it for Pot-plants and a border in a verandah, and I have never seen Plants grow and bloom so well before.*"

From S. H. NEVITT, Esq., Holly House.
"*I have been using the tin of Compound Manure for Flowers only—principally for Roses, and I have had greater success this year than ever, and of course give the Compound the credit of it. I have a splendid lot of blooms.*"

From F. C. B. CAVE, Esq., Woodfield.
"*I like your Compound Manure very much indeed, both for Vegetables and Flowers. My gardeners and I agree that it is the best Manure we have ever used, as we have wonderfully good results from its use. Please send me another bag.*"

From the Rev. F. B. LEONARD, Llandervand.
"*I have the satisfaction of informing you that the Crops to which your Compound Manure was applied were very productive, and I had great reason to be satisfied with the result.*"

From Mr. W. SHINGLER, Gardener to the Right Hon. Lord Harlech.
"*I consider your Compound Manure very good for Vegetables and Flowers,—especially for Pot-plants.*"

From Mrs. E. GILBERT, Grove Hill House.
"*Having used your Compound Manure, I have found it most efficient in promoting the growth of the Plants and the bloom of the Flowers.*"

From T. S. BUCKNALL, Esq., Summer Bank.
"*The Compound Manure I had from you last spring gave me every satisfaction, and I can highly recommend it for Flowers.*"

From JOSEPH GRAY, Esq., Elmhurst.
"*Your Compound Manure is most useful in pushing through early crops, and is far superior to any Manures I have had from other firms.*"

From the Rev. E. GATES, Pytchley Vicarage.
"*Your Compound Manure was most satisfactory. Some Rhubarb to which I applied it grew to an immense size.*"

DIRECTIONS FOR USE.

In preparing potting material, mix well together 1 lb. of the Manure and each bushel of soil. When Pot-plants have fairly started into growth, the Manure may be used to advantage by sprinkling a small quantity on the surface of the soil, after which water the plants, care being taken not to wash the Manure out; the application may be repeated at intervals of 14 days. For Vegetables, Flowers, etc., in the open garden, and also for Vine-borders, sprinkle 4 ozs. of the Manure on every square yard of ground; after which fork in and give a good watering. For Lawns, mix the Manure with a small portion of soil and spread evenly over the surface at the rate of 1 oz. of Manure to the square yard. A solution of the Manure may be made by dissolving 5 ozs. in a gallon of water, which should be well stirred; it may then be applied with advantage as a liquid Manure.

STRONG GALVANIZED

MANURE GUARDS AND CARTS.

Fulfilling the requirements of the **Bye-laws** of the **London County Council** and a necessity in every **well-kept Stable.**

All our Manure Guards are made with strong wrought-iron frames, with half round top rails, strong flat bottom rails, strong round iron upright bars and covered with strong diamond pattern lattice 1½ inch mesh.

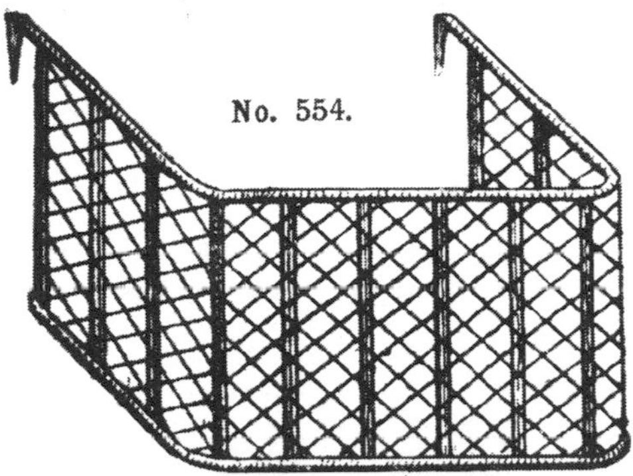

No. 554.

Length ft. in.	Height ft. in.	Projection ft. in.	Capacity Cubic Feet	Strong £ s. d.	Extra Strong £ s. d.	
4 0	2 9	2 3	24¾	1 18 6	2 8 0	each.
4 0	3 0	2 6	30	2 3 6	2 13 0	,,
4 3	3 3	3 0	41½	2 12 0	3 6 6	,,
4 6	3 0	2 6	33¾	2 6 6	2 18 0	,,
4 6	3 6	3 0	44¼	3 1 6	3 14 0	,,
4 6	3 6	3 3	48¼	3 5 0	3 19 6	,,
5 0	3 0	2 6	37½	2 10 6	3 0 0	,,
5 0	3 6	3 0	52½	3 4 6	3 18 0	,,
5 0	3 9	3 6	65½	3 11 6	4 7 0	,,
5 6	3 6	3 0	57¾	3 7 6	4 0 0	,,
6 0	4 0	3 0	72	4 0 0	4 16 0	,,

Other sizes can be made at proportionate prices, and with Skirting Band if required extra. 9 in. high, **1/-**; 12 in. high, **1/4** per lineal foot. If with handle each end for lifting, **4/-** each guard extra.

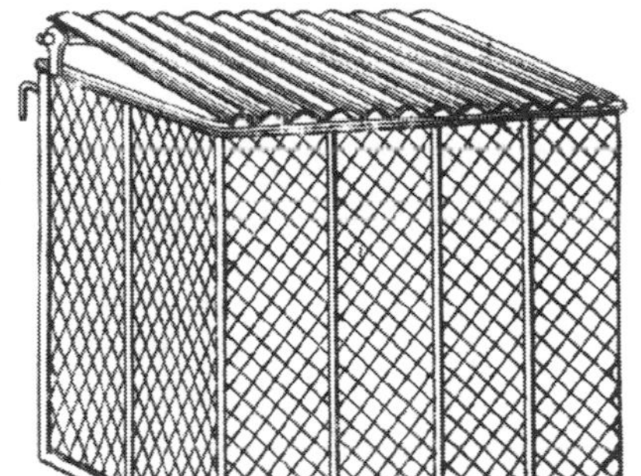

No. 1334. STRONG MANURE GUARDS. As above.

With strong corrugated iron covers on top.

Length ft. in.	Height ft. in.	Projection ft. in.	Capacity Cubic Feet	Strong £ s. d.	Extra Strong £ s. d.	
4 0	3 0	2 6	30	4 0 0	4 4 0	each.
4 6	3 0	2 6	33¾	4 3 0	4 6 0	,,
4 6	3 6	3 0	44¼	4 14 0	4 14 6	,,
5 0	3 0	2 6	37½	4 2 0	4 7 0	,,
5 0	3 6	3 0	52½	4 15 0	4 19 6	,,
6 0	4 0	3 0	72	5 10 0	6 0 0	,,

Other sizes at proportionate prices, and with Skirting Band if required extra, same price as above. Also **handles** if required, same price as above.

No. 1335. EXTRA STRONG GALVANIZED MANURE CARTS.

With self-fastening Hinged Doors, Perforated Sheet Iron Bottoms, and mounted on 4 wheels.

Length ft. in.	Height exclusive of wheels ft. in.	Width ft. in.	Capacity Cubic Feet	Without Skirting Band £ s. d.	With Skirting Band 9 in. deep, as No. 1336 £ s. d.	
3 0	3 0	2 0	18	6 10 0	7 0 0	each.
4 0	3 0	2 0	24	7 0 0	7 13 0	,,
4 0	3 0	2 6	30	7 12 0	8 5 6	,,
4 0	4 0	2 6	40	9 10 0	10 3 0	,,
4 6	4 0	3 0	54	11 0 0	11 14 0	,,
5 0	4 0	3 0	60	12 0 0	12 16 0	,,
5 6	4 0	3 6	77	14 17 0	16 0 0	,,

Other sizes at proportionate prices and with Skirting Band, if required extra, same price as above. Extra Pivot Wheel, if required, as shown below, **10/-** extra.

No. 1336. EXTRA STRONG GALVANIZED MANURE CARTS.

With Corrugated Iron Roofs, Pivot Wheel and Skirting Band, self-fastening Hinged Door, &c.

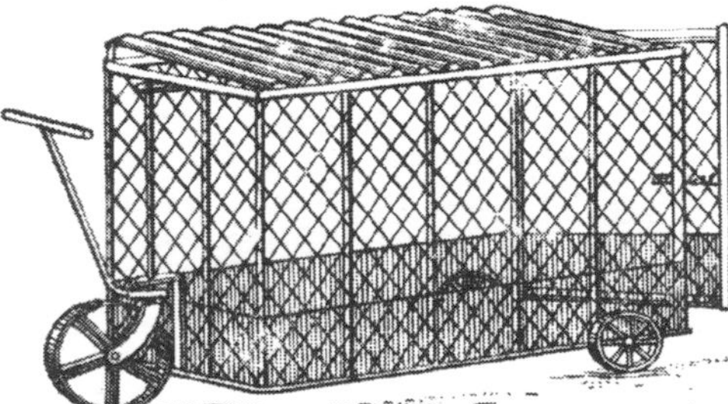

Length ft. in.	Height. exclusive of wheels. ft. in.	Width ft. in.	Capacity Cubic Feet	Without Skirting Band £ s. d.	With 9 in. Skirting Band as shown. £ s. d.	
3 0	3 0	2 0	18	8 0 0	8 10 0	each.
4 0	3 0	2 0	24	8 13 0	9 6 0	,,
4 0	3 0	2 6	30	8 16 0	9 9 0	,,
4 0	4 0	2 6	40	10 19 0	11 12 0	,,
4 6	4 0	3 0	54	13 0 0	13 15 0	,,
5 0	4 0	3 0	60	13 15 0	14 12 0	,,
5 6	4 0	3 6	77	16 10 0	17 10 0	,,

Can be had with **4** wheels as shown above, instead of Pivot wheel, at a reduction of **10/-** each, and this plan is much more recommended for Hard Wear.

Any of the above Manure Guards and Carts can be made to special size at a few days' notice.

MESSRS. WEBB & SONS' ROYAL SEED ESTABLISHMENT,

WORDSLEY, STOURBRIDGE.

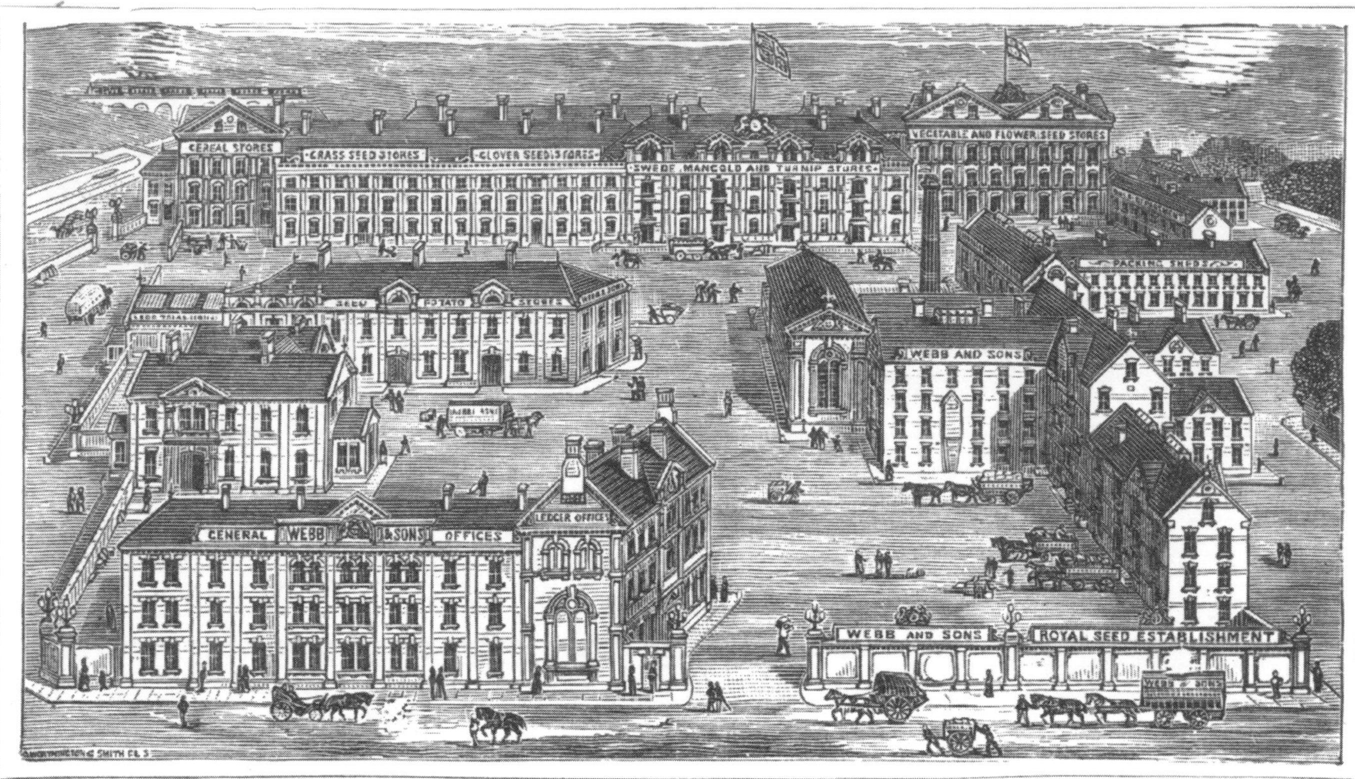

MESSRS. WEBB & SONS' SEED FARMS AT KINVER.

☞ *The largest Seed Farms in the Kingdom.*

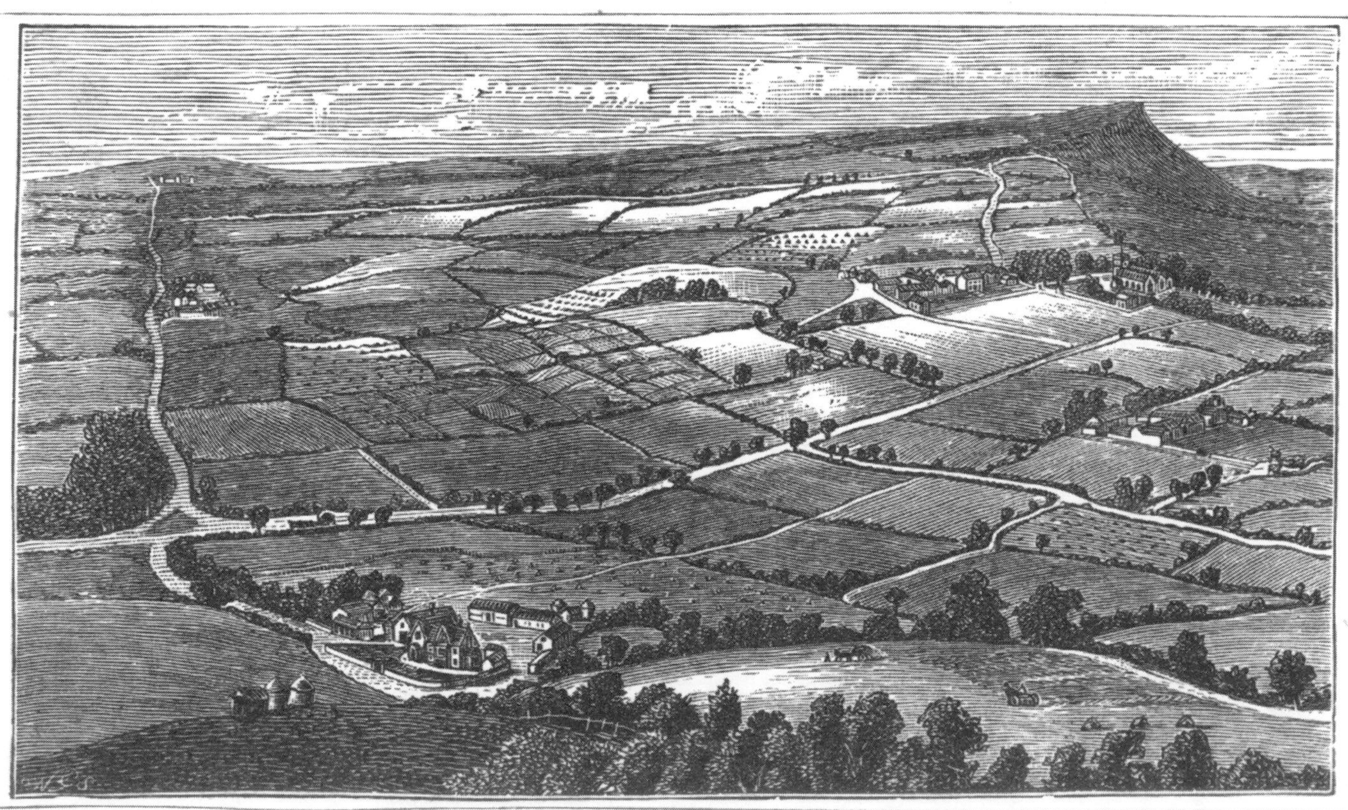

Proprietors :—**WILLIAM GEORGE WEBB AND EDWARD WEBB.**

THE GARDENER AS FARMER

One of the greatest revolutions over the last hundred years has been in the world of farming and professional horticulture. The smallholder and local farmer is becoming a rare breed as field divisions are removed to form large single tracts of land under cultivation, and multinational organisations and pension funds buy up adjoining parcels of land to create huge farming concerns. These changes in scale necessitate increasingly scientific and centralised methods of management, where farmers are businessmen, farm workers are technicians and engineers and farming practice is dictated by agronomists and politicians.

The Victorian farmer and smallholder was generally an individual landworker aiming to create a reasonable living for himself and his family. Farming practices had much in common with those of kitchen gardening, to the point where agricultural seed lists and cultivation recommendations then included as a matter of course were sometimes contained in catalogues aimed primarily at the amateur market.

With a much higher farm animal population, a wide range of sowing mixtures for pastures was readily available, and with concentrated feeding stuffs yet to revolutionise stock husbandry, there was always a good selection of seed for fodder crops and forage on offer.

While most farmers and amateur growers still relied heavily on farmyard and stable manure for land improvement, it can be seen from the catalogues of the day that other manures, often made from processed animal remains, spent hops or 'shoddy' (wood waste) were available. The quest for ever-higher yields was in its infancy.

At the same time, seed companies were encouraging their customers, especially amateur growers, to purchase collections of flower and vegetable seed to send abroad, especially to the British colonies. This is possibly the biggest single factor that dates their catalogues. Today's strict, international health regulations preclude the unmonitored exchange of plants and seeds between countries, and bring home the differences in communications that underscores these intriguing documents of garden history.

SUTTON'S IMPROVED PRIZE STOCKS
OF
HOME-GROWN FARM SEEDS
Sutton's Farmer's Year Book will be published early in the year.
Sutton's Farmer's Year Book will be published early in the year.
SUTTON'S LINCOLNSHIRE TURNIP
SUTTON'S IMPERIAL GREEN GLOBE TURNIP
SUTTON'S INTERMEDIATE MANGEL
SUTTON'S GREEN KOHL RABI
SUTTON'S OXHEART MANGEL
SUTTON'S MAMMOTH MANGEL
SUTTON'S LARGE DRUMHEAD CABBAGE
SUTTON'S BERKSHIRE PRIZE MANGEL
SUTTON'S GOLDEN TANKARD MANGEL
SUTTON'S CHAMPION SWEDE
SUTTON'S POMERANIAN TURNIP
SUTTON'S PURPLE TOP MAMMOTH TURNIP
SUTTON'S WHITE BELGIAN CARROT
PRODUCE THE HEAVIEST CROPS PER ACRE WITH THE LEAST POSSIBLE WASTE.
At the principal local Agricultural Meetings held during the past Autumn, the leading prizes for Field Crops and Pulled Specimens of Roots have been awarded to Messrs. SUTTON'S customers.

85

24 *Webbs' Seed Farms are by far the largest in the Kingdom.*

Successfully used in every County of England and Wales, also in Scotland and Ireland.

CERTIFICATES OF QUALITY.

ENGLAND.
From ARCH. CAMPBELL, Esq., Estate Office, Blenheim Palace.

'I am authorised by His Grace the Duke of Marlborough to say that the Grass Seeds supplied by you last season FOR OVER A THOUSAND ACRES on the farms in hand gave general satisfaction upon the whole.'

SCOTLAND.
From Major-General DAVID BRIGGS, Lathallan Farm.

'The 132 acres of Grass and Clover Seeds I got from you last year have brairded well, and present a much better sole of grass than seeds I got from local dealers. I shall send you an order for this season's Seeds shortly.'

IRELAND.
From T. L. CAMBIE, Esq., Kilboran Farm.

'The Mixture of Grass and Clover Seeds has given me great satisfaction, and I expect a very good crop, as it is looking splendid at present. In fact, all Seeds you have supplied me with have done well.'

WALES.
From EDWD. JONES, Esq., Bank Farm.

'As regards the (Permanent) Seeds, nothing can do better; I have grazed them with calves and sheep up to now, and they look like a gentleman's lawn at present.'

Webbs' Essay 'The Formation of Permanent Pastures'
is the best work on the subject ever written. *Post free 1s. Gratis to Customers.*

WEBBS' ANNUAL CATALOGUE OF FARM SEEDS. *Gratis & post free.*

Part Third.
AGRICULTURAL SEEDS.

For TERMS, *see page* 6 *of this* CATALOGUE.

WE DELIVER OUR SEEDS CARRIAGE FREE.

The custom, so prevalent in the Seed Trade, of delaying the issue of the Agricultural Seed Lists until the month of March, is found inconvenient to Agriculturists who wish to order *"once for all,"* the Seeds they expect to require for the ensuing season. Doubtless it is difficult, in January, to ascertain the market value of every article, or to quote *prices for the whole season;* but, to meet the difficulty, we have here presented a list with prices for *January* and *February only,* and hope to issue a second edition on the 1st of March. Wishing to encourage the practice of ordering Agricultural Seeds early, we have quoted PRICES AS LOW AS POSSIBLE FOR THESE TWO MONTHS, and shall also be happy to allow the discount for cash payment if preferred, as stated at page 6.

In consequence of the unprecedented fine summer and autumn, the samples and condition of Seeds generally are superior to what they have been for the last few years, although the yield in some instances is smaller than previous seasons.

We beg to draw attention to the fact, that although we have affixed such prices to each article as we (and we trust you will also) think fair and very reasonable, **we are yet determined not to be undersold by any house whose Goods are to be depended on.** We beg, therefore, that, should any lower offers be made, they may be communicated to us, that we may if possible meet them.

***** Early purchasers will have the advantage of being supplied with the very best articles; some kinds of seeds being scarce, will probably be all sold or raised in price before the sowing season.**

QUANTITIES OF SEED TO THE ACRE.

The quantity of Seed sown per acre varies greatly in different localities, but the following table may be taken as a guide in ordering Seeds. If guano is drilled with it, the quantity of Seed must be increased, as some will be destroyed by the guano.

	Per Acre.		Per Acre.		Per Acre.
Swedish Turnips	2 to 3 lbs.	Cow Cabbage (to transpl.)	1 lb.	Italian Rye Grass	3 bushels.
Early large Turnips	2 to 3 lbs.	Kohl Rabi, ditto	1 lb.	Vetches	2 bushels.
Stubble Turnips	4 lbs.	Ditto, drilled	4 lbs.	Buck Wheat	3 to 4 pecks.
Rape	4 lbs.	Trifolium incarnatum	24 lbs.	Saintfoin, common	4 bushels.
Mustard	16 to 24 lbs.	Lucerne	16 to 20 lbs.	Ditto, giant	5 bushels.
Mangel Wurzel	4 to 6 lbs.	Furze, for feed	12 lbs.	Linseed, for flax	2½ bushels.
Carrot	6 to 8 lbs.	Chicory	4 lbs.	Ditto, for seed	3 to 4 pecks.
Parsnip	6 lbs.	Rye	2½ bushels.	Beet	8 lbs.

CAUTION.—We are often requested to appoint Agents for the sale of our Seeds in remote parts of the Kingdom, but as it would be impossible for us to insure the correct execution of orders by that practice, **we never appoint Agents.** We, however, deliver our seeds carriage free to most parts of the kingdom.

Sutton's Spring Catalogue and Amateur's Guide for 1858. 41

NOT BOUND BY THESE PRICES AFTER THE FIRST OF FEBRUARY.

CARROT.

Extra large quantities will be charged lower, and very small quantities somewhat higher.
*** The quality of our Carrot Seed is particularly good.

	Pound. s. d.
WHITE BELGIAN; a very heavy Cropper, and very certain	1 0
" " Imported Seed (1s. 6d.)	
Large Green-top Yellow Belgian, similar to White Belgian in size, and far more nutritious (we strongly recommend this sort)	1 6
RED ALTRINGHAM; highly nutritious, and the largest *red* Carrot	1 6
INTERMEDIATE; excellent for shallow soils, or for late sowing on any soil, producing a very great weight per acre of short thick Carrots, which are easily pulled (strongly recommended)	1 6

From the Rev. J. F. Moor, jun., Ampfield Parsonage, Romsey, Feb. 16, 1856.—"I had some excellent Green-top Yellow Belgian Carrot from your seeds. I consider the sort to be a very superior one."

INSTRUCTIONS.—Carrot Seed should not be sown in open fields before the third week of April, as it will not germinate until the temperature of the earth is considerably raised, and, consequently, the weeds indigenous to the soil are liable to get a-head of the Carrots, and seriously injure the crop. It is advisable to sow a little Rape or Mustard Seed in the drills with the Carrot, which coming up quickly, will show plainly where the drills are, and allow of early hoeing, which is a most important point in the cultivation of this crop. Another mode now frequently adopted for attaining the above objects, is to sprout the Seed by steeping it in moist sand before sowing: this is advantageous for several reasons, but care must be taken to turn the sand and seed over every day, to prevent its heating, and also not to sow in very dry weather, as the germ of the Seed will suffer so much by the sudden check as not to recover. When this practice is adopted, the Seed should not be put into the sand earlier than the second week in April, or the plants will be too forward, and liable to run to blossom, which spoils the root. Upon the whole, we consider the former plan of sowing in the open ground (not earlier than the third week in April) is the safest. A funnel-shaped piece of tin, held in the hand, is the best means of depositing the Seed; but where this is considered too tedious, a drill may be used, sawdust being mixed with the seed.

COW CABBAGE.

	Pound. s. d.
LARGE DRUMHEAD; from fine selected plants (very superior stock)	3 0
Thousand-headed; very productive, tall, branching	2 6
SUTTON'S EARLY CATTLE: this, if planted eighteen inches asunder in the row, and two feet from row to row, produces a very heavy crop, and in a short time. Sow in March and August, and transplant at several seasons of the year when land is ready. (This is not of the *Drumhead shape,* but very solid)	3 6
Swedenburgh Cattle; a new sort of Drumhead for spring sowing	3 6
St. John's Early Drumhead; very early, but small (sow March and September)	3 6
Drumhead Savoy, very large	4 0

☞ Several of the principal Flockmasters and Exhibitors of Stock have lately informed us that they find "Sutton's Early Cattle Cabbage" invaluable, as it comes in at certain seasons when food is generally scarce.

KOHL RABI (or Turnip-rooted Cabbage).

	Pound. s. d.
LARGE GREEN, very large and early	3 6
LARGE PURPLE, not so large as the preceding	3 6

INSTRUCTIONS.—The Seed should be sown in April for transplanting as Cabbage Plants are (which mode produces the heaviest crop), or it may be drilled as Swedes, in May, and hoed out to the same distance from plant to plant as Swedes. This plan however requires 4lbs. of Seed per acre, while for the former 1lb. of Seed per acre will be abundant.

☞ KOHL RABI is eaten with avidity by all kinds of Stock—is very hardy, and may be left out all winter, however severe. It is useful for transplanting to mend other crops.

Sutton's Spring Catalogue and Amateur's Guide for 1858. 43

MANGEL WURZEL—*continued.*

We have carefully adjusted our prices with a desire to charge as low as possible for really good Seeds; if, however, it should happen that any one article is higher in our List than in others, we shall be glad to be informed of the circumstance, that we may, if possible, meet it.— PRICE PER CWT. MAY BE HAD ON APPLICATION.

	Pound. s. d.
Large Yellow Globe (from selected roots). This will thrive on any soil. Many roots at our show weighed over 40lbs. each	1 0
Orange Globe, fine shape, dark orange colour	1 0
Red Globe, fine shape differing only in colour	1 0
Long Red (old sort, good stock)	1 0
Elvetham Long Red: a very superior new large variety, weighing from 30lbs. to 40lbs. each, being not only long, but very thick	1 6
Long Yellow; this sort is preferred in some districts; it is very fine	1 0

Mangel Wurzel Seed may be had cheaper, in quantities of half a cwt. and upwards, if ordered immediately (except the Elvetham).

Very small quantities will be charged somewhat higher than these prices.

Mangel Seed is a short Crop this season, **and will probably be dearer.**

INSTRUCTIONS ON SOWING, &c.

*** A good distance for Mangel is 2 feet 6 inches from row to row, and 20 inches from plant to plant in the rows. This will produce a greater weight per acre than can be obtained when the drills are 3 feet apart. The best mode of sowing is with the drill. Dibbling is more economical as to the quantity of seed required; but if this plan is adopted, care must be taken not to set the Seed more than half an inch below the surface or it will not germinate. *After sowing, the land should be rolled, especially if light land or dry weather.* It may be sown from middle of April to middle of May, but the end of April is best. If sown earlier, and the summer should be hot, it is liable to be too forward, and run to seed.

FURZE OR GORSE (Ulex Europæus).

	Pound. s. d.
Very useful for making hedges or covers; also for cutting while young for horse feed. Time of sowing, March, April, and May (very scarce)	2 6

CATTLE PARSNIP.

Large quantities will be charged at a reduced price.

	s. d.
NEW LARGE GUERNSEY; altogether a superior kind, the roots weighing 4 to 6 pounds each	1 6

This is a valuable Crop for Cows; increasing greatly the quantity of Milk.

INSTRUCTIONS:—*Parsnip Seed may be sown in February, March, or April. In other respects Parsnips may be cultivated much the same as Carrots.*

MUSTARD.

Very useful for sheep feed, as also for ploughing in as manure.
Sow in June, July, and August. Quantity required per acre, 3 gallons or 22 pounds.
Price 7d. per pound, 4s. per gallon, or 28s. per bushel.

---

44 *Sutton's Spring Catalogue and Amateur's Guide for* 1858.

RAPE OR COLE.

Of this there are several varieties, the best and most productive of which is the Essex Dwarf Rape, of which we have an excellent true stock.
New Seed, price 16s. per bushel, 2s. 6d. per gallon, or 5d. per pound.
Quantity required per acre, 4 pounds.

SHEEP PARSLEY (Petroselinum Sativum).

This is an excellent feed not only for sheep; horses and cows are equally fond of it. A few pounds of Seed sown over any Pasture in the months of February, March, or April, will be very useful. Price 1s. per pound.

AGRICULTURAL BEET.

NEW LARGE CRIMSON; nearly as large as Mangel Wurzel, and much more nutritious. Quantity of Seed required, 8 pounds per acre. Price 3s. 6d. per pound.
WHITE SILESIAN SUGAR (fresh imported), present price, 1s. 6d. per pound.

FEEDING LETTUCES.

"SUTTON'S SUPERB WHITE COS," and "SUTTON'S SUPERB GREEN COS," are the heaviest Cropping Lettuces in existence. Price of Seed, 2s. 6d. per ounce. We have also several other good sorts which we can supply in mixture, at 1s. per ounce, or 10s. per pound.

YARROW or MILFOIL (Achillea Millefolium).

This plant is remarkable for its excellent fattening properties; Oxen and Sheep grazing in pastures where Yarrow abounds, have been observed to thrive exceedingly. It should be sown with Grass Seeds in laying down land to pasture, or may be sown over old swards in March. Price of Seed, 2s. per pound.

LUCERNE.

Fine new fresh-imported Seed . . . . . . 1s. per pound.

INSTRUCTIONS:—*This is a most useful plant for green food for Horses. It should be sown in April, in drills 12 inches apart; and may be cut four or five times a year. It should be hoed after each time of cutting, and manured every spring. It thrives in any soil, and especially in chalky land.* (See also Calendar of Operations.)

EARLY PEA FOR AGRICULTURE.

EARLY RACEHORSE: the quickest white Field Pea. Comes off in good time to get a good crop of Turnips the same season. Price 15s. per bushel.

MISCELLANEOUS.

LINSEED OR FLAX.
MAIZE OR INDIAN CORN.
BROOM (FOR COVER), 1s. per pound.
RADISH SEED; to sow with Turnip Crops, to save from Fly.
BURNET.
CHICORY.
BUCK WHEAT OR BRANK.
DIOSCOREA BATATAS, OR CHINESE POTATO.
SUNFLOWER SEED (FOR OIL, OR FOR POULTRY).

Sutton's Spring Catalogue and Amateur's Guide for 1858. 53

SUTTON'S MIXTURES

OF

PERMANENT PASTURE GRASS SEEDS.

In these Mixtures, the large and small Seeds are thoroughly incorporated, so as to insure proper combination of sorts throughout the land sown; but, if it should be preferred, the large Seeds may be had in one mixture and the small in another, to be sown at two casts.

MIXTURES FOR LAYING DOWN LAND TO PERMANENT MEADOW OR PASTURE.

The sorts contained in these Mixtures are grown in different localities, and gathered separately by the hand expressly for this purpose, by which means all noxious weeds are excluded; they consist of the most nutritive kinds of Fescues, Poas, Sweet Vernal, Perennial Clovers, Loliums, &c., and each sort being kept separate, they are subsequently mixed in such sorts and proportions as are most suitable to the soil to be laid down. The *quantity* we usually supply is 2 Bushels of light Seeds and 12 lbs. heavy Seeds per Acre. *Price* **24s.** *to* **30s.** *per Acre.*

*** *For large quantities, special contracts may be made at reduced prices.*

MIXTURES FOR RECLAIMED MARSHES AND HEATH LANDS.

Many acres of Land of this description have been successfully laid down to Permanent Pasture by us, with Seeds which we have found invariably to thrive on such soil; and *the cost for this purpose is very little.*

MIXTURES FOR LAYING DOWN CHALKY OR GRAVELLY UPLANDS AND SHEEP DOWNS.

For this purpose Grass Seeds are annually collected from dry and hilly districts, where they are found growing spontaneously; and, after many years' experience, we can confidently assure our friends that a *good and permanent* sward may be obtained on *any* upland from this mixture. Price **30s.** per Acre.

MIXTURES FOR LAYING DOWN WATER MEADOWS.

In this department also we have been very successful, many customers having expressed their great gratification at the effect of these Seeds. Price **22s.** to **25s.** per Acre.

MIXTURES TO LAY DOWN NEW PARK LAWNS.

For this purpose, all coarse growing kinds are carefully excluded; and the sward will, at all seasons, present a luxuriant verdure so desirable in parks contiguous to the Mansion. The cost of Seeds for this purpose will be **16s.** per bushel.

MIXTURES OF FESCUES, AND OTHER GRASSES, CLOVERS, &c.

For one, two, or three years' Pasture or Hay.

These we can supply of best quality, at 20s. to 24s. per Acre. In ordering these mixtures it is necessary to state whether they are required principally for Pasture or Hay.

PERMANENT EVERGREEN GRASSES FOR CHURCHYARDS AND CEMETERIES.

We have had the honour of supplying His Grace the Archbishop of Canterbury and many others of the Clergy, with Grass Seeds, for Churchyards and Cemeteries, which have given great satisfaction. Price of Seed, 1s. per lb. or 18s. per Bushel.

54 *Sutton's Spring Catalogue and Amateur's Guide for 1858.*

RENOVATING MIXTURES FOR IMPROVING OLD PASTURES.

Our Renovating Mixture consists of the finest Grasses and Perennial Clovers. If the seeds are sown *early in the season*, the improvement in the Pasture will be very great, and at a small expense. *Quantity of seed required, 8 to 12 lbs. per Acre.* Price reduced to **9d.** per lb. or 80s. per cwt. Sow in March and April, or after hay cart at Midsummer.

From SHAFTESBURY WALMSLEY, Esq., *Mottistone, Isle of Wight, Oct. 1st*, 1856.

"The Grass Seeds were extremely good and answered my purpose uncommonly well; they gave me a famous crop of Hay last summer, 2½ tons per acre, where I never saw anything but bents and rubbish grow before. I strongly recommend your Renovating Seeds; they are clean, and I believe safely to be depended upon."

From the REV. JOHN GUTHRIE, *Vicarage, Calne, Sept. 30th*, 1856.

"I have no hesitation in expressing my great satisfaction at the *manifest improvement* both to lawn and *pasture* from the seeds which I received from you, though I was somewhat late in the sowing."

From Mr. W. MEEKINS, *Gardener to the Dowager Lady Truro, Bowes Manor, Southgate, Sept. 30th*, 1856.

"I am much pleased with the Renovating Seeds I got last season from you, as in every meadow where I sowed it I found great improvement both in quantity and quality, also the Lawn was very much improved by the mixture you sent me, and my employer was much gratified with the results both in our Pasturage and on the Lawns, and wishes me again to procure mixtures from you when the time arrives for sowing."

From the REV. ALEXANDER WATSON, *Rectory, Bridestowe, Exeter, Oct. 2nd*, 1856.

"I am very much pleased with your Grass Seeds and Renovating Mixture. Your Beet also is a most brilliant and deep colour."

From Mr. J. HALLETT, *Blackford Farm, Highclere, Oct. 3rd*, 1856.

"The Grass Seeds you sent me last season have given me the greatest satisfaction, inasmuch as the plot of ground where they were sown, which before seemed almost past growing anything, is now growing as beautiful a plant of herbage as any one could wish to see."

From Miss ANDREWS, *Norton Villa, near Swansea, Oct. 6th*, 1856.

"Your Renovating Mixture w last yea e had r more than answered our expectatio ns."

From ALEXANDER C. FORBES, Esq. *[illegible]ton House, Swansea, Whitchurch, Feb. 16th*, 1856.

"You will be pleased to hear that the Renovating Seeds I sowed, and which I thought had failed, are now coming up in great abundance."

From Mr. G. NORRINGTON, *Rectory Farm, Taplow.*

"Five years ago I wrote to you to send to me a mixture of Grass Seeds to sow upon ten acres of old pasture. At the time I took the farm the ten acres of meadow were almost useless. I now have a most excellent pasture."

From C. F. THRUSTON, Esq., *Talgarth.*

"Your Seeds have answered admirably. They were sown in spring, under rather unfavourable circumstances. The After-Grass is remarkable; Clover and other Seeds springing up where nothing but the poorest pasture had been previously, and I think that a field of nine acres sown with your RENOVATING MIXTURE, is now one of the finest in our neighbourhood."

INSTRUCTIONS FOR IMPROVING OLD PASTURES.

Having, as far as possible, eradicated the strong growing Weeds and coarse Grasses, and improved the condition of the land according to its requirements, if any, heavy harrows should be drawn over the old turf early in the Spring, to loosen the soil for the admission of Seeds of the finest and most nutritive kinds of Perennial Natural Grasses and Clovers, which, if sown freely, will occupy the numerous small interstices between the plants of grasses already growing, and thereby prevent the luxuriant growth of coarse grasses and noxious weeds. It is a good practice to sow these Seeds at the same time as the top-dressing is applied, but this is by no means necessary.

☞ *Having greatly reduced the Price of our "*RENOVATING MIXTURE*" we doubt not that our liberal terms will encourage the more extensive use of the same for the improvement of Grass Lands.*

Meadows and Upland Pastures may be increased in value 50 per cent. by sowing these Seeds.—Vide numerous Letters continually received by us.

50 *Sutton's Spring Catalogue and Amateur's Guide for 1858.*

ITALIAN RYE GRASSES.

(Lolium Italicum.)

Italian Rye Grass deserves to be more generally cultivated. It will thrive in any soil, and may be sown any time between February and September, with a certainty of success. One of the best seasons, however, for sowing, is the month of August. Liquid Manure applied as often as the crop is cut, greatly increases the produce, but this is unnecessary. Italian Rye Grass is also very useful for sowing with Clovers instead of common Rye Grass; it rises early in the Spring above the Clover, and protecting it from the frosts, brings the crop forwarder and heavier.

Instructions on cultivation will be sent post-free if desired.

	Per Bushel.	Per lb. under 14 lbs.	Per lb. above 14 lbs.
	s. d.	*s. d.*	*s. d.*
1. TRUE ITALIAN RYE GRASS SEED	7 0	0 8	0 7
2. SUTTON'S IMPROVED ITALIAN ditto	7 6	0 8	0 7
3. DICKENSON'S IMPROVED ditto	7 0	0 8	0 7
4. FRESH IMPORTED SEED FROM LOMBARDY	7 6	0 8	0 7

We can recommend with confidence the sorts Nos. 1. and 2. The others are also good, and we keep true stocks of both for those who prefer them. *The Foreign Seed is generally exceedingly foul when it comes to hand, and we clean it thoroughly before selling, which reduces the bulk and necessarily increases the price; but we can supply it cheaper than the above quotations, if sent out just as we receive it in the bales unopened.*

ENGLISH AND SCOTCH RYE GRASSES.

(Lolium perenne.)

	Per Bushel.	Per lb. under 14 lbs.	Per lb. 14 lbs.
	s. d.	*s. d.*	*s. d.*
PERENNIAL RYE GRASS (Lolium perenne), fine clean	7 0	0 5	0 4½
PACEY'S PERENNIAL RYE GRASS, extra fine heavy	8 0	0 5	0 4½
STICKNEY'S HEAVY SCOTCH PERENNIAL RYE GRASS	8 6	0 5	0 4½
EVERGREEN RYE GRASS, or PERENNIAL DEVON EAVER, true; *excellent with other kinds of Grasses for Permanent Pasture*	8 6	0 5	0 4½
ANNUAL, or COMMON, for alternate husbandry, best quality	6 6	0 5	0 4½
Ditto ditto lighter Seed	5 6	0 5	0 4½

FINE GRASS SEEDS FOR LAWNS

IN

FLOWER-GARDENS, ETC.

Price 1s. per lb., 2s. 6d. per gallon, or 20s. per bushel. Quantity required per Acre, 60 lbs. or 3 bushels.

N.B.—Our mixtures of Grass Seeds for Permanent Pasture, at 24s. to 30s. per Acre, include a full supply of Perennial Clovers.

Sutton's Spring Catalogue and Amateur's Guide for 1858. 57

USEFUL TABLES, &c.

GENERAL TABLE OF LAND MEASURE.

627264 Sq. In. =1 Sq. Link.
144= 22956= 1=Sq. Foot.
1296=206611= 9= 1 Sq. Yard.
39204= 625=27225=3025= 1 Perch.
627264= 10000= 4356= 484= 16= 1 Sq. Chain.
1568160= 25000=10890=1210= 40=25=1 Rood.
6272640=100000=43560=4840=160=10=4=1 Acre.

The *English* statute acre contains 4840 square yards; the *Scotch*, 5760; the *Irish*, 7840; the *Devonshire* customary, 4000; the *Cornish*, 5760; the *Lancashire*, 7840; the *Cheshire* and *Staffordshire*, 10,240; the *Wiltshire* tenantry, 3630.

The *French* arpent is an English acre and ¾ths of a rood. The *Strasburg* acre is nearly half an English acre; the *Prussian* morgen is not quite ⅔ths of an acre.

MEASURE OF LENGTH.

12	Inches	equal to	1 Foot.
3	Feet	,,	1 Yard.
5½	Yards	,,	1 Pole or Perch.
40	Poles	,,	1 Furlong.
8	Furlongs or 1760 yards	,,	1 Mile.

RULE FOR ASCERTAINING THE SOLIDITY OF TIMBER.

To compute the solidity of round timber when the tree is straight and its ends equal or nearly—multiply the square of ¼ of the circumference by the length, and the product will be the solidity or contents.

To compute the solidity of round timber when the tree tapers, or is unequally thick, girt the tree in so many places as is thought necessary, then the sum of the several girts, divided by their number, will give a mean circumference, the fourth part of which being squared and multiplied by the length will give the solid contents.

A load of timber, unhewn, is	40	cubic feet.
A load of timber, squared, is	50	,,
A load of 1 inch plank is	600	square feet.
A load of 1½ ,,	400	,,
A load of 2 ,,	300	,,
A load of 2½ ,,	240	,,
A load of 3 ,,	200	,,
A load of 3½ ,,	170	,,
A load of 4 ,,	150	,,

INTEREST TABLE.

AT FIVE PER CENT.

Days.	100*l.*	50*l.*	40*l.*	30*l.*	20*l.*	10*l.*	9*l.*
	s. d.	*s. d.*	*s. d.*	*s. d.*	*s. d.*	*s. d.*	*s. d.*
100	27 5	13 8	11 0	8 3	5 6	2 9	2 6
50	13 8	6 10	5 6	4 1	2 9	1 4	1 3
40	11 0	5 6	4 5	3 3	2 2	1 1	1 0
30	8 3	4 1	3 3	2 6	1 8	10	9
20	5 6	2 9	2 2	1 8	1 1	7	6
10	2 9	1 4	1 1	10	7	3	3
9	2 6	1 3	1 0	9	6	3	3
8	2 2	1 1	11	8	5	3	2
7	1 11	1 0	9	7	5	2	2
6	1 8	10	8	6	4	2	2
5	1 4	8	7	5	3	2	1
4	1 1	7	5	4	3	1	1
2	10	5	4	3	2	1	1
3	7	3	3	2	1	1	1
1	3	2	1	1	1		

Days.	8*l.*	7*l.*	6*l.*	5*l.*	4*l.*	3*l.*	2*l.*	1*l.*
	s. d.	*s. d.*	*s. d.*	*s. d.*	*s. d.*	*d.*	*d.*	*d.*
100	1 2	1 11	1 8	1 4	1 1	10	7	3
50	2 1	11	10	8	7	5	3	2
40	11	9	8	7	5	4	3	1
30	8	7	6	5	4	3	2	1
20	5	5	4	3	3	2	1	1
10	3	2	2	2	1	1	1	
9	2	2	2	1	1	1	1	
8	2	2	2	1	1	1		
7	2	2	1	1	1	1		
6	2	1	1	1	1	1		
5	1	1	1	1	1			
4	1	1	1	1	1			
3	1	1	1					

INTEREST TABLE.

Of £100 for all the several days in the first column at the rates of 3, 3½, 4, 4½, and 5 per cent. in the other five columns.

Days.	3 per Cent.	3½ per Cent.	4 per Cent.	4½ per Cent.	5 per Cent.
	s. d.	*s. d.*	*s. d.*	*s. d.*	*s. d.*
1	0 1¾	0 2¼	0 2½	0 3	0 3¼
2	0 3¾	0 4½	0 5¼	0 6	0 6½
3	0 5¾	0 6¾	0 7¾	0 8¾	0 9¾
4	0 7¾	0 9	0 10½	0 11¾	1 1¼
5	0 9¾	0 11½	1 1	1 2¾	1 4
6	0 11¾	1 1¾	1 3¾	1 5¾	1 7½
7	1 1¾	1 4	1 6½	1 8¾	1 11
8	1 3¾	1 6¼	1 9	1 11	2 2½
9	1 5¾	1 8¼	1 11½	2 2½	2 5½
10	1 7½	1 11	2 2¼	2 5½	2 8¾
20	3 3½	3 10	4 4½	4 11	5 5¾
30	4 11	5 9	6 6¾	7 4	8 2½
40	6 6¾	7 8	8 9	9 10½	10 11¼
50	8 2½	9 7	10 11½	12 3¾	13 8½
60	9 10½	11 6	13 1¾	14 9½	16 5½
70	11 6	13 5	15 4	17 3	19 2
80	13 1¾	15 4	17 6¼	19 8½	21 11
90	14 9½	17 3	19 8¼	22 2¼	24 7¾
100	16 5½	19 2	21 11	24 8	27 4½
200	32 10½	38 0¼	43 10	49 3½	54 9½
300	49 3¾	57 4½	65 9	73 11¾	82 2¼

WAGES TABLE.

Y.	Per Mo.	Per Week.	Pr. D.
£	£ *s. d.*	£ *s. d.*	*s. d.*
1	0 1 8	0 0 4½	0 0½
2	0 3 4	0 0 9¼	0 1
3	0 5 0	0 1 1¾	0 2¾
4	0 6 8	0 1 6½	0 2¼
5	0 8 4	0 1 11	0 3
6	0 10 0	0 2 3¾	0 4½
7	0 11 8	0 2 8¼	0 4¼
8	0 13 4	0 3 0¾	0 5
9	0 15 0	0 3 5½	0 6¼
10	0 16 8	0 3 10	0 6
11	0 18 4	0 4 2¾	0 7
12	1 0 0	0 4 7¼	0 8
13	1 1 8	0 5 0	0 8
14	1 3 4	0 5 4¼	0 9
15	1 5 0	0 5 9	0 10
16	1 6 8	0 6 1¾	0 10½
17	1 8 4	0 6 6¼	0 11¼
18	1 10 0	0 6 10¾	0 11¾
19	1 11 8	0 7 3½	1 0½
20	1 13 4	0 7 8	1 1¼
30	2 10 0	0 11 6	1 7¾
40	3 6 8	0 15 4	2 2½
50	4 3 4	0 19 2	2 9
60	5 0 0	1 3 0¼	3 3
70	5 16 8	1 6 10¾	3 10
80	6 13 4	1 10 8½	4 4½
90	7 10 0	1 14 6¼	4 11½
100	8 6 8	1 18 4½	5 5¾

If the Wages be Guineas instead of Pounds, for each Guinea add 1d. to the Month, or ¼d. to the week.

LONDON, 1884.

VERSAILLES, 1881.

PARIS, 1878.

LIVERPOOL, 1886.

FRANCE, 1882.

WEBBS' PURE GRASS SEEDS

FOR ALL SOILS.

PURITY AND GROWTH GUARANTEED.

Prices on application. Reduced rates for large quantities.

Webb & Sons' Illustrated Essay—

"THE FORMATION OF PERMANENT PASTURES,"

New Edition. The most practical work of the kind yet issued.

1s. post free; gratis to Customers and intending purchasers.

Webbs' Prize Swede, Mangold & Turnip Seeds

PRODUCE ROOTS THAT ARE SUCCESSFUL IN ALL OPEN COMPETITIONS OF THE KINGDOM.

Webbs' Annual Catalogue of Grass and Farm Seeds for 1888 will be issued in February next (gratis and post free), containing prices and full particulars. In the meantime the lowest possible prices will be charged. Grass and Farm Seeds of 20s. value Carriage Free; Five per cent. (1s. in the £) Discount for Cash.

Webbs' Selected Seed Corn.

Awarded the Gold Medal of France, 1882; the Prize Medal of Versailles, 1881; the Champion Prize, *open to the World,* and First Prize Silver Medal, London, 1887; and Premier Honours at all other leading Shows.

☞ See WEBBS' CATALOGUE OF SELECTED SEED CORN for 1887-8; gratis and post free.

Seed Corn of 40s. value Carriage Free. Five per cent. Discount for Cash.

WEBBS' POTATOES FOR FIELD CULTIVATION.

Prices on application.

WEBBS' SPECIAL MANURES

FOR ALL CROPS.

MANUFACTURED AT WEBBS' MANURE WORKS, WIDNES, LANCASHIRE.

All Manures delivered Carriage Free, and Analyses guaranteed.

☞ See WEBBS' ANNUAL CATALOGUE OF SPECIAL MANURES; gratis and post free.

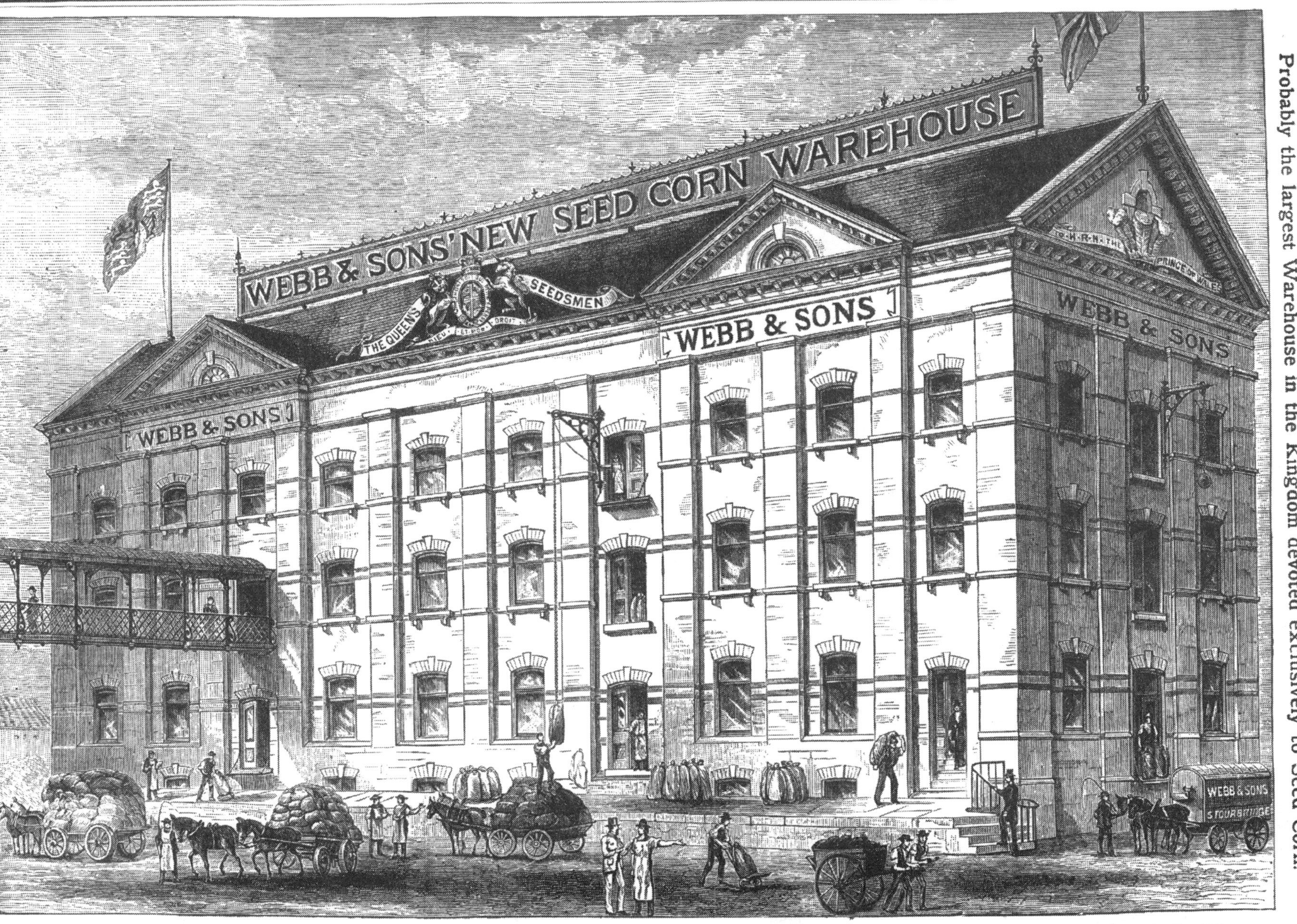
Probably the largest Warehouse in the Kingdom devoted exclusively to Seed Corn.
WEBB & SONS' NEW SEED CORN WAREHOUSE
SEEDSMEN
THE QUEENS
WEBB & SONS
WEBB & SONS
WEBB & SONS
WEBB & SONS
STOURBRIDGE
This new Warehouse contains the most approved machinery and appliances.
WEBB & SONS' NEW SEED CORN WAREHOUSE.
We have just completed the erection of another Warehouse, as illustrated above, which will be devoted exclusively to our Seed Corn trade.
It is probably the largest building for the purpose in the Kingdom, being 120 ft. long × 45 ft. wide, and occupying 198,296 cubic feet.

The Medals of Paris

for Farm Seeds.

WEBBS' SPECIAL MANURES—Continued.

The Medals of Paris

for Farm Seeds.

BEAN AND PEA MANURE.

Price £8 per Ton.

A VERY valuable manure, and one that answers admirably for these crops, which will well repay a liberal application; it should be sown broadcast, and harrowed in, at the rate of **4 to 6 cwt. per acre.**

HOP MANURE.—*Price £8 per Ton.*

THE HOP manure can be applied either at or after digging or ploughing time; it stimulates the growth of the bine, making it strong and healthy, and increases the production of Hops, which are thereby much improved in quality. Use, according to the character and condition of the land, **4 to 8 cwt. per acre.**

MANURE FOR GRASS OR PASTURE LAND.

Price £8 per Ton.

THIS bone manure is specially prepared for enriching poor pastures, and for the purpose of restoring to the soil those invaluable properties of nutrition which are taken from it in the process of grazing, etc. The importance of its application on Grass Land in Dairy-farming is obvious, not only by the yield of milk being greatly improved in quality and quantity, but from the fact that cattle thrive so much better on grass manured with it. On Pasture Land the advantage of applying a dressing of this valuable manure will be apparent for years in the increased luxuriance of the grass crop; and on grass land that has been inundated, or lying under water, it has a wonderfully beneficial effect.

On mowing grass and clover a liberal use of it will *double*, and in some instances *treble* the crop. **For Permanent Pasture use 6 to 10 cwt. per acre; for Mowing Grass and Clover use 4 to 6 cwt. per acre.**

POTATO MANURE.—*Price £8 per Ton.*

PREPARED specially for this particular crop; the liberal use of it will increase the yield, improve the quality of the tubers, and render them less liable to disease. At our Seed Farms the heaviest and best crops of Potatoes were raised by the aid of this Manure. **Apply 5 to 10 cwt. per acre.**

DISSOLVED BONES.—*Price £8, 10s. per Ton.*

GUARANTEED as made entirely from bone,—containing a large proportion of phosphates, the greater part of which are soluble, the remaining part being mellowed and softened, gradually dissolve, nourishing and supporting the plant up to its fullest maturity, and leaving the land in a highly fertilised and enriched condition for the subsequent crop. This manure is most excellent for Corn and Root Crops, to be applied broadcast **3 to 5 cwt. per acre**, or it is a capital 'top-dressing' for the Clover-root, or for Grass Land.

SUPERPHOSPHATE OF LIME.—*Price £7 per Ton.*

THIS is a cheap and generally useful manure, containing a high percentage of soluble phosphates, and is excellent for roots or white straw crops. It is usually applied at the rate of **4 to 6 cwt. per acre.**

PREPARED BONES.—*Prices on application.*

THE value of Prepared Bones as a manure cannot be over-estimated; they contain a great proportion of soluble phosphates of lime, are quick in acting, and thoroughly efficacious.

SHODDY (OR WOOL-WASTE) MANURE.

SPECIALLY PREPARED FOR THE VARIOUS CROPS.

Price £3, 10s. per Ton.

☞ ALL MANURES CARRIAGE FREE. FIVE PER CENT. DISCOUNT FOR CASH.

From J. A. COOKE, Esq., Bellington Farm.—'The manure I had from you for Barley produced a good crop, and the quality was the best I grew out of 140 acres.'

22 *All Manures Carriage Free. Ten per cent. Discount for Cash.*

WEBBS' SPECIAL MANURES

FOR ALL CROPS.

Carriage Free.

For particulars see **WEBBS' CATALOGUE OF SPECIAL MANURES,** *Gratis and Post Free.*

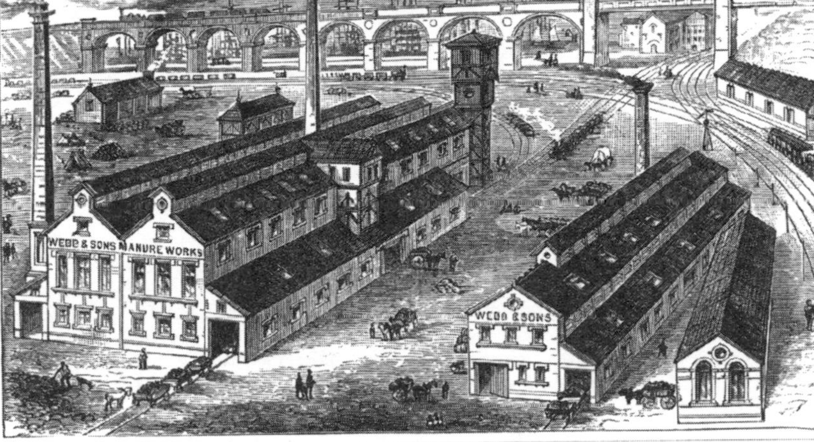

FOR ALL CROPS.

Carriage Free.

For particulars see **WEBBS' CATALOGUE OF SPECIAL MANURES,** *Gratis and Post Free.*

Manure Works, Widnes, Lancashire.

THE great and continued success of Webbs' Special Manures has caused an enormous increase in the demand for them, and we have found it necessary to considerably enlarge the Works erected for their manufacture. The facilities we have on all hands—sea, canal, and rail—for despatching Manures of our usual high standard of quality and condition, enable us to ensure the prompt delivery of all Orders with which we may be favoured.

WEBBS' WHEAT MANURE.—£8 per Ton.

THIS Manure is suitable for Spring or Autumn use, and answers admirably as a top-dressing on young corn which has been injured by excessive moisture or frost. It contains in a highly concentrated form the nourishment necessary for this all-important crop, as it strengthens the plant, increases the yield, and improves the quality of the grain to a very considerable degree. A judicious application of this Manure will be found very beneficial, as, in manufacturing it, we have included those elements which will both promote a rapid fertilisation and permanently enrich the soil. It should be applied as follows:—**with Autumn or Spring sowing, 4 to 6 cwt. per acre; for Top-dressing, 2 to 4 cwt. per acre.**

WEBBS' BARLEY AND OAT MANURE.—£8 per Ton.

THIS excellent and lasting Manure contains in well-proportioned quantities the various requisites for producing strong root-fibre, stiff clear straw, and an abundant yield of well-developed grain. We strongly recommend the use of this Manure at the rate of **3 to 5 cwt. per acre.**

WEBBS' BEAN, PEA, & VETCH MANURE.—£8 per Ton.

A VERY valuable Manure, and one that answers admirably for these crops. It will well repay a liberal application, and should be sown broadcast, and harrowed in, at the rate of **4 to 6 cwt. per acre.**

Webbs' Turnip Manure, . *per Ton.*	£8
Webbs' Mangold Manure, . . .	£8
Webbs' Manure for Grazing Land, .	£8
Webbs' Manure for Newly-formed Permanent Pasture, . .	£7, 15s.
Webbs' Manure for Mowing Grass and Clover, ...	£8
Webbs' Superphosphate, .	*Prices on application.*
Webbs' Bone Superphosphate, *per Ton.*	£7
Webbs' Cabbage Manure, . . .	£8
Webbs' Hop Manure, ...	£8
Webbs' Potato Manure, . . .	£8
Webbs' Dissolved Bones, No. 1, .	£8, 10s.
Webbs' Dissolved Bones, No. 2, . .	£8
Webbs' Prepared Bones,	*Prices on application.*

WEBBS' "CHALLENGE" WHITE WHEAT.

NEW SELECTION. (See Coloured Illustration facing page 6.)

As grown on the

Farms of Her Majesty the Queen.

The best White Wheat in cultivation.

As grown on the

Farms of H.R.H. The Prince of Wales.

THIS splendid variety—introduced by us in 1874—has given the highest satisfaction both at home and abroad, it having been grown with the greatest success by the leading Agriculturists of the Kingdom, as well as by a large number of our foreign customers. Its habit of growth is robust and vigorous,—straw long and clear,—ear of great length, finely developed, with moderate chaff,—grain closely set, medium in length, broad, plump, and remarkably white,—yield from thin seeding enormous. It is suitable for all soils, either spring or winter planting, and unsurpassed for milling purposes. This ennobled wheat has been awarded First Prizes at Birmingham, Abingdon, Hull, Woodstock, Severn Valley Farmers' Club, etc. etc.

Price **11s.** *per Bushel.* *Sow* **6** *to* **8** *Pecks per Acre.* **40s.** *value Carriage Free.*

AWARDED THE

GOLD MEDAL

OF FRANCE, 1882

Also the

PRIZE MEDAL

OF VERSAILLES, 1881.

From Mons. A. G. MIGNOT, Bois-Gauthier, France, February 28th, 1882.

'I have much pleasure in telling you that I have obtained the Gold Medal of France for your Challenge Wheat. I won it in competition with exhibitors from all parts of France—agriculturists who exhibit every year, and who are accustomed to obtain prizes. I must tell you that my wheat was superior to all the others in yielding, straw and grain.'

From Mr. GEO. WILLOCKS, Agent to the Right Hon. Viscount Dillon, Ditchley.

'I have a splendid crop of "Challenge" White Wheat from the seed supplied by you last year.'

From JAS. LONG, Esq., Henlow.

'Your "Challenge" White Wheat promises to be of excellent quality, and is very true.'

From EDWD. HEADINGTON, Esq., Holly Port.

'I have an excellent crop of "Challenge" White Wheat from seed supplied by you last autumn. It surpasses anything else I have, and I intend to sow a great deal more of it another time.'

From MILES NEWMAN, Esq., Farm Steward to the Right Hon. Lord Aveland, Empingham.

'The "Challenge" White Wheat supplied by you looks grand. I have seen none in the neighbourhood to approach it. It is very much admired.'

From "THE AGRICULTURAL GAZETTE,"

September 18th.

'The lowest price paid for wheat this year was 16s., and for one piece I was obliged to pay 20s. per acre. It was a splendid crop of Webbs' "Challenge," drilled after mangel, 1 bushel to the acre, 15 inches between the rows. It grew to 6 feet high, and when cut was a fine upstanding crop. I had it threshed on Monday last, the yield being 46 bushels of 66 lbs. per acre.—*W. T., South Bucks.*'

From R. TAYLOR, Esq., Duns Tew.

'I am really pleased with Webbs' "Challenge" Wheat. I exhibited it at Woodstock Show and won a First Prize, and it was greatly admired by several gentlemen there.'

From SAML. ROBERTS, Esq., Cotton Hall.

'I consider your "Challenge" White Wheat the best variety I ever saw. It is very prolific, and of beautiful quality. I cannot speak too highly of it.'

All Vegetable Seeds, Flower Seeds, and Bulbs delivered Free. 5

From Mr. J. JONES, Little Brompton.

'It is with great pleasure I have to inform you that the White Challenge Wheat you sent me in November last looks beautiful. Nearly every corn has grown, and this severe winter does not seem to have taken the least effect upon it. My neighbours are almost all sowing their land over again.'

18 *Reduced Rates for large quantities of Seed Corn.*

WEBBS' SELECTED FIELD PEAS.

WEBBS' KINVER MARROW.

Awarded First and Second Prizes at the Birmingham Show.

This superior second early Pea was introduced by us ten years ago, and the excellent results of the many trials of it confirm our statement that it is an invaluable general cropping and exhibition Pea. It is remarkably productive, with robust habit of growth; height from 3 to 3½ feet. The pods are handsome, of a bright green colour, very long, curved, and closely filled with Peas of the finest flavour.

'WEBBS' PERFECTION.

The earliest and most prolific white round Pea in cultivation.

This splendid variety is an extraordinary cropper, with vigorous habit of growth; height about 2½ feet. It bears very handsome well-filled pods, which, as well as the foliage, are of a beautiful bright green colour, and the flavour of the Peas is all that can be desired. The valuable qualities of this distinct variety entitle it to the highest recommendation.

WEBBS' SELECTED PRIZETAKER.

A great improvement upon the old variety of Prizetaker.

This green marrow Pea grows about 4 feet high, producing long well-filled pods. It is extensively cultivated, and a general favourite. We have most carefully selected the stock, and the great demand we have experienced is satisfactory evidence of its superiority.

WEBBS' IMPROVED SANGSTER'S No. 1.

New Selection.

We have selected a very choice stock of this well-known early and prolific Pea, which is far superior to the old kind; it grows from 2½ to 3 feet high.

The above-named Peas are specially suitable for Market purposes.

Blue Prussian.
Bedman's Imperial.
Champion of England.
Ringwood Marrow.

Prizetaker.
Fillbasket.
Veitch's Perfection.
Kentish Invicta.

Forty-fold.
Partridge.
Maple.
Common Grey.

Laxton's Supreme.
Prince of Wales.
Blue Scimitar.
Etc. Etc.

Any other Variety can be supplied. Lowest Prices on application.

Mr. GEORGE PARSONS writes :—

'Your Kinver Marrow Pea is without doubt one of the best in cultivation; my crop this year was superb. I have counted upwards of eleven Peas in a pod.'

From Mr. JOHN KING, Colne.

'Webbs' Perfection Pea is undoubtedly superior to any I have yet grown. It is an abundant cropper, and the Peas are of a beautiful green colour and delicious flavour.'

Important Notice.—Webbs' Seeds can only be obtained direct from Wordsley. 41

WEBBS' LARGE-PODDING PEAS

TO PICK GREEN FOR MARKET.

NOTE:—We are not bound by these prices after 14 days from date of issue (February 1st).

	Per bushel.
Prince of Wales, . .	15s.
Laxton's Supreme, . .	
Kentish Invicta, . .	14s.
Champion of England, .	18s.
Fortyfold, ...	16s.
Telegraph, ...	20s.
Veitch's Perfection, . .	20s.
Leicester Defiance, . .	13s.
Fillbasket, ...	
Telephone, ...	20s.
First and Best, . . .	15s.
Early Sunrise, . . .	16s.
Pride of the Market, .	24s.
Duke of Albany, . .	24s.
Ringleader, ...	14s.
Harrison's Glory, . .	16s.
Dr. McLean, ...	16s.
Yorkshire Hero, . .	16s.
Hundredfold, or Cook's Favourite,	14s.

See page 52 for
WEBBS' SPECIAL PEA MANURE.

Any other variety of Pea can be supplied.

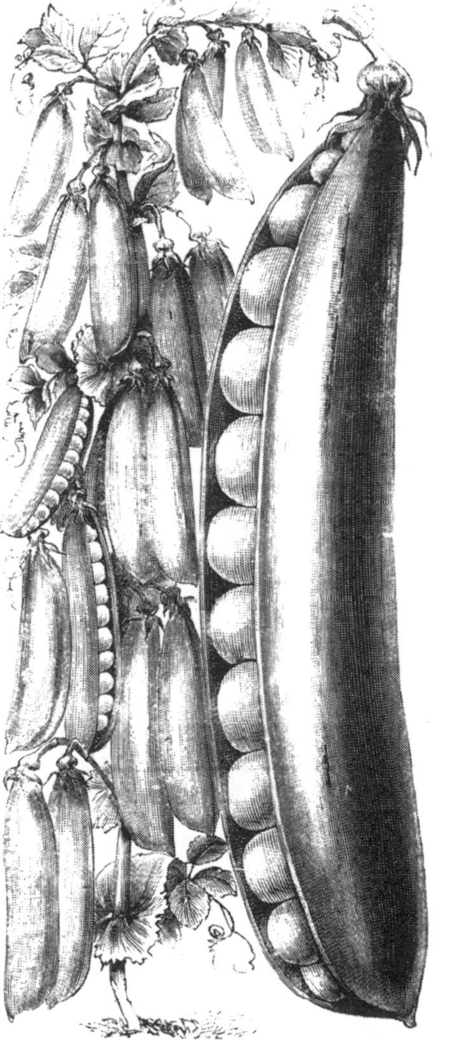

Bedman's Imperial. Eclipse. Blue Scimitar. Partridge. American Wonder.
Ringwood Marrow. Maple. Blue Prussian. Prizetaker. Common Grey. Etc.

Lowest prices of Beans, Onions, Etc., for Market Garden purposes may be obtained on application.

Drill **5** *to* **6** *lbs. per acre, or sow* **1** *to* **2** *lbs. per acre for transplanting*

FIELD CABBAGE.

For Webbs' article—*'The Field Cultivation of Cabbage,'* see page 20.

Webbs' New Early Cabbage—'FLOCKMASTER.'

4s. 6d. per pound.

THIS splendid new Cabbage, offered in 1886 for the first time, after being under trial for some years at our Kinver Seed Farms, has rapidly become very popular. It grows to a large size, with a firm heart, and few outer leaves; while its extreme earliness renders it valuable for sheep and lambs, as, like Webbs' New Early Drumhead, seed sown in March, and planted out in May, will produce a grand crop in September.

FROM MR. W. H. HELLIAR, ILMINSTER.

'The Flockmaster Cabbage is true to sort, and comes to feed very quickly.'

FROM MR. W. COOKSON, HALLOWSGATE FARM.

'I sowed the Early Drumhead Cabbage in March, and have plenty 5 feet round the solid heart; beautiful quality.'

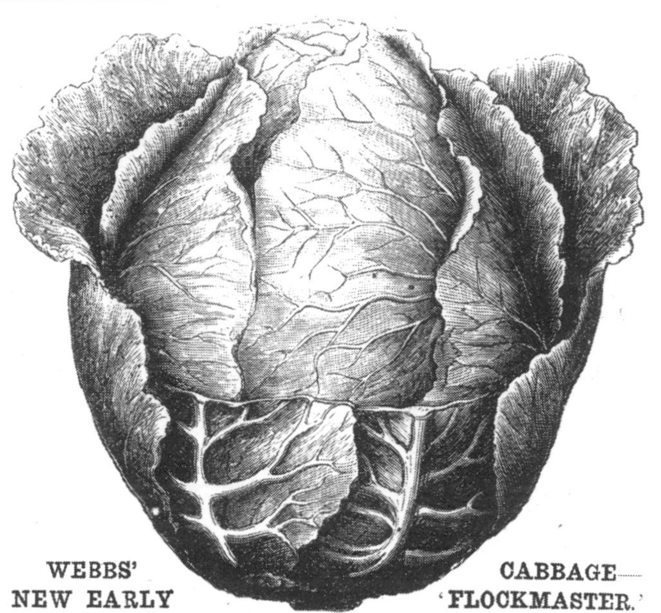

WEBBS' NEW EARLY CABBAGE—'FLOCKMASTER.'

WEBBS' NEW EARLY DRUMHEAD CABBAGE.

Webbs' New Early Drumhead Cabbage.

(See ILLUSTRATION annexed.)

5s. 6d. per pound.

THIS variety is invaluable to sheep-breeders and others who require an early crop of Cabbage, as it grows to a great size, and is very solid. Repeated experiments made at our Seed Farms, with the many varieties of Field Cabbage now before the public, have proved that, with the exception of Webbs' New Early 'Flockmaster,' this variety invariably comes to maturity fully two to three months earlier than any other kind, a splendid crop being ready for consumption in September, from seed sown at the beginning of March, and planted out in May.

FROM T. WARREN, ESQ., BRANSTONE.

'I have a wonderful crop of your Early Drumhead Cabbage *drilled* in April, beating my late Cabbage *set* this spring.'

The Field Cultivation of Cabbage.

NO green crop on the farm is more grateful to a farmer's eye than a heavy one of Cabbage, especially if they are fine, sound-hearted, solid, and weighing, as they often do, from 30 to 60 lbs. each, for almost all kinds of stock are remarkably partial to Cabbage, which appears to be a health-giving and most nutritious food for them.

This kind of produce was extended to field culture in the last century, but the farmers of that day had no such rapid-growing, high-bred varieties as Webbs' New Early Drumhead and Webbs' New Early 'Flockmaster,' the seed of which, if sown early in March, will develop into plants fit for setting out into the open field in May, and produce a highly nutritious green crop for feeding in September.

In the culture of such Cabbages, preference is sometimes given to the system of drilling the seed into the land which is to grow the crop, instead of raising the plants in nursery-beds and transplanting them by hand. When the former mode is adopted, the land has to be prepared the same as for mangold. The stubbles should be surface-cleaned as soon after harvest as possible in the previous autumn, and manured with from ten to twenty tons of farm-yard manure per acre. This material, when spread on the land, should be ploughed in deeply, and the rough furrows left exposed to atmospheric influence during the entire winter. The fallow being sufficiently dry, should be worked across by a scarifier in March, and in April the tillage should be completed, and the seed deposited by the manure drill, with Webbs' Special Cabbage Manure, which is acknowledged to be the most efficient chemical fertiliser for the object in view. The quantity of this manure to be applied depends very much on the original fertility of the soil, and to what extent dung was laid on in the autumn. From 5 to 6 lbs. of seed would be wanted in cultivating after this method, if the drilling were effected for rows from 20 inches to 24 inches apart. Horse-hoeing is as beneficial in a field of young cabbages as in the culture of mangolds or turnips, and should be assiduously attended to, as well as the singling out of the plants in the rows at the proper time with the hand-hoe, leaving them about 20 inches apart.

The cabbage-fly is sometimes found quite as destructive as the turnip-fly in clearing off young plants wholesale at their very first appearance, which has been held by some growers as a sufficient reason for adhering to the usual method of raising the plants in nursery-beds, where they can be more attentively watched, and the customary remedy more easily applied of sowing powdered lime, flour of sulphur, or wood ashes on them early in the morning, when the substance strewn will adhere to the tender leaflets wet with dew. Probably the best means of any in saving a field of young cabbages from the destructive ravages of this insect-pest, is to deposit a sufficient quantity of Webbs' Special Cabbage Manure at the time of drilling the seed, which would have the effect of forcing the plants so rapidly into rough leaf that they would grow away from their enemies.

There are two advantages in the other system of planting, *i.e.* by hand, which ought not to be lost sight of. As the planting is not required to take place until May, and for late autumn consumption not until June, it would be possible to feed off a previous green crop of rye, winter barley, or trifolium, before the cabbage plants would be required to be set out, and if this spring green crop were consumed with artificial food, there would be a considerable addition to the fertility of the field in consequence. The land could also be marked out previous to the setting, by a steerage horse-hoe having its tines reversed. This, drawn up and down the field, would leave it marked out in straight lines at even widths from one another. Then, by drawing the same implement across the field, the reverse way, a series of perfect squares would appear all over it. The work-people would then have to set the plants at every point where the lines were found to intersect, with the result of having them at equal distances on all sides.

The culture of lands required for cabbage-planting in November may now be described. These should be surface-cleaned immediately after harvest, and from 15 to 20 loads of farm-yard dung spread over and ploughed in. A well-prepared seed-bed should have been previously got ready for a stock of plants to be reared. The best varieties for this purpose are Webbs' Champion Drumhead, Webbs' New Early 'Flockmaster,' and Webbs' Emperor. The sowing being effected during the first or second week in August, the plants would be fit to draw out early in November. From 1 to 2 lbs. of seed sufficient plants can often be grown to set out an acre of land. The field in most cases admits of being marked out for planting as in the spring, though some growers prefer to make slight furrows with a ridge-plough the distance the rows are required to be apart. The cabbages are then planted in the furrows instead of on the ridges, because by being so placed they are more sheltered, and stand the winter better.

Although the advantages of extending the cabbage to field culture are generally admitted, two erroneous impressions commonly prevail. Most people believe cabbage-growing to be very costly, only well adapted to weighty purses and high farming; while others take it for granted that there would be little use in attempting to grow a crop unless large quantities of farm-yard manure can be spared for application. The farmer will, however, find just the thing he wants already provided to his hands in Webbs' Special Manure for Cabbages, which may be applied either solely or in combination with a small quantity of dung, with the full certainty of the elements having been perfectly supplied to ensure a heavy crop. And there is one reason why this fertiliser would be found far superior to the employment of so much farm-yard dung, as the crop would be less liable to the disease known as 'clubbing.' This was, until recently, thought to be produced by an insect, but is now generally accepted as of fungus origin, perhaps aided by an excess of organic matter in the soil. Thus, field cabbages are less liable to the disease than those in the garden, and it has often been noticed that gardens which, when highly manured, produced clubbed cabbages, after being neglected for a time grew perfectly healthy ones. Young cabbages, when affected, should be pulled up to have the club removed with a knife, and the incised part dipped into a solution of soot, after which the plant will be likely to grow healthy if re-set.

The high utility of cabbages, both in summer and autumn, will be sure to lead to a more extensive culture. Ram-breeders find that their lambs will progress during June, July, and August on cabbage better than on anything else; and those who rear wether-lambs for mutton will soon discover that a considerably enhanced profit in this branch of husbandry is obtainable by more extensive reliance on this crop. Considering also that cabbages are admitted to be pre-eminently serviceable to dairy cows, grazing cattle, and pigs, not only in exceptionally dry summers, but through-out autumn (as a rule), no one can doubt that extensive cabbage-growing is destined to be a feature of the farming of the future.

VARIETIES.	Distance between the rows.	Distance between the plants.	DRILLING.	SOWING ON SEED-BED.		TO COME IN.
			Time to drill.	Time to sow.	Time to trans-plant.	
WEBBS' NEW EARLY DRUMHEAD,	24 to 30 ins.	24 to 30 ins.	April and May.	March and April.	May and June.	Sept., Oct., and Nov.
WEBBS' NEW EARLY 'FLOCKMASTER,'	20 to 24 ins.	20 ins.	April and May. August.	March. August.	May and June. Oct. and Nov.	Sept. and Oct. July.
WEBBS' EMPEROR,	20 to 24 ins.	20 ins.	April and May. August.	March. August.	June. Oct. and Nov.	Oct. July and Aug.
WEBBS' CHAMPION DRUMHEAD,	30 to 36 ins.	30 to 36 ins.	April and May. August.	March and April. August.	June and July. Oct. and Nov.	Nov., Dec., and Jan. Aug. and Sept.
WEBBS' SELECTED THOUSAND-HEADED KALE,	24 to 30 ins.	24 to 30 ins.	April and May. July and August.	March and April.	June and July.	Oct., Nov., and Dec. Spring and Summer.

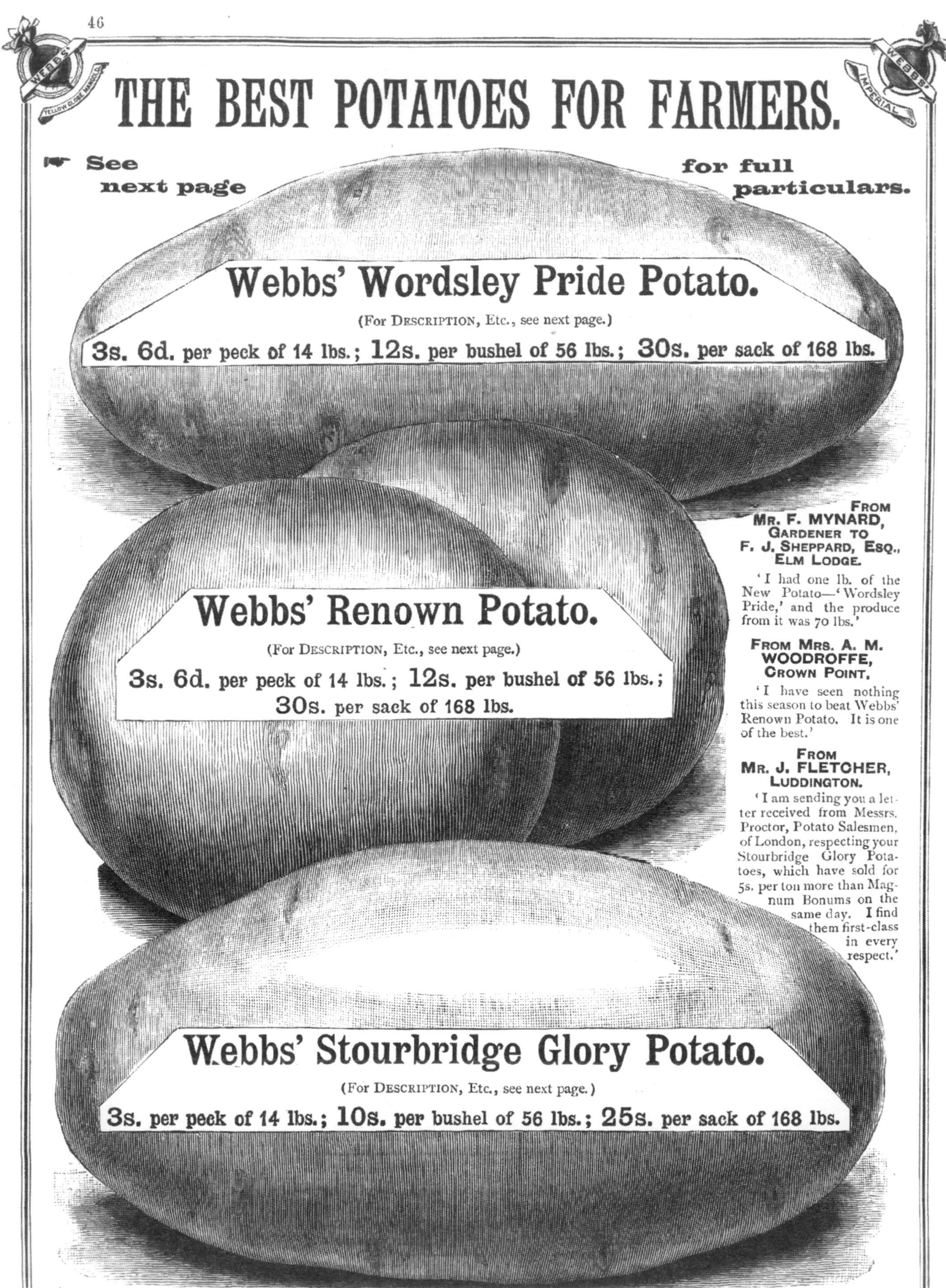
46
WEBBS' YELLOW GLOBE MANGOLD
WEBBS' IMPERIAL
THE BEST POTATOES FOR FARMERS.
See next page for full particulars.
Webbs' Wordsley Pride Potato.
(For Description, Etc., see next page.)
3s. 6d. per peck of 14 lbs.; 12s. per bushel of 56 lbs.; 30s. per sack of 168 lbs.
Webbs' Renown Potato.
(For Description, Etc., see next page.)
3s. 6d. per peck of 14 lbs.; 12s. per bushel of 56 lbs.; 30s. per sack of 168 lbs.
From Mr. F. Mynard, Gardener to F. J. Sheppard, Esq., Elm Lodge.
'I had one lb. of the New Potato—'Wordsley Pride,' and the produce from it was 70 lbs.'
From Mrs. A. M. Woodroffe, Crown Point.
'I have seen nothing this season to beat Webbs' Renown Potato. It is one of the best.'
From Mr. J. Fletcher, Luddington.
'I am sending you a letter received from Messrs. Proctor, Potato Salesmen, of London, respecting your Stourbridge Glory Potatoes, which have sold for 5s. per ton more than Magnum Bonums on the same day. I find them first-class in every respect.'
Webbs' Stourbridge Glory Potato.
(For Description, Etc., see next page.)
3s. per peck of 14 lbs.; 10s. per bushel of 56 lbs.; 25s. per sack of 168 lbs.

Webbs' Seed Potatoes are much cheaper by the half-ton or ton. 47

WEBBS' STOURBRIDGE GLORY POTATO.

Unsurpassed for both quality and productiveness.

The Banksian Medal, awarded by The Royal Horticultural Society.

3s. *per peck of* 14 *lbs.;*
10s. *per bushel of* 56 *lbs.;*
25s. *per sack of* 168 *lbs.*

The Banksian Medal, awarded by The Royal Horticultural Society.

THIS superior Potato is a seedling from Woodstock Kidney, and it has rapidly become one of the leading main crop varieties, both for field and garden use. The haulm is strong and branching in growth, and the tubers are long, but somewhat inclined to oval in shape, of very handsome appearance, and exceedingly valuable for exhibition purposes. The flesh is pure white, firm and floury when cooked, and of unequalled quality. This variety keeps fit for use a remarkably long time, and hitherto it has been perfectly free from disease. (See ILLUSTRATION, page 46.)

Extract from **'THE FIELD,'** April 25, 1891.

'Webbs' Stourbridge Glory has stood all the tests to which Potatoes are subject; it shines on the Show bench, and also as a Farmer's Potato in the field.'

WEBBS' RENOWN POTATO.

3s. 6d. *per peck of* 14 *lbs.;* 12s. *per bushel of* 56 *lbs.;* 30s. *per sack of* 168 *lbs.*

This handsome Potato is second early, of dwarf and neat appearance when growing, and a prodigious cropper. The tubers are very large, solid, and of fine shape, being nearly round; they are fit for use as soon as lifted, and will keep sound long over the winter. Its flesh is white, very dry and floury, and of unequalled flavour—(see ILLUSTRATION, page 46.)

FROM MR. F. JACKLIN, TRING.

'I exhibited Webbs' Renown Potato, taking First Prize in the round class against over 50 competitors. The 12 specimens I showed weighed 10 lbs.—all handsome tubers; the cooking quality is splendid—dry, and white as snow.'

WEBBS' WORDSLEY PRIDE POTATO.

3s. 6d. *per peck of* 14 *lbs.;* 12s. *per bushel of* 56 *lbs.;* 30s. *per sack of* 168 *lbs.*

A very superior second early kidney, and an extraordinary cropper, producing an abundance of large handsome tubers suitable for exhibition purposes, and equally valuable for table use. The skin is white, very smooth, with few eyes, whilst the flesh is fine-grained, exceedingly white, and of first-class quality. Awarded a Certificate of Merit at the National Vegetable Conference, Chiswick, 1889—(see ILLUSTRATION, page 46).

FROM MR. J. W. PARTRIDGE, BOZEAT.

'I am very pleased with Webbs' Competitor Potato. They turned out well, some of them weighing 14 ounces each. It is a splendid cooking variety.'

	Per peck of 14 lbs.		Per bushel of 56 lbs.		Per sack of 168 lbs.	
	s.	d.	s.	d.	s.	d.
WEBBS' NEW POTATO—'COMPETITOR.'—*A splendid main crop variety,*	4	0	14	0	36	0
WEBBS' EARLY ASHLEAF POTATO.—*The earliest Potato in cultivation,*	4	0	14	0	36	0
WEBBS' 'SURPRISE' POTATO.—*One of the best second early kidneys,*	3	0	10	0	25	0
WEBBS' IMPROVED SCHOOLMASTER POTATO.— *Well-known*	2	6	8	0	20	0
WEBBS' IMPROVED MAGNUM BONUM POTATO.— *varieties,*	2	0	7	0	18	0
IMPERATOR POTATO.—*A superior main crop variety; for either field or garden use,*	2	6	9	0	23	0

Webb & Sons charge reduced prices for large quantities, whether requested to do so or not.

MYATT'S ASHLEAF POTATO.
READING RUSSET POTATO.
WHITE ELEPHANT POTATO.
ADIRONDACK POTATO.
VICAR OF LALEHAM POTATO.
PATERSON'S VICTORIA POTATO.
READING HERO POTATO.
BEAUTY OF HEBRON POTATO.
SCOTCH CHAMPION POTATO.
EARLY REGENT POTATO.
EARLY ROSE POTATO.
SNOWDROP POTATO. Etc.

Prices per bushel of 56 lbs., sack of 168 lbs., half-ton, or ton, on application.

☛ *For particulars of* **WEBBS' SPECIAL POTATO MANURE,** *see page 54.*

FLOWER SEEDS.

All Flower Seeds are sent free by Post, *except* SWEET PEAS AND LUPINS.

We have endeavoured to present, this season, a more convenient Flower Seed List, by inserting each kind in the English or other name by which it is most generally known, rather than giving both names, whereby the bulk of the Catalogue would be unnecessarily increased. The *best only* of the *new sorts* are inserted here; and the old favourites are retained; our object being to present the most useful rather than the most comprehensive Catalogue.

COLLECTIONS FREE BY POST.

(THE SELECTION BEING LEFT TO MESSRS. SUTTON.)

Ladies and gentlemen requiring showy kinds of Flower Seeds, and who are not well acquainted with the sorts, are respectfully recommended to leave the selection to us, and we will supply those which we know to be really worthy of cultivation. **If the Newest Sorts only are required, they will be found in this Catalogue distinguished thus*.** Many other kinds of Flower Seeds are kept in stock, but it would increase the size of this Catalogue too much if they were included in this List.

Annuals.

		£	s.	d.
1.	The best 100 sorts (hardy, half-hardy, and tender), with instructions	£1	1	0
2.	The best 50 sorts ditto ditto with instructions	0	10	6
3.	The best 36 sorts ditto ditto with instructions	0	7	6
4.	The best 24 sorts ditto ditto with instructions	0	5	0
5.	The best 24 sorts (hardy sorts only)	0	5	0

Perennials.

6.	The best 50 sorts (hardy, half-hardy, and tender)	0	10	6
7.	The best 36 sorts ditto ditto	0	7	6
8.	The best 24 sorts ditto ditto	0	5	0
9.	The best 12 sorts (hardy sorts only)	0	3	0

Climbers.

10.	The best 12 sorts (hardy, half-hardy, and tender)	0	3	6
11.	The best 6 sorts (hardy sorts only)	0	2	0

Suitable for Rock Work.

12.	The best 12 sorts	0	3	6
13.	The best 6 sorts	0	2	0

Ornamental Grasses.

14.	Sixty fine selected sorts	1	0	0
15.	Thirty ditto	0	10	0
16.	Twelve ditto	0	4	0

Hardy, with Ornamental Foliage.

17.	Twelve fine varieties	0	5	0
18.	Six fine varieties	0	2	6

Everlasting Flowers.

19.	The best 12 sorts	0	3	6
20.	The best 6 sorts	0	2	0

Annuals for forming Large Beds.

21.	Twelve large packets	0	9	0
22.	Six large packets	0	5	0

Greenhouse Seeds.

23.	The best 12 sorts	0	6	0
24.	The best 6 sorts	0	3	6

Sweet Scented Flowers.

25.	The best 12 sorts	0	3	6
26.	The best 6 sorts	0	2	0

Dwarf Flowers suitable for Edgings.

27.	The best 12 sorts	0	3	6
28.	The best 6 sorts	0	2	0

The Seeds are of last summer's growth, and many of them are quite NEW SORTS.

*** *One of these Collections of Choice Flower Seeds will prove an acceptable present to a friend, and may be conveniently transmitted by post.*

ASSORTMENTS OF GERMAN FLOWER SEEDS—continued.

		s.	d.
38. Six varieties extra fine **Double Hollyhocks,** from named sorts	separate	2	6
The above choice sorts in mixture	*per packet*	1	0
39. Ten varieties double dwarf **Rocket Larkspur**	separate	2	6
40. Six ditto ditto ditto	ditto	1	6
The above choice sorts in mixture	*per packet*	1	0
41. Ten varieties dwarf double **Hyacinth-flowered Larkspur**	separate	2	6
42. Six ditto ditto ditto	ditto	1	6
The above choice sorts in mixture	*per packet*	1	0
43. Twelve varieties **Rose-flowered Balsam**	separate	2	6
44. Six ditto ditto ditto	ditto	1	6
The above choice sorts in mixture	*per packet*	1	0
45. Twelve varieties fine new **Camellia-flowered Balsam**	separate	2	6
46. Six ditto ditto ditto	ditto	1	6
The above choice sorts in mixture	*per packet*	1	0
47. Eight varieties new **Miniature Balsam**	separate	2	0
The above choice sorts in mixture	*per packet*	1	0
48. Twelve extra fine varieties **German Zinnia**	separate	2	6
49. Six ditto ditto	ditto	1	6
The above choice sorts in mixture	*per packet*	1	0
50. Six splendid varieties new **Double Zinnia**	separate	2	6
The above choice sorts in mixture	*per packet*	1	0
51. Ten splendid varieties **Double Wallflower** from Erfurt	separate	3	0
52. Six ditto ditto	ditto	2	0
The above choice sorts in mixture	*per packet*	1	0

Fresh imported German Seeds produce finer Blooms, and more Double, than any English Seed, however carefully selected; and the assortments named in the foregoing list are genuine German Seeds just imported. WE WOULD ESPECIALLY RECOMMEND THE ASSORTMENTS Nos. 4, 8, 12, 14, 15, 22, 27, 37, 39, 45, 48, 50, 51, which we would supply (post-free) for £1 10s.

ASSORTMENTS OF ENGLISH FLOWER SEEDS.

	s.	d.
Antirrhinum, in twelve varieties	4	0
,, in six varieties	2	6
Aquilegia, in four choice varieties	1	6
Balsam (Ward's) in seven colours	3	6
,, (Smith's) in nine colours	2	6
Candytuft, six varieties, separate	1	6
Carnation, Flake, twelve sorts	3	6
,, Bizarre, twelve sorts	3	6
,, Yellow, twelve sorts	3	6
,, Perpetual, twelve sorts	3	6
Chrysanthemum, in six varieties	1	6
Clarkia, in ten distinct varieties	3	0
,, in six ,, varieties	2	0
Collinsia, in eight sorts	2	0
Convolvulus major, in six colours	1	6
,, minor, in six colours	1	6
Coreopsis, in ten choice varieties	2	6
,, in six choice varieties	1	6
Delphinium, in five sorts	1	0
Dianthus, in ten choice varieties	3	6
,, in six choice varieties	2	0
Eschscholtzia, in five sorts	1	0
Gilia, in four sorts	1	0
Globe Amaranthus, in four colours	1	0
Godetia, in five sorts	1	0
Ipomæa, (Climbers) in six varieties	2	0
Jacobæa, double, nine colours	2	0
,, ,, in six colours	1	6
Larkspur, stock flowering, in ten varieties	2	6
,, double branching, in six varieties	1	6
Larkspur, Tall Rocket, in eight varieties	2	6
Leptosiphon, in six choice varieties	1	6
Linaria, in eight sorts	1	6
Lobelia (dwarf), in twelve varieties	3	6
,, ,, six ,,	2	0
Lupinus, in twelve distinct varieties	3	6
,, six ,,	2	0
Marigold, double, in six sorts	1	6
Marvel of Peru, in eight colours	2	0
Nasturtium, dwarf, in six varieties	2	0
,, tall, in four sorts	1	0
Nemophila, in twelve varieties	2	6
,, in six varieties	1	6
Œnothera, in twelve distinct varieties	3	6
,, in six distinct varieties	2	0
Petunia, in eight choice varieties	2	6
Phlox Drummondii, in twelve sorts	3	6
,, ,, in six sorts	2	0
Picotee, white ground, twelve varieties	3	6
,, yellow ,, twelve varieties	3	6
Portulacca, in ten varieties	3	0
,, in six varieties	2	0
Schizanthus, in six sorts	1	6
Silene, in ten varieties	2	0
,, in six varieties	1	6
Sweet Peas, in six colours	1	6
Thunbergia, in four distinct sorts	1	6
Tropæolum, in ten choice varieties	2	6
,, in six choice varieties	1	6
Viscaria, in eight sorts	2	0

The Seeds are all of last summer's growth, and many of them are quite NEW SORTS.

*** One of these Collections of Choice Flower Seeds will prove an acceptable Present to a friend, and may be conveniently transmitted by post.

CHOICE COLLECTIONS OF KITCHEN GARDEN SEEDS

FOR ONE YEAR'S SUPPLY OF VEGETABLES.

CARRIAGE FREE.—(See page 2.)

The following liberal collections are carefully made up with a view to their furnishing a supply of Vegetables throughout the year. We annually send great numbers of these to different parts of the British Isles, and would especially recommend them to the notice of those who may not have sufficient time or experience for making their own selection. These collections contain only seeds of the finest quality; each packet has a label attached, giving description, time of sowing, &c.; and to ensure safety in travelling, each collection is **carefully packed, free of extra charge, in a box or case.** Customers ordering in this way, by stating the size of garden, will be supplied with the collection suited to that size, and may rely on the articles sent giving entire satisfaction.

	£	s.	d.
No. 1.—A complete Collection, consisting of 18 quarts of the best kinds of Peas, and all other seeds in proportion, of the best varieties	3	3	0
No. 2.—Ditto, in smaller quantities but equally choice in quality	2	2	0
No. 3.—Ditto, for a medium size garden	1	11	6
No. 4.—Ditto, for a smaller garden	1	1	0
No. 5.—Ditto, for a small garden	0	12	6
No. 6.—The cottagers' packet, containing a liberal supply of Peas, Broccoli, Cabbage, Savoy, Carrot, Celery, Cress, Cucumber, Lettuce, Onion, Parsnip, Radish, Turnip, and Vegetable Marrow	0	2	6

NAME.	No. 1. £3 3 0	No. 2. £2 2 0	No. 3. £1 11 6	No. 4. £1 1 0	No. 5. £0 12 6
Peas, finest sorts for succession	18 quarts	10 quarts	8 quarts	4 quarts	2 quarts
Beans, for succession, Windsor, &c.	8 ,,	6 ,,	4 ,,	2 ,,	3 pints
French Beans, Runners and Dwarfs	6 pints	4 pints	3 pints	2 pints	1 pint
Beet, a variety of sorts	2 ounces	1 ounce	2 packets	1 packet	1 packet
Borecole, or Sprouting Kale, of best sorts ...	3 packets	2 packets	2 ,,	3 packets	2 packets
Brussels Sprouts, fresh imported seed ...	1 packet	1 packet	1 packet	1 packet	1 packet
Broccoli, the best sorts for succession	8 packets	6 packets	4 packets	4 packets	2 packets
Cabbage, best sorts for succession	6 ,,	4 ,,	3 ,,	3 ,,	2 ,,
Savoy, finest curled	2 ounces	1 ounce	½ ounce	½ ounce	¼ ounce
Carrot, best sorts for Summer and Winter use ...	12 ,,	8 ounces	6 ounces	4 ounces	2 ounces
Cauliflower, Walcheren, &c.	2 packets	2 packets	2 packets	1 packet	1 packet
Celery, white and red	2 ,,	2 ,,	2 ,,	2 packets	1 ,,
Couve Tronchuda, a most delicious vegetable ...	1 packet	1 packet	1 packet	1 packet	1 ,,
Cress, plain, curled, &c.	1½ pint and 2 packets	8 ozs. and 2 packets	6 ozs. and 1 packet	4 ozs. and 1 packet	3 packets
Cucumber, the best sorts for frame or ridge ...	4 ,,	3 ,,	2 packets	2 packets	2 packets
Endive, best sorts	1½ ounce	2 ,,	2 ,,	2 ,,	1 packet
Gourd, or Pumpkin of sorts	3 packets	2 ,,	1 packet	1 packet	1 ,,
Leek, Musselburgh	1 ounce	½ ounce	½ ounce	1 ,,	1 ,,
Lettuce, for Winter and Summer use	5 packets	4 packets	3 packets	3 packets	2 packets
Mustard, white	1 quart	1 pint	8 ounces	4 ounces	2 ounces
Melon, choicest sorts	3 packets	2 packets	1 packet	1 packet	
Onion, in variety, including James' Keeping ...	10 ounces	6 ounces	4 ounces	4 ounces	2 ounces
Parsley, extra curled	3 ,,	2 ,,	1 ounce	1 ounce	1 packet
Parsnip, true hollow-crown	6 ,,	4 ,,	3 ounces	2 ounces	1 ,,
Radish, best sorts for succession	2 pints	1 pint	8 ,,	6 ,,	3 ounces
Spinach, Summer and Winter use	2 ,,	1 ,,	1 pint	4 ,,	2 ,,
Salsafy, } mild, sweet flavoured roots, boiled as	1 large pkt.	1 packet	1 packet		
Scorzonera, } Parsnips	1 ,,	1 ,,	1 ,,	1 packet	
Turnip, fine sorts for succession	12 ounces	6 ounces	4 ounces	3 ounces	2 ounces
Vegetable Marrow, best sort	2 packets	2 packets	2 packets	1 packet	1 packet
Sweet and Pot Herbs, of all the useful kinds ...	8 ,,	6 ,,	4 ,,	4 packets	2 packets
Rampion, a useful salad	1 packet	1 packet	1 packet		
Tomato, large red, or Keye's early	1 ,,	1 ,,	1 ,,	1 packet	1 packet
Capsicum and Chili	2 packets	2 packets	1 ,,	1 ,,	1 ,,

From Mr. JAMES FRASER, Gardener to the Earl of Albemarle, Quidenham Park, Attleborough.

October 1st, 1875.

"I wish to express how greatly I am obliged for the good quality of all the Seeds your firm supplied me with last Spring, they, as you are aware, have given equal satisfaction to my employers."

DANIELS BROS.' COLLECTIONS OF FLOWER SEEDS.

We have much confidence and pleasure in offering the following choice collections of English and Foreign Flower Seeds, which we would especially recommend to the notice of those who have not sufficient time or experience for making their own selection. In each class only the most beautiful and distinct will be sent.

Collection A, Price 10/6. Carriage Free.

12 Splendid varieties Pæony Aster
12 Beautiful „ Dwarf German Ten-week Stock
6 „ „ New double Zinnia Elegans
3 „ „ Everlasting Flowers } for Winter
3 „ „ Ornamental Grasses } bouquets

12 Choice Hardy Annuals, the most useful and showy kinds, including Nemophila, Sweet Peas, Tom Thumb Nasturtium, Viscaria, &c.
6 Choice Half-hardy Annuals for bedding out, including Phlox, Marigold, &c.

Collection B, Price 15/. Carriage Free.

12 Splendid varieties Pæony Aster
12 Beautiful „ Dwarf German Ten-week Stock
6 „ „ New double Zinnia Elegans
12 Choice Hardy Annuals, the most useful and showy kinds, including Nemophila, Sweet Pea, Dwarf Nasturtium, &c.

12 Choice Half-hardy Annuals for bedding out, including Phlox, Balsam, Marigold, &c.
6 Hardy Perennials, including Pansies, Hollyhock, &c.
8 Choice Everlasting Flowers } for Winter bouquets.
3 „ Ornamental Grasses }

Collection C, Price 21/. Carriage Free.

12 Splendid varieties Pæony Aster
12 Beautiful „ Dwarf German Ten-week Stock
12 „ „ New Double Zinnia Elegans
8 „ „ Phlox Drummondi
12 Choice „ Hardy Annuals, the most useful and showy kinds, including Dwarf Nasturtium, Nemophila, Saponaria, Viscaria, &c.

12 Choice varieties Half-hardy Annuals for bedding out, including Marigolds, Balsams, Portulacca, &c.
6 Choice varieties Hardy Perennials, including Pansy, Hollyhock, &c.
6 Choice varieties Everlasting Flowers } for Winter
6 „ „ Ornamental Grasses } bouquets.
1 Packet each Calceolaria, Cineraria, Geranium, and Petunia

Collection D, Price 42/. Carriage Free.

6 Beautiful varieties Victoria Aster
8 „ „ Dwarf Chrysanthemum Aster
12 Choice „ Pæony Aster
12 „ „ Dwarf German Ten-week Stock
6 „ „ Giant or Tree „
8 Splendid „ Phlox Drummondi
12 „ „ New Double Zinnia Elegans
8 „ „ Camellia Balsam
4 „ „ Brompton Stock
6 „ „ Double German Wallflower
12 „ „ Everlasting Flowers } for Winter
12 „ „ Ornamental Grasses } bouquets.

25 Choice Hardy Annuals, the most useful and showy sorts, including Saponaria, Nemophila, Dwarf Nasturtium, Sweet Peas, &c.
12 Choice Half-hardy Annuals for bedding out, including Marigolds, Portulacca, Amaranthus, &c.
12 Choice Perennials, including Pansy, Polyanthus, Hollyhock, &c.
6 Choice Greenhouse Perennials and Biennials, including Calceolaria, Cineraria, Primula, Geranium, &c.
6 New or very Choice Annuals

Annuals, Perennials, and Biennials. Post or Carriage Free.

Hardy Annuals.

100 Choice showy and useful varieties, including Nemophila, Viscaria, Clarkia, Collinsia, Convolvulus, Sweet Peas, &c., 16s.; 50 ditto, 8s. 6d.; 25 ditto, 5s.; 12 ditto, 2s. 6d.

Hardy and Half-hardy Annuals.

100 Choice varieties, including Aster, Stock, Nemophila, Marigold, Phlox, Sweet Peas, &c., 21s.; 50 ditto, 11s. 6d.; 25 ditto, 6s.; 12 ditto, 3s. 6d.

Hardy Perennials and Biennials.

25 Choice varieties, including Pansy, Carnation, Hollyhock, Polyanthus, &c., 7s. 6d.; 12 ditto, 4s.

Hardy and Half-hardy Perennials and Biennials.

50 Best Hardy, Greenhouse and Stove varieties, 20s.; 25 ditto, 10s. 6d.; 12 ditto, 6s.

Stove and Greenhouse Perennials and Biennials.

25 Choice varieties, including Calceolaria, Primula, Cineraria, &c., 12s. 6d.; 12 ditto, 7s. 6d.

Ornamental Foliaged Plants.

6 Choice varieties, 2s. 6d.

Sweet Scented Annuals.

12 Fine varieties, 3s.

"The Farmers' Boxes" of Vegetable Seeds,

Contain a liberal and choice assortment of the most useful Vegetables for One Year's supply.

PRICE
12s. 6d. and 21s.
Each. Carriage Free.

Arranged to produce a constant supply of the best Vegetables all the Year round.

BOXES OF VEGETABLE SEEDS FOR COUNTRY GENTLEMEN & AMATEURS,
at 12s. 6d., 15s., 21s., 31s. 6d., 42s., 63s., 105s., *and* 210s. *each.*

COLLECTIONS OF VEGETABLE SEEDS FOR COTTAGE GARDENS *at* 2s. 6d., 5s., *and* 7s. 6d. *each.*

WEBBS' SEEDS OF BEAUTIFUL FLOWERS.

POST FREE.

WEBBS' DOUBLE ZINNIA ELEGANS.
1s. *per Packet.*

For prices and full particulars see

Issued in December next.
Price 1s., Post Free,
(which will be allowed off subsequent orders.)
Gratis to Customers.

WEBBS' NEW PRIZE PETUNIA.
2s. 6d. *per Packet.*

Webbs' Popular Boxes of Floral Gems

contain liberal and choice assortments of Flower Seeds that are specially recommended for the Gardens of Ladies or Amateurs.

2s. 6d., 5s., 7s. 6d., 10s. 6d., 15s., 21s., 31s. 6d., 42s., *and* **63s.**
Each. Free by Post or Rail to all parts of the Kingdom.

Webbs' Special Manures—*Continued.*

WEBBS' TURNIP MANURE.—£8 per Ton.

We have every confidence in recommending this valuable Manure, which contains a large percentage of phosphates, the greater portion being soluble, and the remainder in a reduced or mellowed state, easily assimilable with the soil, which is thereby enriched throughout the whole rotation course. This Manure also contains, in a highly concentrated form, a large quantity of other essential components. **Use per acre—for Swedes,** *with* **farm-yard manure, 3 to 4 cwt.;** *without*, **5 to 6 cwt. For Turnips,** *with* **farm-yard manure, 3 cwt.;** *without*, **4 to 5 cwt.**

WEBBS' MANGOLD MANURE.—£8 per Ton.

This Manure is rich in animal organic matter, ammonia, phosphates, and other constituents most calculated to enhance the quality of this valuable root, and at the same time to bring the land into a high state of fertility for the succeeding crops. **Apply,** *with* **farm-yard manure, 3 to 5 cwt. per acre;** *without*, **5 to 10 cwt. per acre.**

WEBBS' KOHL RABI MANURE.—£8 per Ton.

As Kohl Rabi is coming into more general cultivation, we have prepared a Special Manure for this particular crop, which contains large proportions of all the desirable elements. **Apply 4 to 8 cwt. per acre.**

WEBBS' GRASS MANURES.—The great benefit to be derived from an application of our Manures for Grass Lands is universally acknowledged, as not only do they improve the quality of the herbage, but, being readily soluble, they have an immediate effect upon the plant, promoting early maturity and heavy crops.

Webbs' Manure for Grazing Land.	*Use 6 to 10 cwt. per acre.*	**Price £8 per Ton.**
Webbs' Manure for Permanent Pasture.	*Use 6 to 10 cwt per acre.*	**Price £8 per Ton.**
Webbs' Manure for Mowing Grass and Clover.	*Use 4 to 6 cwt. per acre.*	**Price £8, 10s. per Ton.**

WEBBS' SUPERPHOSPHATE of LIME.—Prices according to Quality.

This cheap and useful Manure is excellent for roots or white straw crops. **Apply 4 to 6 cwt. per acre.**

WEBBS' BONE SUPERPHOSPHATE of LIME.—£7 per Ton.

This Manure contains soluble and insoluble phosphates, etc., and is suitable for use on all soils. **Use per acre—for Swedes, 5 to 6 cwt. For Turnips, 4 to 5 cwt.**

WEBBS' PREPARED BONES.—Prices on application.

The value of Prepared Bones as a Manure cannot be over-estimated; they contain a great proportion of soluble phosphates of lime, are quick in acting, and thoroughly efficacious. **Use 6 to 10 cwt. per acre.**

WEBBS' HOP MANURE.—£8 per Ton.

This high-class fertiliser stimulates the growth of the bine, making it strong and healthy, and increases the production of Hops. Use, according to the character and condition of the land, **4 to 8 cwt. per acre.**

WEBBS' POTATO MANURE.—£8 per Ton.

Our Special Potato Manure is rich in the fertilising elements necessary for the successful cultivation of this important tuber. **Apply 5 to 10 cwt. per acre.**

WEBBS' CABBAGE MANURE.—£8 per Ton.

An application of this Manure at the rate of **6 to 10 cwt. per acre** will be well repaid in the increased size and superior quality of the Cabbages.

WEBBS' DISSOLVED BONES.—£8 per Ton.

Contain a large proportion of soluble and insoluble phosphates, which nourish and support the plant up to its fullest maturity, leaving the land in a highly fertilised and enriched condition for the subsequent crop. This Manure is most excellent for Corn and Root Crops, to be applied broadcast **3 to 5 cwt per acre.**

For further particulars see WEBBS' MANURE CATALOGUE, which may be had gratis and post free on application.

WEBBS' SELECT ASSORTMENTS OF

Annual, Biennial, & Perennial Flower Seeds.

WEBBS' SPECIAL COLLECTIONS OF SEEDS TO PRODUCE FLOWERS, ETC., SUITABLE FOR CHURCH DECORATION AT HARVEST THANKSGIVING SERVICES, ETC.

	s.	d.
11. 6 splendid varieties,	2	6
12. 12 ,, ,,	5	0

Webbs' "Kinver" Collections of Hardy Annuals—

	s.	d.
13. 50 beautiful varieties,	10	0
14. 36 ,, ,,	7	6
15. 25 ,, ,,	5	0
16. 12 ,, ,,	2	6

Webbs' "Kinver" Collections of Half-hardy Annuals—

	s.	d.
17. 50 beautiful varieties,	12	6
18. 36 ,, ,,	10	6
19. 25 ,, ,,	7	6
20. 12 ,, ,,	4	0

Webbs' "Kinver" Collections of Sweet-scented Annuals—

	s.	d.
21. 12 best varieties,	3	0
22. 6 ,, ,,	1	6

Webbs' "Kinver" Collections of Annuals to produce Flowers useful for Bees—

	s.	d.
23. 12 choice varieties,	3	6
24. 6 ,, ,,	2	0

Webbs' "Kinver" Collections of Hardy Annuals for Rock-work—

	s.	d.
25. 12 best varieties,	3	0
26. 6 ,, ,,	1	6

Webbs' "Kinver" Collections of Hardy Annuals specially selected to produce Flowers for Bouquets—

	s.	d.
27. 12 finest varieties,	3	6
28. 6 ,, ,,	2	0

Webbs' "Kinver" Collections of Biennials and Perennials—

	s.	d.
29. 50 beautiful varieties,	12	6
30. 36 ,, ,,	9	6
31. 25 ,, ,,	6	6
32. 12 ,, ,,	3	6

Webbs' "Kinver" Collections of Ornamental Grass Seeds—

	s.	d.
33. 36 fine varieties,	8	0
34. 24 ,, ,,	5	6
35. 12 ,, ,,	3	0
36. 6 ,, ,,	1	9

Webbs' "Kinver" Collections of Everlasting Flower Seeds—

	s.	d.
37. 18 splendid varieties,	5	0
38. 12 ,, ,,	3	6
39. 6 ,, ,,	2	0

Webbs' Choice Collections of Seeds to produce plants valuable for Table Decoration—

	s.	d.
40. 6 superb varieties,	5	0
41. 3 ,, ,,	2	6

Webbs' Choice Collections of Climbing Plant Seeds—

	s.	d.
42. 12 extra fine varieties,	3	6
43. 6 ,, ,,	2	0

Webbs' Choice Collections of Green-house Plant Seeds—

	s.	d.
44. 12 best varieties,	7	6
45. 6 ,, ,,	4	0

Webbs' Choice Collections of Seeds specially selected to supply plants for the Sub-tropical Garden—

	s.	d.
46. 12 fine varieties,	5	0
47. 6 ,, ,,	2	6

Webbs' Choice Collections of the Seeds of Plants suitable for edgings of beds in the Sub-tropical Garden—

	s.	d.
48. 12 fine varieties,	3	6
49. 6 ,, ,,	2	0

☞ *See pages 4 and 5 for List of Special Prizes offered by Webb & Sons in 1888.*

SUTTON'S FLOWER SEEDS—COMPLETE LIST for 1892.

All Flower Seeds are sent free by post or rail to any address in the United Kingdom.

HALF-PACKETS CANNOT BE SUPPLIED, NOR ANY SMALLER PACKETS THAN THOSE OFFERED.

SUTTON'S FLOWER SEED ORDER ROOM, engraved from a Photograph. Two large Stores supply this room daily. COPYRIGHT S. & S.

Our Flower Seeds are saved from the finest strains in existence, and the germinating power of every parcel of seed is proved by reliable tests. Subsequent trials are made in our experimental houses and grounds, and the plants are grown to full development in order that we may personally observe the characteristics of each stock. These experimental trials are of so much interest that every year we are honoured with calls from an increasing number of visitors, who in some instances come from long distances for the purpose of inspecting our displays of flowers. We cordially invite all our customers to do this, in the full persuasion that those who can conveniently arrange such a visit will feel amply repaid for their trouble. The Calceolarias at our Seed Grounds in Reading are generally in perfection about May 20; Cinerarias during March and April; Cyclamens all through the winter; Begonias in May, June, and July; Gloxinias from May to July; and Primulas from November to March. There is also a brilliant display of Asters, Stocks, Verbenas, Lobelias, Phlox Drummondii, Polyanthus, Petunias, Zinnias, &c., at the usual times of flowering.

SUTTON'S COLLECTIONS OF FLOWER SEEDS

For sowing in the United Kingdom. Export Collections are offered on page 126.

SUTTON'S COMPLETE COLLECTION OF FLOWER SEEDS, price 63s., contains—

12 varieties Truffaut's French Pæony-flowered Aster.
12 ,, Chrysanthemum-flowered Aster.
6 ,, Victoria Aster.
6 ,, Sutton's Little Gem Aster.
6 ,, German Globe (Quilled) Aster.
12 ,, Dwarf German Ten-week Stock.
6 ,, Sutton's Perfection Stock.
6 ,, Autumnal-flowering Stock.
6 ,, Improved Queen (Biennial) Stock.
6 ,, Sutton's Prize Hollyhock.
10 ,, Improved Rose-flowered Balsam.
6 ,, Double Zinnia.
6 ,, Double German Wallflower.
6 varieties Phlox Drummondii.
8 oz. Mixed Sweet Peas.
1 packet Sutton's Pot Mignonette.
4 oz. Large-flowered Mignonette.
6 ,, Tom Thumb Nasturtium, 6 sorts.
2 ,, Tall Nasturtium, 2 sorts.
1 packet Miniature Sunflower.
1 oz. Tall Sunflower.
24 varieties showy Hardy Annuals, including Nemophila, Clarkia, Candytuft, Lupinus, Coreopsis, Larkspur, &c.
12 choice Half-hardy Annuals, including Marigold, Lobelia, Ageratum, Ice Plant, Linum rubrum, Portulaca, &c.
12 choice Perennials and Biennials, including Golden Feather, Viola, Myosotis, Petunia, Verbena, Single Dahlia, &c.
6 varieties for greenhouse and conservatory cultivation, including Begonia, Primula, Calceolaria, Cineraria, Cyclamen, &c.
6 varieties Everlasting Flowers, suitable for winter bouquets.
6 varieties Climbers, suitable for covering trellis-work, &c.
6 varieties Ornamental-foliaged Plant Seeds.
6 ,, Ornamental Grasses.

SUTTON'S COMPLETE COLLECTION OF FLOWER SEEDS, price 42s., contains—

12 varieties Truffaut's French Pæony-flowered Aster.
6 ,, Chrysanthemum-flowered Aster.
6 ,, Sutton's Little Gem Aster.
6 ,, Victoria Aster.
12 ,, Dwarf German Ten-week Stock.
1 packet Improved Queen (Biennial) Stock.
6 varieties Double Balsam.
6 ,, Double Zinnia.
6 ,, Double German Wallflower.
6 ,, Phlox Drummondii.
4 oz. Mixed Sweet Peas.
2 ,, Large-flowered Mignonette.
4 ,, Tom Thumb Nasturtium, 4 sorts.
2 ,, Tall Nasturtium, 2 sorts.
1 ,, Tall Sunflower.
12 varieties showy Hardy Annuals, including Nemophila, Clarkia, Candytuft, Larkspur, Coreopsis, &c.
12 choice Half-hardy Annuals, including Portulaca, Lobelia, Marigold, Linum, &c.
12 choice Perennials and Biennials, including Delphinium, Golden Feather, Viola, Petunia, Single Dahlia, &c.
6 varieties for greenhouse and conservatory cultivation, including Begonia, Calceolaria, Cineraria, Cyclamen, Primula, &c.
6 varieties Everlasting Flowers, suitable for winter bouquets.
6 varieties Climbers, suitable for covering trellis-work, &c.
6 varieties Ornamental-foliaged Plant Seeds.

SUTTON'S COMPLETE COLLECTION OF FLOWER SEEDS, price 31s. 6d., contains—

12 varieties Truffaut's French Pæony-flowered Aster.
6 ,, German Globe (Quilled) Aster.
12 ,, Dwarf German Ten-week Stock.
6 ,, Double Balsam.
6 ,, Double Zinnia.
6 ,, Double German Wallflower.
3 ,, Phlox Drummondii.
3 oz. Mixed Sweet Peas.
2 oz. Large-flowered Mignonette.
2 ,, Tom Thumb Nasturtium, 2 sorts.
1 ,, Mixed Tall Nasturtium.
12 varieties showy Hardy Annuals, including Nemophila, Candytuft, Lupinus, Larkspur, Sunflower, &c.
12 choice Half-hardy Annuals, including Portulaca, Lobelia, Convolvulus major, Marigold, &c.
12 choice Perennials and Biennials, including Canterbury Bells, Delphinium, Golden Feather, &c.
6 varieties for greenhouse and conservatory cultivation, including Calceolaria, Cineraria, Cyclamen, Primula, &c.
6 varieties Everlasting Flowers, suitable for winter bouquets.

SUTTON & SONS, Seed Growers and Merchants, READING, ENGLAND.

70

☛ **Webb and Sons send all Flower Seeds free by Post or Rail to all parts of the Kingdom.**

HARDY ANNUALS.

	s.	d.
No. 11. 50 beautiful varieties,	10	0
No. 12. 36 do. do.,	7	6
No. 13. 25 do. do.,	5	0
No. 14. 12 do. do.,	2	6

HALF-HARDY ANNUALS.

	s.	d.
No. 15. 50 beautiful varieties,	12	6
No. 16. 36 do. do.,	10	6
No. 17. 25 do. do.,	7	6
No. 18. 12 do. do.,	4	0

FLOWERS USEFUL FOR BEES.

	s.	d.
No. 19. 12 choice varieties,	3	6
No. 20. 6 do. do.,	2	0

HARDY FLOWERS FOR ROCK-WORK.

	s.	d.
No. 21. 12 best varieties,	3	0
No. 22. 6 do. do.,	1	6

FLOWERS FOR BOUQUETS.

	s.	d.
No. 23. 12 finest varieties,	3	6
No. 24. 6 do. do.,	2	0

BIENNIALS AND PERENNIALS.

	s.	d.
No. 25. 50 beautiful varieties,	12	6
No. 26. 36 do. do.,	9	6
No. 27. 25 do. do.,	6	6
No. 28. 12 do. do.,	3	6

SWEET-SCENTED FLOWERS.

	s.	d.
No. 29. 12 best varieties,	3	0
No. 30. 6 do. do.,	1	6

PLANTS FOR TABLE DECORATION.

	s.	d.
No. 31. 6 superb varieties,	5	0
No. 32. 3 do. do.,	2	6

CLIMBING PLANTS.

	s.	d.
No. 33. 12 extra fine varieties,	3	6
No. 34. 6 do. do.,	2	0

ORNAMENTAL GRASSES.

	s.	d.
No. 35. 36 fine varieties,	8	0
No. 36. 24 do. do.,	5	6
No. 37. 12 do. do.,	3	0
No. 38. 6 do. do.,	1	9

EVERLASTING FLOWERS.

	s.	d.
No. 39. 18 splendid varieties,	5	0
No. 40. 12 do. do.,	3	6
No. 41. 6 do. do.,	2	0

PLANTS FOR GREENHOUSE DECORATION.

	s.	d.
No. 42. 12 best varieties,	6	0
No. 43. 6 do. do.,	3	6

PLANTS FOR SUB-TROPICAL GARDENS.

	s.	d.
No. 44. 12 fine varieties,	5	0
No. 45. 6 do. do.,	2	6

PLANTS FOR EDGINGS OF BEDS IN THE SUB-TROPICAL GARDEN.

	s.	d.
No. 46. 12 fine varieties,	3	6
No. 47. 6 do. do.,	2	0

FLOWERS, GRASSES, ETC., FOR CHURCH DECORATION AT HARVEST FESTIVALS, ETC.

No. 48. 6 splendid varieties. . . . . 2s. 6d. | No. 49. 12 splendid varieties, ... 5s.

54

WEBBS' POPULAR COLLECTIONS OF VEGETABLE SEEDS.

☛ NO CHARGE IS MADE FOR THE BOXES THAT CONTAIN COLLECTIONS.

SPECIAL NOTICE.—We cannot allow any reduction in the prices of our Collections of Vegetable Seeds, but slight alterations will be made in the contents, if desired.

All Collections are sent Carriage Free.

CONTENTS FOR 1897:—

	A.	B.	C.	D.	E.	F.	G.	H.
	£10 10 0 Collection.	£5 5 0 Collection.	£3 3 0 Collection.	£2 2 0 Collection.	£1 11 6 Collection.	£1 1 0 Collection.	15s. Collection.	12s. 6d. Collection.
PEAS, including **Webbs' Perfection**, **Webbs' Kinver Marrow**, and other superior sorts for succession, as tested at our Kinver Seed Farms,	36 quarts.	24 quarts.	18 quarts.	10 quarts.	8 quarts.	6 quarts.	6 pints.	4 pints.
ASPARAGUS,	2 ounces.	1 ounce.	1 packet.	1 packet.	1 packet.			
BEANS, BROAD, the best varieties,	16 quarts.	9 quarts.	5 quarts.	7 pints.	5 pints.	4 pints.	2 pints.	1½ pints.
BEANS, FRENCH, DWARF, best varieties,	4 quarts.	4 pints.	2 pints.	2 pints.	1 pint.	½ pint.	½ pint.	½ pint.
BEANS, FRENCH, RUNNERS, the best,	3 quarts.	4 pints.	2 pints.	1 pint.	1 pint.	1 pint.	½ pint.	½ pint.
BEET, the best, including **Webbs' Dark Red**,	6 ounces.	4 ounces.	3 ounces.	2 ounces.	2 packets.	1 packet.	1 packet.	1 packet.
BORECOLE, or KALE, the best varieties,	6 packets.	4 packets.	3 packets.	3 packets.	2 packets.	1 packet.	1 packet.	1 packet.
BROCCOLI, the best sorts for succession,	8 packets.	6 packets.	5 packets.	4 packets.	3 packets.	3 packets.	2 packets.	2 packets
BRUSSELS SPROUTS, including **Webbs' Matchless**,	4 packets.	3 packets.	2 packets.	2 packets.	1 packet.	1 packet.	1 packet.	1 packet.
CABBAGE, the best sorts for succession,	8 packets	6 packets.	5 packets.	4 packets.	3 packets.	3 packets.	2 packets.	2 packets.
CAPSICUM, choice mixed,	4 packets.	2 packets.	1 packet.	1 packet.	1 packet.			
CARROT, the best sorts for succession,	20 ounces.	12 ounces.	7 ounces.	5 ounces.	3 ounces.	2 ounces.	3 packets.	2 packets.
CAULIFLOWER, the best for succession,	4 ounces.	4 packets.	3 packets.	2 packets.	1 packet.	1 packet.	1 packet.	1 packet.
CELERY, selected varieties,	4 packets.	3 packets.	2 packets.	2 packets.	2 packets.	2 packets.	1 packet.	1 packet.
CORN SALAD,	2 ounces.	1 ounce.	1 ounce.	1 packet.	1 packet.	1 packet.		
COUVE TRONCHUDA,	1 ounce.	1 packet.	1 packet.	1 packet.	1 packet.	1 packet.		
CRESS, PLAIN, CURLED, Etc., the best,	3 quarts & 4 ounces.	3 pints & 2 ounces.	1½ pints & 2 packets.	8 ounces & 2 packets.	4 ounces & 1 packet.	3 ounces & 1 packet.	2 ounces.	2 ounces.
CUCUMBER, the best for frame and ridge,	7 packets.	5 packets.	4 packets.	3 packets.	2 packets.	2 packets.	2 packets.	1 packet.
EGG PLANT, mixed,	1 packet.	1 packet.	1 packet.	1 packet.	1 packet.			
ENDIVE, the best varieties,	4 ounces.	4 packets.	3 packets.	2 packets.	1 packet.	1 packet.	1 packet.	1 packet.
GOURDS, mixed,	1 packet.	1 packet.	1 packet.	1 packet.				
HERBS, POT and **SWEET**,	12 packets.	10 packets.	8 packets.	6 packets.	4 packets.	3 packets.	2 packets.	2 packets.
LEEK,	4 ounces.	2 ounces.	1 ounce.	1 packet.	1 packet.	1 packet.	1 packet.	1 packet.
LETTUCE, COS and **CABBAGE**, the best sorts for succession,	8 packets.	6 packets.	5 packets.	4 packets.	4 packets.	3 packets.	2 packets.	2 packets.
MELON, choice varieties,	6 packets.	4 packets.	3 packets.	2 packets.	1 packet.	1 packet.	1 packet.	
MUSTARD,	4 quarts.	2 quarts.	1 quart.	1 pint.	½ pint.	4 ounces.	2 ounces.	2 ounces.
ONION, the best for summer and winter use,	20 ounces.	12 ounces.	8 ounces.	6 ounces.	5 ounces.	4 ounces.	3 packets.	3 packets.
ORACHE,	1 packet.	1 packet.	1 packet.	1 packet.	1 packet.			
PARSLEY, **Webbs' Giant Curled**,	6 ounces.	4 ounces.	2 ounces.	1 ounce.	1 packet	1 packet.	1 packet.	1 packet.
PARSNIP, the best sorts,	10 ounces.	6 ounces.	4 ounces.	3 ounces.	2 ounces.	1 ounce.	1 ource.	1 packet.
RADISH, the best sorts for succession,	4 pints.	2 pints.	14 ounces.	8 ounces.	5 ounces.	3 ounces.	2 ounces.	2 packets.
RAMPION,	1 packet.	1 packet.	1 packet.	1 packet.	1 packet.			
SALSAFY,	2 ounces.	1 ounce.	1 ounce.	1 packet.	1 packet.	1 packet.		
SAVOY CABBAGE, the best varieties,	4 ounces.	4 packets.	3 packets.	2 packets.	2 packets.	1 packet.	1 packet.	1 packet.
SCORZONERA,	2 ounces.	1 ounce.	1 ounce.	1 packet.	1 packet.	1 packet.		
SPINACH, ROUND and **PRICKLY**,	2 quarts.	3 pints.	2 pints.	1½ pints.	1 pint.	4 ounces.	3 ounces.	2 ounces.
TOMATO, the best varieties,	4 packets.	3 packets.	2 packets.	1 packet.	1 packet.	1 packet.	1 packet.	1 packet.
TURNIP, the best sorts for succession,	3 pints.	1½ pints.	8 ounces.	6 ounces.	4 ounces.	3 ounces.	2 ounces.	2 packets.
VEGETABLE MARROW,	4 packets.	3 packets.	2 packets.	2 packets.	1 packet.	1 packet.	1 packet.	1 packet.

		s.	*d.*
I. Webbs' Collection of Vegetable Seeds for a Cottage Garden,		**7**	**6**
J. Do. do. do.		**5**	**0**
K. Do. do. do.	**(25s.** *per dozen*),	**2**	**6**
L. Webbs' "Farmer's" Complete Collection of Vegetable Seeds,		**21**	**0**
M. Do. do. do.	*smaller size,*	**12**	**6**
N. Webbs' Collection of Seeds to produce Vegetables for Exhibition, *comprising 30 of the best varieties, one packet of each,*		**21**	**0**
O. Webbs' "United" Collection of Vegetable and Flower Seeds,		**21**	**0**
P. Do. do. do. do.	*smaller size,*	**10**	**6**

51

SUTTON'S SEEDS

SPECIALLY PACKED for INDIA and the COLONIES.

MORE HONOURS.

Gold Medal, Ceylon, 1891; Gold Medal, Jamaica, 1891; New Zealand, 1890, a Special Award and Eight Firsts.

Quality.—All Seeds packed for exportation are of the same high quality as those we supply to our Customers at home.

Germination.—The germinating power of each variety is tested with great care by us, and no Seed of any kind is allowed to be packed until we have proved the growth to be thoroughly satisfactory.

Caution.—To protect our Indian and Colonial Customers from being imposed upon with Seeds called by our name, but which have not been grown or exported by us, we have adopted the practice of sending out our Vegetable and Flower Seeds in packets and collections of convenient size, each one bearing our label and Registered Trade Mark.

REGISTERED

TRADE MARK

Beans and Peas are supplied in half-pint, pint, and quart packets. Seeds quoted in our Lists by the ounce, in ¼ oz., ½ oz., and 1 oz. packets. Of the varieties offered in our Lists by the packet only, no smaller quantity can be supplied than the packets quoted.

Loose Garden Seeds, or Seeds in packets which do not bear our Trade Mark, should not be accepted as our goods. Purchasers should carefully note if the seals of our packets have been tampered with or broken.

Deterioration prevented.—Our method of supplying Seeds will save much trouble, and has the additional advantage of preventing the deterioration in germinating power which invariably occurs when large parcels are opened and small portions are occasionally drawn from them.

Screw-caps to Tin Boxes.—Vegetable and Flower Seeds are sent out in hermetically sealed cases, which should not be opened until the Seeds are wanted. The caps should always be screwed down after a packet has been taken out.

Tanks and Cases.—Farm Seeds are usually despatched in iron tanks, or in zinc-lined wooden cases.

Drying.—Certain varieties of Seeds require special drying to ensure their passing with safety through the tropics in hermetically sealed cases, and we possess unique facilities for this work. When the process is considered necessary, a small extra charge is made.

Carriage.—We pay Carriage to the Docks at any Port in Great Britain.

Postage.—We forward Flower Seeds post-free to India, Ceylon, Victoria, New South Wales, Western and South Australia, New Zealand, Tasmania, and all Countries where the Parcel Post is in operation.

Insurance.—We gladly effect Insurance when desired, at Customer's expense.

Prepayment.—All orders for goods to be shipped should be accompanied with a remittance for the value of the goods, packages, and shipping expenses.

Responsibility.—After packages are delivered at the Dock for shipment our responsibility ceases.

SUTTON'S SPECIAL EXPORT COLLECTIONS,

Adapted for the Countries in which they are to be sown, form

ACCEPTABLE PRESENTS FOR FRIENDS ABROAD.

The Illustration below is a reduced facsimile of the design on the lid of Messrs. Sutton's Special Export Box of Seeds.

COMPLETE COLLECTIONS OF

VEGETABLE SEEDS.

£	s.	d.
10	10	0
5	5	0
4	4	0
3	3	0
2	2	0
1	1	0
0	10	6
0	7	6
0	5	0

COMPLETE COLLECTIONS OF

FLOWER SEEDS.

£	s.	d.
5	5	0
4	4	0
3	3	0
2	2	0
1	11	6
1	1	0
0	10	6
0	7	6
0	5	0

SUTTON'S COMPOSITE COLLECTION, containing a supply of **VEGETABLE AND FLOWER SEEDS, 10s. 6d.**

The price of each Collection includes an air-tight case, which will be found useful for many purposes after the seeds have been sown.

We shall also be happy to supply any selection of Vegetable or Flower Seeds desired by Customers.

From S. JENNINGS, Esq.,
Late Vice-President of the Agri-Horti Society of India.

'With reference to your mode of packing seeds for export, I must say how much I was gratified with the system you were so good as to show me. During the whole of my long Indian experience it was my constant regret that English packed seeds were almost invariably lower in germinating power than the American. After seeing the elaborate precautions you take in executing such orders as that of the Agri-Horti Society of India, I am by no means surprised to hear that you have been gratified by the receipt of so much testimony from the tropics as to the condition of your seeds upon arrival. If your correspondents are only careful *not* to open their tin cases until the seed is to be sown, I have no doubt the contents will be found in excellent condition.'

From C. FORD, Esq.,
Superintendent, Botanic Gardens, Hong Kong.

'Your system of packing seeds for exportation to tropical climates, where it is so difficult to keep seeds, is perfect. No seeds from anywhere else than your establishment, I believe, ever arrive in Hong Kong in such excellent condition. In directions to foreign customers I think you might with advantage request them to be careful not to open the seed boxes except on a perfectly dry day, or in a closed room before a fire, and then to immediately place the packets in stoppered bottles until the seeds are sown. This is the practice which I have adopted, as I have found that even a few hours' exposure to the saturated atmosphere prevailing here from May to October is sufficient to destroy the vitality of a great many seeds.'

SUTTON & SONS, Seed Growers and Merchants, READING, ENGLAND.

126

Webbs' system of packing Seeds and Bulbs for Export is unequalled. 109

WEBBS' SEEDS FOR EXPORT.

Webbs' Home-Grown Seeds are annually exported, in immense quantities, to
NEW ZEALAND, AUSTRALIA, INDIA, BRAZIL, VAN DIEMEN'S LAND, UNITED STATES, CANADA, CHINA, JAPAN, WEST INDIES, AFRICA, INCLUDING THE CAPE OF GOOD HOPE, ETC. ETC.

WEBBS' EXPORT COLLECTIONS OF VEGETABLE SEEDS.

No.			£	s.	d.
A1.	Complete Collection,		5	0	
A2.	Do.	do.,		12	6
A3.	Do.	do.,	1	1	0
A4.	Do.	do.,	1	11	6
A5.	Do.	do.,	2	2	0
A6.	Do.	do.,	3	3	0
A7.	Do.	do.,	4	4	0
A8.	Do.	do.,	5	5	0
A9.	Do.	do.,	10	10	0
A10.	"United" Collection of Vegetable & Flower Seeds,		1	1	0
A11.	Do.	do.,		10	6

(☛ *These prices include air-tight cases.*)

THIS is a very important branch of our business, as we are probably the largest Exporters of Seeds in the Kingdom. GRASS, FARM, VEGETABLE, and FLOWER SEEDS, and also BULBS, are carefully packed, by a new process, in hermetically-sealed cases, *for all parts of the World,* delivered free *to the ship's side at any Port in the United Kingdom, and insurance is effected when desired. ORDERS must reach us some days before the sailing of the vessels destined to carry them, and a remittance or satisfactory reference should accompany each order.* ☛ *Special terms to Shippers of large quantities of Seeds.*

WEBBS' EXPORT COLLECTIONS OF FLOWER SEEDS.

No.			£	s.	d.
A12.	Complete Collection,			2	6
A13.	Do.	do.,		5	0
A14.	Do.	do.,		7	6
A15.	Do.	do.,		10	6
A16.	Do.	do.,		15	0
A17.	Do.	do.,	1	1	0
A18.	Do.	do.,	1	11	6
A19.	Do.	do.,	2	2	0
A20.	Do.	do.,	3	3	0
A21.	Do.	do.,	4	4	0
A22.	Do.	do.,	5	5	0

(☛ *These prices include air-tight cases.*)

INDIA.

From WM. ACKWORTH, Esq., Bangalore, India.

"The Seeds I received from you produced very satisfactory results. I consider them better than any I have hitherto had from England."

RUSSIA.

From W. PALMER, Esq., Government of St. Petersburgh, Russia.

"I have much pleasure in stating that your Turnip, Swede, and Mangold Seeds forwarded to me last spring, answered remarkably well."

CEYLON.

From Mons. E. DE FONBLANQUE, Kinloch Estate, Ceylon.

"Your Seeds came up well, and the Bulbs were also very good."

BRITISH GUIANA.

From S. BELLAIRS, Esq., Plantation Met-en-Merrzorg, British Guiana, South America.

"The Cucumbers that won the First Prize at the Horticultural Show held in Georgetown, Demerara, this year, were Webbs' Perpetual Bearer, grown from Seeds imported from Messrs. Webb & Sons. None of the other exhibits approached them."

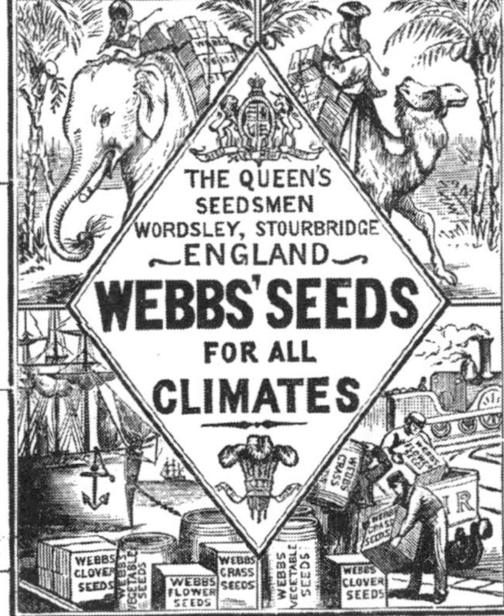

WEBB & SONS' BRANCH ESTABLISHMENT:—
65 QUEEN STREET, AUCKLAND, NEW ZEALAND.

NEW ZEALAND.

From Mr. JOHN CARPENTER, Canterbury, New Zealand.

"The Seeds and Bulbs arrived safely and in good sound condition. I have had a splendid show of Ranunculus, and the Hollyhocks were the admiration of all who saw them."

UNITED STATES.

From J. H. WOODFORD, Esq., Kenrick Park, United States.

"Your Spring Catalogue is very beautiful. The Seeds I had last year were good, and produced superior Vegetables and Flowers."

FRANCE.

From Mons. A. G. MIGNOT, Bois-Gauthier, France. February 28, 1882.

"I have much pleasure in telling you that I have obtained the Gold Medal of France for your Challenge Wheat."

CANADA.

From Messrs. McLEOD & STEWART, Charlottetown, Canada.

"Your Imperial Swede is a perfectly-shaped Turnip, and we have not the least hesitation in saying that it is going to take the lead here. It is most marketable, being so clean, free from coarseness of neck, and clear-skinned."

Economy in the Garden.

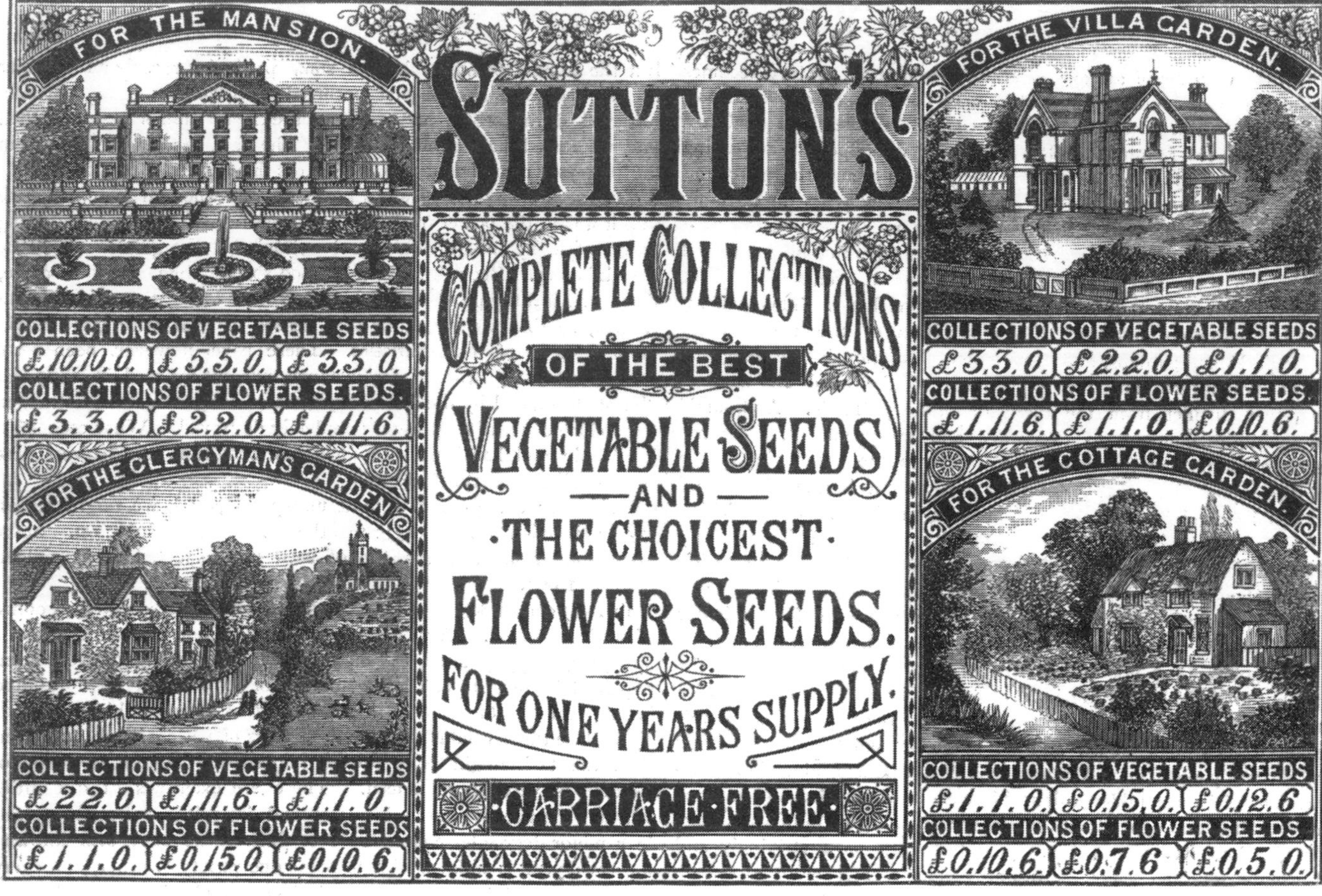

We were the originators of the system, now generally followed, of supplying Collections of Seeds for gardens of various sizes, from that of the Mansion to the plot attached to the Cottage. We are able to give to purchasers of Collections great advantages, by proving in our Trial Grounds which are the best and most productive kinds of Vegetables, and by growing these particular sorts on a very large scale. As we sell none but GENUINE and unadulterated Seeds, and the very liberal supply for the small sums specified can only be afforded by special previous arrangements on our part, we would respectfully intimate that we can make NO ALTERATIONS OR SUBSTITUTIONS.

For particulars of Collections of Flower Seeds see pages 48 and 49.

From the Rev. E. S. DODD, Elmore.

'Your Seeds, both Vegetable and Flower, which I had in the spring, have, as usual, proved most prolific; in fact, the only fault is that we have more Vegetables and Plants than we know what to do with. I had your Guinea Collection this year, and in several cases I only sowed half the seed sent.'

From the Rev. W. J. PAYNE, South Elmham.

'I was delighted with the liberal amount of Garden Seeds sent to me in the Two Guinea Collection.'

From Mr. W. FARMER, Stanthorpe Villa, Bexley Heath.

'Your Guinea Collection of Seeds sent last year was so good that I took three prizes at our local show for Marrows, Cucumbers, and Beans. The Annuals were much admired—in fact, one mass of bloom.'

From the Rev. R. G. BOODLE, Cloford Vicarage.

'The Collection sent last year gave entire satisfaction. The selection of Peas was especially good.'

From A. A. PADLEY, Esq., Market Rasen.

'The Guinea Collection of Garden Seeds was in every way excellent.'

From Mr. W. SALCOMBE, Gardener to M. de Murietta, Esq., Southover.

'You are most liberal in the size of your packets, both of Garden and Flower Seeds.'

From JAS. BLYTH, Esq., Weasenham.

'I continue, as I have been for the last 20 years, perfectly satisfied with your Seeds.'

Highest Distinction.—'THE LEGION OF HONOUR.' Paris, 1878.

SPECIAL NOTICE.

SUTTON'S SEEDS—POST FREE

ALL
VEGETABLE SEEDS
SENT
POST FREE
(EXCEPT PEAS & BEANS).

ALL
FLOWER SEEDS
SENT
POST FREE
(WITHOUT EXCEPTION).

LARGE PARCELS
AND
HEAVY GOODS
WILL STILL BE
FORWARDED
FREE BY RAIL.
FOR PARTICULARS
SEE PAGE 102.

The remarkable success which has attended our introduction of the system of sending Seeds post-free induces us again to remind those of our patrons who may not have availed themselves of this convenient mode of transmitting small parcels, that both Vegetable and Flower Seeds (excepting Peas and Beans) can be forwarded and delivered with a promptitude not possible by rail.

The postal regulations limit each parcel to 12 ounces in weight, but an order can be made up in two or more packets.

As a rule we cannot book these orders, for the system is only practicable when reduced to the most simple treatment. We must therefore ask Correspondents to be kind enough to accompany every order with a remittance for the full value of the goods, unless they already have an account open with us.

As everyone may have a call from the postman at least once each day, we feel sure that customers will find this to be a most speedy and convenient method of obtaining small quantities of Seeds.

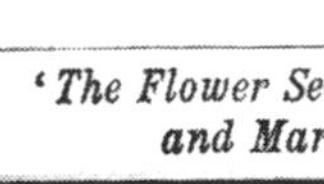

'The Flower Seeds I had [illegible] you last year gave the utmost satisfaction. I had a splendid display of Asters and Marigolds, [illegible] Pansies I don't think could be beaten.'—MR. A. MCLAUCHLAN, *Coupar-Angus.*

101

ACKNOWLEDGEMENTS & SOURCES

In the following listing, the number of each page of *The Victorian Garden Catalogue*, **in bold type**, is listed alongside the page reference of its original source. The original catalogues from which material was taken appear in alphabetical order.

BLACK AND WHITE:

Boulton & Paul, Manufacturers & Galvanizers, Rose Lane Works, Norwich, March 1890 (48th edition)
62 - 47; **66** - 26; **67** - 25; **68** - 19; **114** - 42; **115** - 43; **116** - 44, 117 - 45; **168** - 72; **169** - 75; **171** - 70; **181** - 76; **183** - 65.

B. S. E. & Co., London, 1887, Illustrated Catalogue of Wire Goods &c. of the Best Quality Only. Manufactured on the Premises.
132 - 40; **133** - 44; **134** - 34; **135** - 36.

A Catalogue of Horticultural Buildings and Heating Apparatus manufactured by Boulton & Paul, Ltd., Horticultural Builders, Heating, Ventilating, Electrical and Sanitary Engineers, Norwich, October 1909, no. 174 (2/6)
2 - cover; **136** - 130 &131; **137** - 177; **163** - 126 & 127; **164** - 128 & 129.

Falkirk Iron Co., Book of Patterns, July 1882 (source nos. refer to plate nos.)
142 - 312; **143** - 312[a]; **166** - 304 A; **167** - 304 B.

The Formation of Permanent Pastures by Webb & Sons, The Queen's Seedsmen, Wordsley, Stourbridge; London and Paris
192 - inside front cover.

Garden Furniture and Ornament by John P. White, The Pyghtle Works, Bedford and 134 New Bond Street, London W, 1906
59 - 90; **61** - 93; **64** - 104; **65** - 103; **119** - 201; **124** - 210; **125** - 211; **126** - 200; **138** - 146; **139** - 149; **140** - 129; **144** - 63; **145** - 160; **146** - 70; **147** - 71; **148** - 96; **149** - 80; **152** - 111; **160** - 166; **161** - 170; **162** - 189; **165** - 26.

Illustrated Catalogue of Garden Furniture & Garden Games, Baxendale & Co., Miller St., Manchester, Summer 1907
6 - 12, nos. s58 & s59.

Illustrated Catalogue of Goods Manufactured and Supplied by W. Cooper, *c.* 1893
111 - 47-49 & 333; **122** - 42-45; **123** - 50, 51, 60, 61; **128** - 29, 32, 37 & 39; **141** - 282-285; **158** - 118, 120, 121 & 124; **159** - 100-102 & 114; **178** - 63, 131, 246 & 332; **179** - 288, 305, 310 & 341.

Illustrated and Descriptive Catalogue by Follows & Bate Ltd., Engineers, Patentees and Manufacturers of Agricultural, Horticultural, Domestic, and Special Labour-Saving Machinery, Gorton, Manchester, "Diamond Jubilee", August 1897, no. 650
129 - 36; **170** - 35; **172** - 12; **182** - 23; **184** - 21; **185** - 31; **186** - 11; **187** - 17; **188** - 22; **189** - 25.

The Illustrated Guide for Amateur Gardeners - Daniels Brothers, Norwich, Spring 1876 (1/-)
12 - 44; **13** - 45; **14** - 46; **15** - 47; **16** - 48; **17** - 49; **22** - 70; **23** - 71; **30** - 62; **31** - 84; **58** - 89; **84** - 4; **85** - 5; **86** - 6; **87** - 7; **88** - 8; **89** - 9; **90** - 10; **91** - 11; **110** - 88; **120** - 94; **121** - 95; **212** - 12; **213** - 63.

S. Ramsey & Co., Manufacturers, Merchants, Patentees, Factors & Importers. General Wireworkers & Weavers, 1906
60 - 69; **63** - 70; **112** - 53; **113** - 54; **130** - 82; **150** - 73; **151** - 76; **153** - 78; **154** - 71; **155** - 72; **156** - 79; **157** - 80; **191** - 92.

William & John Richards, Manufacturers of Best Iron, Brass, and Copper Wire, *c.* 1870-80 (source nos. refer to design nos.)
118 - 70,72,74 & 75; **131** - 300 - 312, **180** - 10-27.

Sutton's Amateur's Guide in Horticulture, 1881
20 - 77; **32** - 46; **49** - 47; **72** - 32; **73** - 33; **82** - 14; **83** - 15; **100** - 24; **101** - 25; **102** - 3; **103** - 30; **174** - 42; **175** - 43; **194** - 85; **222** - 4; **223** - 101.

Sutton's Amateur's Guide in Horticulture for 1892
18 - 76; **19** - 77; **21** - 103; **28** - 80; **29** - 95; **50** - 69; **51** - 120; **71** - 68; **98** - 38; **99** - 39; **108** - 57; **109** - 58; **217** - 70; **220** - 126.

Sutton's Amateur's Guide in Horticulture for 1895
24 - 104; **25** - 113; **80** - 9; **81** - 21; **104** - 54; **105** - 59; **106** - 60; **107** - 61.

Sutton's Amateur's Guide in Horticulture for 1897
176 - 86; **177** - 87.

Sutton's Spring Catalogue and Amateur's Guide for 1858. Containing much useful instruction in Horticulture & Agriculture
69 - 52; **196** - 40, 41, 43, 44; **197** - 50, 53, 54 & 57.

Sutton's Spring Catalogue and Amateur's Guide for 1863. Containing much useful Instruction in Horticulture & Agriculture
70 - 32; **78** - 21 & 22 plus tipped-in illustration; **79** - 26-29; **210** - 37; **211** - 40.

Webb & Sons' Catalogue for Farm Seeds for 1879
200 - 37.

Webbs' Annual Catalogue - Farm Seeds, 1892
205 - 41; **206** - 18; **207** - 20; **208** - 46; **209** - 47.

Webbs' Catalogue of Selected Seed Corn, 1883-4
202 - 4; **203** - 5; **204** - 18; **214** - 21.

Webbs' Catalogue of Selected Seed Corn, 1884-5
195 - 24; **199** - frontispiece; **201** - 22; **215** - 23.

Webbs' Spring Catalogue for 1888
26 - 78; **27** - 79; **52** - 86; **53** - 64; **56** - 96; **57** - 59; **74** - 100; **75** - 101; **76** - 23; **92** - 29; **93** - 30; **94** - 48; **95** - 49; **96** - 38; **97** - 39; **190** - 105; **198** - 108; **216** - 99; **221** - 109.

Webbs' Spring Catalogue for 1895
10 - cover.

Webbs' Spring Catalogue, 1897
54 - 88; **55** - 99; **218** - 54; **219** - 51.

COLOUR:

A Catalogue of Horticultural Buildings and Heating Apparatus manufactured by Boulton & Paul, Ltd., Horticultural Builders, Heating, Ventilating, Electrical and Sanitary Engineers, Norwich, October 1909, no. 174 (2/6)
45.

The Formation of Permanent Pastures by Webb & Sons, The Queen's Seedsmen, Wordsley, Stourbridge; London and Paris
48.

Garden Furniture and Ornament by John P. White, The Pyghtle Works, Bedford and 134 New Bond Street, London W, 1906
43, 44.

The Illustrated Guide for Amateur Gardeners - Daniels Brothers, Norwich, Spring 1876 (1/-)
37, 41.

Sutton's Amateur Guide in Horticulture, 1881
42 - cover.

Sutton's Amateur Guide in Horticulture for 1892
36, 38, 39.

Webbs' Catalogue of Selected Seed Corn, 1883-4
46.

Webbs' Catalogue of Selected Seed Corn, 1884-5
47.

Webbs' Spring Catalogue for 1888
33 - cover; **34, 35, 40**.